HANDBOOK OF WORK AND ORGANIZATIONAL PSYCHOLOGY

Volume 3: Personnel Psychology

HANDBOOK OF WORK AND ORGANIZATIONAL PSYCHOLOGY

(Second Edition)

Volume 3: Personnel Psychology

Edited by

Pieter J.D. Drenth

Vrije Universiteit,

Amsterdam,

The Netherlands

Henk Thierry

Tilburg University,

The Netherlands

Charles J. de Wolff

Catholic University,

Nijmegen,

The Netherlands

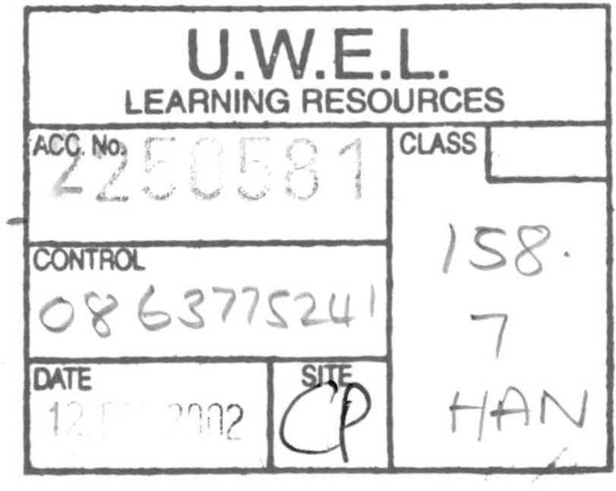

Psychology Press Ltd
27 Church Road
Hove
East Sussex, BN3 2FA, UK

British Library Cataloguing in Publication Data
A catalogue record for this title is available from the British Library

Volume 3
ISBN 0–86377–524–1 (Hbk)
ISBN 0–86377–525–X (Pbk)

Cover illustration by Clive Goodyer
Cover design by Rachael Adams
Typeset by Mendip Communications Ltd, Frome, Somerset
Printed and bound in the United Kingdom by Redwood Books Ltd,
Trowbridge, Wilts, UK

Contents

Contributors to Volume 3

Jen A. Algera, Technische Universiteit Eindhoven, Faculteit Technische Bedrijfskunde, Postbus 513, 5600 MB Eindhoven, The Netherlands.

Giel van den Bosch, Hoogovens Groep B.V., Postbus 10000, 1970 CA IJmuiden, The Netherlands.

Johannes Gerrit Boerlijst, Rupperink 4, 7491GR Delden, The Netherlands.

René F.W. Diekstra, Universiteit Leiden, Faculteit Psychologie, Wassenaarseweg 52, 2333 AK Leiden, The Netherlands.

Pieter J.D. Drenth, Vrije Universiteit, Faculteit Psychologie en Pedagogiek, Van der Boechorststraat 1, 1081 BT Amsterdam, The Netherlands.

Jan A. Feij, Vrije Universiteit, Faculteit Psychologie en Pedagogiek, Van der Boechorststraat 1, 1081 BT Amsterdam, The Netherlands.

Martin A.M. Greuter died after a prolonged illness. Many colleagues at the University of Amsterdam and at Psychotechniek/SHL, Utrecht, are very much indebted to him.

John R. de Jong was attached to the Raadgevend Bureau Berenschot, Utrecht, but sadly passed away in 1995. Among many others, Henk Thierry is indebted to him.

Paul L. Koopman, Vrije Universiteit, Faculteit Psychologie en Pedagogiek, Van der Boechorststraat 1, 1081 BT Amsterdam, The Netherlands.

Gary P. Latham, Faculty of Management, University of Toronto, 246 Bloor Street West, Toronto, Ontario N5S 1V4, Canada.

Willem F.G. Mastenbroek, Anton Mauvestraat 2, 2102 BA Heemstede, The Netherlands.

Henriette Miedema (now van den Heuvel), Berenschot, Bernadottelaan, 13, PO Box 8039, 3503 RA Utrecht, The Netherlands.

Zeeva Millman, Faculty of Management, University of Toronto, 246 Bloor Street West, Toronto, Ontario N5S 1V4, Canada.

Marlies Ott, SHL Psychotechniek, Arthur van Schendelstraat 612, Postbus 1047, 3500 BA Utrecht, The Netherlands.

Robert A. Roe, Katholieke Universiteit Brabant, Faculteit Sociale Wetenschappen, Warandelaan 2, 5037 AB Teilburg, The Netherlands.

Gerard H. Seijts, Faculty of Management, University of Toronto, 246 Bloor Street West, Toronto, Ontario N5S 1V4, Canada.

Henk Thierry, Katholieke Universiteit Brabant, Faculteit Sociale Wetenschappen, Postbus 90153, 5000 LE Tilburg, The Netherlands.

Evert van de Vliert, Universiteit Groningen, Faculteit Psychologische, Pedagogische, Sociologische Wetenschappen, Grote Kruisstraat 2/1, 9712 TS Groningen, The Netherlands.

André F.M. Wierdsma, Universiteit Nijenrode, Straatweg 25, 3621 AG Harmelen, The Netherlands.

Jacques Winnubst, Universiteit Utrecht, Projectorganisatie Verplegingswetenschappen, Postbus 80 036, 3508 TA Utrecht, The Netherlands.

Charles J. de Wolff, Gomarius Messtraat 19, Alverna, 6603 CS Wijchen, The Netherlands.

Jac N. Zaal, Gemeenschappelijk Instituut voor Toegepaste Psychologie, J.J. Viottastraat 52, 1071 JT Amsterdam, The Netherlands.

1

Introduction

Charles J. de Wolff

When the editors of this handbook planned its content, they had in mind four sections. The first section was to contain introductory chapters, such as the history of W&O psychology, and methodology. This would be followed by three sections, each focusing on a particular relationship. The first would concentrate on the relationship between the individual person and his or her task. The second would focus on the individual as a member of a social group, and the third would look at the relationship between the individual and the organization and the organizational environment. Later we decided to add some chapters which could not easily be included in these four sections, but which we thought to be of interest to readers.

The Dutch version of our handbook was structured in this way, and was a loose-leaf edition. Every year, two or three chunks, each containing four or five chapters, appeared. In this way the editors did not need to worry about the size of the sections. This was different for the English version. Taking into account the overall size of the handbook it was decided to have four volumes, and it became necessary to regroup the chapters. In particular, the section on the relationship between the individual and his or her task was too long to fit into one volume. So it was decided to split this section in two: to have one volume on work psychology and another on personnel psychology. In this respect the editors followed the recommendations of the European Reference Model, proposed by a group of European W&O psychology professors (Roe, Coetsier, Lévy-Leboyer, Peiro, & Wilpert, 1994), for structuring the W&O psychology training programme. Roe et al. (pp. 358–359) give a description of the domain of personnel psychology:

> Personnel psychology concerns the relationship between persons and the organization, in particular the establishment of the relationship, its development and its termination. The focus is on "employees", i.e. those with whom the organization has a temporal relationship. Important subjects are: choice processes of individuals and organizations, abilities and capabilities, needs, and need fulfilment, commitment, methods of selection, career development, appraisal, pay, training, etc.

This is different from work psychology where the focus is on "workers who have to perform tasks that are derived from the work processes taking place in the organization".

Roe et al. have chosen their points of focus very well, and these force W&O psychologists to occupy themselves with a set of related issues, all having to do with the relationship between the individual and organization, and prevent them from limiting themselves to only one particular issue. For personnel psychology it means that one has to concentrate on a satisfactory relationship between the employee and the employer, which can only be achieved by looking at many issues, such as those mentioned by Roe et al. in their description of the domain. For example, it is not sufficient to look at personnel selection in isolation, because neglecting issues like training and career management may result in an unsatisfactory relationship.

The focus on the relationship between the employee and the employer reflects a development in the attitudes of W&O psychology over the last 25 years. Prior to this, a more limited point of view was adopted. For example, studies on personnel selection concentrated on maximizing the output of a job incumbent and the utility for the organization. For a long time it was assumed that what was good for the organization was also beneficial to the individual. But such a limited approach overlooked the possibility of hidden costs, such a turnover, restriction of output, whistle-blowing, resistance to change, and so on. By concentrating on the relationship between the employee and the employer, the W&O psychologist is stimulated to adopt a broader approach to the issues she or he is studying.

Personnel psychology has a long history. Some studies had already been performed by the end of the nineteenth century. Many of the issues discussed in this volume were also taken up in early textbooks such as Meijers (1920) and Viteles (1932). Viteles spends some 200 pages on the subject of personnel selection, showing that at that time there was already a substantial body of knowledge. But one also finds chapters on movement studies, fatigue, payment, restriction of output, industrial unrest, safety, training, monotony, motives, supervision, and maladjusted workers. Most of these subjects are also covered in this handbook.

It is interesting to see how broad the domain of W&O psychology already was in that early period. Since then, numerous studies have been carried out. Each year hundreds of articles appear in scientific journals, and many books are published. This has resulted in an even more substantial body of knowledge. As one may expect from a well-developed discipline this body of knowledge is on the one hand stable, but on the other hand new aspects are constantly being added and new approaches developed. This is the way a discipline adapts to a changing environment.

W&O psychology is a scientific discipline, but it is also a field of application. There are now numerous W&O psychologists trained in the subject and applying the knowledge accumulated over the past century. They work in organizations and in consultancy agencies where they are confronted with all kind of problems. Clients pose questions, and these psychologists try to find answers. This in turn might lead to new research questions.

Furthermore, W&O psychologists come up against regulations enforced by governments wanting to stimulate employment, protect workers from health risks, help minorities to stand a better chance on the labour market, and provide employees with more influence on the decision-making processes in organizations. This confrontation with client demands and government regulations has given the domain a special kind of dynamism and has enriched the discipline. While there is a set of basic issues, like how to select applicants and how to train workers, there are also all kinds of new issues which demand the attention of the W&O psychologist. In the period when Meijers and Viteles wrote their textbooks, industrial organizations introduced Tayloristic methods for effecting mass production. So it is not surprising to find chapters in their books on movement studies, fatigue, restriction of output, systems of payment (piece work!), and industrial unrest. These were the issues that clients had to struggle with. Today we have other issues, such as participative management, ethnic minorities and absenteeism. Also, in a well-developed field like personnel selection, W&O psychologists are confronted with new demands from clients, and government interventions (see Chapter 2 in Volume 4 of this handbook.

There are differences between periods, but also between countries, as a result of different socio-economic systems and cultures. This makes W&O psychology and personnel psychology more complex but also more interesting disciplines. Personnel psychology is nowadays a well-developed discipline. One may expect that in the next century there will be plenty of new questions that it will be required to answer.

REFERENCES

Meijers, C.S. (1920). *Mind and work.* London: University of London Press.

Roe, R.A., Coetsier, P., Lévy-Leboyer, C., Peiro, J.M., & Wilpert, B. (1994). The teaching of work and organizational psychology in Europe: Towards the development of a reference model. *The European Work and Organizational Psychologist, 4*, 355–365.

Viteles, M.S. (1932). *Industrial Psychology.* New York: Norton.

2

Personnel Selection: Principles, Models and Techniques

Robert A. Roe

INTRODUCTION

What is personnel selection?

Personnel selection can be defined as an organization's activities aimed at choosing people for the fulfilment of jobs. It comprises both choices concerning the decision to admit people to the organization and the decision about a change of position inside the organization. The choice typically aims at achieving an "optimal" result defined by some kind of objective. While formerly the objective has been to find "suitable candidates", nowadays it is to optimize "utility", defined in terms of the interests of the organization. Utility refers to the overall result of selection evaluated against the background of the goals and resources of the organization, and to its success in the organization's environment.

Personnel selection is part of a larger set of activities called either personnel management, human resources management, or social policy. It has connections with personnel planning, recruitment, training, career development and so on. In modern views of management, centring around the notion of human capital, selection is seen as the cornerstone of a policy that tries to acquire and accumulate human capital.

Personnel selection is a phenomenon with many facets, which can be looked upon from many perspectives. Economically it is a process in which the demand for labour and the supply of labour meet. Legally it is a process in which two parties establish a labour contract in a mutually satisfying way. In this connection special attention is being paid to the power inequality between the two parties, and the risk of harming the weakest party. From a sociological perspective, selection is seen as a mechanism for reproducing and modifying the relationships between social classes and other social entities in society. However, personnel selection is most of all known to be a subject for psychology. Since psychologists have dealt with selection problems for almost a century it is not surprising to see that they have generated a large variety of different approaches to selection.

Initially much attention was given to the notion of "suitability" or "fitness" and the methods for its assessment. In later years attention has shifted towards cut-off scores, utility, ethical aspects, discrimination, the impact of selection on the individual and so on (Roe, 1996a).

This chapter deals with the methodological side of personnel selection[1]. The focus is on the "how" of selection. Unlike in the earlier days (i.e. before the 1990s) the question is not how to assess the qualities of a candidate but how to structure the selection process in such a way that the parties involved can achieve an optimal result. Central is the notion of "selection procedure" which will be defined later. The point of departure is that selection procedures can be designed intentionally (Roe, 1989). Until the 1990s this subject received little methodological attention. The psychological literature has mainly favoured the "classical model", a recipe for a linear procedure to compose predictive test batteries. In practice it was left to the ingenuity of personnel managers and psychologists to invent procedures. The notion of "selection procedure" as such has played hardly any role. The attention was primarily devoted to tests, interviews and other diagnostic instruments. Of course, these are important as elementary building blocks, but they are insufficient to solve selection problems satisfactorily. One also needs methods for processing information and decision making, as well as methods for building up the procedure as a whole.

In this chapter we will first discuss the notion of selection procedure (1) and the methodology of design (2). Next, we will deal with two important functions of selection procedures: the prediction of work performance (3) and decision making about admission and career (4). We will give an overview of the principles for realizing such functions, the models based on these principles, and the methods and instruments to be used in implementation. Our emphasis will be on 'formal' methods which can be fully explicated. In a final section we will discuss 'informal' or clinical methods and the role they can play in selection procedures.

The selection procedure

Organizations are recurrently faced with selection problems. Expansion and restructuring create a demand for new jobs to be taken by people, while innovations and automation produce job changes which call for incumbents with different qualifications. Also, employees leave the organization and move to other positions, thus leaving vacancies to be filled. In all these cases there are jobs for which one or more vacancies exist and one or more candidates (applicants) ready to fulfil these vacancies. The selection problem to be solved consists of making a choice in such a manner that the result satisfies certain standards.

Selection problems can be resolved *ad hoc* by recruiting a number of candidates and finding out which of them seem most suitable for the job. In practice, this is often done without a thorough analysis of the job and by using simple methods such as letters, interviews, and reference checks which require little preparation and elaboration. Usually there is not sufficient time for another approach. This is the common approach to selection in many smaller firms.

An alternative is to proceed in a systematic manner and to design a selection procedure before starting the actual recruitment and selection process. The procedure indicates which steps should be taken, in which order, which people should be involved, which roles they have to fulfil, which tools have to be employed, how they must be used, and so on. In short, it specifies the what, when, by whom, what with and how of selection. Thus, a "selection procedure" is a set of instructions regarding the course of action in selecting people for a job or career. Of course, selection procedures don't have to prescribe everything in detail. They can also be of a general nature or indicate possible options regarding certain decision points. When opting for using selection procedures it is recommended to put them down in writing, e.g. in a procedure manual (cf. Roe, 1983, 1989). This is not only useful for guiding the actual selection process but might also help in meeting the ISO 9000 standard for quality assurance, at least in cases of more sophisticated procedures. In simple cases a short note indicating the steps to take and the criteria to use will suffice.

Seen from an analytic perspective, selection procedures have multiple functions to fulfil. There are minimally four such functions (Roe, 1989; Roe & Greuter, 1991):

1. Information gathering: obtaining information about job openings , job content, job requirements, etc. and on physical, behavioural and biographical characteristics of applicants.
2. Prediction: transforming information on (past or present) applicant characteristics into predictions about their future behaviour, and the resulting contributions to organizational goals.
3. Decision making: transforming predictive information on applicants into a preferred action.
4. Information supply: producing information on applicant characteristics, predicted behaviours, plans for action (decisions), etc.

There are also other functions, such as conveying a certain image of the firm to applicants, establishing positive relationships with candidates, some of whom become future employees, negotiating the terms of a labour contract and so on.

Personnel psychology offers many methods and techniques to fulfil these functions. They can be used to compose a great variety of procedures. A short overview of the options has been presented by Roe (1989). An example of the steps in a simple procedure is presented in Table 2.1. For each step the major functions are indicated. The content of the steps, in terms of job requirements, topics to cover in the interview, etc. have not been specified, but they belong to the procedure as well. Data on the use of different types of selection procedures in practice has been published by Schuler et al. (1993), Shackleton and Newell (1989), Van Eijck et al. (1988), Greuter and Roe (1982).

The next section deals with the question of how selection procedures can be designed.

The design of selection procedures

It has already been noted that the design of selection procedures is a neglected topic in the literature on personnel selection. The only model that found widespread application is the "classical model" which dates back to Thorndike (1949). It comprises steps such as: analyzing the job, choosing criteria to predict, choosing predictors, carrying out a validation study, and composing a predictive test battery. Since it is confined to the predictive function the model is not suitable for the design of selection procedures as a whole. Roe (1984, 1989) has proposed to design selection procedures according to design methodology as developed in the technical sciences (Eekels, 1983; Roozenburg & Eekels, 1991). This opens the possibility to design procedures that cover the whole set of activities and tools implied in selection in a manner that satisfies the differing requirements put by the parties involved. In this way the design gets a systematic character and a recurrent evaluation indicates whether the procedure is acceptable or whether the design process should be continued.

A central notion in design methodology is "design cycle" (Eekels, 1983). It embodies the idea that design activity should proceed in a certain way, following a cyclic sequence of steps. Here we present only the basic variant of the design cycle. By applying the design cycle notion to the several parts of the overall design process, more complex, nested models can be developed. In the case of a product that consists of various independent components, one can apply the basic cycle to each of the components, thus producing a higher order cycle model. The design cycle is a generic notion that can be applied to the design of any artifact. The description of steps given in Figure 2.1, based on Roe (1989), addresses the design of selection procedures.

The basic design cycle presented in Figure 2.1 entails the following steps:

1. *Definition of functions*
   As a first step, one should determine the functions which the selection procedure should fulfil in its given context. Generally speaking selection procedures should serve to collect relevant information, make predictions of performance, evaluate performance, take decisions, and finally inform people involved. These functions must be specified with reference to the particular case, for example the job of system analyst. Thus, the functions the procedure should fulfil are context-dependent. They may be different for procedures to be used within companies and those to be used in a consultancy agency. In order to identify the

TABLE 2.1

Steps in a simple selection procedure.

Steps	*Function*
Application letter	Information gathering
Interview with selection committee	Information gathering
Reference checks	Information gathering
Looking at data for making a prognosis	Prediction
Discussing candidates and making a choice	Decision making
Contacting the selected candidate	Information supply Negotiation
Talking about labour terms (wage, working hours etc.)	Negotiation
Medical examination of the candidate	Information gathering Prediction Decision
Writing to rejected candidates	Information supply

functions one should interview future users of the procedure, and other people that are involved.

2. *Analysis of requirements and constraints*
From the functions to be fulfilled one has to derive requirements that the procedure should meet. These may relate to the input data (what is and is not available), the prediction, the decision (or recommendation), the communication with the people involved, and so on. Furthermore the constraints should be specified. Usually there are limitations regarding time and use of resources, but there may be other constraints as well. For example, with regard to the nature and duration of the transformation process, the interface to organizations overall employment policies, ethical standards, and so on. In principle the requirements and constraints should be set by the future users of the procedures, and other people involved. They belong to the conceptual world of the organization, not to that of the selection specialist. The selection specialist however, can assist to operationalize the requirements and constraints into design criteria. The result of this step may be written down in a document, called the "programme of requirements".

3. *Synthesis*
The next step is making a design, i.e. creating a preliminary selection procedure or adapting an existing procedure in such a way that it can fulfil the desired functions while staying within the limits of the constraints. Synthesis is essentially a creative activity, as the solution that is produced cannot be derived from available knowledge by deduction. However, it certainly requires an intensive use of both substantive knowledge about people and their behaviour, as well as methodological knowledge about tools and techniques, and designing as such (choosing or constructing elements, assembling parts, etc.). The result of synthesis is a draft description of the selection procedure.

4. *Simulation*
This step consists of testing the operational,

FIGURE 2.1

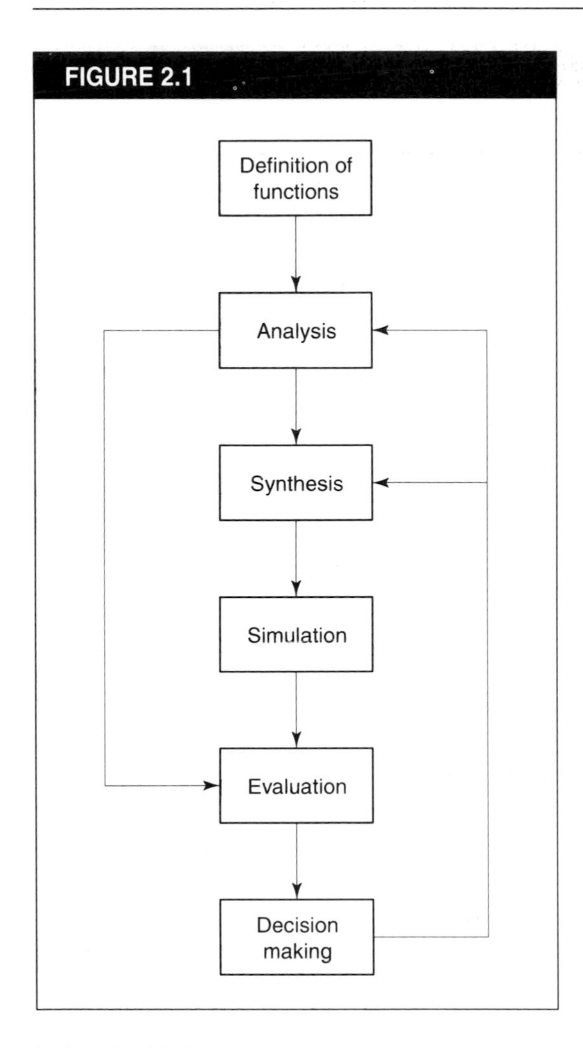

Basic cycle of design.

predictive, and economic properties of the selection procedure, i.e. duration, capacity, validity, effectiveness, utility and cut-off scores, and so on. Simulation can either be done on an empirical basis by running experimental try-outs, such as validation, or by using models. Examples of simulation models are the Taylor-Russell tables, the Curtis and Alf tables, and the Cronbach-Gleser formulae for estimating utility (see e.g. Roe, 1983). The result is laid down in so-called "specifications".

5. *Evaluation*
   Once the properties of the selection procedure are known, one can proceed to assess their value for the user, taking the requirements and constraints as a reference point. This step should answer the question whether the procedure as a whole is or is not satisfactory. The result of this step is a judgement about the value of the proposed procedure.
6. *Decision making*
   Finally, a decision has to be made, either accepting the selection procedure for operational use, or rejecting it. In case of rejection one may continue with step 3 (synthesis), trying to modify and thereby improve the previous solution. Eventually, when errors or insufficiencies in the programme of requirements and constraints show up, one may return to step 2 (analysis) and reformulate requirements and constraints first. When the proposed design has finally been accepted it should still be elaborated in manuals, directions, tools, materials, forms, personnel specifications and so on.

The cycle as described here shows that designing is a combination of a reductive process and a deductive process (Eekels, 1983). The "best" solution cannot simply be found by deduction from existing knowledge. One first has to generate a number of possible solutions (reduction), of which there can be many, before testing them in a deductive way. As it is not certain that an acceptable solution can be found in one single run, it is necessary to *iterate*, i.e. to return to the synthesis or even to the analysis, and have another trial. Central in the design process is a "programme of requirements". Some examples of items which can figure in a programme of requirements are given in Table 2.2.

In the personnel selection literature of the last 15 years much attention has been given to the notion of "utility". It is seen as one of the most important standards for evaluating a selection procedure. This is probably the reason why many models have been published for estimating the accumulated utility, i.e. the utility accruing from a series of decisions taken on the basis of a particular selection procedure (e.g. Boudreau, 1983a, 1983b; Cronshaw & Alexander, 1985; Schmidt et al., 1979; also Boudreau, 1989). We

TABLE 2.2

Some items from a programme of requirements.

Requirements

The procedure shall be suitable for higher commercial jobs.

Job requirements the candidates shall minimally meet are: . . .

The procedure shall yield candidates who keep performing well under stressful conditions.

The procedure shall provide tangible recommendations for the candidates' career opportunities.

A minimal number of suitable candidates shall be rejected.

Candidates with improper expectations about the job shall be identified as quickly as possible and removed from the file.

The final decision about admission shall reside with the immediate supervisor.

Candidates must get a clear picture of the job and how they are going to be selected.

Constraints

Data on the candidates shall be treated with full confidentiality.

Such data shall be destroyed within one month after the moment of collection.

Candidates shall have the opportunity to check the advance of the selection process.

It shall be possible to take decisions within one week.

Candidates shall receive a confirmation of their application within . . . days.

The total gain of selection according to the procedure during the first two years shall not be lower than the total costs of recruitment and selection.

The costs of selection shall be less than ECU 500 per candidate.

Candidates from minority groups shall not be discriminated against.

Candidates shall have the opportunity to read the report on their psychological assessment before the final decision is made.

consider the emphasis on utility to be appropriate provided that this notion is defined broadly and not confined to financial gain. Our example of the "programme of requirements" shows that there are many facets of selection which are not covered by financial utility.

The design cycle is a *model* intended as a tool for a designer or design team. The implicit assumption, however, is that several others can be involved in the design process. There should be at least a "commissioner", possibly a manager, a personnel department, or a consultancy bureau, on whose behalf the design is being made. Often there is also a group of potential users, like selection psychologists or personnel officers, whom we will refer to as "selectors". Other people or organizations can be involved as well: managers who call for selection advice, candidates, labour unions, government bodies. The division of roles implied in the design cycle is the following:

- The commissioner sets the goal of the design; together with users and other stakeholders he (she) points out the requirements and constraints; he (she) evaluates the outcomes of the design, and takes a decision about acceptance or rejection.
- The designer assists in all this; he (she) elaborates the requirements and constraints into criteria, takes care of synthesis and simulation—the actual core of the sign activity; he (she) organizes and monitors the whole process and provides adequate documentation during all phases.

Generally speaking, the success of the design process is dependent upon the interplay between designer, commissioner, users and other stakeholders. This also holds for the domain of personnel selection, where practice provides numerous examples of "design errors": psychometric procedures that are difficult to use by users (psychologists), commissioners (heads of personnel departments or psychological consultancies) changing their mind about how to select, customers (departments or firms) which do not get the right answer to their questions about future employees, candidates who are dissatisfied about the way in which they have been treated, including discrimination. But it should be recalled that systematic design of procedures according to the design approach has hardly found application yet.

There have been a number of publications describing a straightforward application of design methodology in psychological selection. Roe (1989) describes the general principles and an application to the redesign of existing procedures in a psychological consultancy. In a study by Ridderbos (1993) the development of a selection procedure for process operators has been described. Koh (1994) has described the development of a decision support system for personnel selection using the design approach.

PREDICTION OF WORK PERFORMANCE

Since the aim of personnel selection is to ensure a certain level of employees' performance in a future job or career, prediction is a crucial function that any selection procedure should fulfil. Prediction means deriving expectations about future events from current data—in our case deriving expectations about future work performance—from characteristics currently displayed by individuals. In the selection literature, variables describing current characteristics are called "predictors", while variables describing performance are referred to as "criteria". Performance should be understood to have two meanings: the activity shown by people when performing work roles, and the results of those activities (Roe, 1996b). Formal selection procedures use "prediction models" to make predictions about criteria from predictor information (Roe, 1983, p. 176). As we will discuss later, clinical prediction does without such models. It derives statements about future performance in a more direct, judgmental way.

The next section first presents two principles for prediction which underlie often used prediction models. Then a brief description is given of the development of prediction models and their application. Finally, a list of instruments is provided that can be used for assessing the characteristics of candidates.

Prediction principles

The psychology of selection gives us two principles for scientific prediction: the "trait approach" and the "behaviour generalization approach". They are also referred to as "sign approach" and "sample approach" (Wernimont & Campbell, 1968).

The first approach starts from the assumption that there exist a number of well-established relationships between people's traits and their activity, laid down in psychological laws. It is based on the "deductive-nomological" principle (DN-principle) from theory of science (Stegmüller, 1974). When, for a given set of people, a certain law states that a relationship exists between a characteristic **A** and a certain type of behaviour **E**, one can deduct from this law the prognostic proposition that a person who possesses characteristic **A** will show behaviour **E**. For a number of reasons this principle cannot be applied to selection situations in this simple form. First of all, the relationships between predictors and criteria are typically probabilistic rather than deterministic. This implies that knowing a person's score on a predictor variable one can only make an inference about his or her criterion score with a particular probability, but not with certainty. Moreover, traits and characteristics of behaviour cannot be ascertained directly but have to be represented by means of measurement methods. Thus, personality traits are commonly assessed by means of tests. Finally, one must specify the laws invoked and the data used in order to avoid logical contradictions. Such a contradiction would appear when one test would lead to the prediction of a good performance of a person, while another test would predict a poor performance.

The following variant of the DN-principle avoids these problems (see Roe, 1983, p. 21):

w : (x) (Ax ~ Ex;p)
h1: (x) (Ax ↔ ax)
h2: (x) (Ex ↔ ex)
ax
----
ex
P(ex|ax, w, h1, h2) = p

The equation gives a probabilistic behaviour law defining a relationship between the presence of a characteristic **A** and activity **E** for all persons **x**, and two operationalization (or observation) hypotheses **h1** and **h2** according to which **A** is expressed in an observable characteristic **a** and **E** in an observable behaviour **e**. When in a given person **x** the characteristic **a** is observed, the prediction follows that the person will display activity **e** with a certain probability **p**, being the conditional probability of **e** given the observation **ax**, the behavioural law and the two operationalization hypotheses. Figure 2.2 presents the principle of DN-prediction in a graphical form. When the law **w** and the operationalization hypotheses **h1** and **h2** are given, it follows that the expected behaviour can be predicted from the observed characteristic.

The sample approach rests on the principle of generalization. The general hypothesis is that when a person behaves in manner **E** at a given occasion $\mathbf{G_1}$ defined by time and place, it is concluded that he or she will behave in an identical manner **E** on another occasion $\mathbf{G_i}$ at another time and place but belonging to the same universe. There is a generalization from behaviour observed in a certain sample (of situations!) to a universe or another sample drawn from it. For this reason one also speaks about the "domain-sample principle" (DS-principle). The operationalization of the sample is referred to as "work sample". Figure 2.3 gives a graphical representation of the principle. There is an obvious analogy with the model in Figure 2.2, but now the prediction is based upon a relationship defined by the sample's representativeness to the universe of situations. In addition it is assumed that both the universe and the sample are operationalized by means of tasks. Once all this is given, observations of behaviour at certain tasks can be used to predict the behaviour in the universe of tasks, i.e. the job.

The two approaches differ in the underlying epistemological base. The trait approach relates a durable property of the person (something a person *has*) to his or her activity (something the person *does*). The behaviour generalization approach does without the notion of trait but relates behaviour to behaviour (something the person *does* to something else he or she *does*). This is considered as an advantage since there is a smaller conceptual distance between the predictor and the criterion, something which might result in a better prediction. This idea is supported by the finding that instruments based on this approach, so-called "content oriented devices", typically obtain higher predictive validities than tests measuring traits (e.g. Schmitt & Noe, 1986).

A point of similarity is that both approaches assume behaviour to be stable, an assumption which is indispensable for making predictions, i.e. bridging the time interval between the "here-and-now" in which the candidate is being assessed and the "there-and-later" of the work situation. In the first approach the stability is implied in the notion of trait, which presupposes transsituational and temporal constancy of behaviour (Roe, 1981). The second approach makes the assumption that behaviour does not change as long as the situation does not change. This is a severe assumption which leads to the practical disadvantage that only that particular type of behaviour can be predicted which has been shown beforehand.

The development of prediction models

A prediction model is a representation of reality in terms of one or more predictors, one or more criteria and the relation(s) between them. It is used to generate a predictive statement about the criteria, on the basis of current information on the predictors. That statement can refer to the expected position on the criterion (point prediction) or to the likelihood that a certain point will be reached (probability prediction). Prediction models can take many different forms, dependent on the variables included, the type of relationship,

FIGURE 2.2

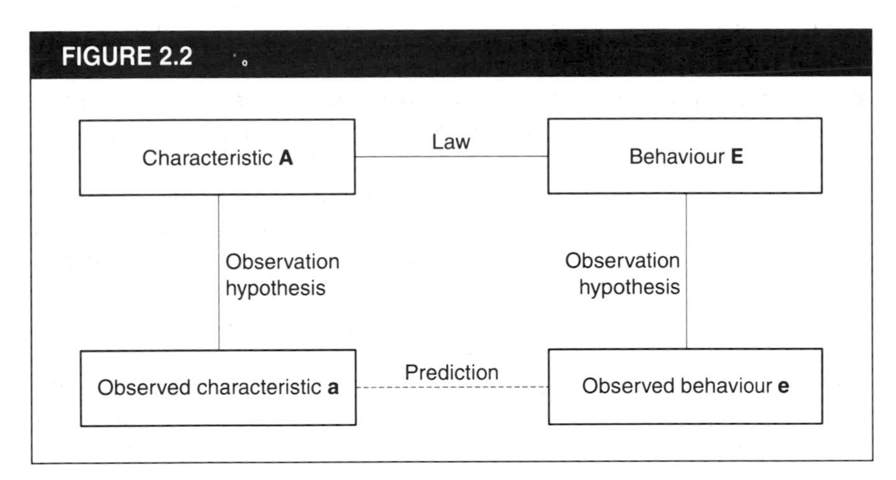

Prediction according to the DN-principle.

and the manner of formalizing it. Since the prediction model can be considered as an independent component of the selection procedure it can also be designed independently (see e.g. Campbell, 1983; Naylor, 1983). Roe (1984; also Greuter, 1989) has developed a stepwise method, which is linked to the design approach. The steps in this method are the following:

1. *Definition of the prediction problem*
   What is the goal of the prediction? What exactly is to be predicted, at which moment, and under which practical conditions?
2. *Identification of model requirements*
   Which requirements and constraints follow from the foregoing? How can they be operationalized in design criteria?
3. *Choice of the model's content*
   Which are the elements of the model, i.e. Which predictors and criteria are to be included?
4. *Choice of the model's structure*
   Which are the relations between the elements? Which elements relate to which? What is the direction (positive or negative) and strength of the relation?
5. *Choice of the model's format*
   How should the model be represented? e.g. in tabular form, regression formulas, algorithms, rules of thumb?
6. *Choice of the model's parameters*
   Which numerical values should be assigned to the various elements and their relations? e.g. means, variances, intercorrelations, regression constants and weights.
7. *Evaluation of the model against the design criteria*
   To what degree does the model under

FIGURE 2.3

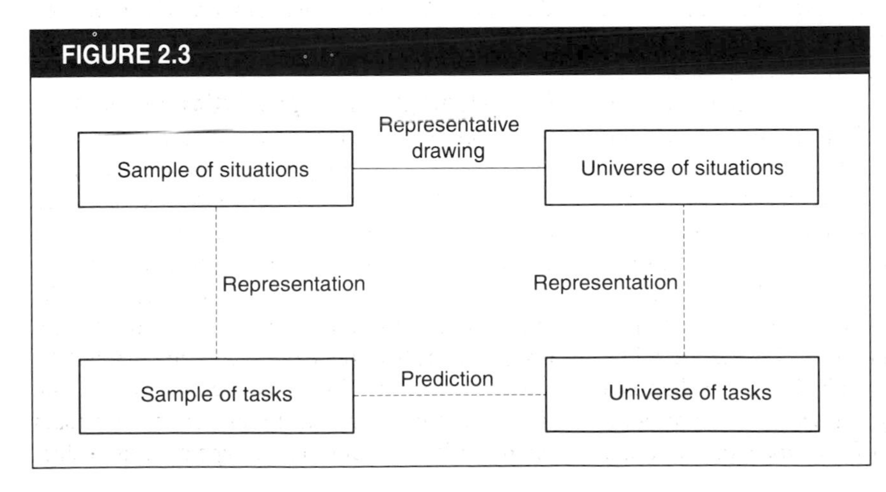

Prediction according to the DS-principle.

construction meet the criteria set beforehand?

8. *Decision on acceptance or rejection*
Is the prediction model acceptable or should it be revised?

Figure 2.4 gives two graphical examples of prediction models. The first model is a simple linear model with one predictor and one criterion variable, the second model is a non-linear model with two predictors and one criterion. This latter model is a so-called "moderator model". Prediction models are often expressed in algebraic form. The predicted criterion score Y' is expressed as function of a number of predictor variables X_i by means of a regression formula. The regression formulas for the two examples presented above are: $Y' = A + BX$ and $Y' = A + X_1X_2$.

Best known are prediction models in the format of a multiple linear regression formula:

$$Y' = A + B_1X_1 + B_2X_2 + B_iX_i + B_mX_m.$$

This model embraces one criterion and a set of m predictors. There are linear relationships expressed in correlations. The parameters of the model are the constant A and the weights B_i. The predictive validity of the model is determined by correlating the predicted scores Y' with the actual criterion scores Y in a sample of candidates.

It is important to note that the parameters of a prediction model can be established in a multitude of ways. The traditional approach is to determine them in a statistical manner, i.e. to estimate them by means of classical regression analysis in a sample of candidates who are actually being hired (see Thorndike, 1949). While undoubtedly the best known, this method is not the best. Unless all needed data are available, which cannot always be ensured, one inevitably runs into the problem of capitalization on chance. The regression parameters are optimal for the particular derivation sample but suboptimal for other samples (and the universe). The multiple correlation as calculated in the sample is consequently too high and shows "shrinkage" when the regression formula is cross-validated in other samples. A better approach is to use data from various samples and to determine the common regression formula using the "m group regression" method (e.g. Molenaar & Lewis, 1979). Another option is to employ so-called "biased" regression methods such as Stein regression and ridge regression (Darlington, 1978; Kennedy, 1988; Pruzek & Lepak, 1992). These methods allow a certain bias when estimating the parameters, which makes the resulting estimates more stable and the multiple correlation more realistic.

Much more simple are the so-called "a priori" methods for parameter estimation, in which the parameter values are chosen by the designer on the basis of published data or theoretical considerations. When using a linear model with multiple predictors good results are obtained with equal weights or weights that are approximately pro-

FIGURE 2.4

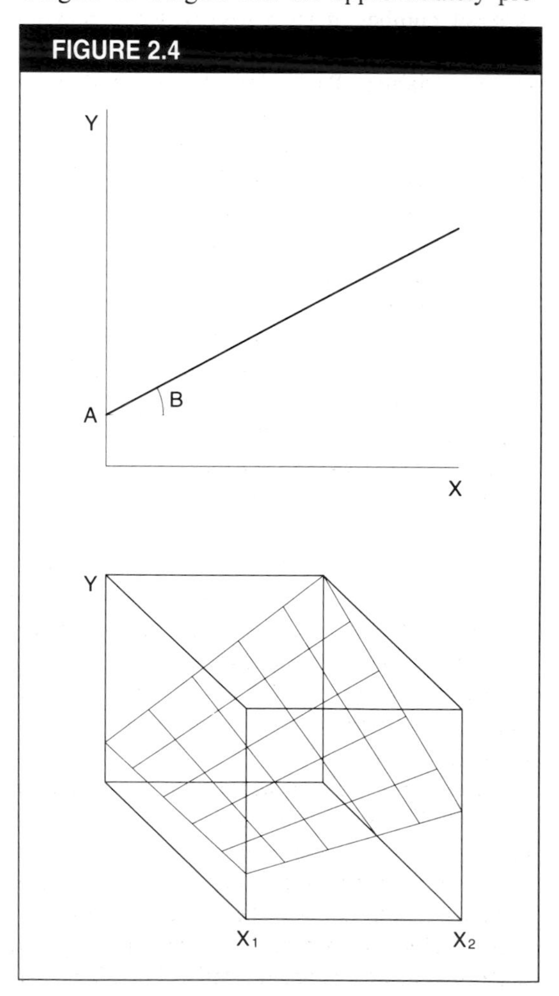

Two examples of prediction models. Bottom: moderator model of the type $Y' = A + BX_1X_2$.

portional to found (or estimated) predictive validities (Pruzek & Frederick, 1978; Wainer & Thissen, 1976). Because of the robustness of the linear model the predictive validity of the total model is only little lower compared to the use of optimal weights (Wainer, 1976). Since no capitalization on chance occurs, rational parameters don't have to be corrected afterwards. Moreover the predictive validity obtained with them shows only fluctuations, no shrinkage. For a more extensive treatment of these steps and methods of parameter estimation, refer to Roe (1983) and Greuter (1988, 1989).

Methods and techniques

A great number of methods and techniques are available for operationalizing predictor and criterion variables. Psychological tests and rating scales are well known examples. The discipline of "psychometrics" has taught us not to consider measurements with such tools as pure indicators of the person's "true" condition or behaviour, but rather as approximations containing a certain degree of error. Generally a distinction is being made between "constructs" and "measures" for operationalizing these or, to quote De Groot (1961), between "constructs as intended" and "constructs as measured". It is important to note the difference between these two types of constructs. As result of an inadequate choice of items, the content of the measure can deviate from what one intended to measure. In such a case one speaks about impaired "construct validity". A set of poorly phrased questions or answer categories can lead to large measurement errors, or deviations from the person's "true score". In this case one speaks about limited "reliability" of the instrument. Often these two types of problems appear at the same time.

Theory of science makes a distinction which is relevant for the field of personnel selection. It distinguishes between "theoretical constructs", which are seen as the building blocks of theories (e.g. traits, skills), and "empirical constructs", which refer to empirical phenomena (e.g. the performance of a particular task). The distinction resembles that between the trait approach and the behaviour-generalization approach mentioned before. It is of importance since it shows a difference in the scope of the two types of construct, which is wider for theoretical constructs than for empirical constructs. Moreover, there is practical difference: theoretical constructs refer to latent attributes of people, which can only be inferred from tests and other measurement instruments. Empirical constructs typically refer to a particular universe or domain of observable behaviour. In the case of empirical constructs the relationship between the "construct as measured" and the "construct as intended" can therefore be seen as the relationship between the sample and the universe. The representativeness of this sample is commonly designated as "content validity", which at the same time can be considered as a form of "construct validity".

The distinction between construct and measure should be carefully kept in mind when choosing methods and techniques for selection. The score on an intelligence test does not show the person's real intelligence, neither does the rated effort at work show the person's real effort. The recommended course of action includes two steps: first, one decides which constructs one wants to use, i.e. conceptual criteria and conceptual predictors. Next, one picks the tools for operationalizing these constructs: operational criteria and predictors.

Step 1

Identifying *conceptual criteria* is a widely discussed issue in selection psychology (e.g. Barret et al., 1985; Drenth, 1976; Fleishman & Quaintance, 1984; Guion, 1991; Ronan & Prien, 1971; Smith, 1976; Thorndike, 1949). The necessary information can be obtained by means of job analysis (Algera & Greuter, 1989; McCormick, 1979). In case of prediction according to the DN-principle one can profit from job analysis methods that analyze the work directly in terms of required traits, such as the Task Abilities Scales (TAS; Fleishman & Quaintance, 1984) and the Threshold Trait Analysis method by Lopez et al. (1981). One might also use "work oriented" methods that support the translation from tasks into personal characteristics, such as the USTES method (United States Training and Employment Service, 1972) and the Occupational Analysis Inventory (OAF; Cunningham et al., 1983). Serious critique (e.g. Harvey & Hayes, 1986; Smith & Hakel, 1979) has made the Position Analysis Questionnaire (PAQ; McCormick et al., 1972) lose much of its popularity. In case of prediction according to the DS-principle one would need methods that give a good description of tasks and task components, like the Systems Task Vocabulary (Miller, 1973) or the task-elements-method (Guion, 1978).

In a number of publications Schmidt and Hunter (e.g. Schmidt & Hunter, 1977; also Pearlman et al., 1980) have argued that detailed methods for job analysis are not required since they do not result in more valid prediction models than more simple, general methods. We consider their position to be based on questionable methods, both with regard to validity generalization (discussed later) and the data set used (validities against overall criteria in very heterogeneous job groups).

Conceptual predictors are to be chosen on the basis of empirical and/or theoretical knowledge about predictor-criterion relationships. Older publications providing results of empirical studies are: Ghiselli (1966, 1973), Lent et al. (1971), Lawshe and Balma (1966), Guion (1965), Bemis (1968) and Asher and Sciarrino (1974). More recent reviews are those by Arvey and Campion (1982; interviews), Reilly and Chao (1982; various predictors), Campion (1983; selection for physically demanding jobs), Sackett and Harris (1984; honesty tests), Hunter and Hunter (1984; various predictors), Schmitt et al. (1984; various predictors), Gaugler et al. (1987; Assessment Centres), Reilly and Israelski (1988) and Robertson and Downs (1989; trainability tests).

During the last decade it has become customary to process validity data by meta-analysis and in particular by the technique known as "validity generalization". This technique, which has been developed by Schmidt & Hunter (1977, 1981) and has been described in more detail by Hunter et al. (1982) and Hunter & Schmidt (1990), offers the opportunity to classify validity data, to test the homogeneity of validity within a given data set, and to correct for a number of "artifacts", thus producing an estimate of a predictor's "true validity". The "artifacts" include restriction of range and unreliability of the criterion and/or predictors. The effects of small sample size are taken into account as well. The operations prescribed by the technique result invariably in one single "true validity" estimate for the predictor-criterion relationship which is usually higher than the raw validities. In our view the technique suffers from a number of conceptual and methodological shortcomings which limit its usefulness and impair the interpretation of estimated "true validities" (see also Algera et al., 1984; Burke, 1984; James et al., 1986; Tenopyr, 1989). The hope is for a new generation of validity generalization techniques which overcomes these limitations (for some proposals see Erez et al., 1996; Jansen et al., 1986; Raju et al., 1991).

It should be kept in mind that the data offered by the sources mentioned above may have lost much of their value, since the empirical domain to which they refer has shown dramatic changes during the last few decades. For example, there have been substantial changes in the nature of work tasks covered by the same or similar job titles, the qualifications and motivational base of the work force have changed, and so have the standards by which management evaluates employee performance (Roe, 1996a). This means that one should not rely on published validity data without serious scrutiny of the setting from which they come. It may also imply that the use of validity generalization techniques will remain restricted to exceptional cases where no change has occurred and large numbers of validity data are available. In all other cases one may have to opt for theoretical methods of analysis which go into the psychological processes and requirements during the execution of tasks (e.g. Koubek et al., 1994; Roe & Zijlstra, 1991).

Step 2

The second step, the operationalization of conceptual criteria and predictors, is based on knowledge of the specific methods and techniques. When dealing with theoretical constructs (e.g. traits, performance dimensions) one has to examine each instrument's construct validity and reliability. In case of empirical constructs (e.g. task performance) the instrument's content validity and reliability are crucial. When time and resources suffice, new instruments can be developed.

Validity and reliability are not the only facets to take into account. Data on predictive validities may be useful as well when focusing on specific criterion-predictor relationships. The aforementioned sources can be used again, but now with a focus on the particular instruments and without abstraction towards the level of underlying constructs. At this stage one should also look at differences between the sexes and ethnic categories, since these may constitute a source of discrimination (e.g. Schmitt & Noe, 1986). Practical aspects of use, such as time and costs of administration of the instruments, or the level of expertise needed in processing and interpretation, are important points to consider as well.

The literature on methods and techniques for predicting performance is very extensive indeed. Here we will confine ourselves to a brief review and refer to other publications.

Operational criteria can be divided into three classes:

1. *Ratings*
   The rating is either given directly on a graphical or numerical scale, or inferred from a rank ordering of subjects.
2. *Objectified measures*[2]
   Again ratings are being given, but the scales carry specific anchors that have been found in a preceding analysis, and there are instructions for limiting the opportunity for making certain types of errors (e.g. forced choice).
3. *Objective measures*
   Performance data are gathered objectively, using production records, administrative records, or bench mark tasks (hands-on testing).

More information can be found in Roe (1983), Landy et al. (1983), Landy and Farr (1983), Latham (1986), and Landy and Rastegary (1989).

Table 2.3 lists types of *operational predictors*, divided according to the principle of prediction they best match, DN or DS. Many methods can be used in connection with both principles. The Assessment Centre embodies a straightforward combination of the two. Generally speaking, ability tests, job samples and Assessment Centres show the highest predictive validities, while personality tests and interviews have a limited predictive power. Much depends, however, on the job, the nature of the criteria, the specific instruments, and the way in which they are deployed. For example, structuring the interview raises its reliability and thereby its predictive capacity (Conway et al., 1995). Some recent publications have pointed at the potential of personality tests to add to the quality of prediction when used in a sophisticated way, i.e. when aiming at particular criteria and leaving aside irrelevant scales and questions (Furnham, 1992; Robertson, 1994). Refer to Schmitt and Noe (1986), Smith and Robertson (1989), Trost and Kirchenkamp (1993), and the publications mentioned earlier for more extensive information.

For many years it has been suggested to include characteristics of the *work situation* as a predictor in the prediction model. Research by Greuter (1988) has opened the opportunity to identify and operationalize relevant situational characteristics. This is done by means of the "critical incidents" technique developed by Flanagan (1954). Applying it to work situations several performance enhancing and performance inhibiting factors are detected. The work situations in which candidates are to be placed are rated by employees who are familiar with them and entered in the prediction equation.

DECISION MAKING ON A JOB AND CAREER

Selection problems cannot be solved without taking a decision about admitting a candidate or about which of several candidates to accept and which to reject. Several types of decision may be distinguished. First of all decisions about admittance (external or entry selection) and decisions about a career (internal selection). Another distinction is between selection decisions proper, i.e. decisions in terms of acceptance or rejection, and placement decisions, i.e. the allocation of candidates to various positions. The distinctive feature of decisions is a choice from a number of options or actions. If one requires selection decisions to be *rational* (Roe, 1983, p. 21), the choice should meet certain standards. In this section we present a number of methods for taking decisions. First we

TABLE 2.3

Review of (operational) predictors.

DN-principle	*DS-principle*
Tests/Probes	
— Ability tests	— Work samples
— Personality tests	— Situational tests (cases)
— Interest & value tests	— Proficiency tests
— Motor tests	— Knowledge tests
— Sensory tests	— Trainability tests
— Tests for mental functions	
Interviews	
— Trait oriented interview	— Criterion oriented interview (situational interview, behavioural consistency interview)
Rating	
of potential	**of performance**
— Self rating	— Peer rating
— Superior rating	— Superior rating
	— References
Biographical techniques	
— Trait-oriented biographical questionnaires	— Diplomas and grades
	— Application form
	— Performance-oriented biographical questionnaires (e.g. accomplishment record)
Assessment centre	

discuss principles for rational decision making in selection. Next, we will go into the design of "decision models". We will also discuss a specific application of decision models, i.e. the setting of cut-off scores. Finally, we will give a brief review of tools for supporting the decision process.

PRINCIPLES OF DECISION MAKING

Normative decision theory, which underlies what follows, starts from the idea that a standard for evaluating the adequacy of a choice can be found in the "utility" resulting from the actions one might take. The utility is a subjective value assigned by the decision maker, in our case someone acting on behalf of the organization. In cases where the effects of actions can be predicted with certainty, as in making a choice among given objects, the decision is not difficult to make. One has only to ascertain the utility of each option and chose the one with the highest utility. In making decisions about people, as in recruiting a candidate for a position in an organization, the effect of the choice is not certain at all. On the contrary, there is a fundamental uncertainty about the outcomes, which one tries to reduce by making predictions. In this kind of situation one needs to:

1. Distinguish between different "conditions" which might occur after the choice has been

made; e.g. the candidate appears to perform poorly, moderately, or well.
2. Account for the likelihood of each of these circumstances.

Decision theory offers the tools for this in the form of schemes for the analysis of decision situations and strategies for taking decisions. We refer to any particular combination of a decision scheme and a decision strategy as a "*decision model*". Decision models provide exhaustive descriptions of actions (options) and circumstances, as well as indicate the utilities and probabilities of each combination. Figure 2.5 presents a well known example from the classical selection literature. It makes a distinction between acceptance and rejection as actions, and between suitability and unsuitability of candidates as circumstances. The four resulting combinations are commonly referred to as: "true positives", "true negatives", "false positives" and "false negatives". One can assign a utility to each of these four outcomes, for example a value between −10 and +10, or a figure on any other type of scale, to express their (un)attractiveness or (un)desirability. Furthermore one can specify the probability that the candidates will appear suitable or unsuitable. In case there is only one candidate this chance is independent of the decision. It follows from the prediction model (see p. 11). In the figure we have inserted fictitious values for the utility (u_{ij}) and the probability of the outcomes (p_j). Decision models are often more complex than the one presented here. How they may look will be discussed in the next section.

Decision strategies are rules for combining utilities and probabilities and for taking a decision, i.e. for determining the best option. There are several possible strategies (e.g. Radford, 1975):

1. Maximization of expected utility (MEU). This means that utilities of the outcomes are weighted with the probabilities of the outcomes and that the choice is for the action with the highest expected utility.
2. Maximization of minimum utility (Maximin). This is equivalent to reducing loss: one compares the actions with regard to the lowest utility and chooses for the action for which this value is highest.
3. Maximization of maximum utility (Maximax). This corresponds to betting for the highest possible gain: one compares actions with regard to the highest utility and chooses for the action for which this value is largest.
4. Minimization of regret (Minimax regret). This is a safe strategy: the actions are being compared with regard to the difference between their highest and lowest utility and one chooses for the action for which this value is minimal.

The strategy most often opted for in personnel selection is *Maximization of expected utility* (e.g.

FIGURE 2.5

Actions	Circumstances: Unsuitable	Circumstances: Suitable
Acceptance	false positive $u_{11} = -8$	true positive $u_{12} = +5$
Rejection	true negative $u_{21} = +2$	false negative $u_{22} = -3$
Probabilities	$p_1 = .19$	$p_2 = .81$

Example of a simple decision scheme.

Cronbach & Gleser, 1965). Since it gives the best results in the long run, it is an attractive strategy for larger organizations which can balance cases of bad and good luck. For smaller organizations or when dealing with particular jobs, it may be better to reduce the risk of a poor outcome, or rather bet for a great gain, and therefore to adopt another strategy.

The design of a decision model

The previous section shows that a decision model can be seen as a representation of reality in terms of possible actions and their outcomes, employed to make a decision about the action to take. Like the prediction model the decision model is a distinct part of the selection procedure which can be designed independently. The design can be carried out in an analogous way. A stepwise method follows (see also Roe & Greuter, 1991).

1. *Definition of the decision problem*
   What is the goal of the decision? What should be decided about and to what purpose? Are the decisions to be made individual decisions about singular candidates or rather collective decisions affecting a group of candidates at the same time?
2. *Identification of model requirements*
   Which requirements and constraints follow from the forgoing? How can they be operationalized in design criteria?
3. *Choice of the model's content*
   Which are the elements of the model, i.e. which utility dimensions, criteria and actions are to be included?
4. *Choice of the model's structure*
   Which are the relations between the elements? How do utilities relate to criteria and actions (utility functions)? In which way is the optimization being determined (strategy)?
5. *Choice of the model's format*
   How should the model be represented? e.g. in tabular form, algorithms, decision rules?
6. *Choice of the model's parameters*
   Which numerical values should be assigned to the various elements and their relations? e.g. means, variances, parameters of utility functions?
7. *Evaluation of the model against the design criteria*
   To what degree does the model under construction meet the criteria set beforehand?
8. *Decision on acceptance or rejection*
   Is the decision model acceptable or should it be revised?

It should be clear at the outset that schemes of the 2×2 type are too simple for many decision situations in personnel selection. Schemes that allow for a continuous criterion scale, with several degrees of suitability, are more appropriate. The relationship between the criterion and the utility variable is expressed as a *utility function*, which can take on many different forms. The simplest form is the linear utility function, which depicts the utility as proportionate to the performance on the criterion. Other well-known utility functions are the threshold function, the normal-ogive function and the parabolic function (see Figure 2.6). The functions for acceptance and rejection often have an opposite sign.

An important distinction is between models for individual and collective decisions (also called "institutional" decisions; (e.g. Drenth & Sijtsma, 1990). The models show a great degree of similarity but they differ on a number of points:

1. Individual decision models depend on predictions about the performance of single individuals, while collective models depend on the performance in a selected group as a whole. This difference is reflected in the distinction between so-called "individual and institutional expectancy tables" (Lawshe & Bolda, 1958).
2. Individual models serve to ascertain whether candidates, considered separately, qualify for being selected or not. Collective models serve to divide the group of candidates into a part that is being selected and a part that is not.
3. Individual models optimize the utility of a single decision, while collective models optimize the total accumulated utility of a number of decisions.

Another important distinction is between

FIGURE 2.6

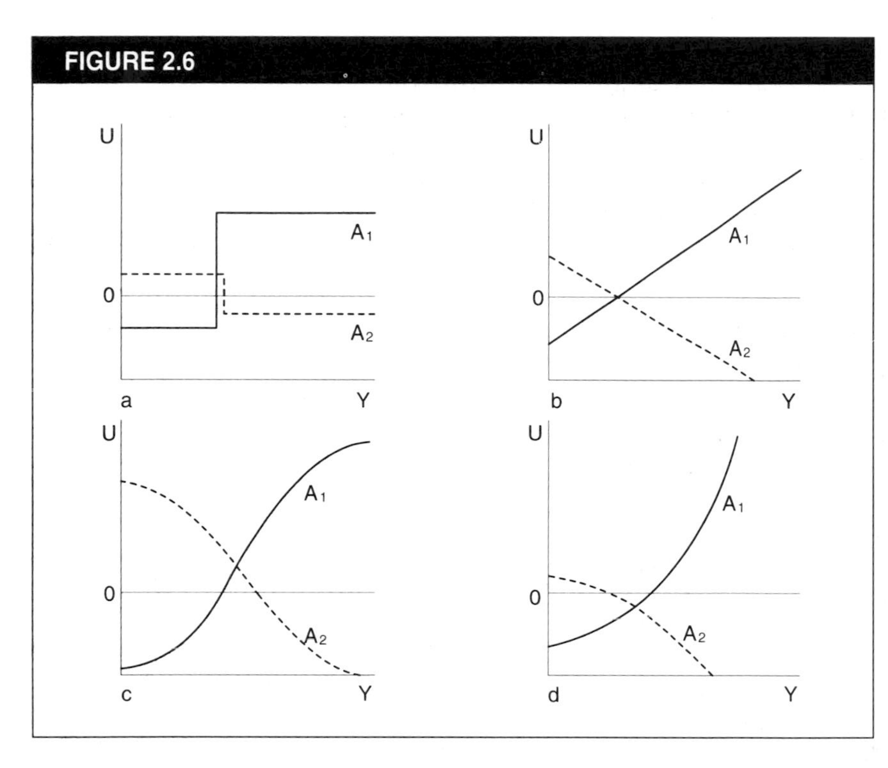

Four types of utility functions in graphical form (based on Roe, 1983);
a. threshold function;
b. linear function;
c. normal ogive function;
d. parabolic function.

models for single moment decisions and those for successive decision moments. In the latter case one also speaks about *sequential decision models.* In sequential models one finds the option of "going on to the next stage" in addition to rejection and acceptance, or options such as "check abilities" or "send to training programme". Each referral to a next stage opens a new set of options to chose from. In this way a whole series of nested outcomes is defined, and for each of which one has to specify the utility and (conditional) probability.

Setting cut-off scores

Decision models can be used to set cut-off scores. A cut-off score is a score on a predictor scale with which the scores of applicants can be compared. Candidates who score higher are admitted while those who score lower are rejected. In order to determine cut-off scores one needs models in which a prediction model has been incorporated. The elements of these models are: utilities, criteria, predictors and options. The cut-off score is set in such a way that the result of selection, as defined by the strategy, produces the highest expected utility.

The literature provides a great number of simplified models which make a direct link between predictors and utility. Such models rest on the assumption of a linear utility function, or a linear relationship between the criterion and the utility variable. Moreover, it is typically assumed that the utility functions for acceptance and rejection have the same form but an opposite sign, or that the utility of rejection is zero. Figure 2.7 demonstrates the principle of setting cut-off scores. It shows the expected utilities of acceptance and rejection, resulting from the use of a single predictor, for two different cases. The cut-off is locate at the point of intersection of the two lines showing the expected utility. In the first case there is a linear relationship between the X-score and the expected utility and there is a single cut-off score X_0, above which acceptance is preferable over rejection. In the second case the relationship is curvilinear and there are two cut-off scores. Between these scores acceptance is preferable over rejection.

A simple *graphical method* suited for individual decisions is the following (Stone & Kendall, 1956). One determines the frequency distributions of the predictor scores in two groups with satisfactory and unsatisfactory criterion scores. In case the

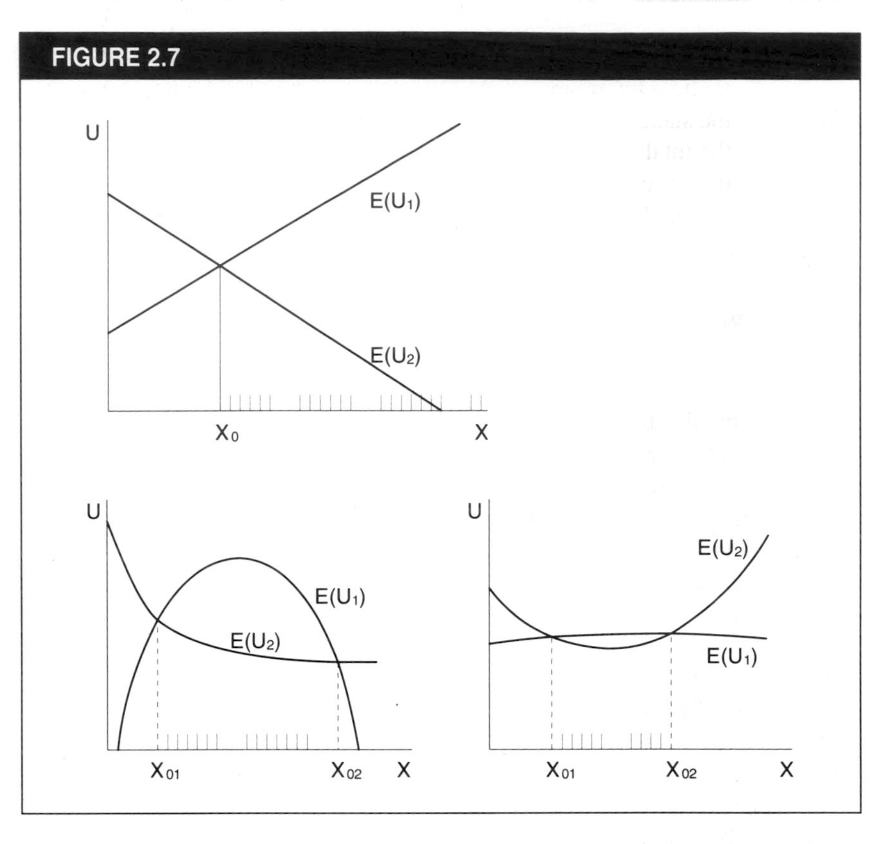

Two examples of deriving cut-off scores from expected utilities. Top: expected utilities of 'acceptance' and 'rejection', $E(U_1)$ and $E(U_2)$ as function of X, with cut-off X_o. Bottom: expected utilities of 'acceptance' and 'rejection', $E(U_1)$ and $E(U_2)$ as function of X, with cut-offs X_{01} and X_{02}.

groups are of equal size the cut-off score is at the point of intersection between the two distribution functions. The decision model underlying this method presupposes threshold utilities with an opposite sign for acceptance and rejection, or: $U_{11} = U_{22}$ and $U_{12} = U_{21}$.

Even more simple is the use of *formulas* that enable one to calculate the cut-off score if certain model parameters are given. Here we mention two formulas to calculate the cut-off score for collective decisions (X_o). The first formula has been described by Guilford (1965). The assumption of the underlying model regarding the utilities is the same as before. It is also assumed that predictor scores are normally distributed. The first formula reads as follows:

$$X_o = M + \left(\frac{Z.Y}{P.Q} \frac{S^2}{M_1 - M_2} \right)$$

In which:

M = the mean of the total group
S^2 = the variance of the total group
M_1 = the mean of X in the group with satisfactory performance
M_2 = the mean of X in the group with unsatisfactory performance
P = the proportion of persons in the group with satisfactory performance
Q = the proportion of persons in the group with unsatisfactory performance
Z = the abcis of the standard normal function corresponding to $P : Q$
Y = the ordinate corresponding to Z.

The second formula, given by Roe (1983), can be derived from a model presented by Cronbach and Gleser (1965). Linear but opposite utilities for acceptance and rejection are assumed, as well as normally distributed predictor scores. The formula reads:

$$X_o = \left(\frac{M(U_1) - M(U_2)}{r(XY)\ \{S(U_1) + S(U_2)\}} \right)$$

In which:

$M(U_1)$ = the mean utility of acceptance in the total group
$M(U_2)$ = the mean utility of rejection in the total group

$S(U_1)$ = the standard deviation of acceptance in the total group
$S(U_2)$ = the standard deviation of rejection in the total group
$r(XY)$ = the product-moment correlation between X and Y.

The literature provides several other formulas for determining cut-off scores. The reader will find a review in Roe (1983) and Cascio et al. (1988). It should be kept in mind that this kind of cut-off score is most easily applied when there are no constraints on the number of candidates to be selected; in other words in case of "*unlimited quota*". Since the use of an ideal cut-off score may result in a larger number of admission decisions than the organization can accommodate, it is not suitable for the case of a "*fixed quota*". Thus, when there is an upper or lower limit to the number of candidates to select (a situation often encountered in practice) another approach has to be followed. Often the so-called "*daily quota*" method is used, i.e. the candidates are rank-ordered according to the expected utility of acceptance (or acceptance minus rejection) and one selects as many people as are needed, beginning at the top of the list. The application of this method leads to a variation of the actual cut-off score over time, depending on the qualification level of the applicants. An alternative for organizations expecting sufficient candidates within a reasonable short time interval is to set a cut-off corresponding to a desired quota and to maintain it during that whole interval. This method is known as the method of *expected yield* (Thorndike, 1949). Other methods, including methods that influence the number of candidates by means of the recruitment process, will not be discussed here.

Tools for decision making

There are relatively few tools for supporting the decision-making process, in any case much less than for the prediction process. For establishing utility functions one may use scaling techniques that quantify decision-makers' judgements about the performance of accepted and rejected candidates. Such techniques have been discussed by Hull et al. (1973), Vrijhoff et al. (1983) and Lamers et al. (1992).

The formal methods which have been published in the literature, for example by Cronbach and Gleser (1965) avoid or reduce the problem of utility assessment by making simplifying assumptions. Typical assumptions are that for accepted candidates the utility is linearly related to the predictor score, and that the utility of rejection is zero. In cases where such assumptions are justified these models and the corresponding formulas are of great use in setting the cut-off score. In other cases they may lead to wrong outcomes, however. This makes a scrutiny of the assumptions in decision models a necessity.

During the last few years several computerized programmes for decision support have been developed and marketed. An example of such a system is SOS, developed by Koh (1994). It is too early to give a review of the usefulness of these programmes. Generally speaking, they may certainly help the adoption of decision theoretical principles in personnel selection.

CLINICAL METHODS

The use of selection procedures comprising prediction models and decision models is still rather exceptional. Much more common is the situation in which the selection expert makes gives a direct interpretation of available data about candidates and jobs, and arrives at a decision in a judgemental way. The exact course of this process is not very clear, but Koh (1994) shows that the thinking process of selection psychologists displays certain intuitive and evaluative episodes.

The popularity of the clinical approach in personnel selection cannot be explained from demonstrated results. The validity and benefit of clinical procedures are often questionable, while the lack of transparency and standardization limit their objectivity. One of the reasons given for the use of informal methods is that it takes *too much time and effort* to structure the prediction and decision-making process by means of formal methods. We consider this to be a point of misunderstanding at the side of practitioners, dating back to the 1950s when the development of selection models and procedures was still in its infancy. Many older selection psychologists believe that the development of a prediction model should be based on an empirical validation study, and that when the opportunities for conducting such a study are absent, clinical prediction is the only feasible alternative. The foregoing has made clear that this view is not longer adequate. Selection procedures can also be designed at a desk or behind a computer, using the theoretical and methodological knowledge that is presently available. And unlike what is commonly assumed, it can be done in a short amount of time, even for a selection situation that involves a single vacancy or candidate.

Another argument for using clinical selection methods is the *expertise* which the selection specialist is supposed to possess. It is argued that, in order to profit from this expertise the specialists should be allowed to follow their own way of collecting and interpreting information. An inconvenience is that this position is difficult to corroborate or disprove. Unlike in other domains, for example, chess, there is a lack of criteria for assessing the performance and hence for testing the expertise of the clinician. There are three sources of doubt concerning the expertise of selection specialists. First, there are studies in which identical data have been processed both formally and informally (see, for a review, Sawyer, 1966; also Roe, 1983). Informal methods did less well than formal methods with regard to predictive validity.

Second, there are studies of "paramorphic representation", the representation of the human reasoning process by a model (Wiggins, 1980). This type of research has shown that the complex reasoning of experts can be replaced by simple models which predict equally well or even better compared to the experts (e.g. Dawes, 1971, 1979).

Third, there are studies concerning the course of affairs in the classical selection interview. These studies are relevant because the interview is a clinical method in optima forma: data that are collected while conducting the interview are being processed in an informal manner. Research has shown that unless strict precautions are being taken the interview suffers from many shortcomings. The major conclusions are that the decision on the candidate is typically taken at an early stage of the interview, on the basis of a limited set of data, that the weights assigned to the information depend on incidental circumstances (moment in the interview, contrast effects), and that the results of the decision process diverge depending on the interviewer, or the match or mismatch between interviewer and interviewee (e.g. Schmitt, 1976; Webster, 1964; Wright, 1969; also Drenth, 1988; Roe, 1983).

Although all these research results can be considered as casting doubt on the expertise of the selection expert, we believe they rather point to the disadvantages of an unsystematic way of working. Our current interpretation is that many selectors do have a certain expertise, but that the visible effect of it is obliterated by a lack of rigorousness in their way of processing information.

Another reason for the popularity of clinical methods—one which might be more important than the reasons most often mentioned—could be called a "*cognitive ergonomic*" one. Clinical methods are compatible with an everyday manner of problem solving, they can be controlled by the selector, and they evoke a sense of certainty. They do possess a high level of "user-friendliness". The effort needed to apply them is less than is the case with formal methods, and the feeling of certainty gives the selector the impression of producing good results.

Thus it seems that there are several reasons for the widespread use of clinical methods, while at the same time they are subject to considerable doubt as far as their scientific base is concerned. We believe it is time to bridge the gap between theory and practice at this point. One way to achieve this (i.e. further research on cognitive processes of the selector) goes beyond the scope of this chapter. The other road is one of a selection practice based on a clinical approach but simultaneously relying on scientific principles and research findings. We will deal with this in the next section.

Development of a clinical procedure

We believe that the use of clinical methods in personnel selection may be justified, provided that three conditions are met:

1. That the selector is indeed an expert; i.e. possesses advanced knowledge of people

and their capacities, jobs and requirements, work activity and performance, and methods and effects of selection.

2. That the methods are sufficiently "user-friendly"; i.e. match with the world view (notions, strategies), the instruments, and the task environment of the selector.
3. That the way of working of the selection professional is sufficiently systematic; i.e. that activities follow a consequential strategy, that wherever possible methods are standardized, etc.

It is obvious that satisfying these requirements simultaneously and in a well-balanced manner is not an easy task to achieve. For example, if too much emphasis is placed on the requirement of user-friendliness, it may mean that there is not sufficient appeal to the professional's expertise, or that the flow of activity is not sufficiently systematic. In fact, a compromise is needed, which can only be found by careful balancing and probing. The expertise of the selector can be improved by means of training. Experience in selecting people is not a guarantee for expertise, since knowledge obtained in practice may be invalid and improper skills can be acquired. A significant finding by Carlson (1967) is that experienced interviewers do not make less errors than inexperienced interviewers.

A method that seems to sufficiently meet the requirements concerning user-friendliness and systematic action is offered by the design approach. Users deliver their contribution in the "programme of requirements" while science offers knowledge and tools for a methodic way of working. In designing the procedure one can largely rely on the same principles and methods that were discussed previously.

Prediction

An important discrepancy between the process of clinical judgement and the use of formal selection methods is the manner of making predictions and taking decisions. Think-aloud protocols show that the clinical process is a complex, segmented process in which the clinician creates images of the job and the candidate (image-building), evaluates data about the candidate, draws conclusions, conducts tests, seeks justifications and so on (Koh 1989, 1994). Two points are important to note:

1. First of all, predictions are not always made in an explicit way; the focus is often on the candidate at the moment of selection rather than on the candidate performing tasks in their future work environment.
2. When predictions are made, they are difficult to discriminate from decisions; both processes seem to be intertwined (see Carlson et al., 1971 on the selection interview).

From a methodological point of view it is desirable to complete the prediction process first. This can help to make sure that all relevant data on the candidate are taken into account, and also that the needed attention is being given to the criteria at which the prediction should be oriented. In other words, the assessment becomes more complete and more focused on the particular selection problem. Moreover, one minimizes the risk of premature conclusions known from studies on the selection interview.

The prediction itself can be made more systematic by using the aforementioned prediction principles. If one opts for the *trait approach* (DN principle), one should focus on traits that are crucial for success. The selector has the task of determining which observations, answers to interview questions, biographical data or test results can be considered as valid indications of these traits, and to collect the required information. Next, these data can be used to generate predictions. The way in which this happens can be left to the selector. The selector's reasoning process can be adapted to the characteristics of the candidates and the situation. A suitable strategy here is "predictor comparison". One compares the predictor scores of candidates and establishes who scores best. As long as there are monotonous relationships between the predictors and the criterion, this technique gives the right conclusion concerning the job performance to be expected. The strategy can also be applied when there is only a single candidate. In this case one makes, in an analogous way, a comparison between that candidate and an ideal candidate of whom one has formed an image beforehand.

The *behaviour generalization approach* (DS principle) opens the possibility to base the prediction on the candidate's earlier work career. The selector looks for similarities between what the candidate has been doing in the past and what is required in the future. One speaks about the strategy of "criterion analogies": conclusions concerning the future performance of the candidate are in fact based on the analogy between the former job and the job to be fulfilled. In order to apply this method one has, of course, to possess the appropriate data, gathered by means of job samples, biographical inventories, interviews, reference checks, and so on.

The application of these approaches, which can of course be combined, can be supported and made more systematic by the use of schemes in which the relevant data can be noted down. Figures 2.8 and 2.9 show examples of such schemes. These kinds of tools can be designed by the selection professional according to their own preference. Most important is that they help to shape the prediction process and to explicate what is happening.

Decision making

A limitation of clinical methods in selection is that the decision process tends to remain implicit. The selection professional does take the consequences of hiring the candidate into consideration, but the evaluation of these consequences and way of dealing with uncertainty remain largely hidden. This creates the risk that the selector introduces their own standards and preferences instead of following the interests of the organization. And it also creates room for arbitrariness.

These problems can be circumvented by introducing decision theoretic principles. First of all, an analysis of the decision situation is needed, i.e. the possible outcomes of selection and courses of action should be identified, and the utility of the various outcomes should be determined. Furthermore, a decision strategy has to be chosen. Once these steps have been taken, one can look at the predictions about the candidates that were made at the previous stage and use them as input for a new reasoning process that leads to a conclusion about whom to select. For this purpose the predictions must be cast in the form of "probability predictions". This means that the selector should not merely indicate how they expect the candidate to perform, but rather also how likely it is that the candidate will perform in that particular way. An illustration of the way in which the selection professional can proceed when taking decisions is given in the last section. There one also finds an integrated scheme which can serve as a practical tool.

An integrated scheme for personnel selection

Earlier (Roe, 1983) we have published a scheme that can be used as a framework for the design of a clinical selection procedure. It actually covers two parts, one relating to prediction, the other relating to decision making. Table 2.4 shows the scheme,

FIGURE 2.8

Job components	Criteria	Predictors	Findings

Scheme to support clinical prediction (1st example).

FIGURE 2.9

Tasks	Requirements	Qualifications	Findings

Scheme to support clinical prediction (2nd example).

filled with some exemplary data showing how it can be used in the case of selection of a single candidate.

The selector first notes (in column A) the relevant criteria for the job and (in column B) which predictive data they intend to use in order to predict each of the criteria. When examining the candidate the findings are noted down (in column C). This can either be done in words, or numbers, or—as shown in the example—with a +/– code. From what has been noted down so far the selector can derive a prognosis concerning each of the criteria. This prognosis is expressed as a subjective probability estimate (in column D). In our example three criterion levels are distinguished (low, average, high), to each of which a probability estimate is assigned. The steps the selector goes through when filling the columns A through D correspond to the design and application of a prediction model. The difference is that the selector has great freedom in their way of gathering data and drawing conclusions. Thus it is possible to add observations that were not envisaged and to take them into account in making the prognosis.

The result of the prediction (in column D) is used as input for decision making. First, the utilities for each of the three criterion levels for accepting the candidate are indicated (column E). Next, the same is done for the rejection of the candidate (column F). This latter step can be discarded when one is not interested in the effects of rejection. In the example we have chosen Maximization of Expected Utility as the decision strategy. As a consequence one can determine the expected utilities in case of acceptance and rejection for each of the three criteria (column G). By adding the values one finds the expected utilities of accepting and rejecting the candidate with reference to the job as a whole. The steps involved in filling the columns E through G correspond to designing and applying a decision model. Again it should be noted that the selector has great freedom in choosing their own way of going about the selection problem.

The significance of the scheme as a whole is that it invites the selector to record their way of working, to proceed through the steps systematically, and to make the data used and the judgements made as explicit as possible. In this way one obtains a result that is open for testing and for justification *vis-à-vis* the candidate or the commissioner. The scheme should not be seen as a prescription that should be applied universally. If the selector is an expert, as we presume, they can determine themself which steps should be taken. The logic of the model underlies the computer system for decision support that we have referred to earlier (Koh, 1994). An evaluation study has shown that selectors using the programme found it useful in the sense of enhancing the transparency of their work and stimulating learning. They did, on the whole, not perceive an improvement in the outcomes of their selection activities. Validation research should be conducted in order to ascertain whether such improvements are or are not obtained.

TABLE 2.4

Scheme for supporting clinical selection (example; based on Roe, 1983; p. 400); L = low, a = average, h = high performance.

A Criteria	B Predictive data	C Findings regarding B	D Prognosis, probability of			E Utility of acceptance if:			F Utility of rejection if:			G Expected utility	H Remarks
			L	A	H	L	A	H	L	A	H		
Able to work independently	experience references	+ +	.10	.20	.70	−5	3	5	4	0	−2	3.6 −1.0	"responsible character"
Pleasant to communicate with	interview application letter references	− + −/+	.30	.40	.30	0	2	5	5	2	−1	2.3 2.0	pedantic experienced no-nonsense
Fast and accurate in typing	diploma typing probe references interview	−/+ −/+ + −	.40	.50	.10	−4	1	4	3	1	0	−0.7 1.7	fast/sloppy "dependable worker" dislikes typing
												$E(U_1) = 5.2$ $E(U_2) = 2.7$	accept!

CONCLUSION

This chapter has offered a general methodology for designing selection procedures which presents the possibility of reconciling the demands from practice with the many opportunities offered by theory. Whether a selection procedure developed according to this methodology meets the demands, and if so to what degree, depends on the one hand on the room for design left by the requirements and on the other hand on the craftsmanship and ingenuity of the designer. Most selection problems can be solved in a multitude of ways, not just one. It is the designer who should find a solution that best matches the particular circumstances of the situation.

The final test of the value of the selection procedure is in its practical application. Only experience and results from practice can demonstrate whether the procedure is adequate or whether it needs adjustment. One would need, in other words, an evaluation to make sure that the procedure is adequate and, at the same time, whether the selection was made in an appropriate way. The programme of requirements offers a suitable instrument for carrying out such an evaluation, since it contains all the points that were considered relevant at the outset. When a procedure is used during a longer period, the evaluation should be repeated after some time, even when the procedure was found to be satisfactory. After all, there can be changes in the nature of the selection problem, the type of people applying for the job, and so on, making the procedure less suited to the situation. Similarly, there can be a change in requirements and constraints, for example, due to new legislation, or a tighter budget for selection activities. By recurrently testing the procedure against the programme of requirements, and checking whether its content is adequate, one can ensure that the selection procedure remains up to date and continues to produce satisfactory results.

NOTES

[1] The author expresses his gratitude to Robert L. Kahn for his helpful comments on an earlier version of this text.

[2] The term "objectified" means: made more objective. It was introduced by Roe (1983; p. 101).

REFERENCES

Algera, J.A., & Greuter, M.A.M. (1989). Job analysis for personnel selection. In M. Smith & I.T. Robertson (Eds.), *Advances in selection and assessment* (pp. 7–30). Chichester: Wiley.

Algera, J.A., Jansen, P.G.W., Roe, R.A., & Vijn, P. (1984). Validity generalization: Some critical remarks on the Schmidt-Hunter procedure. *Journal of Occupational Psychology*, *57*, 197–210.

Arvey, R.D., & Campion, J.E. (1982). The employment interview: A summary and review of recent research. *Personnel Psychology*, *35*, 281–322.

Asher, J.J., & Sciarrino, J.A. (1974). Realistic work sample tests. *Personnel Psychology*, *27*, 519–533.

Barrett, G.V., Caldwell, M.S., & Alexander, R.A. (1985). The concept of dynamic criteria: A critical reanalysis. *Personnel Psychology*, *38*, 41–56.

Bemis, S.E. (1968). Occupational validity of the general aptitude test battery. *Personnel Psychology*, *68*, 396–407.

Boudreau, J.W. (1983a). Economic considerations in estimating the utility of human resource productivity programs. *Personnel Psychology*, *36*, 551–557.

Boudreau, J.W. (1983b). Effects of employee flows on utility analysis of human resource productivity improvement programs. *Personnel Psychology*, *68*, 396–407.

Boudreau, J.W. (1989). Selection utility analysis: a review and agenda for future research. In M. Smith, & I.T. Robertson (Eds.), *Advances in selection and assessment* (pp. 227–258). Chichester: Wiley.

Burke, M.J. (1984). Validity generalization: A review and critique of the correlation model. *Personnel Psychology*, *37*(1) 93–115.

Campbell, J.P. (1983). Some possible implications of "modeling" for the conceptualization of measurement. In F. Landy, S. Zedeck, J. Cleveland (Eds.), *Performance Measurement and Theory* (pp. 277–298). Hillsdale, NJ: Lawrence Erlbaum Associates Inc.

Campion, M.A. (1983). Personnel selection for physically demanding jobs: Review and recommendations. *Personnel Psychology*, *36*, 527–550.

Carlson, R.E. (1967). Selection interview decisions: the effect of interviewer experience, relative quota situation, and applicant sample on interviewer decisions. *Personnel Psychology, 20*, 259–280.

Carlson, R.E., Thayer, P.W., Mayfield, E.C., & Peterson, D.A. (1971). Improvements in the selection interview. *Personnel Journal, 50*(4), 268–275.

Cascio, W.F., Alexander, R.A., & Barrett, G.V. (1988). Setting cutoff scores: Legal, psychometric, and professional issues and guidelines. *Personnel Psychology, 41*(1), 1–24.

Conway, J.M., Jako, R.A., & Goodman, D.F. (1995). A meta-analysis of interrater and internal consistency reliability of selection interviews. *Journal of Applied Psychology, 80*(5), 565–579.

Cronbach, L.J., & Gleser, G.C. (1965). *Psychological tests and personnel decisions.* Urbana, IL: University of Illinois Press.

Cronshaw, S.F., & Alexander, R.A. (1985). One answer to the demand for accountability: Selection utility as an investment decision. *Organizational Behavior and Human Decision Processes, 35*, 102–118.

Cunningham, J.W., Boese, R.R., Neeb, R.W., & Pass, J.J. (1983). Systematically derived work dimensions: Factor analysis of the occupation analysis inventory. *Journal of Applied Psychology, 68*, 232–252.

Darlington, R. (1978). Reduced-variance regression. *Psychological Bulletin, 85*, 1238–1255.

Dawes, R.M. (1971). A case study of graduate admissions: Application of three principles of human decision making. *American Psychologist, 26*(2), 180–188.

Dawes, R.M. (1979). The robust beauty of improper linear models in decision making. *American Psychologist, 34*(7), 571–582

Drenth, P.J. (1976). *Inleiding in de testtheorie.* Deventer: Van Loghum Slaterus.

Drenth, P.J. (1988). De waarde van het selectie-interview. *Gedrag en Organisatie, 2*, 18–26.

Drenth, P.J., & Sijtsma, K. (1990). *Testtheorie.* Deventer: Van Loghum Slaterus.

Eekels, J. (1983). Design procesesses seen as decision chains: Their intuitive and discursive aspects. *Proceedings of the international conference on engineering design*, Copenhagen.

Eijck, M.H. van, Andriessen, J.H.T.H., & Van de Ven, J.W.P.M. (1988). *Werving en selectie in de praktijk.* Den Haag: COB/SER.

Erez, A., Bloom, M.C., & Wells, M.T. (1996). Using random rather than fixed effect models in meta-analysis. Implications for situational specificity and validity generalization. *Personnel Psychology, 49*, 295–306.

Flanagan, J.C. (1954). The critical incident technique. *Psychological Bulletin, 51*(4), 327–358.

Fleishman, E.A., & Quaintance, M.K. (1984). *Taxonomies of human performance.* New York: Academic Press.

Furnham, A. (1992). *Personality at work: The role of individual differences in the work place.* London: Routledge.

Gaugler, B.B., Rosenthal, D.B., Thornton, G.C., & Bentson, C. (1987). Meta-analysis of assessment center validity. *Journal of Applied Psychology, Monograph, 72*(3), 493–511.

Ghiselli, E.E. (1966). *The validity of occupational aptitude tests.* New York: Wiley.

Ghiselli, E.E. (1973). The validity of aptitude tests in personnel selection. *Personnel Psychology, 26*, 461–477.

Greuter, M.A.M. (1988). *Personeelsselektie in perspektief (Dissertatie TU Delft).* Haarlem: Uitgeverij thesis.

Greuter, M.A.M. (1989). Performance modelling for personnel selection. In P. Herriot (Ed.), *Assessment and selection in organizations: Methods and practice for recruitment and appraisal* (pp 183–204). Chichester: Wiley.

Greuter, M.A.M., & Roe, R.A. (1982). Met het oog op selektie. *Gids voor Personeelbeleid, Arbeidsvraagstukken en Sociale Verzekering, 61*(16), 21–26.

Groot, A.D. de (1961). *Methodologie.* Den Haag: Mouton.

Guilford, J.P. (1965). *Fundamental statistics in psychology and education.* New York: McGraw-Hill.

Guion, R.M. (1965). Personnel testing. New York: McGraw Hill.

Guion, R.M. (1978). Scoring of content domain samples: The problem of fairness. *Journal of Applied Psychology, 63*(4), 499–506.

Guion, R.M. (1991). Personnel assessment, selection and placement. In M.D. Dunnette, & L.M. Hough (Eds.), *Handbook of industrial and organizational psychology* (pp. 327–397). Palo Alto, CA: Consulting Psychologists Press.

Harvey, R.J., & Hayes, T.L. (1986). Monte Carlo baselines for interrater reliability correlations using the position analysis questionnaire. *Personnel Psychology, 39*(2), 345–358.

Hull, J.C., Moore, P.G., & Thomas, H. Utility and its measurement. *Journal of the Royal Statistical Society*, series A, 226–247.

Hunter, J.E., & Hunter, R.F. (1984). Validity and utility of alternative predictors of job performance. *Psychological Bulletin, 96*(1), 72–98.

Hunter, J.E., & Schmidt, F.L. (1990). *Methods of meta-analysis: Correcting for bias in research findings.* Newbury Park, CA: Sage.

Hunter, J.E., Schmidt, F.L., & Jackson, G.B. (1982). *Meta-analysis: Cumulating research findings across studies.* Beverly Hills, CA: Sage.

James, L.R., Demaree, R.G., & Mulaik, S.A. (1986). A note on validity generalization procedures. *Journal of Applied Psychology, 71*(3) 440–450.

Jansen, P.G.W., Roe, R.A., Vijn, P., & Algera, J.A. (1986). *Validity generalization revisited.* Delft: University Press.

Kennedy, E. (1988). Estimation of the squared cross-validity coefficient in the context of best subset regression. *Applied Psychological Measurement, 12*(3), 231–237.

Koh, I.S.Y. (1989). *Development of an experimental decision support system for personnel selection. Human thought processes and computer simulation: a good combination.* Tilburg: Tilburg University Press.

Koh, I.S.Y. (1994). *Human assessment and computer support.* Tilburg: Tilburg University Press.

Koubek, R.J., Salvendy, G., & Noland, S. (1994). The use of protocol analysis for determining ability requirements for personnel selection on a computer-based task. Special issue: Cognitive ergonomics. *Ergonomics, 37*(11), 1787–1800.

Lamers, L.M., Van der Gaag, N.L., & Mellenbergh, G.J. (1992). Empirical utility functions for selection. *Methodika, 6*(1) 13–29.

Landy, F.J., & Farr, J.L. (1983). *The measurement of work performance.* Orlando, FL: Academic Press.

Landy, F.L., & Rastegary, H. (1989). Criteria for selection. In M. Smith & I.T. Robertson (Eds.), *Advances in selection and assessment* (pp. 89–112). Chichester: Wiley.

Landy, F., Zedeck, S., & Cleveland, J. (Eds.) (1983). *Performance measurement and theory.* Hillsdale, NJ: Lawrence Erlbaum Associates Inc.

Latham, G.P. (1986). Job Performance and appraisal. In C.L. Cooper & I. Robertson (Eds.), *International review of industrial and organizational psychology* (pp. 118–155). Chichester, UK:Wiley.

Lawshe, C.H., & Balma, M.J. (1966). *Principles of personnel testing.* New York: McGraw-Hill.

Lawshe, C.H., & Bolda, R.A. (1958). Expectancy charts I: their use and empirical development. *Personnel Psychology, 11*, 353–365.

Lent, R.H., Aurbach, H.A., & Levin, L.S. (1971). Predictors, criteria and significant results. *Personnel Psychology, 24*, 519–533.

Lopez, F.M., Kesselman G.A., & Lopez, F.E. (1981). An empirical test of a trait oriented job analysis technique. *Personnel Psychology, 34*, 479–502.

McCormick, E.J. (1979). *Job analysis: methods and applications.* New York: Amacom.

McCormick, E.J., Jeanneret, R.R., & Mecham, R.C. (1972). A study of job characteristics and job dimensions as based on the position analysis questionnaire. *Journal of Applied Psychology, Monograph, 56*(4), 347–368.

Meehl, P. (1954). *Clinical versus statistical prediction.* Minneapolis, MN: University of Minneapolis Press.

Miller, R.B. (1973). Development of a taxonomy of human performance: A user oriented approach. *JSAS Catalogue of Selected Documents in Psychology, 26* (Ms 322).

Molenaar, I.W., & Lewis, Ch. (1979). Bayesian m-group regression: A survey and an improval model. *Methoden en Data Nieuwsbrief. Vereniging voor Statistiek, SWS, 4*(1), 62–72.

Naylor, J.C. (1983). Modeling performance. In F. Landy, S. Zedeck & J. Cleveland (Eds.), *Performance measurement and theory* (pp. 299–305). Hillsdale, NJ: Lawrence Erlbaum Associates Inc.

Pearlman, K., Schmidt, F.L., & Hunter, J.E. (1980). Validity generalization results for tests used to predict job proficiency and training succes in clerical occupations. *Journal of Applied Psychology, 65*, 373–406.

Pruzek, R.M., & Frederick, B.C. (1978). Weighting predictors in linear models: Alternatives to least squares and limitations of equal weights. *Psychological Bulletin, 85*, 254–266.

Pruzek, R.M., & Lepak, G.M. (1992). Weighted structural regression: A broad class of adaptive methods for improving linear prediction. *Multivariate Behavioral Research, 27 1*, 95–129.

Radford, K.J. (1975). *Managerial decision making.* Reston, VA: Reston Publishing Co.

Raju, N.S., Steinhaus, S.D., Edwards, J.E., & DeLessio, J. (1991). A logistic regression model for personnel selection. *Applied Psychological Measurement, 15*(2), 139–152.

Reilly, R.R., & Chao, G.T. (1982). Validity and fairness of some alternative employee selection procedures. *Personnel Psychology, 35*, 1–62.

Reilly, R.R., & Israelski, E. (1988). Development and validation of minicourses in the telecommunication industry. *Journal of applied Psychology, 73*(4), 721–726.

Ridderbos, A. (1993). *Selection by simulation.* Eindhoven University of Technology.

Robertson, I.T. (1994). Personality and personnel selection. In C.L. Cooper & D.M. Rousseau (Eds.), *Trends in organizational behavior* (Vol. 1, pp. 75–89). Chichester: Wiley.

Robertson, I.T., & Downs, S. (1989). Work-sample tests of trainability: A meta-analysis. *Journal of Applied Psychology, 74*(3), 402–410.

Roe, R.A. (1981). Persoonskenmerken. In P.J. Drenth, H. Thierry, P.J. Williams, & Ch. J. de Wolff (Eds.), *Handboek Arbeids-en Organisatiepsychologie.* Deventer: Van Loghum Slaterus.

Roe, R.A. (1983). *Grondslagen der personeelsselektie.* Assen: Van Gorcum.

Roe, R.A. (1984). *Advances in performance modeling: The case of validity generalization.* Paper presented at the symposium 'Advances in Testing'. Acapulco, Mexico, 6 September.

Roe, R.A. (1989). Designing selection procedures. In P. Herriot (Ed.), *Assessment and selection in organizations: Methods and practice for recruitment and appraisal* (pp. 127–142). Chichester: Wiley.

Roe, R.A. (1996a). Naar een nieuw paradigma voor

personeelsselectie. In R. Bouwen, K. de Witte, & J. Verboven (Eds.) *Organiseren en veranderen* (pp. 287–312). Leuven: Garant.

Roe, R.A. (1996b), Arbeidsprestaties. In P.J.D. Drenth, H. Thierry, P.J. Williams, & Ch. J. de Wolff (Eds.), *Handboek Arbeids-en Organisatiepsychologie* (pp. 1–103). Deventer: Kluwer.

Roe, R.A., & Greuter, M.A.M. (1991). Developments in personnel selection methodology. In R.K. Hambleton & J. Zaal (Eds.), *Advances in educational and psychological testing: Theory and applications* (pp. 178–226). Boston: Kluwer Academic Publishers.

Roe, R.A., & Zijlstra, F.R.H. (1991). Arbeidsanalyse voor functie(her)ontwerp: Een handelingstheoretische invalshoek. In J.A. Algera (Ed.), *Analyse van arbeid vanuit verschillende perspectieven* (pp. 179–243). Amsterdam/Lisse: Swets and Zeitlinger.

Ronan, W.W., & Prien, E.P. (Eds.) (1971). *Perspectives on the measurement of human performance.* New York: Appleton Century Crofts.

Roozenburg, N.F.M., & Eekels, J. (1991). *Produktontwerpen, structuur en methoden.* Utrecht: Lemma.

Sackett, P.R., & Harris, M.M. (1984). Honesty testing for personnel selection: A review and critique. *Personnel Psychology, 37,* 221–245.

Sawyer, J. (1966). Measurement and prediction, clinical and statistical. *Psychological Bulletin, 66*(3), 178–200.

Schmidt, F.L., & Hunter, J.E. (1977). Development of a general solution to the problem of validity generalization. *Journal of Applied Psychology, 62,* 529–540.

Schmidt, F.L., & Hunter, J.E. (1981). Old theories and new research findings. *American Psychologist, 36*(10), 1128–1137.

Schmidt, F.L., Hunter, J.E., Pearlman, K., & Shane, G.S. (1979). Further tests of the Schmidt-Hunter bayesian validity generalization procedure. *Personnel Psychology, 32,* 257–281.

Schmitt, N. (1976). Social and situational determinants of interview decisions: Implications for the employment interview. *Personnel psychology, 29,* 79–101.

Schmitt, N., & Noe, R.A. (1986). On shifting standards for conclusions regarding validity generalization. *Personnel Psychology, 39,* 849–851.

Schmitt, N., Gooding, R.Z., & Kirsch, M. (1984). Meta-analysis of validity studies published between 1964 and 1982 and the investigation of study characteristics. *Personnel Psychology, 37,* 407–422.

Schuler, H., Frier, D., & Kauffmann, M. (1993). *Personalauswahl im europäischen Vergleich.* Göttingen: Verlag für Angewandte Psychologie.

Shackleton, V.J., & Newell, S. (1989). Selection procedures in pratice. In P. Herriot (Ed.), *Assessment and selection in organizations: Methods and practice for recruitment and appraisal* (pp. 245–256). Chichester: Wiley.

Smith, J.E. & Hakel, M.D. (1979). Convergence among data source, response bias and reliability and validity of a structured job analysis questionnaire. *Personnel psychology, 32,* 677–692.

Smith, M., & Robertson, I.T. (Eds.) (1989). Advances in selection and assessment. Chichester: Wiley.

Smith, P.C. (1976). Behavior, results, and organizational effectiveness: The problem of criteria. In M.D. Dunnette (Ed.), *Handbook of Industrial and Organizational Psychology* (pp. 745–775). Chicago: Rand McNally.

Stegmüller, W. (1974). *Probleme und Resultate der Wissenschaftstheorie und Aanalytischen Philosophie. Band I: Wissenschaftliche Erklärung und Begründung. Studienausgabe Teil 5.* New York: Springer.

Stone, C.H., & Kendall, W.E. (1956). *Effective personnel selection procedures.* Englewood Cliffs, NJ.: Prentice Hall.

Tenopyr, M. (1989). Comment on meta-analysis: Facts and theories. In M. Smith & I.T. Robertson (Eds.), *Advances in selection and assessment* (pp. 217–224). Chichester: Wiley.

Thorndike, R.L. (1949). *Personnel selection.* New York: Wiley.

Trost, G., & Kirchenkamp, T. (1993). Predictive validity of cognitive and noncognitive variables with respect to choice of occupation and job success. In H. Schulder, J.L. Farr, & M. Smith (Eds.), *Personnel selection and assessment* (pp. 303–314). Hillsdale, NJ: Lawrence Erlbaum Associates Inc.

United States Training and Employment Service (Department of Labor and Manpower Administration). (1972). *Handbook for analyzing jobs.* Washington D.C.: US Government Printing Office.

Vrijhoff, B.J., Mellenbergh, G. & Brink. W.P. (1983). Assessing and studying utility functions in psychometric decision theory. *Applied Psychological Measurement, 7*(3), 341–357.

Wainer, H. (1976). Estimating coefficients in linear models: It dont make no nevermind. *Psychological Bulletin, 86,* 213–217.

Wainer, H., & Thissen, D. (1976). Three steps toward robust regression. *Psychometrika, 41,* 9–34.

Webster, E.C. (1964). *Decision making in the employment interview.* Montreal: Eagle.

Wernimont, R.F., & Campbell, J. (1968). Signs, samples and criteria. *Journal of Applied Psychology,* 52, 372–376.

Wiggins, J.S. (1980). *Personality and prediction.* Reading, MA: Addison Wesley.

Wright, O.R. (1969). Summary of research on the selection interview since 1964. *Personnel Psychology, 22*(4), 391–413.

3

The Selection Process

Charles J. de Wolff and Giel van den Bosch

1 INTRODUCTION

Personnel selection is a subject with a long history. The first involvements of psychologists date from around the turn of the century. There is no other subject within W&O psychology about which so many studies have been conducted. There was even a period that industrial psychology and personnel selection were seen as synonymous by the general public.

Personnel selection is also a subject of great controversies. Heated discussions have been held about how selection should be executed, and advocates and opponents of particular approaches have attacked each other vigorously. History shows that the discussions focus on two points: *effectiveness* and *dignity*. Even today these subjects are still very much alive.

In the past, psychologists mainly chose the prediction paradigm. That is to say, they tried to predict the contribution an employee would make to the organization. Moreover, they were thinking in terms of individual differences: aptitudes and personality characteristics. Selection therefore implies choosing the applicant one expects will contribute most to the organization. In many respects this seems self-evident. Everyone knows that some people achieve more than others, and attempts to identify such people with the aid of selection methods seem highly attractive. During the Second World War, the prediction paradigm yielded spectacular results in, among other things, the selection of pilots (Thorndike, 1949).

Yet doubts have also been raised. The prediction paradigm was said to be useful under certain conditions only. There are other approaches as well, which sometimes seem more appropriate. Career management approaches in particular depart from other basic principles. That does not alter the fact that on the basis of the prediction paradigm numerous methods were developed for personnel selection, such as job analysis, test construction and validation research which belong in the arsenal of a professionally working psychologist.

In this book the following set-up has been chosen. The methods and techniques which belong to the predictive approach are discussed in Chapter 2. This chapter deals with harmonization between the individual and the organization, as is the case during the selection procedure. Questions that go with it are: "What can an organization do to improve harmonization" and "What are the effects of good harmonization". Both "effectiveness" and "dignity" will be looked into, as well as the attunement to other procedures, such as recruitment, training, introduction and career guidance.

2 EFFECTIVENESS

The discussion concerning effectiveness mainly took place in the 1940s and 1950s. In that period a polemic between the advocates of the "clinical" method and proponents of the "statistical" or "actuarian" method (Van der Giessen, 1957). The proponents of the clinical method based their case on phenomenology and "verstehende Psychologie" (Dilthey, 1923). In Germany, this trend played first fiddle in the period preceding the Second World War. The line of reasoning was that clients (applicants, but also the patients of the clinical psychologist) were not capable of rendering a good account of their qualities and experiences. By using indirect methods the psychologist had to bring them to reveal themselves to him. The "verstehende Psychologie" is a holistic approach, and aims understand the other intuitively. It rejects a "measuring" approach in which one tries to measure properties of applicants on the basis of analysis.

The clinical method makes use of interview and observation as well as "projective techniques". In the 1930s and 1940s many observation tests were circulated. Although performance was also assessed (e.g. the number of answers and the amount of time needed to complete the task were registered), the primary concern was *how* the task was accomplished. This constituted the basis on which the psychologist formed an opinion about the applicant's qualities. In this way, a picture was formed of both the applicant's talent and character. Consequently, it was a qualitative approach.

In that period numerous projection tests were developed, such as the Rorschach-test, the Szondi-test and the tree test (De Zeeuw, 1971; Drenth, 1976). The applicants had to execute relatively unstructured tasks with ambiguous and vaguely defined material. When implementing those tasks the applicant usually had the choice of a great number of possibilities, in the course of which the applicant attached a meaning to the offered stimuli. By this process of choosing from the many alternatives regarding structuring and interpreting the material, it was assumed that the applicant would give away significant and fundamental aspects about themself in the process (Drenth, 1975; Lindsey & Thorpe, 1968).

Tasks in this respect are *apperception* (Rohrschach-test: what does this blot mean?), *interpretation* (Thematic Apperception Test: what is going on in the situation as depicted on the plate?), *complementing* (incomplete sentences test: complete the sentence), *choice* (Szondi-test: arrange the photographs according to sympathy), *construction* (village test: build a village with the blocks provided) and *expression* (tree test: draw a tree). The authors of these tests provided all kinds of interpretation rules. Thus, Koch (1954) mentions numerous ways in which a tree can be drawn, and for each he presents a list of characteristics as to what they might signify.

Besides these projective tests, graphology also has to be mentioned in this respect since it can be seen as a form of expression and, like the tree test, may be "interpreted" (see, for meaning and practicability Jansen, 1963).

The clinical method usually led to an exhaustive description of the candidate. Character in particular was elucidated, but also statements were made about intelligence and cognitive skills. On the basis of this description the psychologist gave a verdict on suitability.

Opposed to this clinical method stood the actuarian method. This method was mainly developed in the United States. Use was also being made of tests, but in a quite different manner. The scientific use of tests started at the end of the nineteenth century. Cattell (1890) describes a number of tests that he used to measure skills. In 1901 Wissler gave an account of the calculation of Pearson-correlations between "mental ability tests" and "academic performance" at the University of Colombia. In the 1920s the first manuals appeared in which the actuarian method was described (Hull, 1928; Link, 1924; Viteles, 1932). The basic assumption was that job suitability is determined by a combination of characteristics ("traits") and that those traits can be measured with the aid of tests. In fact, such tests are standardized measuring instruments: the testees are offered standard stimuli. On the basis of their reactions, it is possible to lay down in a score to what extent they possess a certain trait.

The qualities that are important for job fulfilment must be determined on the basis of a thorough job analysis. Whether there exists a relationship between a test score and job performance (validity) has to be verified accordingly, for example with the aid of a correlation calculation.

Viteles (1932) mentions four types of skill: "proficiency" (the skill someone has already acquired to fulfil the job); "competency" (the ability to learn, also referred to as "aptitude"); "temperament and character" and "interests". He notices that general intelligence has only a restricted predictive value; better predictions can only be achieved in combination with other skills. Which combination of skills is the best can be ascertained with the aid of regression equations.

At the beginning of this century the foundation was already laid for the actuarian method. During the Second World War this selection method was applied on a large scale by the American forces. More than 14 million soldiers were tested and classified and, as already mentioned, the programme for pilots became well-known. Thanks to the actuarian method the output of the training could be raised considerably. Of those candidates who scored a 9 for the test, 4% failed the training; of those candidates for the pilot selection with a score of 1, 77% failed the training (Van der Giessen, 1957).

After the war, in 1947, the airmen selection programme was elaborately described in a series of books "The Army Aviation Psychology Program". One volume in this series, *Personnel Selection*, written by Thorndike, was edited separately in 1949. This book renders a detailed description of the actuarian method and, as a textbook, had a great impact on the further development of the field of study.

The successes attracted a lot of attention in the United States as well as in Europe. Attractive was the fact that, apart from the obvious success, selection according to the actuarian method was a skill and not an art as was the case with the clinical method. The actuarian method could be learned whereas the clinical method required a special talent.

Proceedings were undertaken to apply the actuarian method on a large scale for personnel selection as well as admission to schools. The clinical method was used less and less, although the relative merits of the two methods still provoked heated discussions.

In The Netherlands the turning point occurred at the end of the 1950s. From a theoretical point of view the controversy concerning the clinical versus the actuarian method was finally settled in favour of the actuarian method. This method was accepted by the universities as the scientifically correct one. Scientific research was further based on the prediction paradigm. In practice, however, clinical methods were still used for a long time; projection tests and graphology remained in use and have not yet disappeared.

From the discussions and research material published at the time several lessons can be drawn:

1. Projection tests appear to show no significant correlations with criteria such as those used within organizations.
2. Appraisal by selectors, based on intuitive comprehension, appears to be invalid or hardly valid.
3. It is necessary to test statements about suitability by means of empirical research.

After much research it appeared that simple "paper and pencil" tests scored better than intuitive appraisals by selectors. It also emerged that providing the selector with test data, with the intention that he or she should use them to express a final opinion, led to poorer results than determining the result by means of a simple formula. Thus, suspicion arose against subjective measuring such as assessments, and against subjective methods like the interview. There was a general trend towards objective measurements, obtained by tests.

Thanks to research it became more clear what qualities are important in personnel selection. Pioneering work was done by Thurstone (1938) and later on by Guilford (1959, 1967), Fleishman (1967) and the United States Employment Service (1977). These investigations showed how qualities and the execution of tasks interrelate. Taxonomies were being developed regarding aptitudes as well as personality characteristics and interests.

Likewise, instruments to measure these qualities were being constructed. Surveys and evaluations of such instruments can be found in the *Mental Measurements Yearbook* compiled by O.K. Buros, published periodically.

3 DIGNITY

In selection practice it regularly occurred that the applicant was seen as a "testee" to be examined in a "laboratory". The applicant was seen as a "system" with "properties" that had to be measured (Ferguson, 1952). This was seen to contribute to a good allocation of personnel. Bingham (1950) summed up this attitude with: 'Persons or guinea pigs?' The applicant becomes an object, but applicants are supposed to conform to this procedure because it is in their interest to do so. It would lead to better decisions, not only for the organization, but also for the applicant.

This objectification of the applicant applied to both the actuarian and the clinical methods. With the clinical method the psychologist's intention was to bring the applicant to reveal themself so that the psychologist could form an opinion about the applicant's character and talent. That impression was then incorporated in the advice given to the client.

In the 1960s and 1970s in particular, personnel selection became the talk of the town. Opposition was mounting. In the United States an anti-test movement came into being which staged demonstrations in which test papers were burned. In 1962 Hoffman published his book *The tyranny of testing* (Hoffman, 1962) and Gross *The brain watchers* (Gross, 1962). In 1964 Packard followed with *The naked society* (Packard, 1964). In these books psychological testing was bitterly attacked. In 1965 the American Senate and the House of Representatives set up a committee with the aim to investigate more closely the use of tests by government institutions. Personality questionnaires in particular were being looked into. There was concern that incursion would be made upon the private life of citizens (for reports of the "hearings" see the special issue of the *American Psychologist* from November, 1965).

It cannot be denied that tests sometimes do enter into the private lives of individuals, though the extent to which they do so should not be overestimated. Conrad (1967) mentions a study which, of the 5300 questions investigated found only 10 to be unacceptable. Psychologists have argued that it was not so much the questions that were at stake but the psychological implications. Van Strien (1966) and Drenth (1967) state that a balancing of interests was involved. From the viewpoint that it was desirable for an organization to make the best possible use of the applicant's qualities, it would be necessary to judge the admissibility of the questions put to applicants. Drenth urged psychologists to be extremely careful, because the applicant's position was usually a dependent one. However, interests had to be weighed against each other and for that reason a too one-sided approach of the privacy problem was rejected.

However, the discussion had not yet ended. In The Netherlands a petition was submitted in 1971 by Member of Parliament Vellinga in which concern was expressed about selection practices, and the government was invited to take this matter into consideration. Examination revealed an unnecessary deep incursion into private life, results not being discussed properly with the persons tested and insufficient guarantees that the examination results would be made available to professional and qualified people only.

The Minister reacted to this by setting up a committee (the Hessel commission) which not only had to analyse the psychological selection methods, but all selection methods ("procedures for recruitment, selection and employment").

In 1973 the Dutch unions research foundation SWOV published a pamphlet *The dependent applicant* (SWOV, 1973) emphasizing the applicant's vulnerability. Mention is made of, among other things, the applicant's ignorance of his or her market value and of his or her dependency on the company, the necessity to find a job at short notice, and the impossibility for one individual to stand up against a well-oiled organization that has carefully designed procedures and expert staff. The relation organization versus applicant is seen as highly unbalanced and a plea is made for strengthening the applicant's position. In 1973, the Association of Banking, Insurance and Administrative Personnel published a report called "Applicant, application, applying", which advocates a more equal position for the applicant. The report concludes by formulating a sample "code of conduct" for the selection procedure.

Jansen, a former member of the Hessel commission, has elaborated many of these points in his *Ethics and practice of personnel selection* (Jansen, 1979). He mentions the result of an inquiry under 808 personnel officers which showed a rather negative response towards psychological testing (24% as compared to 11% of negative reactions to the employment interview). Many incidents were reported. Negative events appeared to be related to insufficient information, lack of clarity and carelessness. Regarding positive incidents, much "openness" and "clarity" was reported. Jansen therefore concludes that applicants also set store by openness and equality in their relationship with the selector and value correct treatment and conscientiously executed procedures.

In 1977, the Hessel commission published its final report under the title: *An applicant is also a human being* (Eindrapport Commissie Selectieprocedure, 1977). This report proceeds from two main principles:

1. The criterion for selection is the applicant's suitability for the job in question.
2. All parts of the entire selection procedure should be consistent with human dignity.

The latter point is elaborated in a number of rights:

- The right to a fair chance to be employed; selection decisions must be reached on the grounds of careful considerations and fairness and it must always be possible to justify them.
- The right to information; both parties in the selection procedure must be informed in such a way that they can arrive at a justified decision. Apparently, this right is inadequately realized in many procedures. Attention is paid to, among other things, information about the procedure, the job itself and the work organization, data about the applicant which the work organization receives from third parties, and the reason for rejection.
- The right to privacy; the commission recognizes the necessity of the applicant supplying information about themself to enable the work organization to judge their capacities and suitability. "If the information asked has a bearing on the job, such a violation of privacy is admissible".
- The right to confidential treatment of personal data; such data are not to be passed on to an unnecessarily large number of persons and are not to be used for other purposes than those they were obtained for.
- The right to an instrumentally efficient procedure; the selection instruments must meet the requirements of validity and reliability.
- The right of complaint; the applicant should have the right to lodge a complaint when they feel that they have been treated carelessly, unfairly, or incorrectly, or if they think the selection decision was not made on solid grounds. In this connection, the commission recommends to make those carrying out psychological selection tests subject to legal disciplinary measures.

To a reasonable extent these rights fit in with those of the lawyer Mendel who, in 1975, devoted a publication to the legal protection of the applicant (Mendel, 1975). Mendel departs from the freedom principle: "The employer is free to take on employees who, by working harmoniously, contribute to the best possible functioning of the entity as coordinated by him". Both parties therefore need to have maximum freedom during the selection process so as to commit themselves to one another or not. Mendel clearly reacts against notions that would want to limit this freedom principle, especially on the part of the employer.

Moreover, Mendel makes use of the relevance principle. The employer raises expectations by putting an advertisement in the papers. Whatever happens during the selection procedure must be relevant and should take into account those expectations. Mendel also recognizes that applicants often find themselves in a relatively defenceless position and are, depending on the labour market, the most vulnerable party. The relevance principle implies "that a prospective employer who causes harm to the applicant because of his conduct which, otherwise than the applicant may reasonably expect, stands in no relationship to the position at hand, commits in principle a wrongful act which obliges compensation for sustained losses".

The third principle mentioned by Mendel is the "principle of confidentiality". "Indiscretion on the part of the prospective employer which causes damage to the applicant will in principle constitute a wrongful act".

Mendel also refers to the Universal Declaration of Human Rights: anyone has the right to be admitted on equal terms to the government service of his country. Consequently, a different juridical position applies to government jobs than to the private sector. Applicants may appeal to this declaration. According to Mendel this does not mean that no suitability demands may be put forward; it means that these must naturally ensue from the positions to be fulfilled.

Psychologists have, in many respects, anticipated this changing attitude towards psychological testing. At the 1970 conference of the Dutch Institute of Psychologists on the theme of "The new role perception of the psychologist regarding the social aspects of his profession", it was decided to revise the code of conduct. In 1975, after long discussions on the committee's draft version, a revised code was accepted, which took effect on 1 January 1976 (NIP, 1975a).

The division of W&O Psychology accepted an even more elaborate code (NIP, 1975b). In formulating this code, use was made of the results of an inquiry among practising psychologists (Van Strien et al., 1973). The general code comprised the following points: the kind of information clients are entitled to, voluntary participation of the subjects, confidentiality and the right of complaint. The code also states that a client may demand that the psychologist refrains from reporting to third parties (NIP, 1975).

The report of the Hessel commission did not result in concrete measures on the part of the government, however, the Dutch Association for Personnel Officers formulated a code of conduct (NVP, 1980) which follows the recommendations of the Hessel commission.

Psychologists were surprised by the discussion about dignity. They had not foreseen the possibility and the readiness of the government to intervene. Futhermore, the attitude of the general public towards management and the "lackey's of management" became rather hostile at the beginning of the 1970s. This resulted in "withdrawal behaviour", not only in The Netherlands but in other European countries as well. There was a turn away from selection and attention was focused on other subjects, such as industrial democracy. As far as scientific research was concerned, selection became a neglected subject. Nowadays, this has clearly changed, and interest in selection issues is mounting.

It appears that selection is not a neutral process. For those involved much is at stake. Applicants have expectations, they try to influence decision-making processes, directly as well as indirectly. They also have views on the selection procedure. They do not want to be treated as an object and prefer more equality in the relationship with the selector. Politics and the government show an intention to intervene if convinced that this may help the underprivileged, boost emancipation, or provide more equal opportunities for those concerned.

Openness, clarity and carefulness are key words in this respect, not only for the psychologist but also for lawyers, applicants and government officials. Professional codes take this up by formulating rules which further this process. Selection is not only a matter of choosing, but one also has to observe the rules of professional ethics and society with great care.

4 DISCRIMINATION

Besides privacy and dependence there is the problem of *discrimination*. To what extent does a selection procedure provide fair opportunities for those concerned? On the one hand, it is clearly accepted that the employer has the right to appoint the most suitable candidate. On the other hand, it is recognized that specific groups have limited opportunities in the labour market (women, ethnic minorities, foreigners, the handicapped, homosexuals, the long-term unemployed). This leads to the question whether selection procedures are fair to these groups. Is it necessary to give such groups a stronger position in the labour market through positive discrimination programmes. Actions in this respect almost always have a political character. The government or other political bodies which may influence the decision-making process are being prevailed upon to interfere with the selection decision. This may take different shapes. Organizations may be persuaded to express a preference for a certain category of applicants. However, it is also possible to apply a quota system in combination with sanctions for not attaining the objectives.

The working-out differs from country to country and in the future substantial differences may occur, depending on governmental interference, legislation, and activities from interest groups. In The Netherlands, for instance, much interest is being taken in chances for women in the labour market and urban authorities are taking measures to ensure that more women are appointed headmistress (see also Chapter 16). In addition, the State Psychological Service in the Netherlands has adjusted its selection battery because women score lower than men in certain areas and because the chances for women to become assigned to certain positions ought to be improved.

In the United States in particular the discussion about discrimination has expanded enormously and has had far-reaching consequences. In 1964, Congress passed the Civil Rights Act in which a separate paragraph was dedicated to "Equal Employment Opportunity" (EEO). This was followed by more detailed prescriptions from the EEO commission and the Office of Federal Contract Compliance (OFCC, 1968, 1974). These created the possibility to exercise sanctions against employers who discriminate against minorities. The effects on selection psychology were enormous and are well documented in the *Annual Reviews*. In 1969, hardly any attention was paid to this subject, but in 1972 Bray and Moses noted that the period described by them had been dominated by the 'Test Fairness Controversy' (Bray & Moses, 1972). In 1975, Ash and Kroecker mention that annually 70,000 claims were lodged with the EEO commission, of which 15–30% concerned discrimination on account of an unfair use of tests (Ash & Kroecker, 1975). Numerous judicial proceedings took place. When setting up a selection procedure employers first and foremost obtained advice from a lawyer and then from a psychologist. For that reason, a book like *Staffing organizations* by Schneider and Schmitt (1986) pays much attention to the juridical aspects of selection. Psychologists turned out to be embarrassed by this development (Bray and Moses, 1972). Not only had they hardly given attention to minority groups, but the quality of research on majority groups left much to be desired as well. This caused a lot of problems when the fairness of the selection procedure had to be proven in court, and also required a huge catch-up manoeuvre. Schneider and Schmitt (1986, p. 14) mention "numerous court cases and tremendous efforts on the part of personnel researchers".

In the USA in 1978, the 'Uniform guidelines on Employees Selection Procedures' were published, a joint document drafted by government authorities such as the Department of Justice, the Department of Labor and the Civil Service Commission (see also Schneider & Schmitt, 1986 pp. 439–465). The document enters at length into definitions, the choice of selection procedures, the obligation to set up a documentation system, and demands to be made on validity studies and instruments.

In 1982, a report drafted by the American National Academy of Sciences concludes:

> The Committee has seen no evidence of alternatives to testing that are equally informative, equally adequate technically, and also economically and politically viable ... and little evidence that well-constructed and competently administered tests are more valid predictors for a population sub-group than for another: individuals with higher scores tend to perform better on the job regardless of group identity.
>
> (National Academy of Sciences, 1982, p. 144, quoted by Schneider & Schmitt, 1986, p. 14.)

Courts in the United States have applied an 80% rule: When the ratio of an appointed minority is less than 80% in relation to the ratio pertaining to the majority, the organization has to prove that selection procedures are based on the capability of individuals to execute significant parts of the set of tasks (Schneider and Schmitt, 1986). (For further discussion of psychological selection and discrimination see Drenth, 1988a, 1989.)

Recently, the European Court of Justice rejected positive discrimination, overruling a decision of a national court (Judgement of the Court of October 1995, Eckhard Kalanke v. Freie Hansestadt Bremen, ECR 1995 p I 3051). In its judgement, the court states:

> "A national rule that, where men and women are candidates for the same promotion and are equally qualified, women are automatically to be given priority in sectors where they are under-represented, involves discrimination on grounds of sex".

In the opinion of the advocati general it is stressed "positive action must ... be directed at removing the obstacles preventing women from having equal opportunities by tackling, for example, educational guidance and vocational training ...". The advocati general opposes "means of quota systems and the like".

> "In the final analysis, measures based on sex and not intended to eliminate an obstacle, to remove a situation of disadvantage, are, in their discriminating aspect, as unlawful today, for the purposes of promotion, as they were in the past."

This shows that legislation in Europe may develop differently from the United States, which in turn will have consequences for approaches.

5 PROBLEMS WITH THE PREDICTION PARADIGM

At present, literature concerning selection is still being dominated by the prediction paradigm. American authors in particular continue to base their case on this paradigm. In books about W&O psychology the chapter about selection is dedicated first and foremost to predictions (e.g. Landy, 1985). Review articles which appear regularly in *Annual Review* are still based on this starting-point. However, the discussion about "dignity" and "discrimination" has already showed that other factors are at issue. Especially in Europe, objections have been raised against the presuppositions on which the paradigm is based (De Wolff, 1989; Herriot, 1989a,b). These objections focus on four points:

1. Can selectors dispose of good criteria?
2. To what extent is it possible to isolate the decision-making process?
3. Are personal characteristics the only determinants for criteria to be predicted?
4. To what extent are organizations capable of executing validation studies?

5.1 Criteria

The prediction paradigm is based on the presupposition that job requirements are known and measureable. One tries to choose the applicant who is deemed to achieve best given his or her personal characteristics. As a consequence, the job requirements must be known—and that for the entire period of appointment—and those achievements must be measureable. Thorndike (1949) realized that this is problematical. He makes a distinction between "the ultimate goal"—the total contribution to the organization during the applicant's term of employment—and "intermediate goals". Thorndike was aware that it would be hardly possible to assess the total contribution. For that reason, he searched for "intermediate goals". In the pilot selection programme either passing or failing in the training programme constituted such an intermediate goal.

The selection practice has concentrated entirely on measuring intermediate goals, out of sheer necessity, because goals that were more representative of the total contribution of the employee were not available or were rendered available too late. However, by confining oneself to measuring what is on hand, a more principal discussion is being avoided. To what extent are intermediate criteria representative of the "complete final goal"? It is quite conceivable that intermediate criteria only dimly reflect requirements to be complied with during the entire term of employment.

In the 1960s a number of critical questions were formulated (De Wolff, 1967; Wallace, 1965). Recently, these were raised again (De Wolff, 1989). The questions focus on two problems: first, how useful are ratings, and second, how stable are the criteria?

5.1.1 Ratings

The criteria most in use are rating appraisals. In addition, much use is being made of training results. Objective criteria are seldom used. Sometimes they are available, but then it is obvious that they are often strongly influenced by situational characteristics. De Wolff (1973) gives an example of crane drivers. If one were to use the tonnage shifted by a crane driver as a criterion score it appears that this is more dependent on the type of crane used than on the characteristics of the crane driver. Some cranes are capable of shifting many tonnes per move, whereas others can only move several hundred kilos.

Hence, much use is being made of appraisals. Mostly, supervisors are asked to give their opinion on the employees' performance. However, such ratings are problematic as well. As early as 1969, Rundquist complained about low validities (Rundquist, 1969). It remained impossible to predict appraisals in a satisfactory manner. Multiple correlations nearly always remained below .35. Training criteria scored slightly better. Here, the upper limit was .50.

De Wolff (1963, 1970) demonstrated that ratings are only predictable to some extent. It appears that a substantial part of the variance cannot be ascribed to the assessed employees. Assessments convey whether the rater finds the assessed sympathetic (Jaspers, 1966). This is not solely dependent on the qualities of the assessed, but also on the combination rater–ratee. That in particular has to do with the general character of many pronouncements. More about that later.

5.1.2 Stability of criteria

The selection model assumes that the requirements remain the same throughout the entire period of employment. However, no account is taken of the fact that organizations operate in a turbulent environment and that individuals pass through a career.

Due to the turbulent environment, organizations must adapt constantly. Production methods and products are changing and restructuring programmes are being executed with the result that the job specification is changing as well. Employees have to acquire new skills (e.g. handling a computer) and other skills become redundant. These changes are often unpredictable and the prediction model does not allow for this. In fact, the model only fits in with a closed system and not in an open one.

This means that it is impossible to have an overall view of the requirements to be met by people during their career. For the short term, those requirements may be clarified, but in the long term they can change drastically.

Furthermore, job requirements change as a result of career developments. Many employees within organizations do not hold just one position but occupy several posts in succession. Depending on their personal development within the organization another job will be fulfilled by the employee after some time. Even though career patterns are available, marked differences between individuals also still exist. This implies that the demands made on the individual are changing as well.

Considering the contribution made by the employee during the entire period of their employment, it is obvious that this is not only subject to individual qualities, but also depends on the way in which the organization adjusts itself to the turbulent environment and on career decisions. This means that in many cases the "ultimate criterion" is unknown. As far as "intermediate criteria" are concerned, these criteria can be representative of a certain period, but do not apply to the entire term of employment.

From this, one could infer that prediction, and with it, selection, is impossible. However, that would be a too rashly-drawn conclusion. People are very goal-oriented and studies aiming at the analysis of the question as to who has a high potential within organizations, show that a number of their charcteristics can be traced (Campbell et al., 1970; De Wolff, 1973). However, tracing such characteristics requires research in which employees are followed for a longer period during their career. This requires great prudence when choosing intermediate criteria. Thus, assessments given after one or two years are often less adequate. Besides, such assessments regarding career development are especially focused on managers and senior personnel. Much less is known about other categories and usually nothing is known about those who perform well in the long run.

It follows from this that the choice of a criterion is a complex issue. The "ultimate criterion" is almost always unknown. There may be good reasons for choosing an "intermediate criterion" to be applied at the outset of the career (e.g. failing or passing an expensive training programme). However, it may even be desirable to choose a criterion at a later stage (employees whose career show clear progress seen over a longer period of time). The choice is subject to analysis and research results.

5.2 The decision-making process

The prediction paradigm focuses on the employer's decision-making process. From the total applicants the most suitable candidates will have to be chosen. As a result, the selection process is seen as detached from other processes such as recruitment and career management. It is questionable whether this is correct. It is quite conceivable that those other processes make demands on the design of the selection process. When discussing "dignity" we came across an example of this. The obligation to offer minorities a fair opportunity also calls for adjustments of the selection process.

Nowadays, filling a vacancy is a complex process. Usually, the first step is to check whether a vacancy has to be filled. Sometimes, it is decided to adjust the organization so that the vacancy can be cancelled.

If it is decided to fill the vacancy then the question arises as to how to go about it in the best possible way. The labour market is dispersed and consists of niche markets. Candidates within or outside the organization, people working part-time or full-time, or employees with a temporary or permanent appointment may all be eligible. Preference can be given to special categories such as the long-term unemployed, women, foreigners, the handicapped, and so on. In addition, an important step is the way in which applicants are searched for: by means of advertisements, "head-hunters", the job centre, the temps agency, and so on.

Decisions such as these have a bearing on the extent and quality of the group of applicants. Furthermore, not only suitability considerations play a role. for instance, the government, the unions or the works council may stimulate extra opportunities for certain categories of employees ("positive discrimination"). Sometimes, the government provides subsidies for the appointment of certain categories of employees (e.g. the long-term unemployed).

That which follows the selection process deserves attention as well. The decision to employ someone is in most cases the beginning of a long-lasting cooperation between the organization and the individual, and for the employee the beginning of a career. Many organizations used to offer lifelong employment. Lately this has changed since, due to global competition, organizations strive for flexibility. But even so in many cases there will still be a long lasting relationship.

The intensive interaction during the selection process between the supervisor and the personnel officers on the one hand and the applicant on the other may be seen as the beginning of a socialization process. The applicant gets an idea of what they may expect of working in the organization and what expectations the company has regarding their contribution. Likewise, the organization tries to form an opinion of what it can expect of the applicant when appointed. This interaction is based on more than just personal characteristics.

It not only involves a contract based on industrial law, but also a psychological contract by which expectations and to what extent those expectations might be fulfilled are made explicit. Selection in this sense is an exploratory process. The interchange will have to lead to "involvement". This involvement will have influence on the applicant's willingness to accept an offer and keep on working for the organization; it will also influence the applicant's readiness to adapt to a changing environment and put up a qualitatively and quantitatively good performance. When candidates perceive the selection procedure to be open, meticulous and aimed at providing them with adequate information, then this will contribute to the advancement of involvement. If the build-up of involvement fails, then this may result in the offer being refused. It may also result in the candidate leaving the organization shortly after commencement of employment (turnover).

The line of thought behind career and selection policy seems to go very much in the direction of harmonizing the individual's expectations and the expectations of the organization. This is founded on a different paradigm in which selection precedes the harmonization process. This point will be elaborated later. Here, it should be noted that within the harmonization constellation, selection forms part of a more elaborate process. It cannot be examined in isolation, but must be seen in relation to other processes such as recruitment and career management.

Falling short on these points will have a negative effect on involvement and will result in different "outcomes". Here, not only selection procedures are involved, but also other steps within the total process, starting off with recruitment and extending into career management.

5.3 Are achievements determined by the applicant's qualities?

The prediction paradigm is based on the assumption that a successful career depends on the qualities of the applicant. In particular, aptitudes and personality variables come to mind. It is assumed that these characteristics remain unchanged and continue to fulfil an important role during the entire term of employment. These characteristics can be measured with the aid of tests. It is then a matter of technique to find the proper combination of test scores.

In the meantime, it has become obvious that being successful in a career depends on numerous factors. Partly, these factors are linked with the individual's characteristics, but often they are also partly bound up with situational characteristics and the interactions between the two. Moreover, characteristics do not always remain stable. Schneider and Schmitt (1986) note that nobody in his right mind would want to fly with a pilot who has been selected solely by means of a selection interview. It is possible to elaborate on this statement and postulate that no one will have faith in a pilot who has been selected exclusively on the basis of an intelligence test battery and personality questionnaire. Certain skills can only be picked up through training. In order to determine whether such skills are available more is required than holding interviews or conducting "paper and pencil tests". Mostly, it is necessary to construct special tests such as "job samples" or "job simulation tests". Similarly, cognitive skills tests do not always suffice when selection is concerned.

The prediction paradigm assumes that for all members of the population the same characteristics are of equal importance. However, the work situation may differ enormously. Many organizations set great store by assessing whether the applicant fits in with the business culture and is capable of contributing to this culture. This is thought to be of importance for executive functions. The developmental stage of the organization plays a role as well. In a rapidly expanding organization other types of managers, having different kinds of skills, are being looked for than in organizations that are slimming down. Greuter (1988) has shown the possibility of expanding the selection model by not restricting it to personal characteristics, but by including situational characteristics as well so as to be able to determine the interaction between both sets of characteristics. This would result in better predictions. However, it involves a complicated method of working which in turn will push up the costs of selection.

The discussion about personal characteristics has gained extra attention because of publications on validity generalization (Gottfredson & Sharf, 1988).

Furthermore, it means that both the organization and the employee have to do many things in order to make sure that a job is well executed. Job holders have to be trained, and need proper experience before they are able to perform well. So looking for particular qualities in applicants is only the beginning of a process which must lead to good performance.

Some psychologists have advocated that employers should let themselves be guided exclusively by test scores. Prediction formulae for the General Aptitude Test Battery, based on approximately 500 jobs, could be used for this. These psychologists expect this will lead to huge improvements of productivity.

Others are more sceptical (e.g. Bentz, 1988). They think that decisions cannot be based on personal characteristics alone. For instance, the culture of an organization and the extent to which an applicant can contribute to it have to be taken into account as well.

Schneider and Schmitt (1986, p. 408) sum it up well: "... any staffing system cannot resolve all organizational problems." "... organizations can be helped through a variety of strategies including hiring people...". It involves a combination of strategies of which selection is just one, but which should also include training, career development, adjustment of jobs and organizations, consultation, and so on. In short, all those subjects that are addressed in this handbook.

5.4 To what extent is it possible to execute validity studies?

Thorndike's model is based on the assumption that the selector constantly tests his procedures. In 1949 (p. 2 & p. 119), he wrote: "... the reputable worker in the field is continuously concerned with testing, verifying and improving the adequacy of his procedures". *Not* testing he finds despicable: "A personnel selection program which does not involve empirical checks of the selection procedures against criteria of job success is at best a static and untested one. At worst it might be outright charlatanism". Consequently, selectors were constantly told that they ought to conduct validity studies. Predictors have to be correlated with criteria.

This approach proved to be successful to some extent. Particularly in the 1950s, a great many validity studies were conducted. For many years, the *Personnel Psychology* journal featured a column under the name of 'Validity exchange information' in which these studies were published. In The Netherlands, the results of validity studies were systematically collected in test documentaries by the "Test Research Committee", the forerunner of the present COTAN (Commissie Testaangelegenheden Nederland). Furthermore, it was noticeable that researchers succeeded in bringing together dozens of studies about relationships between predictors and criteria for one specific job or group of jobs when conducting meta-analyses. These include a good number of studies that were not published in professional journals. Thanks to this huge number of studies, insight into the validity of predictors increased considerably.

However, it is remarkable that a great many of these studies emanate from big (government) institutions, such as the United States Employment Service, the military forces and large companies. Smaller organizations seem much less capable of conducting this kind of research. The problems focus on two issues: the size of the samples, and the costs. In many institutions and businesses it appears to be difficult to conduct validation studies, due to limited samples. The number of vacancies is too limited for that purpose. By way of illustration, when in the late 1960s some Dutch firms became interested in the use of tests for creativity prediction, it appeared that research could only be carried out by grouping together the efforts of five large selection departments. Only in this way could a sufficiently large sample be obtained (Elshout et al., 1973). For many jobs it is impossible to follow the mode of operation as prescribed by Thorndike.

The costs constitute the second problem. A complete validation study inquiry, including the construction of a workable criterion, requires a substantial investment. Such an inquiry is time-consuming. In many instances, such an investment cannot be turned into a paying proposition. Furthermore, institutions and services usually do not have the resources available to carry out such investigations. Consequently, it is not surprising that in many cases no validity studies were conducted.

Further, attention has to be paid to the construction of selection instruments. Test construction is time-consuming and expensive. In the 1950s and 1960s European universities were active in this field. In the 1970s and 1980s this work came largely to a standstill. It does not look as if the 1990s will bring about many changes in this respect. For selection consultancies and functional organizations this work requires too large an investment. As a result, instruments that were developed many years ago are still being used in large measure.

6. THE ORIENTATION OF ORGANIZATIONAL CONSULTANTS

In 1964, Leavitt wrote an article on the different modes of operation being used by consultants (Leavitt, 1964). He distinguished technological, structural and people approaches. Each one of those approaches is based on value orientation; the adherents have their own vision as to how social problems can be dealt with in the best possible way. As an example of a technological approach he gives a description of "scientific management". Technological approaches objectively seek the best solution, mainly by using techniques. *Rationality* plays a central role in this approach. The tragedy of the case is that rational solutions are not always accepted, and often provoke resistance. The proponents of the technological approach usually attribute this to poor training of the employees involved. People should be trained so as to learn how to appreciate the quality of a solution. More radical adherents prefer the idea of compulsion. Those involved must be coerced into applying the rational solution. Adherents to the rational approach have been reproached as being naive by advisors who take a strong interest in the people approach. Leavitt concludes that "they can point, in evidence, to a monotonously long list of cases in which technological innovations ... have fallen short, because they ignored the human side of enterprise".

The prediction approach to selection appears to be a good example of a rational approach.

Structural approaches concentrate on tasks, competences and responsibilities which they try to regulate and define. The central value here is *legitimacy*. Who has the duty and the competence to do something and in what way are those actions going to be answered for?

This approach can also be recognized in the selection practice. Legislation and instructions that were discussed before ("equal employment opportunities", the Hessel commission, professional ethics) must be classed with this category. Problems are being dealt with by formulating rules and procedures. Interests are protected by determining the desired or compulsory procedures.

The third category, the people approach, concentrates on relations between people. Here, the central value is *involvement*. Only when involved in something are people prepared to seek a solution. Without involvement there can be no cooperation. Although this approach has received less attention in the selection issue, some examples may yet be mentioned. The LIAMA programme (a programme for the selection of life insurance agents that was developed in the United States in the 1960s) attaches great value to "joint exploration" and "mutual decision-making" (LIAMA, 1968). The psychologist's role in this programme is to facilitate these processes by analysing job requirements, structuring the interaction process between supervisor and applicant, and training supervisors to conduct selection interviews. Leavitt wrote his article in 1964, at a moment when only the technological approach within the selection process received attention. His article had no bearing on selection whatsoever, but was much more aimed at "organizational change". His remark about adherents of the rational approach who "ignored the human side of enterprise" was thrown into sharp relief in the years to come, because of the many reactions to the existing selection approach such as those mentioned in the section about "dignity". Since then, the other two approaches have received more attention.

Leavitt concludes that of the three approaches each one is useful to some extent and even necessary. Consequently, he favours some sort of "mixture". However, how such a mixture should come about remains unclear.

A combination also seems to be appropriate for selection. Rationality, legitimacy and involvement are each important values, and none of them can be neglected. The technological approach has yielded useful methods. The structural approach has resulted in rules and procedures which must be observed, and the human approach points out the importance of involvement. Although this has been worked out the least in selection theory there are other areas in W&O psychology which deal specifically with this subject such as participation and motivation.

7. OTHER APPROACHES TO PERSONNEL SELECTION

Literature on selection has been dominated by the prediction programme to a great extent. However, there are other approaches as well. These can be classed under three headings: improvement of the assessment process formation; improvement of decision-making processes; and career approaches.

7.1 The improvement of the assessment process

In most cases the decision to engage or reject a candidate is founded on the judgement of company officials (usually the supervisor). Extensive research has been conducted into ratings (see Chapter 4) in business as well as in selection situations. On the basis of that research serious doubts have arisen about the predictive value of assessments. Inter-rater agreement is often modest. Because of these findings, many psychologists have developed a profound distrust of the use of ratings, which mainly became manifest in the 1950s and 1960s. Even the selection interview enjoyed a dubious reputation. In 1965, Guion observed that "interviews and interviewing procedures are notoriously fallible".

New investigations have altered this view (see Drenth, 1988b for a review, and Harris, 1989). A selection interview may indeed lead to valid statements, provided it is well-structured. Research carried out by Mayfield et al. (1964) and Carlson et al. (1971) in particular has shown that the validity of assessments may be acceptable, if carefully constructed interview schemes are used to work with instead of impressions.

Mayfield and Carlson have worked out their findings in a selection procedure for life insurance agents (Carlson et al., 1971 and Mayfield et al., 1980). Their procedure did not include any psychological tests because, among other things, it seemed virtually impossible to hold these tests under standardized circumstances. They concentrated on a detailed interview scheme based on extensive job analysis. The scheme enters into experience acquired during preliminary training and in social contacts, and the way in which financial matters are being treated. Variables that must be assessed are: "ability to plan", "past sales related experience", "ability to keep financial situations under control", and "interest in people related activities".

The interviewers receive a comprehensive training in the use of this scheme. Mayfield shows that assessments based on this approach measure different factors. It is not just a "halo effect" that is involved, but also assessments of behavioural aspects which indeed represent characteristics of the applicants.

Another method to arrive at more valid assessments is described by Latham et al. (1975). Here, use is being made of the "critical incidents" approach. Latham's approach is in conformity with methods as described by Campbell et al. (1970). Raters are asked to bring forward both excellent and inadequate examples of job fulfilment. The incidents are then rubricated and the question is asked which behaviour is of important relevance to adequate job fulfilment. Latham used these incidents for drawing up "behavioral observation scales" (see Chapter 4). This method lends itself to determining what has to be assessed, as well as to the development of assessment scales. An advantage seems to be that the method can be applied to large numbers of applicants as well as small groups, and even to individual positions.

The LIAMA programme pays particular attention to new requirements being formulated in the jobs. If life insurance agents want to make promotion and become inspector, then the extent to which job requirements differ from former requirements is looked into, as well as the way psychological rewards will change. To what extent a new job requires different "coping" strategies is investigated in other programmes. When assessing suitability special attention is given to these changes.

Likewise, *assessment centers* constitute a

method with which to obtain a more valid judgement formation concerning suitability. With this method raters are called in who have, as a result of their position, a good understanding of the job requirements. This method pays much attention to the creation of situations that facilitate assessment. This is done by letting applicants participate in exercises such as "leaderless group discussions" (see for a description, Thornton & Byham, 1982). This gives raters the opportunity to assess dimensions like "flexibility", "leadership", "planning and organisation", "human relations", "oral communication", and so on. Candidates are confronted with situations in which relevant behaviour is provoked. This behaviour is observed by the raters who are thus able to assess these dimensions appropriately.

The assessment center method often makes a distinction between assessment dimensions that are relevant at the outset of the career, and dimensions that become relevant later on (Thornton & Byham, 1982). Likewise, applicants are distinguished into, for example, first line supervisors, middle managers and top managers. For each category separate assessment dimensions are determined.

It appears that in the 1970s and 1980s much was set in motion to improve the assessment of applicants. The validity of ratings can be improved by bringing in more raters, careful analysis of job requirements, creating situations that facilitate assessments, determining assessment dimensions and construing assessment scales to provide adequate bench marks, and by setting up interview schemes.

Contrary to impressionistic assessments, which psychologists distrust with good reason, these assessments—based on carefully construed procedures—are usable. Key issues are the careful analysis of job requirements and the scrutinizing of the experience of the applicants.

7.2 The decision-making process

Several authors pay attention about the interaction process between employer and applicant, the information both parties need, and the way in which the decision is made.

The prediction model is concerned with the decision-making process of the employer who should base his decision on calculation. Those applicants who score best should be engaged.

This approach is set off by another that stresses that both the organization and the applicant bear their own responsibility. The decision to employ someone should only be taken after ample consultation in which the parties carefully examine what the consequences of the decision will be and whether they are capable of meeting accepted commitments. That consultation should deal with job requirements, capacities and terms of employment.

The adherents to this approach hold principle as well as suitability arguments. The principle argument bears on responsibility which should be dealt with carefully. Individuals and organizations are responsible for their decisions and can be sued for their acts. The implication is that when both parties enter into a relationship they ought to examine from both sides what the possible consequences of such a step may be. Responsibility has to be accepted explicitly for tasks and results.

Usually, the suitability argument is upheld by the idea that ample consultation will result in better insight into job requirements and realistic expectations regarding the results which, in turn, may lead to more involvement. This would manifest itself in a greater willingness to accept a job, less wastage and absence, and better performance (Wanous, 1980). Decision making only on the basis of calculation is rejected by many because it reduces the applicant to an object.

Other approaches have also received attention in scientific literature. The Minnesota studies (Lofquist & Dawis, 1969) focus mainly on the adjustment between function ("job") and individual. At first, these studies had more influence on "career counselling" than selection, but are highly relevant to selection. Lofquist and Dawis recognize that there are two adjustment processes: there is relation between job requirements and abilities on the one hand, and between "needs" and "rewards" on the other. For both relations it is a matter of balance. Lack of balance between requirements and abilities would lead to "unsatisfactoriness" which may urge the organization to look for another solution (dismissal, transfer). Lack of balance between "needs" and "rewards" would lead to dissatisfaction. This may stimulate the employee to look for another solution, for example, to look for another job (see Figure 3.1).

Lofquist and Dawis base their research on a "fit" model: too much as well as too little leads to instability. If someone can do more than the job requires, then this is also a matter of lack of correspondence which requires action to be undertaken so as to change the situation (e.g. by promotion or by searching for a job with more responsibilities). Another important feature of this model is that it departs from dynamic balances. Both job requirements and suitability are susceptible to change, as is the case with "reward" and "needs". That happens as a consequence of the turbulent environment in which organizations operate, but also because of, for example, people growing into their job and acquiring new skills and knowledge as a result of it. Dynamic balances require constant adjustment. The organization as well as the employee have to turn their thoughts to this adjustment process. This is possible by, for example, accepting other jobs or by adjusting those jobs. Consequently, this model differs markedly from that developed by Thorndike.

Another method of decision making presents itself in the LIAMA study already mentioned (LIAMA, 1968). Here, much attention is paid to consultation. During the recruitment and selection period the applicant is informed in great detail about their job and the terms of employment. Furthermore, the extent to which the work meets the applicant's psychological needs are examined. The potential load that comes with the work is discussed as well (LIAMA, 1968). In an explanatory note the authors point out that selection should no longer be regarded as a unilateral decision taken by the organization, but as part of a personnel development programme. It should form an integrated entity together with recruitment, introduction, training and supervision. The parts should not be seen as independent of each other. What is done in the framework of one part should be coordinated with what takes place in other parts.

For that reason, "mutual consent" as regards career decisions and "joint exploration" for the realization of such decisions are held in great account. The complete procedure, especially the selection interview, is structured in such a way that all aspects of the jobs in question are covered by supervisor and applicant. The interview is meant to investigate whether the applicant can be expected to fulfil the job requirements and whether the job will satisfy them. Supervisors must be trained carefully so that they know how to conduct such selection interviews. This entirely different approach towards the applicant also resulted in the notion that applicants have a need

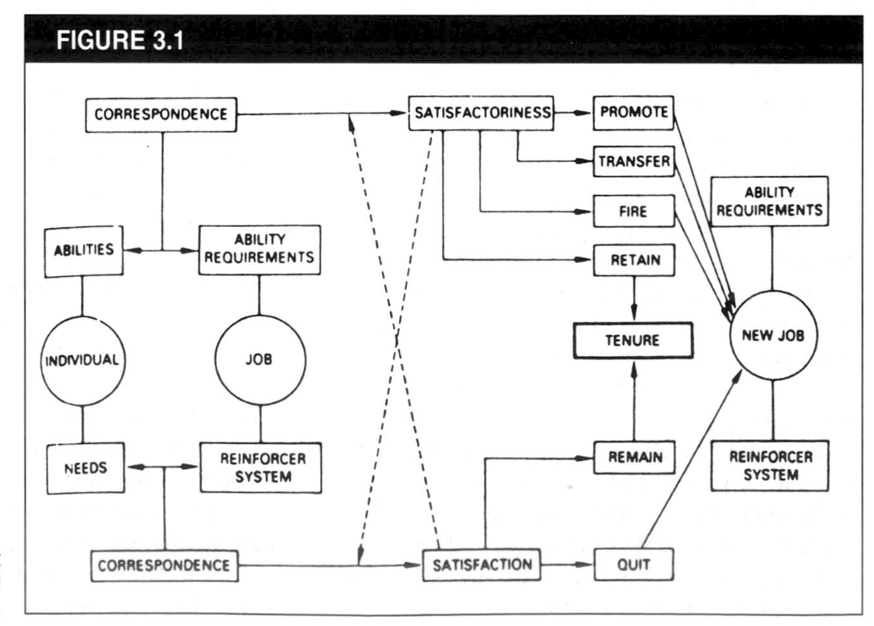

The Work Adjustment Model (Lofquist and Dawis, 1969).

for information concerning the job. In order to take a sound decision about whether or not to accept an offer, good insight into the job requirements and the rewards is first of all required.

In recent years much attention has been paid to "realistic previews" (Wanous, 1980, 1989). The intention is to provide the candidate with the most realistic information possible about what the job has in store for them. By doing so, it is hoped that wastage can be prevented. Latham (Latham et al., 1975) states that information collected by means of a "critical incident" method lends itself very well to setting up such previews. The assessment scales which he developed can be discussed with the candidates in an excellent manner. Figure 3.2 presents an example of a scale developed for the selection of medical consultants based on critical incidents collected from role sets (De Wolff & Schopman-Geurts van Kessel, 1992).

"Realistic previews" indicate what the organization expects of the applicant. It is possible to interpret it as a way of "goal setting". Research shows that goal setting leads to greater commitment and better performance (Locke et al., 1981; Locke & Latham, 1990).

Psychologists have spent quite some time on job analyses. Fleishman has spent a lifetime on developing a taxonomy of human abilities. Much of his work is condensed in his *Job Analysis Survey* (Fleishman, 1992). In this survey 52 human abilities in four major areas (cognitive, psychomotor, physical and sensory/perceptual) are defined. In addition there are 20 other scales on interactive/social and knowledge/skills requirements which are still under development. For each requirement Fleishman has constructed a scale, using specific examples as anchors. The scale can be used by supervisors and by job incumbents. The reliability is high. Using these scales one acquires a good overview of the requirements. This can be discussed with applicants. For each requirement Fleishman mentions test examples (Fleishman & Reilly, 1992).

Fleishman's scales appear to be quite useful in the mutual exploration process. One can discuss with applicants to what extent they are able to meet the expectations of the organization.

Several authors point out that the interaction process between supervisor and applicant is not a neutral one (Herriot, 1989a,b). Levinson et al. (1962) and Gellerman (1968) show that implicit processes also play a role during this process. They state that when entering into a relationship interdependency comes into play. Each party expects that the relation will result in certain outcomes which makes the continuation of the relationship worthwhile. In the interaction process the parties build up the implicit expectation that the other party will do anything to keep the relationship satisfactory. Should the other party fail to meet this expectation, then this will lead to distrust and dissatisfaction. In this view, the selection process is an introduction in which both parties weigh up what to expect of the other party. It not only involves the outcomes in the short term, but also those in the long term. The long-term outcomes may be so important that they provide the incentive for continuing the relationship and contributing to the organization's objectives. This (p. 51) ". . . refers to the tendency by an employee to assume that his organization has tacitly accepted the responsibility for enabling him to fulfil his unstated aspirations as the 'psychological contract' ".

In the case of non-observance of the contract, it does not always mean that an employee will hand in his resignation. It does mean, however, that the employee will adopt a more noncommittal attitude and will identify less with the organization's objectives.

Gellerman explains that not only explicit matters are involved when it comes to selection processes. Parties make estimates of what they may reasonably expect. If this leads to mistakes, then this may seriously affect "commitment". Such implicit processes seem difficult to avoid completely. It seems useful, however, to structure the procedures in such a way that misunderstandings can be avoided as much as possible.

A special aspect constitutes participation in appointments. In the 1970s, there was much discussion on this issue in The Netherlands. For one thing, the idea was to provide prospective colleagues with more influence on the decision-making process. For another, it was also considered to involve subordinates in this process. Since then, the discussion has subsided. On

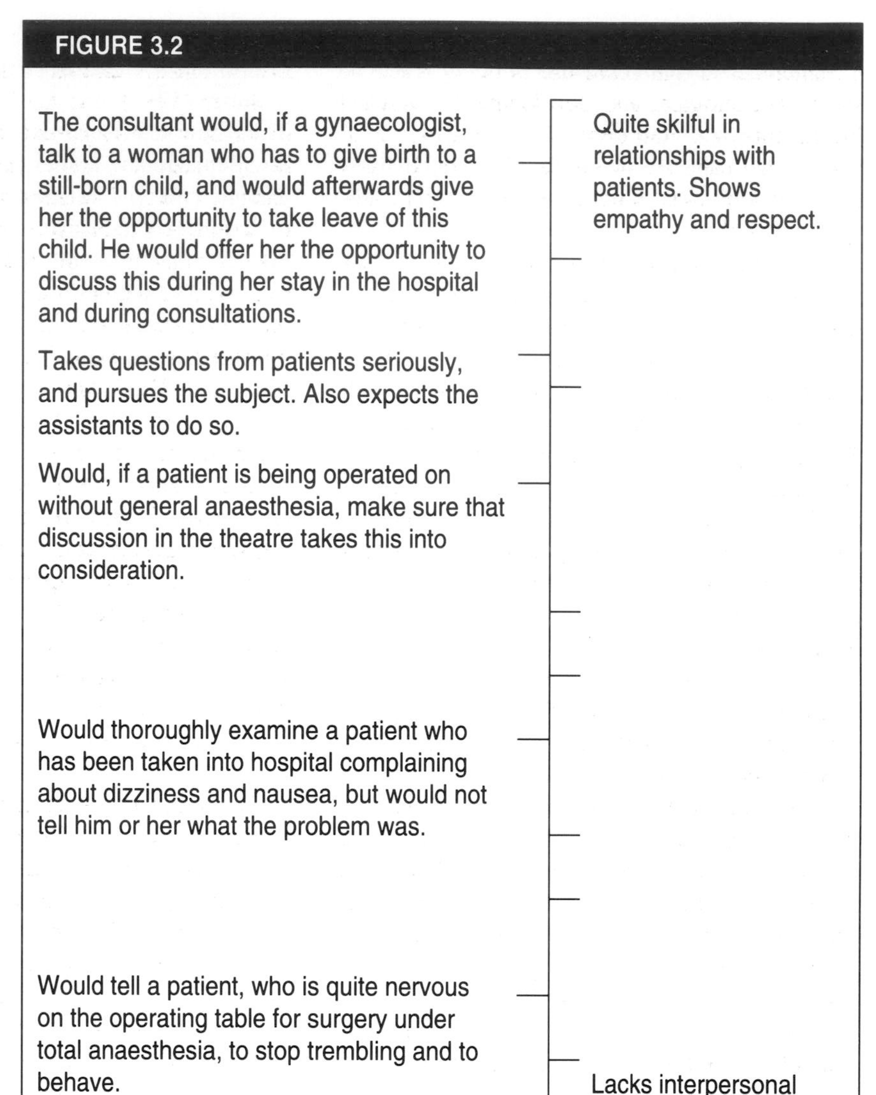

Interpersonal skills of a consultant in relation to patients.

condition that such participation is well-structured, an advantage may be that a clearer formulation of the job requirements and expectations takes place. The applicants as well as the employees involved obtain more opportunities to assess what expectations exist and can ascertain for themselves to what extent they can meet those expectations.

7.3 The career approach

Over the past two decades, interest in career development boomed. Special attention was given to the career development of senior personnel (see Chapters 11 and 12 in this handbook). This development is also of vast concern to selection. Selection and career-guidance have an identical objective: the build up of an adequate work force.

What is striking in literature concerning career management is that more use is being made of socio-psychological and developmental psychological theories. Hall (Hall & Associates, 1986) notices that there are two lines of approach. Seen from the individual's point of view career management is about:

"... attempting to plan his or her career in a personally satisfying and productive manner". Conversely, from an organizational point of view it needs to: "... effectively select, assess, assign and develop employees to provide a pool of qualified people to meet future corporate needs". This description is in accordance with the "work adjustment theory" of Lofquist and Dawis (1969) in which two lines of approach are mentioned as well. The applicant or employee aims at a development that will meet their own needs and the organization is looking for candidates who meet its requirements.

There is a vast difference in views and methodology between career theoreticians and adepts of the selection paradigm regarding the issue as to how a workforce should be set up. The selection paradigm concentrates on predictions based on stable characteristics of the candidates. The career approach concentrates on "development". Employees (and applicants) are regarded as people who are developing and who have to find a place within a changing organization with a changing workforce. Not "predicting" but "developing" and "harmonizing" are the key words here. Hall (1986) emphasizes that it is an "ongoing process". There is no once-only decision, but a continuous occupation with preparing, implementing and following critically.

In career theories the life-story perspective plays an important role. Following Erikson (1968), Schein (1978), Hall (1976) and Super (1980) distinguish stages in the course of life and career. Each stage is characterized by specific assignments which in turn result in specific attitudes. At the outset of the career a position has to be conquered; having found a position a search for characteristic features has to be conducted. Hall describes this process as "identity development through personal choice". He realizes that such a growth process is also a matter of "adult socialization". The new employee is confronted with the values of the organization which he adopts and makes himself familiar with.

Super (1980) and Hall (1986) point out the different transition periods in which new roles are being taken on, and that identity undergoes changes as well. The transition from school-leaver to "employee" constitutes such a transformation. Socialization processes require intensive interaction with the organization. The demands made by the organization should in fact be in accordance with the developmental stage one is in ("Life cycle matching", Hall 1986).

This is not the place to enlarge on career theories. For that the reader is referred to Chapter 12 and to Hall (1986). On the basis of this short description it may be clear that although the objectives of selection and career management go well together their approach differs markedly. This is also evident from the instruments used. Activities in the field of career development are seminars, "workshops", career interviews and "assessment centers".

Characteristic features that go with them are:

- The employee is seen as someone who develops and acquires an identity as a result of the choices he or she makes and the responsibilities taken on. In order to make choices the employee must have information at his or her disposal. Consequently, many activities in the field of career development are geared to the exchange of information and the acquisition of communicative skills so that the employee is capable of acquiring information.
- The supervisor has an important task in providing information, in giving feedback and social support.
- The procedures leave much room for participation. Prior to taking any decisions intensive interaction between the organization and the employee takes place.
- Age and the course of life are important aspects for development and thus for suitability. The course of life goes hand in hand with development which implies that capacities change. Accordingly, suitability is not a stable factor. It is possible to become more suitable—or less suitable—depending on that development. Age constitutes an important variable in this respect.

This has far-reaching consequences for selection. When selecting, not only personal characteristics should be taken into account but the developmental process as well. Selection becomes an "organizational entry", i.e. a means for entering the organization, and constitutes the beginning of an "ongoing process", an intensive process between organization and employee. The responsibility for a smooth proceeding of this process rests with the organization as well as the employee. In this approach the employee is subject and not object, as was the case in the prediction model.

8 PROFESSIONAL DEVELOPMENTS

For a long time W&O psychologists have taken up a unique position with regard to personnel selection. They were considered to be outstanding experts who had to cope with hardly any serious competition. In recent years this has changed rapidly. More and more, customers avail themselves of the services of other experts.

Staffing has become a complicated trouble spot. We already mentioned the juridical problems which arose in the United States as a consequence of stringent legislation. That's why lawyers got more and more involved in selection problems. But employment-finding acquired additional significance as well.

The labour market has become much more complex and is nowadays less transparent. Organizations make much use of temp agencies and headhunters. The number of employment-finding bureaus has increased rapidly and with this, specialization. Certain sectors of the labour market are being focused on. When starting with the search for suitable candidates it only takes a short step to giving advice on appointment. With employment-finding the suitability question is always under consideration, either implicitly or explicitly.

Through this development the position of W&O psychologists has changed. They are no longer the only experts working in the field of personnel selection. Furthermore, the question arises as to which services they should deliver. Because of the increasing complexity there is a growing tendency not to limit oneself to selection in the narrow sense of the word. At present, there are psychologists who busy themselves with recruitment and employment-finding as well.

The psychologist's customer is usually a company official who has only limited experience in recruitment and employment-finding. Bigger companies do indeed have specialized services, but in most organizations the number of vacancies to be fulfilled is often small. Many supervisors and directors are involved in a selection procedure only a few times per year.

Given the problematic nature of the issue, a need for expert support makes itself felt. In addition, there is a growing need for a professional who can take a comprehensive view of the entire field; not only the question of selection, but also recruitment and career problems. That forces psychologists to reflect on the question of job demarcation: what services do they want to offer? With which other experts do they want to cooperate? There is clearly a tendency towards extension of the service package and specialization in sectors of the labour market.

Another trend is internationalization. In the 1960s many northwest-European companies decided to recruit candidates for production jobs in the Mediterranean. With the fast growth of international organizations the need for recruitment abroad increases. In addition, the possibilities that result from the Treaty of Rome for working in one of the associated countries are being used more and more. Consequently, the labour market is no longer a national market exclusively, but has gradually acquired a more international character. This forces recruitment and selection professionals to look at the issue in a wider perspective and intensifies the tendency towards specialization. This development will have even more impact as a result of the further integration of the European market.

It also leads to other research questions. What are the consequences of appointing foreigners who speak a different language and who have to adapt to another culture? Test values for foreigners may differ considerably. For example as a consequence of differences in education. Thus, it appeared that foreign workers who applied for a job with a Dutch firm in the 1960s, scored remarkably lower on tests from the General Test Aptitude Battery. It turned out that they had had only a few years of primary education.

In short, selection psychologists' *domain* is changing. They must allow for questions of a different nature and with other competitors.

9 THE SELECTION PSYCHOLOGIST'S ROLE

The three different approaches regarding selection lead to differences in role interpretation.

The *technological approach* may easily lead to identification with the client. Thorndike (1949) gives a clear example of this. In the last part of his book he enters into the role of the psychologist. First of all, he underlines that selection programmes can only be executed if there is explicit support on the part of the "top management". "It is of critical importance to sell the program to those members of top management who have the power of life and death over the program" (p. 312). When working out the psychologist's role Thorndike not only points out the research and developmental tasks, but he also sees a task reserved for the psychologist in determining policy: "he should participate in determining policy and administrative routines for the utilization of test results" (p. 310). The ultimate possibility, he realizes (p. 311) is that "the psychologist may be given final responsibility for the administrative decision on the placement of each man".

Rational approaches are aimed at technical solutions and continuous improvement thereof. Deviation from an advice based on the best solution is hard to accept. Non-observance of the advice will then be interpreted as dissipation. Therefore, some psychologists want to give the advice an obligatory nature. Supervisors and personnel officers should not be able to back out of it.

The *structural approach* is particularly popular with the government and the labour unions. In the Netherlands, psychologists did try to formulate rules within their professional ethics concerning the responsibilities of the selection psychologist and the rights of the applicants. There exists, for example, a right of complaint and it is laid down that psychologists are obliged to inform the applicant in detail about the selection procedure. Adherents of the structural approach are inclined to think that the applicant's position is too weak. They also have an eye for the weak position of minorities in the labour market. They often plead for instructions so as to improve this position. To that effect, psychologists have paid attention to such matters as participation in an appointment. They also focused their attention on interests and procedures. Examples can be found in Jansen's book (1979) in which the interests of applicants, labour organizations and selectors are discussed as well as the demands made on selection procedures. As already mentioned, Jansen also considers the rights of applicants and organizations. It is here that we find most clearly role perceptions of psychologists that fit in with the structural approach.

The *people approach* underlines the negotiating character of selection procedures, albeit not so much in a juridical as well as a psychological sense. In principle, there are two parties who freely negotiate with one another and who try to reach agreement. The role of the selection psychologist in particular is aimed at facilitating this negotiation process. This can be achieved in several ways. First of all, the psychologist can contribute by helping parties to formulate the issue at hand, for example, by formulating the job requirements or the applicants' needs. The psychologist can make use of such methods as job analysis, critical incidents and questionnaires. Further, the psychologist may help by structuring procedures, for example, by drafting interview schemes and assessment scales.

Contrary to the technological approach the problems of the client as well as those of the applicant are being dealt with and the mutuality is underlined. Concepts such as "mutual exploration" and "joint decision making", as formulated in the LIAMA procedure, fit in with this approach. The build-up of involvement is stressed in particular. Here, in contrast with their technically oriented colleague, the psychologist does not think of him or herself as a decider but as a helper. It is the parties themselves who must decide and who bear the responsibility for the consequences.

10 WHY A PSYCHOLOGICAL EXAMINATION?

The prediction model has nearly always been defended on the basis of its rationality. It was supposed to contribute to a better operating result. Therefore, it should be accepted first and foremost on economic grounds. Consequently, many selectors legitimized their services by virtue of their conviction that this would lead to better operating results. However, the question remains whether this is the only or even the most important reason for the attractiveness of psychological research.

Selection has another bearing as well. Great interests are at stake for all those involved. In most cases, it is a question of sought-after positions for which a number of people wish to be considered. Being elected not only yields material benefits, such as an income, but also immaterial profits such as acknowledgement and esteem. The organization's interest should be the only issue that comes into play in the decision-making process, but in practice this is not always the case. Other considerations may come into play as a result of which persons and groups are either favoured or put at a disadvantage. There are many of these "other" considerations. Some of them are partly legal, others are partly illegal. Some considerations are accepted socially, some are controversial and others are rejected. Mendels' statement, already cited, that "the employer is free to take on employees who, by working harmoniously, contribute to the best possible functioning of the entity as coordinated by him" (Mendel, 1975), leaves a wide latitude for the decider. Especially, the phrase "by working harmoniously" lends to a diversity of interpretations. In family businesses it could mean that a son is to follow in his father's shoes. In certain cultures it is common practice to give relatives and friends in particular the opportunity to profit from vacancies (nepotism).

In western society governments exert more and more influence so as to enable minorities and "the underprivileged" to come better into their own. By issuing rules, companies are obliged to apply positive discrimination, i.e. give preference to those that belong to a minority group.

In other cultures it is customary for the decider to demand a special kind of loyalty in exchange for their support. The decider tries to surround themself with employees that are loyal to them. According to a certain organization theory (Thompson, 1967) in every organization a dominant coalition can be found with a vision of its own on reality. Important vacancies are filled by people who join this coalition.

Therefore, selection is not just a rational process but often a political one. People and parties try to exert influence on the decision-making process. Calling in a rationally-working psychologist introduces objectivity into the procedure. The prediction approach does not depart from interests, but from abilities and performance. Little is known about the question as to why customers call in psychologists for personnel selection. However, it may very well be that the element of objectivity plays an important role. Since interests loom large, the decider may be charged with not having been guided by general organizational interests exclusively. Being able to refer to the contribution of a psychologist and with it to the rationality of the procedure is then a great point gained.

11 PERSONNEL SELECTION IN THE FUTURE

It is clear there is no "best" way to do personnel selection. An organization has to take into account many considerations when setting up a selection procedure. When there are many applicants for a training programme, the organization may select a different procedure than when it selects an executive who should do a turn-around project in a large organization. There are legal aspects, differences in positions, competition with other organizations who want to employ the same applicants, expectation in the past of the applicants and the organization, availability of validity information and many other variables which have to be taken into account.

An important aspect is the psychological contract which has to be established between the new employee and the organization. What is it that the organization expects the new employee to do, and what is it they are prepared to do in return? And what is it the employee expects from the organization, and will the employee be able to meet the expectations of the organization? Exploring such questions is likely to be even more important in the future. In the past years there have been profound changes in the relationships between organizations and employees (Offerman & Gowing, 1993). Organizations used to offer a substantial amount of security, particularly related to labour conditions. There were many organizations offering lifelong employment, promotion from within, income guarantees, pension schemes, and so on. Organizations preferred to recruit young people, who were socialized, and offered a career. In return the organizations expected loyalty and a high degree of commitment. Labour contracts, both collectively and individually, were tailored to such an approach.

Nowadays flexibility is stressed. Organizations want to be able to adapt rapidly to changes in the task environment and offering security is now often seen as incompatible with the need for flexibility.

Organizations have to down-size and to become lean. Many contracts are now temporary. The consequence is that there is now more ambiguity. Will one still have a job next year? Should one look for a job elsewhere? This means that discussing the terms of the psychological contract becomes even more important. To reduce ambiguity, more explicit discussion of the terms of the contract is necessary.

Another change is the composition of the workforce. In many countries there was a baby boom after the Second World War. The effect was that during the 1970s and 1980s many young and well-educated applicants were seeking employment. But over the next few decades it is expected that there will be many older applicants and fewer young applicants. Organizations will have to change their hiring policies, and will also have to find out how they can retain their older employees.

Furthermore there are marked changes in the ethnic composition of the workforce. Many people from Mediterranean countries have moved to the north and west of Europe. In addition many women now seek employment. Again this requires organizations to discuss carefully the terms of psychological contracts. Labour conditions may have to be tailored to the specific needs of these applicants.

Nowadays organizations often have to work on a global scale. Employees may have to work in other countries, and new employees may have to be recruited abroad. In order to meet the competition new organizational structures are introduced. Organizations have to be flat; workers have to work in teams. New technologies are introduced (e.g. multi-media, teleworking). In this post industrial period we will have a service economy, where meeting the demands of customers will have top priority. On the other hand, employees will ask for more autonomy and will be more self-development oriented.

This all leads to more personalized relationship between the organization and the individual. Both will feel a need to specify more explicitly what they expect from each other. This also means that personnel selection cannot be isolated from other instruments such as performance appraisal, career management, and training.

12 REVIEW AND CONCLUSIONS

This chapter started off with the observation that selection has had an eventful history, characterized by many conflicts. In the last two decades clear changes became noticeable. The most characteristic developments have been: the renewed European interest in selection; the erosion of the prediction paradigm and the rise of the career counselling approach; and changing professional attitudes as a result of changes in domain and increasing competition. These changes have created new possibilities on the one hand, but also entail obvious risks. The possibilities are related to the application of knowledge in particular; the risks lie mainly in the quality of the service.

Following Leavitt, we distinguished three approaches in this chapter that are all identifiable in theory and practice. It is the technological approach which has dominated the history of selection. However, the people approach has become more prominent in the last two decades. By showing that such approaches go hand in hand with value orientation, the impression could be conveyed that a choice between these three is arbitrary from a scientific point of view. That is incorrect. Leavitt himself pleads for a mixture; he considers the theories to be complementary. Nor is it a coincidence that this shift took place exactly in the latter period. The technological approach reached its culminating point in the first half of this century, a period in which attention was mainly focused on mass production. The human approach emerged in a period in which "human resources management" became central and in which having to adjust continuously to a turbulent task environment constitutes the most important strategic assignment.

The prediction paradigm is especially useful if one is not to worry about involvement and the setting of tasks. A strategy aimed at the capitalization on individual differences is then highly appropriate. This can be accomplished when one selects for training programmes in which a great number of applicants are involved and the criterion is known and measurable. However, where tasks change as a result of a turbulent environment, where the adequacy of knowledge and experience must be judged, and where identification with and acceptance by the organization play a major role, the career management approach is more appropriate by far. In any case, the structural approach merits constant attention. Employment is a scarce item. Not only the government but pressure groups as well will constantly occupy themselves with the distribution of it.

The risks are related to the providing of services. Due to extensive research there is now much knowledge available which can be used for personnel selection. But there have been changes among service providers, and it is questionable if the available knowledge is adequately used. In the period where psychologists dominated personnel selection there was strong colleague surveillance. This could clearly be seen in the discussions on the code of conduct during the 1970s.

In the years that followed, many psychologists lost interest in the subject. In university training programmes there is less space for selection. As a consequence professionals enlisting this field are less familiar with the subject, and there is less surveillance. One of the strongest aspects of the Thorndike approach was the strong identification with quality. For the development of personnel selection a continuous concern for quality of services is essential.

REFERENCES

Army Air Force Aviation psychology program research reports (1947). US Government Printing Office.

Ash, P., & Kroecker, L.P. (1975). Personnel selection, classification and placement. *Annual Review, 26.*

Bentz, V.J. (1988). Comments on papers concerning fairness in employment testing. *Journal of Vocational Behavior, 33*(3), 388–398.

Bingham, W.V. (1950). Persons or guinea pigs? *Personnel Psychology, 3,* 305–400.

Bray, D.W., & Moses, J.L. (1972). Personnel selection. *Annual Review, 23,* 545–576.

Buros, O.K. (Ed.) (1938). *The mental measurements yearbook.* New York: Gryphon Press, 1938–39.

Campbell, J.P., Dunnette, M.D., Lawler, E.E., & Weick, K.E. (1970). *Managerial behavior, performance and effectiveness.* New York: McGraw-Hill.

Carlson, R.E., Thayer, P.W., Mayfield, E.C. & Peterson, D.A. (1971). Improvements in the selection interview. *Personnel Journal, 50,* 268–275.

Cattel, J. Mck. (1890). Mental tests and measurements. *Mind, 15,* 373–380.

Conrad, H.S. (1967). Clearance of questionnaires with respect to invasion of privacy, public sensitiveness, ethical standards, etc. *American Psychologist, 22,* 356–359.

Dilthey, W. (1923). *Einleitung in die geistes wissenschaften: Versuch einer Grundlegung für dem Studieren des Gesellschaft und der Geschichte.* Leipzig: Groethuysen.

Drenth, P.J.D. (1967). *Protesten contra testen.* Amsterdam: Swets en Zeitlinger.

Drenth, P.J.D. (1975). *Inleiding in de test theorie.* Deventer: Van Loghum Slaterus.

Drenth, P.J.D. (1988a). Psychologische selectie en discriminatie. *Gedrag & Organisatie, 1*(3), 12–22.

Drenth, P.J.D. (1988b). De waarde van het selectie-interview. *Gedrag & Organisatie, 3*(2), 18–26.

Drenth, P.J.D. (1989). Psychological testing and discrimination. In: P. Herriot, (Ed.) *Assessment and selection in organizations* (pp. 71–80). Chichester, Wiley.

Eindrapport Commissie (1977). *Selectieprocedure: Eensollicitant is œk een mens. Sociale Zaken Verslagen en Rapporten, 1977–5.* Den Haag: Sociale Zaken.

Elshout, J.J., Boselie, F., Van de Berg, J., Boerlijst, G. & Schaake, B. (1973). De validatie van een test batterij voor de selectie van wetenschappelijke onderzoekers. In: P.J.D. Drenth, P.J.Willems, & C.J. de Wolff, (Eds.). *Arbeids en Organisatiepsychologie*. Deventer: Kluwer.
Equal Employment Opportunity Commission (1966). *Guidelines on employment testing procedures*. Equal Employment Opportunity Commission.
Equal Employment Opportunity Commission (1970). *Guidelines on employee selection procedures*.Federal Register.
Erikson, E.H. (1968). *Identity, youth and crisis*. New York: Norton.
Ferguson, L.W. (1952). *Personality measurement*. New York: McGraw-Hill.
Fleishman, E.A. (1967a). Performance assessment based on an empirically derived task taxonomy. *Human Factors*, *9*, 349–366.
Fleishman, E.A. (1967b). The development of a behavior taxonomy for describing human tasks: A correlational experimental approach. *Journal of Applied Psychology*, *51*, 1–10.
Fleishman, A. (1992). *Job Analysis Survey*. Palo Alto, CA: Consulting Psychologists Press Inc.
Fleishman, A., & Reilly, M.E. (1992). *Handbook of human abilities*. Palo Alto, CA: Consulting Psychologists Press Inc.
Gellerman, S.W. (1968). *Management by Motivation*. American Management Association.
Giessen, R.W. van der (1957). *Enkele aspecten van het probleem der predictie in de psychologie*. Amsterdam: Sweets & Zeitlinger.
Gottfredson L.S., & Sharf, J.C. (1988). Fairness in employment testing. *Journal of Vocational Behavior*, *33*(3), 225–231.
Greuter, M.A.M. (1988). *Personeelsselectie in perspectief*. Amsterdam: Uitgeverij Thesi.
Gross, M.L. (1962). *The brain watchers*. New York: Random House.
Guilford, J.P. (1959). *Personality*. New York: McGraw-Hill.
Guilford, J.P. (1967). *The nature of human intelligence*. New York: McGraw-Hill.
Guion, R.M. (1965). *Personnel testing*. New York: McGraw-Hill.
Hall, D.T. (1976). *Careers in organizations*. Glenview, IL: Scott Foresman.
Hall, D.T. & Associates (1986). *Career development in organizations*. San Francisco: Jossey Bass.
Harris, M.M. (1989). Reconsidering the employment interview: A review of recent literature and suggestions for future research. *Personnel Psychology*, *42*, 691–726.
Herriot, P. (1989a). Selection as a social process. In M. Smith, & I.T. Robertson (Eds.), *Advances in personnel selection and assessment*. Chichester: Wiley.
Herriot, P. (1989b). Interactions with clients in personnel selections. In P. Herriot (Ed.), *Assessment and selection in organizations* (pp. 219–228). Chichester: Wiley.
Hoffmann, B. (1962). *The tyranny of testing*. New York: Crowell, Collier.
Hull, C.L. (1928). *Aptitude Testing*. New York: World Books.
Jansen, A. (1963). *Toetsing van grafologische uitspraken*. Amsterdam: van Rossen.
Jansen, A. (1979). *Ethiek en praktijk van personeelsselectie*. Deventer: Kluwer.
Jaspers, J.F.M. (1966). *On social perception*. Leiden:
Koch, K. (1954). *Der Baumtest*. Bern: Huber (Zweite Anlage)
Landy, F.J. (1985). *Psychology of work behavior*. Homewood: Dorsey Press.
Latham, G.P., Wexley, K.N., & Rand, T.M. (1975). The relevance of behavioral criteria developed from the critical incident technique. *Canadian Journal of Behavioral Science*, *7*, 349–358.
Latham, G.P., Saari, L.M., Pursell, E.D., & Campion, M.A. (1980). The situational interview. *Journal of Applied Psychology*, *65*, 422–424.
Leavitt, H.J. (1964). Applied organization change in industry: Structural, technical and human approaches. In W.W. Cooper, H.J. Leavitt, & M.W. Shelley (Eds.), *New perspectives in organizational research*. New York: Wiley.
Levinson, H., Price, C.R., Munden, K.L., Mendl, H.J., & Solley, C.M. (1962). *Men, management and mental health*. Cambridge, MA: Harvard University Press.
LIAMA (1968). *Agent selection kit*. Hartfort, CT.
Lindsey, G., & Thorpe, J.S. (1968). Projective methods. In D.L. Sills (Ed.), *An international encyclopedia of the social sciences*. New York: McMillan & Free Press.
Link, H.C. (1924). *Employment psychology*. New York: McMillan.
Locke, E.A., Shaw, K.N., Saari, L.M., & Latham, G.P. (1981). Goal setting and task performance: 1969–1980. *Psychological Bulletin*, *90*, 125–152.
Locke, E.A., & Latham, G.P. (1990). *A theory of goal setting and task performance*. Englewood Cliffs, NJ: Prentice Hall.
Lofquist, L.H., & Dawis, R.V. (1969). *Adjustment to work*. New York: Appleton.
Mayfield, E.C. (1964). The selection interview: A re-evaluation of published research. *Personnel Psychology*, *19*, 239–260.
Mayfield, E.C., Brown, S.H., & Hamstra, B.W. (1980). Selection interviewing in the life insurance industry: An update of research and practice. *Personnel Psychology*, *33*, 527–739.
Mendel, M.M. (1975). *De rechtsbescherming van de sollicitant, mede in verband met het psychologisch onderzoek waaraan hij zich onderwerpt*. Deventer: Kluwer.

National Academy of Sciences (1982). *Ability testing: Uses, consequences, and controversies* (Vol. 1). Washington DC: National Academy Press.

NIP (1975a). *Gedragsregels voor de bedrijfs- en organisatiepsychologie*. Amsterdam: Nederlander Instituut van Psychologen.

NIP (1975b). Beroepscode voor psychologen. *De Psycholoog, 10*, 279–285.

NVP (1980). *Solliciatiecode*. Den Haag: Nederlandse Vereniging voor Personeelsbeleid.

Offerman, L.R., & Gowing, M.K. (1993). Personnel selection in the future: The impact of changing demographics and the nature of work. In N. Schmitt, W.C. Borman, & Ass. (Eds.), *Personnel selection in organizations* (pp. 385–417). San Francisco, CA: Jossey-Bass Publishers.

Office of Federal Contract Compliance (1968). Validation of employment tests by contracters and subcontracters subject to the provisions of executive order. *Federal Register, 33*, 14,392–14,394.

Office of Federal Contract Compliance (1974). Employee testing and other selection procedures. *Federal Register, 39*, 2094–2096.

Packard, V. (1964). *The naked society*. New York: McKay.

Rundquist, E.A. (1969). The prediction ceiling. *Personnel Psychology, 22*, 109–116.

Schein, E.H. (1978). *Career dynamics: Matching individual and organizational needs*. Reading, MA: Addison Wesley.

Schneider, B., & Schmitt, N. (1986). *Staffing organizations*. Glenview: Scott Foresman.

Strien, P.J. van (1966). *Kennis en communicatie in de psychologische praktijk*. Utrecht: Bijleveld.

Strien, P.J., van, Cools, E. (1973). *Speelruimte en spelregels: Verslag van een enquete over beroepspraktijk en beroepsethiek onder de bedrijfspsychologen in Nederland*. Groningen-Utrecht.

Super, D.E. (1980). A life-span, life-space approach to career development. *Journal of Vocational Behavior, 16*, 282–298.

SWOV (Stichting Wetenschappelijk Onderzoek Vakcentrales) (1973). *De afhankelijke sollicitant*. Utrecht: Lumax.

Thompson, J.D. (1967). *Organizations in action*. New York: McGraw-Hill.

Thorndike, R.L. (1949). *Personnel selection: Tests and measurement technique*. New York: Wiley.

Thornton, G.C., & Byham, W.C. (1982). *Assessment-centers and managerial performance*. New York: Academic Press.

Thurstone, L.L. (1938). Primary mental abilities. *Psychometric Monograph, 1*.

Uniform Guidelines on Selection Procedures (1978). *Federal Register, 43*(166), 38,290–28,309.

U.S. Department of Labor, Employment & Training (1977). *Administration dictionary of occupational titles* (4th Edn.). Washington DC: US Government Printing Office.

Vereniging van Werknemers in het Bank- en Verzekeringsbedrijf en Administratieve Kantoren (1973). *Sollicitant, Sollicitatie, Solliciteren*. Utrecht.

Viteles, M. (1932). *Industrial psychology*. New York: Norton.

Wallace, S.R. (1965). Criteria for what? *American Psychologist, 20*, 411–417.

Wanous, J.P. (1980). *Organizational entry: Recruitment, selection and socialization of newcomers*. Reading, MA: Addison Wesley.

Wanous, J.P. (1989). Installing a realistic job preview: Ten tough choices. *Personnel Journal, 42*, 117–134.

Wissler, C. (1901). The correlation of mental and physical tests. *Psychological Review Monograph. Supplement* (Vol. 3).

Wolff, C.J. de (1963). *Personeelsbeoordeling*. Amsterdam: Swets & Zeitlinger.

Wolff, C.J. de (1967). *Het criteriumprobleem*. Deventer: Kluwer.

Wolff, C.J. de (1970). Beoordelingen als criteria. In P.J.D. Drenth, P.J. Willems, & C.J. de Wolff (Eds.), *Bedrijfspsychologie*. Deventer: Kluwer.

Wolff, C.J. de (1973). Selectie van managers. In P.J.D. Drenth, P.J. Willems & C.J. de Wolff, *Arbeids- en Organisatiepsychologie*. Deventer, Kluwer.

Wolff, C.J. de (1989). The changing role of psychologists in selection. In P. Herriot (Ed.), *Assessment and selection in organizations* (pp. 81–92). Chichester: Wiley.

Wolff, C.J. de, & Schopmann-Geurts van Kessel, J.G. (1992). The recruitment and selection of hospital medical consultants. *Work and Stress, 6*(3), 327–338.

Zeeuw, J. de, (1971). *Algemene psychodiagnostiek*. Amsterdam: Swets & Zeitlinger.

4

Personnel Appraisal

Pieter J.D. Drenth

1 INTRODUCTION

In many respects, the appraisal of employees is a constant source of concern for the personnel department. Appraising others is, and will remain, a sensitive matter, especially if this appraisal is negative, and this has to be communicated to the person in question. This may activate all kinds of psychological mechanisms (resistance, denial, aggression, discouragement) in the person appraised which can seriously upset the relationship between the assessor and the assessed. Consequently, or in fear of these consequences, the assessor too may be subject to all kinds of psychological mechanisms, which in turn fail to do justice to the objectivity and fairness of the assessment.

These problems may be partly traced to the applied system, which does not adequately meet certain technical or psychometric requirements. It is hard to play billiards with a bent cue, though a surprisingly artful shot will always be a possibility. They are probably much more importantly due to the organizational and social context in which the appraisal process and its implementation take place. Employee appraisals are part of the system of employee monitoring and stimulation and cannot be isolated from that system. If the personnel management system is unsound, or if a number of important organizational or social prerequisites for its functioning are not met, the appraisal system, however good in itself, will not work.

In this chapter we shall systematically discuss some of the above-mentioned topics. The goals of appraisals, the question of what should be appraised, and the criteria an appraisal system should meet will be discussed, in that order. We shall then present a brief review of the various systems in use, together with their respective pros and cons. The chapter will be concluded by a discussion of what preconditions have to be met or are beneficial for an appraisal system to work well.

Before we actually begin discussing the subject, we should like to address two general issues. First, the introduction referred several times to an "appraisal system". One might well ask whether appraisal actually needs a system, and whether part of the problem would disappear if the often impersonal and bureaucratic "put-a-cross-in-the-square" forms were not used.

Clearly, the larger and more complex an organization becomes, the harder it is for someone making personnel decisions and therefore evaluating employees to draw on his or her own experience to gain insight into the employees' actual and potential performance. Yet such insight should be the basis of such measures and decisions. If one has to go by the experiences and observations of others, it is difficult to see how it can be done without the information having been recorded in a fair and comparative manner. In fact, this is the justification for the use of an appraisal system.

This is why larger companies and organizations show a distinct preference for, and an increasing use of, appraisal systems. In an earlier study in The Netherlands (COP/SER, 1955) it was found that both supervisors and subordinates appreciated the use of a system. "Some sort of system is better than none", was the general reaction. According to a survey we performed among middle and higher staff in the early 1970s, it appeared that appraisals of managers took place systematically in 88 of the 127 companies who responded to an industrial questionnaire (Van Ginniken, 1974, p. 89). An in-depth survey of middle managers in four large organizations (private, semi-governmental and governmental) revealed that appraisals do not take place as often and as regularly as was suggested by the first industrial survey; in only half of these cases did appraisals take place annually (Van Dam & Drenth, 1976).

The frequencies are about the same as those for managers in the UK and in the USA. The developments for the rank and file do not, however, run quite parallel with those with managerial responsibilities. Rowe concluded that 74% of the 460 UK companies he questioned used a system of employee appraisal (Rowe, 1970). Surveying the trends between 1950 and 1957, Whistler and Harper (1962) showed that the percentage of companies in the USA claiming to use an appraisal system fell from 95.3% to 77% for the rank and file and rose from 45.6% to 58% for management. According to the conclusion drawn by Campbell et al. (1970), this trend has continued for middle and upper-level personnel in the USA. Only a few companies use no system at all, but the type of system and the frequency of its use varies from company to company. On the basis of a later review, Lazer and Wikstrom (1978) set the percentages for lower management at 74%, for middle management at 71%, and for upper management at 55%.

All this applies in particular to regular, generally full-time posts. As changes in the composition of staff and in the nature of the job become more sweeping, traditions and procedures in appraisals will change accordingly. It is clear that regular appraisals are carried out less and less with regard to temporary and part-time workers, home workers, advisors, and consultants working only semi-permanently within the company. Nevertheless this category of employees is going to play an increasingly important role in business in the future.

The second issue has to do with a philosophical or, if you will, a political point. Personnel appraisal adopts the paradigm of individual differences; it accepts that these differences exist and considers it prudent to make them known. But the motive for doing so is a separate issue. Goldman (1983) argues, from a Marxist viewpoint, that the real purpose can only be the wish to weaken "labour" and to intimidate employees into toeing the line. An altogether different view is also possible, as Schmidt (1983) demonstrated and as will be seen later in this chapter. It remains true to say, however, that the detection and appreciation of individual differences typifies capitalism rather than socialism (Locke, 1983).

Still, appraisals also have varying degrees of popularity in non-socialist countries, and they seem to have become especially widespread within the Anglo-Saxon and northern European tradition. It is surprising, for instance, to find that a comprehensive and quite exhaustive handbook on industrial psychology (Levy-Leboyer & Sperandio, 1987) contains no chapter on personnel appraisal!

2 THE GOALS OF EMPLOYEE APPRAISALS

In his "uneasy look at performance appraisal" McGregor (1957) expressed what many a practitioner had already experienced: it is difficult to combine the roles of judge and counsellor. In other words, the goal "control and management" is somewhat incompatible with the goal "guidance and development". Indeed, McGregor (1957,

1960) and Maier (1963) strongly oppose this dual role of appraisals.

These two main goals do appear regularly in the literature on the goals of appraisals (Anstey et al., 1978; Cummings & Schwab, 1973; Landy, Zedeck, & Cleveland, 1983; Neubauer & Von Rosenstiel, 1980). At a more specific level, one could make still more refined distinctions which even more clearly delineate the "multi-purpose" character of appraisals. Spriegel (1962) cites guidance, promotion, training and development, dismissal and remuneration, and in that order of frequency, based on a random sample of nearly 400 companies in the USA. Lazer and Wikstrom (1978) use other terms again: management development, performance measurement, performance improvement, remuneration, potential assessment, feedback, personnel planning, and improvement in communications and relations, also in that order of frequency. These classifications overlap somewhat, but on the other hand not all the goals listed in Lazer and Wikstrom's classification are coordinate. One could successfully argue, for instance, that performance measurement has to precede performance improvement and that feedback is one of the means for improving both development and communication.

Something that does not become immediately apparent in the company surveys, because it is not usually an operational objective, but which researchers within the organization certainly do regard as an important function of appraisals, is their use as criteria, for instance for selection (validation of selection instruments) and training.

In trying to identify the main elements of the foregoing paragraph, the purposes of appraisals can be divided into four main categories:

1. Use in decisions concerning the administration and management of personnel; e.g. measures in the area of salaries and wages, allowances and extra allowances, promotions, tenure appointments, transfers, dismissals, and the like.
2. Use with a view to the improvement of performance, motivation, and development. These effects will occur mainly through feedback and the appraisal interview.
3. Use in the attempted identification of potential candidates for upper and management posts, often referred to as management potential assessment.
4. Use as a criterion, for example in selection and training.

In Table 4.1 these four aims have been arrayed on the horizontal axis and the various aspects and characteristics of appraisal systems on the vertical, with the scheme itself showing typologies of features for the different aims. In this presentation the differences have been somewhat sharpened while in reality there are more gradual transitions between them, but the differences in orientation and emphasis are so distinct that one suspects it will not be easy to combine them all into one coherent programme.

The first type of appraisal, oriented towards personnel administration, will be based primarily on actual performance and results. This applies to awards of assessment allowances or increments, for instance, but also to decisions on transfers and promotions in the staff. The basic idea of incentive wages, for example, is that a remuneration is felt to be unfair unless it is somehow coupled to "output" (either directly or in relation to one's own "input"; see Lawler, 1981, and Volume 4 Chapter 12 of this Handbook). This involves the relation between ends and means, or costs and benefits, and the extent to which the person appraised manages to optimize them. Here, the appraiser turns to the past: it is an assessment of what has been achieved so far, without considering all kinds of possibilities of development or aspects of expected growth[1]. The emphasis, to be sure, is on positive aspects: what was achieved by the person concerned, was has he or she managed to do?

Two aspects are of importance: first whether the achievement is rated in a reliable manner (preferably in measurable or numerical form) and second whether the information can be consolidated into one overall rating. Ultimately, decisions regarding promotions, bonus allowances and dismissals should be based on "unidimensional" information, and in practice this will often amount to the requirement of a single, comprehensive appraisal.

Matters are quite different with respect to the majority of these characteristics if the purpose is *guidance and development.* Employee appraisal,

TABLE 4.1

Goals and characteristics of employee appraisals.

Characteristics \ Goal	Personnel management	Guidance, development	Potential assessment	Criterion
What is appraised	Results	Work behaviour	Personality characteristics and capacities	Performance behaviour
Point of view	Relation goal-means	Qualitative aspects	Predictive aspects	Quantitative aspects
Time orientation	Previous period	Past and near future	(Far) future	Present
Emphasis	Positive and negative aspects	Expected growth	Neutral representation	
Important requirements	Comprehensive-ness, objectivity	Specificity, clarity for person concerned	Predictive validity	Objectivity, relevance

in this context often called "job appraisal", is then mainly concerned with work behaviour, especially its qualitative aspects. Naturally, here too one will turn first to the immediate past. However, and particularly during the appraisal interview, the near and more distant future will be frequently discussed. In fact an attempt by superior and subordinate to jointly formulate new objectives and behavioural guidelines based on the results of the preceding period is one of the most important characteristics of the appraisal methods proposed by both McGregor (1957) and Drucker (1954) ("Management by Objectives"). For an effective evaluation and discussion, both positive and negative aspects will have to be raised. For those who abide by the adage that one learns most from one's mistakes, the emphasis will probably be on the less positive and the improvable aspects of work behaviour. This is a timely moment to remember the experiences of Meyer and his colleagues (Meyer, 1977; Meyer, Kay, & French, 1965) at General Electric, where it appeared that criticism provoked many defensive reactions but few behavioural changes!

The extent to which the appraised person is given clear insights into the appraisal itself is very important. The appraisal will only be a useful guide for an employee's self-improvement if he or she is able to understand it fully and to relate behaviour to appraisal. As a guide for readjustment and improvement, an overall appraisal is not good enough: it must be specific and concrete.

A sound *potential assessment*, on the other hand, is another story altogether. Here, the appraisal is aimed at the anticipation of future developments, with the emphasis lying on the aspects of behaviour and performance likely to affect such predictions and extrapolations. Since these predictions nearly always concern future behaviour in a situation and context very different from the current ones (this sort of appraisal is often carried out in connection with the assessment of "management potential"), there is little room for the literal extrapolation of current behaviour. Rather, the emphasis will be on constant determinants in the behaviour of the appraised person, that is, factors like personality and personal abilities. Clearly, the near and more distant future are in mind. The appraisal is part of a search for indicators of further growth; the issues are expected growth and development possibilities. The only criterion for the quality of a potential assessment is, in fact, its predictive power (predictive validity). The effectiveness of the system is measured by the extent to which it can accurately identify future successful managers, judges, professors, field officers, and so on.

In using appraisals as *criteria* for the evaluation of selection procedures or training, the particular requirements are for objectivity and relevance: objectivity, as the standard requirement of any evaluation criterion, and relevance, because such a gauge of selection and training should adequately reflect the goals and objectives of the organization. Here, the emphasis is on aspects crucial to the aims of the organization, and it is these aims that generate the objectives of the appraisal. In many cases this will be performance or output, but can also concern behaviour (medical care, social work).

Since the assessment must be as objective as possible it is clear that the emphasis will be on quantitative aspects. The assessment will be as objective, representative, and neutral as possible and will not, in contrast with salary awarding or job appraisal, emphasize rather positive or negative aspects.

The descriptions of these four goals, and the different requirements that are thereby made on the appraisal system on the one hand and the different orientations of the appraisers on the other hand, would seem to be sufficient arguments against the integration of these goals into one single appraisal system and procedure. The literature, too, displays an increasing tendency to advise the use of separate systems, procedures and moments for these different purposes. We see, for example, the splitting up of "salary appraisal" and "job appraisal" (Kane & Lawler, 1979; Meyer et al., 1965); the separation of "job or salary appraisal" and "potential assessment" (De Quay, 1973). Such divisions attempt to disentangle all kinds of undesirable confusions such as the determination of "current salary" by means of "future growth", or "intelligence" becoming an issue in a discussion about work. At the same time these separations try to avoid various conflicts that may arise from combining incompatible aims; think of the conflict within the individual between the desire for fair feedback about what went wrong (work improvement) and the desire for the most positive possible appraisal (salary increase), or the conflict within the appraiser between the desire for an objective and comprehensive evaluation (dismissal) and the desire for an insightful, specific and discussable appraisal for a guidance interview.

We fear that in practice these goals are often confused and that they are not adequately separated in the system, the procedure, or the appraisal interview. Too often, one sees that part of a salary is directly linked to a job appraisal and the results of an appraisal interview; too often, one sees a job appraisal form with a series of questions on performance, attitudes and the like, and a last question on "future development possibilities": a "potential assessment" element hidden in an ordinary job appraisal. In all likelihood, various practical considerations (cost, time, effort) determine this practice.

It is probably not that easy to keep the issues separated, either. In a survey of 33 large companies in the USA, Campbell et al. (1970) found that most were characterized by a concentration on one of three policy orientations: selection, training, or motivation and development. In the selection-oriented cases, potential assessments and appraisals supporting appointments and placement decisions played the most important role. In the training-oriented cases, emphasis was on training and development and also on the identification of these needs in individuals and organizations. In the motivation and development-oriented cases, administrative and selection purposes had faded into the background altogether; the issues here were both the stimulation and the guidance of managers and supervisors. The authors found only one company in which these three orientations were well integrated and where the instruments (including appraisals) used for the various "roles" were adequately developed.

It seems useful, at the end of this section, to note the difference between the *goal* and the *function* of an appraisal. If an appraisal is designed for a certain goal, this does not necessarily mean that it functions exclusively as such. An appraisal can have numerous side-effects; the confirmation of given power relations, the adaptation of employees to an existing structure, the management of a power struggle or the prevention of unrest. Grunow (1976) speaks of the "latent functions" of appraisals. Where these are unintended, Grunow's suggestion that they be made clear is worth following up. In case there is a deliberate use of such latent functions, it would seem that reformation is desired if the long-term credibility of appraisals is not to be impugned.

3 WHAT SHOULD BE APPRAISED?

One aspect mentioned in the scheme previously discussed needs further elaboration: the issue of what should be appraised. In fact we can choose from three categories: *results*, *work behaviour* and *personality traits*.

The advantages of selecting *personality traits* seem obvious: one is dealing with more or less stable characteristics, so appraisals offer the possibility of making predictions. This also meets the needs of personnel promotion and transfer decisions. Furthermore, personality traits are highly abstracted from incidental events and facts, and since they can be generalized seem to carry more weight. Furthermore it is safer for the appraiser to talk about personality traits, illustrating them with specific incidents, than it is to discuss the incidents themselves, about which the appraised person will be inclined to argue. We should not be surprised, therefore, that appraisal forms are so often filled with "personality traits" like reliability, flexibility, independence, decisiveness, self-confidence, and so on.

At the same time the psychological literature (see for example Hofstee, 1974) prompts us to be very wary of judging "personality traits". In the first place, we know that determining the strength of personality traits by observational methods, without these being founded on a large number of concrete behaviour observations, is neither very reliable nor valid. This is partly due to the fact that it often involves rather complex concepts that do not easily and unequivocally refer to distinct behaviour, which means that appraisers can give free rein to their own various theories and conceptual systems of human behaviour (see Borman, 1983).

It is also due to the fact that the concepts used are often situation-dependent and not unequivocally defined. The concept of reliability may serve as an example. What is meant by an unreliable person? Someone who does not return borrowed books, someone who does not keep appointments, someone who fills out his or her tax forms rather carelessly or someone who cannot be trusted when in charge of the cash register? The relations between these various forms of unreliability are very weak (Mischel, 1968). Appraisers with different ideas about "reliability" will reach different conclusions about one and the same person.

Moreover, discussions about personality traits will not be all that fruitful, partly because of the semantic and conceptual obscurities mentioned above and partly because many characteristics, being part of the *habitus* of the individual, are hard to change. Such "feedback discussions" therefore often lead to irritation, defensiveness, denial, or a sort of passive resignation—hardly useful starting-points for coaching or improvement.

Kavanagh, MacKinney, and Wollins (1971) attempted to salvage personality traits by pointing out that some do possess "construct validity" and as such have a place in the nomological network in which the ultimate criterion for work performance is embedded. Kane and Lawler's response (1979) seems devastating: this may be so, they say, but they are at best the causes of, or limiting factors for, the performance with which the organization is ultimately concerned. They are surrogates for performance criteria just as much as intelligence tests are surrogates for the appraisal of school performance. They describe a person rather than his or her performance and as such can have no place in an appraisal system.

We should, however, make one exception. In the previous section it appeared that, for the purposes of *potential assessment*, the emphasis is in fact on personality traits and personal capacities. In potential assessment two forces are at work which enhance this emphasis. First, prediction is often oriented towards behaviour in a very different context and under completely different conditions. Here, attention has to be paid to those aspects that determine behaviour in all kinds of situations, and this need for generalization causes a shift in emphasis towards more trans-situationally constant capacities and personality traits.

Second, it is not only generalizations over situations that are involved but also generalizations over time. Assessments of growth and development often have to cover a considerable period of time. Here, again, the emphasis tends to shift towards more constant personality factors. This is why well-known potential assessment systems usually include aspects such as analytic ability, realism, ability to anticipate, bird's-eye view, cooperation, self-esteem, effectiveness, expressive skills, initiative, self-control, tenacity, and the like.

Of course, the above-mentioned objections to the appraisal of personality factors still stand. It is an illusion to suppose that one can effortlessly compile a list of such personality factors and then decide that one has a workable system for personality appraisals. The construction of a potential assessment system requires extensive and careful empirical research. From an analysis of the ultimate job requirements it should be deduced which characteristics and traits are involved. Next, one should compile a sufficiently large number of items for these factors, which should be selected on the basis of their inter-correlations and validity, and if necessary fashioned into scales. These scales should then be tested for reliability and predictive validity.

Validity may be tested against two kinds of criteria, i.e. subjective and objective. Muller's study (1970) provides an example of a validity study using subjective criteria. He compared his items and scales with the criterion "expected ultimate level" of the person in the organization, operationalized as the probable attainable salary scale estimated on the basis of an extrapolation of the person's existing salary curve. The problem in Muller's research is that in all likelihood the subjective criterion rating was known to the appraisers, so that the risk of contamination cannot be excluded. As a result, we have here not so much an external validity study but rather an analysis of the grounds on which overall subjective potential assessments are based.

An example of validation using an objective criterion is provided by Tigchelaar (1974): he validated his items and scales against the criterion "salary growth corrected for age and length of service". After careful selection of the items and scales, 40% to 50% of the variance in career success could be predicted by means of such potential assessments.

A warning is not out of place at this point. From the above it might appear that one could conclude that the validity of items and scales is the most important criterion for potential assessments, and this is correct. But this does not mean that all valid items are equally useful. It should be remembered that, for instance, selecting future managers on the basis of a validation of the predictors using a criterion based on the behaviour and performance of *current* management leads to the continuation of current policies and methods. In any case, a critical analysis of "valid" predictors seems appropriate. Is it desired to continue (or, more harshly, to "freeze") current management policy—or is it better to make room for innovation or an altered approach?

For the sake of completeness, we wish to point out that procedures for identifying future management should, of course, never be based on just one source of information, the potential assessment. The traditional literature mentions a variety of methods, such as noting interests, biographical information, cognitive tests and personality inventories, situational tests and clinical interviews, whether or not carried out in a special "assessment centre" (for a survey, see Campbell et al., 1970). Assessment centres have been enjoying a recent resurgence in popularity (see Finkle, 1976; Robertson & Martin, 1986; Schuler & Stehle, 1983, 1987). More actuarial approaches, such as the EIMP study employed by the Standard Oil Co., New Jersey (Laurent, 1962, 1970) or the study of the Industrial Relations Center at the University of Minnesota (Mahoney et al., 1960), and more clinical approaches, such as the well-known management progress study at AT&T (American Telephone & Telegraph Company; Bray, 1964) have also been fruitful in identifying management potential.

Appraisals that do not aim at assessing potential are left with the choice between *performance/results* and work *behaviour/activities*. It was noted in the previous section that in using appraisals as a criterion as well as for personnel decisions (remuneration, tenure, dismissal), objective results are considered the most just. In guidance and coaching, however, one should pay greater attention to activities and behaviour, as these provide the best starting point and the best basis for an appraisal interview.

In fact, emphasizing either performance or behaviour too strongly should be avoided. It should be acknowledged, as was also suggested by Kane and Lawler (1979), that sometimes more than one road leads to the same goal, and that from a qualitative point of view one can be as good as the other. The appraisal of a job that can be characterized by, in their term, "equifinality" (having more than one acceptable road) must emphasize results; the appraisal of a job without equifinality must emphasize work behaviour.

Porter et al. (1975) also note the importance of both aspects. They suggest that appraisal systems have a distinct directional influence. The appraised are influenced by the fact that certain aspects of their work and performance are either positively or negatively judged, just as tests and exams at school determine the nature of learning behaviour. An appraisal that exclusively emphasizes results may well evoke behaviour that clashes with other goals important to the organization: high production at the cost of morale, increased quantity at the cost of quality, high sales at the cost of consumer satisfaction, and so on. Conversely, sole emphasis on work behaviour may also have undesirable influences in the sense that activities rather than achievements are stimulated. For instance, a manager's people-oriented behaviour may be rather unproductive, and working strictly according to rules or agreements may, in emergency situations, have disastrous effects.

It must be admitted that in many (and with current automation and computerization rates in industry, a rising number of) cases, the choice is simplified by the fact that no directly measurable indices are available (service functions, control functions, panel watching). In such cases, there is little choice but to assess work behaviour and activities. This poses two not unrelated dilemmas: how concrete or abstract should such behaviour assessments be, and how many factors should be included in the procedure?

The first problem involves weighing up the pros and cons of divergent alternatives. Table 4.2 gives a number of examples at three levels of abstraction.

TABLE 4.2

A number of (random) examples of three levels of behaviour descriptions.

Incidental activities	Habitual behaviour	Abstract factors
—is always on time	—keeps agreements	—attention to duty
—takes too long breaks	—quality of work preparation	—independence
—has reports ready in time	—dealings with clients	—sociability
—desk is a mess	—prepared to put in extra effort	—motivation
—cannot stand criticism	—work speed	—flexibility
—is sloppily dressed	—technical competence	—analytic ability
—has difficulty finding words in cases of disagreement	—openness to new ideas	—ability to organize
	—stimulation of subordinates	—leadership
—admits mistakes	—prepared to delegate	—creativity
—is able to chair meetings of Works Council well	—being able to make decisions when necessary	
—argues with maintenance mechanics	—knows own shortcomings	
	—way of formulating problems	
—is too buddy-buddy with the secretaries	—is knowledgeable in his/her professional field	

The advantage of emphasizing more concrete behaviour factors (left-hand column in Table 4.2, "Incidental activities") is that they can be perceived more objectively, are closer to observable behaviour, and do not presuppose any personality theory. The dangers, on the other hand, are that behavioural factors are too incidental and do not lend themselves to generalization, with the result that the assessment becomes irrelevant. These objections do not apply to the most abstracted factors in the right-hand column. However, here a problem arises (already mentioned in connection with personality traits as a basis for performance appraisal) with semantic opacity and a lack of clear-cut definitions because the traits are too far removed from observable behaviour. This results in insufficient agreement between appraisers (Borman, 1983) but also between appraiser and appraised, with all the unpleasant consequences this may entail for the appraisal interview.

Somehow, a path has to be steered between the Scylla of excessive tangibility and the Charybdis of excessive abstraction, a path whose course takes us into the area of *habitual behaviour*. One does not, as it were, dive so deeply into the personality structure that one loses touch with reality, neither does one stay so near the surface that one becomes lost in irrelevant details. The middle column in Table 4.2 lists several examples of such habitual behaviour, and indicates the direction in which we think the course should be steered.

The optimum *number* of aspects to be rated is the second problem here. A survey of the various systems of performance appraisal is presented in Section 5. This will include some systems in which the number of factors is not problematic (overall appraisals, free interview), but most systems contain a number of specific factors or aspects which are subject to appraisal. The question, then, is what is the optimum number?

The answer depends partly on the job of the person being appraised. If a job has many relevant aspects (head of a department, academic staff member, independent agent), these should be reflected in the appraisal form.

The question of optimum number is also associated with the problem of abstraction just discussed. To the extent that one works with more abstract, "summary" characteristics or traits (those according to the right-hand column of Table 4.2), fewer factors will be available and fewer needed. By contrast, the number of concrete incidental-behaviour descriptions (of the left-hand column type in Table 4.2) that could be considered is, in principle, inexhaustible.

There have been frequent attempts to solve this problem by factor analysis. This method, however, depends on so many assumptions (use of items or scales, which items/scales, how are they rotated, what criterion is used to stop extraction, what types of communalities are selected) that a conclusive criterion for answering the question posed is not easily found in factor analysis.

Besides, the results of various factor analyses of appraisal systems do not yield much that can be used in practice. In the relevant literature, it has been repeatedly demonstrated that factor analyses of appraisals yield only a very limited number of factors, the first factor generally accounting for by far the greatest part of the variance. This first factor can generally be explained as a kind of general, overall indicator of "performance level"; in most cases it is followed by factors much less likely to explain variance, such as "quality of performance" (see Tiffin & McCormick, 1966, p. 231) or personality traits like motivation or adaptation (see De Wolff, 1963, p. 97). At any rate, factor analysis of existing appraisal scales leads to a poorly differentiated basis for guidance or coaching. A slightly more differentiated picture may occasionally be obtained if the rating list is compiled very carefully and specifically for a homogenous group (see Andriessen & Drenth, 1973; Elshout et al., 1973), but even this does not simply mean that one should confine oneself to the factors detected.

Factor analysis or cluster analysis can, however, be helpful in removing all kinds of unrealistic assumptions. It is an illusion to think that an appraisal system covering 20 work aspects actually represents 20 separate, discernable facets of work behaviour. The analyses mentioned can certainly help to identify a smaller number of factors than there are items and thus to reduce the number of characteristics involved in the appraisal. This kind of analysis can also help select possible items intended to measure those various aspects, or items that should constitute a global rating dimension (e.g. items loading highest on the first non-rotated factor). Again, factor or cluster analysis does not provide definite answers to the questions of "how much and which". An understanding of the behaviour to be appraised and other metric criteria (See section 4) must co-determine the choice as well.

The same holds for potential problems in *weighting* the various aspects in order to reach an overall appraisal. Here too, factor analysis may be helpful, but in the end it is the subjective evaluation of what is important to a particular position that forms the basis for this weighting.[2]

4 CRITERIA FOR APPRAISAL SYSTEMS

In this section we will discuss criteria for evaluating appraisal systems. Two categories of criteria may be distinguished: psychometric criteria and utilization criteria (see Table 4.3).

The *psychometric* criteria can be further differentiated into four groups: relevance, validity, generalizability, and discriminating power.

Relevance

By relevance is meant the degree to which the system provides an adequate representation of the domain of the behaviour to be appraised. We are here concerned with the question as to how adequate the system is in facilitating a reflection of the behaviour to be appraised. Two issues are of importance here: the first is whether all significant parts of this domain are adequately considered. If this is not the case, we speak of *deficiency*. The second is whether care has been taken that the system does not include aspects that are irrelevant to the behaviour to be appraised. If these are included, we speak of *excessiveness*. Thus relevance is primarily determined by the extent to which both deficiency and excessiveness are avoided.

This concept is related to content validity, as known from test theory. Like content validity, relevance is ultimately based on subjective judgement and not on empirical testing (Drenth, 1975), although the latter may provide some support for this judgement (see Cronbach, 1971).

Validity

The concept of validity is drawn directly from test theory and is used in this context in exactly the same sense. A distinction is drawn between

TABLE 4.3

Criteria for rating systems.

Psychometric criteria:	
—Relevance	—Deficiency (−) —Excessiveness (−)
—Validity	—Predictive validity —Construct validity
—Generalizability	—Across methods —Across raters —Across situations —Across items
—Discriminating power	
Utilization criteria:	
—Transparency	
—Acceptability	
—Informational value	

predictive validity and construct validity (Drenth & Sijtsma, 1990). The *predictive validity* of an appraisal is the degree to which it is capable of predicting future performance or behaviour. Predictive validity is a relevant criterion only when there is something which has to be predicted. This occurs primarily in potential assessments, in which case it may even involve a criterion lying in the fairly remote future. In addition, carrying out personnel changes on the basis of performance appraisals also involves a more or less implicit prediction; for it is alleged, on the basis of an assumed matching of individual qualities with the job requirements, that those involved will satisfactorily fulfil the new positions.

As with psychological tests, predictive validity should be tested by empirical correlational research. We discussed this criterion in the previous section in connection with potential assessments. De Wolff (1963) presents an extensive survey of predictive validities against external criteria (other appraisals, training results or performance criteria, as the case may be) of the appraisals currently used in organizations. From this survey it may be concluded that although there is considerable variance (depending also on the nature of the appraisal and the criterion), there is no particular reason for enthusiasm about the predictive powers of most of the appraisal systems currently in use (see also Borman, 1978; Latham & Wexley, 1981).

Regarding *construct validity*, the question is whether an item or scale does indeed cover the underlying characteristic. As in test theory, the question of construct validity of appraisal systems can be answered only through empirical research. Construct validity is higher as the correlation between the appraisal and the other indices of the same work performance is higher; this is the so-called *convergence validity*. Construct validity is also higher as the appraisal has a lower correlation with indices of behaviour aspects which are assumed to have no connection with the characteristic to be appraised, the so-called *discriminant validity*.

It comes as no surprise that the validity of "overall appraisals" or global ratings is lower than that of more specifically defined attributes. Nearly all work that people perform is complex and multidimensional (Ronan & Prein, 1966); it is next to impossible to adequately represent the various aspects, to weigh them properly and to integrate them in one overall appraisal in a subjective manner. Without one being aware of it, some aspects are weighted too heavily and others forgotten. In an appraisal of effectiveness in the United States Air Force, Thorndike (1949) found that it correlated highest with sympathy for the person involved, although this aspect was given the lowest score for importance by the appraisers themselves. More specific appraisals, however, are often not valid enough either. Batz and Schindler (1983) analysed a large number of different systems; the results were discouraging. Brandstätter (1970) had found large differences in quality years before. In their summary, Ronan and Schwartz (1974) reported that such validity was seldom above 0.40, and where it was, the criterion was often contaminated: the appraisers were informed about the objective performance scores, which were being used as the criterion for validation. Objections may be raised against a number of these studies, in the sense that, conceptually, the criterion is too far removed from the behaviour rated. In such a case, a low correlation is to be expected and is even desirable in view of the requirement of discriminant validity. This is true, for example, of Fleishman et al.'s (1955) study in which performance appraisals are compared with absenteeism, accidents, and personnel turnover. In a sense it also holds for the many validity studies relating appraisals with the results of psychological tests (e.g. Woodworth & McKinnon, 1957) or vocational tests (Whitla & Tirrel, 1953).

None of this alters the fact that the validity of appraisals is generally unimpressive, even in those cases where the aspects rated and the criteria are closer to one another. When appraisals are required to be as correct and as just as possible, a preference for objective performance criteria on these grounds seems well justified.

Generalizability

The criterion of generalizability or consistency applies across methods, appraisers, situations, and items.

The first form, generalizability across *methods*, is tested by constructing two parallel forms of the instrument and intercorrelating them. The specific, instrument-bound variance is thereby eliminated.

This method of assessing generalizability is seldom encountered in personnel appraisals. This is not only because few parallel forms of appraisal systems would exist in practice; these could be constructed somehow. The main difficulty is that it is impossible to separate the consistency of the instrument and the consistency of the appraiser. By definition, registration of behaviour takes place via the double channel of system and appraiser, and the appraiser is probably a much more important source of variance than is the instrument. If it was tried to remove the method—variance by having one and the same person carry out the two parallel appraisals—the resulting agreement between the two appraisals would be spurious.

Because of this problem, more attention has been paid to the second form—consistency across *appraisers*—than to the first. On the whole, the literature is not overly positive about the degree of agreement between different appraisers as measured by correlational studies or analysis of variance; Ronan and Schwartz (1974) summarize a large number of titles in this field and conclude that, in general, appraisers show little agreement in their assessments of performance and behaviour. This was found to hold for a variety of appraisers, tasks and appraisal instruments. In truly independent appraisals the correlations rarely exceeded 0.20.

Some critical remarks can be made at this point. First, this kind of research needs different appraisers who are equally well acquainted with the person concerned. This requirement is not often met, at least not in business practice. Second, and more importantly, we may doubt whether a low level of agreement between two different appraisals may legitimately be called error variance. In a series of studies, De Wolff (1965a, b, 1970) demonstrated that appraisals are strongly interactional in nature. In other words, the person appraised actually behaves differently with different appraisers, and different appraisals do reflect some true variance. An important consequence of this finding is the difficulty of using an appraisal to predict how someone will behave/be rated under another superior/appraiser!

A similar problem occurs with the third criterion, generalizability across *situations* and, possibly, across *time*. The coefficient indicating this consistency is the stability coefficient. People actually behave differently under different conditions and at different times. It is not surprising that these differences are also reflected in the appraisals, and these differences cannot be explained away as error variance. For this reason, Kane and Lawler (1979) consider stability an unsuitable measure of reliability for appraisal systems.

They go further, and argue that most systems take insufficient account of the fact that people exhibit large variations in the degree of consistency of their behaviour and that this fact should be a major aspect of the appraisal. They advocate what they call a completely new paradigm in appraising that takes into account the "distributional" aspects of behaviour or performance rated over a given appraisal period.[3] The question still remains whether the advantages of this more informative "distributional measurement" counterbalance the drawbacks of its construction (it is complicated) and in particular of its application (how should this information be utilized for decisions, for instance, about remuneration and placement?). Kane's more recent paper on the subject (1986) still has a hypothetical character. Empirical data are as yet unavailable.

The fourth form of consistency, across *items*, should not be used too formally either. The usefulness of this criterion, also known as the homogeneity criterion, as indexed by the inter-item-consistency formulae or Cronbach's alpha, depends on the homogeneity or heterogeneity of the characteristic being rated. In appraising a complex concept or a heterogenous field, homogeneity would lead to lower construct validity or lower relevance. It remains true, of course, that given homogeneous attributes the inter-item consistency of the scales measuring these attributes should be as high as possible. This is enhanced by having a sufficient number of items with high inter-correlations.

Discriminating power

The fourth psychometric aspect that can be used as a criterion for the quality of appraisal systems is the discriminating power of the scales: the extent to which the scales permit adequate expression of the actual differences between people. This is dependent on three conditions.

First, the extent to which the scales themselves offer enough possibilities for variation (sufficient scale positions) to reflect variations in behaviour. If, for example, there were ten clearly distinguishable performance levels, a scale with only three or four scale positions would be inadequate.

Second, the extent to which the various scale positions are actually used. There are scales whose extreme positions are formulated in such a way that these are hardly ever chosen; choices then accumulate in a few categories in the middle, and mostly on the positive side of the scale. Although the same thing is also caused by other psychological mechanisms (central tendency error, see Section 5.4 of this chapter) it can certainly be affected by the form of the list and the formulation of the behavioural alternatives.

Third, one may think of the context in which the appraisal takes place rather than of the technical aspects of the scale itself. A possible cause of diminishing discriminating power occurs when a reference group is being used which is not very comparable with the persons being appraised. As an example we can take Glickman's (1955) description of United States Army appraisals, where 97% of the colonels were judged to be "superior" or "excellent"; clearly, the reference group was the total population of officers. Incidentally, this is why the Army switched to another appraisal system in which the desired differentiation could be obtained (the "forced-choice" system, see under 5.1, this chapter).

As was mentioned earlier, besides these psychometric criteria exist the utilization criteria. As the term indicates, these criteria are coupled to specific goals of the appraisal system. Unlike the psychometric criteria, the utilization criteria will not have general applicability because, as was explained in Section 2, the goals are diverse. The goal of "guidance and coaching" in particular has its specific requirements, above all in the area of its discussibility and its usefulness for opening an interview. In general there are three utilization criteria, namely:

1. *Transparency*
   The degree to which the relationship between behaviour or performance and the appraisal itself is transparent, especially to the person appraised.
2. *Acceptability*
   To both appraiser and appraised: this criterion is, for example, a very negative point in peer ratings that can otherwise (on metric grounds) be considered positive (see Love, 1981; Domsch et al., 1983);
3. *Information value*
   Particularly focusing on the guidance and improvement of work behaviour.

In the following evaluation of various systems in current use, these criteria, as well as the psychometric criteria, will be applied.

5 SYSTEMS

In this section, we will present a discussion and evaluation of the various systems currently in use or advocated. There are numerous types and the space available here does not allow a detailed discussion of them all. For a discussion of the specific characteristics and qualities we refer the reader to the relevant literature (Berk, 1986; Bernardin & Beatty, 1984; Cummings & Schwab, 1973; Landy & Farr, 1983; Landy & Trumbo, 1980; McCormick & Ilgen, 1980; Smith, 1976). The choice of an optimal system is also decided by many practical issues such as frequency, confidentiality, confidence in and attitudes towards the appraisal process, and so on. We cannot cover all these aspects here either, but refer the reader to Bernardin (1986).

A systematic survey is given in Table 4.4.

The main distinction is made between the *overall* systems, in which the appraisal is eventually summarized in one single score or overall appraisal, systems based on *objective* data, *differentiated* systems which provide a profile or typology of the appraised person, and finally other systems which differ somewhat in character, for

TABLE 4.4

Classification of appraisal systems.

Overall appraisal systems	—Overall ratings —Rank-order systems —Forced-choice systems —Critical incident systems
Systems based on objective data	—Output, cost/benefit figures —Behavioural indices —Comprehensive index systems
Differentiated systems	—Graphic/numerical scales —Descriptive scales —Anchored scales —Checklists
Other systems	—Free interview —Free-written description —Goal-setting interviews

example, the open interview, the free-form essay, or goal-setting interviews. We will now pass these systems in review.

5.1 Overall systems

Into this category fall first of all the *global* ratings and the *rank-order* systems. The global rating leads to an overall appraisal reported on an absolute scale (e.g. from "adequate" to "excellent"). In the rank-order systems, the ranking may be obtained by asking the appraiser directly to rank-order the subjects in the group or by having the appraiser choose first the best, then the worst, then the best and the worst from the remaining group, and so on (alternate ranking). With a larger group, one can also use facilitating procedures, such as rank comparison (form a number of random groups, establish the rank-order within each, and select the best from those at the top at every turn) and paired comparisons (make all possible pairs and compare two at a time). When a larger number of appraisers are available, nomination techniques can also be applied (choose the best 5, 20%, half . . . from a group; the total score then gives the subject's rank-order score).

The third overall system, the *forced-choice* system, was developed in the United States army in order to stop the positive bias in appraisals of higher officers mentioned previously. Sisson (1948) was the first to describe the system, which received considerable attention in the literature during the early 1950s because of the psychometric qualities it professed to have (Baier, 1951; Berkshire & Highland, 1953; Taylor & Wherry, 1951; Travers, 1951). This appraisal system consists of a number of "blocks" of descriptive statements (their number varying from two to five), from which the subject must choose one or two of the most applicable statements. Variations in the compositions of the block are discussed in the literature (see Berkshire & Highland, 1953). An example of a block with four positive statements is shown in Figure 4.1.

The statements are followed by two rows of figures. These are two indices regarding the statements, based on preliminary research. The first index, the preference index, indicates how pleasant it is for the subject if the statement is thought to apply to him or her. The index is actually the average appreciation of this "pleasantness" of a sample of appraisers.[4] The second column, the discrimination index, indicates the validity of the statement, and is based on the differences between the mean ratings of a group of high-performing employees and those of a group of low-performing employees. These difference-scores are to be found in previous experimental research.

FIGURE 4.1

	PI	DI
Reads his/her professional literature	3.8	1.3
Is good at designing research	3.9	2.9
Is able to distinguish good ideas from bad ones	3.8	3.1
Is an accurate experimenter	3.7	1.2

Forced-choice block from an appraisal system of the "Research and Development" department.

In our example, the statements are more or less equivalent with respect to the preference index, but are diverse as far as the discrimination index is concerned. If, in an actual appraisal situation, two statements must be selected from the four in the block, the appraiser will find it difficult to express a positive or a negative bias because all four statements appear equally "favourable". The idea is that the appraiser will then choose the two statements that best apply to the behaviour or the performance of the subject. The system consists of, say, 30 such blocks. The overall (comprehensive) appraisal is determined by the number of times that positively discriminating statements were chosen from the blocks.

Finally, a second empirical method belonging in the overall systems category is the *critical incident* method developed by Flanagan (Flanagan, 1954; Flanagan & Burns, 1955). This system concentrates not on the "how" but on the "what". Instead of a subjective judgement about the degree to which the subject is assumed to possess a given trait or characteristic, the system establishes the frequency of the occurrence of certain critical incidents. Which incidents are critical, whether good or bad, is determined in preliminary empirical research of successful and unsuccessful performances. This system started life as a function analysis method in which the subjective assessments of a number of job characteristics were replaced by the positive or negative incidents reported. The appraisal method was developed from this function analysis system. The incidents are condensed into a (still large) number of categories, and the actual appraisal consists of registering the number of critical performances during the period to be appraised. This results in one score, the sum total of positive and negative incidents.

In connection with the evaluation of these overall appraisal systems, the following may be noted: if the goal of the appraisals requires the subjects to be compared on a single dimension (using the appraisal as a unidimensional criterion for selection or for yes/no decisions) one has to depend on overall appraisals. But it should be remembered that the psychometric qualities of the various systems within this category are not equally satisfactory In Section 3 it was noted that the reliability and validity of global ratings are very poor. Moreover it is not at all clear what is hidden behind such an overall, implicit appraisal; in other words, the appraisal may well be invalid of irrelevant, without this being noticed and without an opportunity to test the fact.

The psychometric qualities (distribution, reliability, validity) of both empirical systems are generally somewhat more favourable than those of the global rating or ranking. The quality of the preliminary empirical research will of course become manifest in the quality of the concrete appraisals. The requirement of empirical research, however, often constitutes a major stumbling block. Often, such research is time-consuming and not always easy to carry out in respect to available test groups and to the necessity of having an "objective" criterion for good and poor performance. With regard to the critical incident method, we may add that the actual appraisal phase is both time-consuming and complicated.

The major objections to the overall systems, however, are in the area of the utilization criteria, particularly if the goal one has in mind is that of guidance, coaching and work improvement. Overall appraisals provide no foothold in this respect because of their lack of diagnostic information. As to the forced-choice method it should be added that, since the "descriptive" and the "rating" elements of the appraisal are split up (so as to avoid bias), the appraiser even does not know whether he is assessing the subject well or badly. This system is defeated, so to speak, by its own qualities.

5.2 Systems based on objective data

To this category belong those systems that primarily emphasize quantifiable results. One may think, for example, of output data, turnover, number of pieces produced, number of arrests (police), number of complaints from clients (service positions) and the like. One can also make use of various kinds of cost/benefit indices.

Next, there are objective data that do not necessarily reflect the immediate output of some person or department, but rather function as an indication of certain attitudes or forms of behaviour. Thus in appraising a manager one might make use of data such as the rate of turnover or absenteeism in his/her department or the morale of subordinates. Merrihue and Katzell (1955) have developed an "employee relations yardstick", a complex framework of indicators regarding atmosphere and climate in the department.

Finally, indicators such as salary, salary growth, and level attained within the organization belong here. The latter two variables are often corrected for factors like age, seniority, educational level and others.

Such objective systems do have their attractions. Because they are often directly linked with organizational goals they seem to have a high degree of validity. The objectivity of the data guarantees the reliability of the indices. For the goal of coaching and guidance an emphasis on output may also be desirable, although as we pointed out earlier, too exclusive an attention to results also has its drawbacks.

The greatest problem with this kind of data, however, concerns its relevance. The kind of measures involved are often both deficient and excessive. They are deficient in so far as many of the goals desired by the organization are not reflected in the objective results; this is true both of the frequently restricted output criteria and of the measures mentioned for morale and atmosphere. The third category (salary, salary growth and job level) may be an exception, because such indices themselves reflect a fairly complex background. They form, so to speak, a summary of the appraisals of a large number of partial aspects of behaviour, often reported or influenced by many different appraisers, and will therefore reflect a rather broad field of behaviour. This is also one of the reasons why this category is assessed positively as a criterion for potential assessments (Tigchelaar, 1974).

These objective measures suffer not only from deficiency but also often from excessiveness, with the probable exception of, again, the third category. A large part of the variance of the measures cannot be attributed to the behaviour of the person concerned but to other factors often beyond his or her sphere of influence. The number of police arrests also depends on the crime rate in the neighbourhood; output depends strongly on, amongst other things, economic conditions and price levels; turnover is determined also by relatively more favourable wage conditions in other companies; morale often depends more on the nature of the work than on the working conditions that can be influenced by the head of the department, and so on.

5.3 Other Systems

In view of our conclusion regarding the most widely used differentiated systems of employee appraisal, we will first discuss the "remaining methods", such as the free-form essay, the open interview, and goal-setting interviews.

In a sense the *free-form essay* is also found in the variable amount of "free space" at the end of many conventional appraisal forms, where the appraiser may formulate an overall impression or add something to the profile "in his/her own words". Such a sketch—often somewhat personal—may be a useful supplement to an otherwise objective form. If, however, the whole appraisal consists of such unstructured descriptions in a personal style, the problems of incomparability, subjectivity and unreliability become so great that this system cannot really compete with more objective systems.

A more or less related method is the *free interview*. Here, the unstructuredness is not in the reporting but rather in the method of assembling the data and impressions, on which subsequently a typology or a person's profile is based. Obviously, this method is realistic only when the appraiser is not the subject's immediate supervisor. The latter should, of course, need no interviews to be able to appraise the work of his or her subordinates. One could think of the independent expert who is commissioned in some systems (e.g. Dutch Civil Service). This method was also favourably evaluated in potential assessments, where the assembling of, on the one hand, information concerning the capacities and desires of the employees and, on the other hand, information about vacancies and placement possibilities (now and in the near future) in the organization is carried out by one person, the careers coordinator (De Quay, 1973).

Finally, we should mention an appraisal system that does not aim to appraise but rather to motivate the person concerned. This system, developed by Drucker (1954) and being in the spirit of McGregor's view of appraisals as described earlier, is the goal-setting interview or *management by objectives* (MBO). The idea is that classic appraisals as such bring about little change and motivate little and should therefore be replaced by an interview in which the goals for the coming period are established by the supervisor and subordinate together. This would motivate the subject much more to reach that goal. An "appraisal interview" would then consist of jointly analysing the question, if appropriate, as to why the goal was not attained and again establishing specified goals and methods for the next period. The Netherlands has several forms of appraisal in which this element is strongly present.

It should be noted that one might argue about the question as to exactly what it is in the goal-setting interview method that is responsible for its possible success. According to McGregor (1957) and Drucker (1954) it is the motivating effect of being personally involved in the goal-setting, but a fairly realistic alternative explanation is that it is simply the fact that specific goals are formulated and established. MBO requires an accurate analysis and assessment of the goals and of the likelihood that they will be attained, as well as a specified plan of the ways in which they are to be realized (see Locke, 1978). It is precisely this element that tends to be lacking in classic appraisals and appraisal interviews.

Undoubtedly, the fact that this kind of interview is not really an appraisal interview any longer also plays a role. When problem behaviour or the failure to meet a norm or deadline are brought up in a discussion, the primary concern is to find ways to prevent problems and to improve working methods, and not to blame people or to saddle them with "insufficient marks". Perhaps the job requirements are too ambitious and have to be adjusted. According to some experts, current appraisal systems are so ineffective in changing behaviour that they consider such goal-setting or problem oriented interviews the only viable option (see Section 6). Of course, in this kind of goal-setting or problem-oriented interviews, the system's psychometric qualities are less important as long as a good and constructive discussion gets under way.

However, the goal-setting interview is tailor-made for the purposes of guidance and coaching. It is very difficult to base, for instance, placement or transfer decisions on it. Nor may this kind of interview be expected to furnish objective measures for the validation of selection and training.

5.4 Differentiated Methods

Among the differentiated methods, which provide a differentiated picture or profile of the subject, are various scale types as well as the so-called checklists. To begin with the latter, *checklists* are lists of statements, of which the appraiser has to indicate whether they are applicable to the subject, mostly in the form of a simple yes/no choice. The statements are listed in random order, although they do refer to a number of underlying factors.

As to this reference, empirical and non-empirical checklists may be distinguished. The latter consist of statements classified on logical grounds. With empirical checklists the classification is achieved on grounds of empirical research; an example of this form is given in Table 4.5. Four factors were established on the basis of a factor analysis of a large number of statements about the work of job analysts. These were: task performance; contacts; know-how with respect to statistics, literature on the subject and technology; and accuracy. The list was compiled using statements which covered as "factor purely" as possible one of the four factors and ordered randomly. The scores on these four dimensions for a given individual are indicated by the number of statements considered applicable.[5]

In the practice of appraising, *graphic and numerical scales* are by far the most frequently used. A number of behaviour aspects, whether or not classified according to main categories—which in their turn may or may not rely on preliminary empirical research—are listed, and the appraiser has to indicate on a graphic or a numerical scale to what extent he or she thinks these characteristics apply (for an example see Figure 4.2).

In *descriptive scales* the positions on the scales are not indicated by a number or place on a continuum but by means of a behaviour description or an indication of intensity (for an example see Figure 4.3). Here the same important distinction obtains as for checklists, i.e. empirically and non-empirically-based descriptions. The non-empirically chosen alternatives are in fact nothing but subjectively indicated scale positions, employing words like excellent, good, adequate, and so on, instead of grades. The apparent communicative gain is often spurious. In fact, the scale positions themselves are, in most cases, less clear than they are in graphic or numerical scales.

One can, however, establish empirically the scale value of the statements beforehand. One of the most elaborate procedures is the method of "equal appearing intervals" devised by Thurstone (see Edwards, 1957, Ch. 4). A large number of statements belonging to a particular category (e.g. quality of the work) is submitted to a number of "expert appraisers" who are asked to indicate how positive or negative the statements rate on the relevant dimension. Next, an average score (usually the median) and the distribution across appraisers are calculated. The statements with the lowest variance (maximizing cross-appraiser item consistency) and with intervals as equal as possible are then selected. In the final appraisal these statements are listed in random order and the appraiser must indicate which of them apply.[6] The score will be the mean scale value of the statements considered applicable.

Anchored scales are constructed following a similarly careful, empirically-based procedure for

TABLE 4.5

A number of items and their factor loadings (×100) from a job analyst's checklist (source: Andriessen & Drenth, 1973).

	I	*II*	*III*	*IV*
—Is not a fast worker	62			
—Knowledge of statistics moderate			66	
—Becomes uncertain when having to carry out instructions independently	56			
—Gets along excellently with superiors		73		
—Is good at explaining technical problems			− 42	
—Careful manner of reporting				62
—Spends much time on details	64			
—Uses statistics a lot			− 60	
—Does not keep up with developments in professional field			59	
—Often does not dare oppose superiors	55			
—Does not associate easily with employees		− 58		
—Quality of work highly fluctuating				− 51
—Insufficient use of ergonomics				− 45
—Able to work well in a team		83		
—Makes clearly arranged graphs and tables			63	
—Occasionally approaches employer unwisely		− 72		

FIGURE 4.2

Teaching		
Content of classes/seminars is of a remarkably high level	□□□□□	Content of classes/seminars can be much improved
Divides up the subject matter clearly and systematically	□□□□□	Divides up the subject matter poorly and hardly systematically
Presentation of subject matter is clear and didactically excellent	□□□□□	Presentation of subject matter is unclear and not very didactic
Presentation is particularly fascinating	□□□□□	Has difficulty holding attention
Coaching students (e.g. with papers and practical training) is remarkably good	□□□□□	Inadequate coaching of students
Leadership		
Is open to ideas; listens attentively	□□□□□	Is not open to ideas of associates
Has very good ability in coaching and helping associates	□□□□□	Coaching leaves things to be desired
Is able to generate enthusiasm and to motivate associates	□□□□□	Lacks ability to inspire or to motivate

Parts of the appraisal form for "academic personnel" Vrije Universiteit, Amsterdam.

selecting behavioural alternatives, the "anchors". In principle, this method, originally developed by Smith and Kendall (1963), starts from the idea of critical incidents. The anchors are derived from a description of a large number of critical behaviour descriptions generated by a group of appraisers, "critical" meaning that they are crucial to good or poor performance. Next, a second group of experts subjects the pool of items to careful formulation and attributes scale values to these items (by group discussion or by the so-called backtranslation method—for a full description of the latter see Campbell et al., 1970, pp. 119–24). This results in a scale whose anchors are not only carefully formulated but also yield an exact level indication of the behavioural aspect to be rated. Campbell et al. (1970, pp. 122–3) give some examples for the dimensions "handling customers' complaints" and "meeting deadlines".

In the so-called "Behaviourally Anchored Rating Scale" (BARS), an assessment is made of the behaviour that is expected of the subject. Another variant of this, in which the frequency of occurrence of the relevant behaviours in the appraisal period is observed and scored, is the so-called "Behavioural Observation Scale" (BOS).

With regard to the sensitivity of both systems to appraiser errors (halo, contrast, etc.), there is not much to choose between the BARS and the BOS. The BOS form is, however, more user-friendly and easier to fill in (Wiersma & Latham, 1986).

Bernardin & Smith (1981) warn against the increasingly sloppy design and use of anchored systems and consider the criticism levelled at them (e.g. Atkins & Conlon, 1978) pertinent but not entirely applicable to the original idea and its implementation.

According to Goodale and Burke (1975), the obvious objection to these systems, that they are rather specific and allow little generalization, is not necessarily always valid. They present a BARS system which can indeed be applied to different jobs. The danger that some "anchors", because of their specific character, attract special attention and will be more easily memorized, but distort the appraisal for the same reason

FIGURE 4.3

I	THEORETICAL PROFESSIONAL KNOWLEDGE	Possesses more knowledge than is required	Sufficient theoretical knowledge to fulfil job satisfactorily	Occasionally lacking in theoretical knowledge	Insufficient theoretical knowledge
II	CAPACITY	Has the job at his fingertips	Fulfils job satisfactorily	Has trouble with certain parts of the job	Has an overall insufficient command of the job
III	INTEREST	Is totally devoted to the job	Does the job with sufficient interest	Does the job with moderate interest	Does not care
IV	INDEPENDENCE	One can leave the work to him or her	Brief instructions will do	Fairly often in need of support	Requires guidance all the time
V	MANNER OF WORKING				
	1. Speed	Works fast	Works at speed required	Does not always attain required speed	Seldom attains required speed
	2. Regularity	Keeps working solidly	Usually attains reasonable regularity	Does not always work regularly	Unable to work regularly
	3. Accuracy	No need to control	Sample controls suffice	Requires regular control	Makes many mistakes, thus requiring constant control

Example of (part of) a descriptive rating scale.

(especially if they are not all that representative of the behaviour being appraised) is real enough (Murphy & Constans, 1987). The "anchors" should therefore be selected with the greatest care.

Considering the great effort required for constructing these anchored scales, the advantage over the good "classic" scales is quite limited—as a review of the literature shows (Schwab et al., 1975), despite the fact that the theory and the ideas behind the system are certainly laudable.

Let us not forget one thing: the comparison of Schwab et al. was made with "good" conventional rating scales. It is no exaggeration to say that these are rare. Because of the subjective and a priori character of these types of scaling, it is in principle possible to construct them off-hand. It takes a lot of discipline and time to construct a good, non-empirical, descriptive scale. The advantage of the empirical systems mentioned is that they are *by definition* carefully constructed. One is forced to concentrate on the careful wording of the aspects to be appraised and the score levels. Inaccurate constructions will come to light of their own accord. This means that, on average, empirically constructed systems will be clearly better than the generally used classic rating scales.

In attempting to evaluate the whole category of "differentiated systems", first of all it should be said that they come out best when judged by utilization criteria. They are transparent, manageable, acceptable to appraiser and subject, and they form a sound basis for an interview or action programme. Because of their informational, differentiated character, moreover, they provide a goal starting point for measures in the areas of training, selection, and organization. As criteria for selection and training research, too, they are usually more satisfactory that other systems.

As to its psychometric characteristics, this category is greatly varied. As was just pointed out, in most cases empirical systems are superior to the do-it-yourself scale systems all too often encountered in practice. As a result of the accuracy inherent to the empirical process of testing chosen aspects, scale positions and weighting factors, they more adequately meet the requirements of relevance, validity and generalizability.

The psychometric qualities of conventional rating scales (graphic, numerical, or descriptive) often leave much to be desired. The most frequently occurring deficiencies are:

1. *Irrelevance.*
   The traits to be rated inadequately reflect the behaviour or performance concerned.
2. *Non-validity.*
   Because the traits are too abstract or the terms used polyvalent, appraisers use their own "psychological theories" as guidelines for assigning scores to particular dimensions (Borman, 1983; Wexley & Youtz, 1985). These private theories are often incorrect and lead to invalid conclusions.

   In addition, the tendency to let appraisals of specific traits be influenced by a conspicuously good or specially bad trait, or more vaguely, by a general good or bad "impression", is often cited as an invalidating appraisal error. The first type of error is called the "halo-effect" and the second the "horn-effect". These two errors often account for a considerable part of the total variance (see Lee et al., 1981). The less familiar the appraiser is with the job and/or with the subject, the more the halo effect increases (Kozlowski & Kirsch, 1987). A statistical control of such halo effects seems to have little positive effect on the validity (Becker & Cardy, 1986), however.

   Cardy and Dobbins (1986) point to an important and often overlooked factor in appraisals: the affective relationship between the appraiser and the subject. The issue of whether the appraiser likes the subject and finds his or her company agreeable is an integral appraisal dimension which has a profound effect on the final appraisal result (see also Alexander & Wilkins, 1982). But too often, subordinates are considered congenial for reasons other than their work performance!
3. *Tendency to reduce variance.*
   In connection with the previous point, amongst other factors, appraisers tend to play it safe and to use only a limited width of the range of scoring possibilities, preferably slightly above the median score. This "central tendency" reduces the variance and thus the differentiating capacity as well as the reliability.
4. *Bias and judgemental errors, coupled to the appraiser.*
   Here, one might think of various social and societal prejudices (sex, age, minorities), the effect of expectations, fear of confrontation with subjects (the "leniency effect"), diverse perceptions of the "good performer", the type of "performer" that the appraiser is, the personal characteristics of the appraiser, the question as to how well one has oneself been appraised, and so on. An example of the effect of individual characteristics on an appraisal is given in the study by Schneider and Bayroff (1953), which demonstrated that an intelligent appraiser appreciates other aspects in his subject than does a less intelligent appraiser. An example of the effect of how an appraiser is appraised is provided by the research of Kirchner and Reisberg (1962); it appeared that an appraiser who was deemed effective appreciated initiative, planning and know-how, whereas another appraiser, deemed less effective, appreciated more cooperation, loyalty to the company, and the like. Mount and Thomson (1987) showed that an appraisal was more accurate when the behaviour displayed by the subject was more in line with the expectations of that behaviour held by the appraiser.
5. *Fluctuation of norms over appraisers.*
   Even if performance or behaviour aspects are correctly rated, the norms for "adequate" or "good" performance may fluctuate so strongly between appraisers as to render the final appraisal arbitrary.

6. *Interaction with various organizational factors.*
Earlier, we saw that generalizability across situations, time and appraisers cannot always easily be acquired and that the variance found in the various consistency measures cannot always simply be labelled as error variance. We saw that people do not always show a stable behavioural pattern and that, under certain circumstances, with certain tasks, and under the supervision of certain people, their reaction will be different from that under other circumstances, tasks, and leaders. This is in fact the major problem in interpreting all kinds of interaction variance: interaction with the company, the department, the job, seniority, age and rank (McCormick & Ilgen, 1980; Mitchell & Liden, 1982) and even with the year of appraisal (De Wolff, 1965). The problem is to distinguish true variance from error variance; it would be mistaken, in any event, to attribute all such differences to errors of judgement.
This means that various technical corrections do not solve the problem either, for these do assume that errors of judgement lie behind the differences. It has been proposed, for instance, to equalize the means and the distributions per department, per year, per appraiser, and so on, by using standard scores within these defined groups—a process which would also eliminate the true differences between groups!

One may find numerous suggestions in the literature for reducing the errors mentioned. They include the technical corrections just mentioned, various practical rules for scale construction (e.g. Lazer & Wikstrom, 1978), the training and coaching of appraisers (Borman, 1979; Bernardin, 1978; Athey & McIntyre, 1987), the use of more than one appraiser or the assistance of a coordinator (the Dutch Civil Service), and many others.

The advice given by Campbell et al. (1970) may well stand as the most realistic. They say that it is most important to set good questions, which the appraiser can answer honestly: questions concerning aspects of behaviour that can be adequately observed and evaluated by the appraiser. Most errors are made because the appraiser does not know what to fill in or how to word it if he or she wishes to be honest. A lack of understanding, and the idea that the traits to be rated are irrelevant, lead to distrust and lack of motivation. These are the main causes of the "errors" of judgement mentioned above. The remedy they suggest is the use of the BARS technique. We would want to put it more broadly: do, in any event, practice the same accuracy as that used in the construction of the BARS, BOS and Equal Appearing Interval scales. Such accuracy appears to be a necessary, though not sufficient, condition for the effectiveness of any appraisal system.

6 CONCLUSION

We should like to conclude this chapter with some remarks about developments in the theory and practice of personnel appraisals.

First, the appraisal of employees is really no more than a paragraph in a chapter entitled "judging people", albeit that it is coloured by the specific context given by a work organization. We deal with the same general principles of human judgement and assessment (Hofstee, 1974; Borman, 1983) and social perception theory (Jaspars, 1964). Curiously enough, however, the contribution of psychology has tended to be mostly of an instrumental and technical nature. There exists a continual flow of studies on the improvement of instruments, the technical sophistication of scales, and methods of avoiding errors of judgement. Their usefulness is clearly beyond doubt, but all too often the relationship with more general psychological theories of judgement and evaluation of human behaviour is lacking. An example of what we consider desirable in this respect is formed by the study carried out by Feldman (1981), which examines individual appraisals from the perspective of attribution theory and the theory of information processing; by Palermo (1983), who argues for an approach in which central importance is given to the ways in which a worker gives meaning to his or her working life, performance appraisal being derived from this model; and by Mohrman and Lawler

(1983), who interpret the behaviour to be appraised from the viewpoint of motivation theory. In our opinion there is an urgent need for more such theoretical foundation in this practical subject.

Second, we wish to draw attention to developments in both the policy and practice of personnel appraisal. Organizations have always considered appraisals primarily a controlling and signalling tool in which higher hierarchical levels make decisions on the basis of information about the performance and behaviour of employees at lower levels. The contribution of psychology, then, has been looked upon mainly from the tradition of measurement: how is the most reliable and valid judgement to be attained?

Another view of appraisal has since come into existence, with its origins in the goals of performance improvement and guidance. It has been realized that personnel appraisal involves the interaction of two adult individuals and that the input of the one being appraised in this interactive process is a condition for the useful effect of this policy instrument. Maier (1958) was one of the first to draw attention to this fact, through an analysis of the appraisal interview. He describes the three well-known forms of interview: Tell and Sell, Tell and Listen, and Problem Solving.

In the first method, the appraiser is also the leader in the appraisal interview. He or she wishes to communicate the appraisal result as accurately as possible to the subject and hopes to convince the subject of its correctness. Confronted with the subject's usual resistance, he or she will tend to start preaching and lecturing, in turn enforcing negative reactions. The underlying view that changes and innovations should be initiated and implemented "top down" is essentially a conservative one.

The Tell and Listen method entails a less directive attitude, at least in the second phase. Once the appraisal has been stated, the appraiser's attitude becomes that of an active listener. The subject may speak out and defend themselves and therefore has the impression of being respected. It is possible, too, that in this way ideas can be generated "bottom up". However, the supervisor is the judge; they determine whether something was well done or inadequate. The only thing that has changed is the way the feedback has been "packaged", which is, indeed, more tolerant and acceptable. Though it often results in a good relationship between supervisor and subordinate, it does not guarantee improvements in performance.

In the third method, the "Problem Solving" approach, the role of the manager is principally different. In this approach it is realized that in essence the process of appraisal is not compatible with one of "helping". In "Problem Solving" we are primarily concerned with the subject's own development. The first thing is to stimulate the subject to think up solutions and improvements themselves, instead of presenting them to the subject ready-made. This requires openness and a complete absence of defensiveness on the part of the subject. Communication should be two-way and attention is strongly focused on problems rather than personal qualities. The basic idea is that real change is achieved only when those concerned participate in it themselves. The now common term "functional appraisal interview" better reflects this intention than the classic term "performance appraisal".

Participation and motivation are central concepts to this approach (Mohrman & Lawler, 1983; Steers & Lee, 1983). In the 1960s a group of researchers supervised by Meyer studied the effects of the classic appraisal process, then characterized by a one-way and top down form of communication (Meyer et al., 1965; French et al., 1966), and were less than positive about the results. They argued in favour not only of separating the two goals "pay determination" and "work improvement" ("split roles in the performance appraisal") but also of a considerable input of the person appraised and of joint goal setting and problem solving. A follow-up publication (Meyer, 1977) restated the central importance of "two-way communication" and "problem-orientation". For suggestions on interviewing technique with regard to the emphasis on "goal" and "problem" aspects, we refer the reader to the literature and to Volume 3 Chapter 11 of the present handbook on management development. A study by Ivancevich and Smith (1981) has demonstrated that such skills can indeed be trained.

Clearly, in this last view the manager is

assigned a very different role. Instead of appraiser he becomes helper; instead of judge, coach. This last role is also cogently stipulated by McGregor (1957), whose views were discussed earlier. The appraisal system of Management By Objectives (MBO), described earlier, is also wholly in this line.

It is remarkable that, despite its sympathetic and—given the research literature—useful elements, MBO has never really taken off. In a sample containing 216 organizations, Locher and Teel (1977) found that MBO was the main appraisal technique in only 13%. In The Netherlands MBO is encountered only sporadically. The objections raised by, for example, Flippo (1976) may be responsible for this. He notes, amongst other things, that often individual results are emphasized at the expense of other important organizational goals. Furthermore, MBO cannot really be applied to jobs where the person concerned has little influence on the concrete output. Finally, MBO does not lead to a comparative rating and is therefore less appropriate for the organization's more administrative purposes.

It is useful at this point to mention a proposal put forward by Teel (1978), which combines the participation of the subject with the desirability of having comparative appraisal scores or profiles at hand. He argues for coupling the supervisor's appraisal with the subject's own. By itself, the self-assessment technique is not very useful; Thornton (1980) showed that as far as its psychometric qualities are concerned, self-assessments are inferior to appraisals by superiors. Their positive aspects, however, are their motivational effect and stimulus for self-development. These elements are picked up in Teel's proposal, in which both appraiser and subject independently complete an appraisal form before the appraisal interview proper begins. The appraisal interview then starts with a discussion of the various aspects, with first the subject explaining his or her opinion and then the appraiser. Next, the previously completed forms are compared. When (on a five-point scale) there is a difference of only one point, the higher score is taken. If the difference is greater, a solution—usually a compromise—is reached through discussion.

Teel's experiences indicated that in two-thirds of the cases there was no difference between appraisals and that only in a very small number of cases was the difference more than one point. The subjects responded very positively to this procedure and they took part in the discussion more freely and more constructively than in the more classic appraisals.

The reason why we have explained this procedure a little more extensively is that, on the one hand, it secures the advantages of the MBO approach, i.e. the subject's participation and active contribution, and on the other hand it also makes available completed appraisal forms, on the basis of which it is possible to make comparisons and administrative decisions.

Finally, and by way of a summing-up, we wish to designate four preconditions for an appraisal system to function well.

First, the *technical qualities* of the system. In this chapter we have formulated a number of requirements that an appraisal should meet. We have also seen that part of the requirements' content varies according to the goal of the appraisal. Here, a close attuning of the technical and utilization aspects to the goal of the appraisal, and the subsequent quantitative optimalization of the system, are of crucial importance.

Second, we should take note of the *organizational conditions* for the design, construction and implementation of the appraisal system. Earlier in this section we noted the importance of participation of the subject in the appraisal process. However, we are now alluding to another aspect of this involvement of both subject and appraiser: involvement in the design and selection of the system as such; the way it functions in the organization, the formulation of the conditions of its application and its secrecy, supervising the observance of these conditions, and so on.

In 1980 a new appraisal system was introduced at the Vrije Universiteit in Amsterdam, whose use extends to academic personnel. It was introduced only after several years of consultation, experimentation and evaluation, in which representative individuals from all levels had a say, and we are convinced that this constituted a major condition for the acceptance and the effective application of the system.

Among the organizational conditions we would

also wish to include the presence of an efficient appeal procedure. From a labour union point of view, Top argued for this in a critical report on "the vulnerable appraisal subject" (Top, 1974). Such an appeal facility has already been realized in government departments and at universities in the Netherlands.

Third, a number of conditions in the area of *organizational structure* may be mentioned. If people are to be appraised on a number of job criteria and performance norms, this can obviously be done better if these criteria and norms are specified, uniform, clear, and accepted by those involved. This means that such a system works better in an organizational structure in which it is clear what everybody's responsibilities are, what goals are being sought, and how information should be gathered about the question as to what extent these goals are being reached. In other words, appraisal systems function better in organizations with clear-cut task structures, distinct goals, and unequivocal measurement procedures.

This is also, not to say especially, true in situations where the organization is undergoing change. Olbrich (1981) correctly urges us to ensure that any discrepancy between expected and actual performance is not the result of organizational conditions and demands having been modified in the meantime. This is a real danger, especially in cases where tasks and contexts are changing rapidly (automation, computerization).

As a final condition, we would suggest a good and open *social climate*. However good the system is, appraisals will never function well if there is no trust, if honest communication is not possible, or if politics or hidden motives determine behaviour. In this connection, Kane and Lawler (1979) mention the importance of the participation of the lower echelons in the setting of goals and the formulation of standards. If this is carried out unilaterally by management, the openness required for the satisfactory functioning of appraisals will never materialize.

If the last two conditions regarding the organizational and social contexts are met, appraisals will be much less a "tool of management" than they used to be. Appraising will then become a rather more continuous activity and an integral part of the leader's task. It will become more closely linked with responsibilities such as task setting and task arrangements, and there will be smooth transition from appraisal to work consultation.

Also, from the employee's perspective, there will be more integration with the other personnel facilities. Work performance appraisal is put into a broader framework, as part of career planning and individual career development. In such a career development plan, as much information as possible is collated: individual wishes and needs, the need for further training or schooling, potential qualities and the possibilities of advancement, and naturally, task fulfilment up to now. Viewed in this way, employee appraisal acquires a central position in personnel policy, both enhancing the stimulation and continuous guidance of employees, and promoting the development of the organization and the management of its human resources.

NOTES

1. This does not in the least mean that remuneration systems are just control systems or that remuneration may not refer to future performance; see also this Handbook, Volume 4, Chapter 12.
2. It is wise not to lose sight of statistical considerations. Weighting is not only determined by the weight factor assigned to a certain trait but also, first, by the number of items per trait in the scale, and second, the variance of the item scores or scale scores.
3. The more or less effective performances or results are rated on a numerical scale. The incidence of these performances or results is then expressed in percentage terms, and the product of this percentage and the scale value forms the basis for the appraisal.
4. There has been considerable research on the question of how these indices should be determined and how the questions should be formulated (Bartlett, 1960; Berkshire, 1958; Waters & Wherry, 1962).
5. In principle it is also possible to weight the statements, for example on the basis of their factor loadings. This does not usually yield much additional value, while its actual implementation becomes much more difficult.
6. In this respect the system is basically a checklist which is why it is sometimes called a "weighted checklist" in the English-language literature on the subject.

REFERENCES

Alexander, E.R., & Wilkins, R.D. (1982). Performance rating validity; the relationship of objective and subjective measures of performance. *Group and Organization Studies, 7*, 485–496.

Andriessen, J.H.T.H., & Drenth, P.J.D. (1973). Een beoordelingslijst van arbeidsanalisten. In P.J.D. Drenth, P.J. Willems, & C.J. de Wolff (Eds.), *Arbeids- en Organisatiepsychologie.* Deventer: Kluwer.

Anstey, E., Fletcher, C., & Walker, J. (1978). *Staff appraisal and development.* London: Allen & Unwin.

Athey, T.R., & McIntryre, R.M. (1987). Effect of rater training on rater accuracy: Levels-of-processing theory and social facilitation theory perspectives. *Journal of Applied Psychology, 72*, 567–572.

Atkins, R.S., & Conlon, D.J. (1978). Behaviorally anchored rating scales: Some theoretical issues. *Academy of Management Review, 3*, 119–128.

Baier, D.E. (1951). Reply to Travers. *Psychological Bulletin, 48*, 421–433.

Bartlett, C.J. (1960). Factors affecting forced-choice response. *Personnel Psychology, 13*, 399–406.

Batz, N., & Schindler, U. (1983). Personalbeurteilungssysteme auf dem Prüfstand. *Zeitschrift für Führung und Organisation, 8*, 424–432.

Becker, B.E., & Cardy, R.L. (1986). Influence of halo error on appraisal effectiveness: A conceptual and empirical reconsideration. *Journal of Applied Psychology, 71*, 662–671.

Berk, R.A. (Ed.) (1986). *Performance assessment: Methods and applications.* Baltimore: Johns Hopkins University Press.

Berkshire, J.R. (1958). Comparisons of five forced choice indices. *Educational and Psychological Measurement, 18*, 553–561.

Berkshire, J.R., & Highland, R.W. (1953). Forced choice performance rating: A methodological study. *Personnel Psychology, 6*, 355–378.

Bernardin, H.J. (1978). Effects of rater training on leniency and halo errors in student ratings of instructors. *Journal of Applied Psychology, 63*, 301–308.

Bernardin, H.J. (1986). A performance appraisal system. In R.A. Berk (Ed.), *Performance assessment: Methods and applications.* Baltimore, MA: Johns Hopkins University Press.

Bernardin, H.J., & Beatty, R.W. (1984). *Performance appraisal: Assessing human behavior at work.* Boston: Kent-Wadsworth.

Bernardin, H.J., & Smith, P.C. (1981). A classification of some issues regarding the development and use of behavioral anchored rating scales (BAS). *Journal of Applied Psychology, 66*, 458–463.

Borman, W.C. (1978). Exploring upper limits of reliability and validity in job performance rating. *Journal of Applied Psychology, 63*, 135–144.

Borman, W.C. (1979). Training raters in performance appraisal. *Journal of Applied Psychology, 69*, 410–420.

Borman, W.C. (1983). Implications of personality theory and research for the rating of work performance in organizations. In F. Landy, S. Zedeck, & J. Cleveland (Eds.), *Performance measurement and theory.* Hillsdale, NJ: Lawrence Erlbaum Associates Inc.

Brandstätter, H. (1970). Die Beurteilung von Mitarbeitern. In A. Mayer & B. Herwig (Eds.), *Handbuch der Psychologie, I,* Göttingen: Hogrefe.

Bray, D.W. (1964). The management progress study. *American Psychologist, 19*, 419–420.

Campbell, J.P., Dunnette, M.D., Lawler, E.E., & Weick, K.W. (1970). *Managerial behavior, performance and effectiveness.* New York: McGraw Hill.

Cardy, R.L., & Dobbins, G.H. (1986). Affect and appraisal accuracy: Liking as an integral dimension in evaluating performance. *Journal of Applied Psychology, 71*, 672–678.

COP/SER (1959). *Bazen in industrie.* Den Haag: COP.

Cronbach, L.J. (1971). Test-validation. In R.L. Thorndike (Ed.), *Educational Measurement.* Washington DC: American Council on Education.

Cummings, L.L., & Schwab, D.P. (1973). *Performance in organizations.* Glenview: Scott, Foresman and Co.

Dam, A.G. van, & Drenth, P.J.D. (1976). *Hoger Beroep.* Amsterdam: COP/Vrije Universiteit.

Domsch, M., Gerpott, T., & Jochum, E. (1983). Personalbeurteilung durch Gleichgestelte in industrieller Forschung und Entwicklung. *Zeitschrift für Arbeits-und Organisationspsychologie, 27*, 173–182.

Drenth, P.J.D. (1975). *Inleiding in de testtheorie.* Deventer: Van Loghum Slaterus.

Drenth, P.J.D., & Sijtsma, K. (1990). *Test theorie.* Holten: Boon, Staflev, Van Loghum Slaterus.

Drucker, P.F. (1954). *The practice of management.* New York: Harper.

Edwards, A.L. (1957). *Techniques of attitude scale construction.* New York: Appleton-Century-Crifts.

Elshout, J.J., Boselie, F.A.J.M., Van de Berg, J., Boerlijst, G., & Schaake, B. (1973). De validatie van een testbatterij voor de selectie van wetenschappelijke onderzoekers. In P.J.D. Drenth, P.J. Willems, & C.J. de Wolff (Eds.), *Arbeids-en Organisatiepsychologie.* Deventer: Kluwer.

Feldman, J.M. (1981). Beyond attribution theory: Cognitive processes in performance appraisal. *Journal of Applied Psychology, 66*, 127–148.

Finkle, R.B. (1976). Managerial assessment centers. In M.D. Dunnette (Ed.), *Handbook of industrial and organizational psychology.* Chicago: Rand McNally.

Flanagan, J.C. (1954). The critical incidents technique. *Psychological Bulletin, 4*, 337–357.

Flanagan, J.C., & Burns, R.K. (1955). The employee performance record: A new appraisal and development tool. *Harvard Business Review, 33*, 95–102.

Fleishman, E.A., Harris, E.F., & Burt, H.E. (1955). *Leadership and supervision in industry.* Bureau of Educational Research Monographs, *33*.

Flippo, E.B. (1976). *Principles of personnel management.* New York: McGraw-Hill.

French, J.R.P., Kay, E., & Meyer, H.H. (1966). Participation and the appraisal system. *Human Relations, 19*, 3–21.

Ginneken, P.J. van (Ed.) (1974). *Verdiensten van hoger personeel.* Deventer: Kluwer.

Glickman, A.S. (1955). Effects of negatively skewed ratings on motivations of the rated. *Personnel Psychology, 8*, 39–47.

Goldman, P. (1983). A sociohistorical perspective on performance assessment. In F.J. Landy, S. Zedeck & J. Cleveland (Eds.), *Performance measurement and theory.* Hillsdale, NJ: Lawrence Erlbaum Associates Inc.

Goodale, J.G., & Burke, R.J. (1975). Behaviorally based rating scales need not be job specific. *Journal of Applied Psychology, 60*, 389–391.

Grunow, D. (1976). *Personalbeurteilung.* Stuttgart: Ferdinand Enke Verlag.

Heinrich, M., & Erndt, H. (1980). Leistungsbeurteilung zur Fundierung personeller Ausleseentscheidungen. *Zeitschrift für Arbeidswissenschaft, 34*, 89–96.

Hofstee, W.K.B. (1974). *Psychologische uitspraken over personen.* Deventer: Van Loghum Slaterus.

Ivancevich, J.M., & Smith, S.V. (1981). Goal setting interview skills training; simulated and on-the-job analyses. *Journal of Applied Psychology, 66*, 697–705.

Jaspars, J.M.F. (1964). *On social perception.* Leiden: R.U. (dissertatie).

Kane, J.S. (1986). Performance distribution assessment. In R.A. Berk (Ed.), *Performance assessment: Methods and applications.* Baltimore, MA: Johns Hopkins University Press.

Kane, J.S., & Lawler, E.E. (1979). Performance appraisal effectiveness. In B.M. Staw (Ed.), *Research in organizational behavior.* Greenwich: Jai Press.

Kavanagh, M.J., MacKinney, A.C., & Wollins, L. (1971). Issues in managerial performance: Multi-trait multi-method analysis of ratings. *Psychological Bulletin, 74*, 34–39.

Kozlowski, S.W.J., & Kirsch, M.P. (1987). The systematic distortion hypothesis, halo and accuracy: An individual-level analysis. *Journal of Applied Psychology, 72*, 252–261.

Krichner, W.K., & Reisberg, D.J. (1962). Differences between better and less effective supervisors in appraisals of subordinates. *Personnel Psychology, 15*, 295–302.

Landy, F.J., & Farr, J.L. (Eds.) (1983). *The measurement of work performance: Methods, theory and applications.* New York: Academic Press.

Landy, F.J., & Trumbo, D. (1980). *Psychology of work-behavior.* Homewood: Dorsey.

Landy, F.J., Zedeck, S., & Cleveland, J. (Eds.) (1983). *Performance measurement and theory.* Hillsdale, NJ: Lawrence Erlbaum Associates Inc.

Latham, G.P., & Wexley, K.N. (1981). *Increasing productivity through performance appraisal.* Reading: Addison–Wesley.

Laurent, H. (1962). *The validation of aids for the identification of management potential.* New York: S.O. NJ.

Laurent, H. (1970). Cross-cultural cross-validation of empirically validated tests. *Journal of Applied Psychology, 54*, 417–324.

Lawler, E.E. (1981). *Pay and organizational development.* Reading: Addison-Wesley.

Lazer, R.I., & Wikstrom, B. (1978). *Appraising managerial performance: Current practices and future directions.* New York: The Conference Board.

Lee, R., Malone, M., & Greco, S. (1981). Multitrait-multirater analysis of performance ratings for law enforcement personnel. *Journal of Applied Psychology, 66*, 625–632.

Levy-Leboyer, C., & Sperandio, J.C. (Eds.) (1987). *Traité de psychologie du travail.* Paris: Presse Universitaire de France.

Locher, A.H., & Teel, K.S. (1977). Performance appraisal—a survey of current practices. *Personnel Journal, 56*, 245–254.

Locke, E.A. (1978). The ubiquity of the technique of goal setting in theories and approaches to employee motivation. *Academy of Management Review, 3*, 594–621.

Locke, E.A. (1983). Performance appraisal under capitalism, socialism, and the mixed economy. In F.J. Landy, S. Zedeck, & J. Cleveland (Eds.) *Performance measurement and theory.* Hillsdale, NJ: Lawrence Erlbaum Associates Inc.

Love, K.G. (1981). Comparison of peer assessment methods; reliability, validity, friendship bias, and user reaction. *Journal of Applied Psychology, 66*, 451–457.

Maier, N.R.F. (1963). *The appraisal interview.* London: Wiley.

Mahoney, T.A., Jerdee, T.H., & Nash, A.N. (1960). Predicting managerial effectiveness. *Personnel Psychology, 13*, 147–163.

McCormick, E.J., & Ilgen, D. (1980). *Industrial psychology.* Englewood Cliffs: Prentice Hall.

McGregor, D. (1957). An uneasy look at performance appraisal. *Harvard Business Review, 35*, 89–94.

McGregor, D. (1960). *The human side of enterprise.* New York: McGraw-Hill.

Merrihue, W.V., & Katzell, R.A. (1955). ERI: Yardstick of employee relations. *Harvard Business Review, 33*, 91–99.
Meyer, H.H. (1977). The annual performance review discussion. *Personnel Journal, 56*, 508–511.
Meyer, H.H., Kay, E. & French, J.R.P. (1965). Split roles in performance appraisal. *Harvard Business Review, 43*, 123–129.
Mischel, W. (1968). *Personality and assessment.* New York: Wiley.
Mitchell, T.R., & Liden, R.C. (1982). The effects of the social context on performance evaluations. *Organizational Behavior and Human Performance, 29*, 241–256.
Mohrman, A.M., & Lawler, E.E. III (1983). Motivation and performance appraisal behavior. In F.J. Landy, S. Zedeck, & J. Cleveland, (Eds.), *Performance measurement and theory* (pp. 173–189). Hillsdale, NJ: Lawrence Erlbaum Associates Inc.
Mount, M.K., & Thomson, D.E. (1987). Cognitive categorization and quality of performance ratings. *Journal of Applied Psychology, 72*, 240–246.
Muller, H. (1970). *The search for the qualities essential to the advancement in a large industrial group.* Utrecht: R.U. (dissertatie).
Murphy, K.R., & Constans, J.I. (1987). Behavioral anchors as a source of bias in rating. *Journal of Applied Psychology, 72*, 573–577.
Neubauer, R., & von Rosenstiel, L. (Eds.) (1980). *Handbuch der Angewandten Psychologie, Vol. 1, Arbeit und Organisation.* München: Moderne Industrie.
Olbrich, E. (1981). Die Beurteilung von Mitarbeitern. In F. Stoll (Ed.), *Die Psychologie des 20 Jahrhunderts, Band XIII, Anwendungen im Berufsleben* (pp. 259–283). Zurich: Kindler Verlag.
Palermo, D.S. (1983). Cognition, concepts, and employees theory of the world. In F.J. Landy, S. Zedeck, & J. Cleveland (Eds.), *Performance measurement and theory* (pp.97–115). Hillsdale, NJ: Lawrence Erlbaum Associates Inc.
Porter, L.W., Lawler, E.E., & Hackman, J.R. (1975). *Behavior in organizations.* New York: McGraw-Hill.
Qua De, C.L.M. (1973). Management development en beoordelingen. In P.J.D. Drenth, P.J. Willems & C.J. de Wolff (Eds.), *Arbeids-en Organisatiepsychologie.* Deventer: Kluwer.
Robertson, I.T., & Martin, P.J. (1986). Management in Britain: A survey and critique. *Journal of Occupational Psychology, 59*, 45–57.
Ronan, W.W., & Prein, E.P. (1966). *Toward a criterion theory: A review and analysis of research and opinion.* Greensboro: Richardson Foundation.
Ronan, W.W., & Schwartz, A.P. (1974). Ratings as performance criteria. *International Review of Applied Psychology, 23*, 71–81.
Rowe, K.H. (1970). An appraisal of appraisal. *Journal of Management Studies, 10*, 1–25.
Schmidt, F.L. (1983). Alternative theories: Comments on Goldman. In F.J. Landy, S. Zedeck & J. Cleveland (Eds.), *Performance measurement and theory.* Hillsdale, NJ: Lawrence Erlbaum Associates Inc.
Schneider, D.E., & Bayroff, A.G. (1953). The relationship between rater characteristics and validity. *Journal of Applied Psychology, 37*, 327–380.
Schuler, H., & Stehle, W. (1983). Neuere Entwicklungen des Assessment-Center-Ansatzes; beurteilt unter dem Aspekt der sociale Validität. *Zeitschrift für Arbeits-und Organisationspsychologie, 27*, 33–44.
Schuler, H., & Stehle, W. (1987). Assessment Center als Methode der Personalentwicklung. *Beitrage zur Organisationpsychology, vol. 3.* Stuttgart: Verlag für Angewandte Psychologie.
Schwab, D., Heneman, H.G., & Decotiis, T. (1975). Behaviorally anchored rating scales: A review of the literature. *Personnel Psychology, 28*, 549–562.
Sisson, E.D. (1948). Forced choice: The new army rating. *Personnel Psychology, 1*, 365–387.
Smith, P.C. (1976). Behaviors, results and organizational effectiveness: The problem of criteria. In M.D. Dunnette (Ed.), *Handbook of industrial and organizational psychology.* Chicago: Rand McNally.
Smith, P.C., & Kendall, L.M. (1963). Retranslation of expectations: An approach to the construction of unambiguous anchors for rating scales. *Journal of Applied Psychology, 47*, 149–155.
Spriegel, W.R. (1962). Company practices in appraisal of managerial performance. *Personnel, 39*, 77–83.
Steers, R.M., & Lee, T.W. (1983). Facilitating effective performance appraisals: The role of commitment and organizational climate. In F.J. Landy, S. Zedeck & J. Cleveland (Eds.) *Performance measurement and theory.* Hillsdale, NJ: Lawrence Erlbaum Associates Inc.
Taylor, E.K., & Wherry, R.J. (1951). A study of leniency in two rating systems. *Personnel Psychology, 4*, 39–47.
Teel, K.S. (1978). Self-appraisal revisited. *Personnel Journal, 57*, 364–367.
Thorndike, R.L. (1949). *Personnel selection.* New York: Wiley.
Thornton, G.C. (1980). Psychometric properties of self-appraisal of job-performance. *Personnel Psychology, 33*, 263–273.
Tiffin, I., & McCormick E.J. (1966). *Industrial psychology.* London: Allen & Unwin.
Tigchelaar, L.S. (1974). *Potentieelbeoordeling en loopbaansucces.* Amsterdam, VU (dissertatie).
Top, W. (1974). *De kwetsbare beoordeelde.* Utrecht: Sociaal Wetenschappelijk Instituut van de Vakcentrales.
Travers, R.M.W. (1951). A critical review of the

validity and rationale of the forced-choice technique. *Psychological Bulletin*, *48*, 62–70,

Waters, L.K., & Wherry, R.J. (1962). The preference index and responses to forced-choice pairs. *Personnel Psychology*, *15*, 99–102.

Wexley, K.N., & Youtz, M.A. (1985). Rater belief about others: Their effects on rating errors and rater accuracy. *Journal of Occupational Psychology*, *58*, 265–275.

Whisler, T.F., & Harper, S.F. (Eds.). (1962). *Performance appraisal: Research and practice.* New York: Holt.

Whitla, D.K., & Tirrel, J.E. (1953). The validity of ratings of several levels of supervisors. *Personnel Psychology*, *6*, 461–466.

Wiersma, U., & Latham, G.P. (1986). The practicality of behavioral observation scales, behavioral expectation scales and trait scales. *Personnel Psychology*, *12*, 619–627.

Wolff, C.J. de (1963). *Personeelsbeoordeling.* Amsterdam: Swets & Zeitlinger.

Wolff, C.J. de (1965a). Factoranalyse van beoordelingen. *Nederlands Tijdschrift voor de Psychologie*, *20*, 95–100.

Wolff, C.J. de (1965b). Een factoranalyse van beoordelingen afkomstig van verschillende beoordelaars. *Nederlands Tijdschrift voor de Psychologie*, *20*, 283–292.

Wolff, C.J. de (1970). Beoordelingen als criteria. In P.J.D. Drenth, P.J. Willems, & C.J. de Wolff (Eds.), *Bedrijfspsychologie.* Deventer: Kluwer.

Woodworth, D.G., & McKinnon, D.W. (1957). The measurement of intellectual efficiency in assessment of 100 Air Force captains. *AFPTRC-TN-57*-128.

5

Assessment Centre Methods

Jac N. Zaal

1 INTRODUCTION[1]

Assessment centre methods (ACM) undoubtedly derive their name from a building where people were invited to participate in all kinds of assignments to determine their suitability for a certain position. How this was done and what experts were involved cannot be deduced from the name. Such centres were probably used by large organizations such as the government, the army, and multinationals. A comparison can be drawn with the refrigerator, which was known as "frigidair" after a well-known brand.

This association has long been superseded and the assessment centre (AC) now has a certain fame among industrial psychologists, human resource management (HRM) professionals, business administrators and their business clients as a method with which to assess leadership qualities. Whether this still relates to the almost classic form in which the AC made its start at the beginning of the 1960s is highly doubtful. If personnel advertisements are an accurate reflection of practice, we can see a colourful collection in which the word "assessment" is the only constant factor in the selection procedure. We may safely assume here that assessment is about something other than the familiar psychological examination. By most of the people concerned, including the applicant, it is by now generally accepted that it will include practical assignments (role plays) relating to the content of the position in question.

Another striking fact nowadays is the number of advertisements announcing that special attention will be given to the assessment of suitability. In most cases higher, and particularly management, positions are involved. Methods associated with and derived from ACM appear to be used increasingly in the assessment of personal qualities, whether in respect of selection, potential appraisal, promotion, career planning or management development (Altink et al., 1992).

In this chapter we offer an outline of the history of ACs, we discuss the method in relation to other selection methods and we subsequently deal with characteristics, basic principles and applications. The chapter concludes with a critical discussion of the qualities and pitfalls of ACMs.

2 WHY ASSESSMENT CENTRES? USE AND EFFICIENCY OF ALTERNATIVE SELECTION METHODS

In many organizations, a great deal of time is spent on the selection, training, counselling, assessment and development of staff. Such activities emphasize the importance of the human factor for the achievement of the organization's goals. Special attention is paid to tracing and developing management talent. Without underestimating the contributions of others, this particular interest is probably caused by the manager's role in the development, management and operational strength of the organization.

The quality of the management is closely linked to the quality of the selection and promotional decisions and, in the long term, with that of adequate training and development efforts.

Assessing someone's leadership qualities is not only time-consuming but, for various reasons, also a difficult task, the result of which, in retrospect, is often capable of improvement.

The absence of a good job analysis probably lies at the root of the problem. An adequate description of the management's tasks and efforts on various levels and the job requirements to be derived from this description forms the basis of an efficient selection.

A second cause can be found in the efficiency of the methods used to ascertain whether someone actually has the required management qualities. This efficiency appears to vary widely for different methods as is illustrated by the information on the utility from a study by Hunter and Hunter (1984). In that study, utility is defined as the annual net productivity increase for the American federal government as employer. The validity coefficients used are based on meta-analysis of a large number of studies in which assessments by supervisors have been used as prediction criterion. Since the absolute value is irrelevant for the separate selection methods in this respect, Table 5.1 shows how much better the utility is than that of the use of ability tests to reject the lowest 20% (low cutoff).

The frequency of use of selection methods in Table 5.1 is derived from various studies. Although the random checks naturally differ and, consequently, these figures should only be interpreted with due reserve, we can conclude that the correspondence between the utility and frequency of usage is remarkably low. The added value of traditional methods such as letter of application, diplomas and the general (application) interview is small, whereas the added value of little-used methods such as worksample tests, peer ratings, ACs and tests of professional knowledge is considerably higher. The figures for worksamples (and ACs) are slightly distorted since the relatively high costs of development and purchase have insufficiently been taken into account. This does not, however, apply to the method with the highest added value: the psychological test. It should be added, however, that this utility only holds true if the test is used to select the best candidates and that if the same tests are used to select candidates who meet certain minimum requirements, their value is quite small.

The figures on the frequency of use of the various methods in Dutch companies, at that time taken from Greuter and Roe (1980), are largely confirmed by recent information from Altink et al. (1992). This particularly applies to the continuing popularity of traditional methods. Naturally, we are not in favour of abandoning the letter of application or the interview but we do have major reservations about their use to assess the suitability of candidates. However, the figures also show hopeful trends. For example, it appears that ACs are being increasingly used, from less than 8% in the 1980s to 28% in 1992.

For the psychological test also, which, according to criticism in the public media and its relatively infrequent use was not very popular in the previous decades, the tide seems to be turning, especially where the selection of middle and higher management is concerned (frequency of use in 1992: 40% and 60% respectively). Yet its reputation remains unstable. When asked for the reason why no use is being made of psychological tests, 28% of the respondents answered that they had no faith in it. As a comparison the most frequent reasons for not using ACs are: "not familiar" (18%) and "too expensive" (28%).

The predictive validity of worksample tests and ACs has been extensively documented (Asher & Sciarrino, 1974; Finkle, 1976; Gaugler et al., 1987; Robertson & Kandola, 1982; Thornton & Byham, 1982). In The Netherlands, we have seen a recent increase in published and unpublished studies (Albers & Altink, 1993; Jansen and Stoop, 1995; Maëla, 1993; Van Opstal, 1994; Wiersma et

TABLE 5.1

The frequency of use (% of users per activity) and the utility of selection activities.

	Frequency of use					*Utility**	
Selection activity	1	2	3			Start	Promotions
			Job level				
			l	m	h		
Application form	57	—	—	—	—	—	—
Letter of application	63	—	—	—	—	—	—
References	50	96	—	—	—	3.0	—
Diplomas	—	—	—	—	—	1.1	—
Worksample	—	—	60	30	22	—	6.1
Antecedents	19	—	—	—	—	—	—
Aptitude test**	25	30	10	40	60	6.2	6.2
Medical examination	71	—	—	—	—	—	—
Interviews	94	100	—	—	—	1.6	—
Other	8	—	—	—	—	—	—
biographical data	—	6	—	—	—	4.2	—
knowledge of the job	—	—	—	—	—	—	5.4
peer ratings	—	—	—	—	—	—	5.6
assessment centres	—	22	—	28	—	—	4.9
probation	—	—	—	—	—	5.0	—

* Taken from Hunter and Hunter (1984). Based on the net utility per year of the use of the psychological tests to reject the lowest 20% (aptitude tests low cutoff: U = 2,500,000) the figures indicate how much better the annual net utility is of the other activities.

** Aptitude tests top-down.

1: Greuter and Roe, 1980

2: Robertson and Makin, 1986

3: Altink et al., 1992

al., 1991) the results of which show a positive though varying picture.

Another advantage of the performance of ACs in comparison to traditional methods such as interviews, references and appraisals is the incorporation of simulation exercises. These components have been specially developed to reveal behavioural skills which are essential for successful future job performance. Managers and other people involved are thus enabled to see with their own eyes what the candidate's performance in those crucial areas is. For the candidates themselves it is a good opportunity to show what they are capable of instead of merely having to verbally express their skills.

The distinction between two approaches plays an important role in the scientific discussion on the use of selection methods. The psychological test aims at measuring psychological qualities and is based on the "sign" approach, whereas work-samples and simulations in ACs are samples of the behaviour which is relevant for the target position. Interpretation is based on the "sample" approach (Van der Flier, 1992; Wernimont & Campbell, 1968; see also Chapter 2 in this volume).

Both approaches have their strong and weak points. The strength of the test lies in the measurement of basic traits and the generalizability of its predictions for various positions, and not in the measurement of more specific leadership skills. The latter aspect is indeed a feature of ACM.

For many users, the choice between the various methods such as the psychological test on the one hand and situational methods on the other is a question of weighing up the costs and benefits. In view of the risks involved in hiring unsuitable managers however, a *combination* of methods resulting in a substantial improvement of the quality of decisions is well worth the money. In that respect both methods can complement each other. We find this vision reflected in the nature and design of assessment centres integrating the contributions of different methods.

The recent discussion on the scientific interpretation of the simulation exercises of assessment centres again hinges on the distinction between "sign" versus "sample" (Herriot, 1986; Jansen, 1991, 1993; Zaal, 1990). In section 5.4 we will discuss this more systematically.

3 HISTORY

The experienced applicant may feel that the practical exercise, the most typical element of an AC, is the most recent development in the selection process, but its first practical applications in the educational and business sector actually date back to the turn of the century, well before the use of psychological tests became successful (Guildford, 1967). Even Binet's well-known intelligence test probably owes its breakthrough mainly to the use of exercises from educational practice and not to specific tasks used in experimental psychology of the day (Cronbach, 1990). But even if we restrict ourselves to ACs in their present form, their history goes back some 50 years.

As for the psychological tests, the developments within ACM are closely linked to military selection. In their excellent monograph on assessment centres, Thornton and Byham (1982) quote Eysenck (1953) and Vernon and Parry (1949) who indicate that the selection procedures of German army officers served as a model for the design of the selection procedures of British officers by the War Office Selection Boards (WOSB). They in turn were the basis of the selection programme for intelligence officers designed by the Office of Strategic Services (OSS) which was specially founded for this purpose by President Roosevelt. Although the original intention was to follow the assessment programmes of the English WOSB closely, the final form and content of the first American ACs were largely determined by the psychologist Henry A. Murray (MacKinnon, 1974). Murray and his colleagues at the Harvard University experimented with a new psychological approach, referred to as "personology", enabling them to "completely" understand the individual in all its unique qualities. One of the features of this approach was that several colleagues were involved in the diagnostic process at the same time, each of them using their own research method and reporting their findings in a joint meeting, the so-called "diagnostic council". Their work, described in the now classic *Explorations in Personality* (Murray, 1938) had a great impact on the development of the early civilian ACs of the Chicago Bell Corporation (Bray, 1987).

Another feature of the OSS's new approach constituted the use of unstructured exercises (situational tests) alongside traditional tests and questionnaires, offering the opportunity to observe candidates in a "natural" situation. One such test was the interrogation of an intelligence officer by the security police after he had been caught searching through a file in an office. The candidate was given 12 minutes to prepare, in which time he must think of all kinds of reasons (innocent excuses) to explain his presence at the scene. This interrogation exercise was followed by a follow-up interview ("post stress" interview) in which a sympathetic officer tried to get the recruit to betray his cover while the latter was explicitly instructed to reveal it under no condition. The dimensions on which the candidates were assessed included emotional stability, holding on to the cover, and motivation for the army unit in question, and were based, as were the other dimensions, on a task analysis of the exercises (Office of Strategic Services, 1948).

The first civilian applications of such integrated assessment methods can be attributed to the British Civil Service Selection Board (CSSB) (Eysenck, 1953; Vernon, 1950; Vernon & Parry, 1949). In the United States the use of ACs is inextricably bound up with the pioneering work of Bray at the Chicago Bell Corporation (Bray, 1964). At the end of the 1960s, ACs were increasingly used in the USA (Cohen et al., 1974) and these methods started to gain in popularity in the Netherlands as well (Bomers & Homan, 1978). At the beginning of the 1980s there was an increase in both the services of private consulting agencies and in the applications within large companies and the government (Seegers & Esser, 1982; Van Vianen, 1991; Zaal, 1990) and, as we have shown before, this development is still continuing. This trend is also reflected in the large number of scientific studies and publications on this subject.

4 FEATURES, METHOD AND APPLICATIONS

Assessment centres manifest themselves in many different forms. This, however, is also true of the earliest applications and is inherent to the very nature of the method (Finkle, 1976). Not surprisingly, the definition has been the subject of international conferences on this method and standards were finally endorsed by the third International Congress on the Assessment Centre Method, in Quebec in 1975 (Moses & Byham, 1982).

Important features are the use of different methods including at least one practical exercise (simulation), and the use of several, specially trained assessors, rating in terms of observed behaviour (behavioural dimensions) which have been defined in advance on the basis of a task analysis. More specifically, ACs are characterized by the fact that the overall rating is reached in a joint assessor meeting in which the reports on the various components are integrated. To ensure clarity, a working party set up specifically for this purpose adds a comment to its report that procedures in which all components are judged by one and the same assessor (so called individual assessments) do not fall within the definition of ACs, even if the components consist of various techniques such as written tests, interviews and simulations. The use of different simulation exercises in which several assessors report only on the separate exercises, instead of making an integrated final report, is not covered by the definition of AC either.

ACs will differ according to the nature and the number of dimensions used and according to the nature and the number of simulations. That goes without saying. They also differ according to assessment objectives such as selection, promotion, career indication and individual development; according to the way in which observations are made, rated and reported; according to the choice and training of assessors; according to the way in which the candidates receive feedback; and according to the degree of preceding research and professional counselling (Finkle, 1976, p. 861).

In our description we will address various aspects separately: behavioural dimensions and simulations, the assessment process, the assessor training and various applications.

4.1 Common elements of assessment centres

Regardless of which form or tradition is adhered to, each assessment contains simulations and behavioural dimensions. Simulations and behavioural dimensions can be considered to be the common element of an AC and determine its content to a major degree. Both must ensure an optimum reflection of the tasks and abilities required of the manager.

Commonly used exercises are: conducting interviews with staff and clients, chairing meetings, and dealing with papers. The behavioural dimensions reflect the crucial skills a manager should possess to be able to function successfully (for example, planning and organizing, social and communication skills). In other words, the content of the AC is geared to the specific tasks and job requirements of certain organizations and to the abilities required for certain management positions. So developing an assessment centre requires extra efforts from the organization, and its content, a matrix of behavioural dimensions and exercises, can vary with each application. Not every skill can be observed in each simulation. However, the assessment programme must contain at least one, and preferably, several components in which all relevant dimensions can be observed. In Figure 5.1 the exercises have been complemented with other much-used methods describing the content of the assessment programme in an integrated application.

FIGURE 5.1

	Methods				
	Structured general interview	Criterion-based interview	Interview simulation (role-playing)	In Basket exercise + interview	Psychological examination
Criteria					
–biographical criteria	x				x
–(professional) training	x				x
–work experience	x				x
–professional knowledge	x				
–planning/organizing		x		x	
–delegation				x	
–problem analysis		x	x	x	x
–judgement			x	x	x
–persuasiveness	x		x		
–listening	x	x	x		x
–flexibility		x	x		x
–cooperation		x			x
–stress tolerance			x	x	x
–achievement motivation	x	x		x	x
–initiative		x	x	x	
Time	1 hour	1 hour depending on the number of criteria	½ hour	2 hours	Depends on the number of tests and the length of interview with the psychologist

Matrix of features/behavioural dimensions and various components of assessment centres (marks in cells indicate which behavioural criteria can be rated in various components).

A much-used method for job analysis is the Critical Incidents Technique (Flanagan, 1954). This method describes situations crucial to successful job performance. Analysis of those situations in terms of actions and their subsequent results must reveal the manager's behaviour and underlying skills which are essential to success and effectiveness. Another approach is based on the Repertory Grid Method (Kelly, 1963) which explores differences between effective (successful) and non-effective managers through assessments (Stewart & Stewart, 1981). The focus of attention is on differences in specific activities and the way in which managers deal with problems.

Theoretically, such methods offer the basis for the formulation of the specific competences required by the organization, and the description of situations in which these competences are of overriding importance for the manager's success or failure. This explains both the wide variety in content of ACs and their divergent quality in terms of acceptance, recognizability and predictive power. Over the years, the design has clearly been standardized. Some authors speak of a second generation of ACs, the development of which has been shortened and streamlined by standardization in the descriptions of behavioural dimensions and the content of exercises. This will probably lead to improved efficiency but it is doubtful whether this is equally true for all applications. Before we go into this, we will first discuss the behavioural dimensions and their interrelation with the manager's task.

4.2 Behavioural dimensions and management roles

The behavioural dimensions are aimed at basic skills which the manager should possess and which he or she should demonstrate in various situations. They play a key role in each part of the assessment process. There is no standard collection of basic skills and neither is there a fixed protocol to gather them from the data of the job analysis. The dimensions which are eventually used within an organization will also be based on the observations and experiences of the management itself, though Jeswald (1977) warns against the danger of too readily following badly defined and invalidated performance criteria which traditionally take root in an organization.

The direct reference to observable and actual behaviour in different situations (behaviour indicators) is essential to the definition of behavioural dimensions in AC applications. However, the definition of behavioural dimensions is on a higher aggregation level than the indicators and the actual behaviour itself, so that, when assessing actual behaviour, interpretation of behaviour plays an inevitable role. These interpretations, however, are of a different nature than the references to the underlying personality attributes or personality traits which are referred to in the interpretation of personality questionnaires. The differences mentioned here are central to the aforementioned distinction between the "sign" and "sample" approach. The distinction between behavioural dimensions and personality traits is further complicated because the names used show much overlap and, in this way, more correspondence in psychological meaning is suggested than is justified on the basis of the various approaches and the psychometric data. We will return to this subject when discussing the results of validation research.

Although behavioural dimensions as crucial skills should in principle be redefined for each position, we see that at the level of the basic dimensions there is a gradual falling back on dimensions found in previous applications. In particular, the list of 40 behavioural dimensions published by Thornton and Byham (1982) often serves as a basis for drawing up a job profile of the 10 to 15 most typical skills.

These vary according to the nature and level of the position. Table 5.2 describes the importance of behavioural dimensions for three management levels: high (board), middle, and low (supervising operational staff), from a recent study among GITP consultants (Laban, 1995). The figures are based on assessments of a number of positions in various sectors by some 20 consultants with the aid of a list containing nearly 200 descriptions of separate management activities (indicators) deduced from the 39 separate behavioural dimensions. A detailed and systematic job description was available for each position. The average scores on the behavioural dimensions are shown on a four-point scale. The ten highest scores per level are in bold type. The other average scores are only shown if there is a significant difference between the groups and this is done only for the level with the highest score. For easy reference these dimensions have been divided into broader categories. Several categorizations are possible. This table uses the categorization of Thornton & Byham (1982).

Differences between job levels include communication skills, impact, problem solving and motivational behaviour. For higher management positions in particular, listening ability and good oral communication is important. In addition, there are strong requirements for performance and sociability, problem analysis, vision and management identification. Group and individual leadership are considered to be more important for success on the lower management levels. Such information can be used as a frame of reference but it will always need to be complemented by relevant information from the organization itself.

The list of common behavioural dimensions can be useful in job analysis alongside the use of other methods including joint discussions with key

TABLE 5.2

Profile of behavioural dimensions for three management levels.

Oral criteria	*High*	*Middle*	*Low*
Communication			
1. Listening	**3.10**	**3.14**	**3.06**
2. Oral communication*	**3.26**	—	—
3. Persuasiveness*	3.09	3.00	—
4. Written communication*	2.76	—	2.19
Steering behaviour			
5. Flexibility	—	—	—
6. Group leadership	**3.16**	**3.46**	**3.42**
7. Individual leadership*	—	**3.34**	**3.43**
8. Development of staff*	—	—	**3.07**
9. Performance*	**3.26**	**3.18**	—
10. Sensitivity	—	**3.09**	**2.95**
11. Sociability*	**3.41**	**3.10**	**2.91**
Administration			
12. Delegation	—	—	—
13. Planning and organizing*	—	2.82	—
14. Progress control	—	**3.14**	**2.93**
Problem solving behaviour			
15. Creativity*	—	2.76	—
16. Learning ability	—	—	—
17. Extra-organizational awareness*	3.07	—	—
18. Judgement*	**3.16**	—	—
19. Organizational awareness*	**3.28**	**3.20**	—
20. Problem analysis*	**3.15**	**3.10**	—
21. Vision*	**3.32**	—	—
Motivational behaviour			
22. Ambition	—	—	—
23. Energy	—	—	—
24. Initiative	—	—	—
25. Customer orientation	—	—	—
26. Management identification*	**3.33**	**3.19**	**2.89**
27. Independence*	2.75	—	—
28. Entrepreneurship*	2.88	—	—
29. Achievement motivation	—	—	2.93
Personal behaviour			
30. Adaptability	—	—	—
31. Decisiveness	—	—	—
32. Discipline	—	—	2.95
33. Daring	—	—	—
34. Handling details	—	—	2.09
35. Stress tolerance	—	—	—
36. Tenacity	—	—	—

* Average rating by GITP consultants of the importance on a four-point scale (Laban, 1995). The 10 highest scores per level are shown in bold type. Furthermore, wherever the difference between the levels is significant, the highest average score is indicated per dimension. See the text for further explanation.

figures, interviews and questionnaires (techniques). A definite advantage of using commonly defined behavioural dimensions is that it then becomes very easy to compare different positions with each other both within and between organizations. This especially plays a part in ACM applications for management development and career planning.

That the specific job content is strongly linked to the manager's concrete activities can be illustrated by relating these behavioural dimensions to the task description of the manager in terms of the roles he has to fulfil.

The tasks performed by the manager have been described in numerous studies. In the well-known Mintzberg study (1980), for example, 10 roles could be distinguished based on an observation of daily activities in which the following aspects are central:

- The social interaction between people (formal behaviour; supervising; functioning as a focal point within the organization).
- Processing complex information (collecting and absorbing information, supplying information to persons within the organization and to outside authorities in the capacity of the organization's spokesman).
- Decision making (entrepreneur/innovator, problem solver, authorizing human/material and financial resources, negotiator).

These descriptions reflect broad behavioural dimensions relating to social interaction and impact, analytical skills and decision making.

The model of competitive values of Quinn (1984, 1988) and Quinn et al., (1996) describes eight roles which are systematically linked to effectiveness criteria for the individual's success at supervision and the company's success. These roles are categorized on the basis of two perspectives: flexibility versus supervision and internal versus external orientation, so that four quadrants are created (see Figure 5.2). In a factor analysis of self-ratings of managers (Verouden, 1994) these quadrants form four independent factors.

As *innovator and negotiator*, managers are alert to the changing environment, recognize important trends, foresee and anticipate necessary changes, tolerate uncertainty and accept risks. They will have to convey this vision in an appealing and convincing way in order to enthuse others and to acquire the means for realizing their plans.

In this role, managers will have to possess skills such as *problem analysis, judgement, extra-organisational awareness* and especially *vision; communication skills* including *persuasiveness*; they will have to be able to deal with objections, resistance and setbacks (*stress tolerance, independence, daring and organizational sensitivity).*

Directors and producers must visualize expectations through processes such as planning and goal setting, and must be resolute initiators who define problems, select alternative solutions, draw up rules and policy. They are able to motivate their staff into higher productivity and quality through their strong task orientation, personal dedication and energy. References to skills such as *planning and organizing, decisiveness, initiative* and *daring* are self-evident, as well as *dedication, energy, achievement motivation, and supervision.* But skills such as *delegation, judgement, flexibility, impact* and *perseverance* are also essential.

In the role of *coordinator and information processor*, managers focus on internal management. They actively inform themselves of daily activities, collect and analyse information, check whether rules are being observed, whether information is correct, report, and make surveys. They provide structure and ensure predictability of the production process, and that it is oriented towards efficiency and making tasks lighter, towards handling crisis situations; they have an eye for technology, logistics and everyday business. In this role, *problem analysis, handling details, written communication, planning and organizing* and *progress control* skills must be drawn on.

As a *mentor* and *teambuilder*, managers focus on cooperation and the personal development of their staff. They will try to solve personal conflicts and reconcile differences of opinion. They encourage participation, offer freedom and invite personal contributions. They adopt an open attitude towards their staff, are approachable and support and appreciate staff. Indispensable skills are *group and individual leadership, communication skills, persuasiveness* and *sensitivity.* An

FIGURE 5.2

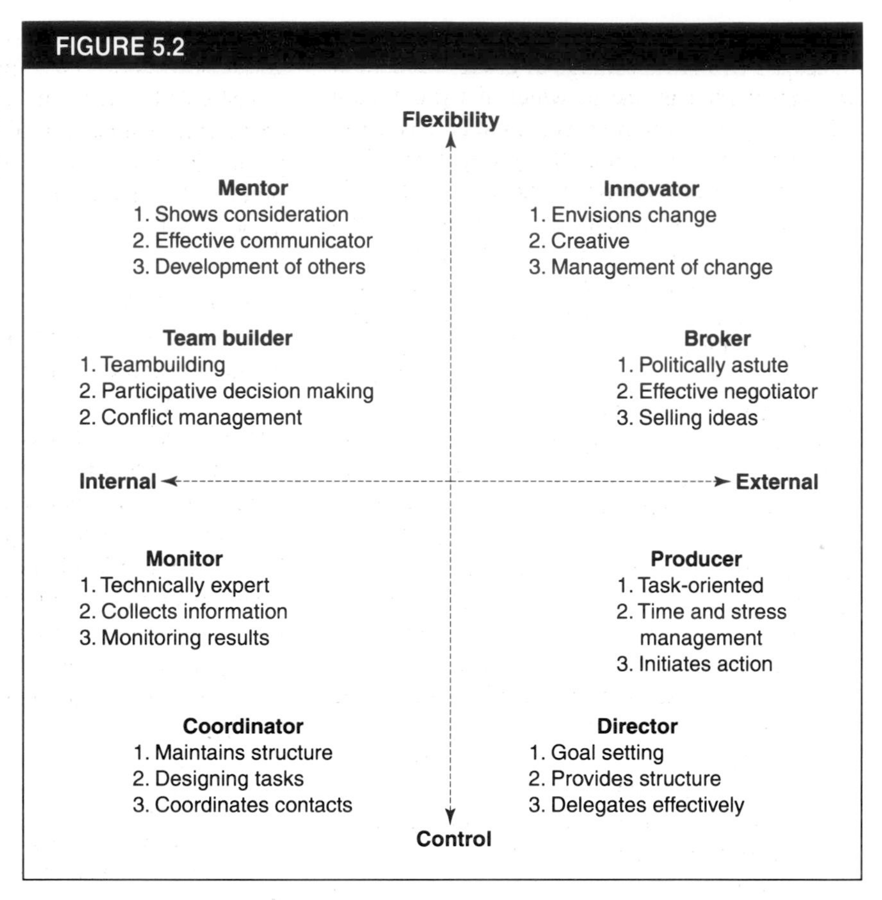

Management roles after the model of competing values framework of leadership roles (Quinn, 1984).

appeal will also be made to their *flexibility* and *cooperation.*

This description illustrates how the performance of basic management tasks and activities, placed within the functional interrelation of role patterns, is supported by more elementary behavioural skills and how, conversely, these skills can be deduced from the activities. It also appears that translation into behavioural dimensions reveals a certain degree of overlap. Relations between tasks (roles) and behavioural dimensions are of a complex nature. We have also noticed such complex relations between behavioural dimensions and components of the assessment. In the roles described here we have not dealt with accents and differentiations in the roles which are related to the management level and the position's specific nature (something which the literature referred to does indeed describe in more detail; see Quinn, 1984, 1988). In general, as with the behavioural dimensions, the weight of the roles is determined on the basis of a job analysis study. Its outcome is specified as the job profile for the position in question.

4.3 Assessment centre exercises

The simulation of specific management situations (the exercises) is even more important for the content of the assessment centre programme than the management profile and the relative values to be attributed to the behavioural dimensions.

These exercises pre-eminently represent the situation in which the future manager has to operate. The candidates are supposed to demonstrate the relevant behavioural skills in situations and circumstances which are characteristic for the organization. The repertoire which has developed over the years shows a large variety of oral and written exercises.

Much-used oral exercises are the group discussion, interviews, presentations and fact finding. We will discuss these successively.

Group discussion

There are two basic variants of group discussion: the first variant is one in which the group as a whole is given a certain assignment and each has an equal position within the group (leaderless group discussion). Assignments can vary according to the extent to which the instruction has been elaborated and structured. The "building of a village" is an example of a free assignment. Apart from some general information about size and number of inhabitants, the participants are granted complete freedom in working out a proposal. Most assignments require the participants to put forward a joint solution (proposal) for a certain problem. Examples of problem definitions are: who qualifies for a certain position (job profile and six CVs are provided); draw up a job profile (task description and a general list of requirements are given); which equipment to take along on an expedition to, for example, the moon. To prevent a non-committal attitude, each participant is asked to draw up a personal preference in advance and participants are sometimes also given explicit instructions to contribute individual ideas to the joint solution as much as possible. However, the emphasis must always be on mutual cooperation in order to reach a joint solution.

In the second variant, each participant gets a specific role. For example, acting as the representative of a certain department at a meeting in which a joint budget has to be allocated; proposing a member of one's own staff during the allocation of a limited number of grants/courses, and so on.

Group discussion techniques sometimes evoke resistance since candidates might feel that they have to "fight" each other, as it were. This especially applies to selection situations relating to internal vacancies. Assuming that cooperation among peers is a situation typical of the future position, it is possible to create conditions under which candidates accept and appreciate these assignments (Zaal, 1990). For example, the instruction will expressly point out the importance of good teamwork and the explanation can provide more details about the assessment criteria that are being used.

Interviews

In an interview simulation the participant is assigned a certain role (sales assistant, executive, assistant customer service, counter clerk etc.). The participant receives background information and is instructed to examine or solve problems or to communicate a negative decision. The discussion partner is a trained and instructed role-player and plays a (preferably demanding) customer, colleague or client.

Presentations

Presentations are mostly brief exercises which are assigned together with an analysis exercise. Relevant situations include presenting and defending policy plans, reorganization, automation or cost-cutting plans before a critical panel which, as part of its role, usually also has the authority to grant orders or to allocate budgets, and so on. An extra handicap which is often included is restricting the time that the participant thought he would need for the presentation. Such exercises emphasize the ability to briefly convey important issues and to assess and anticipate the wishes and priorities of the audience.

Fact finding

This exercise generally has the briefest instruction. The participant has to find out the relevant data on a certain case from an informer. The latter functions as a database; he merely knows facts and the opinions of others, but does not have an opinion of his own.

Naturally, problem definition and analytical skills play an important role here. The ability to overview the problem and timely switch to the level of details, awareness of the difference between facts and one's own interpretations and distancing one's own interpretations and presuppositions are important for successfully performing this kind of exercise.

The exercise is usually followed by a second part in which the findings, sometimes in the form of a consultation, are presented and the candidate is questioned critically about them by a "client".

Written exercises consist of drawing up or evaluating policy plans, staff reports and so on (analysis exercise) and dealing with the mail of a department manager ("In Basket").

Analysis exercise

In such exercises the candidate is provided with extensive information about a certain difficult subject that is sometimes also statistically complex. A well-known type of exercise is the comparison of given alternatives (location of a new plant, traffic, merger partner). This adds more structure to the exercise. These exercises are often characterized by great pressure of time. Problem analysis, judgement and written communication must be drawn upon equally here.

In Basket

The "In Basket" exercise is the simulation most commonly used in assessments in the United States (Thornton & Byham, 1982). Although there are no representative figures for the Dutch situation, the programmes of the government and those of a few large consulting agencies (personal communication) suggest that they are similar to those found in the United States. The reason is probably twofold. The content of the exercise has a strong face-validity, and it is easy to use.

In Baskets come in all kinds and sizes. They can correlate to a wide range of organizations (central and local government, administrative and manufacturing companies, production, commercial and personnel departments), and different management levels ranging from department head to division manager.

The problems that are presented in written form (memos) are of a varying nature: requests from staff needing advice, instruction, information for the performance of their duties; instructions from superiors; customer complaints; requests for information from the accounts department; personal problems of staff, personnel problems, planning problems caused by illness of staff; supplies becoming exhausted; scheduling problems and so on.

The overload of information requires quick processing of information and assessment of the gravity of the problems, decisiveness and the planning and organizing of one's own work and that of others. In addition, the exercise also calls on written communication skills.

In an interview after completion of the exercise, the candidate can explain his or her actions. Essential to the rating is whether information has been overlooked and which objectives or effects the candidate sought to achieve with the actions or measures chosen/taken.

Exercises requiring the management of a company within a group where business information, market information and so on is periodically provided (management games) are rarely used but could, however, be appropriate for certain assessment programmes aiming at specific groups or objectives.

So, exercises can aim at individuals or groups and can be both oral or written. Written exercises such as analysis exercises and In Baskets may take several hours, depending on the level of the position in question. Other exercises, regardless of their level, last no more than 20 minutes, as in the case of interview simulations and fact finding exercises. All exercises allow the participant far less time than would be needed for the equivalent situations in the manager's everyday work. That restriction is founded primarily on practical considerations. But apart from that, the AC's efficiency will also depend on the extent to which problems must be solved in too little time, thereby forcing participants to be as effective as possible.

The above examples show that corporate ACs take place in a simulated business setting and that those for government take place in a simulated government setting. Exercises differ according to the organizational level to which they correspond: junior management, middle management or executive level. Furthermore, disciplines and type of organization are distinguished. Exercises are often specially geared to the needs of certain organizations. The AC's strength mainly lies in its ability to develop exercises such that they embody the entrepreneur, the team manager or director in such a way as to suit a particular organization's wishes. The condition that the crucial skills must be observable and assessable in the AC can only be fulfilled in this way. There is no system or prescription to represent the most characteristic situations. Both the intuition and the experience of the developer, in cooperation with the customer, must lead to a satisfactory result. Still, it would mean a major improvement for the efficient use of ACM if there was a better understanding of the situational determinants of ACM. A question directly related to this is how far one should go in customization in order to ensure effectiveness. Should the situational nature of assessment centre exercises, and even more so with regard to the worksample, be more prototypical for task elements disregarding the content of the job? In any case, an AC exercise should represent a broad range of situations rather than being an exact job replica.

In answering that question, it must be realized that AC exercises are not objective in themselves, but primarily aim to create opportunities for assessing behavioural skills (dimensions) that generalize about various settings and exercises. Apart from aspects such as face value and acceptance (the organization wants it and the candidate expects it) the answer to the above question will mainly depend on the possibility to evoke and assess relevant behavioural skills. As long as the setting is equally accessible and acceptable to each candidate it is not relevant whether the role-playing takes place in a hospital, bank, ministry or machine factory. The objective of the AC may make specific demands upon the setting. In the case of regular personnel selection, more freedom can be allowed with respect to setting whereas adherence to the appropriate level and discipline (commercial, financial, general management) will be more critical for the assessment of the required behavioural skills. For assessment programmes developed and organized within one's own organization and intended for potential assessment of one's own staff, the organizational setting with its specific regulations, procedures and content areas will be of more importance and will be more specifically aimed at the level of the participants and the intended career perspective. However, as said before, it must be borne in mind that simulations are primarily meant for creating appealing situations representing relevant problems on the appropriate level so that the desired skills can be demonstrated and assessed. An important prerequisite here is the creation of equivalent conditions for the candidates. For example, the solution of exercise problems should not require professional knowledge, or knowledge of procedures and rules which may not be taken to be common knowledge in the target group. The specific setting of the exercises therefore often constitutes a less relevant consideration. Whether the intended generalization about situations can be demonstrated in empirical research will be discussed later in this chapter.

4.4 Assessment procedure

The way in which behavioural dimensions are rated differs according to the style of the assessment centre method. In the original AC developed by the American company AT&T and the subsequent developments in the United States based upon this AC (described in Moses & Byham, 1982; Thornton & Byham, 1982) the assessors make a report for each exercise which contains the relevant behavioural observations for the behavioural skills in question. In doing so, the assessor can use the rating instructions which have been discussed during the assessor training. These instructions generally serve as an example, with the exception of the In Basket (see Born et al., 1986). The allocation of assessors over exercises and candidates should preferably be such that each assessor only assesses the candidate in a single exercise. In this way, the reports on the various exercises per candidate come from different assessors and together they form the basis on which the observations per behavioural dimension can be integrated and subsequently evaluated. The reports are supplemented with the information from the post interviews held with the candidate after completion of each exercise. So dimension ratings are awarded only at the end of the programme over the whole of actions in all exercises. During the final interview, a so-called overall rating is drawn up (OAR: Overall Assessment Rating) which is an indication of the candidate's management potential. This overall rating can never be an arithmetic sum of the dimension ratings (Byham, 1982). The use of scales, checklists and techniques, other than the 5-point Likert scale on which the dimension and overall rating are indicated, is generally restricted as a result of this procedure.

The ACs developed by the Dutch government and KPN (The Netherlands Postal and Telecommunications Services) distinguish themselves by the use of anchored behaviour scales (Van Vianen, 1991; Zaal & Van Vianen, 1991). An important feature of the method used is that the relevant management (behavioural) dimensions are rated separately for each exercise. Only in the case of differences larger than, for example, two points on a 7-point scale, is the rating explained and discussed on the basis of observations and is followed by a final rating of the relevant dimension. So the result of the assessment centre can best be described by the matrix of exercises × dimensions (Zaal, 1990). A general judgement about the candidate's management potential may be reached by simply adding the ratings. This way of integrating results could be characterized as an actuarial method as opposed to the clinical method used in the final evaluation of the ACs based on American tradition. Apart from that, the ratings on the separate exercises can certainly lead to an evaluative discussion in which the observations made during the exercises are also brought forward and weighed intuitively, as are the observations from other components. Such a discussion will not be held for each candidate, but only if there is reason to do so. This could be the case where there are notable differences between assessor and/or exercise ratings.

An additional advantage of the above method is that the task of the assessors is more structured. As a result, a shorter training generally suffices. In this way, the implementation of the assessment centre takes less time and the objectivity of the ratings is simultaneously increased.

The major difference between the two approaches is the emphasis on observations and the behavioural dimensions. The exercises can reveal important situational styles and these are indeed mentioned in the final report but the exercises as such are not rated separately.

4.5 The assessor training

An essential component of the assessment centre method is the assessor training. The simulations and interviews, by definition, provide only subjective ratings and it is generally known that consensus among assessors is often hard to achieve.

The most common pitfalls are: rating more kindly than someone deserves (leniency); rating everyone equally good or bad (central tendency); rating a person's characteristics and skills equally good or bad (halo or horn effect); and lack of disagreement as to the meaning of characteristics, features, and skills (for a discussion of these rating errors, see also Chapter 4 of this volume.

There is no single prescription for the prevention of these errors, neither can the solution be found within the assessment centre approach. This aspect has also been somewhat neglected in research. In a few key publications however (Byham, 1982; Thornton & Byham, 1982), we can find clear indications about some of the essential components of assessor training.

The most important skills that the assessor will have to learn can be summarized by the term 'ORCWE':

- Observing behaviour during the exercises.
- Recording the observations.
- Classifying behaviour into the behavioural dimensions.
- Weighing behavioural dimensions.
- Evaluating the final, overall judgement.

In these steps we can also recognize the possible solutions to the pitfalls mentioned earlier. The purpose of the assessor training both relates to content (how do we define the behavioural dimensions for our organization and how do they become visible in the exercises) and to method (following certain observation procedures, consequent searching for translation into specific behaviours and systematic postponement of interpretations while recording behaviour, refraining from interpretations of feelings and meanings, refraining from mutual comparisons). The latter (methodical) element in particular is new to the manager and runs counter to the customary way of judging, which focuses on results.

The time-consuming nature of judging according to these rules also evokes resistance. In this respect, professional assessors who are psychologists can rely heavily on their education. Conversely, the manager has an advantage where assessing and understanding the relevance of the behavioural dimensions for successful future job performance are concerned. These components should be supported by training material, specifically for the observance of behavioural dimensions with the aid of clear and short definitions based on a good job analysis and examples of positive and negative behaviour indications worked out for each exercise. Some examples follow.

Sensitivity

Definition: the ability to recognize the feelings and needs of others and to allow for them in one's own behaviour. Awareness of the way in which one's own behaviour and decisions come across.

Positive indications

- Shows understanding for the position of "x".
- Enquires after the feelings of "x".
- Is patient.
- Mentions aspects that are valuable to "x".

Negative indications

- Pays no attention to the personal position of "x".
- Does not respond to reactions of a personal and emotional nature.
- Opposes reactions of a personal and emotional nature.

Decisiveness

Definition: being willing and able to take quick decisions if sufficient information is available. Expressing an opinion, defining one's position and taking action should not be unnecessarily postponed by waiting for or collecting even more information.

Positive indications

- Takes a clear standpoint.
- Presents action plan in case of certain bottlenecks.
- Does not reconsider decisions if no new information is given.
- Is the first to offer suggestions and tries to enthuse others.

Negative indications

- Does not usually adopt a standpoint.
- Suggests a solution but does not make a personal choice.
- Waits for others to suggest standpoints and concurs.
- Makes repeated requests for new information.
- Requests postponement of decisions.

In the same way, examples will help to work towards a standard which will be based on experience and subjective judgements rather than on objective standards. Developing and subsequently using anchored behaviour scales also fits into this stage of the assessment process. These will, however, rarely be based on extensive empirical and psychometric research. Rather, they must be considered as an aid alongside a proper observation protocol.

This protocol constitutes the basis for the final evaluation and the assessment centre report. Candidates, like the organization, are not solely interested in the final rating as such, however far-reaching it may be. Both parties want an assessment of achievements and activities which will serve not only as explanation and justification of the conclusions but will also form a basis for planning the candidate's future personal development.

It goes without saying that the content of the assessor training, like the content of the assessment centre itself, is tailor-made and should be adjusted to the specific job content for each assessment. Assessor training is mainly based on the principle of "learning by doing". As a consequence, a permanent component of the programme consists of actually doing/performing the exercises. Being rated by colleagues in the process often leads to understandable resistance, even if only the first steps of the assessment process are involved. The solution may be found in hiring role-players for the initial try-out.

The description of the assessment process and the assessor training will have made it clear that the quality of the assessment centre depends even more on the quality of the assessors than on the quality of the exercises.

4.6 Integral assessment procedures (IAP)

In the description so far, we have restricted ourselves to the practical exercises, the most typical components of the assessment centre methods. These are also the components which receive most or even sole attention in the literature.

However, considering the origin, the first applications and the definition of ACM, this is not so self-evident. The definition mentions various methods which not only include criterion-based interviews but also psychological tests and questionnaires and even projective techniques (Bray, 1987). The way in which ratings of behavioural dimensions and information on personality and intelligence from the psychological examination could be integrated into the final report of an AC is hardly discussed in literature. This situation probably illustrates the preference—based on the American and Anglo-Saxon tradition—or using managers from the organization itself for internal AC applications. The use of psychologists as external advisors is common practice in Dutch assessment centres. This offers the scope and conditions for ACM applications that truly integrate psychodiagnostic assessment and behaviour-oriented situational assessment.

Personality traits and abilities such as intelligence are characteristics that are not easily reducible to concrete behaviour in specific situations. They are a predisposition or a tendency towards certain behaviour, the occurrence of which also depends on situational circumstances. This does not alter the fact that after initial scepticism, the predictive value of personality traits for the manager's success is supported by recent studies (Barrik & Mount, 1991; Tett et al., 1991; Zaal & Van Vianen, 1991). The predictive value not only applies to the factors responsibility and achievement orientation but also to extrovertedness and, up to a certain degree, to kindness. This fact alone makes the input relevant from a psychological point of view but does not necessarily provide a simple prescription for the integration of the results of psychological examination and the ratings of behavioural dimensions into the practical exercises. It is obvious, however, that a description of a personality in which traits such as firmness, contact orientation, neurotic vulnerability, orderliness and so on, emerge, is a relevant supplement to the qualities of decisiveness, leadership, customer orientation, persuasiveness and so on, whether or not these are demonstrated in the practical exercises. They can underpin and complete the picture that emerges from the ratings and can also shed light on possible contradictions in the ratings of behavioural dimensions, either in ratings of different exercises or in ratings of different dimensions within the same exercise. Naturally, this completion and underpinning also applies in reverse order from behavioural dimensions to personality.

That integration can be supported by making relationships between personality and behavioural dimensions more clear, doing so in advance and in a systematic way. A useful tool here is the taxonomy of adjectives according to the model of the Big Five (Hofstee & De Raad, 1991). It offers many concepts that refer directly to behavioural dimensions and provides ample opportunities for placing them in this personality model through the use of similar descriptions. This may subsequently lead to the deduction, perhaps by means of a few intermediate steps, of the specific expectations about the relationship between behavioural dimensions and the specific scales of various personality questionnaires.

4.7 Organizational, technical and logistic aspects

The use of ACs involves a great deal of work for an organization, even if the preparation and implementation are (partly) contracted out to an external agency. An exception to this is the sole use of an AC for selection of external candidates. The use of ACs for potential assessment or for determination of the developmental needs of staff has important organizational, technical and logistic consequences. The significance lies in the repercussions for existing policies, the commitment of the management and the consequences for future participants.

First, the use of ACs must be sufficiently supported within the organization. Other than with the request for external psychological advice, the personnel department must start by achieving harmonization of the various functions; not only recruitment and selection but also training and development, performance appraisals and promotions. In addition, broader support will have to be acquired from managers who face new appointment criteria for their staff, involvement in personal development plans and possible participation as assessors.

Finally, the board's permission is required since this body is directly responsible for appointments to key positions. Using ACM is more than simply the introduction of a new technique. The very nature of the method can trigger a process of cultural and organizational change because of the openness and directness with which personal success factors within the company are being discussed, the intensity and the objectivity of the assessment procedures and the commitment with a view to personal growth and development. At the same time, these implications reflect the added value of ACM which cannot be easily expressed in money terms and which is rarely dealt with in utility studies.

The first steps on the way to implementation of ACM mainly consist of information and consultation. The next steps consist of creating steering committees and working parties and drawing up a schedule. We will not describe a detailed scenario here but restrict ourselves to mentioning some points that are specific to the use of ACM:

- Choice of assessors: external or internal; which departments, which level and how many?
- Administrative procedures for determining who is allowed to participate, when, and on the basis of which criteria.
- Procedures for follow-up, especially the development/training efforts and results.
- The organization and implementation of assessment centres itself also has its own dynamics and logistics, described in more detail in Seegers (1989) and Jansen and De Jongh (1993).

4.8 Applications

Each application primarily aims to reveal skills which are not quite necessary in the present position but which will indeed be essential for a subsequent position: assessing the leadership qualities of staff workers, commercial qualities of clerical workers and management qualities of junior managers at senior executive level, for example.

Considering this general objective, three specific objectives are distinguished determining the form, content and procedures of an assessment centre:

1. Selection decisions.
2. Individual development requirements.
3. Assessment of management potential.

Design and implementation of programmes will differ according to the motives for use and the grounds on which candidates are invited. These differences may relate to the behavioural dimensions being assessed, to the scope and length of the AC programme, to the level of difficulty and complexity of the exercises, to the nature of the decision (recommendations), to the nature of the feedback to both participants and organization, to the form of the written report and to the necessary scientific research (Jeswald, 1977). Figure 5.3 illustrates these differences schematically.

Differences not only concern the number of dimensions but also the scope of the simulations, the extensiveness of the report and the follow-up. The commitment of management and the management development department is a prerequisite in assessment centres for individual development and potential assessment. Assessment centres aimed at individual development, also called development centres, will be most effective if information is combined with self-rating and peer-ratings. Registration of progress might be added here (Seegers, 1989). As far as the scientific basis of such applications is concerned, measuring differences between behavioural dimensions (differential validity) and measuring behaviour change during the training and development process deserves special attention. As the next section will show, these are aspects the scientific quality that have not yet been sufficiently proved. The continuing check on reliability and, more widely, the constant efforts to adhere closely to the prescribed procedures, generally receives little attention in scientific research.

In the United States, encouraging the social acceptance of ACs means trying to meet the demands of equal treatment (employment opportunity). Jurisprudence emphasises the demonstrable link with the content of the job (job relatedness, see Byham, 1982, p. 34). As a result, examination of the equal treatment of minorities in assessment centres has received a great deal of attention in the United States. The next section will discuss the results of reliability and validity research.

FIGURE 5.3

Procedure	Selection	Development	Potential
Motivation	Immediate need for new staff	Immediate need to upgrade skills of present management (potential)	Identification/ development of long-term management potential
Participants	Qualified by education, experience and position	Identification of skills, deficiencies or narrow experience	Those performing well on supervisory or staff specialist jobs
Behavioural dimensions	Restricted to crucial, specific job requirements	Specific and general	General
Scope and length	Minimum of simulations and components aimed at crucial tasks, in view of valid decision	Minimum necessary to stimulate critical tasks, provide immediate feedback and counselling	*idem*
Difficulty level	No more difficult than the most difficult tasks of the target job	Various levels of difficulty to challenge participants with different degrees of competence	Various levels of difficulty to identify participants with different degrees of competence
Type of decision	Select/reject	Developmental needs in specific dimensions	Eligibility for future promotions, specific management needs
Feedback	Limited; on request	Detailed; may include peer and self-evaluations	Detailed; emphasis on career planning and self-development
Reports	Limited; participant, personnel department	Detailed; participant, MD department, supervisors	Detailed; participant, personnel department
Scientific research	■ Predictive validity final rating (OAR) ■ Continuous monitoring of reliability ■ Social acceptance	■ Differential validity of dimensions ■ Measurement of behaviour change	■ Predictive validity (OAR); acceptance ■ Continuous monitoring of reliability ■ Differential validity of dimensions ■ Measurement of behaviour change

Aspects of design and objective of assessment centres (according to Jeswald, 1977).

5 EVALUATION: ACCEPTANCE, RELIABILITY AND VALIDITY

The scientific quality of methods for assessing individual differences is generally associated with psychometric qualities such as reliability and validity. The guidelines for the development and use of psychological tests and achievement tests of the Dutch Association of Psychologists (NIP) reflect that opinion. Social and (professional) ethical aspects are still not integrated into these guidelines.

The working party that published the standards for assessment centres in 1977 made the explicit choice to include such aspects. From the very first edition, the standard work in The Netherlands on the theory of testing and its applications has dedicated a separate chapter to the ethics of testing (Drenth, 1980). The following section will address the reactions of users and the aspect "fairness" (impartiality). Reliability and validity will be dealt with next.

5.1 Acceptance

Information about the opinions of Dutch users is scarce. Maybe the acceptance of ACM is so self-evident that research is considered as an unnecessary luxury rather than as a self-evident, social and scientific justification of their use. Possibly social pressure is lacking. But this pressure does indeed exist for government appointments. This could explain the fact that information is restricted to ACs developed for the government. Detailed information is published in a number of internal reports and conference papers (Baker, 1986; Pieters et al., 1985; Pieters & Zaal, 1984; Zaal, 1986a, b, 1990). Tables 5.3 and 5.4 summarize the results for two ACs, in this instance two applications for groups of varying level and age. The assessment centre for qualification for the National Fire Brigade Academy is aimed at College/university graduates who are in the initial stages of their careers. The assessors are senior fire brigade officers and commanders. The participants in the AC for top positions in national government consist of senior staff executives and department heads who are being assessed for possible appointments to positions at board level or higher. They are assessed by top government officials.

After completion of the assessment centre, the participants could fill in an evaluation form giving their judgements by means of bipolar 5-point rating scales on the degree of reality of the simulations, the level of difficulty, the job-relatedness and the degree to which the content had been experienced as interesting. Naturally, the judgements cannot be detached from the actual content of the exercises and that detailed information is of

TABLE 5.3

Average ratings of quality aspects of assessment centre exercises of the national government (adapted by Zaal, 1990).

*Quality aspects**	*National Fire Brigade Academy*		*Top civil servants*	
	Participants (n = 35)	Assessors (n = 11)	Participants (n = 12)	Assessors (n = 9)
Realistic	4.0	3.9	4.8	4.4
Interesting	4.3	4.1	4.0	3.8
Clear	4.2	3.4	4.4	4.5
Relevant	4.3	4.0	4.3	4.4
Demonstration of skills	3.7	4.4	3.9	4.3
Difficulty	2.9	2.6	2.8	2.6

* Bipolar scale 1 to 5 (= high score); for a description of exercises see Table 5.4.
See text for further explanation.

TABLE 5.4

Average ratings of assessment centre exercises of the national government with regard to various quality aspects* by participants and assessors (adapted by Zaal, 1990)

Assessment centre exercises	*Top civil servants*		*National Fire Brigade Academy*	
	Assessors (n = 11)	Participants (n = 35)	Participants (n = 12)	Assessors (n = 9)
In Basket	—	3.8	3.9	—
Analysis	3.8	3.9	3.6	—
Leaderless group discussion	3.3	3.6	3.9	3.7
Group discussion with leader	—	3.7	—	—
Presentation	—	4.2	4.2	—
Interview	3.9	4.2	3.9	4.3

* Ratings on a bipolar 5-point scale; see Table 5.3 for the description of the quality aspects.
See text for further explanation.
NB: average scores include the rating of the difficulty level of the exercises.

special interest to the developers (suppliers) and their clients. Information that has wider implications is the level of difficulty of the exercises. The judgement of both the assessors and the participants confirms that the level of the exercises is geared to that of the participants. It is remarkable that the participants are more likely to underestimate the opportunities to demonstrate their abilities than are the assessors. The valuation of the exercises varies. Usually, the interview simulation (discussing problems with an employee) and the presentation (choosing a new location for a fire station or presentation of a policy document) are rated highest. The group discussion is rated rather low, though adequate by both groups. In both assessment centres the content of this exercise corresponds least closely to the target position which may partly explain the discrepancy with the evaluations of the other exercises.

The results generally correspond to what has been documented elsewhere in the literature (Baker & Martin, 1974; Boche, 1977; Kraut, 1973; Robertson and Kandola, 1982; Slivinsky & Bourgeois, 1977; Stewart & Stewart 1981). So we may conclude that the judgement of those concerned, especially that of managers as experts, provides the empirical confirmation of the content validity of the exercises used in assessment centres as described before.

"Fairness" or impartiality towards minority and gender groups has been thoroughly studied in the United States (Huck, 1973; Huck & Bray, 1976; Ritchie & Moses, 1983; Shore, 1992; Thornton & Byham, 1982; Walsh et al., 1987). The results show that opportunities for minorities and for men and women do not differ and, in so far as this should be the case, some positive discrimination towards women can be noticed (Walsh et al., 1987). In The Netherlands, there is at least one study on cultural bias (Lamers, 1993). This was an inquiry into an assessment centre for business consultants of employment exchanges. Although the small numbers do not permit a definite conclusion, the results do indicate a fair rating of performance in the exercises. There is, however, a tendency towards positive discrimination in the overall assessment rating concerning those belonging to a cultural minority.

5.2 Reliability: consensus among assessors

Considering the method's nature, the reliability of assessment centres mainly depends on whether consensus can be achieved among the assessors.

Sometimes, relationships between dimension ratings of certain exercises are reported in terms of internal consistency (Thornton & Byham, 1982) but most authors consider this to be an element of construct validity. This also applies to assessor errors that are not reflected in the degree of consensus such as the halo or horn effect. Consequently, when evaluating the reliability and construct validity of assessment centres one should take into consideration their mutual dependability. The section on the psychological meaning of behavioural dimensions will deal with this.

The interrater reliability of the ratings concerning the management dimensions strongly depends on the number of independent assessors participating, the amount of training they have received, and the method used in rating. The effect of training can be illustrated by a survey taken from Zaal (1990). The information in Table 5.5 relates to some national government AC programmes.

The results of the interrater reliability study show that values exceeding 0.80 are a rule rather than an exception. The use of anchored behaviour scales might have contributed to this but these values do not deviate positively from the findings of Thornton & Byham (1982). Thornton and Byham do not indicate how many dimensions had to be rated in each exercise. In the national government assessment programmes they are limited (up to about seven). It goes without saying that the more dimensions have to be rated, the heavier the assessor's task, a fact which puts some pressure on the reliability of the ratings (Gaugler & Thornton, 1989). For reasons of efficiency it is also advisable to pay attention to the unique and crucial contribution rather than to completeness when selecting the nature and number of dimensions.

It is remarkable that the reliabilities of the separate management dimensions in assessment centres reach similar and even better levels than the average sub-section of various capability tests, regardless of the assessment style.

5.3 Predictive validity

The reputation of the predictive validity of ACs is firmly rooted in the legendary Management Progress Study of AT&T in 1957 (Bray, 1982, 1987; Bray & Grant, 1966). The target group in question consisted of recent graduates (academic and non-academic). All recruits were assessed and the results of the assessment centre kept secret. Ten years later, it was found that between 75 and 82% of those having reached middle management positions had been correctly identified by the assessors. The reverse was also true. Of the number of managers stuck in first-level management positions, 94% had been correctly predicted.

Numerous studies have since demonstrated the predictive validity and its generalizability. The most well-known and most extensive is the meta-analysis of Gaugler et al. (1987). The corrected average validity was 0.37. Several factors appeared to have an effect on validity. The predictability of potential ratings appeared to be better than that of performance or dimension

TABLE 5.5

Reliability coefficients (interrater reliability) of separate behavioural dimensions in assessment centre programmes of the national government classified according to amount of training and the level of reliability (in brackets percentages over column totals) adapted by Zaal (1990).

*Level**	*Amount of training*							
	None		0.5 day		1 day		Total	
	n	%	n	%	n	%	n	%
Weak	8	(30)	4	(22)	5	(26)	17	(31)
Reasonable	12	(44)	7	(39)	5	(26)	14	(26)
Good	7	(26)	7	(39)	9	(47)	23	(43)

* Weak: r: < .70; reasonable: r < .80 –> .69; good: r > .79

ratings (0.53, 0.36 and 0.33 respectively). The objective of ACs also played a role. ACs for potential rating (development of assessees who have already been hired) or for hiring decisions (selection) have a higher validity than ACs for promotional decisions (0.46, 0.41 and 0.30 respectively). Also, the kind of assessor was found to have an effect. Contrary to prevailing opinions, the validity for psychologists proved to be significantly better than that for managers. The length of the training, however, had no effect. This could be indicative of a ceiling effect but Gaugler et al. (1987) do not indicate the average length. The number of exercises, the quality of the assessment centres (internal and external validity) and the use of peer ratings also have a positive effect on the predictive validity of the OAR.

The predictive validity of dimension ratings has been less extensively documented, but appeared to be predominantly positive also, with the relatively strong dimensions being aspects of personal communication (leadership, being commercially persuasive, persuasiveness), aspects related to decision-making (judgement, decisiveness, and taking decisions) administrative skills and other aspects such as initiative, flexibility and self-confidence (Thornton & Byham, 1982). In a recent study by Tziner et al. (1993) the predictive validity of behaviour dimensions was examined over a period of four years. This study used separate and joint ratings of psychologists and managers. The joint rating of planning and organizational skills proved to be the most consistent predictor.

More recently, some Dutch studies on the predictive validity of assessment centre applications have been published. Wiersma et al. (1991) report a 0.48 predictive validity of the overall rating for the prediction of potential ratings by supervisors after a period of 6 to 24 months.

Three out of the nineteen unpublished studies described by Albers & Altink (1993) contain predictive information. One of these studies investigated later performance assessments by both the commander and colleagues (Tersmette, 1991). The information is taken from the AC for qualification for the National Fire Brigade Academy. The commander's judgement appears to be strongly influenced by the overall rating of two exercises but, curiously enough, the correlations are negative. It concerns the In Basket ($r = -0.55$) and the interview with a subordinate ($r = -0.58$). It is hard to give an explanation but perhaps one can be found in the emphasis on certain behavioural dimensions in the rating of both exercises. For example, the possible emphasis on aspects of sensitivity (compare Cronbach, 1990) instead of on planning skills and decisiveness. In the same study, the information—unique for The Netherlands—regarding the ratings by colleagues is indeed predicted by the assessment centre ratings of dimensions such as insight ($r = 0.32$), decisiveness ($r = 0.39$) and oral communication ($r = 0.41$). Of the overall ratings of the exercises, presentation ($r = 0.49$) and group discussion ($r = 0.33$) predict best. Van Opstal (1994) reports a predictive validity of $r = 0.25$, $N = 70$ of a selection assessment for the position of intermediary at an employment agency (OAR with performance ratings by the supervisor after one or two years). According to a multiple regression analysis of components of the assessment centre, the variance of the overall assessment rating is determined by two factors from the exercise "Interview with a client" (sensitivity/listening and persuasiveness/impression upon first appearance), two factors from the In Basket (judgement/problem analysis/decisiveness and planning/organizing), two personality traits (being carefree and dominance) and the total score of the intelligence test.

A second validity publication also concerns a GITP study of an assessment centre for the promotion of executives in a public service company (Maëla, 1993). The validity of the overall rating in relation to performance assessments by the supervisor is 0.51 ($N = 25$). The high, negative correlations with the behavioural dimension of individual leadership on both interview simulations are remarkable here. Apparently the supervisor does not think of a people-oriented leadership style, as opposed to a task-oriented leadership style, as being conducive to effectiveness in this executive position. This is indeed true for dimensions such as decisiveness, oral communication and persuasiveness and for the In Basket-based dimension, judgement. These results, like those of Tersmette (1991), raise questions about the job analysis preceding the design of the assessment centre and the choice of behavioural dimensions. Possibly, managers were insufficiently involved in gathering these data. Another explanation could be the assessors focusing on intended or preferred managerial behaviour instead of on less popular or less accepted styles which, as a matter of fact, could be the effective daily practice. It indeed stresses the vital importance of an effective job analysis to minimize surprises, as described previously.

Finally, we would like to mention a recent study of an assessment centre for promotion (Jansen & Stoop, 1995). The predictive validity is 0.42 (0.56 after correction for restriction of range) with the criterion "present salary level".

In a multiple regression analysis with the criterion "subsequent increase in salary" various dimensions from several components play a part. Others include "ambition" and "firmness" as assessed in a personnel interview, the dimension "firmness" from the group discussion, "firmness" assessed in an interview with the line manager and two intelligence factors namely numerical reasoning and divergent thinking (multiple regression analysis = 0.39). Of these predictors, only "ambition" from the personnel interview bears a significant first order correlation to the criterion (r = 19; 0.30 after correction for attenuation).

Ambition and firmness appear to be the most consistent simultaneous and predictive predictors of present salary and annual increase in salary. Both criteria, however, constitute one common factor with loadings of 0.89 and 0.93. An interesting question here is why firmness assessed in different settings contributes to the prediction of differences in salary as an independent and therefore uncorrelated factor.

The above validity studies confirm the predictive strength or, rather, the potency of ACs. However, this is something which will always have to be confirmed again and again by empirical studies. At the same time, we face the necessity of searching for psychological explanations to tell us which personal competences contribute to the prediction of future success and why. It is natural to base the explanation of the predictive validity primarily on the fact that the ACM measures the relevant management skills in an adequate way. However, alternative explanations cannot be ruled out. The study of Jansen and Stoop in which the present salary level is used as a prediction criterion and which may have been known to (some) assessors illustrates that we should be alert to alternative explanations undermining the predictive validity claimed such as:

- Criterion contamination: the AC rating itself contributes to successful job performance.
- Indirect criterion contamination: the assessors actually assess the candidates on the basis of their knowledge of the factors that can affect future promotion opportunities.
- Self-fulfilling prophecy: the selected candidates derive a sense of self-respect from the AC rating that can benefit their entire career (Klimoski & Brickner, 1987).

These alternative explanations deserve more attention in predictive studies. The study design should allow for measurement of possibly contaminating factors, for example through questionnaires (in advance and afterwards) so that possible effects on the predictive validity may be assessed.

5.4 The psychological meaning of behavioural dimensions

According to Thornton and Byham (1982), the question of the psychological meaning of ratings of behavioural dimensions should be clearly distinguished from that of the meaning of personality traits. Behavioural dimensions were said not to refer to underlying characteristics. They are bases on a worksample approach (Wernimont & Campbell (1968). There is no nomologic network on the basis of which predictions can be made that are the subject of empirical study in support of the construct validity. If behavioural dimensions represent management skills that may be interpreted as a domain of behaviours, examination of the meaning will mainly focus on determination of the content validity. Such a study could be especially aimed at the assessment of the job-relatedness of behavioural dimensions by experts in this field (see, for example, the study of acceptability discussed in Section 5.1).

A compelling question in this respect is the one concerning the generalizability of behavioural dimensions over situations. Behavioural exercises on which dimension ratings are based only constitute a limited sample from the extensive domain of daily situations that the manager is confronted with. First, the question will have to deal with the generalizability over the restricted number of situations in the assessment centre itself but this will ultimately lead to the generalizability over the numerous situations in which the manager must prove his or her effectiveness. If behavioural dimensions fail to show sufficient generalizability over situations, should it imply that behavioural dimensions are too strongly linked to situation-specific exercises and should these findings imply that behavioural dimensions are meaningless as constructs for understanding assessment centre ratings? The alternative interpretation would then be an overall effectiveness rating for exercises. This discussion is at the heart of the so-called "sign versus sample" debate of assessment centre validity.

In this context, other relevant questions have to do with the interrelationship of different behavioural dimensions and with the question how many and which behaviour clusters or factors can be distinguished. Examination of meaning will also have to focus on the insight into the situational influences on behaviour (or behavioural dimensions) and on the way in which behavioural dimensions are interrelated, also in view of the effectiveness of behaviour in certain situations. That insight is essential to a better understanding of the lack of generalizability of behavioural dimensions.

Finally, the meaning of behavioural dimensions as measured in ACs will also have to be discussed with regard to their interrelatedness with personality and capabilities.

Generalizability of behavioural dimensions

Examination of the generalizability of behavioural dimensions has mainly been conducted through multitrait multimethod analysis (Campbell & Fiske, 1959), (confirmative) factor analyses (Bycio et al., 1987; Van der Velde et al., 1994; Zaal & Van Vianen 1991) and structural covariance analyses (Fennekels, 1987; Zaal & Pieters, 1985). A condition for this design, as opposed to the rating procedure as proposed by Thorndike and Byham (1982), is that dimensions are rated on the level of exercises. The results invariably show

TABLE 5.6

Results of the multi-trait/multi-method analysis of GDR and LGD ratings for the AC of the Dutch Police Academy (Zaal & Pieters, 1985).

		Trait factors					*Method factors*	
Exercise*	Dimension**	MO	OC	P	PI	ST	GDR	LGD
GDR	MO	0.709	—	—	—	—	0.741	—(***)
	OC	—(***)	0.285	—	—	—	0.875	—
	P	—	—	0.327	—	—	0.808	—
	PI	—	—	—	0.724	—	0.477	—
	ST	—	—	—	—	0.425	0.756	—
LGD	MO	0.226	—	—	—	—	—(***)	1.023
	OC	—(***)	0.704	—	—	—	—	0.690
	P	—	—	0.359	—	—	—	0.888
	PI	—	—	—	0.384	—	—	0.825
	ST	—	—	—	—	0.536	—	0.791

* GDR = Group Discussion with Roles; LGD = Leaderless Group Discussion
** MO = Motivation; OC = Oral communication; P = Persistence; PI = Personal interaction; ST = Stress tolerance
(***) zeroed for the assessment of parameters; corresponding variance components have been calculated on the basis of ACOVS parameter assessments from the ACOVS programme (Jöreskog, 1974).

TABLE 5.7

The variance components of the behavioural dimensions of the GDR and LGD (Zaal & Pieters, 1985)*

Exercise	*Dimension*	*Trait*	*Method*	*Error*
GDR	MO	0.503	0.549	0.0
	OC	0.081	0.766	0.127
	P	0.107	0.633	0.232
	PI	0.551	0.228	0.270
	ST	0.181	0.572	0.247
LGD	MO	0.501	1.047	0.0
	OC	0.496	0.476	0.019
	P	0.129	0.789	0.183
	PI	0.147	0.681	0.284
	ST	0.287	0.626	0.080

* See explanation in Table 5.6.

a dominant effect of the method (or exercises). The average correlations between different dimensions within the same exercise are higher than the average correlation of the same behavioural dimension rated in several exercises. For comparison see Tables 5.6 and 5.7 which show the results for the assessment centre for the National Fire Brigade.

As an aside, it should be mentioned that the method effect is indeed predominant but that for some dimensions such as oral communication and personal interaction (sensitivity) and, to a lesser degree, stress tolerance, fairly high trait coefficients are found.

The results of Zaal and Pieters (1985) and Van der Velde et al. (1994) are based on national government assessment centres. In these assessment centres, the ratings of the oral exercises are given by managers and those of the written exercises by psychologists. Such findings, however, are also reported by Sackett and Dreher (1982), Turnage and Muchinsky (1982), Robertson et al. (1987), Herriot (1986) and Silverman et al. (1986). In other words, it is a phenomenon which is systematically found. The differences between the low homogeneity of behavioural dimensions (spread over exercises!) and the high interrater reliabilities reported by Thornton and Byham (1982) also point in that direction. One might notice, however, the marked difference between homogeneity coefficients for different behavioural dimensions (Thornton & Byham, 1982, pp. 206–207). It must therefore be concluded that although behaviour assessed in assessment centres is determined to situationally to a considerable extent one is easily inclined to overlook signs for, be it limited, generalizability of particular dimensions. The impact of situational determinants in ratings of behaviour is a common fact which, for example, is also found in measuring diagnostic skills of the physician by means of role-playing. (Nu Viet Vu & Barrows, 1994; Pieters et al., 1994; Swanson et al., 1995; Van der Vleuten & Swanson, 1990). Some, including Jansen (1991, 1993) draw the conclusion that behavioural dimensions must be abandoned and that assessment centres should preferably be rated and interpreted as a collection of separate work-samples. The assessment process would then have to be supported by behaviour indicators per exercise and this would lead to a reliable judgement of effectiveness in the various exercises. The understandable reasoning behind this is that it does more justice to the empirical data. We do not believe, however, that full justice is done to the outcome in this way. As we have seen, there are indeed indications for generalizability, albeit limited, of (some) behavioural dimensions. Apart from that, this proposed method introduces another, not purely semantic, problem: how to report and communicate on performance and development needs in various situations (compare the uncorrelated rating of firmness by the personnel manager, the line manager and the assessors in the study of Jansen & Stoop, 1995). Others, like Joyce et al. (1994) propose to (assess and) report on task elements that are closely tied to exercises. One might wonder, however, whether "work-sample" or task ratings would be less loaded with situational variance as seems to be the case with behavioural dimension ratings.

Before leaving this subject let us turn to alternative explanations for the lack of generalizability of dimension ratings.

Alternative explanations and supplementary information

With regard to the measurement of diagnostic skills, Messick (1994) argues that skills do not always manifest themselves in the same way in different situations, but that these changes are not entirely arbitrary and therefore correlate to construct-relevant variables. The meaning of these constructs for the selection and construction of tasks is too important to abandon them as a directive concept.

In the light of this perception it is important to search for alternative explanations for the high interrelationship of dimensions within exercises. A possible explanation could be the assessor's inclination to pay special attention to the effectiveness of behaviour and to pay too little attention to the distinction of separate dimensions. Another explanation could be the occurrence of the well-known halo or horn effect. This halo effect refers to the assessor's inclination to base his or her ratings of the separate dimensions on a single general impression of the candidate involved (either good or bad). The result is that ratings of separate behavioural dimensions correlate with each other to a higher degree than the interrelationship between behaviours would actually justify. Empirical study on the tenability of these explanations would have to use experimentally manipulated rating instructions and a method of study in which halo effects can be directly assessed and corrected (Guilford, 1954). Studies based on applications in the consulting practice do not generally reveal data that lend themselves to this kind of analysis. The study on the group discussion technique as described by Fokkema and Dirkzwager (1960) is an appropriate example, however, of a method which could well have incorporated such an analysis. It is also an example of the effect of objective assessment methods on the validity of ratings. Following Bales (1951) these authors restrict themselves to the dimensions prominence, sociability and effectiveness. Table 5.8 is based on average correlations over a number of sessions. Subjective ratings are based on a checklist of 10 indicators per behavioural dimension. Objective ratings are based on the scoring of a large number of indicators per behavioural dimension (60–140) during the exercise. The criterion consisted of mutual sociometric ratings by the participants.

The subjective ratings of effectiveness and prominence predict sociometric leadership choices (as was to be expected), but no more than that. However, the objective rating of only prominence predicts better and, in addition, predicts sociometric sympathy choices which may indicate that sympathy choice also determines who you choose as a leader (a relationship not demonstrated by the subjective ratings). The study of Reilly et al. (1990) also mentions the possibility to improve the generalizability by using other rating methods such as "behaviour checklist". In addition, including the ratings by role-players and other participants might contribute to a better empirical embedding of behavioural dimensions.

There is, furthermore, also sufficient empirical evidence that well-trained assessors can distinguish different dimensions within the same exercise (Kruithoed, 1993; Schut, 1995). These studies also show, however, that the factor structure of behavioural dimensions within the exercises varies according to the nature of the tasks. For example, in a planning exercise, decisiveness may go hand in hand with planning and organizing, judgement and problem solving while in an interview with the employee, decisiveness goes together with initiative and achievement/result orientation.

The way in which the role of employee is played also has an effect on correlations between ratings of the behavioural dimensions (Tan, 1996). This

TABLE 5.8

Average validities for different sessions of leaderless group discussion (according to Fokkema & Dirkzwager, 1960)

Predictor	*Criterion: Sociometric choices*	
	Leader	Friend
Subjective rating		
prominence	.37	.10
effectiveness	.37	—
sociability	—	—
Objective rating		
prominence	.53	.26
effectiveness	—	—
sociability	—	—

study systematically varies instructions for role-players according to the degree to which resistance can be offered. If the employee plays his or her role in a self-confident way, gives many opinions of his or her own and uses counter arguments, the correlation between decisiveness and leadership appears to be positive (r = 0.33). If, on the other hand, the employee is passive and uncertain, then the same behavioural dimensions appear to correlate negatively with each other (r = −0.57). Poor monitoring of this kind of situational influences may reduce the generalizability of behavioural dimensions for exercises. These findings illustrate the systematic influence of situational variables on the meaning of behaviour assessments.

The disappointing correlations between the same dimensions rated in several exercises may furthermore arise from the fact that the candidate's behaviour with respect to a specific dimension cannot always be evoked equally adequately in each exercise. A dimension such as interpersonal sensitivity, for example, can be assessed better in a situational test than in an In Basket. A study by Smith and Blackham (1988) showed that the candidate's behaviour in a group discussion and presentation exercise mainly had an effect on the rating of the dimensions leadership, communication skills and self-confidence and that the In Basket mainly affected the rating of the candidate's methodical and analytical capabilities In other words, even if the behavioural dimensions are valid constructs, the generalizability for exercises will not necessarily be high because of the situational dynamics of behaviour.

Examination of the generalizability of behavioural dimensions shows that broad behavioural dimensions such as personal interaction and performance level (Shore et al., 1990) can be generalized. For certain behavioural dimensions, substantial correlations are also found between exercises whose findings are at least partly supported by correlations with personality traits (Kruithoed, 1993). Certain behavioural dimensions appear to be more affected by the specific exercises than others (Schut, 1995, see Table 5.9). Higher correlations over different exercises are, for example, found for dimensions referring to impact such as sociability (r = 0.54, n = 15) and persuasiveness (r = 0.33; n = 33) and to relational behaviour such as flexible behaviour, customer orientation and listening. For achievement-oriented attitude to work and leadership no interrelationships are found (see Table 5.9 for more details).

Although management skills cannot be simply interpreted as general dimensions that can be generalized over various situations, the opinion that management skills completely coincide with the exercise is not sufficiently supported either.

TABLE 5.9

Average correlations between behavioural dimensions and behavioural clusters for different exercises (convergent validities) (according to Schut, 1995)

	Correlation	*n*
Personal strength	.11	244
Decisiveness	.06	108
Daring*	.38	18
Initiative*	.40	55
Entrepreneurship	.05	26
Impact*	.20	118
Stress tolerance	.00	139
Oral communication	.12	102
Persuasiveness*	.33	49
Sociability*	.54	15
Leadership	.01	106
Delegation	.00	22
Individual leadership	.00	43
Relational behaviour*	.26	262
Flexibility*	.21	25
Customer orientation*	.28	123
Listening*	.23	49
Organizational sensitivity	.00	14
Cooperation*	.36	32
Sensitivity	.22	169
Achievement-oriented attitude to work	.07	145
Achievement motivation	.07	145
Planning, organization and control	.13	80
Planning and organizing	.04	53
Progress control*	.26	33
Judgement	.02	134
Problem analysis*	.22	142

* Behavioural dimensions and clusters the average correlation of which is significant ($P < .05$ unilateral). See text for further explanation.

We believe that behavioural dimensions are useful constructs which should, however, be interpreted as being dependent on situational constraints to varying degrees.

Behavioural dimensions, capabilities and personality

The meaning of behavioural dimensions as more than merely situationally determined qualities can also be supported by examination of the relationship between personality and intelligence. We have already pointed out that there is a remarkable similarity between adjectives used to describe circumplex models of personality factors (Hofstee & De Raad, 1991). Is this similarity also supported by empirical study? Hardly any relationships were found in previous studies of information stemming from national government ACs (Zaal &

Pieters, 1984; see also Zaal and Vianen, 1991). More recent studies do indeed report systematic relationships with personality. For example, Shore et al. (1990) found relationships between intelligence and final ratings of achievement-oriented behavioural dimensions on the one hand, and between personality scales and final ratings of behavioural dimensions relating to participation, impact and personal acceptance on the other. Van Opstal (1994) also found significant correlations between intelligence and the rating of problem analysis from the In Basket exercise while Kruithoed (1993) reports relationships between ratings of behavioural dimensions in interview simulations and personality. Behavioural dimensions do not show the expected relationships to the same extent. Sensitivity, decisiveness, organizational sensitivity, flexibility, listening, progress control and stress tolerance assessed in oral exercises belong to the dimensions which scored better in that respect than, for example, oral communication, persuasiveness, problem analysis, judgement, development of staff and individual leadership.

However, it must be added that the number of relationships found fell well short of the expectations based on the analysis of the similarity of the content description of personality scales and behavioural dimensions. Obviously, personality models invite higher expectations than are, on reflection, justified on theoretical grounds. In particular, compare the factor "culture" or "openness to experience" from the "Big Five" model.

The study by Shore et al. (1990) does not relate to the rating of behavioural dimensions in exercises so that, all in all, the empirical basis of the behavioural dimensions as broader and more general skills as assessed in AC exercises is rather poor. On the level of the exercises, the situational variance seems to be too strong to expect substantial relationships with underlying variables.

It seems logical that situation effects can only be sufficiently averaged at the aggregation level of the final ratings of the AC so that it is possible to speak of broader skills in terms of management competences, which are also expected to be related to underlying characteristics of personality and intellectual capacities. However, it may be clear that assessment centre ratings will not meet the desired qualities in a cheap way. Assessment centres should be developed and run by the book. Research to date has made it clear that without maximum efforts to assess behavioural dimensions already at the level of the exercises, one should not have high expectations of the validity of measurement of the target competencies on an overall assessment centre level.

Future studies into the meaning of personality for behavioural dimensions may benefit from new developments in personality study as described in Born (1995) who systematically integrates situational variables into the measurement of personality traits by means of questionnaires.

6 CONCLUSION: FURTHER RESEARCH

Increasing the insight into the whys and wherefores of the predictive value of ACMs is not of merely scientific interest. Blind prediction can hardly lead to a productive application in psychological consulting practice.

Spearheads of a study programme will have to be aimed at several aspects of applying ACM methods, such as the definition of behavioural dimensions and the assessment process, the identification and the "functionality" of dimensions in the social and situational context, the predictive validity, and the construct validity of behavioural dimensions themselves.

In the assessment process, besides the use of the scale techniques already mentioned, use can also, for example, be made of techniques resulting in a compulsory division of ratings of different qualities of the same person ("ipsatisering") to avoid halo effects, thereby also dealing with the artificially high relationships of behavioural dimensions within the same exercise. Studies will also have to focus on effects of the rating instruction aimed at effectiveness of behaviour, or on more objective observance and, in consequence, the effect of the type of assessor (managers versus psychologists; see Gaugler et al. (1987). The influence of the situational factors themselves (the nature of the exercises) also deserves systematic study. Attention will have to be paid to both the effectiveness and the interrelationship of behavioural dimensions. The use of detailed rating scales and objective rating methods is important, as is including the judgement of role-players and participants in the study. Both self-ratings and the rating of other participants seem to provide useful information, although in the case of self-ratings one should be aware of the fact that the predictive validity might be very low (Hunter & Hunter, 1984).

Predictive components in the assessment process will have to be studied with the aid of multivariate techniques. The results of the use of multitrait multimethod techniques in validation studies of ACs are by now well-known and it even remains to be seen whether this will promote a black and white reasoning—sample or sign—and will sufficiently stimulate creative hypotheses that invite subsequent study.

Most studies are based on information from the consulting practice. In this case, the possibilities to vary conditions experimentally are of course limited. Therefore, a better insight into the whys and wherefores of the working of ACs also depends on study in a "laboratory setting" in which important aspects of task, situation, rating and role instructions can be experimentally varied.

Finally, more weight will have to be attributed to conceptualization of behavioural dimensions in broad factors. At the moment it is difficult to say what these factors will have to look like. One of the reasons for this is that factors based on (assessed) behaviour do not produce an unequivocal picture. Possibly, given the complex interactions between competences and situations, the results of the ratings in assessment exercises should be less decisive when determining someone's competences. More weight could be attributed to factors found in the assessment of tasks and activities (job analysis) and to performance ratings (see, for example, Yukl, 1994 for the development of the Management Behaviour Survey).

Any attempt to improve the validity of and increase the theoretical insight into ACM is well worth the effort, considering the importance of wide applicability of convergent judgements in terms of suitability dimensions for personnel psychology.

NOTES

1. The author wishes to express his acknowledgement for the editors' comments on an earlier version. The Dutch version was translated by Dr C.M.H. Hermans.

REFERENCES

Albers, M.B.M., & Altink, W.M.M. (1993). Assessment centers in Nederland. *Gedrag en Organisatie, 6*, 241–251.

Altink, W.M.M., Roe, R.A., Greuter, M.A.M., & Candel, C.J. (1992). Oplossen van problemen bij werving en selectie. *Gids voor Personeelsmanagement. 12*, 33–38.

American Psychological Association. (1966). *Standards for educational and psychological tests and manuals,* Washington DC: A.P.A.

Asher, J.J., & Sciarino, J.A. (1974). Realistic work-sample tests: A review. *Personnel Psychology, 27*, 519–533.

Baker, D. (1986). *Assessment center for Dutch top level civil servants.* Paper presented at 14th international congress on the assessment center method, Dearborn, Michigan.

Baker, D. R., & Martin, C.G. (1974). *Evaluation of the federal executive development program assessment center.* Washington, DC: US Civil Service Commission, Applied Psychology Section, Personnel Research and Development Center.

Bales, R.F. (1951). *Interaction process analysis.* Cambridge, MA: Addison-Wesley.

Barrik, M.R., & Mount, M.K. (1991). The big five personality dimensions and job performance: A meta analysis. *Personnel Psychology, 44*, 1–26.

Boche, A. (1977). Management concerns about assessment centers. In J.L. Moses & W.C. Byham (Eds.), *Applying the assessment center method* (pp. 243–260). New York: Pergamon Press.

Bomers, G.B.J., & Homan, T.H. (1978). Assessment Centers. *Intermediair*.

Born, M.P. (1995). *Het meten van prestatiegerichtheid.* Academisch proefschrift, Vrije Universiteit, Ridderkerk: Ridderprint B.V.

Born, M.P., Algera, J.A., & Hoolwerf, G. (1986). *Management potentieel beoordeling.* Den Haag: Rijks Psychologische Dienst.

Bray, D.W. (1964). The management process study. *American Psychologist, 19*, 419–429.

Bray, D.W. (1982). The assessment center and the study of lives. *American Psychologist, 37*(2): 180–189.

Bray, D.W. (1987). *The assessment centers in the United States.* Paper presented at the first European conference on assessment centers, Amsterdam.

Bray, D.W., & Grant, D.L. (1966). The assessment center in the measurement of potential for business management. *Psychological Monographs, 80* (17, Whole No 625).

Bycio, P., Alvares, K.M., & Hahn, J. (1987). Situational specificity in assessment center ratings: A confirmatory factor analysis. *Journal of Applied Psychology, 72*, (3), 463–474.

Byham, W.C. (1977). Application of the assessment center method. In J.L. Moses & W.C. Byham (Eds.), *Applying the assessment center method*. New York: Pergamon Press.

Byham, W.C. (1982). *Dimensions of managerial competence*. Monograph VI. Pittsburgh, PA: Developmental Dimensions Press.

Campbell, D.T., & Fiske, D.W. (1959). Convergent and disciminant validation by the multitrait-multimethod matrix. *Psychological Bulletin, 56*, 81–105.

Cohen, B.M., Moses, J.L., & Byham, W.C. (1974). *The validity of assessment centers: A literature review*. Monograph II. Pittsburg, PA: Developmental Dimensions Press.

Cronbach, L.J. (1990). *Essentials of psychological testing*. New York. Harper & Row.

Cronbach, L.J., & Gleser, G. (1965). *Psychological tests and personnel decisions*. Curbana, IL: University of Illinois Press.

Drenth, P.J.D. (1980). *Inleiding in de testtheorie*. Deventer: Van Logum Slaterus.

Eysenck, H.J. (1953). *Uses and abuses of psychology*. Baltimore: Penguin Books.

Feltman, R. (1988). Validity of a police assessment center: A 1–19 year follow up. *Journal of Occupational Psychology, 61*, 129–144.

Fennekels, G. (1987). *Validität des Assessment-Centers bei Führungskräfteauswahl und Entwicklung*. Bonn: Reinische Friedrich-Wilhelms Universität.

Finkle, R.B. (1976). Managerial assessment centers. In M.D. Dunnette (Ed.), *Handbook of industrial and organizational psychology* pp. 888–891. Chicago, IL: Rand McNally.

Flanagan J.C. (1954). The critical incident technique. *Psychological Bullletin, 51*, 327–349.

Flier, H. van der (1992). *Hebben wij eigenschappen nodig? "Signs" en "Samples" in het psychologische selectie-onderzoek*. Inangurale oratie. Amsterdam: Vrije Universiteit.

Fokkema, S.D., & Dirkzwager, A. (1960). A comparison of subjective and objective methods for observation of discussion-groups in personnel selection. *Acta Psychologica, xvii*, (1), 55–79.

Gaugler, B.B., & Thornton, G.C. (1989). Number of assessment center dimensions as a determinant of assessor accuracy. *Journal of Applied Psychology, 74*, 611–618.

Gaugler, B.B., Rosenthal, D.B., Thornton, G.C., & Bentson, C. (1987). Meta-Analysis of assessment center validity. *Journal of Applied Psychology, 72*, 493–511.

Greuter, M., & Roe, R. (1980). *Personeelsselectie in Nederland*. Amsterdam: Universiteit van Amsterdam.

Guilford, J.P. (1954). *Psychometric methods*. New York: McGraw-Hill.

Guilford, J.P. (1967). *Nature of human intelligence*. New York: McGraw-Hill.

Herriot, P. (1986). Assessment Centers: Dimensions or job samples. Paper presented at the European Conference on the Benefits of Psychology, Lausanne.

Hofstee, W.K.B., & Raad, B. de (1991). Persoonlijkheidssctructuur: de AB5C-taxonomie van Nederlandse eigenschapstermen. *Nederlands Tijdschrift voor de Psychologie, 46*, 262–274.

Huck, J.R. (1973). Assessment centers: A review of external and internal validities. *Personnel Psychology, 26*, 191–212.

Huck, J.R. (1974). *Determinants of assessment center ratings for white and black females and the relations of these dimensions to subsequent performance effectiveness*. Unpublished doctoral dissertation, Wayne State University, Detroit, MI.

Huck, J.R., & Bray, D.W. (1976). Management assessment center evaluations and subsequent job performance of white and black females. *Personnel Psychology, 2*, 13–30.

Hunter, J.E., & Hunter, R.F. (1984). The validity and utility of alternative predictors of job performance. *Psychological Bulletin, 96*, 72–98.

Jansen, P.G.W. (1991). *Het beoordelen van Managers. Effectiviteit van assessment center methoden bij selectie en ontwikkeling van managers*. Baarn: Nelissen.

Jansen, P.G.W. (1993). De werking van het assessment center. "Zurück zu den Sachen" (Husserl). *Gedrag en Organisatie, 6*, (1), 10.

Jansen, P.G.W., & Stoop, B. (1995). Validiteit van een Nederlandse assessment center selectie procedure. *Gedrag en Organisatie, 8*, 189.

Jansen, P.G.W., & Jongh, F. de (Eds.) (1993). *Het Assessment Center: Een open boek*. Utrecht: Het Spectrum.

Jeswald, T.A. (1977). Issues in establishing an assessment center. In J.L. Moses & W.C. Byham (Eds.), *Applying the assessment center method* (pp. 45–68). New York: Pergamon Press.

Jöreskog, K.G. (1974). Analyzing psychological data by structural analysis of covariance matrices. In D.H. Krantz, R.D. Luce, R.C. Atkinson and P. Uppes (Eds.), *Contemporary development in mathematical psychology* (Vol. 2). San Francisco, CA: Freeman.

Joyce, L.W., Thayer P.W. & Pond, S.B. (1994). Managerial functions: An alternative to traditional assessment center dimensions. *Personnel Psychology, 47*, 109–121.

Kelly, G.A. (1963). *A Theory of Personality*. New York: Holt, Rinehart & Winston Inc.

Klimoski, R., & Brickner, M. (1987). Why do assessment centers work? The puzzle of assessment center validity. *Personnel Psychology, 40*, 243–260.

Korps Rijks Politie (1988). *Management profiel en assessment center Korps Rijks Politie*. Den Haag : Korps Rijks Politie Personeel Opleiding en Vorming/ Rijks Psychologische Dienst.

Kraut, A.I. (1973). Management assessment in international organizations. *Industrial Relations, 12*, 172–182.

Kruithoed, L. (1993). *Twee assessment oefeningen nader bekeken*. Doctoraal scriptie, Rijks Universiteit Leiden. Rotterdam: GITP.

Laban, T.F. (1995). *Management Profielen. Analyse van management functies en het opstellen van functieprofielen in termen van selectiecriteria*. Doctoraalscriptie, Rijks Universiteit Groningen. Amsterdam: GITP.

Lamers, M. (1993). *Effect van cultuur op assessment-center-methoden*. Project Arbeidsvoorziening, Onderzoeksverslag, Katholieke Universiteit Brabant. Nijmegen: GITP.

MacKinnon, D.W. (1974). *How assessment centers were started in the United States*. Pittsburgh, PA: Developmental Dimensions Press.

Maëla, M. (1993). *De voorspellende waarde van het individueel assessment programma*. Onderzoeksverslag, Vrije Universiteit Amsterdam. Amsterdam: GITP.

Messick, S. (1994). The interplay of evidence and consequences in the validation of performance assessments. *Educational Researcher, 23*, (3), 13–23.

Mintzberg, H. (1980). *The nature of managerial work*. Englewood Cliffs, NJ: Prentice Hall.

Moses, J.L., & Byham, W.C. (1982). *Applying the assessment center method*. New York: Pergamon Press.

Murray, H. (1938). *Explorations in personality*. Cambridge: Oxford University Press.

Nu Viet Vu, & Barrows, H.S. (1994). Use of standardized patients in clinical assessment: Recent developments and measurement findings. *Educational Researcher, 23*, 23–30.

Office of Strategic Services, Assessment Staff (1948). *Assessment of men*. New York: Rinehart.

Opstal, I. van (1994). *Rapport voorspellende waarde van het Individueel Assessment Programma voor uitzendconsulenten*. Amsterdam: GITP.

Pieters, H.M., Touw-Otten, F.W.W.M., & Melker, R.A. de (1994). Simulated patients in assessing consultation skills of trainees in general practice vocational training: A validity study. *Medical Education, 28*, 226–233.

Pieters, J.P.M., & Zaal, J.N. (1984). *Evaluatie van assessment center methoden als selectie instrument bij de R.P.D.* Den Haag: Rijks Psychologische Dienst.

Pieters, J.P.M., Hollenberg, W.H., Roosbroeck, H.F.M. van, & Zaal, J.N. (1985). *Selectie van Brandweerofficieren: Toepassing van assessment center methode*. Den Haag: Rijks Psychologische Dienst.

Quinn, R.E. (1984). Applying the competing values approach to leadership: Towards an integrative framework. In J.G. Hunt, D. Hosking, C. Schriesheim, & R. Steward (Eds.), *Leaders and managers: International perspectives on managerial behavior and leadership*. Elmsford, NY: Pergamon Press.

Quinn, R.E. (1988). *Beyond Rational Management: Mastering the paradoxes and competing demands of high performance*. San Francisco: Jossey-Bass.

Quinn, R.E., Fearman, S.R., Thompson, M.P., & McGrath, M.R. (1996). *Handboek managementvaardigheden*. Schoonhoven: Academic Service.

Reilly, R.R., Henry, S., & Smither, J.W. (1990). An examination of the effects of using behaviour checklist on the construct validity of assessment center dimensions. *Personnel Psychology, 43*, 71–84.

Ritchie, R.J., & Moses, J.L. (1983). Assessment center correlates of womens advancement into middle management: A 7-year longitudinal analysis. *Journal of Applied Psychology, 68*, 227–231.

Robertson, I.T., & Kandola, R.S. (1982). Worksample tests: Validity, advers impact and applicant reactions. *Journal of Occupational Psychology, 55*, 171–183.

Robertson, I.T. & Makin, P.J. (1986). Management selection in Britain: A survey and critique. *Journal of Ocupational Psychology, 59*, 45–57.

Robertson, I.T., Gratton, L., & Sharpley, D. (1987). The psychometric properties and design of managerial assessment centers: Dimensions into exercises won't go. *Journal of Applied Psychology, 60*, 187–195.

Sackett, P.R. (1987). Assessment centers and content validity: Some neglected issues. *Personnel Psychology, 40*, 13–25.

Sackett, P.R., & Dreher, G.F. (1982). Constructs and assessment center dimensions: Some troubling empirical findings. *Journal of Applied Psychology, 69*, 187–190.

Schippmann, J.S., & Prien E.P. (1986). Psychometric evaluation of an integrated assessment procedure. *Psychological Reports, 59*, 111–122.

Schneider, J.R., & Schmitt, N. (1992). An exercise design approach to understanding assessment center dimensions and exercise constructs. *Journal of Applied Psychology, 77*, 32–41.

Schut, P. (1995). *De bruikbaarheid van gedragscategorieën en gedragsdimensies bij assessment oefeningen*. Doctoraal scriptie Rijks Univeriteit Groningen. Groningen: GITP.

Seegers, H.J.J.L. (1989). Assessment centers for identifying long-term potential. In P. Herriot (Ed.),

Handbook of assessment in organizations (pp. 745–772). London: Wiley.

Seegers, H.J.J.L., & Esser, J.I. (1982). *Talenten van vandaag voor organisaties van morgen: De assessment center methode.* Deventer: Kluwer.

Shore, T.H. (1992). *Subtle gender bias in the assessment of managerial potential.* New York: Plenum Publishing Corporation.

Shore, T.H., Thornton, T.H., & McFarlane-Shore, L. (1990). Construct validity of two categories of assessment center dimensions ratings. *Personnel Psychology, 43,* 100–116.

Silverman, W.H., Dalessio, A., Woods, S.B., & Johnson, R.L. (1986). Influence of assessment center methods on assessor ratings. *Personnel Psychology, 39,* 565–579.

Slivinsky, L.W., & Bourgeois, R.P. (1977). Feedback of assessment centers results. In: J.L. Moses, & W.C. Byham (Eds.), *Applying the assessment center method* (pp. 143–160). New York: Pergamont Press.

Smith, P.B., & Blackham, B. (1988). The measurement of managerial abilities in an assessment centre. *Personnel Review, 17,* 15–21.

Stewart, A., & Stewart, V. (1981). *Tomorrow's managers today.* Southampton: The Camelot Press Ltd.

Swanson, D.B., Norman, G.R., & Linn, R.L. (1995). Performance-based assessment: Lessons from the health professions. *Educational Researcher, 24,* 5–11.

Tan, M. (1996). *Het effect van rolstandaardisatie op de begripsvaliditeit van de gedragscriteria in assessment-oefeningen.* Stage verslag/Doctoraal afstudeerscriptie Universiteit van Amsterdam. Amsterdam: GITP.

Tersmette, M. (1991). *Follow up van aspirant brandweer officieren: De predictieve validiteit van assessment centers.* Doctoraal scriptie Katholieke Universiteit Nijmegen. Den Haag: Rijks Psychologische Dienst

Tett, R.P., Jackson, D.N., & Rothstein, M. (1991). Personality measures as predictors of job performance: A meta-analytic review. *Personnel Psychology, 44,* 703–742.

Thornton, G.C., & Byham, W.C. (1982). *Assessment centers and managerial performance.* New York: Academic Press.

Turnage, J.J., & Muchinsky, P.M. (1982). Transsituational variability in performance within assessment centers. *Organizational Behaviour and Human Performance, 30,* 274–300.

Tziner, A., Ronen, S., & Hacohen, D. (1993). A four-year validation study of an assessment center in a financial corporation. *Journal of Organizational Behaviour, 14,* 225–237.

Velde, E.G. van der, Born, M.P., & Hofkes, K. (1994). Begripsvalidering van een assessment center met behulp van confirmatieve factoranalyse. *Gedrag & Organisatie, 1,* 18–25.

Vernon, P.E. (1950). The validation of Civil Service Selection board procedures. *Occupational Psychology, 24,* 25–95.

Vernon, P.E., & Parry, J.B. (1949). *Personnel selection in the British forces.* London: University of London Press.

Verouden, H. (1994). Ontwikkeling en validiteit van een vragenlijst voor leiderschapstijlen. Onderzoeksverslag, Katholieke Universiteit Brabant. Amsterdam: GITP.

Vianen, A.E.M. van (1991). Een getrapte assessment procedure: Bijdrage van de situatietest voor de functie van adviseur. In H. van de Flier, P.G.W. Jansen, & J.N. Zaal, *Selectieresearch in de praktijk* (pp. 221–236). Lisse: Swets en Zeitlinger B.V.

Vleuten, C.P.M. van der, & Swanson, D.B. (1990). Assessment of clinical skills with standardized patients: State of the art. *Teaching and Learning in Medicine, 2,* 58–76.

Walsh, J.P., Weinberg, R.M., & Fairfield, M.L. (1987). The effects of gender on assessment center evaluations. *Journal of Occupational Psychology, 80,* 305–309.

Wernimont, P.F., & Campbell, J.P. (1968). Signs, samples and criteria. *Journal of Applied Psychology, 52,* 372–376.

Wiersma, U.J., Leest, P.F. van, Nienhuis, T., & Maas, R. (1991). Validiteit van een Nederlands assessment center. *Gedrag & Organisatie, 4,* 218–225.

Winer, B.J. (1971). *Statistical principles in experimental design.* New York: McGraw-Hill.

Yukl, G.A. (1994). *Leadership in organizations* (3rd Edn). Englewood-Cliffs, NJ: Prentice-Hall.

Zaal, J.N. (1986a). *Assessment centers topfuncties: Eindverslag.* Den Haag: Rijks Psychologische Dienst.

Zaal, J.N. (1986b). *Ac Dutch.* Paper presented at the conference of European Foundation of Management Development, Nürnberg.

Zaal, J.N. (1990). Assessment Centers at the Dutch Central Goverment. In R.K. Hambleton & J.N. Zaal (Eds.), *Advances in Educational and Psychological testing.* Boston: Kluwer Academic Publishers.

Zaal J.N., & Pieters, J.P.M. (1984). *Evaluatie van assessment center methoden bij de eindselectie van de Nederlandse Politie Academie 1984.* Den Haag: Rijks Psychologische Dienst.

Zaal, J.N., & Pieters, J.P.M. (1985). *Assessment Centers at the Rijks Psychologische Dienst.* Paper Presented at the West European Conference on the Psychology of Work and Organization, Aachen.

Zaal, J.N., & Vianen, A.E.M. van (1991). Assement van leidinggevend talent. *Gedrag en Organisatie, 5,* 358–375.

6

Task Characteristics

Jen A. Algera

INTRODUCTION

The work task as the determinant of work motivation and satisfaction is the central topic for this chapter. The focus is on task characteristics that refer to the content of the work and the way in which work tasks are structured. First of all we will discuss the motivational implications of job design and second we will indicate to what extent scientific knowledge in this field can be useful in the design or redesign of production systems.

After a short description of the social context in which the scientific interest for job content has developed this century, a discussion of the theoretical notions and the empirical research in this field will follow. Next, we will go into the applications of these notions with regard to task characteristics in job design and organization design. Finally, task characteristics will be considered as dependent variables, as being the result of technology, the organization structure and management systems.

SOCIAL CONTEXT

At the beginning of this century, the leading principle for the design of production organizations was to split up the work into as many simple tasks as possible. These principles of scientific management (Taylor, 1911) were aimed at raising productivity, a better control of the production process, and lower production costs.

Already during the introduction of production systems based on these principles, people recognized that this method of production would not be satisfying from the perspective of the job incumbent. Ford, for instance, had many problems with his personnel (turnover) in his car factory, despite the high rate of unemployment and the high wages. However, people felt that this was the price one had to pay to achieve the mass production of goods that would raise the general level of prosperity, so that workers too could profit as consumers. Fry (1976) points out that scientific management was discredited early on by some, due to the improper use of Taylor's ideas. Instead of determining the best work method and a reasonable work pace, time and motion studies were used only as a means to increase work pace and to further erode tasks. This misuse was so clear that the American Congress passed a bill in 1915, in which the use of time recording instruments for the measurement of work performance was prohibited within government institutions. Nevertheless, Tayloristic ideas have had an enormous influence on the designers of industrial production installations, the engineers, and the work analysts.

Willems (1970) notes that the interest in the design of human work within the social sciences is of a relatively recent date. Initially, the work of industrial psychologists was concentrated on the selection and placement of personnel on the basis of individual differences between people, in which the job to be done was accepted as given. Later on, questions of a social psychological nature entered into the picture, such as for instance the role of leadership and relations within a group. It was only in the 1950s and 1960s that behavioural scientists started to have an interest in the design of production systems and the content of work as a determinant of (negative) reactions from job incumbents.

In accordance with this line of thought developments have taken place during the past 40 years, which are indicated by terms like work enrichment, job design, quality of work, humanization of work, etc. What is common to these trends is a reaction to the problems that occur in organizations that were designed according to the scientific management approach. Problems such as low productivity, high rates of absenteeism, low job satisfaction, and high turnover are attributed to the Tayloristic type of work organization and the related management systems.

In the Netherlands social discussion of this theme led to the inclusion of a number of articles in the Working Conditions Act (1996).

SCIENTIFIC BACKGROUND

There are several theories—more or less detailed—that can provide a basis for research into relations between aspects of the work situation, and the behaviour and attitude of task performers. Here, we shall restrict ourselves to an evaluation of task attributes. Other determinants of behaviour and attitude in the work situation, such as the style of leadership, are treated elsewhere.

For a proper understanding of the terms used we will refer to Hackman (1969, p. 113). He proposes the following for the term *task*: "A task may be assigned to a person (or group) by an external agent or may be self-generated. It consists of a stimulus complex and a set of instructions which specify what is to be done *vis-à-vis* the stimuli. The instructions indicate what operations are to be performed by the subject(s) with respect to the stimuli and/or what goal is to be achieved." Furthermore, Hackman points out that a distinction can be made between the objective task elements and they way they are perceived by the task performer (redefined task input), which can differ from person to person.

One can choose various points of departure for the description or measurement of tasks and jobs. In the literature (Companion & Corso, 1982; Fleishman & Quaintance, 1984; Hackman, 1969) four different approaches are distinguished:

1. *Behaviour description*. In this approach task analysis is based on a description of the behaviour that task performers actually display while doing a task. Most emphasis is placed on the visible behaviour of the task performer, such as the adjusting of switches or the reading of instruments.
2. *Behaviour requirements*. This point of departure looks into the reactions a task performer should have to be successful in carrying out his or her duties. Such a viewpoint occurs in systems analysis, where the question is what function a particular system component has. Attention is focused mainly on intervening processes between stimulus and response, such as scanning or short-term memory.
3. *Ability requirements*. Tasks are analysed in this approach in terms of the human abilities necessary to carry out a task. One example of a model that is related to this approach is the well-known Structure-of-Intellect Model by Guilford (1967). The model distinguishes a large number of components of intelligence, which correspond to elementary tasks that can be further divided into three basic dimensions (operation, e.g. memory; content, e.g. visual information; product, e.g. relations).
4. *Task characteristics*. Task analysis in terms of objective characteristics of the task, independent of the reactions that are

required (behaviour requirements), that are actually given (behaviour description), or the necessary human abilities (ability requirements). The attention in this approach is focused on the intrinsic, objective characteristics of tasks, such as the physical characteristics of the stimuli. Hackman (1969) also includes characteristics such as goal clarity in this category (any aspect of the actual task materials presented to a subject or group), besides the physical nature of the stimuli.

If one regards task characteristics as the determinants of behaviour and attitudes of task performers, points 1 and 3 (behaviour description and ability requirements, respectively) are less applicable. These two approaches refer more to characteristics of the task performer than to those of the task. Points 2 and 4 (behaviour requirements and task characteristics, respectively) have more to offer because of the strong emphasis on characteristics of the task to be carried out. Hackman (1969) is greatly in favour of measuring the intrinsic characteristics of tasks. The most important argument against this approach (task characteristics) is that it can be very difficult in practice, because of the large number of possible characteristics.

To operationalize the reactions of task performers to various task characteristics, the following dependent variables are used in research: performance, absenteeism, turnover, and reactions to the job such as work satisfaction, satisfaction with opportunities for development, and psychosomatic complaints. While discussing the various models we will take a more detailed look at the relation between the specific task characteristics and specific dependent variables.

Theoretical notions on relations between task characteristics and reactions from task performers

Over 20 years ago Turner and Lawrence (1965) published *Industrial jobs and the worker: An investigation of response to task attributes*. This study was the basis for a research paradigm leading to a great number of empirical studies in recent years. With the choice of a descriptive framework to describe jobs, Turner and Lawrence provided a number of criteria that such a descriptive framework has to meet:

- The opportunity to describe jobs in all branches of industry.
- Giving quantitative data.
- The description of jobs in terms of behaviour: what concrete human behaviour is required for task performance. These have to comprise both motoric activities and social and cognitive components of behaviour too.
- The practical usability of the descriptive framework. Moreover, it has to meet the requirement of inter-judge reliability.

The shortcoming of existing frameworks for job description (from a technical, organizational, or job-evaluation perspective, for instance) was that they were not focused enough on the description of the human behaviour needed for task performance, according to Turner and Lawrence.

In the development of a new descriptive framework, Turner and Lawrence chose a two-fold classification scheme: categorization of behaviour in activities, interactions, and mental states on the one hand and categorization of task elements in prescribed and discretionary on the other (Fig. 6.1).

The term prescribed refers to the completely predetermined parts of the task. Turner and Lawrence, by the term *discretionary*, indicate that, within the boundaries of a prescribed task, an individual has to make his/her own choices or decisions. In both cases we are talking about behaviour that is needed to perform a task. The term *autonomy* for instance refers to the discretion a task performer is expected to need to make a decision (which is built into the design of the task) upon carrying out the task assigned. The six requisite task attributes corresponding to the cells from Fig. 6.1 are:

1. Variety (e.g. variety of tools, equipment, prescribed work pace).
2. Autonomy (e.g. amount of latitude in determining the work method).
3. Required interaction (necessary contacts).
4. Optional interaction (opportunity to make contacts or restrictions, e.g. because of noise, both on and off the job).

FIGURE 6.1

		Elements of behaviour		
		activities	interactions	mental states
Elements of task	prescribed	variety (object and motor)	required interactions	knowledge and skill
	discretionary	autonomy	optional interaction (on or off the job)	responsibility

Source: Turner, A.N., & Lawrence, P.R. (1965). *Industrial jobs and the worker: An investigation of response to task attributes.* Boston: Division of Research, Harvard University Graduate School of Business Administration. Reprinted by permission.

5. Knowledge and skill (required learning time).
6. Responsibility (e.g. the ambiguity of remedial action).

Besides these six task attributes, Turner and Lawrence distinguish a number of additional attributes that are closely associated to the nature of the job, but are not required for task performance—the so-called Associated Task Attributes. The most important of these task attributes is the Task Identity index, described as the degree to which a task results in a personal and visible contribution. The other Associated Task Attributes are pay, working conditions, cycle time, degree of mechanization, and capital investment.

Most attributes are measured by determining the average score on different scales, which are considered indicators for the attribute in question. As these attributes are highly interrelated, a total score is calculated (the so-called Requisite Task Attributes or RTA index) on the basis of the score of the six attributes. The RTA index is a measure of the task complexity.

An important contribution to theory about task attributes was made by Cooper (1973). On the basis of a hierarchical cluster analysis Cooper reduced the task attributes of Turner and Lawrence to two underlying concepts: physical variety and skill variety. Next to that he introduced two new terms: *transformations* and *goal structure*. While the first term is related to Turner and Lawrence's task identity, the latter can be viewed as an extension of the domain of task attributes that have an effect on the reactions of task performers.

An essential characteristic of most tasks is that the task performer has to transform one situation into another. For instance, he or she has to transform a problem into a solution. Transformations represent operations with regard to the stimulus material of the task and imply movement towards a goal, in the view of Cooper. Transformations draw their motivational force from the fact that they bring about changes in the structure of the total task. The greater the contribution of a transformation to the total task, the greater its motivational value will be. On top of this, the effects of transformations have to be observed unambiguously by the task performer to maximalize their motivational value. According to Cooper, therefore, transformations can be considered in terms of (1) the contribution to the total task (transformational value) and (2) the visibility of their effects (transformation feedback).

The transformational value depends whether a certain task has a central or peripheral position within the final product (or service). The motivational value of transformation feedback is determined by two aspects of the transformation according to Cooper: distance and direction. Distance is the total amount of activity required for the transformation. Cooper refers to research in which it appears that the efforts of subjects show an inverse relation with distance. The aspect of direction has to do with information regarding the progress towards (or away from) the goal. Cooper adds that the concept of task identity of Turner and Lawrence (1965) is a composite of both transformational value and transformation feedback, which is described as the ability to distinguish a task as a unique and visible work assignment.

The concept goal structure introduced by Cooper is made up of two components, in his view (separate from the goal content): (1) goal clarity and (2) goal difficulty. Goal clarity has to do with the specificity with which performance criteria are defined. Goal difficulty in Cooper's view is closely related to the concept level of aspiration, which also plays an important role in achievement motivation theory. The level of aspiration refers to the future achievement level that an individual is striving for, given his or her past achievements.

Other authors also include goal structure in the domain of the task attributes that influence the motivation and performance of task performers. Carnall, Birchall, and Wild (1976) distinguish the following three components in the concept goal structure: clarity of goal, goal difficulty, and feedback of results. Umstot, Bell, and Mitchell (1976) mention two task characteristics that are related to goal structure, namely goal specificity and goal difficulty. This line of thought ties in with goal-setting theory, which has enjoyed a great deal of attention in recent years. From the many empirical studies it has become clear that specific and difficult goals lead to higher performance than vague and easy goals. Besides specific goals, specific feedback is necessary to reach higher levels of performance (Algera, 1990).

Based on the studies of Turner and Lawrence (1965) and Hackman and Lawler (1971), Hackman and Oldham (1975, 1976, 1980) developed the so-called Job Characteristics Model of work motivation. This model has stimulated empirical studies on the one hand and has operationalized the theoretical notions regarding the role of task attributes in the context of work motivation on the other. We shall discuss the empirical findings and theoretical points of discussion with respect to the relation between task attributes and dependent variables, against the background of this model. Essentially the model (Fig. 6.2) predicts positive results (high degree of motivation, high amount of

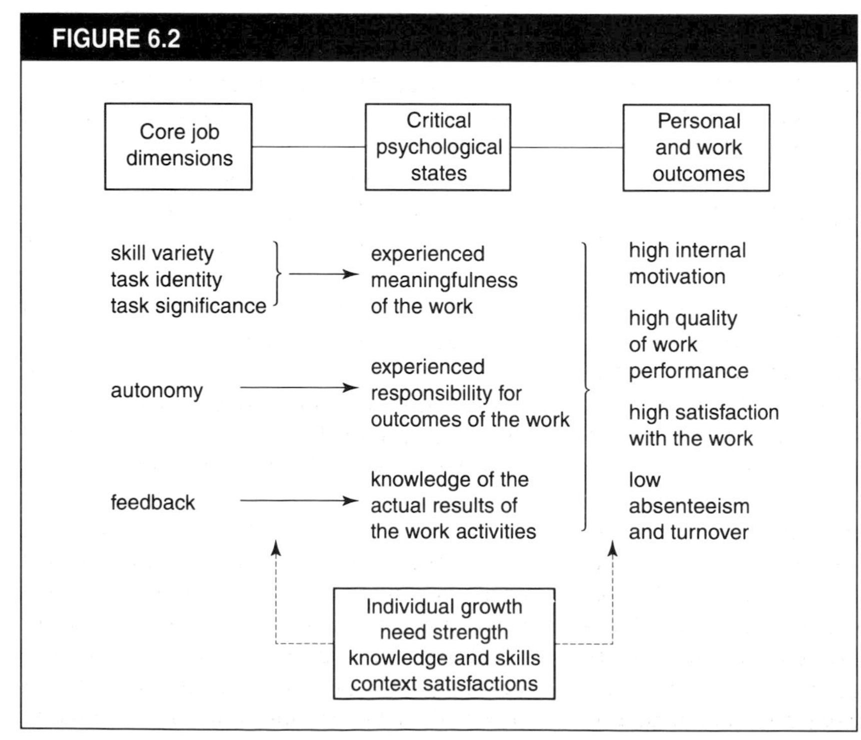

Job characteristics model (Hackman & Oldham, 1975, 1976, 1980). © 1975 American Psychological Association. Reprinted/adapted by permission of the author.

satisfaction, high level of performance, low absenteeism and turnover), if three critical psychological states are present in the individual: experienced meaningfulness, experienced responsibility, and knowledge of results. The model further states that these critical psychological states are caused by the presence of five task attributes, namely skill variety, task identity, task significance (mainly responsible for experienced meaningfulness), autonomy (related to experienced responsibility), and feedback (related to knowledge of results). As each individual reacts differently to a job with a high motivating potential, the variable individual growth need strength works as a moderator between the relation core job dimensions and critical psychological states and between the relation critical psychological states and outcomes. At a later stage (Hackman & Oldham, 1980) other moderator variables were added, i.e. knowledge and skills and context satisfactions.

Hackman and Oldham (1975) devised a measuring instrument specially for the purpose of this model: the Job Diagnostic Survey (JDS). Besides that, a single score can be gained for the five task attributes by combining in a multiplicative formula. The resulting score, the motivating potential score (MPS), is regarded as an indicator for task complexity. The JDS and the model are explicitly meant to support the (re)design of tasks (Hackman, Oldham, Janson, & Purdy, 1975).

During the early 1980s various review articles appeared (Aldag, Barr, and Brief, 1981; Roberts & Glick, 1981) and more recently four meta-analysis studies were published (Fried & Ferris, 1987; Loher, Noe, Moeller, & Fitzgerald, 1985; Spector, 1985; Stone, 1986). Here, we shall restrict ourselves to the most important points of discussion that are raised in these review studies.

Objective or perceived task attributes

Many discussion in the literature regarding the Job Characteristics Model are focused on the question whether task attributes should be measured objectively or subjectively. In the original study by Turner and Lawrence (1965, p. 10), the task attributes were considered to be determined by technology: "By intrinsic task attributes we meant such characteristics of the job as the amount of variety, autonomy, responsibility and interaction with others built into its design." In their research design the task attributes were primarily viewed as objective characteristics of tasks, to be measured by means of ratings by the researchers on the basis of observations and discussions with heads of departments. In later studies, however, task attributes are usually measured by means of ratings by the task performers themselves. Hackman and Oldham's vision (1975, 1976, 1980) is that the task attributes, as they are perceived by the task performers themselves, are the most important determinants of the behaviour and attitudes of the task performers. On the other hand, there is the simultaneous assumption that perceived task attributes nevertheless also reflect the objective characteristics of the tasks. This dilemma is clearly illustrated by the following quotation from Hackman and Oldham (1980, p. 97):

> Yet the job characteristics model in its present form does not differentiate between objective and perceived properties of tasks, and it is not known whether the motivational benefits of "enriched" work derive primarily from objective task characteristics (even if those characteristics are not perceived by the performer) or from employee perceptions of task characteristics (even if those perceptions are influenced by non-job factors).

In a critical review of the research on task attributes, Roberts and Glick (1981) state that it has not moved beyond an exploratory stage. The main objection to much of the research in this field is that researchers do not make a clear distinction between *within-person* relations, *situation–person*, relations and *situational* relations. In many studies within-person relations are the only ones dealt with because the observations regarding both the independent variables (task characteristics) and the dependent variables (behaviour and attitude of task performers) stem from the same source of information. This can result in common method variance. A possible alternative explanation for the (high) correlations between task characteristics and behaviour/attitudes, being the cognitive consistency within the person, cannot be excluded in such a design.

In the discussion on whether objective task characteristics are the most important determinants of the behaviour and attitudes of task performers, Salancik and Pfeffer (1978) argue against the Job Characteristics Model (JCM). In their view it is not so much the objective task characteristics but the social environment of the individual that has to be considered as the most important determinant of task perceptions and attitudes. The social environment of the individual—and colleagues in particular—contains signals and information that determine the reaction of the task performer with respect to a task. In other words, task perceptions and attitudes are mainly a socially constructed reality. Salancik and Pfeffer (1978) present an alternative model, the Social Information Processing (SIP) model, to explain the relations between attitudes and task perceptions.

The most important difference between these two models lies in the mutual relation between objective and perceived task characteristics. Two different types of research designs have been used to get more insight into this question.

First, objective manipulation of task characteristics and quasi-experimental studies questioned whether changes in task characteristics lead to changes in task perceptions in the direction of objective change. Take for example the experimental manipulation of the amount of autonomy, which should have consequences for the perceived amount of autonomy. This discussion about the effects of objective task changes and the social environment on task perceptions was continued later too (Caldwell & O'Reilly, 1982; Griffin, 1983; Salancik, 1984; Stone, 1984; Stone & Gueutal, 1984). In a review article by Thomas and Griffin (1983), the results of a dozen studies are summarized that concentrate on this question. The answer is that both the objective task and the social environment can be considered as determinants of task perceptions. The authors conclude that both determinants influence the perception of tasks. There is more support for a combined model than for superiority of one of the two models.

Second, research was done by means of correlations between the task perceptions of task performers themselves and of those of others (i.e. supervisors or researchers) to see whether these task perceptions can be regarded as a reflection of the objective task characteristics. Fried and Ferris (1987) present data from 15 studies. The median correlation turns out to be .63, while the median of the median correlations in studies with more than one task characteristic is .56. In studies where the Job Diagnostic Survey was used the latter value is .54. From this kind of research we can conclude that a considerable degree of agreement exists between the task perceptions of task performers themselves and those of others.

Results from both types of research in which either experimental or correlational designs were used show that though the objective and perceived task characteristics are strongly related, this correspondence is not perfect and leaves room for other determinants of task perceptions, such as the social environment.

Construction of objective indicators

Besides attempts to raise objectivity by ratings of task characteristics by supervisors and researchers, objective indicators were sporadically developed. Globerson and Crossman (1976), for instance, proposed an objective indicator that supposedly corresponds with the subjective perception of the variety of work. They designed a measure, the so-called NRT (non-repetitive time), as an indicator of variety, based on the total time spent on different task elements within the cycle time. This means that the score for variety of work becomes higher when more different task elements occur within the cycle time of the task and when the time spent on each of the task elements is longer. Globerson and Crossman (1976) indeed find a positive correlation between the NRT and the subjective perception of variety. However, the question remains to what extent the NRT truly is an objective measure, as the determination of the cycle time of a task is rather arbitrary.

It is no doubt clear in experiments in psychophysics what physical stimulus is responsible for a particular psychological reaction. But in a concrete and more complex work situation this will be more ambiguous. Hill (1969) points out that no properly defined physical correlate exists for perceived variety. In other words, it is not possible to specify directly the nature of the physical stimulus that results in the perception of variety. All one can say is that it is related to the structure of the work. On the basis of a series of experiments, Hill (1969) concludes that the entropy (a measure for the differentiation within a system) of the task structure could perhaps serve as an objective measure for the perceived variety.

More recently, Wood (1986) proposed an interesting approach to objectively determine task complexity. This approach is based on a model in which three essential components from each task are postulated: products, (required) actions, and sources of information. First, the product is identified; next, the required input at the level of specific actions is determined; and, finally, the sources of information that are important to carry out the actions are identified. Wood presents a number of complicated formulas to calculate the task complexity. No data are available with respect to the validity of this measurement procedure. Wood (1986) does provide a number of illustrations for the use of the proposed formulas. One of his examples is related to the task of air traffic controller. He distinguishes six different actions in this task, e.g. "landing instructions for the pilot". For each action a number of sources of information are distinguished. In this case these would be: weather conditions, visibility of the runway, runway conditions, and the quality of the landing manoeuvre.

Wood (1986) notes that it is not always possible to calculate a score for task complexity using the formulas he provides, and certainly not for some work situations in the field. This again illustrates how difficult it is to develop and validate real objective indicators of task characteristics. Moreover, Wood's approach leaves open the question to what extent the identification of actions and the related sources of information can be determined in an objective way.

A second remark regarding the relevance of objectively measured task characteristics in the light of work motivation and work satisfaction has to be made here. It concerns the aggregation level at which a task characteristic is defined. In the quoted attempts to develop objective indicators, it concerned tasks or subtasks that were part of a job. However, if we look at the level dependent variables refer to (e.g. work satisfaction, psychological complaints, absenteeism, etc.), it is obvious that the independent variables should be defined at the aggregation level of the job. In an approach such as Wood's (1986), this could be realized by combining the scores for the separate tasks into one total score for the job as a whole.

The dimensional structure of task attributes

The number of task dimensions that can be distinguished has been the subject of many empirical studies. In the original study of Turner and Lawrence (1965), a single index was used: the Requisite Task Attributes (RTA) index. It comprised the weighed sum of six moderately intercorrelated task attributes (responsibility, autonomy, required interactions, optional interactions, variety, and knowledge and skill). No information is available, however, regarding the internal consistency of the items that belong to each of the six task attributes. As mentioned earlier in this section, five a priori task attributes are postulated in the Job Characteristics Model. Besides that, a single index (MPS) is proposed as an indicator of task complexity.

Many studies have been done concerning the a priori structure of the Job Diagnostic Survey (JDS) and similar instruments, for example the Job Characteristics Inventory (JCI; Sims, Szilagyi, & Keller, 1976). Dunham, Aldag, and Brief (1977) investigated the factor structure of the JDS in 20 different samples. The result of this study clearly demonstrates that the underlying dimensional structure of the JDS is inconsistent across different samples. The postulated five-factor structure was only found in two of the twenty samples. Usually a smaller number of dimensions (four, three, or even two) is found. In a more recent study by Fried and Ferris (1986), in which the original JDS database was reanalysed, a three-factor structure was found. The task attributes "task identity" and "job feedback" were identified as separate factors, but "skill variety", "task significance", and "autonomy" corresponded to one factor. In a factor analysis of subgroups, a five-factor structure was found, particularly in samples of respondents with higher levels of education. In samples of respondents with lower levels of education factor structures with four, three, or two factors were found. In another study, Idaszak and Drasgow (1987) point out an artefact in measurements, caused by the negative formulation of items. They state that it is the main reason for the inconsistent results of the empirical research on the factor structure of the JDS.

The are three problems with the evaluation of the results of research concerning the dimensional structure of task attributes.

First, the measuring instruments used in the various studies are not identical. This hampers comparisons between the studies.

Second, there is quite a difference in the variance of jobs in the various samples. On the one hand, correlations between task attributes are determined on the basis of a sample of jobs from different branches of industry and at different levels in the organization. On the other hand, there are studies in which the sample of jobs is far more homogeneous, and is restricted to jobs in a certain department of a factory (Wall, Clegg, & Jackson, 1978).

Third, we have to consider whether the basic data refer to differences between jobs or whether they refer to differences between jobs and/or differences between individual perceptions of the same job. In the major part of the studies, the database comprises individual task perceptions of different jobs. Fried and Ferris's study (1986) included a database with nearly 7000 respondents working in nearly 700 different jobs. In an analysis of such a database, the variance between scores can be partially attributed to objective differences between jobs and partially to differences between perceptions of the same job.

The role of the critical psychological states

The assumed mediating role of the critical psychological states in the JCM has been subjected to relatively little empirical testing. In the rare studies in which this is the case, various methods for testing have been used, for example partial correlation (Hackman & Oldham, 1976), path analysis (Wall et al., 1978), and the analysis of linear structural relations (Algera, van der Flier, & van der Kamp, 1986). The results of these analyses give little support to the model. Inspection of the correlation patterns reveals that the direct relations specified between task characteristics and critical psychological states do not occur as the model predicts. Besides that, research is very scarce in which the predicted causal effects are tested by means of the appropriate statistical techniques.

Wall et al. (1978) tested the model using path analysis, a statistical method to test causal relations postulated a priori between variables. The empirical data did not agree with the model on many points. This particularly applied to the presumed role of the critical psychological states. While testing the JCM against an alternative model, in which direct relations between task characteristics and outcome variables were postulated, the alternative model proved to explain a significantly larger proportion of the variance than the JCM. As the direct relations between task characteristics and outcome variables would have the same implications for task redesign if the critical psychological states had behaved according to the model, the JCM was not rejected as a whole by Wall et al. (1978). They do propose a number of reformulations for the model, such as mediating role for internal work motivation as a critical psychological state. In the path analysis of Wall et al. (1978), path coefficients were estimated by a series of regression analyses. This means that the relations in the model were not tested at the same time.

More recent research, by Algera et al. (1986) among others, does make use of simultaneous testing of the causal relations between the variables in the model. For such testing the LISREL analysis method (Jöreskog & Sörbom, 1978) was used. This method of analysis was used for causal modelling, i.e. the testing of hypotheses with respect to non-experimental data. The word "modelling" refers to the point that the analysis of data starts from a theoretical specification. The word "causal" refers to the fact that such a specification is intended to explain the data instead of describe them. In the study of Algera et al. (1986), the JCM and a number of modifications of the JCM were tested in two different samples. The results show a poor fit between the empirical data and the JCM and the modifications of the JCM. The conclusion is that it is nearly impossible to model the exact causal relations between the many variables in one comprehensive model. Although the correlation patterns of the attitude variables (e.g. satisfaction) allow for a mediating role of the critical psychological states, the correlation patterns regarding behavioural variables (see for instance Fried & Ferris, 1987) are such that a mediating role for critical psychological states is out of the question.

Hogan and Martell (1987) also tested a number of causal relations from the JCM using the same method of analysis, in a sample of office workers. Among other things the JCM was compared to an alternative model lacking critical psychological states in this study. Here, too, the alternative model showed a better fit with the empirical data than the original JCM.

The effects of moderator variables

In the original JCM the variable growth need strength (GNS) is considered as a moderator variable, while in a later publication (Hackman & Oldham, 1980) knowledge and skills and context satisfactions are postulated as moderator variables too. In most studies the moderating effect of GNS was investigated, but the other variables with respect to individual differences were also analysed. White (1978) published a review study and concluded that the generalizability of the effects of individual differences is limited. Shepard and Hougland (1978) also point out that the research results in this field are inconsistent. Roberts and Glick (1981) state that there is little support from empirical research for GNS as a moderator variable.

In a number of later publications, where meta-analysis was used, the evaluation of GNS as a moderator variable was less negative. The results of different studies are combined in the meta-analysis method, in which statistical artefacts are removed to determine the true relation between variables. Loher et al. (1985) applied meta-analysis to determine the true relation between task characteristics and satisfaction, and also investigated GNS as a possible moderator variable. They found a correlation between a task characteristics index and satisfaction of .39. The correlation between satisfaction and separate task characteristics varied from .32 (task identity) to .46 (autonomy). For the high GNS group, the correlation between task characteristics and satisfaction was much higher than for the low GNS group. One interesting finding is that the variance observed for the high GNS group across the studies disappears after correction for sampling error and measurement unreliability. But this variance is still quite considerable for the low GNS group after correction for these statistical artefacts. On the basis of this finding, Loher et al. (1985) suggest that factors without influence on the relation between task characteristics and satisfaction for high GNS people, do play a role with people that have low scores for GNS. In their view the success of task enrichment for low GNS individuals depends on factors such as support from management or appreciation of the working group of these kinds of interventions.

Spector (1985) presents the results of a meta-analysis across 20 samples with regard to the moderating effect of GNS and similar variables on the relation between task complexity and outcome variables. He finds higher correlations for people who score high on GNS than for people who have a low score. This effect was stronger for satisfaction than for other outcome variables, like work performance. Spector (1985) concludes that research on moderator effects is still worthwhile.

Fried and Ferris (1987) report the results of a meta-analysis across five studies with regard to the moderating effect of GNS on the relation between MPS (Motivating Potential Score, the single index for task complexity from the JDS) and work performance. They found a far stronger relation between MPS and work performance for high GNS people than for low GNS people. The 90% credibility value (the 90% cutting point of the distribution cleaned of statistical artefacts) between MPS and work performance for the high GNS group was .45 and .10 for the low GNS group. The meta-analysis studies mentioned offer some correction for the initial negative findings concerning the moderating effect of individual differences on the relation between task characteristics and outcome variables.

The relation between task characteristics and outcome variables

As has been mentioned earlier, studies that test the JCM as a whole, including the mediating role of the critical psychological states, are relatively rare. In the larger part of the empirical research, direct correlations between task characteristics and outcome variables are presented.

Although by far the most studies use perceived task characteristics, such as those measured by the JDS or JCI, to determine the relation between task characteristics and outcome variables, in a small number of studies the difference between objective and perceived task characteristics is taken into account while explaining variance in the outcome variables. The relations between objective or perceived task characteristics respectively and outcome variables were investigated in these studies. Algera (1981, 1983), for example, found substantial agreement in the correlation patterns between 24 task characteristics and 17 outcome variables. This was done with scores on the 24 task characteristics given by the task performers themselves (perceived task characteristics) on the one hand, and by non-task performers on the other (objective task characteristics). Also in a number of other studies (e.g. Oldham, Hackman, & Pearce, 1976; Stone & Porter, 1978), correlations between objective and perceived task characteristics respectively and outcome variables have the same pattern. The only exception seems to be the study of Brief and Aldag (1978), in which very different correlation patterns are found for scores from supervisors in comparison to those of task performers.

Fried and Ferris (1987) refer to a number of studies (Ganster, 1979; Orpen, 1979; Umstot et al., 1976) in which the effect of objective manipulations of task characteristics on attitudes is compared to that of perceived task characteristics. The results of these studies demonstrate comparable effects. Fried and Ferris (1987) reach the conclusion that scores for task characteristics given by task performers themselves can be useful as independent variables. The problem of within-person relations as indicated by Roberts and Glick (1981) seem to be less dramatic than was originally presumed (see also Taber & Taylor, 1990). However, from a methodological perspective objective task characteristics are preferable to perceived task characteristics if one is dealing with situation–person relations.

As regards the relation between task characteristics, measured by means of the JDS, and outcome variables, the meta-analysis of Fried and Ferris (1987) offers the most complete review.

The results of this study indicate moderate to strong relations between task characteristics and outcome variables that refer to attitudes. After correction for statistical artefacts, it appears that the task characteristic feedback is most strongly related to the overall job satisfaction (90% credibility value .43). The task characteristic autonomy has its highest correlation with growth satisfaction (90% credibility value .71) and the task characteristic skill variety is most closely related to internal work motivation (90% credibility value .52).

The relations between task characteristics and behavioural variables, however, are considerably lower. The task characteristics task identity and feedback have the highest correlation with the variable work performance, with a 90% credibility value of .13 and .09 respectively. The relations with absenteeism are a little higher (90% credibility value for the task characteristics autonomy and feedback are −.29 and −.19 respectively).

Another classic discussion treated by Fried and Ferris (1987) is the comparison between the multiplicative formula of the MPS and a simple additive formula for the combination of scores for five task characteristics of the JDS. The latter index proves to give the best results, both for attitudinal variables and behavioural variables. However, the differences in 90% credibility values are not very large (.74 versus .63, .88 versus .77, .66 versus .53, and .27 versus .23 respectively for overall job satisfaction, growth satisfaction, internal work motivation, and work performance).

The dependent variables

In the original JCM (Hackman & Oldham, 1975, 1976) a number of dependent variables are mentioned (see Fig. 6.2): internal work motivation, satisfaction, quality of work performance, absenteeism, and turnover. In later publications, absenteeism and turnover are no longer mentioned as dependent variables by Hackman and Oldham (1980), and the quality of work performance is replaced by the variable work effectiveness. Besides that, the collection of dependent variables that is believed to be related to task characteristics has been extended by other authors (e.g. Algera, 1983; Broadbent, 1985). The extension particularly concerns variables that refer to personal effects such as psychological and psychosomatic complaints (Algera, 1983), or anxiety and depression (Broadbent, 1985). In empirical research some dependent variables are used more often than others. On the whole, there are more studies that have used attitudinal variables, for example satisfaction, than have used behavioural variables, such as work performance, absenteeism, and turnover.

Broadbent (1985) stresses the clinical effects of the task design, in his view specific task characteristics are related to specific neurotic symptoms. He emphasizes the interactive effects of task characteristics and individual personality traits that determine the stress reactions of the individual. As regards the first point, Broadbent refers to data from a number of studies that demonstrate specific task characteristics indeed have specific effects. It appears, for instance, that work pace has more effect on anxiety than on depression, and has no effect at all on work satisfaction. He defends the view that the determinants of satisfaction, anxiety, and depression are different. It is for this reason that he opposes the combining of different task characteristics if one wants to predict stress reactions.

The evaluation of the JCM

In view of the research findings regarding distinct parts of the JCM, we can now evaluate the JCM as a whole. The most critical part of the JCM is no doubt the relation between objective and perceived task characteristics. It can be shown that there is a reasonable degree of correspondence between objective and perceived task characteristics. On the one hand, proof can be found in studies where objective task characteristics have been manipulated. On the other, it can be found in studies in which the correlations between the ratings of task characteristics have been made by task performers and non-task performers, and where the respective correlation patterns with dependent variables show a large degree of agreement. However, there are other factors, such as the social environment and method variance, that partly explain the relation between task characteristics and dependent variables. This means that ratings made by task performers can be used as indicators for objective task characteristics, although there is not a perfect correspondence. In more recent comparative studies, a number of authors argue for an integration of the JCM and the SIP approach. The empirical research results indeed lend support to an integration of both models, rather than a preference for one or the other (see, for instance, Fried & Ferris, 1987; Glick, Jenkins, & Gupta, 1986; Thomas & Griffin, 1983; Vance & Biddle, 1985). Vance and Biddle (1985), for example, found very interesting results with respect to the interaction between the social environment and the objective task characteristics in the situation wherein task performers are confronted with a new task. In this study the effect of the social environment on the task perception only appeared to occur if the influences from the social environment took place before the task performer came into contact with the objective task characteristics. Vance and Biddle conclude that both the direct experience with objective task characteristics as well as the social environment influence the task perceptions.

Regarding the correlations between task characteristics and dependent variables, the relations with attitudinal variables, such as satisfaction, generally seems considerably stronger than the relations with behavioural variables, such as work performance. Furthermore, it would appear that specific dependent variables are linked to specific task characteristics (Fried & Ferris, 1987; Glick et al., 1986). This means that if one wants to influence specific dependent variables, interventions would have to focus on particular task characteristics. However, if one is interested to influence a broad range of dependent variables, the task characteristic feedback is the most promising, according to Fried and Ferris (1987). The task characteristic feedback turns out to be related to both attitudinal and behavioural variables. From empirical findings in goal-setting theory, it has been found that feedback plays an important role in improving performance (Algera, 1990).

An important shortcoming of the JCM of a more general nature is that the model is static. The model does indicate which relations exist between task characteristics and dependent variables, but says nothing about the role of the factor time. Indeed, there are very few research results regarding the effect of the factor time. One exception is the research of Katz (1978a, 1978b), where it is suggested that the factor time operates as a moderator of the relation between task characteristics and satisfaction. He investigated the effect of the time of experience with a job on the relation between task characteristics and satisfaction. It turned out that the correlation between the task characteristic autonomy and satisfaction was negative for new task performers (0–3 months on the job). For task performers who had been working on the job for longer periods the correlation was positive. The highest correlation was found where people had been working on their job for about a year, after which there was a slow decrease that tailed off to nearly zero for people who had been working for over 15 years in the same job. Kozlowski and Hults (1986) made an analysis of the time one had been working in the same job and its effect on the relation between task complexity and work performance in a sample of engineers. They found an extremely strong moderating effect for the time one had spent working in the same job for engineers working in research and development departments. The relation between task complexity and work performance is low in the period 0–1.5 years in the job. It rises during the period 1.5–4.5 years in the job and then decreases considerably if one works in the same job for over 4.5 years. For engineers working in staff departments a very gradual decreasing correlation was found between task complexity and work performance the longer people are working in the same job. Griffin (1991) presents a longitudinal study that shows an improvement of the quality of work performance, but only a year after the job redesign intervention. This also illustrates that job redesign takes time to have its effects on work performance.

Summarizing, we may conclude that the JCM as an integral model finds no overall support in the results from empirical research. This particularly holds for the precise causal relations postulated in the model and for the mediating role of the critical psychological states. On the other hand, there is much empirical support for the effect of task characteristics on dependent variables, although these effects are stronger for the way people experience work (e.g. satisfaction) than for work performance. Vogelaar and van der Vlist (1995) conclude that job redesign on the basis of JCM has an immediate effect on attitudinal variables and a delayed effect on behavioural variables. That is why it can be expected that modifications of the JCM will be developed in future research into the effects of task characteristics.

THE JCM AS AN INTERVENTION STRATEGY FOR JOB (RE)DESIGN

As mentioned earlier, the JCM and the corresponding instrument (the JDS) were introduced to help in job (re)design (Hackman et al., 1975). From an overview of the empirical research regarding this model it turns out that the major part of the research is focused on testing (parts of) the model. Few studies are aimed at the JCM as a guideline for interventions in actual practice. Loher et al. (1985) express their concern about the small number of studies in professional literature that report on actual interventions. Basically, the emphasis is placed on the JCM as a model that diagnoses a situation rather than the JCM as a vehicle to implement actual changes in tasks.

In later publications, Hackman and Oldham (1980) presented five principles for implementation:

1. Combining of tasks.
2. Forming of natural work units.
3. Establishing client relationships.
4. Vertical loading.
5. Opening feedback channels.

In addition, an indication was given for each of the five principles of implementation on which of the specific task characteristics the principle is expected to have an effect. However, this supplement to the JCM has not been worked out carefully or in any detail up to now.

We can pose a number of questions relevant to this issue. For example: What is the relation between task characteristics at the level of the individual task and higher organizational levels? As most jobs are not independent of other jobs, but are related to them, one has to take the mutual relations between jobs into account during interventions. The same applies to relations with higher organization levels. In short, intervention strategies based on the JCM must be embedded in a broad approach to organization design.

Another question we can ask concerns the way the principles of implementation are exactly worked out in practice. Take, for example, the way in which people are supposed to form natural work units in a specific situation. These questions illustrate that for practical implementation more attention has to be paid to the task structure as a dependent variable—depending on technology, organization structure, and management systems—than to the task structure as an independent variable. There is a limited number of studies in which the relations between variables at various organization levels have been mapped. Rousseau (1978), for instance, studied the relation between technological differentiation at a departmental level, task characteristics at the level of individual jobs, and the reactions of task performers. Hackman and Oldham (1980) discuss that desirable changes in task structure are hindered by the rigid nature of the technology or by management systems used. They refer to the effects of an increase in feedback on the management systems. Data on work performance are used by managers to decide which interventions have to take place. The change of feedback information structures can have a considerable impact on the existing management systems. This means that changes in task structure on the shop-floor in existing organizations also have consequences for the way management and supporting departments work.

Brass (1985) presented a number of concepts and research findings on the relations between technology, interdependency of tasks and task characteristics, and the effects of these on satisfaction, work performance, and power. His idea is that technological uncertainty (unpredictability) is an important determinant of task structure. He defines technology as a process that consists of three phases: input, conversion, and output (cf. Veen, 1980). The degree of uncertainty can be determined for each phase. Besides that, he sees the interdependency of tasks as an essential aspect of technology. Thus, he presumes the reciprocal interdependency of tasks (cf. Thompson, 1967) is related to a high degree of uncertainty in the conversion phase. Conversely, sequential interdependency of tasks is related to a low degree of uncertainty in the conversion phase. Brass (1985) proposes a number of relations between technology and task structure that are based on the idea that organizations try to reduce uncertainty. This would mean that flexibility in task structure is required to cope with uncertainty. He does indeed find empirical support for a number of his hypotheses. Brass (1985) advocates the integration of theories at an individual and organizational level in the study of task and organization design, referring to notions from the socio-technical systems approach as a possible conceptual framework.

An interesting view on task characteristics as dependent variables was put forward by Clegg (1984). He follows Perrow's (1967) notions on technology as a variable that contains a greater or smaller degree of uncertainty. The organization structure is viewed as a reaction to uncertainty. In his concept of task complexity, Clegg (1984) makes a distinction between tasks and roles. The first aspect is predominantly determined by technology, like for example the degree of automation. The latter aspect is determined by the management system used and refers to the discretion task performers have to make decisions in their daily work (i.e. determining work pace, the allocation of tasks within a group, and determining rest periods). The distinction between roles and tasks has a number of consequences (Clegg, 1984): (1) tasks and roles can be designed relatively independently from each other, (2) this distinction is not made in the literature on task design, which makes a proper interpretation of research on task complexity difficult, (3) in practice there may be ways to redesign roles without the necessity of having to change technology, (4) in most examples of task redesign there is only redesign of roles, while the tasks are hardly changed, and (5) the central proposition of the socio-technical approach (joint optimization) has been a myth up to now.

According to Clegg (1984), there are two important reasons why it is difficult to redesign more complex task structures. The first is that more complex task structures, such as self-managing groups, are viewed by engineers and managers as task structures that have a number of risks which are difficult to control. The second reason is that more complex task structures influence the balance of power in an organization, not only for management but also for supporting departments, for example maintenance.

Cordery and Wall (1985) also emphasize that managers and supervisors directly influence how autonomy and feedback in job redesign are actually improved.

CONCLUSIONS

It is evident that there are sufficient studies on task characteristics as independent variables. The large amount of empirical research proves that task characteristics have effects on the attitudes and the behaviour of task performers, although individual differences moderate these effects and relations with work experience (e.g. satisfaction) are stronger than with work performance or other behavioural variables. There is a greater need for research on the relations between technology, organization structure, and management processes on the one hand and task characteristics on the other. In other words, research on the JCM or SIP approach should be placed in a broader perspective.

The introduction of new technologies and information systems in factories and offices is partially aimed at the integration of different organization processes. Integrated logistic systems bring about greater cohesion in various production processes which in turn increases the interdependency between departments. A broader theoretical perspective, including both task characteristics and characteristics of technology, information systems, and management control systems may stimulate future research on task and organisation design.

REFERENCES

Aldag, R.J., Barr, S.H., & Brief, A.P. (1981). Measurement of perceived task characteristics. *Psychological Bulletin*, *90*, 415–431.

Algera, J.A. (1981). *Kenmerken van werk*. Lisse, Netherlands: Swets & Zeitlinger.

Algera, J.A. (1983). "Objective" and perceived task characteristics as a determinant of reactions by task performers. *Journal of Occupational Psychology*, *56*, 95–105.

Algera, J.A. (1990). Feedback systems in organizations, in C.L. Cooper & I.T. Robertson (Eds.), *International review of industrial and organizational psychology* (Vol. 5; pp. 169–193). Chichester, UK: John Wiley & Sons.

Algera, J.A., Flier, H. van der, & Kamp, L.J.T. van der (1986). Causal modeling of quality of work. In G. Debus & H.W. Schroiff (Eds.), *The psychology of work and organisation* (pp. 175–182). Amsterdam: Elsevier Science Publishers.

Brass, D.J. (1985). Technology and the structuring of jobs: Employee satisfaction, performance, and influence. *Organizational Behavior and Human Decision Processes*, *35*, 216–240.

Brief, A.P., & Aldag, R.J. (1978). The job characteristics inventory: An examination. *Academy of Management Journal*, *21*, 659–670.

Broadbent, D.E. (1985). The clinical impact of job design. *British Journal of Clinical Psychology*, *24*, 33–44.

Caldwell, D.F., & O'Reilly, C.A. (1982). Task perceptions and job satisfaction: A question of causality. *Journal of Applied Psychology*, 67, 361–369.

Carnall, C.A., Birchall, D.W., & Wild, R. (1976). The design of jobs—an outline strategy for diagnosis and change. *Management Services*, *20*(6), 48–51.

Clegg, C.W. (1984). The derivation of job designs. *Journal of Occupational Behavior*, *5*, 131–146.

Companion, M.A., & Corso, G.M. (1982). Task taxonomies: A general review and evaluation. *International Journal of Man–Machine Studies*, *7*, 459–472.

Cooper, R. (1973). Task characteristics and intrinsic motivation. *Human Relations*, *26*, 387–413.

Cordery, J.L., & Wall, T.D. (1985). Work design and supervisory practice: A model. *Human Relations*, *38*(5), 425–441.

Dunham, R.B., Aldag, R.J., & Brief, A.P. (1977). Dimensionality of task design as measured by the Job Diagnostic Survey. *Academy of Management Journal*, *20*, 209–223.

Fleishman, E.A., & Quaintance, M.K. (1984). *Taxonomies of human performance*. Orlando, FL: Academic Press.

Fried, Y., & Ferris, G.R. (1986). The dimensionality of job characteristics: Some neglected issues. *Journal of Applied Psychology*, *71*, 419–426.

Fried, Y., & Ferris, G.R. (1987). The validity of the Job Characteristics Model: A review and meta-analysis. *Personnel Psychology*, *40*, 287–322.

Fry, L.W. (1976). The maligned F.W. Taylor: A reply to his many critics. *Academy of Management Review*, *1*, 124–129.

Ganster, D.C. (1979). The effects of individual differences and objective task scope on task perceptions and satisfaction: A laboratory investigation. *Proceedings of the Academy of Management, 39*, 59–63.

Glick, W.H., Jenkins, G.D., & Gupta, N. (1986). Method versus substance: How strong are underlying relationships between job characteristics and attitudinal outcomes? *Academy of Management Journal, 29*, 441–464.

Globerson, S., & Crossman, E.R.F.W. (1976). Nonrepetitive time: An objective index of job variety. *Organizational Behavior and Human Performance, 17*, 231–240.

Griffin, R.W. (1983). Objective and social sources of information in task redesign: A field experiment. *Administrative Science Quarterly, 28*, 184–200.

Griffin, R.W. (1991). Effect of work redesign on employee perceptions, attitudes and behaviours: A long-term investigation. *Academy of Management Journal, 34*(2), 425–435.

Guilford, J.P. (1967). *The nature of human intelligence.* New York: McGraw-Hill.

Hackman, J.R. (1969). Toward understanding the role of tasks in behavioral research. *Acta Psychologica, 31*, 97–128.

Hackman, J.R., & Lawler, E.E. III. (1971). Employee reactions to job characteristics (Monograph). *Journal of Applied Psychology, 55*, 259–286.

Hackman, J.R., & Oldham, G.R. (1975). Development of the Job Diagnostic Survey. *Journal of Applied Psychology, 60*, 159–170.

Hackman, J.R., & Oldham, G.R. (1976). Motivation through the design of work: Test of a theory. *Organizational Behavior and Human Performance, 16*, 250–279.

Hackman, J.R., & Oldham. G.R. (1980). *Work redesign.* Reading, MA: Addison-Wesley.

Hackman, J.R., Oldham, G.R., Janson, R., & Purdy, K. (1975). A new strategy for job enrichment. *California Management Review, 17*, 57–71.

Hill, A.B. (1969). The measurement of work variety. *The International Journal of Production Research, 84*(1), 25–39.

Hogan, E.A., & Martell, D.A. (1987). A confirmatory structural equations analysis of the Job Characteristics Model. *Organizational Behavior and Human Decision Processes, 39*, 242–263.

Idaszak, J.R., & Drasgow, F. (1987). A revision of the Job Diagnostic Survey: Elimination of a measurement artifact. *Journal of Applied Psychology, 72*, 69–74.

Jöreskog, K.G., & Sörbom, D. (1978). LISREL IV: *A general computer program for estimation of linear structural equation systems by maximum likelihood methods.* Uppsala, Sweden: University of Uppsala.

Katz, R. (1978a). Job longevity as a situational factor in job satisfaction. *Administrative Science Quarterly, 23*, 204–223.

Katz, R. (1978b). The influence of job longevity on employee reactions to task characteristics. *Human Relations, 31*, 703–725.

Kozlowski, S.W., & Hults, B.M. (1986). Joint moderation of the relation between task complexity and job performance for engineers. *Journal of Applied Psychology, 71*, 196–202.

Loher, B.T., Noe, R.A., Moeller, N.L., & Fitzgerald, M.P. (1985). A metaanalysis of the relation of job characteristics to job satisfaction. *Journal of Applied Psychology, 70*, 280–289.

Oldham, G.R., Hackman, J.R., & Pearce, J.L. (1976). Conditions under which employees respond positively to enriched work. *Journal of Applied Psychology, 61*, 395–403.

Orpen, C. (1979). The effects of job enrichment on employee satisfaction, motivation, involvement, and performance: A field experiment. *Human Relations, 32*, 189–217.

Perrow, C. (1967). A framework for the comparative analysis of organization. *American Sociological Review, 32*, 194–208.

Roberts, K.H., & Glick, W.H. (1981). The job characteristics approach to task design: A critical review. *Journal of Applied Psychology, 66*, 193–217.

Rousseau, D.M. (1978). Measures of technology as predictors of employee attitude. *Journal of Applied Psychology, 63*, 213–218.

Salancik, G.R. (1984). On priming, consistency, and order effects in job attitude assessment: With a note on current research. *Journal of Management, 10*, 250–254.

Salancik, G.R., & Pfeffer, J. (1978). A social information processing approach to job attitudes and job design. *Administrative Science Quarterly, 23*, 224–253.

Shepard, J.M., & Hougland, J.C. (1978). Contingency theory: "Complex man" or "Complex organization"? *Academy of Management Review, 1*(2), 23–35.

Sims, H.P., Szilagyi, A.D., & Keller, R.T. (1976). The measurement of job characteristics. *Academy of Management Journal, 19*(2), 195–212.

Spector, P.E. (1985). Higher-order need strength as a moderator of the job scope-employee outcome relationship: A meta-analysis. *Journal of Occupational Psychology, 58*, 119–127.

Stone, E.F. (1984). Misperceiving and/or misrepresenting the facts: A reply to Salancik. *Journal of Management, 10*, 255–258.

Stone, E.F. (1986). Job scope–job satisfaction and job scope–job performance relationships. In E.A. Locke (Ed.), *Generalizing from laboratory to field settings* (pp. 189–206). Lexington, MA: Lexington Books.

Stone, E.F., & Gueutal, H.G. (1984). On the premature death of need satisfaction models: An investigation of Salancik and Pfeffer's views on priming and consistency artifacts. *Journal of Management, 10*, 237–258.

Stone, E.F., & Porter, L.W. (1978). On the use of incumbent-supplied job characteristics data. *Perceptual and Motor Skills, 46*, 751–758.

Taber, T.D., & Taylor, E. (1990). A review and evaluation of the psychometric properties of the Job Diagnostic Survey. *Personnel Psychology, 43*, 467–500.

Taylor, F.W. (1911). *The principles of scientific management*. New York: Harper & Row.

Thomas, J., & Griffin, R. (1983). The social information processing model of task design: A review of the literature. *Academy of Management Review, 8*, 672–682.

Thompson, J.D. (1967). *Organizations in action*. New York: McGraw-Hill.

Turner, A.N., & Lawrence, P.R. (1965). *Industrial jobs and the worker: An investigation of response to task attributes*. Boston: Harvard Graduate School of Business Administration.

Umstot, D.D., Bell, C.H., & Mitchell, T.R. (1976). Effects of job enrichment and task goals on satisfaction and productivity: Implications for job design. *Journal of Applied Psychology, 61*, 379–394.

Vance, R.J., & Biddle, T.F. (1985). Task experience and social cues: Interactive effects on attitudinal reactions. *Organizational Behavior and Human Decision Processes, 35*, 252–265.

Veen, P. (1980). Kenmerkenvan organisaties. In P.J.D. Drenth, H. Thierry, P.J. Willems, & C.J. de Wolff (Eds.), *Handboek Arbeids- en Organisatiepsychologie*. Deventer, Netherlands: Van Loghum Slaterus.

Vogelaar, A.L.W., & van der Vlist, R. (1995). Het Job Characteristics Model en taakherontwerp. *Gedrag en Organisatie, 8*(2), 65–87.

Wall, T.D., Clegg, C.W., & Jackson, P.R. (1978). An evaluation of the Job Characteristics Model. *Journal of Occupational Psychology, 51*, 183–196.

White, J.K. (1978). Individual differences and the job quality–worker response relationship: Review, integration, and comments. *Academy of Management Review, 3*, 267–280.

Willems, P.J. (1970). Werk ontwerpen. In P.J.D. Drenth, P.J. Willems, & C.J. de Wolff (Eds.), *Bedrijfspsychologie, onderzoek en evaluatie* (pp. 273–289). Deventer, Netherlands: Van Loghum Slaterus.

Wood, R.E. (1986). Task complexity: Definition of the construct. *Organizational Behavior and Human Decision Processes, 37*, 60–82.

7

Job Analysis

Jen A. Algera and Martin A.M. Greuter

1 INTRODUCTION

The description and analysis of human work is important for interventions in practice that are based on insights and theories from industrial and organizational psychology. In this chapter the role of job analysis is discussed from different objectives of personnel management, such as personnel selection, personnel appraisal and reward systems.

First, a global survey is given of the ways job analysis is used in the area of personnel management (Section 2). Section 3 aims to provide the reader who has little knowledge about the subject of job analysis with a further introduction by means of an overview of the subjects usually found in job analysis. In Section 4 attention is paid to the way in which data about the job is collected. Besides a general overview of data collection methods, there is a specific focus on the use of questionnaires for the purposes of job analysis.

Section 5 goes into the various fields of application, but as job analysis is mostly applied to personnel selection, this field of application is given more extensive treatment. Besides this, the section shows how job analysis can be applied to the design of personnel appraisal systems, job evaluation systems and to new technology environments.

Research on job analysis and the development of new methods mostly takes place in (very) large organizations. In the United States much research has been carried out in military organizations, such as the army, the navy and the air force. In particular, studies in the American air force carried out by the Air Force Human Resources Laboratory have become widely known. The specific significance of the research in American military organizations is extensively described in the handbook edited by Gael (1988). Some methods were later applied in non-military organizations too.

2 JOB ANALYSIS AND ITS USES

Levine (1983) mentions no less than 11 different objectives within the broad field of the management of human resources in work organizations in which information on tasks and jobs is used. Given the great number of objectives, it is not all that surprising that many methods and techniques for job analysis and work analysis have been developed. These existing methods can be divided into various categories depending on your point of view. McCormick (1976), for example, mentions four points of view, from which to distinguish job analysis methods:

1. The type of information (i.e. referring to work activities, work performance or the context of a job).
2. The form of information (qualitative versus quantitative).
3. The method for collecting data (i.e. observation, interview, questionnaire).
4. The person supplying the information (i.e. task performer, job analyst).

In actual practice many combinations of possibilities from each of the four categories can be found. Different methods can lead to different results however. This is illustrated, for instance, in a study by Cornelius, Carron, and Collins (1979), who tried to define job clusters for supervisory jobs in the chemical process industry. They made use of two different approaches to describe jobs: descriptions in terms of work activities and in terms of personal characteristics. These two approaches turn out to result in strongly differing clusters.

Ash (1988) points out that it is not very probable that one method of work analysis is usable for all the objectives of personnel management mentioned. This view is supported by Levine, Thomas, and Sistrunk (1988). These authors noted that there is no encompassing theory (as yet), from which links can be made between human work behaviour and certain characteristics of the work situation. A classic publication in this context is Dunnette's statement (1976) about the world of work on the one hand and the world of human attributes on the other. He makes it clear that there are taxonomies of human behaviour and taxonomies of work tasks, but translating the one type of taxonomy to the other is a major problem.

The lack of such an encompassing theory means that there are no theoretical indications available that dictate which work analysis method should be chosen. Therefore, a pragmatic approach is the most suitable. This means that the usability of a certain work analysis method particularly depends on the degree to which it contributes to the specific objective (selection, training, etc.) involved.

Pearn and Kandola (1988) point out that the importance of job analysis has greatly increased in recent years. In particular, the rapid technological changes and the related questions about the skills and competences people need as a consequence, have led to an increased focus on task and job analysis.

Various underlying concepts can be used for the description and analysis of human work. The type of job information that serves as a basis for the description makes the major difference between various approaches. In the literature (Algera, 1987, 1989, 1991; Fleishman & Quaintance, 1984) four different approaches are usually distinguished:

1. Behaviour description. In this approach the focus is the behaviour the task performers actually display in executing the task, like reading instruments or adjusting control switches.
2. Behaviour requirements. This approach is aimed at the behaviour the task performer should display to perform a task successfully. This viewpoint is dominant in systems analysis, in which the crucial question is what function a particular system component fulfils. The emphasis is especially placed on the intervening processes between stimulus and response, like, for example, short term memory.
3. Ability requirements. Here, tasks are analysed in terms of the human abilities and personal traits needed to properly perform a task.
4. Task characteristics. The focus here is on task analysis in terms of the objective characteristics of the task, separate from the behaviour that should be displayed (behaviour requirements), or is actually displayed (behaviour description), or the required human abilities (ability requirements). The emphasis in this approach is placed on the actual objective characteristics of tasks. This approach is important if one wishes to consider the content of the work itself as a factor that influences job motivation and job satisfaction. In such a case, it is necessary to define the task in terms that refer to characteristics of the task itself.

In Section 4, several examples will be discussed with respect to job analysis methods and instruments, grouped according to these approaches.

3 SUBJECTS OF JOB ANALYSIS

In Figure 7.1 an overview is shown of the type of information related to job analysis: the categories are those usually found in the literature.

Most categories in the figure need no further explanation, with the exception of the fifth category "critical human characteristics". In this category an indication is given of the necessary human characteristics to do one's job properly.

Where desired use can be made of a checklist for the identification of these human characteristics. The list contains (nearly) all the characteristics needed to describe the entire spectrum of work activities (approximately 50 to 60 characteristics). The reader is referred to Dunnette (1976) and Greuter (1991).

In Figure 7.2 an example is given of a job description based on the scheme from Figure 7.1 (general information, nature of the organization, job content, job context). The various categories have been worked out in narrative terms, but evidently a different, more quantitative report is a possibility too, for example in the form of profiles.

It should be noted that the example given is a collage of very diverse instruments; these subjects are not all covered in one and the same job analysis instrument (although there are instruments that seem to come close to this ideal perspective: e.g. the 1989 Work Profiling System by Saville and Holdsworth).

One can understand why it is not plausible that a general job analysis instrument could be developed with which the entire occupational field could be covered. Attempts to do so always prove to have a more restricted use than was originally intended. One example is the Position Analysis Questionnaire (PAQ) by McCormick, Jeanneret, and Mecham (1972). In practice it proves to be less suitable for management jobs and other jobs in which cognitive activities are dominant, because insufficient differentiation occurs within these job categories.

Yet the authors initially intended the PAQ to be useful for a wide range of jobs, from simple low-level jobs to high-level management jobs. Another example is the Dictionary of Occupational Titles (DOT), which describes nearly all jobs in the American economy. In this system, one can also find a translation of job demands to psychological tests.

A closer look at various job analysis methods tells us that they suffer from systematic deficiencies. In the first place, most methods pay little attention to the description of cognitive activities, i.e. thought processes like decision making, planning, organizing, assessing, problem-solving, deciding priorities, and so on. As these thought processes are typically a main ingredient for management and executive jobs, this is clearly an important restriction of most job analysis instruments. The now classic exception to the rule is the Task Strategies Approach (TSA) by Miller (1973: see for a description Fleishman & Quaintance, 1984). This approach is based on the information processing paradigm. The person doing the job is considered as an information processor with four system functions: the information processor receives input information, records and remembers information (short- and long-term), processes information (interpretation) and selects and executes a certain action. Within each of these categories a further subdivision has been made with the help of which the cognitive activities to be carried out can be described fairly accurately. Examples of these subcriteria are: input selection, filtering of information, detection, searching, identification, coding, interpretation, categorization, storing, passing on information, short term memory, and mathematical processes like addition, solving equations, and so on.

A second objection is that most job analysis methods only touch very briefly upon the context of the job. Often, only a minimal indication is given of some context characteristics, which have been grouped under the category "job context" in Figure 7.1. Here, we are dealing with aspects like degree of responsibility, structuring of activities and amount of authority. The other context characteristics are usually left unmentioned, although it is reasonable to assume that these may be relevant in job analysis for the selection of personnel or the

FIGURE 7.1

I **General data regarding the job**
Among others the name of the job and the company, etc.

II **Nature of the organization**
Among others important products/services, company size (turnover, number of employees), company history, organization environment (market conditions and the like), future developments.

III **Job content**

1. Job situation within the organization. For example, indicated by means of an organization chart.
2. Important work activities
   - Physical activities: walking, standing, bending, lifting; use of equipment, tools, machines; tooling activities as applied to materials (manual tooling of material, assembly work, disassembly work, hand/arm and finger movements, adjusting/tuning, etc.).
   - Cognitive activities: collecting and interpreting information, decision making, planning and organizing, assessing, problem solving, etc.
3. Internal and external contacts. Parties involved, the nature of contacts and the frequency they take place.
4. Use of job aids. Material aids, PC, machines, equipment, tools.
5. Managerial tasks. Number of employees that are supervised directly or indirectly; style of leadership (e.g. person or task-oriented).

IV **Job context**

- Presence of stressors, like peak workload, time pressure, deadlines, role ambiguity, role conflict, monotony, interpersonal conflicts, traumatizing events.
- Performance conditions, like required accuracy, number of degrees of freedom (room for action or decision making), authority, responsibility, availability of resources.
- Work atmosphere, like degree of cooperation, degree of collegiality, informal social contact (social talk).
- Leadership climate (leadership received). What kind of leadership is used by the manager? (e.g. person or task-oriented).
- Organization culture/climate: among others aspects like power distance, individualistic versus collectivistic, masculine (oriented towards assertivity, aggression, macho behaviour) versus feminine (person and relation-oriented), short versus long-term, formal versus informal.

V **Critical characteristics**
Characteristics relevant for work like skills and cognitive capacities, traits, psychomotoric and sensory capacities.

A cross-section of job analysis subjects.

FIGURE 7.2

1 Name of job	Personnel consultant.
2 Aim of job	Consultant advises the line management concerning HRM policy, recruits/selects personnel in consultation with management, mediates in problems with labour or training, and is involved in organization change processes.
3 Place within organization	Reports hierarchically to the head of HRM and functionally to the division chiefs belonging to the field of work, has no managerial duties.
4 Knowledge required	– Higher professional education in Human Resources Management and personnel work. – Additional courses in organization science.
5 Main characteristics of work activities	
Professional Activities	– Analyses problems of an individual or organizational nature. – Applies instruments of HRM management. – Makes contribution to HRM development policy. – Introduces/evaluates new developments.
Contacts	– Many contacts with managerial staff, co-workers, job applicants; nature of contacts is informative and influential. – Contacts are both individual and in a group setting. – Contacts often involve confidential information and require a position of trust.
Organizational and managerial activities	– Planning/continuation of recruitment/selection activities in division(s). – Instructs secretariat. – Coordination discussions on salaries, appraisal and the like. – Takes the lead in specific projects.
6 Job level	Mostly administrative; develops policy regarding specific aspects of own field of work.
7 Method of cooperation	– Works independently, does not need to make decisions on the spur of the moment. – Cooperation concerns various actors.
8 Responsibility for results	– Quality of advice given to management. – Coordination of HRM activities (personnel supply, salary discussions, etc.).
9 Type of activities	– Professional: 20% – Contacts: 50% – Organizational: 30%

Example of a job description.

design of new jobs. Take for example the aspects mentioned under the category "stressors" (workload, time pressure, role ambiguity, role conflict, etc.), but also look at work atmosphere and culture characteristics, such as cooperation, leadership climate, an individualist versus collectivist culture, and so on.

4 COLLECTING INFORMATION IN JOB ANALYSIS

Though there is a great diversity of job analysis methods, a reasonable comparison can generally be made regarding the procedure for collecting job information in each method. In Section 4.1 an overview is presented of the most important data collection methods from the perspective of job analysis. Next, in Section 4.2, we look at more formalized systems of job analysis, such as the use of questionnaires.

4.1 A concise overview of methods

The first step in the analysis of jobs is the collecting of data. Different methods are available for this purpose, each with its own specific advantages and disadvantages (Greuter, 1991).

Interview

The most frequently used method for the collection of data is the interview. Questions are put to one or several employees, the manager or experts. There are variants on this theme, like the group interview or conference. Mostly the interview is not structured or only semi-structured. The interview usually results in much information, but it is labour intensive, expensive and time-consuming.

Observation

By carefully observing work activities and by attempting to understand the employee's situation, one learns several specific requirements needed for the job and related types of behaviour. This method is only suitable for short cycle jobs that are fairly stable and in which an emphasis is placed on visible activities. As the chance is quite high that infrequent or irregular occurrences fall outside the period of observation, there is no guarantee of a complete picture. Occasionally, the presence of an observer interferes with the work. The use of non-obtrusive methods like video-taping or filming should then be considered. Other restrictions are mistakes made by the observer with respect to interpretation.

Combined with other methods (interview), the disadvantages just mentioned are not so great and therefore observation can be a meaningful supplement to information gained orally or in writing. Besides the observation of specific work activities, this method can be applied more broadly, especially for the registration of elements of the context of the job.

Written questionnaire

One can also collect data by questioning one or several employees in writing. This can be done in a number of ways. One possibility is the semi-structured questionnaire that can be distributed to those involved (by post if necessary). Participants are asked to supply data on themselves and their work in their own words.

The use of the questionnaire has to be restricted to people who can verbalize matters well. This latter objection is less applicable to a completely structured questionnaire with precoded answer categories. As a structured questionnaire offers advantages in processing too (computer processing, statistical techniques), this method is often more suitable than other approaches.

One variant on the structured questionnaire is the so-called checklist. This is usually made up of a large number of dichotomous items (i.e. does occur / does not occur) that are related to activities or other aspects of the job. Checklists can easily be used with large groups of job incumbents and processing the data takes little effort. However, it is necessary to make extensive preparations.

Finally, there is the journal method that requires employees to keep track of their activities from hour to hour during a set period. This is a systematic method of data collection that can result in much information, but the employee has to make a considerable effort.

Experience

The so-called experience method means the analyst has to do the work of the job incumbent and if necessary has to train themselves by following a course. The idea behind this is that personal experience and careful study of the learning process help one to trace critical difficulties in the job. From these experiences it is possible to deduce the capacities one needs for the job. This method is expensive and time-consuming and is only worthwhile in simple jobs. Against the considerable face validity there are the objections that learning experiences cannot be generalized just like that, that there is a danger of over-estimation of novice's problems and that the analyst identifies with the job too little or too much.

Documentation

Besides the methods mentioned there are other possibilities, among which is the study of various sources of data, like working instructions, work reports, teaching material, maintenance records, instructions for use, and so on. By themselves these sources of information are too superficial, but combined with other methods they can provide usable angles.

The information that the different methods provide varies between qualitative and quantitative. This depends on the degree of structuring one has realized in the application of the method. Though it is true that the interview, the observation method and the written questionnaire can be further elaborated upon (i.e. the structured interview, structured observation methods) that result in quantitative information, these methods are often used to gain a qualitative, verbal and descriptive picture of the job in practice. The experience method and the documentation analysis nearly always lead to a qualitative report. For experience analysis this is a condition to arrive at a proper description, considering its introspective nature. In document analysis the opportunities for quantitive processing are restricted, because the analyst very much depends on the information present. Sometimes (ad hoc) answer categories can be determined in retrospect with which the information can be summarized, or a certain degree of quantification can be achieved another way.

The result of data collection has to be such that a proper representation of the job can be constructed. It is a representation in the sense that all critical job aspects have to be covered. What we should call "critical" in this context is rather difficult to define. In fact one can only reach a conclusion on this issue based on a complete survey of work activities, consequences and the related positive or negative results, the latter being decided in the light of the objective of the job. This requires even more precise information than turns out to be present in most situations. It is recommended that the final product be checked for completeness and relevance by different judges, preferably from different perspectives: job incumbent, colleagues, the head of the department, and so on.

Critical elements can also be traced by experts (by simulation if necessary).

4.2 Questionnaires and other systematic methods

In what follows we will discuss some well-known job analysis instruments in which the process of data collection is worked out in a very structured manner by means of (mostly extremely extensive) questionnaires. On top of this, we will be dealing with methods that nearly always provide quantitative job data in some shape or another.

In dealing with these instruments, we will use the scheme discussed earlier: Behaviour description, Behaviour requirements and Ability requirements.

See Chapter 6 for details on the task characteristics method.

Behaviour description

The majority of job analysis instruments developed in the last three decades fall within the category of behaviour description. They refer to questionnaires in which many diverse work activities are rated as to their relative importance to the job (how *important* is activity X for the job?) or for the degree to which the activity in question occurs (how *often* does activity X occur in the job?).

Position Analysis Questionnaire (PAQ)

The PAQ (McCormick et al., 1972) is one of the best-known methods of job analysis.

It consists of a worker-oriented questionnaire made up of 189 items each related to an independent work activity in general terms (McCormick defines these items as "job elements").

The questions are divided into six sections:

1. Information input: items relating to the kinds of information one has to process or handle in a job. Example: written material, quantitive data, etc.
2. Mental processes: items on the required mental processes. Example: taking decisions, solving problems, degree of planning.
3. Work output: items that have to do with the execution of work, and more particularly the use of machines and tools. Example: drawing tools, measuring instruments, keyboards, etc.
4. Relation with other persons: items about contacts that are necessary to do the work. Example: contacts with the public, salespersons, representatives.
5. Job context: items on the work environment and work situation. Example: outside work, high temperatures, dirty work.
6. Other job characteristics: category for miscellaneous items about shift work, clothing, responsibilities for materials, etc.

Parallel to this descriptive part (called job data), attribute requirements (attribute data) were developed: for each job element judges (psychologists) were asked to indicate which human characteristics (attributes) are relevant from a fixed list of 68 characteristics. The judges used a 6-point scale from 0 to 5 (0 = not applicable, 5 = high degree of importance). The rating of at least eight and a maximum of eighteen judges was asked for each human characteristic (reliability coefficients around 0.90). The profile of required human characteristics (attribute profile) was determined for each job element, by calculating the median for each of the 68 characteristics.

As far as PAQ is concerned, quite a lot of research was carried out in Europe too. A German version was developed, called the Fragebogen zur Arbeitsanalyse (FAA) by Frieling (1975; see also Frieling & Hoyos, 1978). Besides this, part of the Arbeitswissenschaftliche Erhebungsverfahren zur Tätigkeitsanalyse (AET) by Rohmert and Landau (1979) was based on PAQ.

A British version is available under the name Job Structure Profile (JSP; Patrick & Moore, 1985). The research on JSP, however, is not (yet) that extensive and only encompasses reliability research. In The Netherlands the Dutch Postal Service (PTT) has an adaptation available called Vragenlijst Functie-Analyse (VFA). However, this differs radically from the original PAQ (Scheltens, 1978; Simmelink, 1979).

Occupation Analysis Inventory (OAI)

OAI was developed by Cunningham, Boese, Neeb, and Pass (1983). It is intended to be an improved variant of PAQ; PAQ proved to give too little specific information on jobs. OAI offers a wider range of possibilities in this respect, first because the questions were formulated a lot more specifically (job-oriented) and second because the number of questions was increased dramatically.

The OAI consists of 617 items that largely describe specific work activities, divided into five sections:

1. Information received.
2. Mental activities.
3. Work behaviour.
4. Work goals.
5. Work context.

In the OAI the weight of the attributes has also been determined, from which it is possible to deduce how important a certain human characteristic is for a certain activity, as described in the job element in question. Moreover, the structure of the research on OAI is identical to that of PAQ: comparisons between dimensional structures of job data and ratings of required characteristics (attribute data), and further research into the relations between the OAI job dimensions and the GATB (General Aptitude Test Battery).

A shortened adaptation of the OAI has been made called the General Work Inventory (GWI). This questionnaire has about two hundred items and is clearly more suitable for practical application than the very extensive OAI.

Work Profiling System (WPS)

Recently, the Work Profiling System (WPS) was developed in England (Saville & Holdsworth, 1989). The WPS has three different questionnaires with more than 800 questions in total, for the following job groups: management and staff; administrative and service personnel; and skilled and technical workers. Each questionnaire is composed of various sections. While filling in the questionnaire, one first decides which sections are important to fill in for the job in question.

In the design of WPS, Human Attribute Profiles (HAP) have been constructed for the activity described in each item. A weighed linear composite of important human characteristics was set up per item.

The WPS can be done entirely on the computer. The output is a short report of the most important tasks, the most important context information and the profile of required characteristics. Besides this, supplementary information can be retrieved about the design of personnel appraisal systems, interview questions in personnel selection, training needs, and job evaluation. As far as the application of WPS in job evaluation is concerned, WPS leads to a total score in points for each job. The score is found after an extensive validation and cross-validation process in which weighing factors for job dimensions are determined. Considering the diverse possibilities for application of WPS, it can be used as a relatively flexible system for various personnel management objectives.

A shortened version of the WPS was constructed called the Direct Attribute Questionnaire. This questionnaire leads to a direct estimate of the HAP. It cannot, however, be qualified as a worker-oriented method, as for WPS, but should be considered as part of the category "ability requirements".

Behaviour requirements

Within the category "behaviour requirements" the supply of job analytical methods is considerably more restricted. In addition, this category usually does not deal with questionnaires, but a semi-structured work method by means of interviews at most.

Critical Incidents Technique

The Critical Incidents Technique (CIT, Flanagan, 1954) is a technique that has been around for some time and that has recently been enjoying renewed attention because of its relevance to assessment centre methods.

The procedure in the CIT has remained the same over the years as far as its main points are concerned. The method comes down to this: people doing the job and others who know the work well are questioned orally or in writing, to provide examples of very effective or ineffective functioning.

For the job of secretary, for instance, we have the following descriptions (Borman, 1974):

Good: – Typing and spelling are such that rereading and correction are not necessary. Letters are signed by the secretary herself/himself.
– Can file a letter so that it can be found again after six months.

Bad: – Types a short letter so that the text is at the top of the page, while the rest of the page is left blank.
– Makes copies so that the words on the left-hand side of the original are unreadable.

After the incidents have been collected (often 200–300 per job!), an effort is made to divide them into a few main categories, generally between 10 and 20. This categorization goes through different phases during which people doing the job, supervisors and others are consulted each time to assess and correct the (intermediate) results. The resulting categories, called behaviourial dimensions, can then be the point of departure for the deduction of the required human characteristics.

In the critical incidents approach it is important to map the entire role set for the job in question by interviewing the various categories of people involved. A good example of this is given by De Wolff and Schopman-Geurts van Kessel (1992) with respect to the job of medical specialist. The role set here is made up of nurses, doctors, other specialists, the head of the outpatients' clinic, secretary of the partnership and others. By means of this approach it is possible to compose an extensive list with specific behaviour requirements, which can be used in the selection of candidates (after a categorization into critical behaviourial dimensions has taken place).

Repertory Grid

The Repertory Grid is an interview method that compares well with the CIT. Here, too, the point is to gain specific examples that indicate successful and less successful performance. The way in which these examples are gained, however, differs from the CIT procedure. The interview starts by asking in what respect a successful person differs from a less successful person: which human characteristics does the one have that the other lacks or does not have enough of?

In the next phase, the interviewee is asked about typical examples from work concerning each human characteristic mentioned. Thus, the human characteristics are related to work behaviour.

Ability requirements

The supply of job analysis methods within the category "Ability requirements" is ample. We will discuss the following methods from all those available: the Task Abilities Scales, Job Analysis Questionnaire for Psychological Selection, Threshold Trait Analysis and the Minnesota Job Requirements Questionnaire.

Task Abilities Scales (TAS)

The Task Abilities Scales of Fleishman et al. (see Fleishman & Quaintance, 1984, pp. 461–464) consists of 52 scales in total to measure the importance of cognitive, sensory and psychomotoric characteristics. By means of graphic 7-point scales the relevance for each characteristic has to be determined to fulfil one's task. In each case three points on the graphic scale (low, medium, high) are anchored by examples of concrete actions. These anchors or standardized tasks were constructed with the help of panels of experts in a scaling procedure; they are kept as factorially pure as possible, i.e. they mainly characterize one aptitude factor. We refer the reader to the classic work of Guilford (1954) for the scale construction methods.

Job Analysis Questionnaire for Psychological Selection

In The Netherlands the Job Analysis Questionnaire for Psychological Selection (Dutch abbreviation FAPS) was developed according to the principle of anchored rating scales, as for the TAS we just discussed.

The point of departure in the FAPS concerns 20 abilities (including reasoning, ingenuity, command of language, etc.) and 19 personal traits (vigour, cooperation, dominance, extroversion, etc.). Rating scales were developed for each of these characteristics with three to six different examples of tasks. For purposes of illustration the scale for creativity is shown in Figure 7.3.

Threshold Trait Analysis (TTA)

The Threshold Trait Analysis (TTA) developed by Lopez (1986) measures the relative importance of 33 different characteristics. The characteristics are divided across five main areas:

1. Physical.
2. Mental.
3. Learned.
4. Motivational.
5. Social.

For each characteristic, short work-oriented definitions have been made. For example cooperation is defined as: work as a member of a team; decision making as: choose a course of action. For every trait the required level of complexity, the importance of the trait as a job requirement and the weight it has for the total work performance is determined in job analysis.

The TTA is achieved by making use of interviews. The choice of 33 characteristics is not based on empirical research by Lopez, but on various findings in the literature (see Lopez, 1988).

Minnesota Job Requirements Questionnaire (MJRQ)

The Minnesota Job Requirements Questionnaire (Desmond & Weiss, 1973, 1975) is a short questionnaire with 45 items. An action or activity is mentioned with each question, like "understanding of words", "precise movement of fingers in the handling of very small objects", "fast and accurate mental arithmetic". The job analyst has to indicate on a 7-point scale how important these actions or activities are to do the job properly.

FIGURE 7.3

Creativity (imagination, originality)

Definition: the capacity to form original ideas or to think of new solutions to problems.

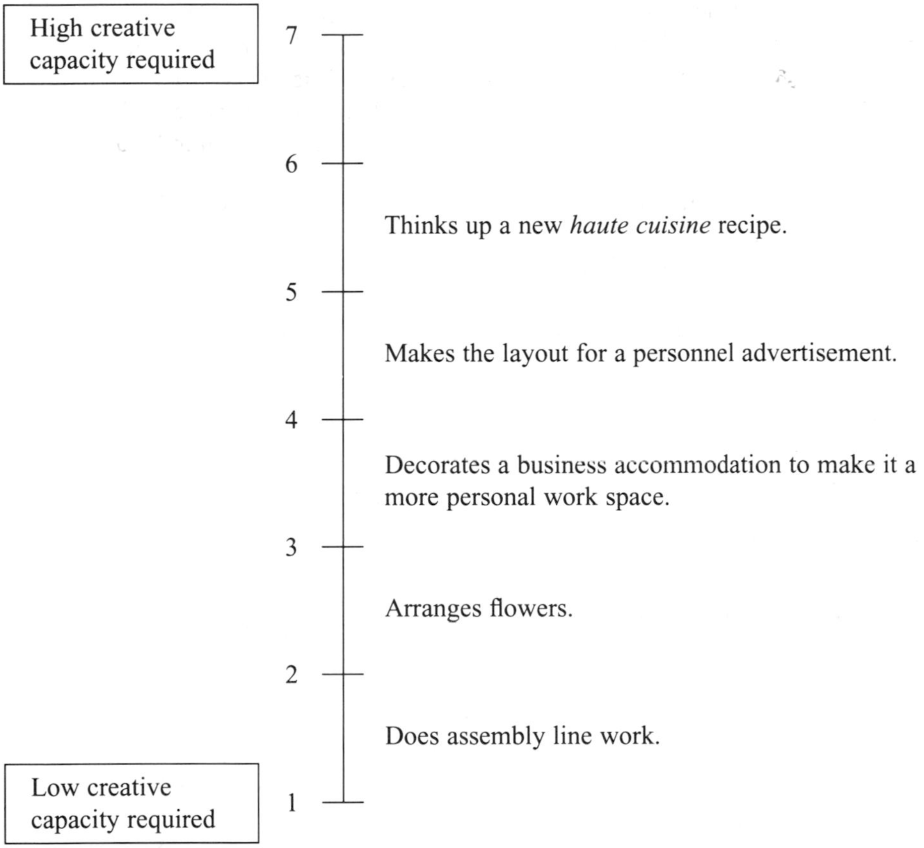

Anchor	Scale	Behavioural example
High creative capacity required	7	
	6	
		Thinks up a new *haute cuisine* recipe.
	5	
		Makes the layout for a personnel advertisement.
	4	
		Decorates a business accommodation to make it a more personal work space.
	3	
		Arranges flowers.
	2	
		Does assembly line work.
Low creative capacity required	1	

Creativity rating scale from the Job Analysis Questionnaire for Psychological Selection (Dutch abbreviation FAPS).

The MJRQ results in a description of the job in terms of a group of seven characteristics, among which are required verbal capacity (V), numeric capacity (N), administrative capacity (Q), and reasoning (R). The factors measured by MJRQ are similar to the factors measured by the GATB (General Aptitude Test Battery). In this way we can span the gap between the job content and the required characteristics on the one hand and the presence of these characteristics in job applicants on the other.

The MJRQ has been translated in The Netherlands by Bovenschen and Esser (1982). This questionnaire seems to be suitable for non-job analysts to fill in, i.e. by the head of a department or the job incumbent.

5 APPLICATIONS

In this section we will pay attention to some fields of application, like job analysis for purposes of personnel selection (5.1), appraisal, job evaluation and new technology (5.2).

Our greatest focus will be on applications

within the field of personnel selection. This choice can be justified by the fact that this perspective has been the most frequent subject of empirical research. For that matter, job evaluation also enjoys scientific and practical interest. As the latter subject is dealt with in more detail elsewhere in this volume (see Chapter 8), we shall restrict ourselves to a relatively brief treatment.

5.1 Job analysis and personnel selection

It is not that easy to follow a recruitment and selection procedure without having previously carried out a further analysis of the job and its requirements. However, the actual practice of recruitment and selection may lead us to think otherwise. By such an analysis, the organization can design the selection procedure that follows. In other words, based on the job profile, the organization can show which criteria, predictors and selection instruments are eligible. Apart from its informative role regarding the design of the selection procedure, the job analysis also provides key information during the procedure. This information may be required by the job applicant or third parties, like external consultants. From the job analysis, the text of the personnel advertisement can be composed, and job applicants can be informed as to the content of the job. Moreover, during job interviews one can take a concrete look at the tasks to be carried out and the expectations of both the company and the job applicant. In addition, consultants involved in the procedure, like the selection psychologist, can be kept up to date as to the most important focal points. Finally, job applicants who are rejected can be given specific focused information regarding the decision at the end of the procedure, expressed through the job profile that formed the basis for the selection. In other words, job analysis functions as the glue in the selection procedure: it gives guidance to the activities of the whole selection process and it is the medium *par excellence* during information transfer between the organization and the job applicant.

The importance of a good job analysis is extensively discussed in various handbooks and in the scientific literature. In 1923, Freyd already recognized the necessity of a proper job analysis. In his voluminous *Measurement in Vocational Selection*, Freyd (1923) distinguishes 10 steps in selection; the first step is job analysis. The aim of this, according to Freyd, is to trace human characteristics that lead to success or failure. Job analysis plays an important role in the rest of the steps mentioned by Freyd too. In Step 2, for instance, one has to identify and operationalize criteria for successful performance. In the next step, the abilities required and other personal traits are specified, an activity that is usually taken to be part of job analysis.

Despite the obvious importance of job analysis, we have the impression that it does not receive the attention it deserves, either in practice or in scientific research. In The Netherlands the Directorate General of Labour of the Ministry for Social Affairs and Employment (1984) instigated research into the recruitment and selection policy of 51 organizations. The sample, that is not claimed to be representative for all Dutch enterprises, encompassed 29 companies in the profit sector (especially the metal industry, food industry and banking) and 22 companies in the non-profit sector (among others, health care, social insurances / National Health Service, and public transport). Thirty-seven of the fifty-one organizations (72.5%) always make a job description before the recruitment and selection procedure. This percentage may seem high, but one should keep in mind that we are talking about a core activity here without which the selection procedure cannot actually be carried out properly. Next, the survey mentions the fact that there are only six cases in which a standard system for job descriptions is used. Besides this, six organizations stated they never made job descriptions, while eight organizations only made descriptions for jobs at high levels.

Recently, Bosch and Samren (1991) reported on an inventory with respect to the use of job analysis, for recruitment and selection among others. The research was aimed at consultancy firms in particular. Within this group nearly 70% of the respondents made use of job analysis. The interview was used most often for the collection of job information. The authors expect an increase of computerized systems for the collection of job information. No doubt this could lead the more frequent use of questionnaires in relation to interviews. The response in the research mentioned was rather poor (21%), which means that the results have only very limited validity.

We can assume that the situation is little different elsewhere. From a survey held by Ryan and Sackett (1987) among members of the American Psychological Association, who are involved in selection procedures, it appears that less than 40% make use of a systematic job analysis method.

In the remaining part of this section, we shall take a closer look at the position job analysis should hold in personnel selection. We start with a brief account of objectives: why is job analysis applied in personnel selection?

5.1.1 Objectives of job analysis in personnel selection

Within the context of personnel selection, job analysis has an informative function and, besides this, it is an aid in the design of selection procedures (see Figure 7.4).

The activities in personnel selection and the role of job analysis can be summarized with four main points:

1. *Collecting information about the vacancy*
   Provides general and specific information for the company, consultants and job applicants.
2. *Design of prediction model*
   Identification of criteria; choice of predictors.
3. *Design of decision model*
   Operationalization of the utility dimension.
4. *Report*
   Gives case specific relevant points for the report.

The following aspects are important for the informative function.

General orientation by the organization on the job and the workplace

As part of job analysis general questions are raised like:

- What are the most important tasks and responsibilities?
- What relationship is there between this job and department objectives respectively? Is it really necessary to continue the existence of the job?
- What relationships are there between this job and other jobs?
- How is the job embedded in the organization?
- Which career opportunities link up with this job?

These and other questions are not exclusively related to the design of the selection procedure, although they do run ahead of it. The organization could bring up this matter at a different time, completely unrelated to the selection procedure as a specific reason. Nevertheless, it is clear that

FIGURE 7.4

Activities in personnel selection	Role of job analysis
Collecting information about the vacancy	Provides general and specific information for the company, consultants, and job applicants
Design of prediction model	Identification of criteria; choice of predictors
Design of decision model	Operationalisation of the utility dimension
Report	Gives case-specific relevant points for the report

An overview of the role of job analysis.

indispensable information is made available to the company, the job applicant and possible consultants.

Information for the job applicant

Often an interested job applicant is sent a job description to provide some insight into the most important tasks of the job. It is understood that providing information about the job and the organization is important for the job applicant, as it helps the applicant to make a balanced assessment of the job, i.e. its pros and cons. In relation with this, Wanous (1980) introduced the notion of Realistic Job Previews. What this means is that realistic information is given about the job and organization during the selection procedure, in which the complete picture is not biased in a positive sense. This kind of facelift could lead to disappointments at the start (reality shock), after which premature turnover may occur.

From research (see, for example, Saks & Cronshaw, 1990) we know that the way in which the (realistic) information is given, either in writing or orally during an interview, in part determines the impression of honesty that the job applicant receives from an organization. Oral information transfer has proved to be more effective in this sense.

Information for consultants

If consultants such as psychologists and medical doctors are involved in the procedure, then information transfer from the department in question to the consultants is necessary to help them set up the procedure and the final report. In practice, bringing in consultants often has the positive side-effect that a job analysis is made after all, either by the company itself or by a consultant. As far as the involvement of the psychologist is concerned, it is a requirement that the procedure and the report are sufficiently related to the job. Consequently, it is hard to believe psychological consultancy is carried out without a job analysis having taken place first.

Design of prediction procedure and instruments

Traditionally, job analysis has been viewed as an aid in the design of the selection procedure. In this, the design of the prediction model in particular is focused upon, i.e. the identification of relevant (behavioural) criteria and the related predictors. Besides this, job analysis can be used to develop selection instruments including the accompanying rating scales. This especially concerns instruments that are constructed according to the principle of work samples. Take, for example, In Basket, role-playing or the situational interview. The rating scales referred to are the Behaviour Observation Scale (BOS), and the Behaviourally Anchored Rating Scale (BARS), or their variants. We shall come back to both design functions in separate sections further on.

5.1.2 Job analysis as an aid in design

In this section we shall first discuss the role job analysis plays in the design of prediction models, the identification of criteria and the choice of predictors. Then we shall discuss in what way job analysis can be used for the purposes of designing selection instruments.

Design of prediction models

In personnel selection use is made of prediction models, whereby work performance is linked to traits or behavioural characteristics of the job incumbent. Predictions can be worked out according to two paradigms, defined as "signs" and "samples" by Wernimont and Campbell (1968).

The sign approach is based on the notion that there is a relation between traits and work performance. This link is of a theoretical nature and can be made more explicit by means of a hypothesis. During selection, measurements are made of these traits. As the traits can be linked to future work performance by hypotheses, the measurements can be taken as expected work performance, i.e. as indicators (signs) for later work performance.

The sample method is characterized by the fact that parts of the job content and context are directly represented in the selection instrument. This can be done by means of worksamples, as these can be seen as a kind of replica of (parts of) the job. Examples of this are a typing test for the selection of secretaries, and an In Basket for the assessment of managers.

There are, however, elaborations of the sample

method conceivable for the interview (compare, for example, the situational interview; Latham, Fay, & Saari, 1980) and biographical questionnaires (Pannone, 1984). The sample method does not refer to traits. The prediction is based on the principle of statistic generalization; from the performance in the worksample (or a different sample instrument) an extrapolation is made into the future towards the performance in the job (see also Ridderbos, 1992).

In what way can job analysis contribute to the development of prediction models according to the sign or sample approach? (See also Greuter, 1991; Greuter & Algera, 1989.)

Identification of criteria

In the sign approach it is necessary for criteria to be of a more abstract nature and therefore more generally applicable. Besides that, an important condition is that the criteria can be linked with a psychological theory regarding the structure of work performance. Without the latter it is not really possible to make a link with relevant traits. So economic performance criteria like turnover and productivity are less suitable if one wishes to work out the sign approach. In the light of the requirements mentioned, worker-oriented job analytical methods are particularly appropriate, like the PAQ. The job dimensions mentioned in this (e.g. decision making, information processing, giving instructions) are of a more general nature and can be translated to the level of required traits without too much difficulty.

To work things out following the sample method, very detailed and complete information is necessary; at a later stage parts of the job have to be simulated at a very concrete level in a worksample, selection interview or biographical questionnaire. For the description of the job an important perspective is to know how the job domain in question is defined: tasks can be ordered according to the degree of importance, frequency, amount of time spent, decisive importance of mistakes made, and so on. In the end the ordering or stratification determines which work activities will be simulated in the work sample. An approach that has proved its merit in sample methodology is the Critical Incidents Technique we discussed earlier. The examples of incidents collected in this are concrete enough to serve as a point of departure for a simulation of a worksample or as an item in a biographical questionnaire or selection interview.

Choice of predictors

Predictors are selected through analysis of the content of the criteria mentioned earlier. For the sample approach this gives no insurmountable problems, as predictors and criteria are related by content: they are focused on the same domain of tasks. After the domain of tasks has been defined with the help of job analysis, a sampling procedure has to be chosen and executed accurately. The result is a sample of tasks that can be converted into a sample of problems: the predictor variable(s).

Things are more complicated for the sign approach: predictors and criteria are not equal regarding content, but belong to different conceptual systems; criteria relate to work behaviour and predictors to required traits.

How can these different taxonomic systems (Dunnette, 1976) be linked to each other?

In part an answer to this has been given in the previous sections: the work or worker-oriented job analytical instruments such as PAQ, OAI and WPS have been discussed. It is possible to generate a profile of required traits with these questionnaires. Next, trait-oriented methods were discussed like TAS, MJRQ and FAPS. What these methods have in common is that they provide a direct estimate of the underlying profile of traits.

Via careful job analysis one can choose the most promising predictors. However, in the end empirical correlation research between predictors and criteria is decisive in answering the question as to whether the predictors chosen are indeed sound.

An example is the research of Elshout, Boselie, Berg, Boerlijst, and Schaake (1973), in which a test series for research engineers was validated. A factor analytical approach was used too in this approach to reduce the large number of criterion aspects to a more limited number of criterion components. Traits do not immediately rise from the job content, but depend on the analyst's interpretation. Stereotypical opinions may influence the choice of traits to a great extent. Research on PAQ, for instance, proved that job analysts base their judgement on common-sense knowledge of the job when setting up a job description, related to general and stereotypical characteristics of the job in question (Arvey, Davis, McGowen, & Dipboye, 1982; Cornelius, Schmidt, & Carron, 1984; DeNisi, Cornelius, & Blencoe, 1987; Jones, Main, Butter, & Johnson, 1982; Smith & Hakel, 1979). Stereotypical opinions can then also influence the translation to traits.

It should be noted that trait-oriented job analyses bring along a greater risk of stereotyping than the methods that belong to the category "behavioural description". In the latter group of methods the job is divided into components (job elements) and then an estimate is made per component of the importance of a series of human characteristics. Such a strategy is preferable, at least from this point of view, to a method in which the job as a whole is taken as the point of departure, like in the trait-oriented job analytical methods (Cornelius & Lyness, 1980).

Design of instruments

Work samples and other selection instruments based on the sample method, as we mentioned earlier, can only be developed if rather extensive job analyses have been made. Instruments like the CIT and the Combination of Job Analysis Methods (C-JAM; see Levine et al., 1988) can be considered.

The following selection instruments can be developed with the aid of job analyses:

- Job application form: special versions of a biographical questionnaire (see Pannone, 1984).
- Interview: situational interview and criterion-oriented interview.
- Assessment exercises: various discussion exercises (group discussion), In Basket, role-playing, and other simulations.
- Psychological test: so-called work sample test. This is a questionnaire with short definitions of problems and multiple choice answers. For each alternative answer a certain weighing factor has been calculated from validation research. An example for the job of prison warder is given in Figure 7.5.

Regarding this example, it should be noted that there was a preference for analogous problems, i.e. definitions of problems that by nature and content are similar to those that may occur in prisons. This

FIGURE 7.5

1. During your sister's holiday you look after her house. Her 16-year-old son, who is somewhat rebellious, did not want to go along and has therefore been left in your care. The strict house rule that he has to be home before twelve o'clock at night is a given fact for both of you. At a quarter to twelve he phones you to ask whether he can come home an hour later ("He's having such a good time"). After you have refused him at first he threatens to stay out all night.

a. You reach a compromise and give him half an hour extra.
b. You do not respond to his threat and persist.
c. You tell him to phone you back in five minutes and phone your sister to consult with her.

2. Assume that you are working in a store. An aggressive customer comes in to complain about goods that still have not been delivered. Luckily you can explain that he has come to the wrong store for his complaint. The man leaves in an even angrier mood to go and find your colleagues in the other store (that is part of the same chain of stores).

a. You make a phone call to your colleagues to warn them about the client who is coming.
b. You phone your colleagues the next day to see how things turned out.
c. You go to the store in question to help your colleagues in case of an emergency.

Example of a work sample test.

was done to get better recognition of the problems by job applicants.

The CIT, Repertory Grid, C-JAM and other techniques can also be used to develop rating scales. First, the various examples of incidents are divided across main categories. Next, the incidents are placed on a scale per main category, according to the principle of Behaviourally Anchored Rating Scales (see, for example, Latham & Wexley, 1981). The resulting rating scales can be used for the assessment of the performance on the sample instrument in question. Naturally, the use of BARS need not be limited to personnel selection alone. The BARS methodology is equally applicable in personnel appraisal. First, relevant behaviour criteria are identified. Next, each criterion is operationalized by means of a graphic scale in which various positions have been anchored from bottom to top with the aid of concrete examples (see Chapter 9).

5.1.3 Discrimination in personnel selection: The wrong conclusions based on job analysis?

In determining job requirements there is a risk of discrimination. That is to say, the choice of job requirements needed occurs in such a way that certain groups of job applicants cannot properly meet them. We can distinguish two cases.

Direct discrimination

Human characteristics are incorrectly marked as relevant job requirements, so in fact the choice is not legitimized by the job content.

For example, in the past one job requirement for the job of policeman was "physical strength", as it was assumed that a policeman would have to physically intervene in a conflict escalating into a fight. Obviously uncurtailed adherence to this job requirement leads to the more frequent rejection of female job applicants in practice. A further analysis tells us that the requirement of physical strength is not a necessary condition for the work: nowadays a greater emphasis is placed on preventing conflicts and non-physical solutions to conflicts (solving problems through discussion), so that the requirement of physical strength has lost part of its relevance.

Discriminating effect

Human characteristics are correctly identified as relevant job requirements, but using these characteristics as requirements means that certain groups are rejected more often.

For example, making demands about intellectual capacities, certainly if this is done concerning the required educational background (i.e. university level), results in the more frequent rejection of members from various minority groups.

Setting job requirements that cause a discriminating effect by the way in which they work out for various groups, can be a great source of discrimination. We believe it is greater than intended or unintended forms of discrimination during selection, that take place in the assessment of job applicants (see Chapter 10).

Paradoxically, direct discrimination is less problematic than the discriminating effect; discrimination in its direct form is a result of an incorrect job analysis. All that has to be done is to correct the job profile. Though this exercise is not without its problems, it nevertheless can be done. With the discriminating effect, however, we are talking about problems of a different level. The postulated job requirement is a legitimate one in principle and can be defended based on the job content, so people will not be that willing to let it go. In so far as a shift in standards is allowed, compensations will be demanded in the form of additional training for candidates with deficiencies (in their prior education, for example). Other measures at the workplace could also be considered, like supervision, task/job design, and so on. Matters like this nearly always involve political considerations, which are essentially focused on the question as to what extent the organization in question wishes to allow the intake of members of minority groups.

5.1.4 Job analysis in actual practice with respect to personnel selection

As we noted before, job analysis is not applied that much in actual practice. In part this has to do with the shortcomings related to each job analysis instrument. Nearly all the instruments give little possibility to describe cognitive processes and characteristics of job context and culture. Evidently no definite solution is offered to transpose the job content to required human characteristics.

However, there are other problems that prevent the frequent application of job analysis.

The first fundamental question is whether a detailed job analysis is really necessary. In the present literature on validity generalization (see Schmidt & Hunter, 1977, 1981) strong doubts are raised with respect to the indispensability of a specific job analysis. Validity generalization refers to the question whether the validity of a test for a specific job can be generalized to various jobs, situations and times. The conclusion of Schmidt & Hunter (1981) is that validity coefficients for various aptitude tests can be generalized across a broad range of job groups; differences in the exact composition of the task between jobs would often have no consequences for the underlying structure of required aptitudes and skills. A "molecular" job analysis would therefore be unnecessary (Pearlman, 1980; Pearlman, Schmidt, & Hunter, 1980). We believe there is a danger that the technique of validity generalization could be applied to the extreme: any cognitive test could be valid for any random job. A more thoughtful position to take is that properly constructed cognitive tests have a certain degree of validity for (nearly) all jobs. Yet simultaneously there is added value (validity) for specific combinations of cognitive dimensions, skills and traits as predictors in relation to job content and context (situational specificity). This means that typically it is worthwhile to determine specific test criterion relations.

It should also be noted that the technique of validity generalization has its own criticism to deal with. Among others there was considerable criticism concerning the way in which jobs were combined in overly heterogeneous job groups for the purposes of validity generalization. Moreover, the role of job analysis is not restricted to model development alone (the viewpoint taken by validity generalization); it is an important source of information for the company, consultant, and the job applicant, as was mentioned earlier.

Even if job analysis is primarily considered from the perspective of model development, implementations following the sample approach do still require extensive job information. What we particularly have in mind is the application of content-based selection devices, like assessment centres. Another reason job analysis is not applied as frequently in practice as might be expected is that there is a noticeable shift from a job-oriented selection approach to a person-oriented approach. Instead of the suitability for one specific job, we now have to look at suitability for a series of jobs (career), where it is uncertain what specific jobs will be done in the future. Rather than having job criteria, organizations prefer to have career criteria and if these are hard to make clear then the choice is made to simply employ "good people". Such a selection without criteria seems to have no need for job analysis. In reality, however, in this situation, criteria are relevant, although not at the level of the job content. They are related to the more general characteristics of the work climate and culture of the department and company that remain relatively constant throughout a career.

The use of formalized job analysis methods may seem unnecessary in practice, when using the "clinical" approach by an expert consultant. Half a word seems to be enough for the consultant to instantly perceive which underlying human characteristics are really relevant. However, this proposition is undermined by the fact that the inter-judge reliability with respect to the deduction of required human characteristics from the job content is generally low. Only with relatively large numbers of judges can sufficient reliability be realised (for TAS about 20 judges are necessary; see Fleishman & Quaintance, 1984).

Looking back on all the problems mentioned concerning job analysis, we nevertheless feel secure enough to say that job analysis is and will remain an indispensable instrument now and in the future for personnel selection. The one condition is that sufficient attention be paid to the role of cognitive processes and context characteristics, and that a transparent expert system is available for the deduction of required traits from the job content.

5.2 Other applications

5.2.1 Job analysis and appraisal

Personnel appraisal is a classic instrument in the management of human resources in an organization. As explained elsewhere in this handbook, there are various objectives for which personnel appraisal is used. In addition, personnel appraisal is not applied to the same degree for different groups of personnel (executives, staff members, management). Managerial staff are paid more attention in many organizations, especially larger ones. Often we see a separate department for Management Development, which is in charge of personnel management and personnel development for the category of managerial staff.

As far as the type of job information is concerned, a distinction can be made in appraisal between sign and sample types of information. In the past, the emphasis was mostly placed on personality traits (sign) in appraisal systems. This has evident disadvantages, certainly where it concerns the appraisal of present job performance. Personality traits provide few clues to the concrete changes in behaviour that may be necessary to achieve an improvement in performance. For this, far more concrete information is needed that directly refers to required behaviour in the job in question. Only where it concerns an estimate of someone's potential for a series of jobs in the (distant) future, which may alter as to their exact content, is appraisal for more general capacities and personality traits inescapable. For all other cases it is advisable to link appraisal to concrete behaviour requirements that stem from the job in question (present or future).

In recent years, there has been a growing interest in appraisal linked to concrete job requirements, which is more in line with the sample approach. For managerial jobs, such an approach is often operationalized by means of an assessment centre (see Seegers, 1989). The core of the assessment centre is a series of simulations and exercises that are a reflection of the tasks in which good performance is felt to be very important in order to function properly in the job in question. The sample approach is used for other jobs too. Ridderbos (1992), for instance, recently developed a series of BOS scales for the job of operator in the (petro)chemical process industry. Originally, these scales were developed as a criterion measure to validate a worksample type of predictor instrument, but they are also excellent as an appraisal instrument for regular personnel appraisal.

5.2.2 Job analysis and job evaluation

An important element in rewarding employees for the work they do is the financial evaluation of the job. Besides rewards for the job as such, an (extra) reward can be given for certain achievements (see Chapter 8 in this volume). Here, we will restrict ourselves to job analysis for job evaluation. Thierry and De Jong (1991, p. 102) define the term as the process of description, analysis and grading of a job up to and including the assignation of the valid salary class.

By means of a system of job evaluation, the balance of reward between various jobs in a work organization is determined, especially in the larger organizations or in certain branches of industry. Since World War Two the use of job evaluation has become more widespread.

What is essential from the perspective of job analysis are the criteria used to place jobs in a certain salary class. In other words, from which viewpoints are jobs weighted, and how are the jobs financially evaluated as a consequence?

Thierry and De Jong (1991) note that in Dutch systems of job evaluation, the various viewpoints are mostly combined into three to seven main characteristics, such as:

- Knowledge and experience.
- Responsibility.
- Problem solving.
- Leadership.
- Social skills.
- Working conditions.

The procedure followed to place a job in a certain scale can vary. If different viewpoints are used, the sum of the scores for the various viewpoints is taken. If necessary a weighing factor is applied to each viewpoint first. The weighing factor gives the relative importance of the viewpoint in question. Eventually, a final score can be calculated by which a job can be placed in a certain salary class. Besides this point system, frequent use is made of the job classification method in The Netherlands. The method allows the job as a whole to be placed in a salary class. This system is used by the government, for example.

From the perspective of job analysis, several psychometric issues are important in job evaluation systems. The first is the inter-judge reliability. Here, the question is to what extent different judges interpret the differences between jobs in the same way.

According to Madigan (1985) an extremely high inter-judge reliability is required, as the consequences are so important for the employees involved. He reports on reliability coefficients that may be high in some cases, but do not always meet these high demands. A second important aspect concerns the independence of the various viewpoints. There is much research from which it appears that the variance between jobs can be explained by a single factor.

The research of Wiegersma (1958) is a classic in this respect. He discovered an extremely high intercorrelation between the viewpoints "knowledge", "independence" and "time span of discretion". Moreover, these viewpoints have a high weighing factor in some job evaluation systems. So, it is not that surprising that the variance between jobs can largely be explained by a single factor.

A third aspect has to do with the role that (global) stereotypical opinions of jobs play in the assessment process that trained job analysts are involved in. There is a relatively large amount of research (for a survey, see Algera, 1987; Smit-Voskuijl, 1992, recently provided a survey of the possible sources of bias in job analysis) from which it appears that stereotypes play a role in the assessment of jobs. It can be even more insidious if one considers that high inter-judge reliability may be the result of (subconscious, common) stereotypes. If this were to be the case then little could be criticized about the *accuracy* of the measurements, but a lot could be criticized about the *validity* of the measurements.

In general we can say that the psychometric objections have had little or no influence on the systems and procedures of job evaluation in practice. This can be explained by the highly political context in which these systems are used. It is not the psychometric qualities, but the acceptability of the results is important to employers and unions.

In incidental cases the result of comparative job evaluation plays a role in a broader political context. Thus, in 1992 there was a public debate in The Netherlands on the backlog in salary for educational staff in schools. An important argument in this discussion was that the research on the weight of jobs showed educational staff earned 10 to 20% less than civil servants with a job of comparable weight. For the salary system of the government the correction for this backlog of 10 to 20% would probably mean the jobs of educational staff would have to be placed in a higher scale.

5.2.3 *Job analysis and new technology*

Through the introduction of new technology and more particularly the use of computers, the nature of work changes. In general a shift can be noted from physical to mental (cognitive) work (see Chapter 17 in this handbook). This applies to manufacturing (computerized process control) and offices (computerized information systems) alike. Ekkers, Brouwers, Pasmooij, and De Vlaming (1980) draw the conclusion that interactive computer use has now become an integral part of the jobs of many people who did not previously have any direct contact with computers. Card, Moran, and Newell (1983) believe this implies a major change. They say there is a fundamental difference between operating machines or devices and the interactive use of computers. Operating machines or devices requires a limited number of operational controls with which people can react to the signals that indicate the status of the process or tool. However, in the interactive use of computers there is an entirely different kind of communication between man and machine. Both the man and the machine can interrupt communication, ask questions and redirect communication in different phases of interaction (see Card et al., 1983). The phenomenon is also observed by Hollnagel and Woods (1983). These authors speak of cognitive systems engineering, i.e. an approach in which an attempt is made to design man/machine (computer) systems from the perspective of cognitive processes.

Regarding the task characteristics that are of influence on the behaviour of task performers (see Chapter 6), a special position is held by the task characteristic "feedback" in the case of man/computer interaction. Communication between people and computers is severely impeded if people do not receive proper information on the (cognitive) actions taken by the computer during communication (see Buchanan & Boddy, 1983; Roe, 1988). Jacoby, Marzursky, Troutman, and Kuss (1984) distinguish two types of feedback:

results feedback and diagnostic feedback. The first type of feedback gives information about the accuracy or correctness of a (human) response. Diagnostic feedback refers to the informational value of the information. Jacoby et al. (1984) state that results feedback is far less usable than diagnostic feedback if we are dealing with cognitive (in contrast to motoric) tasks. It is clear from these considerations that the translucence of the computer's actions is of vital importance for smooth communication in interactive computer use.

From the perspective of task and job analysis, the most striking characteristic of new technology is that there is a shift from observable to non-observable behaviour of the task performer. This shift is important for the development of training programmes (Verhoef, 1991) and the design of man/machine interfaces (see Roe, 1988). As for the conceptual basis for task analysis, this means that methods from the category behaviour description are less relevant, because the emphasis is on observable rather than non-observable behaviour. Existing methods and instruments, like the PAQ (McCormick et al., 1972) or the AET (Rohmert & Landau, 1979) have therefore become less usable.

The behaviour requirements approach (see section 2 of this chapter) is aimed at the mental processes between stimulus and response and thus is more suitable in principle. Fleishman and Quaintance (1984) discuss among others the task strategies approach of Miller. In this method 24 different cognitive process functions are distinguished (e.g. short-term memory), which sometimes partially overlap. For each of the 24 process functions an indication is given of which task strategies can be followed, to bring about an effective and efficient task execution. Fleishman and Quaintance (1984) believe that this approach can be useful for systems design.

Besides this, they give an example of the development of training programmes based on the 24 process functions, for several tasks in which the cognitive aspects of task execution are dominant.

Another approach, based on a model of people as information processing systems, was brought forward by some Danish researchers (Hollnagel, Pederson, & Rasmussen, 1981; Rasmussen, 1983). This approach is focused on a distinction between various levels of information processing. Rasmussen (1983) works with three levels of information processing: skill-based (use of fixed routines), rule-based (use of a repertory of fixed rules for known situations) and knowledge-based (use of strategies for unforeseen situations, in which argumentations for cause and effect relations are (implicitly) applied). The model was applied by Hollnagel et al. (1981), for example, in studies concerning high risk-systems like nuclear power stations. The key question was whether operational errors made by operators in nuclear power stations could be traced back to skill-based, rule-based or knowledge-based levels of information processing. Based on the results from such analyses, training programmes were developed that focused on the level of information processing that corresponded to certain operational errors.

An approach related to Rasmussen's approach (1983) is the 'Handlungstheorie" of the German researcher Hacker (1986). In this theory various psychological regulation levels are distinguished as well. Hacker's theory has spread into Europe (see Roe, 1988; Roe and Zijlstra, 1991).

Another way of gaining information about the non-observable behaviour of task performers is by making use of verbatim protocols of the task performer themselves. Leplat and Hoc (1981) note a rise in the use of the verbatim protocol method, at least in some European countries, especially aimed at the analysis of tasks in which the cognitive component is important. Verbatim protocols can be used by having the task performer think aloud during the execution of the task. Alternatively, this can be done afterwards (subsequent verbatim protocolling). However, Leplat and Hoc (1981) point out that the validity of the latter method (subsequent) is not without problems. The question of validity is important as it appears from research (Hoc & Leplat, 1983) that differences can exist between the cognitive processes during the execution of a task and the verbatim protocols of the task performer.

Other researchers have also made use of the method of verbatim protocols for task analysis. Drury (1983), for instance, studied the task of stock market analysts. Extremely complex diagrams were constructed based on the results from which many suggestions could be deduced for task design. Card et al. (1983) used the verbatim protocol method combined with video recordings in the study of man/machine interaction. The verbatim protocols provided very useful information about the mental breaks and the phased structure of task execution. Hollnagel et al. (1981) advocate the use of data from different sources of information, like training simulators, research simulators and interviews with operators, in their study of operator behaviour in nuclear power stations.

The introduction of new technology has led to a change in the type of skills necessary to successfully go about one's tasks. As a result, there is a need for methods of task and job analysis that have a greater focus on the underlying cognitive processes during task execution than is present in traditional instruments, like the PAQ or the AET. Though several approaches have been developed, as described, there are still many questions regarding the reliability and validity that have not yet been answered.

6 CONCLUSION

In this chapter a general overview has been given of the role and the importance of job analysis, with a strong emphasis on applications in the field of personnel selection.

One remarkable observation is that job analysis would appear to be an indispensable part of systems and procedures (selection, appraisal, job evaluation, etc.) in many fields of personnel management on the one hand, but that on the other it is not often applied systematically or professionally and scientifically in actual practice. Various explanations can be given for this, like the labour-intensive nature of many methods, the lack of validity and/or reliability, and the prevalence of practical and political viewpoints.

Many methods are available in which specific areas of application (selection, job evaluation, etc.) have their own specific requirements. Obviously the multipurpose nature of existing methods (PAQ, AET, etc.) is often a lot more restricted than the authors had intended it to be. In short, job analysis is a complex subject, in which many conceptual questions have yet to be answered.

Besides the classic applications of job analysis, new questions have arisen in practice. From the context of new technology, the key is to have methods for cognitive task analysis and the allocation of tasks to people and the computer. Next to this, we find that work by individuals more and more is done as part of a group task rather than as an individual task, making job and task analysis at the level of group tasks increasingly important. Thus, many unanswered questions still exist in the field of job and task analysis for work and organization psychologists.

REFERENCES

Algera, J.A. (1987). Job and task analysis. In B.M. Bass, & P.J.D Drenth (Eds.), *Advances in organizational psychology: An international review*. Newbury Park, CA: Sage.

Algera, J.A. (1989). Taakkenmerken. In P.J.D. Drenth, Hk. Thierry, & Ch.J. de Wolff (Eds.), *Nieuw handboek arbeids-en organisatiepsychologie*, 2.2, (pp. 1–30). Deventer: Van Loghum Slaterus.

Algera, J.A. (1991). Arbeidsanalyse ten behoeve van motivatie en satisfactie. In J.A. Algera (Ed.), *Analyse van arbeid vanuit verschillende perspectieven*, (pp. 143–177). Amsterdam/Lisse: Swets & Zeitlinger.

Arvey, R.D., Davis, G.A., McGowen, S.L., & Dipboye, R.L. (1982). Potential sources of bias in job analytical processes. *Academy of Management Journal*, *25*(3), 618–629.

Ash, R.A. (1988). Job analysis in the world of work. In S. Gael, (Ed.), *The job analysis handbook for business, industry and government* (pp. 3–13). New York: Wiley.

Borman, W.C. (1974). The rating of individuals in organizations: An alternate approach. *Organizational Behavior and Human Performance*, *12*, 105–124.

Bosch, J. & Samren, J. (1991). Functie-analyse voor personeelsselectie. *Gids voor Personeelsmanagement*, *3*, 44–47.

Bovenschen, P., & Esser, H. (1982). *Invloed van automatisering op het gebruik van kundigheden*, (Doctoral thesis), Psychologisch Laboratorium, Amsterdam.

Buchanan, D.A., & Boddy, D. (1983). Advanced technology and the quality of working life: The effects of computerized controls on biscuit-making operators. *Journal of Occupational Psychology*, *56*, 109–119.

Card, K., Moran, T.P., & Newell, A. (1983). *The psychology of human-computer interaction*. Hillsdale, NJ: Lawrence Erlbaum Associates Inc.

Cornelius III, E.T., & Lyness, K.S. (1980). A comparison of holistic and decomposed judgement strategies in job analysis by job incumbents. *Journal of Applied Psychology*, *65*(2), 155–163.

Cornelius III, E.T., Carron, T.J., & Collins, M.N. (1979). Job analysis models and job classification. *Personnel Psychology*, *32*, 693–708.

Cornelius III, E.T., Schmidt, F.L., & Carron, Th.J. (1984). Job classification approaches and the implementation of validity generalization results. *Personnel Psychology*, *37*(2), 247–261.

Cunningham, J.W., Boese, R.R., Neeb, R.W., & Pass, J.J. (1983). Systematically derived work dimensions: Factor analysis of the occupational analysis inventory. *Journal of Applied Psychology*, *68*, 232–252.

DeNisi, A.S., Cornelius III, E.T., & Blencoe, A.G. (1987). Further investigation of common knowledge effects on job analysis ratings. *Journal of Applied Psychology*, *72(2), 262–268.*

Dcsmond, R.E., & Weiss, D.J. (1973). Superior estimation of abilities required in jobs. *Journal of Vocational Behavior*, *7*, 13–29.

Desmond, R.E., & Weiss, D.J. (1975). Worker estimation of ability requirements of their jobs. *Journal of Vocational Behavior*, *7*, 13–29.

Drury, C.G. (1983). Task analysis methods in industry. *Applied Ergonomics*, *14*(1), 19–28.

Dunnette, M.D. (1976). Aptitudes, abilities, and skills. In M.D. Dunnette (Ed.), *Handbook of industrial and organizational psychology*, 473–520. Chicago: Rand McNally.

Ekkers, C.L., Brouwers, A.A.F., Pasmooij, C.K., & Vlaming, P.M. de (1980). *Menselijke stuur-en regeltaken* (Human control tasks). Leiden: NIPG/TNO.

Elshout, J.J., Boselie, F.A.J.M., Berg, J.J. van den, Boerlijst, G.J. & Schaake, B. (1973). De validatie van een testbatterij voor de selectie van wetenschappelijke onderzoekers. In P.J.D. Drenth, P.J. Willems, & Ch.J. de Wolff (Eds.), *Arbeids-en Organisatiepsychologie* (pp. 39–48). Deventer: Kluwer.

Flanagan, J.C. (1954). The critical incidents technique. *Psychological Bulletin*, *51*, 327–358.

Fleishman, E.A., & Quintance, M.K. (1984). *Taxonomies of human performance*. Orlando: Academic Press.

Freyd, M. (1923). Measurement in vocational selection: An outline of a research procedure. *Journal of Personnel Research*, *2*, 215–249, 377–385.

Frieling, E. (1975). *Psychologische Arbeitsanalyse*. Stuttgart: Kohlhammer.

Frieling, E., & Hoyos, C.G. (1978). *Fragebogen zur arbeitsanalyse* (FAA). Bern: Hans Huber.

Gael, S. (Ed.) (1988). *The job analysis handbook for business, industry, and government* (Vols. I & II). New York: Wiley.

Greuter, M.A.M. (1991). Arbeidsanalyse ten behoeve van personeelsselectie. In J.A. Algera, (Ed.), *Analyse van arbeid vanuit verschillende perspectieven* (pp. 17–60). Amsterdam/Lisse: Swets & Zeitlinger.

Greuter, M.A.M., & Algera, J.A. (1989). Criterion development and job analysis. In P. Herriot (Ed.), *Assessment and selection in organizations*, Chichester, UK: John Wiley.

Guilford, J.P: (1954). *Psychometric methods*. New York: McGraw-Hill.

Hacker, W. (1986). *Arbeitspsychologie-psychische regulation von arbeitstatigkeiten*. Berlin: VEB Deutscher Verlag der Wissenschaften.

Hoc, J.M., & Leplat, J. (1983). Evaluation of different modilities of verbalization in a sorting task. *International Journal of Man-Machine Studies*, *18*, 283–306.

Hollnagel, E., Pederson, O.M., & Rasmussen, J. (1981). *Notes on human performance analysis*. Roskilde: Riso National Laboratory.

Hollnagel, E., & Woods, D.D. (1983). Cognitive systems engineering: New wine in new bottles. *International Journal of Man-Machine Studies*, *18*, 583–600.

Jacoby, J., Marzursky, D., Troutman, T., & Kuss, A. (1984). When feedback is ignored: Disutility of outcome feedback. *Journal of Applied Psychology*, *69*, 531–545.

Jones, A.P., Main, D.S., Butter, M.C., & Johnson, L.A. (1982). Narrative job descriptions as potential sources of job analysis ratings. *Personnel Psychology*, *35*, 813–828.

Latham, G.P., Fay, C., & Saari, L.M. (1980). BOS, BES and baloney: raising kane with Bernardin. *Personnel Psychology*, *65*(4), 422–427.

Latham, G.P., & Wexley, K.N. (1981). *Increasing productivity through performance appraisal*. Reading, MA: Addison-Wesley.

Leplat, J., & Hoc, J.M. (1981). Subsequent verbalization in the study of cognitive processes. *Ergonomics*, *24*, 743–755.

Levine, E.L. (1983). *Everything you always wanted to know about job analysis*. Tampa, FL: Mariner.

Levine, E.L., Thomas, J.N., & Sistrunk, F. (1988). Selecting a job analysis approach. In S. Gael (Ed.), *The job analysis handbook for business, industry and government* (pp. 339–352). New York: Wiley.

Lopez, F.M. (1986). *The threshold traits analysis*. Port Washington, NY: Lopez & Associates.

Lopez, M. (1988). Threshold traits analysis system. In S. Gael (Ed.), *The Job Analysis Handbook for business, industry and government* (pp. 880–901). New York: Wiley.

Madigan, R.M. (1985). Comparable worth judgments: A measurement properties analysis. *Journal of Applied Psychology*, *70*, 137–147.

McCormick, E.J. (1976). Job and task analysis. In M.D. Dunnette (Ed.) *Handbook of industrial and organizational psychology* (pp. 651–696). Chicago: Rand McNally.

McCormick, E.J., Jeanneret, P.R., & Mecham, R.C. (1972). A study of job characteristics and job dimensions as based on the Position Analysis Questionnaire. *Journal of Applied Psychology*, *56*, 347–368.

Miller, R.B. (1973). Development of a taxonomy of human performance: Design of a systems task vocabulary. *JSAS Catalog of Selected Documents in Psychology*, *3*, 29–30 (Ms No. 327).

Ministerie van Sociale Zaken en Werkgelegenheid (1984). *Werving en selectie in 51 Nederlandse arbeidsorganisaties*. Den Haag.

Pannone, R.D. (1984). Predicting test performance: A content valid approach to screening applicants. *Personnel Psychology*, *37*(3), 507–515.

Patrick, J., & Moore, A.K. (1985). Development and reliability of a job analysis technique. *Journal of Occupational Psychology*, *58*, 149–158.

Pearlman, K. (1980). Job families: A review and discussion of their implications for personnel selection. *Psychology Bulletin*, *87*, 1–28.

Pearlman, K., Schmidt, F.L., & Hunter, J.E. (1980). Validity generalization results for tests used to predict job proficiency and training success in clerical occupations. *Journal of Applied Psychology*, *65*, 373–406.

Pearn, M. & Kandola, R. (1988). Job analysis, a practical guide for managers. London: Institute of Personnel Management.

Rasmussen, J. (1983). Skills, rules and knowledge: Signals, signs and symbols and other distinctions in human performance. *IEEE Transactions on Systems, Man and Cybernetics*, *13*, 257–266.

Ridderbos, A. (1992). *Selection by simulation: A work sample approach to the selection of process operators*. Ph thesis. Eindhoven: Technische Universiteit Eindhoven.

Roe, R.A. (1988). Acting systems design: An action theoretical approach to the design of man-computer systems. In V. de Keyser, T. Quale, B. Wilpert, & S.A.R. Quintanilla (Eds.), *The meaning of work and technological options*. Chichester: Wiley.

Roe, R.A., & Zijlstra, R.F.H. (1991). Arbeidsanalyse ten behoeve van (her)ontwerp van functies: Een handelingstheoretische invalshoek. In: J.A. Algera (Ed.), *Analyse van arbeid vanuit verschillende perspectieven* (pp. 143–177). Amsterdam/Lisse: Swets & Zeitlinger.

Rohmert, W., & Landau, K. (1979). *Das Arbeitswissenschaftliche Erhebungsverfahren zur Tätigkeitsanalyse (AET)*. Bern-Stuttgart-Wien: Verlag Hans Huber (English edition published 1983 by Taylor & Francis, London.)

Ryan, A.M., & Sackett, P.R. (1987). A survey of individual assessment practices by I/O psychologists. *Personnel Psychology*, *40*, 455–487.

Saks, A.M., & Cronshaw, S.F. (1990). A process investigation of realistic job previews: Mediating variables and channels of communication. *Journal of Organizational Behavior*, *11*, 221–236.

Saville & Holdsworth Ltd. (1989). *Work Profiling System (WPS)*. London: Saville & Holdsworth Ltd.

Scheltens, R. (1978). *Vragenlijst voor Functie-analyse*. Verslag van een onderzoek onder 1350 PTT-ers. PTT, SWI-1, rapport 590/2.

Schmidt, F.L., & Hunter, J.E. (1977). Development of a general solution to the problem of validity generalization. *Journal of Applied Psychology*, *62*, 529–540.

Schmidt, F.L., & Hunter, J.E. (1981). Old theories and new research findings. *American Psychologist*, *36*(10), 1128–1137.

Seegers, J.J.J.L. (1989). Assessment centres for identifying long-term potential and for self-development. In P. Herriot (Ed.). *Assessment and selection in organizations* (pp. 745–771). Chichester: Wiley.

Simmelink, J.T. (1979). *De VFA: Ter afsluiting. Onderzoek naar de waarde van de Vragenlijst voor Functie-analyse*. Den Haag: PTT.

Smit-Voskuijl, O.F. (1992). Mogelijke bronnen van vertekening bij functie-analyse. *Gedrag en Organisatie*, *5*(1), 11–37.

Smith, J.E., & Hakel, M.D. (1979). Convergence among data source, response bias, and reliability of a structured job analysis questionnaire. *Personnel Psychology*, *32*, 677–692.

Thierry, H., & Jong, J.R. de (1991). Arbeidsanalyse ten behoeve van beloning. In J.A. Algera (Ed.), *Analyse van arbeid vanuit verschillende perspectieven*, (pp. 99–141), Amsterdam: Swets & Zeitlinger.

Verhoef, L.W.M. (1991). Arbeidsanalyse ten behoeve van training van cognitieve vaardigheden. In J. A. Algera (Ed.), *Analyse van arbeid vanuit verschillende perspectieven* (pp. 61–97), Amsterdam: Swets & Zeitlinger.

Wanous, J.P. (1980). *Organizational entry: Recruitment, selection and socialization of newcomers*. Reading, MA: Addison-Wesley.

Wernimont, P.F., & Campbell, J.P. (1968). Signs, samples and criteria. *Journal of Applied Psychology*, *52*, 372–376.

Wiegersma, S. (1958). Gezichtspunten en factoren in de genormaliseerde werkclassificatie. *Mens en Onderneming*, *12*, 200–208.

Wolff, C.J. de, & Schopman-Geurts van Kessel, J.G. (1992). The recruitment and selection of hospital medical consultants. *Work & Stress*, *6*(3), 327–338.

8

Job Evaluation

Henk Thierry and John R. de Jong

1 INTRODUCTION

In many Dutch work organizations—private industries as well as government institutions—systems of job evaluation (JE) are used for the majority of personnel. These systems are often seen as ways of establishing salary levels for a variety of different jobs. This qualification is understandable, but the core of job evaluation lies in the preceding procedures. Job evaluation scrutinizes the activities involved in a job and the work conditions usually associated with it. Usually, jobs are described first. These are then analysed in terms of particular characteristics (for example, the level of knowledge required) and during the process of grading, a value is given to each characteristic. Finally, jobs are ordered and categorized into groups and classes on the basis of their total value. Eventually salaries for each salary class are negotiated by employers, federations and unions of employees. Salary surveys can play a useful role in this process by showing the average salary paid and the distribution of salaries within a particular sector or group of jobs. In countries where *Collective Labour Agreements* apply, these agreements usually specify the starting and end salary in each class.

The concept of "job" has a specific meaning in this context. It refers to "all the tasks that must be performed by an employee, the responsibility he or she bears and the working conditions associated with the job" (De Jong, Gaillard, & Kamp, 1977; Voskuijl, 1996). The content an employee gives to a job and the way he or she actually carries it out are not taken into consideration. Job evaluation eventually determines the salary *class* of a job. In Chapter 12, Volume 4 of this Handbook, factors that influence *individual* fixed and variable incomes are gone into in more detail. These include such factors as experience, performance (appraisal) and irregular working hours. It is important to note here that a substantial number of companies and institutions in various countries express the (yearly) appraisal of individual performance in terms of the salary scale appropriate to that employee's job. This may imply that in addition to the annual "increment" (experience bonus), there is also an extra increase in the form of a "step" up the salary scale. This helps explain why many employees still see job evaluation as a way of determining individual salaries.

In this chapter we will first look at why job evaluation has developed in the way it has, and consider a few often-used systems of JE. In Section 3 we discuss the use of job evaluation and, after examining the procedures that usually accompany it, we will consider whether the data that becomes available during the course of JE and which is used to establish appropriate rates of remuneration can be used in other ways as well. Section 4 gives an overview of recent research and also draws on older research findings that have particular relevance to the reliability and validity of JE. Finally, we conclude by looking into the future in an attempt to identify trends that may emerge.

2 APPLYING JE

2.1 Purpose of JE

Terms such as "trained", "experienced", and "untrained" do have a familiar ring. They recall a time when industrial labour appeared less differentiated and specialized. This was one reason why a worker's *skills* could be used as an unambiguous measure of remuneration.

There are very few companies that maintain this tripartite division today. First, labour is extremely differentiated. This is a continuing trend and has led to a growing desire for greater refinement in classification. Second, it is also clear that workers' skills (and degree of training) are not necessarily relevant for all the work they are expected to do or for the conditions under which they work (for example, physically heavy work in difficult or risky conditions). Both these factors have led to a shift in emphasis: criteria for a fair equitable remuneration should no longer depend on a worker's qualifications but on the *demands of each job*.

Another phenomenon has also affected this change. In large work organizations it had become increasingly difficult to establish whether the relationship between wages and salaries[1] were *appropriate*. An instrument was needed that was capable of evaluating jobs systematically or—as is sometimes said—objectively. Here we encounter the criterion "internal equity": *inside* a company the relationship between salaries should be fair. In this way, the United States' Civil Service Commission introduced one of the earliest forms of JE in 1871 and in 1909 the city of Chicago also adopted JE.

Over the course of time different methods of job evaluation have been developed. The so-called *point system*, dating from 1925, eventually emerged as the one most often used. A well-known example of such a system was that of the American National Electrical Manufacturers Association. By 1945 this system had been adopted by some 1200 to 1500 companies (Smith & Murphy, 1946). Table 8.1 shows the job characteristics used in this method and an accompanying description gives job requirements and the corresponding number of points. Five points, for example, were awarded for work involving a relatively light mental or visual load: "Limited mental load and sporadic visual attention because the work is almost completely automated or because it only needs attention from time to time". The maximum of 25 points was awarded for work requiring "Concentrated attention and precise observation normally involving the determination, planning and preparation of extremely complex activities" (Smith & Murphy, 1946).

These were somewhat global specifications. Therefore, in the companies concerned, the characteristics of a number of "*key jobs*" were described in fairly great detail together with the number of points that should be awarded. "Key jobs" are jobs that differ considerably from one another, whose activities are often performed. This information was intended as a reference that would allow comparisons to be made when other jobs were being analysed (we will briefly return to the use of "key jobs"—sometimes also called exemplary jobs—in Section 3). Finally, a table was constructed showing the total number of points and the corresponding wage or *salary class*.

The JE system was only used on a comparatively small scale in The Netherlands and in other parts of Europe before the mid-1930s. During the Second World War it attracted attention and after 1945 there was a growing interest in JE in The Netherlands. A wide range of systems were developed; some were designed for individual companies, others for a particular branch of industry. Most of these systems did not survive long and in the early 1950s they were replaced by two systems that had come to be very widely used: the "*Normalized Method of Work Classification*" (GM) and the "*Metal Method*". Typically, these

TABLE 8.1

Characteristics and points in the National Electrical Manufacturers Association's system.

Characteristics	*Steps*				
Skills					
Education	14	28	42	56	70
Experience	22	44	66	88	110
Initiative and innovativeness	14	28	42	56	70
Work load					
Physical load	10	20	30	40	50
Mental/visual load	5	10	15	20	25
Responsibility					
For company assets or processes	5	10	15	20	25
For materials or product	5	10	15	20	25
For the safety of others	5	10	15	20	25
For the work of others	5	10	15	20	25
Working conditions					
Working conditions	10	20	30	40	50
Danger	5	10	15	20	25

were both *point systems* in which exemplary jobs (key jobs) played an important role. They were used almost exclusively for manual jobs and were unsatisfactory for clerical, managerial or other functions.

The GM was published in 1952 and was accompanied by about 100 examples of *job descriptions* and gradings from various branches of industry (exemplary jobs). It got its final form in 1959. The GM has 10 characteristics with accompanying tables to enable points to be established for every job. Each characteristic (or each associated sub-characteristic) is first graded on the basis of a job description. In most cases use is made of an 8-point scale of three steps (0–2p, 2–4p, etc.). The score derived shows the extent to which a (sub) characteristic is present in a particular job. This result is then multiplied by a weighting factor (or a weighting coefficient) which reflects the relative importance of that characteristic in the general picture. Weighting factors do not vary with the jobs to be evaluated; rather they reflect a societal evaluation of the importance of each characteristic. The appropriate wage or salary class is determined for the whole job on the basis of the total number of points awarded.

Table 8.2 shows aspects of the GM together with weighting factors. An example is included relevant to the job of "Chauffeur with extra duties".

The *Metal Method* for manual workers was introduced in 1954. It has 5 characteristics and 21 sub-characteristics. Later, an FC system (the system for clerical, technical and supervisory personnel) was implemented for white-collar workers.

The *Integral System for Job Evaluation (ISR)* and the *System for Labor Conditions (SAO)* developed from the FC. The ISF/SAO system has been in use since 1981 and is used to evaluate all jobs usually found in a company. The ISF/SAO, like the American system mentioned earlier, does not have a weighting factor; the weight of a characteristic emerges from the maximum number of points it can receive. The characteristics and sub-characteristics of ISF/SAO are shown in Table 8.3. The length and intensity of the workload is evaluated for each characteristic.

Examples of evaluations have also been compiled for the ISF/SAO in order to facilitate a uniform interpretation of the table of analysis.

Because it was thought that labour conditions should not influence job level, a separate system

TABLE 8.2

An example of how the GM calculates the total number of points for a job (a chauffeur with extra duties).

	Characteristics (aspects)	*Figures*	*Weighting factor*	*Points*
1	Knowledge (nature and degree)			
2	Independence			
3	Contact (nature and intensity)			
4	Authority (demands and circumstances)			
5	Communication and expression skills			
6	Dexterity			
7	Feeling for machinery and material			
8	Inconveniences associated with the work			
8a	Workload			
8b	Tension in posture, one type of movement			
8c	Aggravating attention			
8d	Work atmosphere			
8e	Personal risk			
9	Special demands			
10	Accident risk (chance and extent)			

was introduced to "weight" them. It was decided to analyse work conditions (and possible compensation) separately. This approach is also used by various other systems. Although the ISF/SAO was developed for the metal industry, it is also used outside this sector.

Government policy may facilitate the use of job evaluation (or, in other cases, impedes it). The first instance applies to the use of a "centralized wage control policy", which emerged in The Netherlands between 1945 and the early 1960s. According to such a policy, the government determines the level of wage increase every year. Because of a shortage of labour, each company tried to offer as high a wage as possible, and job evaluation was a condition for this. From the early 1960s to the present day increasing use has been made of JE particularly for non-manual jobs, such as office work and managerial jobs. Initially, separate systems were developed for different categories of work but later on an increasing number of integrated JE systems were designed to grade and classifying *all* jobs normally found in a work organization. The desire to "harmonize" conditions of work for "manual workers" and white-collar employees played an important role in this process (Colenbrander & Buningh, 1982; De Jong et al., 1977).

Originally there were many differences in the labour conditions of these two categories of personnel including the remuneration period (weekly wage rather than monthly salary), the rules applying to the first days of sickness, pension provisions, clothing, and so on. In the mid-1960s, there was a strong feeling that such differences could no longer be reasonably defended, especially because the pace of technical development had made the old distinction between physical and mental labour increasingly much less useful. The movement towards harmonization began earlier in The Netherlands than in most other industrial countries and led to the use of one range of *salary classes* for all company employees.

We now return to the question raised in the title to this section: the applications of JE. We have already mentioned one of these: it is used as an instrument to compare jobs in order to evaluate whether the relationship between (wages or) salaries is appropriate. This theme—the underlying relationship—is found to varying degrees in many definitions of JE. Thus De Jong et al. (1977)

TABLE 8.3

Characteristics of the Integral System for Job Evaluation (ISF) and the System for Labour Conditions (SAO).

Characteristics ISF	*Sub-characteristics*	*Values*
1. Knowledge	Job-related knowledge and experience	40–340
	Manual skills	0–75
	Expression skills	5–50
2. Complexity	Nature of work and degree of independence	40–255
3. Responsibility		5–165
4. Contact		5–125
5. Administration/Leadership	Hierarchical	10–130
	Non-hierarchical	5–90

Characteristics SAO	*Sub-characteristics*	*Values*
1. Atmosphere	Noise, vibrations	
	Weather conditions	0–22
2. Body posture		
3. Use of force		
4. Personal risk		0–18
5. Monotony		

conclude that JE is a way of helping to establish the *relative value* of particular jobs in order to determine wages or salaries. Schuler and Youngblood (1986) saw the issue as one of determining relative value within a labour organization (the so-called internal criterion). McCormick (1976), however, put the accent on the external criterion: there should be an appropriate relationship between the salaries emerging from JE and what is considered acceptable on the labour market (see also ILO, 1977; Sayles & Strauss, 1977).

A second aspect of JE is to use job evaluation data for organizational and personnel policy decisions. This involves making decisions about selection, education, training, performance appraisal, career planning and the (re)structuring of jobs. We return to the theme of the potential application of data generated by *job analysis* in more detail in Section 3.

Scholten (1979) focused attention on a third aspect. He considered it significant that in The Netherlands after 1945, although there was often a conflict of interests between government, employers' organizations and labour unions, there was, nevertheless, consensus about JE. The government wanted an instrument that could differentiate wages more precisely, because it believed increased differentiation would stimulate an increase in productivity and such an instrument was extremely appropriate for the centralized wage control policy. Employers also wanted more wage differentiation, partly because this would increase promotion possibilities. The trade union leadership saw JE as a way of ensuring that job content rather than the supply and demand of the market place would be the remuneration criterium. Furthermore, wage differentiation was appropriate in a situation of growing job differentiation and was capable of signalling when one group of employees (for example, in agriculture) lagged behind in wage development (for a more detailed account of post-war wage politics see Fase, 1980; Koopman-Iwema & Thierry, 1981). Now, Scholten (1979, 1981) suggests that JE played an important role in *controlling societal problems,* particularly as far as issues such as status and remuneration were concerned. JE was an example of regulation: with its help both management and trade unions were able to keep their employees and members in line.

A fourth aspect concerns the role of JE in the *income politics* concerning the professions in The Netherlands. This "application possibility" can be seen as a particularization of the above: it makes social problems manageable. Describing, analysing, valuing and accrediting an income norm to such professional groups as surgeons with their own practice, for example, was made possible by selecting a comparable job in government service. We will return to this topic again in Section 3.

More and more countries are using JE in connection with *equal pay for men and women* doing jobs of comparable value. In this fifth use—referred to in the Anglo-American part of the world as "*comparable worth*" or "equal opportunities"—JE can play a role if a female member of staff (or group of employees) complains her salary is lower than that of men in comparable jobs. This theme is also discussed in more detail in Section 3.

A sixth use of JE has been identified by Katz and Kahn (1978) among others. *Job descriptions*, they observe, are one way a work organization can communicate its values to its personnel and in doing so help ensure more predictable behaviour. JE has a *socialization role* here and helps increase the *predictability* of work behaviour.

It is possible to summarize this overview by suggesting that the objectives of JE involve on the one hand setting *wage or salary relationships* within an institution or company. Once access has been acquired to the data generated by developing and applying JE, it may become possible to use it in another way, for example, to solve staffing and organizational problems. This process, however, does not work the other way round: if, for example, a system to appraise job performance has to be established in a company or career planning has to be improved, these measures are usually not tailored to introducing a JE system. There are cheaper, more appropriate (and often better) ways available.

On the other hand, The Netherlands is an example of a country that uses JE data for other "purposes" as well. Formulated in sociological terms, JE is embedded in an "institutional framework": JE is instrumental in preventing social "conflicts" (or, if they occur, in keeping them in line). JE is applied to a greater extent in The Netherlands than probably in any other country. Estimations are that up to around 70% of all salaries are directly or indirectly determined through JE. Of course, in some sectors JE is applied more (e.g. the service industry) than in other sectors. Although quite a variety of JE systems is in use, some five or six systems are very dominant (e.g. Poels, 1996).

2.2 Types of JE system

In this section we begin by classifying JE systems and then go on to examine a few types in more detail. The first criterion refers to the *number of job characteristics to be evaluated*. Differentiations are:

1a. Various characteristics (see GM, for example).
1b. One characteristic (see the Jaques time-span, for example).
1c. The whole job.

The second criterion refers to *the method of grading:*

2a. Rank ordering.
2b. Setting various categories or classes (remember the term "work classification").
2c. Assigning points using a scale of one or more dimensions.

Each JE system can be "coded" in this way. The designation for the *point system* is 1a/2c, for example. We have characterized the methods known to us in Figure 8.1.

More or less detailed information on the structure and nature of many JE systems can be found in McCormick (1976); De Jong et al. (1977); ILO (1977); Wing Easton (1980); Scholten (1981); Colenbrander and Buningh (1982); Hazekamp, Hisken and Hoogstad (1985); Spector, Brannick, and Coovert (1989); Harvey (1991); Poels (1996). Here we will discuss three somewhat "unusual" methods in more detail. Job classification (as used

FIGURE 8.1

		2. Way of grading		
		2a. Ranking of jobs	**2b.** Jobs divided into classes	**2c.** Scale or scheme
1. Assessed characteristics or job as a whole	**1a.** Various characteristics	**1a/2a.** Ranking per characteristic (factor comparison)	**1a/2b.**	**1a/2c.** Points given per characteristic (point method)
	1b. One characteristic	**1b/2a.**	**1b/2b.** Decision band method (Paterson)	**1b/2c.** Time-span method (Jacques)
	1c. Job as a whole	**1c/2a.** Ranking of jobs	**1c/2b.** Job classification	**1c/2c.**

Methods of job evaluation.

by, for example, the government), time-span (Jaques) and decision band (Paterson).

From Figure 8.1 it appears that job classification includes assigning jobs to pre-defined classes on the basis of an evaluation of the jobs in their totality. This is a method used in the Dutch civil service up to and including the rank of director general. The so-called "reasoning by comparison" estimate has six main categories and between three to seven levels. These overlap each other to some extent. The "calculation" involves knowledge required, communication skills and the degree of responsibility associated with the job. In higher jobs such factors as the complexity of problems, the management input and possible stress also become relevant.

Jaques' *time-span method* was developed during the course of his long association with the Glacier Metal Company in London (see Jaques, 1956, 1961 and 1964). Jaques believed that during wage negotiations objectives and logical arguments were more apparent than real. In his view, emotional considerations played a major role. The problem with the job evaluation systems of that time was that non-comparable and non-quantifiable criteria were used for different jobs. Jaques observed that the time factor played a critical role as far as an individual's job and salary level was concerned. For example, the higher the job level, the longer the period over which a wage/salary is paid (hour/week/month), the longer the working-in period and the longer the period of notice given with dismissal. This observation lies at the core of the measurement system Jaques developed to evaluate job level: responsibility. In this respect his identification of two different types of task-activities within each rank is important. Each task involves:

1. "Discretionary content": the part of a task in which an employee must act according to his or her own judgement and choice;
2. "Prescribed limits": the written and unwritten rules, signals and customs, etc. which the job-holder must use as his or her guide.

These prescribe the limits within which the job-holder can use his or her own insights to make decisions.

The higher the job level, the more extensive the discretionary content. Typical of this responsibility is the maximum time-span in which the job holder acts according to his or her own insight before his or her boss can evaluate the quality of these actions. A *job analysis* shows that the maximum *time-span* for lower-skilled and clerical work is between one hour and one month, for example. For higher level jobs it can be two years or more. In this connection, Jaques developed a method for analysing salary differentials within a company and for the progress of an employee's salary over a number of years.

The instrument constructed by Jaques is a good example of a multi-purpose system, given that it can also be applied in such areas as career and staff planning (see Section 3). Comparative research on the subject has been carried out by Kvålseth and Crosmann (1974), Wijnberg (1965), Hazekamp (1966; 1970), Atchison and French (1967), Goodman (1967), and Richardson (1971).

Jaques contributed other significant theoretical assumptions. He believed, for example, that each individual is *unconsciously* aware of his or her job-level capacity, the job level he or she actually occupies and what constitutes a fair wage. Under certain conditions these beliefs can be made "*conscious*". For a more detailed discussion we direct our readers to the literature on the subject (see, for example, critical discussions such as Thierry, 1969).

Paterson, like Jaques, also concluded that one characteristic could become the basis for evaluating jobs of all types and at a variety of levels. For him this characteristic is *decision making*. In his view it is possible to differentiate six decision bands. These differ from each other essentially in both type and level of decision. The highest band (E) is characterized by the policy decisions of top management; band (C) involves the interpretation of these decisions at middle-management level within the boundaries set by the higher band (D); band (A)—the second to lowest level—involves "automatic" decisions concerning the when, how and where of process operationalization and implementation. Each band—except the lowest (O)—also consists of two levels in which the higher level coordinates the activities of the lower level. In this way a hierarchical structure of authority is built up consisting of 11 levels. Sub-levels can also be identified (for more detailed discussion see Paterson, 1972, 1981). In The Netherlands this method is only used in a very small number of organizations. Many more examples can be found in England, Canada and South Africa, for example. There is, however, very little research on this issue.

3 USES OF JE

3.1 From *job description* to job evaluation

In the previous section we gave a brief description of a frequently followed procedure in connection with the GM. Here we look in more detail at the different stages involved in this procedure (see Colenbrander & Buningh, 1982; De Jong et al., 1977; Harvey, 1991; Hazekamp et al., 1985; Livy, 1975; McCormick, 1976; Scholten, 1981; Schuler & Youngblood, 1986; Spector et al., 1989; Wing Easton, 1980). There can be more or less radical deviations from this procedure in practice. These deviations depend, however, on the JE system involved and include such aspects as job classification, the views of the system holder (often a consultancy firm), the industrial sector, local customs, experience gained in foreign branches, and guidelines from a headquarters located elsewhere.

As we have already mentioned, use is often made of exemplary or *key jobs*. If these are not readily available, the company concerned must select them in such a way that the jobs to be described and evaluated can be compared satisfactorily.

The first stage is to *describe* the job, and here the following distinctions are usually made:

- Defining the name of the job, the department concerned, the objective of the job and its place in the organization (in relation to higher jobs, jobs at the same level and lower jobs).
- Describing sub-tasks, contacts and responsibilities, etc.
- Describing these further—in most cases according to the "characteristics" of the system being applied.

Generally speaking, use is made of a questionnaire and/or of interviews with job-holders and their bosses. Sometimes colleagues and subordinates are also involved. Because *job description* is of critical importance for the ultimate evaluation, many types of conflicts and tensions can arise. The reasons for this can often be found in events in the recent past: for example, a job has gradually changed in content but this has not been adequately taken into account in the way the job has been evaluated. Problems associated with reorganizations and mergers also have the tendency to crop up when job descriptions are being made.

Objections to proposed job descriptions can sometimes be traced to the way information was assembled. Thus, it is often helpful to recommend that observation, a diary kept by the job-holder, or the "critical incident" technique (we will return to this later) be used next to or instead of questionnaires and interviews. Another reason for resistance can be the decision to select a detailed rather than a more global job description. The former is more encompassing, although in practice it becomes quickly outdated. Global job descriptions, on the other hand, remain valid longer but are less precise. As changes in technology are occurring more frequently—and, as a consequence, job requirements are redefined time and again—short global descriptions of a normative nature increasingly apply to key jobs. Often, it is held that a short profile suffices for all other jobs (see also Cascio, 1995). The question of whether the information collected on the route from description to classification will be used for other purposes (for example, performance appraisal) can also cause tension. Because of these (potential) sources of conflict, the stage of *job description* can, in practice, prove to be one of the weakest links in the JE cycle.

The second stage is *job analysis*. In principle there are various instruments available for this (see, for example, Harvey, 1991; Schuler & Youngblood, 1986; Spector et al., 1989; Chapter 7 of this volume). Such techniques analyse jobs in terms of the activities they involve, such as drilling, cleaning, re-stocking stores, and so on. Some examples are:

- Functional Job Analysis (FJA) (US Department of Labor, 1972) developed by the United States Training & Employment Service (USTES). This instrument is the basis of the widely recognized Directory of Occupational Titles. Applying the FJA requires considerable training (Fine & Wiley, 1971).
- Management Position Description Questionnaire (Tornow & Pinto, 1976). A checklist of 197 items.
- Executive Position Description Questionnaire (Hemphill, 1960).
- Work Profiling System (Saville & Holdsworth, 1989).

Various other methods are "worker oriented"; that is to say they describe jobs in terms of required work behaviours (like observing, acting, combining data). These methods include:

- Position Analysis Questionnaire (PAQ) (McCormick, Jeanneret, & Mecham, 1969). The PAQ consists of 187 elements. These can be evaluated using six scales. Much research has been done on this list, e.g. in The Netherlands. Also, a German version has been developed (the FAA: Frieling, Kannheiser, & Hoyos, 1973; Hoyos, Graf, & Frieling, 1977; and the AET: Landau & Rohmert, 1989).
- Critical Incident Technique (KIT): for each job various events or incidents are collected that show very effective or very ineffective performance. In addition, causes, circumstances and consequences that recur are studied as well as the extent to which a job-holder has the situation under control. The frequency with which these incidents occur are then registered, together with the competences required to deal with them. These are then grouped on particular dimensions along which it is possible to arrive at a job description. With the help of such details—and in situations where performance appraisal is necessary—Behavioural Anchored Rating Scales (BARS) and Behaviour Observation Scales (BOS) can be constructed (see Chapter 4).
- Elaborated Critical Incident Technique: the difference between this technique and KIT is that not only is extremely (in)effective performance studied, but also the reasons for, circumstances and consequences of "ordinary" average performance.

We have spent some time on this section for two

reasons. First, these instruments can probably strengthen JE (we return to this in Section 4). In the much-used *point system*, analysis and grading involve establishing the extent to which each characteristic of a system is found in a job, subsequent to which a total is set. In the older systems grades were multiplied by the weighting factor per characteristic. In most modern systems the weighting factors have already been worked into the grading. The total number of points awarded to a job are eventually calculated using simple addition. Second, when these particular systems are referred to in the literature, mention is also made of possible multi-purpose applications (see also Section 3.3).

After the point total for the job has been calculated, the rank order for a number of "evaluated" jobs is established. Independent judges are frequently involved here. These results are then compared with the results of the point total. If there are no discrepancies, then the job group or the job class is considered defined. Wage negotiation between the employer and the trade union can then establish the appropriate wage or *salary class*.

3.2 Parties involved

Many interest groups are involved in the preparation and implementation of JE, or in introducing changes in the way it is applied. In addition to the job-holders concerned, there is the Works Council, as well as management, the personnel and organization department, trade unions, employers' federations and often a consultancy agency.

Resistance and objections characterize the process of preparing, implementing and applying JE because of the many different interests and interest groups that can become involved. Committees are usually set up either to deal with these problems directly, or to prevent them. In practice, the committees themselves also vary considerably in such matters as composition and degree of authority. Among other things it is important to establish an advisory committee. The work of such a committee involves coordinating various tasks (for which separate committees may have been established) and monitoring progress in general. The committee's first task may well be to select a JE system from those available, unless there is a particular system for the sector concerned, a prior agreement with the unions, or a particular tradition to be followed. It is important that the committee informs personnel about the nature of the system to be used.

Committees can also perform an important function in subsequent stages and in situations where personnel appeal against the job descriptions made or the job evaluation ultimately suggested.

3.3 Multi-purpose applications

We use this concept rather broadly. First, we examine JE in a non-remunerative context: personnel and organizational policy. Second, we assess the significance of JE for *equal pay* for female personnel.

3.3.1 Personnel policy and organizational matters

Terms such as "multi-purpose", "job profiling", and "management tools" are often used when referring to the application of JE in areas where, as Kleinendorst (1982) observed, there is a systematic and planned use of data collected with the help of JE for objectives other than remuneration. These include: recruitment, selection, performance appraisal, career planning, education and training, job structuring and organizational design (see also Hazekamp, 1982).

Dutch surveys in the 1980s (LTD, 1982, 1987) show that larger companies used JE as a multi-purpose instrument more frequently than smaller companies.

Table 8.4 shows some examples of these other applications.

There is remarkably little literature on experiences with these types of application or on the results of research. Exceptions include Kleinendorst (1982); Bindels (1982); Zwarts (1982); Brons (1987) and Harvey (1991). Kleinendorst suggests that the renewed—certainly not new (see also Lawshe & Satter, 1944; Lijftogt, 1966)—interest in the subject reflects a tendency towards a decentralization of labour negotiations and the high cost of developing and implementing a JE system. Kleinendorst's own research relates to four "cases". These show that task structuring is

TABLE 8.4

Application of job evaluation for purposes other than remuneration.

Way JE is used
Recruitment and selection
Performance appraisal
Education and training
Career planning
Organization analysis
Work structuring

the most sophisticated application of JE. *Job descriptions* were reduced to extremely small components of a task, for example, and new (enriched) jobs were subsequently created with the help of certain "combination" rules. This process may be necessary, for example, because mergers or reorganizations have taken place, or because of a need to improve opportunities for upward mobility within the organization. Another example is the development of a policy on staffing structure. Brons (1987) noted, for example, that when jobs are qualified according to characteristics they share (such as knowledge, problem solving), a profile can be developed that allows the identification of any imbalance present in the organizational structure. This can happen, for example, when relatively less weight is given to problem solving in jobs at higher levels of the job hierarchy than at lower levels.

In his research Kleinendorst emphasized that the multi-purpose character of JE in the companies he had studied should be seen as a bonus, a side effect. JE would not have been implemented if it had not been necessary to structure wage and salary relationships.

There are two practical reasons why we are a little reticent about this. First, Hazekamp pointed out as early as 1982 that, when a system designed for a particular industrial sector is applied without any adaptation to the specific conditions of an institution or company, the JE data generated are too global to make multi-purpose application possible (Hazekamp, 1982). When, in addition, shortened procedures such as those used in the normative job series are employed—as is increasingly the case nowadays—then the data collected lacks sufficient detail and focus for other applications (for example, performance appraisal). Second, we believe that there must be greater emphasis at an earlier stage on the extent to which JE data can be regarded as being *congruent* with the data required for making decisions on such matters as selection, training, performance appraisal, and so on. This congruence is often—and unjustifiably—taken as self-evident. From this perspective it is easy to understand why the literature on methods of job analysis reviewed earlier in this section contain practical examples and results of investigations into multi-purpose applications of JE (see Latham, 1986, among others, on job performance). There is little research into the effectiveness of the methods of job analysis generally used within the context of JE, although such research would be very desirable.

3.3.2 JE and equal pay for female personnel

If a female employee (or a group or category of staff working in a particular sector) believes she is earning less than a male colleague (group or category) doing work of similar value, she is entitled to lodge a complaint on the basis of the laws relating to equal wages and equal treatment. In The Netherlands, the Commission for Equal Treatment (Smit-Voskuijl, 1987) has then to use JE. Although it can give advice, its advice is not binding. If an employer does not follow it, a salary claim can either be brought to the local court or to one of the arbitration commissions provided for in a Collective Labour Agreement (see also Schoute, 1982).

In Great Britain (the Equal Opportunities Commission, for example) and the United States (Bellace, 1987; Elizur & Thierry, 1987) the *point method* is advocated for such cases. In these countries a shift in terminology—namely from equal opportunities to "*comparable worth*"—reflects the fact that female staff no longer have to limit their comparisons to men filling the same functions as themselves. They can now make a comparison between their jobs and those of men in jobs of *comparable significance.* This means heavier demands are put on JE systems.

Unlike The Netherlands, it is quite customary in Great Britain and North America to involve the civil courts for this type of complaint. This means that lawyers and members of the judiciary must have some degree of familiarity with JE and, because of this, psychologists are among those who have become involved in these cases as expert witnesses in recent years. An increasing amount of empirical research is also being done into JE in these countries and its results have definite implications for the way JE is used. We will spend some time examining this in what follows.

When the question of discrimination against female personnel is being discussed, the main issue becomes which job characteristics (and other possible variables) actually influence the value of a job. In this context tracking sources of "bias" has priority (see also Voskuijl, 1996). First, bias can reside in the *name* associated with a job. The Equal Opportunities Commission (1981), for example, observed that a woman is called a "shop assistant" and a man a "salesman"; a woman "a secretary" and a man an "administrator", although the content of their jobs is the same. In The Netherlands *verkoper* (salesman) carries other associations than "*verkoopster*" (saleswoman): the salesman not only sells, he also has a leadership function. Second, job *characteristics* can be chosen in such a way that jobs usually done by men score more points than jobs that are mainly done by women. In this sense women can be discriminated against if the lifting of objects is evaluated rather than manual dexterity, negotiating rather than counselling, skill rather than responsibility, leadership rather than organizing, and so on. (Doverspike & Barrett, 1984). Both authors let four assessors use the *point method* to evaluate 105 "female dominated" and 105 "male dominated" jobs. Calculations were then made of interrater reliability, the correlation between the score per characteristic and the total score, the structure of factors analysed, and the partial correlations between a characteristic and male/female dominated job where the total score is held constant. A slightly different definition of bias applies to each of these statistical tests. Remarkably, there was quite a degree of similarity between the results—showing that "bias" did not result in a systematic discrimination against women—while the method of partial correlation gave rise to most corrections (for men and women). Mahoney and Blake (1987) added a fifteenth characteristic to the fourteen already in use: masculinity and femininity. Factor analysis results showed that this characteristic did not play an independent role.

A third source of bias can be traced to the JE *method* (although in practice it can be difficult to distinguish this from the above). Madigan and Hoover (1986) suggest that its criterion does not necessarily lie in the level of mutual correlations among methods, but in the extent of agreement about the class to which a job has been assigned. Six metric computations of data from about 200 jobs evaluated by both the Position Analysis Questionnaire and a point method showed a recurrent, statistically significant, discrimination to the disadvantage of women.

Fourth, bias can occur when jobs are being *described* and, more generally, in sub-sections of the JE process (Schwab & Wichern, 1983). Shimmin (1987) gives various examples, including the selection of *key jobs*, the (very limited) number of women in advisory committees, and so on.

The sources of bias that have been mentioned so far are "internal" in nature: they are related to the quality of JE and to some of its procedures. But "bias" can also have an "external" character and lie in the *criterion*, namely the salary for a job. Its direct manifestation is apparent when jobs filled mainly by women receive lower pay than comparable jobs filled mainly by men. Furthermore, we cannot exclude the fact that there may be a "pro-male bias" in performance appraisal (Nieva & Gutek, 1980). In a laboratory study, Dobbins, Cardy, and Truxilly (1988) found that judges with traditional attitudes (stereotypes) towards women were less precise in their differentiation of the average performance level of women than judges with non-traditional attitudes. It is interesting to note that this difference was only evident when performance appraisal referred to personnel decisions (such as promotion or salary) and not when the object of evaluation had "something to do with research". Thus, "bias" in performance appraisal could work through into the salary level through tying the (e.g. annual) performance result to a pay increase as set in the relevant salary scale. We must leave this issue here. On the basis of research in the United States, Latham (1986), however, believed this effect to be quite negligible.

Van Schaaijk (1987), referring to Dutch data in the 1970s, came to the conclusion that age and degree of education are critical factors. In Dutch industry, women in lower-level jobs earn about the same as men; at higher levels they earn very much less (see also Schippers, 1982). From an analysis of the wages of 10,000 randomly chosen Dutch men and women, Van Driel and Israëls (1987) came to the conclusion that men, on average, earned 33.3% more than women. When other variables were held constant, the variable that made the greatest contribution (11.8%) was gender. In an indirect sense age also played a particularly important role: working men were in general older than working women.

Other studies (Grams & Schwab, 1985; Mahoney & Blake, 1987; Mount & Ellis, 1987; Schwab & Grams, 1985) have shown that *indirect* rather than direct discrimination is significant here. To the extent that "female dominated" jobs are more poorly paid in practice, this seemed to work as a reference point and to negatively influence the ultimate evaluation of specific jobs held by women. It made little difference whether the assessor was a man or a woman.

Multiple regression is often used to establish whether men and women holding comparable jobs are remunerated differently. Job salaries are the dependent variable and various characteristics are input as independent variables (in inverse multiple regression—which is sometimes recommended—in this context job salaries are used as an independent variable). A separate analysis is made for men and women. If the results over the whole spectrum are lower for women than for men, it can be said that there is evidence of discrimination. Various legal judgements have concluded that if this is the case, then the "male" regression comparison is binding for these female jobs. However, Arvey, Maxwell, and Abraham (1985) suggested that these conclusions may have been drawn too quickly: the unreliability of JE as an instrument of measurement can also be either wholly or partly responsible for differences in regression (see Section 4). On the basis of simulated data they show that in the absence of any "sex bias", unreliable job values do indeed lead to unequal lines of regression.

Finding a solution to these problems is far from simple. If an effort is made to make JE more reliable, then any sex bias present can lead to it being estimated too highly. De Corte (1989) has developed a model for solving this type of problem.

4 RELIABILITY AND VALIDITY

4.1 Reliability

In discussing the way in which grading data and weighting factors are combined in the GM and most other analytical JE systems, a certain degree of measurement imprecision has been observed. Grading data are often assumed to have interval properties, although generally speaking this is not explained. Thus, grading data should be considered as having rank order properties, as also applies to weighting factors. In the strict sense they should not be multiplied with each other (Hazewinkel, 1967). More generally, Elizur (1980) suggests that the way data are used in many JE methods—and here he includes ranking, classification and the point system—assumes a degree of precision that is frequently unjustified, both theoretically and statistically. A variety of subjective factors can intervene during the process of describing and classifying jobs and these play an important role (see Section 3.1).

Madigan (1985) points out that the indices most frequently used to assess the reliability of JE data concern interrater consistency. Whilst some studies have produced reliability estimates of more than 0.90, these are often lower. Madigan observes that the bottom line as far as level of reliability is concerned has never been established. This is critical, for example, when making decisions about job categorization and *salary class*. Even an interrater reliability of 0.95 is too low, Madigan argues, because—as his research shows—there can be considerable variation in salary classification.[2]

Hazewinkel (1967) has pointed to another vulnerable part of the evaluation procedure. In an ingeniously constructed experiment, he showed that experienced job analysts can be led astray during job evaluation by *global data* on the level of remuneration for a job (that were partly incorrect). Hazewinkel presumed that other data, such as, for example, the hierarchical position of a job or its status, that in themselves have little to do with the content of a job, could also be misleading in a similar way.

Since Smith and Hakel's (1979) study, the themes discussed above—*precision* in job evaluation and the role of *information and training*—have played an important role in research. Smith and Hakel found that there was little difference between the PAQ scores of on the one hand untrained students who scarcely knew the names of 25 jobs and on the other those of students who had received information on job content, job holders, experienced job analysts, and managers. In addition, the correlations between the PAQ profiles of these five groups of judges were extremely high. Comparable results have also been reported by Arvey, McGowen, and Dipboye (1982), but not by Cornelius, DeNisi, and Blencoe (1984). Following Cronbach (1955), Harvey and Lozoda-Larsen (1988) suggest, however, that global degrees of correspondence between judges are not very indicative and that measures such as "elevation" and "differential accuracy" are of more importance. The first measure represents possible "leniency"—the degree to which the average evaluation of a judge deviates from that of an expert. The second measure reflects the precision with which the judge (compared to the expert) can predict differences between various jobs along the dimensions in question.

Harvey and Lozoda-Larsen (1988) used a "job-oriented" instrument in their research and not the PAQ. Job holders' scores were used as the norm. Judges who were given extensive information about the jobs were found to be much more accurate in their evaluation than those who only knew the name of the job. Hahn and Dipboye (1988), using the PAQ, recorded very similar results. From their research it also appeared that prior training in precision of evaluation had an additional and positive effect on precision. In this connection Schwab and Heneman (1986) also advocate the use of a consensus procedure. They found that trained evaluators who used a variety of sources of information and who had to reach a consensus had a high degree of interrater consistency.

Methods of *job analysis* can also be unreliable. However, there are very few comparative studies where the same judges use different systems to evaluate the same set of jobs. In Madigan and Hoover's (1986) study, two analysts repeatedly evaluated jobs with the help of a *point method* and the PAQ. The results showed that there was a 54% agreement between both systems as far as scaling in the salary for the job was concerned. Levine, Ash, Hall, and Sistrunk (1983) asked 93 JE experts to evaluate 7 methods of analysis and indicate their usefulness for 11 organizational applications (for example, *job description*) and 11 practical aspects (for example, acceptability). Not one of the methods scored high on all measures.

If we summarize the research results discussed in this section, we have to conclude that, in as far as the reliability of aspects of JE systems has been investigated, there is no reason for great optimism.

4.2 Validity

The comparative research referred to above could also have been cited in this section. We begin by examining the *discriminant validity* of the JE system. The point total given to a job is seen as the composite score on a number of independent dimensions each of which has a different weight. The results of factor analysis show that, in JE systems with 10–12 characteristics, two to five factors often explain total job scores (see, among others, Belcher, 1975; Burckhardt & Kallina, 1967; Hazewinkel, 1967; Lawshe, 1945; Lawshe & Alessi, 1946; Lawshe & Maleski, 1946; Lawshe & Satter, 1944; Madigan, 1985; Mahoney &

Blake, 1987; Rogers, 1946; Wiegersma, 1958; Young, 1981). In this connection Belcher refers to four "universal factors": skill, effort, responsibility and work conditions. There are also examples where one factor is almost sufficient to explain the entire variation (Madigan, 1985; Dutch data in Van Sliedregt's Ph. D. study; Wiegersma, 1958), even though the PAQ involves 13 different dimensions (McCormick, Jeanneret, & Mecham, 1969). Obviously the particular method of factor analysis adopted and the method of rotation play a role here, and of equal importance is the selection of the sample of jobs analysed. However, in almost all cases, evaluating a small number of dimensions seems to be sufficient.

On this bases it is appropriate to query the *construct validity* of JE systems: which dimensions—to be operationalized in characteristics—are actually used when jobs are compared? In The Netherlands, the various characteristics have been combined into between three and seven major characteristics in most systems (see, for example, Colenbrander & Buningh, 1982; Hazekamp, 1982; Poels, 1996). These are:

- Knowledge and experience.
- Responsibility.
- Handling of problems.
- Leadership.
- Social skills.
- Work conditions.

But why have these concepts been selected in preference to others? Why has it been assumed that these characteristics represent the construct "job value"? Elizur (1980) notes that it is far from clear why certain dimensions and characteristics have been chosen and there is no evidence of any theoretical base. He advocates adopting one dimension as a point of departure—for example, the discretion job holders have in performing their job (see Jaques, 1956; Paterson, 1972)—and that facet analysis (Guttman, 1959) should be used to define characteristics that have a "positive monotonous" relationship with each other. If we confront this approach with the results of factor analysis on the total scores for jobs that we discussed earlier, then we must conclude that most JE systems do not have a unidimensional structure. What is more important, however, is the second conclusion that little is known about the construct validity of many JE systems.

This conclusion is, alas, also true for the *predictive validity* of JE data. Often, criteria are suggested relating to "perceived societal fairness", or current wage and salary relationships in as far as these are considered as fair. As early as 1953, De Groot pointed out that only systematic empirical testing could show how far the total values obtained for jobs do in fact correspond to such yardsticks (De Groot, 1953). Regrettably, no such testing materialized. In addition, there is a particularly difficult problem associated with these criteria. As has already been stated, weighting factors, in combination with grading data, are used to determine the value of a job. Weighting factors indicate the relative importance of a characteristic, that is to say the importance that is attached to it in practice, especially in terms of existing market relationships. If existing relationships are chosen as criteria—and the total scores of jobs evaluated are consequently correlated with the salaries paid for these and similar functions—then *criterion contamination* occurs. The same variable, after all, affects both the predictor and the criterion. This difficulty can, however, be countered when a number of salaries which are considered equitable constitute the criterion and the weighting factors or scales derived from them are used to determine scores for other jobs.

The custom in various companies of "checking" the validity of a series of jobs evaluated by a *point system* by using rank orders of all these jobs (or some of them) developed by a third party, does not solve the problem. This would require data on the predictive validity of the "ranking" of jobs being made available. The custom of continuing to make changes (in the *description*, *analysis*, evaluation and/or classification of jobs) until those involved find the results acceptable is understandable but, nevertheless, carries all the trademarks of a convenience solution.

The implications of the research into the reliability and validity of JE data summarized in this section give no cause for satisfaction (see also Voskuijl, 1996). In the first place, there are still many gaps. This does not mean that "more research is desirable"—which is the conclusion usually drawn in research reviews. Rather, we wish to stress the fact that there is surprisingly little research on the psychometric qualities of the systems on which these important decisions are based (see, for example, Hahn & Dipboye, 1988). We believe that the subject—wage and salary relationships amongst large numbers of employees—is of sufficient importance to warrant the stimulation of an intensive research programme. Those involved in labour politics should also give encouragement to such an undertaking.

In the second place the research results available suggest caution as far as the multi-purpose application of JE data is concerned. If we look at decisions made in the context of personnel and organization, then—in an extension of the comments made in Section 3.3.1 on congruency of data—a critical issue becomes the degree to which the dimensions basic to a JE system correspond with those considered essential in performance appraisal and organization design. This type of analysis has been carried out, for example, on PAQ data. We do not know of any comparable research that is relevant to other systems of job analysis that were mentioned earlier. Empirical research carried out in the area of "*comparable worth*" (Section 3.3.2), has also led to results similar to those we have discussed here. In general, results of scientific research should be available to justify using an instrument for a particular goal. Using an instrument in this way cannot simply be considered as proper until research proves otherwise.

5 CONCLUSION

At the end of Section 4 we referred to a number of themes that should be examined more fully in future research. Here we make several comments about the use and the usefulness of JE in the near future. The more enterprises and institutions are faced with incisive change, the more there is the need to tailor JE to particular "local" conditions and specific "company-internal" objectives. This development is also known as giving "managerial objectives" a higher priority, or making the use of JE more "flexible". Also, companies now consider skipping the use of JE, introducing "skill-based" evaluation (or competency-based evaluation) instead. This method of remuneration involves rewarding each member of staff individually for each extra skill or capacity acquired through training, education or practical experience. These forms of remuneration can be very useful when increasing and different capacities and skills are being demanded of staff in situations of rapid technological change.

Yet, employees and managers tend to *compare* the salaries they earn to others from time to time. Increasingly, it is recognized that JE-systems may provide a proper tool to assess the extent of both *distributive* and *procedural* justice (e.g. Hermkens, 1995; Thierry, in press). Obviously, tools other than JE may fulfil that role; nonetheless, many organizations lack these tools (Thierry, 1997). Consequently, the use of JE, and tailoring it slightly to the particular conditions of a company, may contribute to (the perception of) justifiable and fair wage and salary conditions.

NOTES

1 Both concepts are used in this chapter without further differentiation.

2 Similar results are reported on the basis of Dutch data in van Sliedregt's current Ph.D. research (University of Amsterdam).

John R. de Jong was attached to the Raadgevend Bureau Berenschot, Utrecht, The Netherlands, but passed away in 1995. During his long professional and scientific life he made invaluable contributions to the science of work, combining the engineering perspective with that of the behavioural scientist in an expert manner. Among many others, Henk Thierry is indebted to him.

REFERENCES

Arvey, R.D., Maxwell, S.E., & Abraham, L.M. (1985). Reliability artifacts in comparable worth procedures. *Journal of Applied Psychology*, *70*, 695–705.

Arvey, R.D., McGowen, S.L., & Dipboye, R.L. (1982). Potential sources of bias in job analytic processes. *Academy of Management Journal*, *25*, 618–629.

Atchison, T., & French, W. (1967). Pay systems for scientists and engineers. *Industrial Relations*, *20*, (1), 44–56.

Belcher, D.W. (1975). Wage and salary administration. In D. Yoder & H. G. Heneman (Eds.), *Motivation and commitment: ASPA Handbook of personnel and industrial relations*. Washington: Bureau of National Affairs.

Bellace, J.R. (1987). The impact of the American and British equal pay guarantee on job evaluation. *Applied Psychology: An International Review*, *36*, 9–24.

Bindels, M.A.F.W. (1982). Multi-purpose gebruik van functieclassificatie. In H. Thierry (Ed.), *Differentiatie in beloning?* (pp. 49–60) Deventer: Kluwer.

Brons, T.K. (1987). *Functiewaardering als instrument van organisatie-en personeelsbeleid*. Congresboek Functiewaardering in non-profit organisaties. Eindhoven: Studiecentrum voor Bedrijfsleven en Overheid.

Burckhardt, F., & Kallina, H. (1967). Eine Faktorenanalyse der analytischen Arbeitsbewertung. *Arbeitswissenchaft*, *6*, 124–126.

Cascio, W.F. (1995). Whither Industrial and Organizational Psychology. *American Psychologist*, *50*, 928–939.

Colenbrander, H.B., & Buningh, C.A. (1982). *Functieclassificatiemethoden. Een onderzoek naar toegankelijkheid, aanvaardbaarheid en openheid van methodieken*. Alphen aan den Rijn: Samsom.

Cornelius, E.T., DeNisi, A.S., & Blencoe, A.G. (1984). Expert and naive raters using the PAQ: Does it matter? *Personnel Psychology*, *37*, 453–464.

Corte, W. de (1989). *Loondiscriminatie en functiewaardering*. Oostende: Inforservice.

Cronbach, L.J. (1955). Processes affecting scores on 'understanding of others' and 'assumed similarity'. *Psychological Bulletin*, *52*, 177–193.

Dobbins, G., Cardy, R., & Truxillo, D. (1988). The effects of purpose of appraisal and individual differences in sterotypes of women on sex differences in performance ratings: A laboratory and field study. *Journal of Applied Psychology*, *73*, 551–558.

Doverspike, D., & Barrett, G.V. (1984). An internal bias analysis of a job evaluation instrument. *Journal of Applied Psychology*, *69*, 648–662.

Driel, J. van, & Israëls, A.Z. (1987). Beloningsverschillen tussen mannen en vrouwen. *Economisch Statistische Berichten*, *72*, 828–832.

Elizur, D. (1980). Job evaluation: A systematic approach. Aldershot: Gower Press.

Elizur, D., & Thierry, H. (1987). Job evaluation, comparable worth and compensation. *Applied Psychology: An International Review*, *36*, 3–7.

Equal Opportunities Commission (1981). *Job evaluation schemes free of sex bias*. Manchester: EOC.

Fase, W.J.P.M. (1980). *Vijfendertig jaar loonbeleid in Nederland: Terugblik en perspectief.* Alphen aan den Rijn: Samsom.

Fine, S.A., & Wiley, W.W. (1971). *An introduction to functional job analysis methods for manpower analysis*. Kalamazoo, MI: W.E. Upjohn Institute.

Frieling, E., Kannheiser, W., & Hoyos, C. (1973). *Untersuchungen zur Position Analysis Questionnaire PAQ*. Regensburg: Lehrstelle für Angewandte Psychologie, Universität Regensburg.

Goodman, P.S. (1967). An empirical examination of Elliot Jaques' concept of time span. *Human Relations*, *20*, 155–167.

Grams, R., & Schwab, D.P. (1985). An investigation of systematic gender related error in job evaluation. *Academy of Management Journal*, *28*, 279–290.

Groot, A.D. de (1953). Genormaliseerde werkclassificatie. *Mens en Onderneming*, *7*, 401–415.

Guttman, L. (1959). A structural theory of intergroup beliefs and action. *American Sociological Review*, *24*, 318–328.

Hahn, D.C., & Dipboye, R.L. (1988). Effects of training and information on the accuracy and reliability of job evaluation. *Journal of Applied Psychology*, *73*, 146–153.

Harvey, R.J. (1991). Job Analysis. In M.D. Dunnette & L.M. Hough (Eds.), *Handbook of Industrial and Organizational Psychology*. (2nd edn, Vol.2, pp. 71–163). Palo Alto: Consulting Psychologists Press.

Harvey, R.J., & Lozoda-Larsen, S.R. (1988). Influence of amount of job descriptive information on job analysis rating accuracy. *Journal of Applied Psychology*, *73*, 457–461.

Hazekamp, F.C. (1966). Werk, capaciteit en beloning in het Glacier project. *Polytechnisch Tijdschrift*, *21*, (11), (447–455), (13), (534–538), (14), (578–582).

Hazekamp, F.C. (1970). Enige ervaringen met de timespan-methode van dr. Elliott Jaques. In P.J.D. Drenth, P.J. Willems, & C.J. de Wolff (Eds.), *Bedrijfspsychologie: Onderzoek en evaluatie*. Deventer: Kluwer.

Hazekamp, F.C. (1982). *De ontwikkeling in techniek en procedures van functiewaardering*. Conferentieboek. Eindhoven: Euroforum.

Hazekamp, F.C., Hisken, A., & Hoogstad, J. (Eds.) (1985). Vizier op functiewaardering. Vlaardingen: Nederlands Studie Centrum.

Hazewinkel, A. (1967). *Werkclassificatie: een wetenschappelijk instrument?* Groningen: Wolters.

Hemphill, J.K. (1960). *Dimensions of executive positions*. Ohio State University: Research monograph.

Hermkens, P. (1995). Sociale vergelijking en rechtvaardigheid in belonen. *Gedrag en Organisatie, 8*, 359–371.

Hoyos, C., Graf, O., & Frieling, E. (1977). Methodik der Arbeits-end Berufsanalyse. In K.H. Siefert, (Ed.), *Berufspsychologie*. Göttingen: Hogrefe.

ILO (International Labour Office) (1977). *Job Evaluation* (9th edn) Geneva: ILO.

Jaques, E. (1956). *Measurement of responsibility. A study of work, payment and individual capacity*. London: Tavistock.

Jaques, E. (1961). *Equitable payment: A general theory of work, differential payment and individual progress*. London: Heineman.

Jaques, E. (1964). *Time-span handbook*. London: Heineman.

Jong, J.R. de, Gaillard, A.W.K., & Kamp, B.D. (1977). *Hernieuwde studie Functiewaardering in Nederland*. 's-Gravenhage: NIVE.

Katz, D., & Kahn, R.L. (1978). *The social psychology of organizations* (2nd edn). New York: Wiley.

Kleinendorst, B.F.M. (1982). *De waarde van functiewaardering*. Den Haag: Ministerie van Sociale Zaken en Werkgelegenheid.

Koopman-Iwema, A.M., & Thierry, H. (1981). *Prestatiebeloning in Nederland: Een analyse*. Dublin: European Foundation for the Improvement of Living and Working Conditions. Amsterdam: Universiteit van Amsterdam, Vakgroep Arbeids-en Organisatiepsychologie.

Kvålseth, T.O., & Crosmann, E.R.F.W. (1974). The Jaquesian-level-of-work estimators: A systematic formulation. *Organizational Behavior and Human Performance, 11*, 303–315.

Landau, K., & Rohmert, W. (1989). Recent developments in job analysis. *Proceedings of the International Symposium on Job Analysis, March, 1989*. Stuttgart, Universität Hohenheim.

Latham, G.P. (1986). Job performance and appraisal. In C.L. Cooper, & I.T. Robertson (Eds.), *International review of industrial and organizational psychology 1986* Chichester: Wiley.

Lawshe, C.H. (1945). Studies in job evaluation, II: The adequacy of abbreviated point ratings for hourly-paid jobs in three industrial plants. *Journal of Applied Psychology, 29*, 177–184.

Lawshe, C.H., & Alessi, S.L. (1946). Studies in job evaluation, IV: Analysis of another point rating scale for hourly-paid jobs and the adequacy of an abbreviated scale. *Journal of Applied Psychology, 30*, 310–319(b).

Lawshe, C.H., & Maleksi, A.A. (1946). Studies in job evaluation, III: An analysis of point ratings for salary paid jobs in an industrial plant. *Journal of Applied Psychology, 30*, 117–128(a).

Lawshe, C.H., & Satter, G.A. (1944). Studies in job evaluation, I: Factor analysis of point ratings for hourly-paid jobs in three industrial plants. *Journal of Applied Psychology, 28*, 189–198.

Levine, E.L., Ash, R.A., Hall, H., & Sistrunk, F. (1983). Evaluation of job analysis methods by experienced job analysts. *Academy of Management Journal, 26*, 339–346.

Livy, B. (1975). *Job evaluation: A critical review*. London: Allen & Unwin.

Lijftogt, S.G. (1966). *Werkclassificatie: Waardering en kritiek*. Den Haag: COP/Sociaal-Economische Raad.

(LTD) Loontechnische Dienst. (1982). *Functiewaardering in Nederland: gebruik en toepassing, 1980*. Den Haag: Ministerie van Sociale Zaken en Werkgelegenheid.

(LTD) Loontechnische Dienst. (1987). *Functiewaardering in Nederland 1984*. Den Haag: Ministerie van Sociale Zaken en Werkgelegenheid.

Madigan, R.M. (1985). Comparable worth judgments: A measurement properties analysis. *Journal of Applied Psychology, 70*, 137–147.

Madigan, R.M., & Hoover, D.J. (1986). Effects of alternative job evaluation methods on decisions involving pay equity. *Academy of Management Journal, 29*, 84–100.

Mahoney, T.A., & Blake, R.H. (1987). Judgements of appropriate occupational pay as influenced by occupational characteristics and sex characteristics. *Applied Psychology: An International Review, 36*, 25–38.

McCormick, E.J. (1976). Job and task analysis. In: M.D. Dunnette (Ed.), *Handbook of Industrial and organizational psychology* (pp. 651–696). Chicago: Rand McNally.

McCormick, E.J., Jeanneret, R.P., & Mechem, R.C. (1969). *A study of job characteristics and job dimensions as based on the Position Analysis Questionnaire*. Lafayette: Occupational Research Center, Purdue University.

Mount, M.K., & Ellis, R.A. (1979). Investigation of bias in job evaluation ratings of comparable worth study participants. *Personnel Psychology, 40*, 85–96.

Nieva, V.F., & Gutek, B.A. (1980). Sex effects on evaluation. *Academy of Management Review, 5*, 267–276.

Paterson, T.T. (1972). *Job evaluation* (Vols 1 & 2). London: Business Books.

Paterson, T.T. (1981). *Pay for making decisions*. Vancouver: Tantalus.

Poels, F.C.M. (1996). *Functiewaardering: Een fundament in beweging*. Vlaardingen: Nederlands Studie Centrum.

Richardson, R. (1971). *Fair pay and work*. London: Heineman.

Rogers, R.C. (1946). Analysis of two point rating job evaluation plans. *Journal of Applied Psychology*, 579–585.

Sayles, L.R., & Strauss, G. (1977). *Managing human resources*. Englewood Cliffs, NJ: Prentice-Hall.

Schaaijk, M. van. (1987). Verdienen vrouwen meer dan mannen? *Economisch Statistische Berichten, 72*, 315–317.

Schippers, J.J. (1982). Beloningsdiscriminatie van de vrouw in Nederland. *Economisch Statistische Berichten, 67*, 452–458.

Scholten, G. (1979). *Functiewaardering met mate*. Alphen aan den Rijn: Samsom.

Scholten, G. (1981). *Passen en meten met functiewaardering*. Alphen aan den Rijn: Samsom.

Schoute, F.J. (1982). *Juridische implicaties van de invoering van functiewaardering*. Conferentieboek. Eindhoven: Euroforum.

Schuler, R.S., & Youngblood, S.A. (1986). *Effective Personnel Management* (2nd edn). New York: West Publishing Company.

Schwab, D.P., & Grams, R. (1985). Sex-related errors in job evaluation: A real world test. *Journal of Applied Psychology, 70*, 533–539.

Schwab, D.P., & Heneman, H.G. (1986). Assessment of a consensus-based multiple information source job evaluation system. *Journal of Applied Psychology, 70*, 533–539.

Schwab, D.P., & Wichern, D.W. (1983). Systematic bias in job evaluation and market wages: Implications for the comparable worth debate. *Journal of Applied Psychology, 68*.

Shimmin, S. (1987). Job evaluation and equal pay for work of equal value. *Applied Psychology: An International Review, 36*, 61–70.

Smith, J.E., & Hakel, M.D. (1979). Convergence among data sources, response bias, and reliability and validity of a structured job analysis questionnaire. *Personnel Psychology, 32*, 677–692.

Smith, R.C., & Murphy, M.J. (1946). *Job evaluation and employee rating*. New York: McGraw-Hill.

Smit-Voskuijl, O.F. (1987). Functiewaardering als maatstaf bij de Wet Gelijk Loon. *Sociaal Maandblad Arbeid*, 295–309.

Spector, P.E., Brannick, M.T., & Coovert, M.D. (1989). Job analysis. In C.L. Cooper & I. Robertson (Eds.) *International review of industrial and organizational psychology 1989* (pp. 281–328). London: Wiley.

Thierry, H. (1969). *Arbeidsinstelling en prestatiebeloning*. Utrecht: Het Spectrum.

Thierry, H. (in press). Theories on compensation: The perspective of the reflection theory. In M. Erez, U. Kleinbeck, & H. Thierry (Eds.), *Work motivation in the context of a globalizing economy*. Mahwah, NJ: Lawrence Erlbaum Associates Inc.

Thierry, H. (1997). Effectief belonen. *Gids voor Personeelsmanagement, 76*, 54–58.

Tornow, W.W., & Pinto, P.R. (1976). The development of a managerial job taxonomy: A system for describing, classifying and evaluating executive positions. *Journal of Applied Psychology, 61*, 410–418.

US Department of Labor, Manpower Administration. (1972). *Handbook for analyzing jobs*. US Government Printing Office.

Voskuijl, O.F. (1996). *Beoordelingsprocessen bij functie-analyse*. Amsterdam: Disseratiereeks Faculteit der Psychologie.

Wiegersma, S. (1958). Gezichtspunten en factoren in de genormaliseerde werkclassificatie. *Mens en Onderneming, 12*, 200–208.

Wijnberg, W.J. (1965). *Capaciteit en inkomen*. Haarlem: Algemene Werkgeversvereniging.

Wing Easton, N.J. (1980). Functiewaardering: Kies zelf uw systeem. Deventer: Kluwer.

Young, A. (1981). *A Comparable worth study of the state of Michigan job classification*. Lansing, MI: Office of Women and Work.

Zwarts, H. (1982). Loon naar werken en werk naar loon. In Thierry, H. (Ed.), *Differentiatie in beloning?* Deventer: Kluwer.

9

Theoretical, Practical and Organizational Issues Affecting Training

Gary P. Latham, Zeeva Millman, and Henriette Miedema

INTRODUCTION

As Wexley and Latham (1991) noted, training and development systems in Europe and North America must be strengthened if their human resources are to be prepared to compete adequately in the future. As the dawn of the 21st century approaches, managers on both continents will have to handle an increase in cultural diversity with sophisticated human resource skills. They will have to understand that employees with different cultural backgrounds do not necessarily think alike about such issues as handling confrontations, or even such basics as to what constitutes a good day's work.

To paraphrase a headline in the *Wall Street Journal Report* in 1990, North America now has smarter jobs and dumber workers. One year later there was widespread indignation in the United States when a Japanese politician, Yoshio Sakurauchi, Speaker of the lower parliamentary house, made headlines in the same newspaper by blaming America's economic problems on its largely illiterate, lazy, overpaid workforce. Although Sakurauchi later apologized and said that he had been misquoted, there was truth in what he allegedly said.

Thirty per cent of unskilled workers in the United States are functionally illiterate, according to the recently published book *Closing the Literacy Gap in American Business*; among semi-skilled workers, the figure is 29%; for managerial, professional and technical employees, it is 11%.

One in eight adults in the United States over 20, in a group of 3400 surveyed by the Census Bureau, could not read.

Among adult Americans finished with school, nearly 60% have never read a single book and most of the rest read only one book a year, according to Alvin Kernan (1990), author of *The Death of Literature*.

In both Europe and North America, workers are often left to themselves when shifts in the economy or foreign competition have affected or eliminated their jobs. Traditional manufacturing industries such as steel, automobiles, and rubber are providing less and less jobs. In these and other blue-collar industries, more than 1 million jobs in North America alone have disappeared since 1978, and these are jobs that will never come back (Karmin & Sheler, 1982). Instead, employment opportunities are growing in the high technology, service and information sectors. Feeling most of the brunt and terribly in need of retraining are the mechanics, assemblers, welders, semi-skilled and unskilled labourers who work in factories. New technology is resulting in the need for ongoing training and retraining. While training at the beginning of one's career was once sufficient to carry a person through their career, the "shelf-life" of even one's education is rapidly decreasing. For example, a decade ago an MBA degree in North America had a shelf-life of approximately twelve years; it is now considered to be current for only seven or eight years (*The Economist*, March 1991).

Implicit in many arguments put forth by the Japanese is the belief that cultural homogeneity currently gives their industries a competitive edge over their European and North American counterparts. A debate on the value of diversity is beyond the scope of this chapter. However, it should be noted that Japan is not without its problems. Employees are now questioning why the country is doing well and they are not, in that they perceive that their nation's prosperity is not trickling down to them; the population is ageing faster than any in the world with one in four becoming 65 or older by the turn of the century; and there is a growing feminist movement due to the lack of career-track positions open to women (Cohen, 1992). Rather than engage in "Japan bashing", it falls to industry in Europe and North America to provide the training and development opportunities necessary for employees to compete effectively in a global economy.

The purpose of this chapter is four-fold. First, theory that can guide training and development is described. Second, practical considerations affecting training are reviewed. Third, organizational issues that can enhance training effectiveness are discussed, specifically with regard to the transfer of what is learned during training to the job. Fourth, the chapter closes with a discussion of research gaps in the training literature.

THEORY

To the extent that theory is absent, there is an absence of understanding of why a training programme worked or failed to work (Latham & Crandall, 1991). As a result, the steps that can be taken to increase training effectiveness are often difficult to discern. Thus, when theory is neglected, it is not surprising that training programmes often waste an organization's time and money. Three theories that can help trainers design programmes that will increase the probability of bringing about a relatively permanent change in an employee's behaviour are behavioural learning theory (Skinner, 1953; Watson, 1913), three stage learning theory (Anderson, 1982), and social cognitive theory (Bandura, 1986).

Behavioural learning theory

Behaviourally based training programmes have their roots in Watson's (1913) philosophy of behaviourism which states that only objectively observable knowledge is valid. Thus Watson argued: "The time seems to have come when psychology must discard all reference to consciousness; when it need no longer delude itself into thinking that it is making mental states the object of observation" (p. 158). Instead, Watson advocated focusing on two specific objectives: to predict the stimulus, knowing the response; and to predict the response knowing the stimulus. A fundamental tenet of behaviourism is that there is an immediate response of some sort to every effective stimulus. Thus there is strict cause-effect determinism in behaviour.

Watson's ideas had a powerful effect on the early work of B.F. Skinner (1938). Skinner showed how voluntary or instrumental behaviour is affected by environmental events that immediately follow a given behaviour. Such spontaneous behaviours, which voluntarily operate on the environment, are called operants. Environmental events that increase the frequency with which an operant behaviour occurs are called reinforcers; those that decrease the frequency are called punishers. The frequency of an operant response can be changed, Skinner showed, by altering the schedule on which a reinforcer is presented. These systematic changes, which affect the frequency of a response, are called operant conditioning or behaviour modification.

Nord (1969) was among the first I/O psychologists to argue that training programmes should be based on operant principles. His argument was repeated two years later in the first chapter on training and development in the prestigious *Annual Review of Psychology*: "The operant conditioning model, in truth, has a great deal of structured similarity to the motivational theories of McGregor, Maslow, and Herzberg. It simply gets to the heart of the matter much more quickly" (Campbell, 1971, p. 571).

The best known training applications of behaviouristic principles are the teaching machine and programmed learning textbooks. Skinner showed that performance is enhanced if information is presented in small increments, which require a response followed immediately by feedback. This has been done through a variety of devices, including electronic machines that display material and whose buttons, when pressed, indicate the correctness of a response, as well as textbooks that provide spaces for responses to questions; the correct answer is usually shown on the next page (see Fiedler, Chemers, & Mahar, 1984).

Goldberg, Dawson, and Barrett (1964) found that slow learners (defined in terms of their low mental ability test scores) performed better when they used programmed textbooks rather than traditional learning textbooks. However, in a review of 213 studies comparing programmed instruction, Nash, Muczyk, and Vettori (1971) found that while programmed instruction consistently reduced training time by about one third, most well-controlled studies were unable to show significant differences in learning between programmed instruction and conventional learning methods. They concluded that the studies that did obtain differences usually compared well thought-out programmed instruction with a company's less organized training programmes. Underlying this conclusion is a fundamental point—namely, the precision of operant methodology. A trainer is required to specify the stimulus, the desired response, and the immediate outcome that will be presented to reinforce this response, as well as the schedule and method for administering it. This level of specification not only lends itself to measurement and evaluation, but also increases the probability that a well thought-out plan will be effective. Measurement provides objective feedback to trainers as to whether the training intervention should be continued, modified, or discontinued. Objective feedback is far superior to basing decisions solely on the subjective reactions of trainees and upper-level managers regarding training effectiveness; subjective reactions often result in the elimination of effective training programmes and the adoption of new fads (Wexley & Latham, 1991).

In addition to the importance placed on feedback, three other fundamental operant principles have influenced training practices: making an outcome immediately contingent on a specific behaviour, so as to increase (reinforce) or decrease (punish) its frequency; altering the schedule by which the outcome is administered; and adhering to the principle of shaping, or successive approximation (the latter term refers to reinforcing successive approximations of a behaviour until the desired behaviour occurs). The simplicity and effectiveness of these basic operant principles prompted Porter (1973) to advocate their use in training marginal workers—those people whose performance in general is considered well below industry standards. Consequently, two field studies (Yukl & Latham, 1975; Yukl, Latham, & Pursell, 1976) were conducted with women employed to plant trees in a rural area of South Carolina. Research on animals (Honig, 1966) and an organizational simulation (Yukl, Wexley, & Seymore, 1972) had led to the hypothesis that high response rates occur with a variable ratio schedule, but cognitive factors explain why the resulting data did not support this hypothesis. Money administered on the variable ratio schedule was interpreted by the women as a form of gambling;

the women did not approve of gambling so they did not approve of the programme. The continuous schedule, however, was interpreted by the employees as piecework pay rather than as a form of gambling; thus, it was perceived as morally acceptable. Contrary to the hypothesis, productivity (number of trees planted per employee hour) was higher on the continuous than on the variable ratio schedule.

In a subsequent study in the state of Washington, Latham and Dossett (1978) repeated the study with high-school and college educated, unionized workers. Consistent with the laboratory research, employees who had already learned the job performed better on a variable ratio schedule than on a continuous one; the converse was true for inexperienced employees.

With regard to reinforcers, Nordhaug (1989) found that training in itself is often perceived by employees to be a reward. This is consistent with surveys which show that employees in the 1990s are attracted to and are retained by organizations that stress a learning culture. Hall and Richter (1990) characterized this as the "pinball" phenomenon (if you win the game, you get to play again) in that today's employees are motivated to do well so that they get another project with greater significance and more resources. The rewards come from learning and solving complex problems so that good performance demands the development of new knowledge and skills.

Today, I/O psychology books on training (e.g. Goldstein, 1986; Wexley & Latham, 1991) acknowledge the importance of taking into account operant methodology in the design of training programmes. In fact, operant methodology is considered to be one of seven milestones in I/O psychology (Dunnette, 1976). Behaviourism, however, as a philosophy of science, has been largely discredited.

Dulaney (1968) showed that even the simplest forms of learning may not occur unless people are conscious of what is being required of them. Kaufman, Baron, and Kopp (1966) showed that cognitive influences can weaken, distort, or nullify the effects of reinforcement schedules. In that experiment, everyone was rewarded on the same schedule. Nevertheless, those who were informed that they would be reinforced once every minute (a fixed interval schedule) produced a very low response rate (mean = 6). Those who were informed that they would be reinforced on a variable ratio schedule maintained an exceedingly high response rate (mean = 259); while those who were correctly informed that their behaviour would be rewarded once every minute, on the average (a variable interval schedule), displayed an intermediate response rate. Thus, it was shown that identical environmental consequences can have different behavioural effects as a result of a person's cognitions.

Both laboratory (e.g. Locke, Cartledge, & Koeppel, 1968) and field experiments (Latham, Mitchell, & Dossett, 1978) have shown that feedback which significantly affects performance cannot be interpreted as supporting behaviourism. This is because feedback affects behaviour only to the extent that it leads to the setting of, and commitment to, a person's conscious goals.

Mitchell (1975) argued that it is irrelevant whether one can see or directly measure cognitions; numerous disciplines (such as physics and astronomy) refer to unobservables as causal variables:

> "These unobservables can be indirectly measured through their effects on other variables and eventually on observables. Through what is called a 'logic of theoretical networks' (Cronbach & Meehl, 1955), we can ascribe meaning to these constraints and through a process of empirical confirmation provide support for their meaning. Thus a logical positivist position is an unnecessary limitation on scientific inquiry and a poor representative of current thought in philosophy of science (Kaplan, 1964)".
>
> (Mitchell, 1975, p. 65.)

Three stage learning theory

Consistent with the philosophy of behaviourism, theories of skill acquisition originally focused on overt motor skills. The concept of skill acquisition was broadened by Bartlett (1958) to include cognitive skills such as problem solving and thinking.

A three stage theory of skill acquisition was proposed by Fitts (1964), and elaborated on by Anderson (1982). Anderson (1982) described the first stage as the declarative stage in which facts and information needed to perform a skill are learned. Knowledge compilation occurs in stage two. It is in this second stage that individuals integrate the sequences of cognitive and motor processes needed to accomplish the task. Thus facts and information acquired in the declarative stage are transformed into useful knowledge. Learning occurs through practice and experimentation. Procedural knowledge occurs in the third and final stage as skills become so automatized that an individual is able to perform the task without placing demands on cognitive resources.

In summary, the three stage theory states that learning occurs in a progressive manner, with each stage of skill acquisition fulfilling a different function. In each subsequent stage, decreasing demands are made on available cognitive resources, leaving increasing amounts of cognitive resources available for other tasks. This theory therefore suggests that different training techniques are appropriate at different stages of the learning process. This is because different tasks are being learned during each stage, and different amounts of cognitive resources are available in each stage.

Kanfer and Ackerman (1989) conducted a series of studies to test the relationship between ability and motivation during the different stages of skill acquisition. Level of ability was found to have a strong influence on performance in the early stages of skill acquisition. With regard to motivation, a myriad of previous studies across tasks and populations had shown that the setting of specific difficult goals resulted in higher performance than setting no goals, or even abstract goals such as "do your best" (Locke & Latham, 1991). But, Kanfer and Ackerman (1989) found that setting a specific outcome goal during stages one and two hindered skill acquisition because it placed too high a demand on a person's cognitive resources. This finding suggests that trainers must distinguish between process (i.e. behavioural) and outcome (i.e. result to be achieved) goals. The effectiveness of outcome goals is moderated by the attentional demands of each specific learning stage. The higher the attentional demands of a learning stage, the less effective the setting of an outcome goal is on the resulting behaviour. This is because in the first phase of learning (declarative knowledge), the trainee must focus on acquiring a basic understanding of what is required to perform the task. During the second phase of learning (knowledge compilation), the trainee must integrate the sequences of cognitive and motor processes required to perform the task. Performance improvement occurs from trying various methods of simplifying or reducing each task component. It is only in the third phase of skill acquisition that procedural knowledge results in automatization of the skill. Thus the trainer can shift the emphasis from ability to motivation. Goal setting is primarily a motivational technique (Locke & Latham, 1984).

Because the declarative knowledge phase involves high attentional demands, it is difficult for trainees to concentrate on additional information-processing demands such as focusing on what they must do to attain an outcome goal. As performance stabilizes during the knowledge compilation and procedural knowledge stages, attentional demands are reduced and attention may be shifted to other areas without substantial decrements in performance. Research is needed on the benefits of setting specific process goals during the first two stages of learning.

Three stage theory may explain why Dugan (1988) found that an enhanced third week of training did not increase the amount of information used by raters in making appraisals relative to those who received two weeks of training. Dugan concluded that cognitive limitations affect the amount of information an appraiser can use regardless of the extra week of training. Moreover, the enhanced week of training may have disrupted an individual's judgment strategies without allowing sufficient time for effective strategies to be inculcated.

To summarize, trainers must ensure an optimal level of arousal during the three stages of learning. Outcome goals should be set only after the person has the requisite ability to perform the task. The setting of outcome goals during the later phases in the learning process directs trainees' attention toward effective performance strategies, and helps to create a robust sense of self-efficacy. Research is needed on the effects of setting process goals (e.g. goals focused on identifying appropriate task strategies) during different phases of the learning process. The issue of optimal levels of arousal, goal setting, and self-efficacy lie at the core of social cognitive theory.

Social Cognitive Theory

According to social cognitive theory (Bandura, 1977, 1986) learning occurs as the result of actual experience, vicarious experience, verbal persuasion and physiological responses. Reinforcers change behaviour through the intervening influence of thought. A reciprocal triadic interaction is hypothesized to exist among an individual's cognitions, the environment and behaviour. Explicit in this view is the notion that behaviour is both determined by and affects environmental consequences, which in turn affect the person's conscious goals or intentions, and vice versa.

Central to social cognitive theory are the concepts of self-regulation, self-efficacy and outcome expectancies (Bandura, 1986). Self-regulation refers to individuals regulating their own behaviour based on self-efficacy perceptions, performance goals, and outcome expectancies. Self-efficacy concerns the individual's belief that he or she can successfully accomplish a course of action (Bandura, 1982). Outcome expectancies are the individual's beliefs about anticipated environmental consequences of their behaviour (Bandura, 1986).

Social cognitive theory has stimulated much empirical research in training during the past decade. For example, Frayne and Latham (1987) trained unionized state government employees in the use of self-regulation techniques to increase their subsequent work attendance. The training consisted of goal setting, the writing of a behavioural contract, self-monitoring, and the selection and self-administration of rewards and punishments. Compared to a control group, training in these self-regulation techniques gave employees the skills to manage personal and social obstacles to job attendance, and it increased their personal self-efficacy to do so. Scores on a measure of self-efficacy correlated positively with subsequent job attendance. In a follow-up study, Latham and Frayne (1989) showed that this increase in job attendance continued over nine months. At that point the control group was given the same training. Both self-efficacy and job attendance increased to that of the original trained group.

Why is it that some trainees do not accept goals or do not respond to training in self-regulation techniques? Social cognitive theory distinguishes between two judgemental sources of futility. Trainees can give up because they do not believe they can do what is being taught. This would be an example of low self-efficacy. Alternatively, trainees high in self-efficacy also may experience feelings of futility because they do not believe the environment will be responsive to their efforts. This belief is referred to as a low outcome expectancy.

Conditions that result in high self-efficacy and low outcome expectancies typically generate resentment, protest, and effort to change existing practices within the organization. If change should prove to be difficult to achieve, the trainees are likely to desert environments they perceive as unresponsive to their efforts, and pursue their activities elsewhere (Bandura, 1982).

Thus a central role of trainers is to teach significant others outside of training (e.g. supervisors, co-workers) to look for and reinforce desired change. For example, if a person who has been labelled as a problem employee begins to exhibit desired behaviours, these new behaviours should be reinforced. If the employee continues to be seen as a problem employee, regardless of their changed actions, the person is unlikely to continue to exert considerable effort to change. In addition, trainers need to teach people strategies for making the environment responsive to ways of effectively coping in a hostile environment.

A second aspect of social cognitive theory that continues to be investigated in the training literature is vicarious learning through behaviour modelling. Fundamental to the effectiveness of behaviour modelling are learning points for the trainee, which are stated in concrete behavioural terms (e.g. "make the praise specific rather than general"). These learning points are usually derived from a job analysis such as the critical incident technique (Flanagan, 1954) which focuses on behaviours that enable people to perform the job effectively.

The importance of learning points for behaviour modelling training was shown in a study by Mann and Decker (1984). They found that attaching learning points to the key behaviours performed by a filmed model enhances both the recall and the acquisition of those behaviours. Subjects were unable to identify key behaviours simply from observing the model. But like Latham and Saari (1979), they also found that giving the learning points in the absence of the model did not bring about a behavioural change.

Latham and Saari (1979) used behaviour modelling to train supervisors how to interact effectively with their employees. Their nine training modules focused on the following topics: (1) orienting a new employee, (2) giving recognition, (3) motivating a poor performer, (4) discussing poor work habits, (5) discussing potential disciplinary action, (6) reducing absenteeism, (7) handling a complaining employee, (8) reducing turnover, and (9) overcoming resistance to change. The training programme was designed to include the components of effective modelling, namely, attentional processes, retentive processes, motor reproduction processes, and motivational processes.

The trainees met for two hours each week for nine weeks. Each training session followed a similar format:

1. Introduction of the topic by the trainers (attentional processes).
2. Presentation of a film that depicts a supervisor modelling effectively a situation based on a set of three to six learning points that were shown in a film immediately before and after the model was presented (retention processes).
3. Group discussion of the effectiveness of the model in exhibiting the desired behaviours (retention processes).
4. Actual practise in role-playing the desired behaviours in front of the training class (retention processes; motor reproduction processes).
5. Feedback from the training class on the effectiveness of each trainee in demonstrating the desired behaviours (motivational processes).

In each practice session, one trainee took the role of supervisor and the other trainee assumed the role of an employee. No set scripts were used. Instead, the two trainees were asked to recreate an incident relevant to the film topic for that week which had occurred to at least one of them within the past year.

The learning points in the film were posted in front of the trainee playing the role of supervisor. For example, the learning points for handling a complaining employee included: (1) avoid responding with hostility or defensiveness, (2) ask for and listen openly to the employee's complaint, (3) restate the complaint for thorough understanding, (4) recognize and acknowledge his or her viewpoint, (5) if necessary, state your position nondefensively, and (6) set a specific date for a follow-up meeting. These learning points provide one of the key components of coding and retention.

At the end of each of the nine training sessions, the supervisors were given copies of the learning points for that session. They were asked to use the supervisory skills they had learned in class with one or more employees on the job within a week's time period. In this way, transfer of training from the classroom to the job was maximized. The supervisors were also asked to report their successes and failures to the training class the following week.

To further ensure that the supervisors would be reinforced for demonstrating on-the-job behaviours that were taught in class, their superintendents attended an accelerated programme designed to teach them the importance of praising a supervisor, regardless of whether he or she was in the training or control group, whenever they saw him or her demonstrate a designated behaviour. This procedure enhanced the motivational processes of the training.

An evaluation of this behaviour modelling training included four types of measures: reaction, learning, behaviour, and performance criteria. The training programme produced highly favourable trainee reactions, which were maintained over an eight-month period. Moreover, the performance of the trainees was significantly better than that of supervisors in a control group on a learning test administered six months after training, and on performance ratings collected on the job one year after training.

The practical significance of this study is that it supports earlier applications of behaviour modelling for training first-line supervisors (e.g. Moses & Ritchie, 1976). These studies taken together indicate that certain leadership skills can be taught, provided that the trainee is given a model to follow, is given a specific set of goals or learning points, is given an opportunity to perfect the skills, is given feedback about the effectiveness of his or her behaviour, and is given reinforcement in the form of verbal praise for applying the acquired skill on the job (Latham & Saari, 1979).

Meyer and Raich (1983) evaluated the outcome of behaviour modelling training in terms of sales performance. Those who received the training increased their sales by an average of 7% during the ensuing six-month period; their counterparts in the control group showed a 3% decrease in average sales.

Davis and Mount (1984) compared the effectiveness in the teaching of performance appraisal skills of (1) using computer-assisted instruction (CAI) and (2) using CAI plus behaviour modelling. The CAI training alone was as effective as the CAI plus modelling in terms of performance on a multiple-choice test. However, the CAI plus modelling was found to improve significantly employee satisfaction with the way their managers conducted the appraisal discussion. The CAI training was no more effective than the control group in this regard.

A meta-analysis of 70 studies on the effectiveness of management training found that behaviour modelling is among the most effective of all training techniques (Burke & Day, 1986). One reason for this superiority is that modelling affects self-efficacy as an intervening variable affecting performance. However, different training methods may be needed for persons with high and low self-efficacy. In a study involving the use of computer software, Gist, Schwoerer, and Rosen (1987) found that modelling increased the performance for people whose pre-test self-efficacy was in the moderate-to-high range. For those with low self-efficacy, a one-on-one tutorial was more effective. This is why a person analysis, discussed subsequently in this chapter, is so important. A person analysis takes into account individual differences among trainees.

Bandura (1982, 1986) identified four informational cues which trainers can use to enhance a trainee's self-efficacy beliefs. In descending order of influence, they are: enactive mastery, vicarious experience, persuasion, and emotional arousal.

The first strategy trainers can use to increase self-efficacy is to focus on the trainee's experiences with the particular task. Positive experiences and success with the task tend to increase self-efficacy; failures lead to a lowering of efficacy. For example, Bandura (1982) found that self-efficacy increases when one's experiences fail to validate one's fears, and when the skills one acquires allow mastery over situations that the person once felt threatening. But, in the process of completing a task, if trainees encounter something that is unexpected and intimidating, or the experience highlights limitations in their present skills, self-efficacy decreases even if the person's performance was "successful". Only as people increase their ability to predict and manage threats do they develop a robust self-assurance that enables them to master subsequent challenges. It would appear imperative that trainers arrange the subject matter in such a way that trainees know in advance what they will be taught, and that they experience success in that area through active participation with the subject matter.

A second way self-efficacy can be increased is through vicarious experience: namely modelling others' behaviour. Observing others exhibit successful performance increases one's own self-efficacy, particularly when the model is someone with whom the trainee can identify (Bandura, 1986).

A third approach trainers can use to increase a trainee's self-efficacy is through verbal persuasion. This involves convincing the trainee of his or her competence at a particular task. For example, Gist (1990) has argued that self-censorship can stifle creativity through the cognitive process of self-judgments (e.g., "my idea is no good"). Thus she hypothesized that cognitive modelling may be more appropriate than behaviour modelling when the performance deficiency is due to inappropriate thought rather than overt behaviour or skill.

Cognitive modelling is a self-instruction technique that involves visualizing one's thoughts as one performs an activity. The results of Gist's study in a federal research and development agency showed that subjects in the cognitive modelling condition had significantly higher self-efficacy than their lecture-trained counterparts following training (Gist, 1989). In addition, the cognitive-modelling subjects were superior to the lecture/practice group in generating divergent (i.e. creative) ideas.

PRACTICAL CONCERNS

Practical as well as theoretical concerns must be taken into account if training is to be effective. Needs assessment has traditionally involved a three step process of identifying an organization's goals, conducting an analysis of the tasks that must be accomplished in order to achieve these goals, and identifying who needs what training in order to perform these tasks (McGehee & Thayer, 1961). Related to person analysis is a fourth step that is macro in nature, namely, demographic analysis, where the training needs of populations of workers (e.g. women, people over 40) are identified.

Organizational Analysis

An underlying theme that emerges from the training literature over the past decade is that training must be linked to an organization's strategy if it is to be viewed by higher management as effective (Latham, 1988). The importance of this step can be found in a paper by Brown and Read (1984). They argued that the productivity gap between UK and Japanese companies could be closed by UK companies taking a strategic view of their training policies. This should be done by ensuring that the training plan is constructed in the same context and by the same process as the business plan, and more importantly, that it be viewed in direct relationship to it. Thus, achievement of training goals should be regularly monitored and subjected to a thorough annual review alongside the business plan.

The need to make training objectives congruent with the organization's goals has also been recognized by the United States' military. The original Instructional Systems Development (ISD) approach to identifying training needs was based on a detailed analysis of input from job incumbents. In other words, training needs were defined on the basis of how often and how well job incumbents were performing their job tasks. The military concluded that this approach focused too narrowly on the job as it was defined, and thus was less useful for analyses of jobs that were being redefined in accordance with new technology. More importantly, the traditional ISD approach did not ensure that military training was compatible with the long-term strategy of the military. The current approach to defining training needs is based on a thorough analysis of the training provider's mission. From this mission-based analysis, training objectives are now derived (Latham & Crandall, 1991).

Recently, researchers have begun to theorize on how corporate strategy should drive training content. For example, Jackson, Schuler, and Rivero (1989) suggested that managers should adopt training programmes that complement their competitive strategies so that the desired employee role behaviours are indicated.

Three types of competitive strategies are: innovation strategy, quality-enhancement strategy, and cost-reduction strategy (Porter, 1973; Schuler & Jackson, 1987). Innovation strategy is used to develop products and services which are new and different from those of competitors. Quality-enhancement strategy focuses on improving the quality of an organization's products or services. Cost-reduction strategy is used as an attempt to gain competitive advantage by being the lowest cost producer.

Training programmes in organizations with an innovation strategy should teach employees how to deal effectively with ambiguity and unpredictability. Moreover, training should focus on the skills required by existing jobs as well as future-oriented skills that are likely to be required when pursuing innovation strategies. Organizations with quality-enhancing strategies should focus on teaching employees to identify ways to improve the process by which goods and services are made or delivered. An organization pursuing a cost reduction strategy should teach people how to implement tight controls without hurting morale. For example, these firms may wish to emphasize cross-training that enriches jobs so that fewer employees can be used to achieve maximum efficiency (Schuler & Jackson, 1987).

Hussey (1985) has argued that training objectives, especially for management development, should be reviewed by top management whenever a major change in strategic emphasis is planned. However, his survey of UK companies revealed that only one third of the respondents saw the necessity for doing so. Most managers felt that training objectives should be tailored to the individual rather than to corporate needs. Hussey argued for a shift in thinking regarding the purpose of training. Training should not be for the sole improvement of the individual with the hope that it will benefit the organization; training should also be for the benefit of the firm knowing that this in turn will benefit the individual.

Task Analysis

Downs (1985) conducted a survey across British industry to determine the most relevant and difficult areas related to retraining. Not surprisingly, the data indicated that the jobs of the future will require less memorizing of facts and procedures, fewer physical skills, and far more conceptual ability. A review of the literature (Fossum, Arvey, Paradise, & Robbins, 1986) showed that while it is replete with descriptions of job change, little has been done to apply existing technology to measure these changes. One such procedure is to compare job descriptions over time. One way to do this is to have managers "nominate" jobs where significant change is likely.

Hall (1986) described ways of strengthening the links among the management succession process, individual executive learning, and business strategy. The first step is to conduct a future-oriented job analysis. The purpose of this analysis is to link future strategic organizational objectives with future executive job requirements. To do this, the future mission and future goals of the organization must be made explicit. Unfortunately, this is often not done.

Arvey, Fossum, Robbins, and Paradise (1984) advocated the concept of updating. This concept is similar to a future-oriented job analysis. However, as Arvey et al. admitted, the concept is a fuzzy one. The authors urged a more comprehensive and precise description and measurement system than currently exists for these kinds of behaviours. From examples provided by Arvey et al., it would appear that a present-oriented critical incident methodology would lend itself to the development of behavioural observation scales for measuring the extent to which a person engages in updating behaviours (e.g. keeps abreast of technical journals, periodicals, and in-house publications; allocates working time for developmental purposes; volunteers for special assignments and tasks that represent a change in present job assignments).

Regardless of whether trainers are focusing on future or present jobs, they should take into account two factors in performing a thorough task analysis, namely, the technical environment and situational constraints (Ostroff & Ford, 1989). With regard to the technical environment, attention must be given to the predominant technology that directly yields a product or service, the equipment used and conditions surrounding a job, the people with whom the job incumbent interacts, the informational requirements of those interactions and the skills required for effective interaction within and across work units.

Situational constraints are those that affect directly organizational, sub-unit or individual performance. Eight such factors are: adequate job related information; tools and equipment; materials and supplies; financial and budgeting support; services and help from others; personnel preparation through education, training or experience; availability of necessary time; and physical comfort and conditions required for performing the job (Peters et al., 1985). As Ostroff and Ford (1989) pointed out, this typology of situational constraints provides a framework for diagnosing a performance deficiency. The solution may not be in increasing a person's skills as much as it is in removing situational barriers to effective job performance. Remaining alert to situational constraints is an effective way by which trainers can prevent trainee outcome expectancies from becoming unnecessarily low.

Person Analysis

Traditionally, person analysis has been studied within a two-step process (Wexley & Latham, 1991). Step one is concerned with how well a specific employee is performing the job. The term performance appraisal is used to refer to the procedure used to measure the person's job proficiency. The results of the performance appraisal determine whether step two is required. If the employee's performance is appraised as inadequate, step two involves determining the specific knowledge and skills the employee needs to correct this situation.

Recently, research interest has expanded to discovering ways to promote the desire for continuous learning on the part of the employee. This trend is due largely to the de-layering and the concomitant downsizing of organizations where the continuous upwardly mobile employee is becoming a thing of the past. Career growth is being redefined as the development and use of new skills and abilities where lateral moves in an organization are no longer to be perceived as a signal that the person has plateaued (Hall & Richter, 1990). Fundamental to this shift in thinking is self-assessment.

McEnrue (1989) found that organizational commitment and perceived opportunities for promotion influence the employee's willingness to participate in self-development. Younger employees and employees with high levels of organizational commitment were found to be most receptive to self-development. It would appear that low outcome expectancies for advancement on the part of young workers, and low levels of perceived self-efficacy among older workers will need to be dealt with before a continuous learning culture can be put in place. And both variables may require attention with regard to employees who view themselves as minorities in the work setting (e.g. Turkish employees in The Netherlands; Francophones in English speaking provinces in Canada).

Consistent with McEnrue's (1989) finding that outcome expectancies influence a person's desire for training, Fishbein and Stasson (1990) found that people who ask to attend a technical skills class are those who perceive that training will teach them ways of saving time as a result of learning optimal ways of doing their work. With regard to assessing who is truly trainable, Robertson and Downs (1989) argued for the use of worksample tests. Two benefits of such tests, as noted by Robertson and Downs, are that they have predictive validity for jobs that involve the learning of simple skills in a formal training programme, and that the method of instruction used for the test simulates actual job requirements. Thus trainability tests allow organizations to assess needs, predict future performance, and at the same time, provide applicants with first-hand understanding of the job for which they are being trained.

Using a large sample of white male high-school graduates, Mumford, Harding, Weeks, and Fleishman (1989) developed a multivariate model of the influence of trainee characteristics and situational variables on training performance. Situational factors included course difficulty and length, length of the training day, instructor quality, and feedback. They found that learning was most influenced by trainee aptitude and reading level. Factors such as the level of difficulty of the course material had more impact on training performance than did course length, instructor quality, or the feedback received.

Demographic Analysis

In addition to identifying the training needs of the person relative to the tasks that must be accomplished in order to achieve the organization's goals, trainers should also examine the training needs of different demographic groups (Latham, 1988). As Latham & Crandall (1991) noted, demographic changes in the workplace will affect training. These changes include: (a) the shortage of skilled entry-level workers, and the increasing number of (b) minorities, (c) women, and (d) people over 40 years of age.

In contrast to the "baby boom" generation (1946–1961) which produced a plentiful supply of workers, the "baby bust" generation (1964–1975) will be unable to fill all the entry level positions that the baby boom generation will be vacating within the next 20 years, let alone the millions of new jobs that will be created annually (Offerman & Gowing, 1990). Compounding this problem is the low level of literacy and lack of basic skills of the many members of the minority groups who are filling this void (Kruger, 1990; Sandroff, 1990). To correct this situation, organizations will have to design and implement basic skills training programmes. For example, the Insurance Society of Philadelphia has instituted a six-week summer internship for non-college bound students which consists of on the job training as well as remedial instruction in mathematics, reading, and analytical thinking (Kruger, 1990). Such training programmes are likely to be a forerunner of what will soon become common practice in Europe and North America on the part of industrial organizations.

There is currently minimal evidence that the task requirements of a managerial job for a female or non-white differs from those for a white male, or that women or non-whites need training which is not required for white males (Goldstein & Gilliam, 1990). However, training which socializes white males to fully accept women and non-whites into the workplace as their subordinates, peers and superiors may indeed be needed.

Observed negative relationships between age and performance may stem from situational constraints in the form of organizations withholding developmental resources from older employees (Goldstein & Gilliam, 1990). This underscores the need to garner full organizational support for older workers participating in training and retraining programs. When organizational support is absent, the self-efficacy of older workers regarding their ability to perform the to-be-trained task is likely to be low. When this occurs, it should not be surprising when it is reported (e.g. Johnston & Porher, 1987) that these older employees are unwilling to retrain for new jobs in contrast to younger inexperienced individuals (McDaniel, McDaniel, & McDaniel, 1988).

ORGANIZATIONAL ISSUES

Transfer of Training

Of primary concern to organizations is that transfer of training occurs. Transfer of training refers to the extent to which what was learned during training is used on the job (Wexley & Latham, 1991). Organizational issues affect the extent to which this takes place. To summarize this chapter thus far, organizations need to conduct a work environment assessment before training begins in order to identify situational constraints to the transfer of training (Robinson & Robinson, 1985). By removing these barriers, employees will develop high outcome expectancies which will help ensure that people will be motivated to attend the training classes.

Once the barriers have been removed, trainers need to focus on theory to guide them in the development of processes that will ensure that this transfer takes place. One such theory, consistent with the behaviourist tradition, is Thorndike and Woodworth's (1901) theory of identical elements. This theory states that transfer is maximized when the stimulus and the response in the training setting are similar, if not identical, to those in the workplace. Emphasis is placed on teaching people to make the same response learned in training to new but similar stimuli on the job. Thus the simplest form of transfer is stimulus generalization (Ellis, 1965).

Individuals improve in their ability to learn new tasks when they have practised a series of related or similar tasks. This progressive increment in performance is a form of transfer known as learning to learn. Knowledge acquisition regarding similarity relationships is a result of learning general approaches or modes of problem solving, becoming familiar with the situation, and learning related classes of materials. For example, Skinner's (1954) programmed instruction represents an efficient way for people to learn related concepts and principles. A key benefit of programmed instruction is that it gives the trainee extensive practice on a series of related problems and carefully leads the trainee to the development of the appropriate concepts.

Consistent with Anderson's (1982) three stage theory, Harlow (1959) found that if practice with a particular type of problem is discontinued before it is reliably learned, little transfer will occur to the next series of problems. Time and effort must be spent on mastering early problems before moving on to more complex ones. As a learning set is formed, relatively few trials are necessary for finding the solution to new problems. Insight is usually the result of extensive prior practice on related problems. It is a phenomenon which occurs as a result of "learning to learn".

In Germany, Van Papstein and Frese (1988) found that task application knowledge mediates the relationship between knowledge gained in training sessions and the transfer of this knowledge to the job. Task application knowledge refers to knowledge of how to apply new material to the work setting.

Harlow's (1959) learning set theory leads to predictions about the effects of motivation on learning. During the early stages of learning a series of problems, learning is slower as the trainee makes a great many errors. Errors may lead the trainee to refuse to make more responses or to engage in relatively random behaviour which is characteristic of responses to frustration. Harlow predicted that there would be fewer emotional responses as a learning set develops if ways could be found to minimize these errors. Finally, his research suggests that the resistance that older employees show to new learning situations might be due more to frustration arising from making errors than to any limitation in learning capacity on the part of these individuals.

Interestingly, research in this regard has been conducted in Germany by Frese and his colleagues on the role of errors in the learning process (Frese & Altmann, 1989; Frese, Brodbeck, Heinbokel, Mooser, Schleiffenbaum, & Thiemann, 1991). They suggested that training programmes should teach trainees how to manage errors. Error management was defined as the process of both learning how to know when errors are likely to arise, as well as how to deal with them. In support of their hypothesis, Frese et al. (1991) found that secretaries who received error management training performed better than those who were provided with detailed instructions on how to minimize errors. In brief, subjects were divided into two groups for the purpose of learning to use a word processing system. In one group, subjects were provided detailed instructions on how to do the word processing tasks. As a result, subjects did not make any errors. In the second "error management" group, subjects were given the same task but were not given detailed instructions as to how to complete the task. As a result, errors were encountered. Subjects in this group were encouraged to try to solve the problems, and learn from the process. This area of error management merits further attention.

Consistent with the work on the learning points which are used in behavioural modelling, research in experimental psychology (Ellis, 1965) shows that labelling or identifying important factors of a task facilitates transfer of learning. This, not surprisingly, is because labelling helps people distinguish important features of the task.

In summary, research in experimental psychology shows that transfer of training is facilitated (1) when the training conditions are highly similar to those that will be encountered on the job; and (2) when cumulative practise with (3) a series of related tasks or problems leads people to learn how to learn, so that (4) general principles are understood. Moreover, (5) important features of the task should be labelled.

Research in industrial organizational psychology shows that what occurs after the training is completed is also important for the transfer of training to the job. For example, Wexley and Baldwin (1986) found that trainees should have specific goals regarding the maintenance of behavioural changes. Gist, Bavetta and Stevens (1990) found that training in self-management resulted in even higher transfer of training than simply setting a specific goal.

Because situational constraints are often beyond the organization's control (e.g. noise levels; uncooperative customers), trainees should also be taught coping strategies. Based on research in clinical psychology, Marx (1982) proposed a relapse prevention model which teaches trainees cognitive (e.g. awareness of non-adaptive thought processes) and behavioural (e.g. anxiety reduction stress management) skills to prevent slips from becoming total relapses. Coping strategies might include time management, assertiveness training, negotiation skills, or interpersonal problem-solving training. In addition to the above factors, such organizational variables as pay and promotion factors, one's peer group, and supervisory support can affect the transfer of training.

Pay and Promotion

Outcome expectancies, as noted throughout this chapter, are beliefs about whether a specific behaviour or behaviours will lead to desired outcomes. Trainees may believe that they are capable of performing a specific behaviour but not choose to do so because they believe it will have little or no positive effect upon them. Thus high outcome expectancies are critical to the transfer of training to the job setting.

Researchers in both the behaviourist and social cognitive traditions have long known that the environment affects behaviour. Nevertheless, environmental reinforcers such as pay, promotion, or the opportunity to receive challenging assignments are often ignored in the training context (Leifer & Newstrom, 1980; Robinson & Robinson, 1985). Newly-acquired knowledge and skills should be incorporated into merit plans in order to increase the probability that these skills will be used on the job.

Caplow (1983) described a study of clerical workers who, following training, were allowed to work without close supervision. The result was lower productivity and morale than those in a control group. Interviews with the employees who had received the training disclosed that after they were given autonomy they thought themselves entitled to higher pay than the other clerks. They became so disgruntled at not receiving a pay increase that their output eventually declined to a much lower level than that of the control group. This study highlights the importance of making certain that the outcome expectancies of management and trainees are in alignment prior to implementing training.

Trainer skills

Trainers must be adept in finding ways to ensure high self-efficacy among trainees. Research from experimental psychology shows that high anxiety has an adverse effect on learning (Ellis, 1965). Thus it is not surprising that Hirschhorn and Gilmore (1989) found that anxiety, fear, uncertainty, and the perception that supervisors are intolerant of mistakes had a deleterious effect on the learning process. This is consistent with Isen's (1984) finding that negative affect harms the normal pattern of behaviour, and suggests that research is needed to determine the role of both negative effect and the environment on the learning process.

The persuasive effect that a trainer can have, directly or indirectly, on a trainee's self-efficacy and subsequent behaviour, has recently been documented under the rubric of the Pygmalion effect (Eden, 1984, 1990). For example, Eden and Shani (1982) conducted a field experiment to investigate the Pygmalion effect on Israeli Defence Force trainees. Boot-camp trainees were randomly assigned to one of three conditions where they were described respectively to their instructors as having high, regular, or unknown command potential. The results of this study showed that those trainees who were designated as having high command potential performed significantly higher than the control group on an objective achievement test. Moreover, trainees in the high potential condition reported greater satisfaction with the course and more motivation to continue with the next training course than did their peers in the control group.

A follow-up study by Eden and Ravid (1982) replicated these results and provided further insight into the nature of the Pygmalion effect. Specifically, these authors tested the influence of the Pygmalion effect when it was manipulated independently of the trainee as well as the trainer. Trainees in clerical courses in the Israeli Defence Force were randomly assigned to one of three conditions where the instructors were informed (a) that the trainees had high potential for success, (b) regular potential for success, or (c) that insufficient information prevented prediction of trainee success. The trainees in the insufficient information condition, unbeknown to the trainers, were then randomly assigned to two groups. Specifically, one group was told that they had high potential for success, while the other was told they had regular potential for success. Success in training was subsequently measured by instructor performance appraisal ratings as well as by an objective performance examination.

The results of this study demonstrated highly significant Pygmalion effects for both the instructor-expectancy and trainee-expectancy conditions. Instructor expectancy accounted for 52% of the variance in mean performance ratings;

trainee expectancy (i.e. self-efficacy) accounted for 35% of the variance. As for the objective performance exam, instructor expectancy accounted for 27% of the variance in scores; trainee-expectancy accounted for 30% of the variance. Interestingly these results persisted despite a change in instructors midway through the training course who were unaware of the Pygmalion manipulation. Thus, the effects of the initial expectancy induction "carried over" to the relief instructors whose expectations had not been experimentally manipulated.

The results of these two studies show the effects of trainer beliefs on trainee beliefs and behaviour. Trainers who have high expectations of trainees can communicate these expectations in a myriad of ways (e.g. attention, verbal persuasion). A trainee who believes that others think highly of his or her capabilities develops a strong sense of self-efficacy and thus exhibits high performance. Taking steps to persuade trainees that they have the capability to perform well would appear to serve as an antidote to a trainer or supervisor who does not think highly of a trainee's performance potential.

Peer Group

A potential force in the socialization process within an organization is the interactive dynamics between the individual and his or her peers. Such interaction can provide support and reinforcement for not only learning what is being taught in the training programme, but also applying what was learned in training to the job. Conversely, failure to secure such support can result in alienation during training and/or on the job. For example, an early study by Lippitt (1949) on training for participation in community affairs found that those people who had been members of training teams were significantly more active in community affairs subsequent to training than those who had been trained alone. In addition, Evan (1963) found that avoidable terminations were significantly lower when a trainee was assigned to a department with two or more trainees than when the person was assigned to a department either alone or with only one other trainee. These findings suggest that a trainee who has the substantive support of other trainees will have higher self-efficacy and superior coping mechanisms to deal with the stresses created by a new or redesigned job than would be the case without such support.

Supervisory Support

Another organizational factor critical to training effectiveness is supervisory support. To increase the probability of transfer of training to the workplace, supervisors need to reinforce the application of what was learned in training to the job. To do this effectively, the supervisors must be fully aware of the training objectives as well as the content of the training for attaining those objectives. Although we know of no research on the subject, it has been our experience that this can be done effectively when a supervisor serves as either the trainer or co-trainer. This not only increases supervisory understanding of and appreciation for the training, but it increases trainee outcome expectancies that demonstrating the learned skills will be valued by the organization.

When the trainee returns to the job, supervisors should adopt the same strategies as those used by trainers in the classroom. That is, early task assignments should be given to allow the employee to experience success in applying the newly acquired skills. The supervisor should continually model skills of exhibiting the verbal and non-verbal cues that connote a positive expectation that the employee will constantly apply the newly acquired knowledge and skills, and that he or she will be able to do this well. As discussed earlier, observational learning and verbal persuasion provided by the supervisor are critical for maintaining high employee self-efficacy. Moreover, the supervisor should coach the employee to set specific difficult but attainable goals. These goals should be made public.

One way to publicize commitment to training objectives is for both the supervisor and the trainee to sign a contract which explicitly lists the long-term goals of the training programme and the conditions under which the learned behaviour will occur on the job (Leifer and Newstrom, 1980). By setting goals in advance, the trainee can focus his or her attention on the important components of the training programme content. In addition, having supervisors publicly commit to the objectives of the training programme helps to increase their investment in the outcome of training. The contracted goals should be specific and measurable so that progress toward the goals can be evaluated through the use of behaviour-based performance appraisals such as behavioural observation scales (Latham and Wexley, 1981).

RESEARCH GAPS

Given the increasing cultural diversity of employees in the European and North American workforce, there is a growing need for studies on the optimal ways an organization can provide them training. With the advent of the Treaty on European Union in 1992, it is puzzling that so little attention is being given to this subject by organizational psychologists in Europe. The extant knowledge comes largely from research conducted by North Americans. Two additional issues embedded in cultural diversity are mentoring and learned helplessness.

Cultural Diversity

Triandis, Brislin, and Hui (1989) identified two dimensions of culture that are a source of differences in employee values, namely beliefs surrounding individualism versus collectivism. People who value primarily individualism place emphasis on their own personal progress. They value autonomy, privacy, individual initiative and achievement. Their identity is based primarily on themselves as individuals. In contrast, people who espouse a collectivist philosophy value group work, derive their identity from the group, and emphasize the importance of group-based decisions. These differences in values should be considered when developing and implementing training programmes. Programmes designed to focus on the individual and his or her autonomy and achievement will be more effective in countries in which the majority of its citizens espouse individualism, such as United States and Canada. Training programmes developed for employees in predominantly collectivistic countries such as Japan, should emphasize group work and development. A more difficult task faces European trainers who must train increasingly culturally diverse groups of employees. Such training programs need to teach people to be adaptable to the different values of the culturally diverse participants.

Hall and Gudykunst (1989) addressed the role of ethnocentric corporate culture in an organization's decision to provide intercultural training. They defined ethnocentrism as the belief that one's own cultural attitudes and values are superior to values and attitudes espoused by members of other cultures. Studying a sample of 65 male and female human resource directors from over 200 multinational corporations, the authors found that the level of ethnocentrism decreased as the amount of cultural awareness training increased. This emphasizes the need for intercultural training in order to maximize cooperation among workers from different cultures.

Schneller (1989) developed a training programme to reduce trainee certainty that a message was understood. The rationale underlying this training was that by reducing certainty, the likelihood of the message sender asking for clarification would be increased, and consequently, communication among members of different cultures would improve. In brief, the training involves using overhead transparencies to show trainees 10 different gestures. The trainees were then asked to answer whether they recognized the gestures as a means of communication, what the message meant to them, and how certain they were of the meaning. The trainees were then given feedback on the correct meaning of the gestures. This was followed by a discussion of the implications of the findings for understanding cultural differences.

The results of the study showed that the training reduced trainee certainty that they had comprehended the message. Consequently, the people who received the training asked for clarification which in turn lead to enhanced communication.

Black and Mendenhall (1991), after reviewing the literature on cross-cultural training concluded that it can be effective for developing skills, facilitating cross-cultural adjustment, and enhancing job performance. However, most of this research is atheoretical. Consequently, the authors presented a framework based on social cognition theory (Bandura, 1986) for guiding subsequent research. In brief, this framework, using social cognitive theory (SCT), shows how individuals receiving cross-cultural training gain increased confidence in their ability to interact with others from different cultures. According to SCT, trainees can learn about different cultures by observing others and subsequently cognitively or behaviourally practising learned behaviours. As a result, individuals experience increased self-efficacy and outcome expectancies which positively influence their retention and reproduction learning processes, and finally, result in better performance in, and adjustment to, the new cultural setting.

Mentoring

Mentoring refers to a one-on-one relationship between an experienced and usually older organizational member, who serves as the mentor, and a less experienced younger employee or protégé (Klaus, 1981) in which the protégé is expected to derive job, career, and psychological benefits (Kram, 1985). Dreher and Ash (1990) reported that individuals who experienced extensive mentoring received more promotions, had higher incomes, and were more satisfied with their pay and benefits than were those people who experienced less extensive mentoring relationships. The linking of mentoring and career success of the protégé is due in part to modelling. Social cognitive theory (Bandura, 1986), described earlier, suggests that the protégé acquires important managerial skills by observing an effective senior manager.

Research to date has focused on existing relationships between a mentor and his or her protégé, and has identified two main roles served by the mentor, namely a career development role in which the mentor facilitates the protégé's upward movement in the organization, and a psychosocial role in which the mentor provides the protégé with personal support and nurturance (Kram, 1985). Thus mentoring may prove invaluable to the integration of women and minority groups into the workforce.

Ragins and McFarlin (1990) found that opposite-sex mentors and protégés were less likely than same-sex mentors and protégés to engage in after-work social activities, leading the authors to conclude that sexual concerns may limit the cross-gender mentor relationship. They suggested that one way for organizations to overcome the limitations on cross-gender mentor-protégé relationships may be by organizing social events that provide sanctioned environments in which protégés and mentors can interact socially.

Another important finding concerns the distinction between mentors that are the protégé's immediate supervisor versus those that do not fulfil a supervisory role. Supervisory mentors were perceived as more effective than non-supervisory mentors in terms of both career development and psychosocial functions (Ragins & McFarlin, 1990). The authors cited accessibility of the supervisory mentor as one possible reason for this. Another reason may be that immediate supervisors are closer to subordinates and therefore more capable of providing guidance in terms that are relevant to the subordinate.

The ways in which one gets selected for mentoring have yet to be thoroughly investigated. One way might be to train employees in ways of demonstrating organizational citizenship behaviour (OCB). OCB refers to spontaneous, discretionary behaviour that although not formally rewarded by the organization, an individual engages in for the benefit of the organization as a whole (Organ, 1988). Such behaviours include helping co-workers when their workload is heavy, taking off less days than most employees, and volunteering to do things for the organization that are not part of one's job description (Organ, 1988). Possible ways to train employees to engage in such behaviours may include modelling on the part of significant others in the organization and teaching these behaviours through a formal behavioural modelling training program.

Learned Helplessness

An important problem that deserves attention, yet to date has been curiously absent from the literature on training and development is overcoming and preventing learned helplessness. Learned helplessness refers to a condition in which individuals become passive and fail to initiate behaviour that will enable them to attain desired outcomes (Abramson, Seligman & Teasdale, 1978; Maier & Seligman, 1967). Explained in terms of an individual's attributional style, learned helplessness can occur when an individual who has failed to achieve a desired outcome attributes failure to global, stable, and internal factors, rather than specific, changing, external factors (Abramson et al., 1978). While attributional style is an important determinant of learned helplessness, individuals in certain occupations where the potential for failure is high may be more susceptible to learned helplessness than employees in less failure-prone occupations.

An example of an occupation in which learned helplessness might be high is life insurance sales (Seligman & Schulman, 1986). This is because individuals in this occupation face failure on a routine basis. In a study of life insurance salespeople, helplessness deficits were operationalized in terms of survival in the organization and productivity (Seligman & Schulman, 1986). Salespeople who exhibited a pessimistic explanatory style sold less insurance and left the organization sooner than did those with an optimistic explanatory style.

Learned helplessness has negative implications for organizations, such as decreased employee motivation and productivity, not to mention little or no OCB. Training programmes designed to alter an individual's attributional style may be one way to combat learned helplessness. As learned helplessness refers to a belief that one's efforts will not produce desired outcomes (Abramson et al., 1978), it may also be related to low levels of self-efficacy. Training to increase perceived self-efficacy may therefore prove to be an effective strategy for reducing, if not preventing, learned helplessness. Finally, learned helplessness may be related to the economy, with its incidence increasing in recessionary times and decreasing in boom years. Learning more about this phenomenon will enable the development of training to reduce its occurrence.

CONCLUSION

This chapter has presented a review of the theories and practices that underlie the field of training and development. From a methodological perspective, the principles of operant learning are still considered important with respect to the development of training programs, however, the philosophy of behaviourism has been rejected by most behavioural scientists. Attention is now being given to cognitive factors that affect the success of training programmes. Anderson's (1982) three stage theory suggests that learning involves a linear component such that individuals go through three successive stages of learning. Finally, social cognitive theory incorporates both the behavioural and cognitive elements of learning, and has gained widespread acceptance from both theoreticians and practitioners.

From a practical perspective, some attention has been devoted to the issues of needs analysis, the relationship between corporate strategy and training needs and content, and transfer of training. Finally, we have identified a number of issues that require further attention. Research on cultural diversity is needed as the workforces in North American and European organizations become increasingly heterogeneous. Mentoring, a method of training and development, is widely used yet research on this topic is relatively scarce. Another important topic warranting additional research is learned helplessness. While this phenomenon influences the success of training programmes, it has been largely overlooked to date by organizational psychologists. Future research efforts should be directed at gaining an understanding of this phenomenon, and ways of designing training programmes to overcome its potentially negative influence.

Investing heavily in worker training and education is a proven pathway to increases in productivity and the productivity of high value-added goods and services. Slashing wages and transferring production to Third World countries may be an interim step for organizations to cut costs and survive in a fiercely competitive world. Long-term gains, however, will go to those organizations that do more by offering high-quality goods, great service, speed, and low prices to customers. Only a well-trained and educated workforce can embrace the kinds of total quality management, just-in-time inventory control, computerized manufacturing, teamwork systems, and other techniques which are crucial to producing the goods that generate First-World level profits and salaries.

Corporate America in particular should take

note. It spends only $30 billion a year on employee training. That works out to about one third of what Europe spends per employee. Worse, most of the American money currently goes to train managers at expensive business schools rather than to train workers at local community colleges, even though experience at Motorola and Ford, for example, shows that grass-roots employee training is what truly pays off. A boost in funding and a redirection of resources would go far to make the bottom half of the workforce more productive and organizations more competitive than is currently the case.

REFERENCES

Abramson, L.Y., Seligman, M.E.P., & Teasdale, J. (1978). Learned helplessness in humans: Critique and reformulation. *Journal of Abnormal Psychology, 87*, 79–74.

Anderson, J.R. (1982). Acquisition of a cognitive skill. *Psychological Review, 89*, 369–406.

Arvey, R.D., Fossum, J.A., Robbins, N., & Paradise, C. (1984). *Skills obsolescence: Psychological and economic perspectives*. Unpublished manuscript.

Bandura, A. (1977). *Social learning theory*. Englewood Cliffs, NJ: Prentice-Hall.

Bandura, A. (1982). Self-efficacy mechanism in human agency. *American Psychologist, 37*, 122–147.

Bandura, A. (1986). *Social foundations of thought and action*. Englewood Cliffs, NJ: Prentice-Hall.

Bartlett, F.C. (1958). *Thinking: An experimental and social study*. London: Allen and Unwin.

Black, J.S., & Mendenhall, M. (1991). Cross-cultural training effectiveness: A review and a theoretical framework for future research. *Academy of Management Review, 15*, 113–36.

Brown, G.F., & Read, A.K. (1984). Personnel training policies—Some lessons for Western companies. *Long Range Planning, 17*,48–57.

Burke, M.J., & Day, R.R. (1986). A cumulative study of the effectiveness of managerial training. *Journal of Applied Psychology, 71*, 232–245.

Campbell, J.P. (1971). Personnel training and development. *Annual Review of Psychology, 22*, 565–602.

Caplow, T. (1983). *Managing an organization*. New York: Holt.

Cohen, E. (1992). Inside Japan. *Akron Bulletin*, Winter, pp. 15–19.

Cronbach, L.J., & Meehl, P.R. (1955). Construct validity in psychological tests. *Psychological Bulletin, 52*, 581–602.

Davis, B.L., and Mount, M.K. (1984). Effectiveness of performance appraisal training using computer-assisted instruction and behavior modeling. *Personnel Psychology, 37*, 439–452.

Downs, S. (1985). Retraining for new shifts. *Ergonomics, 28*, 1205–1211.

Dreher, G.F., & Ash, R.A. (1990). A comparative study of mentoring among men and women in managerial, professional, and technical positions. *Journal of Applied Psychology, 5*, 539–546.

Dugan, B. (1988). Effects of assessor training on information use. *Journal of Applied Psychology, 73*, 743–748.

Dulaney, D.E. (1968). Awareness, rules and propositional control: A confrontation with S-R Behavior Theory. In T.R. Dixon & D.L. Horton (Eds.), *Verbal behavior and general behavior theory* (pp. 340–387). Englewood Cliffs, NJ: Prentice-Hall.

Dunnette, M.D. (1976). Mishmash, mush, and milestones in organizational psychology. In H. Meltzer and F.R. Wickert (Eds.), *Humanizing organizational behavior*. Springfield, IL: Chas C. Thomas (pp. 86–102).

Eden, D. (1984). Self-fulfilling prophecy as a management tool: Harnessing Pygmalion. *Academy of Management Review, 9*, 64–73.

Eden, D. (1990). *Pygmalion in management*. Lexington, MA: Lexington Books.

Eden, D., & Ravid, G. (1982). Pygmalion v. self-expectancy effects of instructor and self-expectancy on trainee performance. *Organizational Behavior and Human Performance, 30*, 351–364.

Eden, D., & Shani, A.B. (1982). Pygmalion goes to boot camp: Expectancy, leadership, and trainee performance. *Journal of Applied Psychology, 67*, 194–199.

Ellis, H.C. (1965). *The transfer of training*. New York: Macmillan.

Evan, W.M. (1963). Peer-group interaction and organizational socialization: A study of employee turnover, *American Sociological Review, 28*, 326–440.

Fiedler, F.E., Chemers, M.M., & Mahar, L. (1984). *Improving leadership effectiveness: The leader match concept*. New York: Wiley.

Fishbein, M. & Stasson, M. (1990). The role of desires, self-predictions, and perceived control in the prediction of training session attendance. *Journal of Applied Social Psychology, 20*, 173–198.

Fitts, P.M. (1964). Perceptual-motor skill learning. In A.W. Melton (Ed.), *Categories of human learning* (pp. 244–283). New York: Academic Press.

Flanagan, J.C. (1954). The critical incident technique. *Psychological Bulletin, 51*, 327–358.

Fossum, J.A., Arvey, R.D., Paradise, C.A., & Robbins, N.E. (1986). Modeling the skills obsolescence process: A psychological/economic integration. *Academy of Management Review, 11*, 362–374.

Frayne, C.A., & Latham, G.P. (1987). Application of

social learning theory to employee self-management of attendance. *Journal of Applied Psychology*, *72*, 387–392.

Frese, M., & Altman, A. (1989). The treatment of errors in learning and training. In L. Bainbridge & S. Antonio Ruiz Quintanilla (Eds.), *Developing skills with information technology*. New York: John Wiley.

Frese, M., Brodbeck, F., Heinbokel, T., Mooser, C., Schleiffenbaum, E., & Thiemann, P. (1991). Errors in training computer skills: On the positive function of errors. *Human Computer Interaction*, *6*, 77–93.

Gist, M. (1989). The influence of training method on self-efficacy and idea generation among managers. *Personnel Psychology*, *42*, 787–805.

Gist, M. (1990). Minorities in media imagery. A social cognitive perspective on journalistic bias. *Newspaper Research Journal*, Summer, 52–63.

Gist, M.E., Bavetta, A.G., & Stevens, C.K. (1990). Transfer training method: Its influence on skill generalization, skill repetition, and performance level. *Personnel Psychology*, *43*, 501–523.

Gist, M.E., Schwoerer, C., & Rosen, B. (1987). Effects of alternative training methods on self-efficacy and performance in computer software training. *Journal of Applied Psychology*, *74*, 884–891.

Goldberg, M.H., Dawson, R.I., & Barrett, R.S. (1964). Comparison of programmed and conventional instruction methods. *Journal of Applied Psychology*, *64*, 110–114.

Goldstein, I.L. (1986). *Training in organizations: needs assessment, development, and evaluation*. Monterey, CA: Brooks/Cole.

Goldstein, I.L., & Gilliam, P. (1990). Training system issues in the year 2000. *American Psychologist*, *45*, 134–143.

Hall, D.T. (1986). Dilemmas in linking succession planning to individual executive learning. *Human Resource Management*, *25*, 235–236.

Hall, P.H., & Gudykunst, W.B. (1989). The relationship of perceived ethnocentrism in corporate cultures to the selection, training and success of international employees. *International Journal of Intercultural Relations*, *13*, (2), 183–201.

Hall, D.T., & Richter, J. (1990). Career gridlock: baby boomers hit the wall. *Academy of Management Executive*, *4*, 7–22.

Harlow, H.F. (1959). Learning set and error factor theory. In S. Koch (Ed.), *Psychology: A study of science* (pp. 492–537). New York: McGraw-Hill.

Hirschhorn, L., & Gilmour, T.N. (1989). The psychodynamics of a cultural change: Learning from a factory. *Human Resource Management*, *28*, 211–233.

Honig, W.K. (1966). *Operant behavior*. New York: Appleton-Century-Croft.

Hussey, D.E. (1985). Implementing corporate strategy: Using management education and training. *Long Range Planning*, *18*, 28–37.

Isen, A.M. (1984). Toward understanding the role of affect in cognition. In R. Wyer & T. Srull (Eds.), *Handbook of social cognition* (Vol. 3, pp. 179–236). Hillsdale, NJ: Lawrence Earlbaum Associates Inc.

Jackson, S.E., Schuler, R.S., & Rivero, J.C. (1989). Organizational characteristics as predictors of personnel practices. *Personnel Psychology*, *42*, 727–785.

Johnston, W.B., & Porher, A.H. (1987). *Workforce 2000: Work and workers for the twenty-first century*. Indianapolis, IN: Hudson Institute.

Kanfer, R. & Ackerman, P.C. (1989). Motivation and cognitive abilities: An integrative aptitude-treatment interaction approach to skill acquisition. *Journal of Applied Psychology*, Monograph, *74*(4), 657–690.

Kaplan, A. (1964). *The conduct of inquiry*. Scranton, PA: Chandler.

Karmin, M.W., and Sheler, J.L. (1982). Jobs: A million that will never come back. *U.S. News and World Report*, 13 September, 53–56.

Kernin, A. (1990). *The death of literature*. New Haven, CT: Yale University Press.

Kaufman, A., Baron, A., & Kopp, R.E. (1966). Some effects of instructions on human operant behavior. *Psychonomic Monograph Supplements*, *1*, 243–250.

Klaus, R. (1981). Formalized mentor relationships for management and executive development programs in the federal government. *Public Administration Review*, *41*, 489–496.

Kram, K.E. (1985). *Mentoring at work: Developmental relationships in organizational life*. Glenview, IL: Scott Foresman.

Kruger, P. (1990). A game plan for the future. *Working Women*, supplement, January.

Latham, G.P. (1988). Human resources training and development. *Annual Review of Psychology*, *39*, 545–582.

Latham, G.P., & Crandall, S.R. (1991). Organizational and social factors affecting training effectiveness. In J.E. Morrison (Ed.), *Training for Performance*. Chichester: Wiley.

Latham, G.P., & Dossett, D.L. (1978). Designing incentive plans for unionized employees. Comparison of continuous and variable ratio reinforcement schedules. *Personnel Psychology*, *31*, 47–61.

Latham, G.P., & Frayne, C.A. (1989). Increasing job attendance through training in self-management: A review of two studies. *Journal of Applied Psychology*, *74*, 411–416.

Latham, G.P., Mitchell, T.R., & Dossett, D.L. (1978). Importance of participative goal setting and anticipated rewards on goal difficulty and job performance. *Journal of Applied Psychology*, *63*, 163–171.

Latham, G.P., & Saari, L.M. (1979). The application of social learning theory to training supervisors through behavior modeling. *Journal of Applied Psychology*, 64, 239–246.

Latham, G.P., & Wexley, K. (1981). *Increasing productivity through performance appraisal.* Don Mills, ONT: Addison-Wesley Publishing Co.

Leifer, M.S., & Newstrom, J.W. (1980). Solving the transfer of training problems. *Training and Development Journal,* August, 34–46.

Lippitt, R. (1949). *Training in community relations: A research exploration toward new group skills.* New York: Harper.

Locke, E.A., Cartledge, N., & Koeppel, J. (1968). Motivational effects of knowledge of results. *Psychological Bulletin, 70,* 474–485.

Locke, E.A., & Latham, G.P. (1984). *Goal setting: a motivational technique that works!* Englewood Cliffs, NJ: Prentice-Hall.

Locke, E.A., & Latham, G.P. (1991). The fallacies of common-sense truths—a reply. *Psychological Science, 2,* 131–132.

Maier, S.F., & Seligman, M.E.P. (1967). Learned helplessness: Theory and evidence. *Journal of Experimental Psychology: General, 105,* 3–46.

Management education, passport to prosperity. (1991, March). *The Economist.*

Mann, R.B., & Decker, P.J. (1984). The effect of key behavior distinctiveness on generalization and recall in behavior modeling training. *Academy of Management Journal, 27,* 900–910.

Marx, R.D. (1982). Relapse prevention for managerial training: A model for maintenance of behavior change. *Academy of Management Review, 7,* 433–441.

McDaniel, C.O. Jr., McDaniel, N.C., McDaniel, A.K. (1988). Transferability of multicultural education from training to practice. *International Journal of Intercultural Relations, 12,* 19–33.

McEnrue, M.P. (1989). Self development as a career management strategy. *Journal of Vocational Behavior, 34,* 57–68.

McGehee, W., & Thayer, P.W. (1961). *Training in business and industry.* New York: Wiley.

Meyer, H.H., & Raich, M.S. (1983). An objective evaluation of a behavior modeling training program. *Personnel Psychology, 36,* 755–762.

Mitchell, T.R. (1975). Cognitions and Skinner: Some questions about behavioral determinism. *Organization and Administrative Sciences, 6,* 63–72.

Moses, J.L., & Ritchie, R.J. (1976). Supervisory relationships training: A behavioral evaluation of a behavior modeling program. *Personnel Psychology, 29,* 337–343.

Mumford, M.D., Harding, F.D., Weeks, J.L., & Fleishman, E.A. (1989). Relations between student characteristics, course content, and training outcomes: An integrative modelling effort. *Journal of Applied Psychology, 75,* 443–456.

Nash, A.N., Muczyk, J.P., & Vettori, F.L. (1971). The relative practical effectiveness of programmed instruction. *Personnel Psychology, 24,* 397–418.

Nord, W.R. (1969). Beyond the teaching machine: The neglected area of operant conditioning in the theory and practice of management. *Organizational Behavior and Human Performance, 4,* 375–401.

Nordhaug, O. (1989). Reward functions of personnel training. *Human Relations, 42,* (5), 373–388.

Offermann, L.R., & Gowing, M.K. (1990). Organizations of the future—Changes and challenges. *American Psychologist, 45,* 95–108.

Organ, D.W. 1988. *Organizational citizenship behavior. The good soldier syndrome.* Toronto: Lexington Books.

Ostroff, C., & Ford, J.K. (1989). Assessing training needs: Critical levels of analysis. In I. L. Goldstein and Associates (Eds.), *Training and development in organizations.* San Francisco: Jossey.

Papstein, P. van, & Frese, M., (1988). Transferring skills from training to the actual work situation: The role of task application knowledge, action styles and job decision latitude. *CHI 88 Proceedings,* 55–60.

Peters, L.H., O'Connor, E.J., & Eulber, J.R. (1985). Situational constraints: Sources, consequences, and future considerations. In J. Ferris & K. Rowland (Eds.), *Research in personnel and human resources management, 3,* 79–114.

Porter, M.E. (1973). Turning work into nonwork: The rewarding environment. In M.D. Dunnette (Ed.), *Work and nonwork in the year 2001* (pp. 113–133). Monterey, CA: Brooks/Cole.

Ragins, B.R., & McFarlin, D.B. (1990). Perceptions of mentor roles in cross gender mentoring relationships. *Journal of Vocational Behavior, 3,* 321–339.

Robertson, I.T., & Downs, S. (1989). Work sample tests of trainability: A meta-analysis. *Journal of Applied Psychology, 74,* (3), 402–410.

Robinson, D.G., & Robinson, J.C. (1985). Breaking barriers to skill transfer. *Training and Development Journal, 39,* 82–83.

Sandroff, R. (1990). Why it won't be business as usual. *Working Woman,* supplement, January.

Schneller, R. (1989). Intercultural and intrapersonal processes and factors of misunderstanding: Implications for multicultural training. *International Journal of Intercultural Relations, 13,* 465–484.

Schuler, R.S., & Jackson, S.E. (1987). Linking competitive strategies with human resource management practices. *Academy of Management Executive, 1,* 207–219.

Seligman, M.E.P. & Schulman, P. (1986). Explanatory style as a predictor of performance as a life insurance sales agent. *Journal of Personality and Social Psychology, 50,* 832–838.

Skinner, B.F. (1938). *The behavior of organisms.* New York: Appleton.

Skinner, B.F. (1953). *Science and human behavior.* New York: Free Press.

Skinner, B.F. (1954). The science of learning and the

art of teaching. *Harvard Educational Review, 24*, 86–97.

Thorndike, E.L., & Woodworth, R.S. (1901). The influence of improvement in one mental function upon the efficiency of other functions. *Psychological Review, 8*, 247–262.

Triandis, H.C., Brislin, R., & Hui, C.H. (1989). Cross cultural training across the individualism-collectivism divide. *International Journal of Intercultural Relations, 12*, 269–289.

Watson, J.B. (1913). Psychology as the behaviorist views it. *Psychology Review, 20*, 159–177.

Wexley, K.N., & Baldwin, T.T. (1986). Posttraining strategies for facilitating positive transfer: An empirical investigation. *Academy of Management Journal, 29*, 503–520.

Wexley, K.N., & Latham, G.P. (1991). *Developing and training human resources in organizations*. New York: Harper & Row.

Yukl, G.A., and Latham, G.P. (1975). Consequences of reinforcement schedules and incentive magnitudes for employee performance: Problems encountered in an industrial setting. *Journal of Applied Psychology, 60*, 294–298.

Yukl, G.A, Latham, G.P., & Pursell, E.D. (1976). The effectiveness of performance incentives under continuous and variable ratio schedules of reinforcement. *Personnel Psychology, 29*, 221–231.

Yukl, G.A., Wexley, K.N., & Seymore, J.D. (1972). Effectiveness of pay incentives under variable ratio and continuous reinforcement schedules. *Journal of Applied Psychology, 56*, 19–23.

10

Work Socialization of Young People

Jan A. Feij

1 INTRODUCTION

In this chapter an outline will be given on the process of the socialization of young people in the work domain: the learning process by which young people acquire the skills, attitudes and values, and behaviour that are needed in order to be able to function as a valuable employee or as a fully integrated member of a working organization. Socialization is also found in other areas of life. Therefore, a distinction can be made between general and more specific definitions of socialization.

Hurrelmann (1988, p. 2) gives the following general definition: "Socialization designates the process in the course of which a human being, with his or her specific biological and psychological dispositions, becomes a socially competent person, endowed with the abilities and capacities for effective action within the larger society and the various segments of society, and dynamically maintains this status throughout the course of his or her life." In more specific definitions, learning or transformation processes have been mentioned which concern the acquisition of roles, opinions, values, skills and patterns of behaviour necessary for successful participation in a particular social system (e.g. in work or in a relationship).

It is not easy to distinguish between "socialization" and "learning" or "development". In any case we want to define "socialization" as an intra-personal concept and to distinguish it from "upbringing", i.e. the behaviour through which one tries to influence another person's development of character. As we will show, many authors make a connection between socialization processes at work and in other areas of life such as in relationships, family and leisure.

In socialization (at work) all kinds of factors play a role in the person and the (working) environment as well as in interactions between these two. If one studies the socialization process, one will inevitably encounter psychological, sociological and economical factors, all of which influence the way young people participate in the various social structures. Furthermore, "life-span developmental" approaches place work socialization in the wider context of career development. Hall (1987), for instance, views a career as a long-term "bundle" of socialization experiences, as the person moves in, through, and out of various work-related roles over the span of his or her work life. Therefore, this chapter has much in common with Chapter 12 in this volume, first published in 1989 (Boerlijst & Aite-Peña, 1989; see also Heesink & Feij, 1992[1]).

Figure 10.1 illustrates the complexity of the development of the occupational role, the different "theatres" in which it takes place and the significance of psychological, social and economical factors for the development of occupational roles. In principle, work socialization is a process that can span a lifetime. This chapter is mainly concerned with the phase in which young people leave school and enter the world of employment. During this period (roughly between the ages of 18 and 30, i.e. late adolescence and early adulthood) other status transitions usually take place as well: becoming economically independent, leaving the parental home, and entering into relationships. This is one of the reasons why this is an important phase in the socialization process, which is very influential in the further course of a person's occupational lifetime.

Work socialization, i.e. the acquisition of roles, attitudes, values and skills, begins in early childhood, continues through the school period and accumulates in adolescence and young adulthood, when a person leaves school and the first steps are taken into the world of employment—the "confrontation" or "encounter phase". Until that time the socialization process is referred to as anticipatory socialization. The process is completed in the "adaptation phase" in which different persons and organizational structures within the company and work group form the most important "socializing agents".

However, many critics regard the distinction within discrete stages of socialization as artificial and unsupported by empirical evidence. In addition, many authors stress the fact that the socialization process never ends. Furthermore, one must realize that the acquisition of social roles does not always occur via conscious, rational choices. The course of life can be drastically altered by small events, and because of this, life often has a "probabilistic" character (Vondracek, Lerner, & Schulenberg, 1986), impeding generalizations about "the socialization of young people".

Only an interdisciplinary approach, in which the diverse, mainly psychological, sociological and economic theories and factors are taken into account, can lead to a proper understanding of work socialization processes. Chapman (1990),

FIGURE 10.1

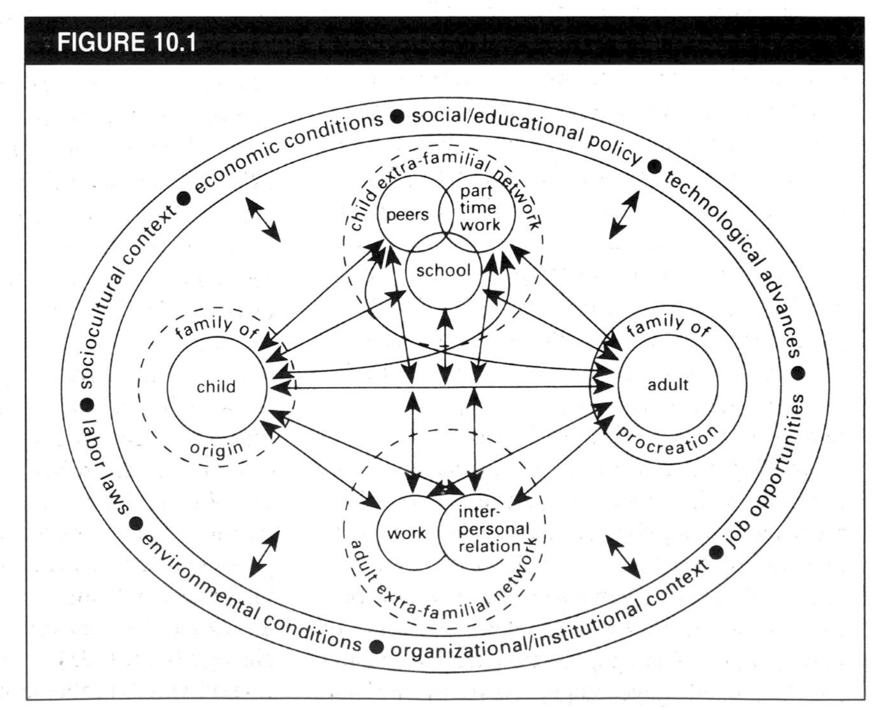

Career development: a dynamic interaction of the person with various types of environment (source: Vondracek et al., 1986, p. 79). Reprinted with permission of the author and publisher.

for example, provides arguments for the integration of developmental psychological and sociological approaches into the study of socialization. An interdisciplinary approach is required because, in order to correctly answer the central question "how does someone become a successful worker?" knowledge concerning three types of factors is needed. First, knowledge concerning factors in the person, such as capacities, interests, values and (role) behaviour, and the way in which these factors develop in combination with an often drastically changing environment. Second, structural factors in the work or school environment. And, finally, the wider social-economic, cultural and political context as it manifests itself in, among other things, employment, union legislation and governmental policy regarding training and work. Therefore, one can, if one wishes, enlarge the enumeration of relevant disciplines with, for example, anthropology, political science and, where past processes of change are concerned, history (Borman & Reisman, 1986).

Does a general all-embracing socialization theory exist? The answer is hardly or not at all. It is more likely to be a question of the application of diverse disciplinary theories to the field of socialization, rather than the existence of a single "umbrella theory". It is impossible to discuss in great detail all these theories in the context of this chapter (for an overview, see Hurrelmann, 1988).

In this chapter the emphasis is placed upon *psychological* theories and factors. Theory formation on and research into the subject of socialization within psychology, receives impulses mainly from developmental psychology, social psychology and the theory of personality. When particularly concerned with work socialization, work and organizational psychology (especially the "vocational psychology", Crites, 1969) obviously needs to be added to this list.

Developmental psychology is relevant because socialization is a process of (personality) development and as many claim, it especially concerns the question of development of the self-concept or "identity": i.e. a person's self-image as a worker (or as a partner, parent, or whatever life role). In particular, the older, psycho-analytically oriented developmental psychology, such as Erikson (1968), has had great influence on socialization theory formation.

Several authors believe that professional career and identity development go hand in hand (Hall, 1976; Kidd, 1984; Marcia, 1980; Super, 1957, 1981; Waterman, 1982). In this context "vocational maturity" and "vocational identity" (Crites, 1973; Super, 1955) are terms that have often been used. However, nowadays an "ecological" developmental psychology or "life-span developmental approach" (Baltes, 1978; Bronfenbrenner, 1979; Super, 1980; Vondracek et al., 1986) has become popular, in which the notion of strict developmental stages has been abandoned and the dynamic interaction with all sorts of context variables is being stressed.

Social psychology is essential because the processes through which people learn the "role of the worker" and develop their self-image or identity, takes place in the social environment (see, for example, Owens, 1992). Processes of social comparison could help to determine which exterior values will be integrated in the self-image (the "social identity"). In socialization literature, one encounters many social-psychological theories: social learning theories (Bandura, 1977; Krumboltz, 1981), role theories (Allen & Van de Vliert, 1984; Graen, 1976; Katz & Kahn, 1978), social comparison and attribution theories (Kelley, 1967; Rosenberg, 1981; Tajfel, 1978; Turner 1984) expectancy-value theories (Feij, 1987; Taris, Heesink, & Feij, 1995a[1]; Wanous, 1992) and attitude-behaviour models (Fishbein & Ajzen, 1975; Van Breukelen, 1990). A general model of newcomer entry and socialization into social groups has been presented by Moreland and Levine (1982); see also Anderson and Thomas (1996).

Personality psychology is also relevant to socialization theory and research. In socialization literature many "personological" terms appear (e.g. "work-personality" or "self-image"; see Van der Werff, 1985). Moreover, in research an attempt is often made to determine how it is possible that socialization is not equally successful for each individual. This interest in "individual differences" is the essence of personality psychology (Feij, 1985). In the influential "choice of career" and "vocational choice" theories of Roe

(1956) and Holland (1973) "personality" justifiably receives a significant place.

Hurrelmann (1988) summarizes the different sociological theories that are relevant to the field of (work) socialization. Sociological theories have a lot in common with the different psychological models. Although "interactionism", stating that socialization is determined by the mutual influence of person and environment, is the predominant movement these days, it is not a matter of one specific theory in which all these approaches are integrated.

The structure of this chapter is based on the chronological course of the work socialization process. In Section 2 a summary will be given of the various stages, processes and research variables mentioned in the literature on work socialization and career development. First of all, the different concepts and definitions used in the literature on (work) socialization as well as their internal relations will be specified. Next, a brief outline of the domain of organizational socialization research—undoubtedly one of the most relevant subjects for readers of this volume—is presented. In this section the taxonomy originally introduced by Fisher (1986) will be followed. Finally, the process of work socialization is placed in the wider array of factors and systems that influence a young adult's career development.

Section 3 will briefly deal with the periods in which young people are prepared for their entrance into "the world of work". Attention will be paid to the following subjects. First, the influence of the family in which a person grows up on the formation of attitudes and values towards work will be described. Second, the significance of the school as an "anticipatory socializing institution" is presented. The transition phase between school and employment (or unemployment) will also be discussed. How do young people choose a suitable organization? Essentially, socialization concerns the entire process of choosing a career, but this subject cannot be dealt with in detail here (see Chapter 12 of this volume).

Section 4, which forms the main part of this chapter, deals with the entrance into the employment process and the many factors which influence the integration of young people in the world of employment in their entrance period. A theoretical perspective of organizational socialization as a communication process will be presented and the close relation between recruitment, selection and socialization will be dealt with, as well as the actual practices used in companies.

In Section 5 the results of these and previous phases and processes will be outlined. A successful socialization implies a satisfactory situation for both employee and organization. From the point of view of the individual this means a stable "identity" as a worker and a balance between capacities and needs, and the values and demands that apply to the social environment (i.e. the employment organization). Good performance, a feeling of commitment to both work and company, a feeling of satisfaction and well-being, and good health can be regarded as a gauge for the above.

From the point of view of the organization, successful socialization means that one can speak of an employee who is well integrated in his or her working environment, who is valuable to the working team of which he or she is a part, and who has attained an equilibrium between adaptation and innovative behaviour, which is optimal to the organization.

So long as such a harmonious situation is not yet attained, further development is possible or necessary, until a point of balance or compromise between demands, wishes and possibilities emerges. Most authors nowadays stress that socialization is not so much a passive process of adaptation, but more an active process of information-seeking and negotiation or "contracting" (Anderson & Thomas, 1996; Heinz, 1991; Whitely, 1986). When development stagnates, in favourable cases a person will start searching for a new job and will be active on the employment market. In less favourable cases demotivation, dissatisfaction and a low degree of well-being is the result, or even dismissal from employment. The outcome of the socialization process is dependent on many factors in both the person and the situation, which influence each other. Therefore, the result is not a static state of affairs. Feedback processes from the outcome back to the person and the situation can lead to a new interaction and a new result (Whitely, Peiró, & Sarchielli, 1992; WOSY-International Research Group, 1989).[2]

Section 6 provides a summary of this chapter

and an evaluation of the present theory and research on work socialization. Important themes, such as the interaction between socialization in employment and in partner relationships or the family, gender-differential socialization and gender differences in the career, or the influence of the working mother as a working role model, unfortunately cannot be discussed in depth here due to the limitations placed on this piece. The reader is referred to reviews of the recent literature on the interface of work and family presented by Swanson (1992) and Watkins and Subich (1995).

2 SOCIALIZATION WITH REGARD TO WORK: STAGES, PROCESSES AND VARIABLES

2.1 Terminology

Although much has been written on the subject, there is little thorough knowledge regarding the way in which young people develop into capable participants in the work process, i.e. how they acquire the values, knowledge and skills needed in the work situation and required for an adequate execution of their task within the organization. This process is indicated by the use of many terms, such as: "work role development", "work personality development", "integration in the world of work", "occupational socialization", "organizational socialization", or more simply "work socialization". Figure 10.2 shows the relation between the different definitions.

The term "work socialization" refers to all socialization processes in the domain of work. The term "anticipatory socialization" is used in various contexts, indicating the preparation for work in general, for a specific occupational role or for a concrete task within a certain organization. Therefore, anticipatory socialization is a rather broad field of research. It does not only involve the influence of "pre-entry socialization" on the assimilation of newcomers in the organizational role, but also subjects from the psychology of occupational choice and selection. After all, the way in which the young employee adapts to the work situation will, to a large extent, depend on the "match" between expectations and capacities and the job a person chose or has been selected for (Van den Berg & Van den Tillaart, 1986; Wanous, 1992). We will return to these points in later sections.

Anticipatory socialization can be defined as "all learning or experience that prepares, either functionally or dysfunctionally, an individual for entry into the organization" (Fisher, 1986, p. 120). In this context Frese (1982) differentiates between *indirect* and *direct* anticipation. The first concerns preparations for the future work situation originating from the family and school. The foundation for successful participation in the occupational process is laid in the parental home, within the circle of friends, during school and in training. In these domains, opinions, expectations and values concerning what work entails and what can be derived from it, are already emerging. It is a matter of "socialization *to* work". Holiday jobs or part-time work also contribute to this process. According to Clarke (1980a) previous work experience improves the chance of finding employment. Direct anticipation concerns preparations by the individual such as the gathering of information on the future job and the weighting of personal opportunities and prospects.

In an outline of the available literature, Fisher (1986) also shows that there are two kinds of studies in the field of anticipatory socialization: (a) literature on the self-identity (as far as work is concerned) and on relatively stable values regarding work in general, for example, the "work ethic" (see MOW International Research Team, 1987) or the occupation in particular (e.g. Holland, 1973); and (b) specific studies on the expectations or beliefs of the young employee with regard to concrete aspects of the new role in the organization, such as the type of work, supervision and promotion chances.

We reserve the term "occupational socialization" for the development of the occupational role in a wider context. Occupational socialization is a matter of values and skills that are generalizable in various organizational contexts.

"Organizational socialization" and "work group socialization" specifically relate to the integration process within the organization (or proximal work group) into which the young employee enters and in which he or she must learn

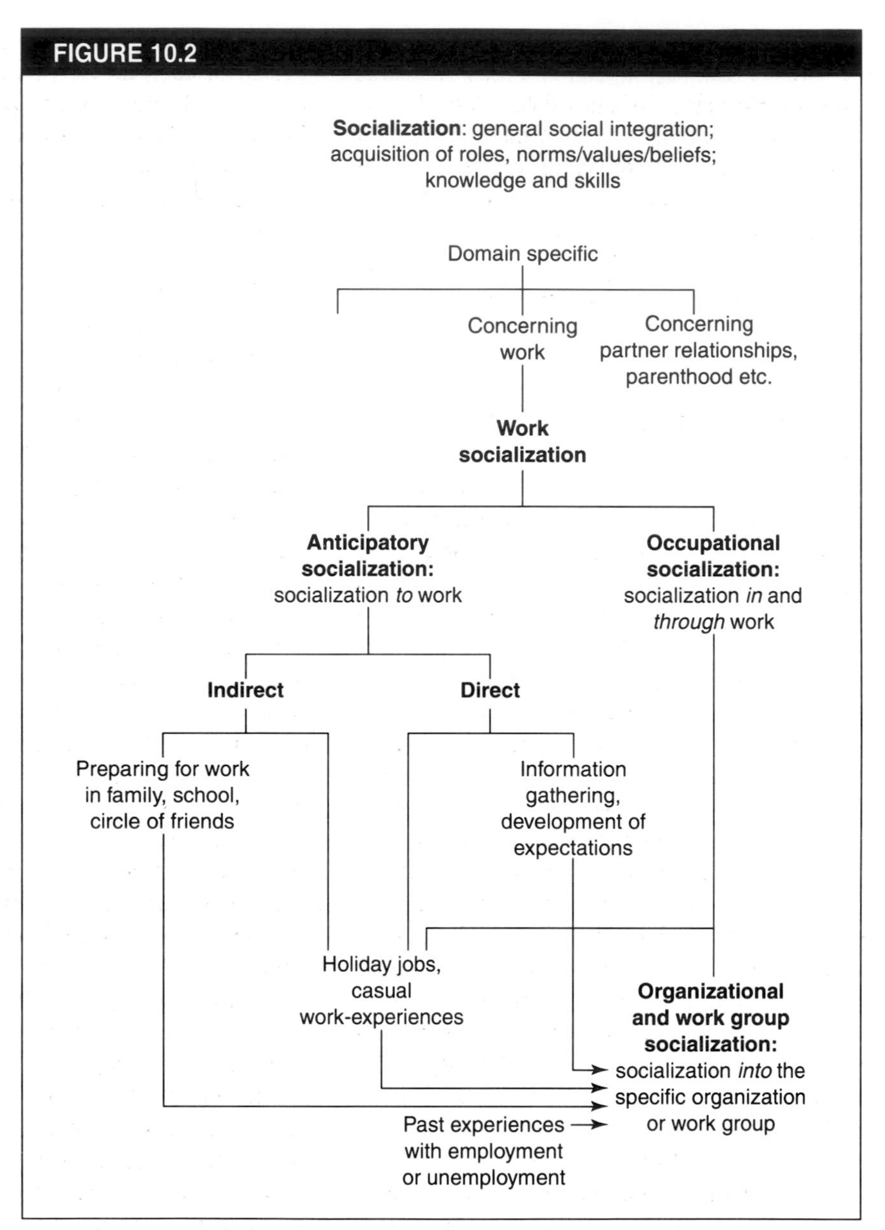

Socialization: terms and their internal relations.

to execute a particular task and adapt to the specific organizational or group climate. This is also called "in role socialization" or "socialization into work".

Furthermore, an often used term in literature on socialization is (status) "transition". This is defined as a period "during which an individual is either changing role (taking a different role) or changing an orientation to a role already held" (Louis, 1980b, p. 202). Socialization, broadly defined, is a long term process pervading an individual's entire career (Feldman, 1989; Hall, 1987; Van Maanen, 1976). In every meaningful transition a process of socialization takes place in the new role and situation. There are many such transitions, for example, the transition from school to work, the transition from unemployment to work or a change in a person's role within the same organization (Chao, O'Leary-Kelly, Wolf, Klein, & Gardner, 1994; Nicholson, 1987; Van der

Velde & Feij, 1995 Van Maanen & Schein, 1979; Van der Velde, Feij, & Taris, 1995). Coetsier, Claes, and Berings (1987) justifiably claim that the process of learning, which forms the core of socialization, does not restrict itself to the moment of transition (where one could speak of an "acute" socialization moment), but begins before and continues afterwards. For a description and empirical test of work-role transition theory the reader is referred to Nicholson (1984) and Ashforth and Saks (1995).

2.2 Organizational socialization: a taxonomy

Organizational socialization is defined as: "the process by which an individual comes to appreciate the values, abilities, expected behaviours, and social knowledge essential for assuming an organizational role and for participating as an organizational member" (Louis, 1980a, pp. 229–230). One of the first publications on this subject is by Bakke (1953). He spoke of a fusion process in which person and organization are being attuned to one another. This fusion consists of the process of socialization of the newcomer by the organization and a simultaneous process, namely the personalization or individualization, whereby the newcomer modifies the organization or workplace (see Hess, 1993). Over the last decade, several authors attempted to review and integrate the large number of studies on organizational socialization that appeared in the different professional journals and books (e.g. Anderson & Thomas, 1996; Fisher, 1986; Hall, 1987; Wanous & Colella, 1989; Whitely, 1986).

In Fisher's (1986) outline it appears that there are three general approaches to the subject "organizational socialization" which can be distinguished in the literature. In the first place authors are concerned with the *content* of socialization. Socialization is a process of learning and change with regard to the newcomer, and a relevant question that one could pose is "what can be learned" or "what changes are made?" A second approach is the study of the *outcomes* of the socialization process. Third, one can analyse the socialization *process*. This third approach entails various stage models. Analysing the socialization process is concerned with understanding the stages through which a newcomer passes as he or she develops into an experienced organizational member. More recent process-research has focused on the information acquisition and feedback-seeking behaviours of organizational newcomers. We will return to this subject later (see Section 4.2).

2.2.1 Content

Socialization researchers (e.g. Feldman, 1976, 1981; Morrison, 1993a) suggest there are four primary tasks which make up the socialization process: (a) *task mastery*—learning how to perform the components of one's job; (b) *role clarification*—developing an understanding of one's role in the organization; (c) *acculturation*—learning about and adjusting to the organization's culture; and (d) *social integration*—developing relationships with co-workers.

Fisher (1986) developed a related but slightly different taxonomy. She mentions four content categories that concern the learning process of the newcomer in the organization: (a) values, goals and culture of the organization; (b) work-group values, norms and friendships within the work-team (see Anderson & Thomas, 1996); (c) knowledge and skills needed for effective task performance; (d) personal development (i.e. possible changes of identity, self-image and motivational structure as a result of experience with the demands posed by the job or the organization). Several studies can be mentioned to illustrate this point. For example, the results of a study among police recruits by Stradling, Crowe, & Tuohy (1993) revealed evidence of identity transformation, i.e. changes in recruits' self-image, during the initial socialization to the police service. These changes were interpreted in terms of adaptation toward a more instrumental and cynical operational style. Similarly, Guimond (1995) observed changes of attitudes and values as a result of socialization processes in the military system.

The newcomer has much to learn (see also Schein, 1968, 1978). Apart from the four previously mentioned "learning tasks", the young employees should be prepared by the socializing organization for the fact that they have to learn something and that they must pay attention to that which they have to learn and from whom. Fisher mentions other topics, important for research, education and training officials. For example, the order in which the various aspects of the organization are learned, the question whether the learning process is primarily concerned with attitudes, values and opinions or overt behaviour, and the legitimacy of the interference of the organization with the various areas of the employee's life.

Although there is a great deal of conceptual overlap among the aforementioned content areas, Chao et al. (1994) argue that there has been virtually no empirical research to verify the hypothetical content of the socialization domain or to relate content areas to socialization processes and outcomes. Chao et al. (1994) presented a new taxonomy of content dimensions of the socialization domain. From a review of the socialization literature, in particular three classic sources (Feldman, 1981; Fisher, 1986; Schein, 1968), the following six dimensions of organizational socialization content were conceptualized and developed: (a) *performance proficiency*; (b) *people*—i.e. establishing successful and satisfying work relationships with organizational members; (c) *politics*—the individual's success in gaining information regarding formal and informal work relationships and power structures within the organization; (d) *language*—the individual's knowledge of the profession's technical language as well as knowledge of the jargon that is unique to the organization; (e) *organizational goals and values*; (f) *history*—i.e. knowledge of the organization's traditions, customs and myths as well as knowledge about the personal backgrounds of particular organizational members. Chao et al. (1994) found support for these socialization dimensions through a factor analysis on questionnaire data from full-time professionals. Furthermore, the results of their study show that three groups of respondents with different career outcomes—i.e. respondents who did not change jobs, changed jobs within their organization, or changed jobs as well as organizations—had significantly different response patterns on all six content dimensions.

2.2.2 Outcomes

Which "outcomes" or criteria can be distinguished regarding the success of the process of organizational socialization? Socialization may be expected to result in an increase of knowledge about the organization, the working team, the job, and particularly knowledge about what the organization expects from the employee (i.e. role clarity). In addition, socialization should result in an increase of skills, and finally in altered attitudes, opinions and personal values. According to Fisher (1986) the emphasis in descriptive literature is placed on somewhat different outcomes than in more empirically-oriented literature.

Fisher concludes that articles in the first category "stress the learning and internalization of organizational norms and values and worry about the problem of overconformity. They suggest that the ideal outcome state is creative individualism (Schein, 1968) or role innovation (Van Maanen & Schein, 1979), which consists of obeying the most central norms, while introducing new ideas by refusing to conform with all norms (Schein, 1968)" (Fisher, 1986, p. 110). We will return to this subject later. Identification and innovations are probably not that important in routine jobs with strict supervision. In contrast, internalization of norms and values in a group of professionals working independently is of utmost importance.

Many outcome variables related to work socialization are mentioned in empirical literature (e.g. Feldman, 1976, 1981, Toffler, 1981), such as:

- Motivation and performance criteria: i.e. the appropriate skills and productivity; role clarity; accurate knowledge of work procedures and work environment; intrinsic motivation, effort and initiative; and the ambition of the employee to build a career.
- Commitment: trustworthiness regarding the realization of the work role; involvement and identification with the values of the company; or, as a negative indication, the tendency to leave the company as soon as the opportunity arises.
- Interpersonal qualities: cooperation; mutual influence; a good relationship with colleagues.
- Well-being and satisfaction: satisfaction with the job in general or facets thereof; self-confidence and feelings of self-efficacy; minimal role insecurity and minimal tension at

work; self-acceptance and acceptance by colleagues as a valuable member of the workforce; an overall feeling of well-being, etc.

Undoubtedly one could add to this list or argue about the classification of the variables in the four categories. (For a critical discussion of the subject of classification of outcomes the reader is referred to Section 5 of this chapter). Empirical research concerning the relationship between the different outcome variables needs to be undertaken. As a researcher, one has to realize what has been emphasized earlier: that socialization is an ongoing learning process that in many cases is never completed. In the words of Chao et al. (1994, p. 731): "... current research is almost exclusively focused on organizational newcomers, yet basic tenets of socialization theory describe it as a lifelong process pervading an individual's entire career". Depending on the specific learning requirements of any new work-role and the degree of similarity or difference between old and new roles, learning can be completed and socialization stabilized in a short time, or learning may continue to progress over prolonged time periods. If the latter is the case, the outcomes at a certain moment can be viewed as "independent variables" influencing later phases in the learning process.

2.2.3 Processes: stage models

A third way to view the organizational socialization is in terms of phases in the adaptation or learning process that young people go through. Many authors have constructed stage models in which they indicate how "naive" newcomers in the organization grow to become complete socialized "insiders" (Feldman, 1976, 1981; Graen, 1976; Louis, 1980a; Schein, 1978; Van Maanen, 1976). Despite differences in terminology these models have much in common. Most are variations of a "three-stage entry" model (Porter et al., 1975). The essence of the three phases will be described here; later on they will be dealt with in more detail.

The "*anticipatory socialization*" or the "pre-entry" phase. This is the period before entering the organization. As we have seen, this phase includes the preparation, in the broader sense, for entering the work process. Whitely (1986) though, prefers the term "market encounter phase" to emphasize that this preparation does not always lead to employment, but for many young people nowadays it unfortunately leads to unemployment. In this phase the school functions as a socializing agent preparing young people for work by providing them with knowledge, skills, attitudes, values and norms, and an idea of what to expect in the future. Furthermore, the parental home and potential supporting agencies such as the job centre and youth organizations play a part in this phase. Also, companies, unions and social activities associated with the firm already contribute to anticipatory socialization; through adequate advice, these institutions can help prevent unrealistic expectations (Coetsier et al., 1987). This will facilitate the transition of young employees.

The "*confrontation phase*". Terms such as "breaking-in period", "encounter", or "accommodation" are also used to describe this phase. We are concerned here with the first, and for effective socialization the most important, confrontation with the organization. In this, as Coetsier et al. (1987, p. 4) describe it, "acute moment of transition from the one role to the other", previously-acquired expectations are tested on reality, personal estimations are compared to the evaluations given by the organization and "reinforcement contingencies" are discovered: i.e. which type of behaviour is preferred and rewarded, and which types of behaviour are seen by the organization as undesirable. In this process, role ambiguity and conflicts can arise, resulting in disorientation (Feldman, 1976). From research cited by Anderson and Thomas (1996) it appears that "unmet expectations" are a major reason for employees' leaving employers in the first few years of employment. A good fit between expectations and the reality of the job, however, is also related to young employees' career-enhancing strategies and attempted job content innovation (Feij, Whitely, Peiró, & Taris, 1995).

These entrance experiences, in which old roles have to be discarded and new ones taken on, are often described as stressful, or as a "reality shock" (Jones, 1983; Nelson, 1987; Nelson, Quick & Joplin, 1991; Saks & Ashforth, 1996a; Wanous, 1992). Accordingly, Schein (1978) introduced the idea that the transition between the various phases requires reorientation and adjustment from many young employees. Other authors, however, strongly doubt that the notion of a "shock" is indeed relevant (Clarke, 1980a). It is evident that the way in which the company receives, informs and guides the newcomer, i.e. applies "socialization tactics" (Jones, 1986), is of great importance to the outcome of this confrontation phase. If there is indeed a "shock", this can be reduced considerably by the socializing organization.

Several writers have suggested that one vehicle for easing the stress of the transition to a new organization and facilitating newcomer adjustment is through effective psychological "contracting" (Anderson & Thomas, 1996; Nelson et al., 1991; Rousseau, 1989). Anderson and Thomas define the psychological contract as the exchange relationship that exists between an employee and his or her organization, meaning that the employee carries out certain actions and behaves in certain ways (e.g. effective performance, loyalty) and expects the organization to fulfil its obligations in return (e.g., salary, job security). They cite Herriot (1984) who argues that one role of the psychological contract is to decrease uncertainty and increase the perceived predictability of organizational actions.

The final phase, in which lasting adjustment evolves and the employee becomes a complete "insider" is the "*adaptation phase*". In socialization literature other terms are also used, such as the "phase of mutual acceptance", "settling in", "change and acquisition", or, "metamorphosis" (for references, see Fisher, 1986). In Section 2.2.1. we described the various types of adjustment demanded of the young employees, for instance, task mastery, integration of the demands of the role and being successful in the new role, and the development of a positive attitude towards the norms and values of the organization, or of the relevant groups therein. The employee has to, as Fisher (1986, p. 116) calls it, "learn to handle conflict both within and external to the organization ... establish an identity perceived as important by both him- or herself and the organization, and settle into new attitudes, values, and behaviours that are consistent with prevailing norms regarding loyalty, commitment, and performance".

The choice of a three stage model is somewhat arbitrary. Wanous (1992) formulated several criteria with which the term "stage" has to meet. First, the experiences that form a particular phase must have more characteristics in common with each other than similarities with experiences in other phases. Furthermore, the sequence from phase to phase must be clear. Accordingly Wanous (1992) comes to an integrated model that has four phases and starts when the newcomer enters the company. These phases and the experiences that can be found within are summarized in Table 10.1.

As previously stated there has been a lot of criticism of late on these phase models, for example, that they are too deterministic and they do not take individual differences into consideration (Reese & Overton, 1970; Whitely, 1986). But the models have not only been criticized on theoretical grounds; phase models are also debatable on empirical grounds: "Stage models, viewed as heuristic devices only, may be helpful in describing some of the types of learning and change which occur during this process. However, whether stage models accurately describe three or four consistently and observable distinct steps containing different content is questionable" (Fisher, 1986, p. 117). Instead of starting from fixed, successive phases with unique "socialization tasks", Fisher argues that an empirical approach is required. This implies that through longitudinal research (and on a variety of research samples) the moments at which the different learning processes take place are mapped. Perhaps there are indeed discrete stages, but it is likely that young employees do not go through these stages at the same pace. Furthermore, one must realize, according to Fisher (1986), that there are not only stages in the individual adjustment, but also the *job* alters as the newcomer learns to meet the demands of the position. In this context, authors like Graen (1976) and Louis (1980a) point out, that a negotiation between the employee and his superiors takes place.

The previously outlined three- and four-stage models concern early phases in the organizational

TABLE 10.1.

Stages in the socialization process.

Stage 1: Confronting and accepting organizational reality
- *a* Confirmation/disconfirmation of expectations
- *b* Conflicts between personal values and needs, and the organizational climates
- *c* Discovering which personal aspects are reinforced, which are not reinforced, and which are punished by the organization

Stage 2: Achieving role clarity
- *a* Being initiated to the tasks in the new job
- *b* Defining one's interpersonal roles
  - *i* with respect to peers
  - *ii* with respect to one's boss
- *c* Learning to cope with resistance to change
- *d* Congruence between a newcomer's own evaluation of performance and the organization's evaluation of performance
- *e* Learning how to work within the given degree of structure and ambiguity

Stage 3: Locating oneself in the organizational context
- *a* Learning which modes of one's own behaviour are congruent with those of the organization
- *b* Resolution of conflicts at work, and between outside interests and work
- *c* Commitment to work and to the organization stimulated by first-year job challenge
- *d* The establishment of an altered self-image, new interpersonal relationships, and the adoption of new values

Stage 4: Detecting signposts of successful socialization
- *a* Achievement of organizational dependability and commitment
- *b* High satisfaction in general
- *c* Feelings of mutual acceptance
- *d* Job involvement and internal work motivation
- *e* The sending of "signals" between newcomers and the organization to indicate mutual acceptance

Source: J.P. Wanous, Organizational Entry, 2nd edition, p. 209. Copyright 1992, Addison-Wesley Publication Company Inc. Reprinted by permission of Addison-Wesley Longman Inc.

socialization process. If one chooses a longer-term perspective, many more phases could be distinguished (see Boerlijst & Aite Peña, 1989). Nicholson (1987) points to the "cyclic" character of the work socialization process: after an individual has gone through the three phases—"preparation", "encounter" and "adjustment"—a certain balance is attained in the work ("stabilization"). After a while the individual will have matured enough to face a new challenge. When a person subsequently changes employment, he or she will find themselves in the first phase again.

2.3 Work socialization in a wider perspective

In the lives of young people the entry into employment is an important event, which is embedded in the course of life in various ways, for example, connected with other transitions, such as leaving the parental home and becoming self-supportive.

At this point, the transition from school to work is the most significant change of status that one encounters when studying the work socialization process. The analysis of this change requires a multi-disciplinary approach (Clarke, 1980a; Fisher, 1986). Whether or not a person finds employment is dependent on many factors: the local labour market, the way in which a person searches for a job, and the extent to which that person applies him- or herself. However, the sort of career advice, selection, information and (when needed) re-schooling, and the policies of government, education and the business community concerning these notions are also important. The transition from school to work is thus decidedly intricate. Heinz (1991) describes the entry into the labour market as a decision-making process that is directed by (a) the structure of possibilities concerning schooling and job opportunities; (b) institutional schemes (e.g. apprenticeship); (c) social referential norms, such as the values of parents and friends; (d) "biographical commitments", i.e. previously-taken decisions and results thereof, such as diplomas and occupational qualifications; and (e) wider aims in life that the person concerned pursues or that are important to him or her.

The nature and the level of the first job that a (high)school or university graduate accepts are also dependent on a great many individual-psychological and social-structural factors. After all, once the young employee starts his or her first job, a complex interaction between personal characteristics and the introduction procedures employed by the company comes into play; as such this interaction can be viewed from a more individual or a more structural perspective.

Clarke (1980a) outlined the contribution that the various scientific disciplines could make to the knowledge of the school–work transition. Naturally, psychology explains the entry into the work process from the perspective of individual characteristics (capacities, needs, personality traits, etc.) and studies the aspirations, choices of career, expectations and attitudes towards work that develop along with these characteristics. In addition, psychology studies the results of guidance, advice and information given to the individual graduate. Sociology mainly studies social, structural and cultural factors, such as social class, domestic background and type of education received. Economics stresses the importance of the structural factors of the labour market. From this perspective, it is of considerable importance whether a person has a job with a relatively low reward, poor working conditions, little job security, and limited promotion and training possibilities, versus a job in a more favourable "primary sector" of the employment market.

Although we will mainly concentrate on the psychological aspects of the work socialization process, the sociological aspects are also essential in this chapter, not least for a good understanding of the psychological factors. Featherman and Sørensen (1984) have, for example, shown that a connection exists between the age at which a person enters the employment process and other significant transitions (marriage, children, etc.). They also argue that this connection differs for people from different cohorts, probably due to large-scale institutional developments, such as industrialization (see Blossfeld & Nuthmann, 1991). Many transitions that are important to the socialization process are apparently not only connected to age ("age-graded"), but also determined by the character of the times ("history-graded").

The many factors that at various moments influence the work socialization process are summarized in a model borrowed from O'Brien (1986), shown in Figure 10.3. In this model the course of the work socialization process is schematically shown. The process begins as anticipatory socialization in the family in which a person grows up and during the period of education. The combination of capacities, values and interests on the one hand, and acquired knowledge and skills on the other, results in an affinity with a certain type of work or job, the "ideal choice of job". However, this ideal job cannot always be obtained. The profession that a person will take up, is, apart from the ideal choice, also dependent on the education received and the local labour market, which in turn depend on the aforementioned structural factors.

Finding a suitable job often requires a considerable investment in the form of searching and being prepared to accept other types of work than the type for which one has been trained. Sociologists therefore stress that for many school-leavers it is not so much a question of choice of profession, but more a question of "allocation" of profession.

FIGURE 10.3

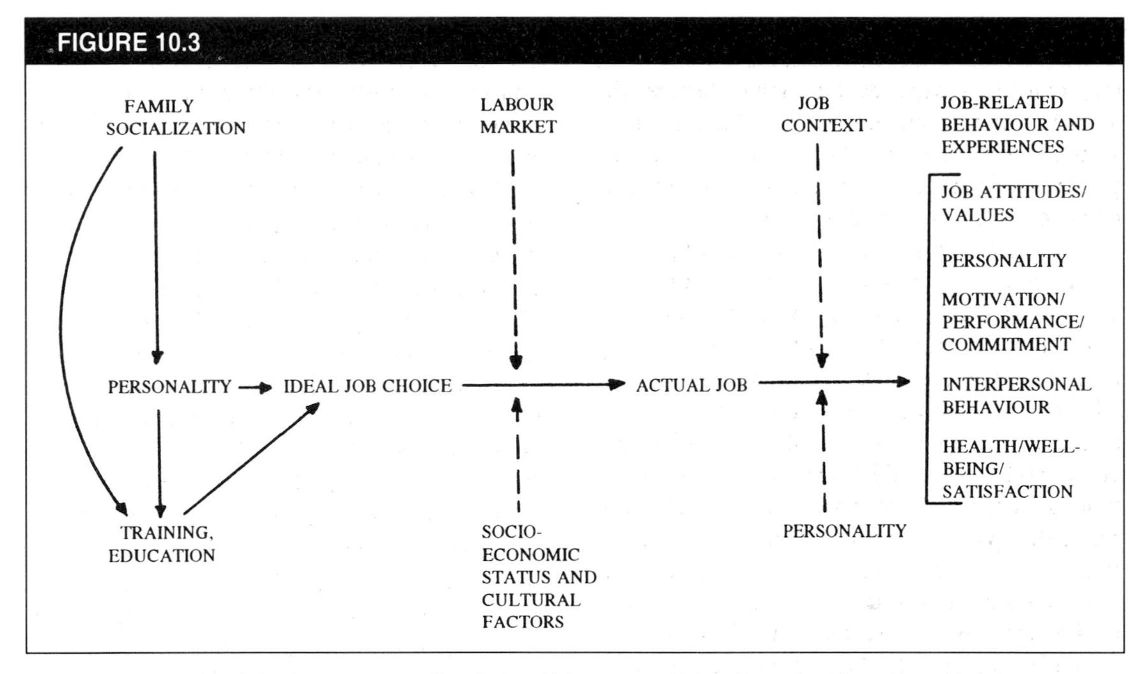

Work socialization: the relation between personality, choice of job, content of job and job-related behaviour with various moderators (modified from Psychology of Work and Unemployment, O'Brien, 1986, p. 100). Copyright John Wiley & Sons Ltd. Reprinted with permission.

A person's social-economic status also influences the job choice and searching process. Not only do many domestic and institutional environmental factors influence the intellectual and personality development, determining the choices that will be made, environmental factors will also exert influence during the search for a job. Parents, family and friends can be both supportive and informative toward the individual during the period in which a suitable job is sought. Usually, the modelling function alone is enough to make the "social network" very influential. An important social-cultural factor is ethnicity: the chance of employment is considerably less favourable for ethnic minorities, even for those with a high level of education, than it is for the indigenous population. Through training, among other things in social skills and (re-)education, this disadvantage can hopefully be reduced (Bleichrodt & Van Leest, 1987).

Once the graduate has found work, he or she starts the "confrontation phase". Many work-related behaviours, experiences and attitudes of the new employee are of course directly dependent on the content of the job (what it actually entails and the qualifications needed) but also on the characteristics of the task, such as the amount of variety and autonomy (Hackman & Oldham 1975) or the extent to which the work entails working with people, data and objects (Fine & Wiley, 1971).

However, as Figure 10.3 shows, the relation between the content of the job and task-related behaviours and evaluations is "moderated" by other factors—namely "personality" and the context in which the task is carried out. The "job context" consists of, among other things, the relations between employees, the quality of the organization or the "organizational climate", and the socialization tactics used, such as providing adequate information about career possibilities within the company. "Personality" as a moderator is meant to represent on the one hand work values, for example, the work ethic or the importance a person attaches to work compared to other areas of life—i.e. the "centrality of work" (MOW International Research Team, 1987). On the other hand, "personality" comprises capacities, interests and needs, self-image and personality traits in the social-emotional sphere.

In summary, Figure 10.3 shows how the dynamic interaction between aspects of the job, the work environment and personal characteristics determines the outcome of the socialization process. Successful socialization thus results in employees who are devoted to their work, satisfied, functioning effectively, and healthy. The model just described corresponds with more recent developments in the personality theory ("interactionism") and more specifically, with vocational and job choice orientated person-environment "fit" theories (e.g. Edwards, 1991; Holland, 1973; Kristof, 1996). It must be said that Figure 10.3 is an "heuristic" model rather than an empirically tested model. O'Brien (1986), for example, concludes that the moderating effect (in the statistical sense) of values in the relation between characteristics of the job and job satisfaction is not strong. According to O'Brien the relation between the content of employment and satisfaction is, in other words, not notably influenced by personality characteristics.

However, a proper harmony or "fit" between the individual's needs and capacities and the rewards and demands of the work(environment) is an essential basis for employee's satisfaction and well-being; see Edwards (1991) for a review. In practice, one attempts to attain this harmony through an adequate "job design" on the one hand and selection of the right personnel on the other. Cases of a clear "mismatch" between the expectations of the newcomer and the reality of the job will often result in dissatisfaction, and lead to health complaints and absenteeism (Feij, Banks, Parkinson, & Whitely, 1992) or the tendency to search for alternative employment (Mobley, Griffith, Hand, & Meglino, 1979; Taris, Heesink, Feij, Van der Velde, & Van Gastel, 1991; Taris, Van der Velde, Feij, & Van Gastel, 1992; Wanous, 1992).

Such a "mismatch" can have various consequences: acceptance of the fact that the position does not live up to expectations, a change of values or searching for alternative employment and hence a change of environment. For socialization theory this means that the "outcomes" of the socialization process feed back to the individual and the environment at a certain time (WOSY International Research Group, 1989). For the sake of clarity such "feedback loops" are not included in Figure 10.3.

In the next Section we will briefly deal with two central subjects in the literature on work socialization: the role of the family in the anticipatory socialization and the transition from school to work.

3 ANTICIPATORY SOCIALIZATION

3.1 Work socialization in the parental home

Work socialization starts as early as the parental home. Here the foundation is laid for later orientations and values with regard to education and work. Children learn a lot from their parents (and brothers and sisters) about the "world of work".

According to Vondracek et al. (1986) the socialization process first of all begins with the activities that the child develops within the family in the form of domestic chores and play (see, for example, Blair, 1992). The method and style of upbringing employed by the parents, such as the extent to which the parents stimulate performance or independence, is very important to this process, as is the (emotional) bond between parents and child (e.g. Greenberger & Goldberg, 1989). Other significant factors in this context are the material and financial support offered by parents, their encouraging and positive attitude towards the career choice of the child, and the relationship with brothers and sisters.

Within the context of the family the child learns a number of important roles and role expectations. In this learning process parents act as the first and perhaps most influential role models: "Through the perception of, identification with, and practice in 'playing' parental work and sex roles, children begin to grasp notions concerning societal role expectations and to fantasize about what work role they might eventually assume" (Vondracek et al., 1986, p. 53).

Furthermore, the socialization process can be influenced by the structural characteristics of the family, such as the size of the family, the order in which the children are born, or whether it is a one-parent home. Finally, material factors linked to the structure and the social-economic status of the family also play a role, for example, the amount of living space, the reading material available, and so on. However, according to Vondracek et al. (1986) the processes in which these sorts of family-ecological factors have influence have hardly been studied.

A significant study on the influence of the family on the work socialization processes was conducted by Mortimer, Lorence, and Kumka (1986), who built on the earlier work of Kohn (1977, 1981). Their theoretical starting point is the so-called "occupational linkage model" (Lueptow, McClendon, & McKeon, 1979). This model assumes that there is a relationship between the social-economic position of the parents and the socialization of the child, and that this connection progresses through three causative lines. First, there is a connection between the work experiences (which are strongly dependent on social class) and the system of values that the father of the family holds. Second, it is assumed that this value system determines the "socialization orientations and practices", i.e. the methods of upbringing employed. In turn, these govern the work values and behaviour of the adolescent and thus are responsible for his or her later performance at work. This model emphasizes "occupational self-direction": parents who experience independence in their employment (mostly a privilege of the higher social classes), value this highly and therefore emphasize independence in the upbringing of their children (Kohn & Schooler, 1983).

Based on this theory Mortimer et al. (1986) conducted a longitudinal survey on the connection between work characteristics, family charcteristics and personality characteristics (mainly attitudes and values). Unfortunately the research was limited to a group of highly educated males. In spite of the one-sided composition of the sample, which had a potential for restriction of range in the research variables, the findings of Kohn and Schooler (1982, 1983) were confirmed.

In accordance with the "occupational linkage model" the extent to which the adolescent felt supported by his father appeared a fundamental socialization factor. This fatherly support influenced the development of competent self-image and a strong involvement with work; these factors in turn influence the forming of the value system regarding work and also the experiences and performance in the career. Furthermore, it was striking that, even in this limited group, more support was experienced from the father when the social-economic status of the family was higher, which is in accordance with Kohn's theory.

Mortimer et al. (1986) also show that at a certain point in the socialization process the role of the parents (or the father) seems to be finished. The further psychological development of young adults seemed to be more determined by personal work experiences. A significant outcome of the study is that the experience of autonomy in the job is a crucial factor in the development of a feeling of competence and a positive work mentality.

In a Dutch survey by Te Grotenhuis and Dronkers (1989) the significance of the socializing role of the father is also apparent, and this time in a negative sense. They found that the children of unemployed fathers function poorer at school and receive higher education less frequently than children of working fathers, even after partialling out differences in milieu. Thus, according to Te Grotenhuis and Dronkers, there is an increase in the already existing inequality of educational opportunities, and the likelihood of unemployment is passed on from one generation to another.

In another Dutch survey, Meijers (1989) studied the socialization process in the family in a qualitative-descriptive manner. Among other things, the influence the parental home has on the "plan of life" of adolescents and the position of work within that plan was studied, as well as both the transfer of values and the manner in which parents direct the behaviour of their children. The results show that almost all young people interviewed had the feeling that adulthood was something that "happened" to them. Also their wishes and ideas regarding work appeared to be either poorly structured, or not exist at all. Boys appeared mostly to hold on to the traditional role of breadwinner, while the majority of girls wanted to combine children and work, something that could lead to conflicts with (future) partners (see Archer, 1985). Furthermore, Meijers (1989) found differences in the way in which parents handle their sons and daughters with regard to work.

Parents negotiated significantly more often with their daughters than they did with their sons about the demands concerning work.

These points show that the socialization regarding work as it takes place in the family has much to do with gender-specific role patterns. The division of roles between the father and the mother, the career of both partners, the emotional climate within the family and the manner in which both parents communicate with their children, form interrelating factors that are probably of great influence on the socialization process and the differences therein that can occur between boys and girls. Many recent studies stress gender as a major determinant of career development and career outcomes, such as salary (Paludi, 1990; Taris, Bok, Feij, & Heesink, 1994; Taris, Heesink, & Feij, 1995b; see also Watkins & Subich, 1995). Several studies suggest that sex differences in vocational structure and career development may be the result of sex-role socialization (Astin, 1984; Neimeyer, Brown, Metzler, Hagans, et al., 1989). Lytton and Romney (1991), however, meta-analysed a large number of studies on whether parents show systematic differences in their rearing of boys and girls, and concluded that most effect sizes were non-significant and small. In North American studies, the only socialization area to display a significant effect for both parents was encouragement of sex-typed activities.

Because work socialization is a constantly developing process, the role patterns, attitudes and values learned in the parental home will be taken into the family that the young adult will create himself or herself ("the family of procreation"): the experience within that family or in more non-committal relationships will influence the further (work) socialization process (see also Figure 10.1). Mortimer et al. (1986), for example, have shown that a relationship exists between experiences at work and experiences in the newly-founded families of the men surveyed.

Thus, the young adult men and women are socialized further and transfer their roles and values to their own children, in as far as the "generation gap" allows them to do so. The intertwinement of socialization in the domains of work and partner relationships and the meaning of gender roles form a complicated subject, which we cannot explore further in this chapter. For a more extensive review see, among others, Watkins & Subich (1995).

3.2 The role of the school and the transition from school to work

The significance of schooling and education for work socialization and career development is evident. The primary task of the school is obviously to convey knowledge. Diplomas and certificates offer entrance into the "world of work". In addition, job orientation, career guidance, and providing information concerning the job market are also tasks of the school system.

Schools are important socializing institutions for yet another reason. The pupil gains experience through various activities, inter-personal relationships, roles and role expectations, which will also be important in the future at work: "It is through the school that the child is provided with his or her first structured social arena within which to encounter and realize the consequences of social and academic competence, competition and power relationships, which may be extremely important to career development" (Vondracek et al., 1986, p. 49). Also, obvious matters such as being able to work at a fixed time and place, are learned at school. In addition, pupils—because they literally "move up" to a higher grade—gain experience through a series of transitions to an increasingly complex context. These "hordes" form a forerunner for the later transition from the school situation to the work situation, and therefore are very educational indeed.

How does the transition from school to work progress and which factors and processes play a facilitating or a hindering role therein? In an outline of the available literature by Clarke (1980a), the widespread misunderstanding that the school–work transition is extremely stressful is disproved. Although this transition usually takes place during a turbulent period in adolescence and young people are often poorly prepared and naive with regard to the work situation that awaits them, the belief that this transition is a "culture shock" (Louis, 1980b) is strongly over-exaggerated and not based on empirical data. Rather, the school–work transition has positive effects on most young people (Tiggemann & Winefield, 1989; Van der Velde et al., 1995).

A general image evolving from the literature (e.g. Clarke, 1980a; Meijers, 1989; Roberts, 1984) is that the influence of "socializing agents"—the school, parents, contemporaries and government—on the ease with which the adolescent makes the school–work transition, is relatively insignificant. New employees will always experience some adaptation problems because once they start work, they have to learn technical and social skills, they have to adjust their prior expectations, and they have to readjust to new daily routines (Coetsier et al., 1987). In spite of this, according to Clarke (1980a) the vast majority is able to make such an adjustment within a few weeks. There is, for that matter, evidence that the quality of the introduction procedure has no strong or lasting effect on the attitudes of young employees, nor on the number of times they change jobs during the first period of their career. However, greater satisfaction is experienced in companies that provide newcomers with a preparatory introduction, but that may be due to the higher level of the positions concerned (Douglas, unpublished, cited in Clarke, 1980a).

The great significance of a good match between education and the job market is generally acknowledged. Companies invest a lot of money in extra schooling and retraining, and the structural integration of education and work is to date also given high priority by the governments of most Western countries. Thus in all Dutch provinces "Contact Centres for Education-Work" have been established. Their task is to facilitate the contact between schools and companies, for example, where work experience is concerned. Various regional institutes had already been founded: apprenticeship-schemes that form a combination of specific occupational training and practical experience in in-company technical schools over a two-year period. Instructors, industry and trade unions participate in these schemes. The aims are quality control of occupational training and work arbitration, exchange of employees, information for graduates, and research into the job market of the particular profession. The Centre for the Development of Occupational Education (CEDEFOP) is a European organization that is primarily concerned with occupational education in various countries and regularly publishes on this subject.

The interest of social institutes and researchers in the school–work transition is partly due to the need for economic recovery in the beginning of the 1980s. It was hoped that a better match between education and the job market would contribute to the fight against the immense unemployment of young people. Unfortunately, even now there is not enough work for graduates. For these people, the transition process consists of a transition of school to *no* work (unemployment) and the transition becomes a gap in their "course of life". Even here one can speak of a socialization process: an "acute" socialization for unemployment and an anticipatory socialization for possible work in the future (Coetsier et al., 1987). Knowledge concerning the influence of unemployment experiences on the attitudes and behaviour of graduates is therefore extremely relevant (see, for example, Fryer, 1989; Schaufeli, 1988; Tiggeman & Winefield, 1984; Warr, 1987). If one wishes to make full use of all "human resources", one should concentrate primarily on high-risk groups among graduates. In particular, groups who are likely to have adaptation problems or to encounter unemployment (like ethnic minorities or women returning to work after having a family) should be trained in how to search for employment, or be given a chance to take part in bridging programmes and help programmes; see, for example, Van den Bergh (1990). The bridges and barriers young adults with (physical) disabilities experience in their transition from school to work, and the potential barriers to their successful organizational socialization have been discussed by McCarthy (1986) and Colella (1994).

A discussion on the transition from school to work without mentioning "school and occupational choice" is incomplete. After all, this choice process is of crucial importance to the socialization to work and the further socialization in the occupation chosen (see Figure 10.3). Whether or not a person is happy and functions effectively at work will be mainly dependent on an optimal choice of occupation, and this, in turn, depends on the type of education chosen earlier.

There is however too much literature on the subject of occupational choice to be able to discuss it fully within this context. In this chapter we will limit ourselves to mentioning the various occupational choice theories: the typological approach (Holland, 1973) and the developmental approach, such as the "vocational maturity" theory (Super, 1983) or the theories of Roe (1956) and Helbing (1987), in which the "matching" of the self-image and the career-image are central. For further information we refer the reader to the work of Clarke (1980b), Roberts (1984), and Verijdt and Diederen (1987) in which attention is especially paid to the relation between occupational choice and structural factors such as the job market, unemployment, and recruitment and selection procedures. A general overview of the field of occupational choice is given by Crites (1981).

The literature shows that young people these days are in general able to make realistic choices, and that they are inclined to accept work based on the idea that their first job will not last for the rest of their working lives. Nowadays, a person searches for a job instead of a career, and the work experience one gains can be a good start to finding a more permanent job. This implies that frequent changing of jobs can be positively interpreted as a rational use of limited possibilities. Research by Heesink (1992) supports this conclusion. She found that the unemployment experiences and the changing of jobs did not have a negative effect on the quality of the position held by the young people in her study. Mobility seemed to have a rather positive effect: the number of hours worked as well as the salary earned in the present job were predicted by the number of prior job changes.

3.3 Anticipation of work: expectations and behaviour when searching for employment

An important aspect of the school–work transition is that the graduate school- or college-leaver is confronted with the job market. Whitely speaks of the "market encounter" phase and shows the significance of market opportunities and market structures, search practices and market-focused individual differences, as influences on the socialization process as well as on outcomes of the socialization process (Whitely, 1986). Many factors influence the socialization in this phase: vocational advice, personal characteristics (the "work-personality" and "vocational maturity"), individual or institutional support from educational institutions and the business community, and possible earlier work experiences. These factors will influence the motivation of the school-leaver to search for work, his or her "locus of control" and the expectations concerning the job market. The aforementioned variables will then determine the "search strategies" of the school-leaver, namely the manner, the frequency and the duration of the search, and the nature of the information sources which he or she consults. Eventually this process will lead to a (desirable or less desirable) "match" between expectations and the reality of the new job. If the new recruit is dissatisfied with the job, he or she is confronted with several possibilities: adapting their prior expectations and values, changing the job-content, or leaving the job altogether.

At this moment, such a socialization model is being empirically tested in an international collaboration (Touzard, 1992; WOSY International Research Group, 1989). The WOSY project is a longitudinal study among young adults, who were interviewed for the first time when they were about six months into their first full-time job. The WOSY panel consists of young people either employed as machine operators in the metal industry or working with office technology; most of them received lower occupational training. Everybody is interviewed three times, with one year intervals (T1, T2 and T3).

The results show that the extent to which the work matches education, interests and expectations, determines the satisfaction and the well-being of the Dutch respondents at T1 (Van Gastel et al., 1991). Feij et al. (1992) found—in an analysis of the entire collection of T1 data from the WOSY project—that a good "match" between work and earlier expectations (i.e. job characteristics better than expected) is an important mediating variable in the relationship between personal characteristics and work characteristics on the one hand, and the health and enthusiasm of the young employee with regard to his or her further career on the other. Moreover, Feij et al. (1995) found—in an analysis of T1 and T2 data—that the correspondence between job characteristics and expectations at the time of job-entry accounted for the development of career-enhancing strategies and job content innovation attempts.

In addition, research quoted by Wanous (1992) and Fisher (1986) shows that a career is determined by the accuracy of the expectations that a person has in advance. That is why it is so important that the information, on which the expectations are based, is correct, so that a realistic "job-preview" can be developed (e.g. Premack & Wanous, 1985). We will return to this later in Section 5.1.

Fisher (1986) mentions the following sources of information on which young people can base their expectations relating to their new job.

The first is personal experiences and perceptions (the "self"). People often base their expectations on earlier experiences, and they can raise their expectations about a new role as a way of reducing the dissonance following a decision. For example, after a job is chosen, it will be evaluated more positively than before. Pre-entry expectations that are inflated in this way could lead to later disappointment.

Taes (1989) studies the expectations of students who have almost graduated in intermediate vocational education concerning their chances in the job market. Those with the most positive self-image should, in theory, be the most optimistic. According to Gecas (1981) and Rosenberg (1981) a positive self-image emerges in childhood under the influence of a warm and stimulating climate of upbringing; this should lead to a child's feelings of "self-efficacy" and the tendency to attribute good performance to his or her own capabilities and behaviour. Taes (1989) was able to confirm her hypothesis: adolescents with a positive self-image do not expect to have to search for a long time to find a suitable position. Feelings of competence, emerging from the estimation of one's performance at school, were also relevant in this context.

Other potential sources of information are:

- *The school, family and friends.* The part that these institutions play in the anticipatory socialization has been discussed earlier.
- *The media.* Radio, television, newspapers and magazines give both specific and more general information about the job market, and determine the prospective employee's conceptualization about the world of work.
- *The organization and job centres.* Before the work process begins these institutions can provide much of information (albeit good or bad).

In the next Section we will further discuss the significance of a realistic "job-preview". Fisher (1986, p. 123) summarizes this as follows: "Possessing such information should increase the quality of applicants' choices of an employer and also facilitate accurate anticipation and minimize the reality shock often experienced by organizational newcomers. Further, realistic job previews may work by increasing applicants' commitment to the decision they make to accept a job".

In summary, the anticipatory socialization process concerns two processes: (a) the development of basic values with regard to work in general (see MOW International Research Team, 1987) and (b) the emergence of concrete expectations about the future work role and work situation. During the school–work transition the second point is of particular importance. This period is usually too short for a fundamental change of values. Fisher (1986) assumes that expectations are significant for the work socialization shortly after the entrance into the job, whereas values influence adaptation and socialization over a longer period of time.

The searching behaviour of young school-leavers does not always result in actually acquiring the desired job (Taris et al., 1995a). After all, many companies employ one method of selection or another. In Section 4 we will return to the interaction between socialization and selection—a less strict selection process usually means that a more extensive socialization is needed.

3.4 Choice of organization

After young people have chosen an occupational area they will at a certain point have to chose an organization in which they can pursue their occupation. It is not always a matter of choice and it is not always a rational choice that is made (Clarke, 1980b). Crites (1969) feels that in general one can speak of a compromise for both the individual and the organization.

Wanous (1992) discusses two alternative visions concerning the process of choice of organization. The first assumes that people choose in a systematic and rational way. The second assumes that usually there is a rather unprogrammed choice.

An example of the "rational" vision is the expectancy theory (for more information see Chapter 11 in Volume 4). This is based on the premise that people choose to make their potential satisfaction as high as possible. Researchers can "calculate" the attractiveness of an organization by asking a person to evaluate all "outcomes" of their chosen organization (to what extent does the work seem agreeable, is there a possibility to enlarge knowledge and skills, etc.?). By weighing up each evaluation with the significance which the person attaches to each outcome, and by then combining the results, an "attractiveness score" for that particular organization is attained. One can compare this score with those of other organizations. The expectancy theory further predicts that the effort a person puts in in order to enter into the organization of his or her choice is determined by multiplying the expectation to be accepted by the attractiveness of the organization.

According to Wanous (1992), both views of organizational choices have received some research support, due to the different research designs used to study each one. More studies of expectancy theory have been carried out, and the evidence supporting that theory is stronger than the evidence for the unprogrammed view of organizational choice.

The previous Sections have shown just how complicated the school–work transition is, and Clarke's complaint (1980a) that there is no complete, generalizing description of this period still seems accurate. More interdisciplinary and longitudinal studies are needed, in which not just the school–work transition is analysed, but also the later career patterns of both men and women. In particular, more knowledge about the *processes* that underlie socialization, i.e. changes in attitudes and behaviour, should be gained.

In the next Section we will describe which factors influence the socialization process after the entry into the "world of work", and which role the various socializing agents play therein.

4 THE ENTRY INTO THE WORKING ENVIRONMENT

From the point of view of the work organization, socialization is the process through which young people are transformed into members of an organization, integrated into the working life of the organization, and committed to the strategic goals and objectives of the company. The entry into the first full-time job in a particular company is an important step in the work socialization process; the "confrontation" in which the young employee tests his or her expectations on reality. After this testing a phase of adaptation follows in which more lasting changes evolve (see the "three stage entry model" described in Section 2.2.).

The newcomer has to acquire three important things: (a) skills that are needed for effective task performance; (b) adequate role behaviour; (c) a positive attitude towards the company's values, or those of the relevant groups therein (Feldman, 1981, see Section 2.2.1.). Socializing tasks for the organization are providing information, education and training, and sometimes also extra training and re-education. Several comments concerning the "adaptations" described by Feldman (1981) that the newcomer has to make, are necessary.

Whether or not the newcomer succeeds in quickly acquiring the skills needed for performing the task (point a), depends on the qualifications that a person has attained before entry into the work process. Nevertheless, a company usually also contributes to these qualifications. Coetsier et al. (1987), for example, state that the majority of young people questioned, who work with new technology, declare that they have not learned this at school, but in the company or through self-tuition. These Belgian authors further observe that companies put little energy, time and money into the selection of young people, especially where young people with vocational training are concerned. The Dutch situation will be discussed thoroughly in Section 4.4.

In order to achieve adequate role behaviour (point b) it is important that the newcomer discovers which tasks he or she has to perform at entry as well as after possible changes in the work situation, what the priorities are and how much time every task is supposed to take. If the newcomer is to develop an accurate image of his or her role in the organization, both a realistic anticipation and good reception into the company are needed. The latter is often lacking (Clarke, 1980a; Coetsier et al., 1987; Fisher, 1986; Van den Berg & Van den Tillaart, 1986). Coetsier et al. (1987) found that the organization's reception is often limited to a brief introduction to immediate colleagues, the machine that one will operate and the job that one will perform, and that the introduction is usually left to the goodwill of older colleagues.

Adjustment to the norms and values of the group (point c) usually occurs during a kind of initiation process. Hautaluoma, Enge, Mitchell, and Rittwager (1991) caution that severe initiation in any social group can have strong negative side-effects and might not be the most effective approach for producing desired outcomes. It is of great importance that the young employee learns the many nuances of the well-defined rules that dictate the job, and learns to have an eye for the informal social network. It is self-evident that the social skills of the newcomer are essential to this process.

Severe criticism has been expressed with regard to the notion of stages (see Section 2.2.). It is beyond dispute that newcomers in the organization have a lot to learn: values, goals and culture of the organization or of a smaller work unit; task skills and matters concerning the development of their personal identity (Fisher, 1986). However, whether all these learning processes occur simultaneously and fit exactly in the aforementioned phases is doubtful, and not really relevant.

Once a company fully accepts the new employee as an insider this is shown by means of certain signals: a positive appreciation of adequate performance; the assignment of new tasks; sharing of inside-information; initiation "rites" (e.g. get-togethers or dinner parties); promotion or increase in salary (Schein, 1978). In turn, the newcomers themselves also send out signals to show that they accept the organization: enthusiasm, motivation (e.g. voluntary overtime) or the pure fact that the person does not leave the company.

4.1 Factors which influence "in-role" socialization

Which factors determine the nature and effectiveness of the process of "in-role" socialization? Or put differently: which factors are responsible for the emergence of the desired change in the attitudes and behaviours of the young employee? Fisher (1986) refers to motivational factors of the persons involved, structural characteristics of the work situation and the conduct of the socializing agents.

4.1.1 Motivational factors

According to Fisher (1986) motivational factors include:

- Anxiety: reduction of anxiety could be one of the basic motives involved in socialization (Nelson, 1987; Saks & Ashforth, 1996; Van Maanen & Schein, 1979).
- Self-efficacy: the belief that one is able to take on a task-situation encourages role-exploration and social learning in the organization (Bandura, 1977; Jones, 1983, 1986).
- Amount of choice: Fisher argues that the more independence the newcomer had, or felt to have had in the creation of his or her own new role, the more he or she will feel motivated to be successful in that role.
- Social rewards.
- Investments: if the newcomer has invested a great deal in his or her work in the form of time, friendships and training, the commitment to the company will probably increase.

Further, many personality characteristics can influence the motivation to become socialized, such as self-respect, the attitude towards authority and the need for control and feedback. Whitely (1986) adds the various norm- and value-dimensions, such as "work duty" and valued work outcomes (see MOW International Research Team, 1987) to the list of relevant personal characteristics. Also, the need for affiliation, and the correspondence or "mismatch" between the expectations of the newcomer and the first work experience might be significant motivational factors. It can be concluded that individual differences between young people in interaction with factors in the social environment determine the nature and the course of the socialization process.

An interesting aspect of this is that the motive to become socialized during the socialization process can change in character (Van Maanen, 1976). Initially the new employee tries to behave as is expected of him or her; later identification with the group with which one is most directly concerned is striven for, and eventually internalization of the value system which prevails in the organization is pursued.

4.1.2 Structural features of the work situation

Fisher (1986) distinguishes between aspects of the socialization setting and aspects of the role itself.

Context factors

Context factors include the procedures distinguished by Van Maanen (1978; see also Van Maanen & Schein, 1979), which the organization can employ (separately or in combination) to mould the newcomer—the "socialization tactics". These are:

- Individual or collective (i.e. in groups) informing and training of the newcomer; "collective" is meant to signify that a number of newcomers follow a course or a period of training together, for example, intensive group training for salesmen or management training.
- Formal versus informal training; is the newcomer assigned a special "learner-status" or is training a "*laissez-faire*" learning process (as is the case with an "on-the-job-training", in which the newcomer is considered as a full member of the working unit from the start)?
- Sequential training through clearly specified stages, versus random training in which the stages are unfamiliar, vague or continually varying.
- A fixed socialization procedure in which the newcomer knows exactly how much time a particular transitional period will take, versus a more variable time schedule, which is based on individual progress.
- Serial versus disjunctive training: training by an experienced employee, with special emphasis on continuity and personal development; or learning independently from the new situation without the help of such an old hand as a role model.
- investiture, in which the value of the personal characteristics of the new employee is stressed ("we value you for what you are"), versus "divestiture", in which the personal identity of the newcomer is placed second to the goals of the introduction period.

Van Maanen and Schein (1979) have formulated a series of hypotheses indicating for which sort of transitions in the organization a particular socialization tactic is most appropriate, and what the reaction will be. The following example illustrates their ideas. According to the authors three types of reactions to the various socialization procedures are possible: (a) "custodianship", in which the newcomer conforms to the traditional role and learns to perform the work as it has always been done; (b) "content innovation", which means that the newcomer changes or improves the knowledge and procedures on which the work role is based; (c) "role innovation"—in this case the newcomer attempts to radically change the work role's goal (e.g. the modern views on the role of the family doctor).

One of the hypotheses of Van Maanen and Schein (1979) is that collective socialization will lead to a conforming attitude in the newcomer, or at best to the pursuit of innovation regarding the content of the job. In this hypothesis the socialization tactic that the company prefers depends on the nature of the transition. Collective socialization is most logical in the case of an employee already employed in the company, who needs to overcome a "functional" barrier (e.g. has to learn a new technique), but also where the orientation of new employees is concerned. However, according to Van Maanen and Schein (1979), individual socialization is the obvious tactic when one has to overcome a "hierarchical" barrier (e.g. in the case of a complex learning process in which an assessment regarding individual capability takes place).

Over the last decade, a number of studies have been done to test such hypotheses. One of the first to conduct empirical research on the influence of the socialization tactics on the adjustment of the newcomer to the organization, was Jones (1986). Jones found support for his hypothesis that "individualized" tactics (i.e. individual, informal, random, variable and disjunctive), more often lead to innovative role orientations where newcomers are concerned. "Institutionalized" tactics (collective, formal, etc.) more often resulted in a conforming manner of performance, and adjustment to the demands of the task. Furthermore, Jones found that feelings of competence (self-efficacy) have a moderating function in this learning process. It also became apparent that compared to individualized procedures, institutionalized socialization procedures lead to less role conflict and ambiguity, to stronger job satisfaction and commitment to the organization, and to minimalization of the inclination to voluntarily leave the company.

Later studies have replicated and extended Jones' work by demonstrating that institutionalized tactics are negatively related to the intention to quit, stress symptoms and self-appraised performance, and positively related to job satisfaction and organizational identification and commitment (Allen & Meyer, 1990b; Ashforth & Saks, 1996; Baker, 1992; Baker, 1995; Baker & Feldman, 1990; Zahrly & Tossi, 1989). Baker and Feldman (1990), for example, studied the different tactics of "people processing" and the impact of these strategies on newcomer adjustment. They analysed the interrelationship among socialization tactic items based on Jones's work, and found two overall patterns: "unit" and "batch" people processing. The "batch" process (formal, collective, fixed, sequential and serial) tended to be associated with more positive attitudinal responses than the "unit" (i.e. the opposite) strategy. In addition, Jones' (1986) finding that institutionalized socialization is related to a custodial orientation, whereas individualized socialization is related to role innovation, has also received support in recent studies (Allen & Meyer, 1990b; Ashforth & Saks, 1996; Black, 1992).

As Anderson and Thomas (1996) pointed out, the focus on organizational tactics of newcomer socialization typifies the conception of the socialization process in the 1970s. In this conception, the newcomer was seen as a passive recipient of people processing strategies. "Critical of this stance, researchers in the 1980s, and even more so in the 1990s, have recognized the proactive role that newcomers necessarily take in any organization socialization and entry process" (Anderson & Thomas, 1996, p. 426). Moreover, Wanous and Colella (1989) suggested a need for research on the *processes* through which socialization procedures influence newcomers. An unpublished study by Saks and Ashforth (1997) was aimed at decreasing the fragmentation of socialization literature by integrating the socialization tactics approach and another, more recent, approach to socialization: the process of information acquisition (see Section 4.2). Saks and Ashforth (1997) argued that socialization tactics set the stage for information acquisition, and information acquisition is a key process that underlies the effects of socialization tactics on socialization outcomes. Consistent with previous research, the results of Saks and Ashforth's (1997) study indicated that socialization tactics and information acquisition (i.e. feedback and observation) were positively related to socialization outcomes. Furthermore, the frequency of newcomers' feedback from and observation of co-workers and supervisors was found to partially mediate the relationship between the tactics and job satisfaction, organizational commitment, and intentions to quit, and completely mediate the relationship between the tactics and task mastery and anxiety.

Wanous (1992) points out that socialization is concerned with making newcomers conform to the organization. It is different from "newcomer orientation", where the fundamental purpose is to help newcomers cope with entry stress during the immediate post-entry period. In his view organizational socialization comprises three basic processes: (a) social learning as the way newcomers learn; (b) new roles, norms, and values as the material that is learned; and (c) conflict as the unique dynamic of this particular learning. Furthermore, the basic psychology of socialization lies in how to persuade newcomers to adopt new organizational norms and values. Persuasion can be directed at the newcomer's attitudes (beliefs, feelings, and intentions) and at their actions. Wanous (1992) describes several ways in which a newcomer's attitudes and behaviour can be changed. For example, the company can use cooptation or seduction, where the newcomer is given the illusion that he or she is able to make several tempting choices. They will then rationalize the choice of the most inviting option, but in so doing also adopt the ideas of the company.

The company can also employ the following method. One makes sure that the newcomer invests a great deal of time and energy in the organization (the attitude-object). In doing this, the attractiveness of the object is increased. Then the employee is rewarded for his or her effort, for example by increasing his or her status ("you are one of the very few who have been employed by our company") and facilities. In receiving these rewards the employee will develop a feeling of obligation, which will cause the aforementioned seduction procedure to provide further commitment to the organization.

Aspects of the working role

Katz and Kahn (1978) have stressed that organizations can be seen as role-systems. Employees perform many roles, which have rights, duties and privileges attached to them. Role dimensions influencing the ease with which the employee is socialized, are, according to Fisher (1986), among other things:

- Desirability: personal or social appreciation of the new role, as well as whether the role was chosen voluntarily by the new incumbents.
- Clarity or institutionalization.
- Level of performance demand: the degree to which the organization appeals to the commitment of the performer of the role. One can also include the degree to which new skills have to be acquired, the concentration required, and the extent to which the employee has to give up his or her identity (Schein, 1978).
- Resemblance of the role to a possible previous role, and its relationship to currently held roles and desired future roles.

Nicholson (1984) presented a theory of work-role transitions. He argues that work-role transitions may involve two independent processes: personal development and role development. Personal development entails adapting oneself to fit the role, while role development entails adapting the role to fit oneself. Personal development and role development are combined to create four modes of work adjustment (replication, absorption, determination and exploration). Furthermore, Nicholson argues that the particular mode of work adjustment that one utilizes is a function of, among other things, motivational orientations and role requirements. The first role requirement, discretion, refers to the latitude individuals have in altering task-related characteristics. The second, novelty, refers to the degree to which the role permits the use of prior knowledge, skills and habits. Personal development is argued to be a function of role novelty and the newcomer's desire for feedback, while role development is argued to be a function of role direction and desire for control. In a longitudinal study of business school graduates, Ashforth and Saks (1995) found mixed support for this model.

According to Whitely (1986), in addition to aspects of the work role, concrete aspects of the task will also influence the course and result of the socialization process. He mentions temporal aspects of the work, and the pattern of life resulting from it (e.g. shift work); the content of the task (see Fine & Wiley, 1971); subjective characteristics of the task (Hackman & Oldham, 1980); the difficulty of the task, i.e. the amount of time needed to learn to perform the task; negative conditions, such as overburdening, role conflict, ambiguity and unsafe or unhealthy working conditions; and flexibility and supervision, i.e. the extent to which the content of the task, the procedure and/or products of the job are specified. However, further research is needed to establish which of these many factors plays the most prominent part.

Furthermore, according to Whitely (1986), features of the working unit are also important for socialization. For instance, the extent to which the members of the working unit have to depend on each other with regard to the "work flow" and the tasks which are shared or the composition of the working unit according to age, career or commitment to the job. After all, group members function as a role model for the newcomer; we will return to this in the next Section. Anderson and Thomas (1996) reviewed existing research into work group socialization. Contrasting newcomers socialization into the wider organization with their assimilation into the proximal work group, the authors argue that the work group often forms the primary medium through which the socialization process is enacted. They view work group socialization as a learning process resulting in two interdependent outcomes: assimilation of the newcomer into the group and the reciprocal impact the newcomer has in changing the group's norms, climate and structure.

Finally, Whitely (1986) mentions the quality of the organization, the attention paid to training and career opportunities, and the manner in which the company allows the newcomer to progress within the job or from function to function.

4.1.3 The socializing agents

In principle, the influence of other people in the working environment, i.e. the "agents of socialization", on the learning process of newcomers is considerable. In terms of social learning theory socializing agents act as a "model", or, because of the power they have over all sorts of reward systems, influence the consolidation of the desired behaviour. The role expectations of the new employee do not only depend on various kinds of formal instructions and a proper task description. Informal contacts with colleagues, either with the boss or with fellow subordinates, are also of great importance. However, Fisher (1986, p. 137) concludes that:

> Relatively few studies have investigated the role of agents in the socialization process, and little is known about how newcomers choose which agents to attend to. I have suggested that power, affectivity, similarity of role, availability, and expertise may contribute to this decision, but there is relatively little empirical evidence for this list to date. The problems of dealing with multiple and conflicting agents have also been inadequately explored.

There are many socializing agents who may serve as a model or source of information to the newcomer, depending on the nature of the job and the phase of the socialization process: peers, superiors or subordinates, training functionaries, clients and representatives of works associations or trade unions. Actually, the "self" is also a socializing institution, since everybody socializes him or herself in the end through a certain selective sensitivity to others and through previous personal experiences (Fisher, 1986).

Obviously the supervisor constitutes a fundamental source of information for the newcomer. Superiors have formal authority, give evaluations and rewards, communicate a particular pattern of expectations, and through these means influence the behaviour of the new employees. (The reverse is also true: subordinates may have a socializing influence on their new boss). Whitely (1986) mentions four relevant aspects of the way in which a boss and his or her subordinates relate to each other in a social context: (a) the intensity of supervision, the frequency with which the boss gives instructions and feedback, and the extent to which the newcomer is checked on or left free; (b) the "developmental function": the extent to which advice is given and clear expectations concerning the future performance are communicated. Is the young employee assigned work enabling him or her to improve his or her skills and from which something can be learned? It seems probable that in the first phase the newcomer will not appreciate a very strong challenge nor too great an amount of freedom (Katz, 1980); (c) the amount of social support that the supervisor provides; a great deal of support is indispensable to the self-appreciation of the newcomer and will prevent or ease conflicts and disappointments, especially in the confrontation phase; (d) the credibility of the boss who after all, functions as a "model" and influences the internalization of the values, views and behaviours by the new employee.

For many newcomers, their "peers" are particularly appealing as a socializing authority; after all, they almost by definition satisfy the criteria mentioned by Fisher: similarity in roles, availability, and expertise. Whitely (1986, p. 69) notes: "Social psychologists have for years recognized the importance of peer or co-workers contact as a core group from which the youth learns new behaviours, values, norms and beliefs and gains a positive sense of self" (see also Kram & Isabella,

1985). Compared with bosses, they are more often available. In addition, there is no hierarchical relationship, stimulating communication and social support. In this context, Whitely mentions relevant variables, such as frequency of contact with each other, support given by colleagues, and also a "developmental function": colleagues provide technical or task-related information and feedback, which is useful to the socialization and career planning of the newcomer.

In spite of Fisher's (1986) rather pessimistic conclusions, there is considerable empirical support for the assumption that feedback from and observation of co-workers and supervisors is particularly important for newcomers' socialization (e.g. Katz, 1980; Louis et al., 1983; Miller & Jablin, 1991; Ostroff & Kozlowski, 1992; Weiss, 1978; see also Section 4.2 of this chapter). Also, Reichers (1987) emphasized the role of interactions between newcomers and insiders as the primary vehicle through which initial socialization occurs. Feij et al. (1995) demonstrated that newcomers' relations with their supervisor and co-workers are related to the career enhancing strategies and attempted content innovation of young employees. This relationship is mediated by the correspondence between characteristics of the work situation and the employees' expectations.

Another important socializing agent is the mentor (Chao et al., 1992; Kram, 1985; Ostroff & Kozlowski, 1993; Pence, 1995). Ostroff and Kozlowski (1993, p. 171) conceptualized mentors as "senior, experienced organizational members, who help young professionals develop technical, interpersonal, and political skills". The authors showed that mentors were most instrumental in helping newcomers learn about the organizational domain relative to other content domains (see Section 2.2.1). Moreover, mentors provided significantly more information about the organizational domain than other sources. The organizational domain reflects an appreciation of the politics, power, and value premises of the organizational system. Its features comprise knowledge of the organization's mission, special languages, key legends, myths, stories, and management's leadership and motivational style.

The various socializing agents are usually of influence simultaneously. The behaviour of the newcomer is therefore the result of various forces, which may differ in direction and intensity (Fisher, 1986). Although a certain overlap will exist between the more general socialization practices employed by the company and the relation of the new employee with his or her boss and colleagues, a discrepancy can also exist between these factors (Whitely, 1986). The employer, for instance, could apply institutional tactics, whereas the colleagues use more individualized practices.

The socialization process can therefore be seen as a process of supply and selection of, at times, contradictory information. This topic will be dealt with in the next Section.

4.2 Organizational socialization as a process of communication

An important goal for newcomers in an organization is to minimize the feeling of insecurity (Jones, 1986; Louis, 1980a; Van Maanen & Schein, 1979; Wanous, 1992). In the beginning the new employee is very much unsure as to what exactly the organization expects of him or her. (The "psychological contract", as discussed in Section 2.2.3, may be helpful in reducing this uncertainty). Van Maanen and Schein (1979, p. 110) accurately observe that: 'Socialization necessarily involves transmission of information'.

Nowadays communication sciences state that the process of role learning is fundamentally of a communicative nature. Miller (1989, p. 2), for example, states: "for the most part newcomers learn organizational and group norms, rules and behaviour through the information, instructions, and feedback they exchange with incumbents in their work environments". This process can be examined through analyzing both the "signals" given by the organization and the search processes through which the new employee seeks to attain information about his or her role (Ashford, 1986; Ashford & Cummings, 1985; Jablin, 1984, 1987).

Miller (1989) outlines a communication model including the following variables: (a) type of information, for example, task instructions, performance-feedback or opinions of the others about the newcomer; (b) the source of information—does the information come from the supervisor, colleagues, or from the task itself?; (c) the perceptions of the new employee, for example, concerning the social "costs" of the search process, or the perceptions with regard to insecurity about the role itself; (d) the information-seeking strategies—how is the information seeking carried out, directly or indirectly? Through observation of a model or through a provocation strategy, i.e. deliberately annoying somebody or breaking a rule followed by observing the reactions of the new "information source"?; (e) the results of the process of information accumulation: role clarity or role ambiguity, and role conflict; (f) various moderating variables: self-confidence, tolerance of ambiguity, social support and socialization tactics applied by the organization.

Miller (1989) tested many possible causal relations between these variables in a quasi-experimental study. The results showed among other things that if newcomers use open and observational strategies when receiving information concerning the task, role ambiguity diminishes. Miller therefore advises new employees to take the initiative to enter into communication with others, to freely pose questions about their tasks, and to take personal observations and experiences seriously. In doing this, the time needed to become a competent employee could be reduced considerably (see Katz, 1985). Miller (1989) also found that role conflicts were linked to provocation strategies. Presumably one can speak of a vicious circle here.

Marsh, Dobos, and Brown Zahn (1988) researched to what extent employees at different stages of the socialization process ("entre/encounter" "metamorphosis" and "post-metamorphosis")[3] use alternative channels of communication to gain information about their organization. In addition, the place of the newcomer in the organizational hierarchy was taken into account. Indeed, employees at a lower level are socialized through different or differently phased procedures (e.g. fixed, collective) than employees with a more complex task and a considerable amount of responsibility, such as managers (see Van Maanen & Schein, 1979).

In the study of Marsh et al. (1988), a distinction was made between two sorts of information: (a) information on how an organization attempts to integrate its members, i.e. attempts to stimulate morale and mutual cooperation; (b) information on the "competitive" strategy adopted by the company in order to improve its position in the market. In addition, various "channels" were distinguished, for example, personal contacts, group meetings, memos, official media or personal opinions (the "self").

From the results of the cross-sectional research by Marsh et al. (1988) it appeared that lower level and higher level new employees held different judgements concerning the amount of effort that the company—viewed proportionally in the three phases—puts into advice and guidance with regard to the "integrative" and the "competitive" dimension of the communication process. According to many new employees, for example, little information was given about competitive strategies in the entry phase, but it was mainly the lower-level personnel who experienced this. The researchers also found disparity in the use of the channels of information. Lower-level personnel tended to name the supervisor as the source of information about the competitive strategies of the company; managers tended to name colleagues as their main source of information regarding the integrative activities of the company. Van Maanen and Schein's (1979) hypothesis that individual and informal channels of information are more important in the socialization process than collective and formal channels was confirmed, however, the authors again found a "status" effect.

Anderson and Thomas (1996) classify the changes in the predominant emphasis of socialization research over time into four distinct eras. The most recent change in outlook on socialization is classified under the heading of the "proactive information acquisition era". Indeed, many recent studies recognize the important role of information seeking in the process of socialization (e.g. Anderson & Thomas, 1996; Ashford & Black, 1996; Comer, 1991; Miller & Jablin, 1991; Morrison, 1993a, b; Ostroff & Kozlowski, 1992; Saks & Ashforth 1996, 1997). These studies all portray newcomers as proactive in adapting to their new environment, and stress that a primary way in which newcomers are proactive during socialization is by seeking information.

Morrison (1993a) mentions three functions of information seeking: it enables newcomers (a) to reduce uncertainty, (b) to understand and master their new environment, and (c) to compensate for the frequent failure of supervisors and co-workers to provide sufficient information. In Morrison's longitudinal study the frequency with which new staff accountants sought specific types of information during their first six months of employment was related to how well they had mastered their job, defined their role, learned about their organization's culture, and become socially integrated. These are the four primary learning tasks that make up the socialization process (Feldman, 1976; see also Section 2.2.1 in this chapter). Morrison (1993a) found that, as hypothesized, task mastery was related to the frequency with which newcomers sought technical information and performance feedback. Role clarity was related to the frequency with which they sought referent information and performance feedback, and social integration was related to the frequency with which newcomers sought normative information. The amount of variance explained, however, was modest. Morrison (1993a) suggests that information seeking is just one of many mechanisms through which socialization occurs; other mechanisms include formal orientation programs, mentoring, the development of social support, and information exchanges initiated by others.

Ostroff and Kozlowski (1992) studied the relationship between information acquisition about organizational contextual domains from different sources and socialization outcomes. They found that newcomers' acquisition of information was related to their knowledge of different organizational contextual domains. Both information and knowledge were related to higher satisfaction, commitment and adjustment, and lower turnover intentions and stress. It further appeared that newcomers rely primarily on the observation of others, and that observation is one of the most useful sources of knowledge. Ostroff and Kozlowski (1992) also found interesting interactions between type and source of information. For example, newcomers used co-workers and supervisors to a similar extent for acquiring task and organizational information, but supervisors were used more for role-related information, whilst co-workers provided more information on the group domain. Furthermore, Mignerey, Rubin, and Gorden (1995) showed that newcomers who *actively* sought information in the early stages of employment were more likely to assume an innovative role profile within the organization.

The effects of mentoring relationships (see also Section 4.1.3 in this chapter) on the learning process of newcomers were investigated by Ostroff and Kozlowski (1993). Their study focused on how newcomers acquired information about the important domains of the work setting (task, role, group, organization) from potential information sources (such as mentor, supervisor, co-workers, observation, experimentation, and objective referents). The results indicate different patterns of information acquisition for newcomers with and without mentors. Those with mentors were able to learn more about organizational issues and practices compared with non-mentored newcomers.

It is clear that the studies quoted still leave many questions unanswered, but the "communication approach" in our opinion does indeed form an important trend in organizational socialization research (see also Bullis, 1993).

In summary, the sources and content dimensions of information, as well as the way newcomers seek information and are provided with feedback emerge as important factors that separately or in an interactive manner influence the process and outcomes of early organizational socialization (see also Morrison, 1993b). Anderson and Thomas (1996, p. 434) argue, however, that the amount of information is not equivalent to its utility. The authors further suggest that:

> ... future research is called for to advance our understanding, not so much of information-seeking, but of information integration and the development of knowledge structures held by newcomers which are paramount in their transition toward becoming effective job performers.

4.3 Recruitment, selection and socialization

Wanous (1992) regards the entry of new employees into an organization as a dual matching process. One match is between the individual's specific job requirements and the capacity of the organization to fulfil them. The other match is between the individual's capabilities or potential and the requirements of a particular job. A *mis*match between the required job outcomes and the capacity of organizational climates to fulfil those requirements will lead to dissatisfaction and insufficient commitment to the company. The young employee will be inclined to leave the company voluntarily. When there is a *mis*match between individual capacities and the demands of the job or the organization, this will result in poor work performance and involuntary "turnover". A large body of literature exists providing support for these hypotheses (Bretz & Judge, 1994; Edwards, 1991; Kristof, 1996).

Wanous (1992) holds that this dual matching model is not only useful to explain "turnover", but also to describe the entry process: the individual chooses an organization based on his or her capabilities and needs; the organization recruits and selects individuals based on the demands of the task and the climate of the organization (Porter, Lawler, & Hackman, 1975). The entry of newcomers is thus a process of mutual attraction and in practice it is of great importance that this process is understood. For a company it is extremely expensive if unsuitable employees are attracted or if competent employees leave the company. Schneider (1987) has further elaborated on these ideas in his attraction-selection-attrition-model.

The matching model presumes an intrinsic relation between recruitment, selection and socialization of new employees. Selection will primarily influence the balance between the job requirements and the individual's capabilities, while the recruiting strategy adopted by the company will primarily influence the match between individual needs and the climates of the organization. The less successful a company is in attracting suitable employees through its recruitment and selection policy, the more important the application of post-entry socialization tactics will become, in order to bring about a good mutual relationship between the individual and the organization.

In a study by Chatman (1991) among recruits in public accounting firms, person-organization fit was shown to be created, in part, by selection (assessments of who the person is when he or she enters the organization) and socialization (how the organization influences the person's values, attitudes, and behaviour during membership). The results of her study support the hypotheses that (a) recruits whose values, when they enter, match those of the firm, adjust to it more quickly; (b) those who experience the most vigorous socialization fit the firm's values better than those who experience less socialization; and (c) recruits whose values most closely match the firm's, feel most satisfied and intend to and actually remain with the firm longer. Caldwell, Chatman, and O'Reilly (1990) found that rigorous recruitment and selection procedures and a strong and clear organizational value system were associated with higher levels of employee commitment based on internationalization and identification (see Section 5.1). Similarly, results of a study by Orpen (1993) indicated that recruitment and socialization practices were positively associated with employee commitment, but only in a firm with relatively strong cultural norms. Van Vianen and Ten Bruggecate (1995) studied the influence of the fit between newcomers' perceptions of the organizational climates and their climate preferences on several outcomes: organizational commitment, intent to leave the organization, and job satisfaction. Seven dimensions of organizational climate were distinguished in their study. The results showed that the assesment of fit was only important for three climate dimensions: work pressure, regulation and effort. For the other dimensions, risk orientation, reward, friendship and peer cohension, the fit measures did not contribute significantly to the prediction of the outcome measures beyond the main effects of the perceived-climate variables.

Wanous (1992) advocates the use of a recruitment policy which is as realistic as possible. This entails that the company supplies realistic information to the "outsiders" before and during the entry, instead of trying to "sell" the organization by only emphasizing its positive facets. This realism has many advantages. First of all, potential newcomers are given more choice. Thus "self-selection" can occur: candidates match their own needs to the organization climate that they perceive, and are able to decide for themselves. This will lead to a greater commitment to the organization chosen, more satisfaction in the long term, and will substantially diminish the necessity to leave the organization voluntarily.

Moreover, realistic recruitment will lead to realistic expectations on the part of the new employee, which will reduce the possibility of disappointment later—with all its disadvantageous consequences. By these means, conflicts between the individual and the organization during the entry phase—which arise due to the fact that one of the parties does not provide complete or correct information about themselves (Porter et al., 1975)—will arise less frequently. The methods employed by the organization may differ considerably; from brochures, audio-visual or oral presentation to realistic "worksample tests" or "assessment centres". These are not just useful as valid methods of selection; they will also provide a realistic "job preview" for the candidate.

In short, realistic recruitment procedures deserve preference, because they result in more realistic expectations of the newcomer, which is beneficial to the development of positive job attitudes. From a review of the literature, Wanous (1992) concluded that realistic recruitment has a small effect on the job performance of newcomers. Realistic recruitment *does*, however, increase the "job survival rate" for newcomers.

In deciding whether or not to use realistic recruitment, an organization must consider the specific situation: (a) the selection ratio for the job; (b) the type of job; and (c) labour market conditions. Moreover, too much realism is not always beneficial; it can, among other things, evoke feelings of despair in the candidates. It should also be noted that, although the realistic job preview literature indicates the importance of developing realistic expectations about the job and the organization for an employee's adjustment to the organization, this assumption is not consistently supported by empirical research. For instance, Bauer and Green (1994) studied the entry of new Ph.D. students in their doctoral programmes. They found that individuals who had collected information that they perceived as realistic, and who had past research experience, were more involved in their doctoral programmes, were more engaged in doctoral research, had less role conflict, felt more accepted and were more productive, as measured by objective outcomes. Adkins (1995), however, found that, in a sample of mental health specialists, realistic expectations about the job and interpersonal relationships on the job, in general did not predict socialization outcomes. In a field experiment with new recruits to entry-level service jobs, Warung (1995) made a comparison between the effects of a realistic orientation with or without additional self-regulatory coping training. In Waung's study, two groups were compared, an experimental and a control group. The control group received information warning candidates that the job had negative aspects and information about specific coping behaviours. The experimental group received the same information as the comparison group, plus training in cognitive restructuring and positive self-talk, and statements to increase self-efficacy. In contrast with expectations, the experimental group exhibited more early turnover (i.e. probably a self-selection effect). Of those remaining after four weeks, candidates from the experimental group were significantly more likely to report intentions to remain for a year or longer, and to report greater satisfaction.

Selection and socialization are thus alternative methods to match the individual's values with those of the organization. If the self-selection of the newcomer or the selection by the organization which is principally based on the capabilities of the applicant is not successful, the company can attempt to influence the values, skills and motivation of the new employee. However, the actual relation between selection and socialization may depend on the type of organization into which the new employee enters.

Etzioni (1964) stated that the mix of selection and socialization varies between companies and is linked to two factors. First, this mix is linked to the mechanisms through which the organization exercises control over its members (physical control, e.g. through coercion; material control, e.g. giving financial incentives; or control via symbolic means, such as prestige, esteem or acceptance). Second, the mix depends on the control over the organization's boundaries, that is, the amount of control possible by a strict admission of newcomers. According to Wanous (1992), the need for socialization will increase as the degree of selectivity in personnel selection decreases. However, little research has been designed to test this idea. In a study by Mulford, Klongan, Beal, and Bohlen (1968) it was found that the effect of further socialization attempts on the performance of the newcomer was nil in the case of organizations with a strict selection policy. However, in the case of average or low-selective organizations the socialization procedures had a positive effect. This is understandable: if selection is so strict that only people who exactly fit the profile are chosen, there will be little need for further indoctrination.

Other factors that play a role are the "pre-entry" experience of the newcomers (their previous work experiences) and the way in which they have selected themselves for a certain job. Self-selection procedures mostly lead to a decreased need for detailed socialization attempts by the organization.

4.4 An example presenting the Dutch situation in the 1980s

Van den Berg and Van den Tillaart (1986) researched—in 24 Dutch organizations from diverse major areas of industry—the attuning process between companies and new employees; i.e. the recruitment and selection and the socialization. Their starting point, like that of Wanous (1992) and Fisher (1986), was that the result of the recruitment and selection determines the further introduction process after entry into employment.

In every company the formal policy regarding recruitment, introduction and fit between the qualifications of the newcomer and the demands of the position were described. Furthermore, the working procedures as used in practice were taken into account. For example, to what extent are facilities in the various companies available to new employees in order that they are able to function optimally in the company and in their own position?

Two separate categories of employees were interviewed: 104 graduates and 131 employees who had recently changed company; all the individuals concerned had been employed by their current companies for between three and thirty months. Among other things they were asked just how well informed they were in matters that could be important to their work situation. An attempt was also made to pinpoint the exact times and methods employed in the transmission of information. Both the behaviour on the job market and the settling-in period were taken into account.

4.4.1 Recruitment policy

Van den Berg and Van den Tillaart (1986) first point out that the rapid increase in the number of graduates entering the job market in The Netherlands since 1980 has had important consequences. Applicants had to be more active than before in their search for employment and in the process they had to adapt their wishes and preferences to the situation at hand. The employees interviewed said they had applied for many jobs and a large percentage of them admitted that the main reason for their acceptance of their current job was purely because they needed some form of employment.

As a result of all the spontaneous job applications, companies did not have to place job advertisements or seek the assistance of the job centre. Recruitment took up less time and energy, and direct selection became possible again. As a result of the rapid technological and organizational changes, recruitment criteria also changed. The criteria for professional knowledge and skills had become increasingly specific to the particular companies; so-called "social-normative" qualifications (personal characteristics, such as the ability to adapt quickly, motivation and loyalty) had, in general, become more important.

Van den Berg and Van den Tillaart (1986) differentiate between two strategies of hiring personnel. First, the "training strategy" in which the company primarily concentrates on the social-normative qualifications of the applicant. Once employed, the newcomer will have to be taught and trained to acquire the necessary specific technical knowledge. Second, the "recruitment strategy", in which one primarily selects applicants with the necessary professional or technical qualifications, so that these individuals can be immediately placed into the structure.

The authors discuss several conditions in which the one strategy would be more appropriate than the other. For example, they mention the availability of sufficiently qualified candidates and the costs involved as factors influencing the choice of strategy. Both strategies have advantages and disadvantages. The authors conclude that although new employees will less frequently be employed without the mandatory qualifications, a certain distance can remain between on the one hand the demands of the position and on the other hand the knowledge, skills and attitudes that have been acquired from an alternative external training scheme.

4.4.2 Problems of fit regarding school–work adjustment

Van den Berg and Van den Tillaart (1986) have only taken stock of the matching problems in the professional technical domain. First of all, actual matching problems were considered. As one might expect, newcomers employed through the training strategy had had more adjustment problems than newcomers employed through the recruitment strategy. After all, in using the training strategy companies concentrated primarily on social-normative qualifications, while specific technical problems were put up with and resolved structurally, if necessary. Subjectively experienced adjustment problems appeared to be clearly related to the more objectively defined problems. Van den Berg and Van den Tillaart (1986) found that all newcomers with an insufficient fit, whether overqualified or underqualified for a particular position, or newcomers who had had training in the wrong field, experienced problems.

In our own research (Van Gastel & Feij, 1989a, 1989b; see also WOSY International Research Group, 1989) newcomers who were trained through apprenticeship schemes (in the Dutch metal industries and in the office computerization sector respectively), were interviewed after being employed by the various companies for approximately six months. A considerable percentage of them also appeared to have experienced adjustment problems.

In the case of the young people working in the metal industry, less than 40% said they had experienced a good fit between the apprentice period and the job. What is more, the judgement given by the young people surveyed on the match between the job and their previous education appeared to be strongly connected to the rating they gave their own performance during the training period. A less than satisfactory apprenticeship therefore cannot just simply be blamed on the apprentice. In addition only a small percentage of the people interviewed had the opinion that the job and its various aspects did not live up to their expectations. Furthermore, the results showed that the (dis)satisfaction with one's work is dependent on the adjustment problems experienced and the discrepancy between the characteristics of the job and the expectations that one had about that job (i.e. unmet expectations). Particularly, those individuals for whom the job itself did not match with their training and their interests, felt that they were taken less seriously at work. The fit experienced between apprenticeship and work and the extent to which the young people felt that they were being taken seriously, eventually appeared to be related to their judgement on the quality of the organization.

Similar results were obtained for the sample of young people with jobs in the office computerization sector. This shows that optimal transition from training to work is important for the experience of the physical work situation in which one finds oneself (Van Gastel & Feij, 1989a, 1989b).

4.4.3 Introduction to the company

How does the process of introduction and becoming familiar with the company, the department or work group and the job itself proceed? Van den Berg and Van den Tillaart (1986) have studied two points: (a) the way in which a company tries to solve possible problems of fit (which are connected to the adopted recruitment strategy); (b) the conveyance of new information to the new employee.

Matching policy

The solution to problems arising when the recruitment strategy fails is usually left to the department involved to resolve, because of a lack of general company policy. The solution can vary considerably, from extra training and/or extra attention and guidance during the initial phase, adaptation of the function, transfer, a *laissez-faire* policy in which the newcomer will have to solve the problems him- or herself, to dismissal.

Usually however, the recruitment strategy produces the desired results; there are no real adaptation problems in technical respects and not much time and effort is needed for the initial training approach, according to Van den Berg and Van den Tillaart (1986). Our own research showed that qualified newcomers in the metal industry were reasonably or well satisfied about the training-work fit concerning the primary aspects "manual dexterity" (almost 80%) and "being able to operate machines" (more than 65%) (Van Gastel & Feij, 1989b). For young people with an apprenticeship in the field of automation the percentage was more than 65%, for both "manual dexterity" and "handling machines" (Van Gastel & Feij, 1989a). Adaptation problems were diagnosed more often in both groups with regard to technical theory and supplementary subjects.

The "training strategy" can, primarily because of the importance given to "social-normative" qualifications, come with adjustment problems, especially in jobs with technical demands. However, Van den Berg and Van den Tillaart (1986) argue that companies have in these cases provided a structural solution. One allows the newcomer to be trained after the selection, by means of a short "on-the-job" training period, participation in an internal training programme, or participation in a recognized vocational training programme, e.g. an apprenticeship scheme. While participating in these schemes, the newcomers usually do not only attain the necessary technical qualifications, they also indirectly attain social-normative qualifications, for example, by allowing them to become accustomed to the prevailing production procedures.

Van den Berg and Van den Tillaart (1986) conclude that not all Dutch companies systematically and carefully deal with problems of mismatches between the qualifications stipulated by the company and the qualifications possessed by the newcomer. The facilities needed to solve these problems are often lacking and a considerable percentage of the newcomers are not pleased with this situation.

The transmission of information

In The Netherlands little empirical research has been conducted into the transmission of information in the introductory period. According to Van den Berg and Van den Tillaart (1986) very little time is spent on this in socialization in any case. Information transmission usually consists of a tour around the company and/or an introductory chat with immediate colleagues. Notwithstanding this, the process of social integration usually goes quite smoothly. (This was also the case in many of foreign research programmes, as we have mentioned earlier.) Van den Berg and Van den Tillaart made an inventory of the information that newcomers have on a series of significant subjects. The results are shown in Table 10.2.

Table 10.2 shows that the new employees mainly indicate that they are well informed about directly relevant matters, for example, the work itself and their days off. Newcomers are clearly less informed about more structural factors, such as provision of health care, or career facilities. Those individuals whose introduction was restricted to the department or the actual place of work only, are usually not very well informed.

Table 10.2 also provides insight into the source of information, i.e. whether information is obtained via formal or informal channels. New employees seem to see the company as the main—formal—source of information for official matters, such as the contract of employment, the rewards and the work schedule. For information on the type of work, safe working practices, the company, the organizational culture, and work relations, the company is less often referred to as being the main source of information. This result gives one food for thought, because the information that the newcomers informally accumulate is often incomplete or incorrect.

The methods of introduction of new employees applied by companies vary immensely. Information is presented in either written or oral form; the offer is active or passive and there is variation in the moment when the introduction takes place, as well as the division and distribution of time;

TABLE 10.2

Results from the process of transmission of information, 235 newcomers from various Dutch companies were surveyed.

		% newcomers broadly informed[1]	% newcomers mentioning the company as a source of information
A	All subjects (65) together	62	67
B	Separate main subjects		
	1. Own task	89	56
	2. Work schedule	87	73
	3. Rules of conduct	83	64
	4. Rewards	82	79
	5. Safety	69	60
	6. Contract of employment	62	80
	7. Company and organizational structure	61	52
	8. Settlements and insurances	49	60
	9. Labour relations	45	29
	10. Health provisions	44	65
	11. Career (facilities)	36	65

[1] "broadly informed": persons who indicate to be informed about more than two thirds of the specific topics within each main subject of the interview.

Source: Van den Berg and Van den Tillaart (1986, p. 46). Reprinted with permission of the publisher.

sometimes there is a teacher or mentor available and sometimes there is not. Van den Berg and Van den Tillaart show that the methods adopted are dependent on the introduction policy and vary immensely in results. Similar to recruitment, the introduction and training of newcomers is especially well provided for in companies who have a clear, well-planned policy with regard to personnel.

Van den Berg and Van den Tillaart (1986) conclude that all too often companies do too little to promote the "social integration" of newcomers, but despite this, the process usually takes place relatively quickly (see Fisher, 1986). The vast majority of newcomers feel "at home" in the company shortly after starting work; furthermore, how well a person is informed does not appear to be connected to matters like absenteeism and behaviour in the job market.

However, Van den Berg and Van den Tillaart also report that problems of fit do appear to lead to exploration of the job market by the employees. In particular, newcomers who feel themselves to be "under-utilized", search for or have searched for another job. How the individual views his or her chances on the job market also plays a role; the more a person viewed his or her chances as favourable, the more active they were in the job market.

The previous Sections illustrate the influences the strategies adopted by companies have on the process of organizational socialization (cf. Jones, 1986; Van Maanen & Schein, 1979). In the next Section we will examine what the results of the socialization process are. In other words, how we can differentiate between those young employees who are successfully socialized and those who are not.

5 OUTCOMES OF THE SOCIALIZATION PROCESS

Many variables have already been mentioned as indicators as to whether work socialization has been successful or not (Coetsier et al., 1987; Feldman, 1981; Fisher, 1986; Schein, 1978; Van Maanen, 1976; Whitely, 1986; see also Section 2.2.2 of this chapter): job satisfaction, satisfactory work performance, loyalty to the organization, intrinsic motivation, job involvement, innovation and spontaneous cooperation. As far as this last point is concerned, strict adherence to the rules prescribed, like exaggerated submission to the norms of the organization, indicates ineffective, misplaced socialization, according to Coetsier et al. (1987).

In essence, almost every characteristic of a well functioning employee could count as an indicator. For instance, high employee-ratings on the traditional four content dimensions mentioned in Section 2.2.1 (namely, task mastery, role clarification, acculturation and social integration) could be viewed as indicators of successful completion of the primary learning tasks, i.e. successful socialization. Chao et al. (1994, p. 737) criticized two traditional indicators of socialization and career development, namely job and organizational tenure. They state that:

> ... the problems with a tenure measure include its flawed assumption that all individuals are socialized at the same rate and its failure to capture the complexities of the socialization construct itself. As a process, organizational socialization occurs over time. However, outcomes from a successful socialization process are better related to the learning of particular content areas than the more passage of time.

Chao et al. (1994) conclude that the identification and measurement of the six content areas (mentioned in Section 2.2.1) can advance the empirical research on organizational socialization by moving away from secondary measures such as job or organizational tenure and focusing on the required content of learning during intense socialization episodes.

Likewise, it is doubtful whether job satisfaction is an adequate measure of socialization outcomes. An employee who has successfully completed his or her learning tasks could be satisfied, however, the reverse is not necessarily the case. Furthermore, as we will argue in Section 5.2, job turnover does not necessarily implicate unsuccessful socialization; well-socialized and fully satisfied employees may also change jobs. In other words, there is no perfect correspondence between tenure, satisfaction and other assumed socialization outcomes.

Perhaps the best way to avoid this kind of confusion is to distinguish *focal* or *direct* socialization outcomes, such as measures of socialization content or results of learning tasks, from *indirect* outcomes such as career effectiveness, job satisfaction and commitment. In the following Sections we will briefly discuss three important topics: (a) how does commitment to the organization originate?; (b) turnover as outcome variable; (c) conformity versus innovation.

5.1 Commitment to the organization

Although we can criticize the concepts of job and organizational commitment and tenure versus turnover as inadequate operationalizations of organizational socialization, knowledge of the determinants of these phenomena clearly has great practical relevance. We therefore devote this short Section to the question "what makes young employees commit themselves to an organization?".

It is impossible to summarize the large body of literature on commitment in this chapter. Thus we will only present some of the main findings here. Research carried out by Meyer and Allen (1988), for example, has shown that experiences employees had immediately after starting in the company played a significant role in the development of commitment. One of the most reliable predictors for the development of commitment was the confirmation of expectations held by the individuals prior to joining the company—a factor that is generally viewed a determinant of satisfaction and commitment (Wanous, 1992). As we already argued in Section 2.2.3, unmet expectations are a major reason for leaving the company in the first few years of employment. Low discretion environments in particular seem to hinder the adjustment to mismatches (West & Rushton, 1989). In a study on the apprenticeship socialization strategy, Blau (1988) found that the quality of working relationship was significantly positively related to met expectations, role clarity, organizational commitment and performance.

In Meyer and Allen's (1988) study, a further favourable factor for the development of commitment was that one could "be oneself" (i.e. self-expression). Mael and Ashforth (1995) found that earlier behaviour and experiences, as embodied in biodata, predisposed new recruits to identify with the US army; these biodata and organizational identification in turn predicted subsequent attrition from the army.

Furthermore, the organizational career and reward systems seem to play an important role in the development of commitment (Caldwell et al., 1990). In general, all the factors discussed in Section 4.3 that determine a good fit between the employee and his or her organization or workplace may also foster commitment.

Van Breukelen (1990) describes the various mechanisms through which the relationship between the individual and the company evolves:

- Identification, as a result of the wish "to be part of the group".
- Internalization; becoming familiar with the organization's values, resulting in a strong agreement between the values of the individual and the organization.
- Flexibility or compliance of the individual as a result of instrumental economic considerations.
- Commitment based on the realization that one has moral obligations toward the company.

Partly based on Fishbein and Ajzen's (1975) attitude-behaviour model, Van Breukelen (1990) classifies different types of commitment. For example, he distinguishes between "calculative commitment" (a careful consideration of the advantages and disadvantages, profits and costs, and the consequences of continued membership of the organization), and affective commitment (a positive attitude towards the concept of "organization", based on identification with the aims and values of the organization and the attraction of the members of the organization, apart from purely instrumental deliberations).

In his research, Van Breukelen found that there was less clarity in the difference between the forms of commitment mentioned (and those not mentioned here), than had been suggested in other publications (e.g. Allen & Meyer, 1990a). Based on the "theory of planned behaviour" (Ajzen, 1985) it was possible to predict the voluntary progression within a group of relatively young navy personnel reasonably accurately.

Caldwell et al. (1990) found that rigorous recruitment and selection procedures and a strong and clear organizational value system were associated with higher levels of employee commitment based on internationalization and identification. Strong organizational career and reward systems were related to higher levels of instrumental or compliance-based commitment.

At this moment, a three component conceptualization of commitment seems promising (Allen & Meyer, 1990a; Meyer & Allen, 1991; 1993). This model distinguishes between affective, continuance, and normative commitment, each of which have their own pattern of antecedents and consequents. This conceptualization is useful for research in many different applied fields and in different kinds of organizations. Kelley (1992), for instance, studied the impact of organizational socialization on the customer orientation of service employees. His study showed that organizational socialization had a positive impact on employee perceptions of the organizational climate, their level of motivation and their organizational commitment. Hellman and McMillin (1994) studied the effect of newcomer socialization on affective commitment, using undergraduates as subjects. The authors found support for their hypothesis that socialization would account for variance in commitment over and above the variance accounted for by overall satisfaction with the organization, i.e. the university.

As stated, the concept of commitment has been criticized as an inadequate measure of socialization. In addition, it should be noted that commitment cannot only be viewed as a socialization *outcome*, but can have different consequences itself, depending on the career stage concerned. Cohen (1991) conducted a meta-analytical review dealing with the relationship between organizational commitment and its outcomes. The findings supported the proposition that the career stage moderated this relationship. For instance, the relationship between commitment and turnover (both actual and intended) was stronger in the early career stages than in the mid and late career stages. The relationship of commitment with performance and absenteeism was strongest in the late career stage using tenure as the career indicator.

5.2 Change of employment as an "outcome"

Once a new employee realizes that several characteristics of the job or the company do not live up to his or her expectations, he or she will begin to show signs of dissatisfaction and will be inclined to leave the company. These may be indications that the process of social integration has not been successful, at least with the company in question (Dunnette, Arvey, & Banis, 1973; Feij et al., 1992).

Many researchers have concentrated on the relation between satisfaction and job mobility—i.e. the intention to leave the company or actually finding a new job (Mobley et al., 1979; Nicholson, 1987; Taris et al., 1991, 1992; Wanous, 1992). It is clear that insight into the factors determining dissatisfaction and turnover is relevant. It is very much in the interest of the company that good employees are retained and satisfied instead of leaving or becoming ill due to discontent. Knowledge of the socialization process and the policy aimed at the integration of newcomers can help in this respect.

As we have seen, a person's choice to leave the company can be explained by a matching model, in combination with expectancy theory. Satisfaction with the job and commitment to the organization are determined by the strength of the agreement between the needs of the individual and the various aspects of the organizational climate. The degree of satisfaction depends on a person's appreciation of the various work outcomes and the estimated importance of these outcomes. Whether dissatisfaction will indeed lead the individual to take action and seek another job, depends on the attractiveness of other organizations and on the motivation of the individuals involved to be employed by another company. This process of comparison can have the following consequences: one is satisfied and stays in the company; one is dissatisfied but does not make a serious attempt to leave; one is dissatisfied and actively searches for another job.

According to Wanous's (1992) matching model, the main reason why newcomers voluntarily leave the organization is low job satisfaction caused by unmet expectations. The results of a review of the literature on "met expectations" were quite consistent with this view. That is, the strongest effects of unmet expectations are found on job satisfaction and organizational commitment, followed by one's intention to remain in the organization, and then by actual job survival (staying or leaving).

Schultz and Buunk (1990) researched which factors determine general dissatisfaction with the present job. Besides negative aspects of the present job, the appreciation of other jobs play a role, for example, regarding use of knowledge and skills, development of initiatives, and so on. However, search behaviour is more strongly connected to dissatisfaction with the present job than to the appreciation of alternatives.

Whether or not it is a question of successful socialization can be seen in the outcome variables, such as the career pattern after starting one's first job, the strategies adopted by the newcomer in order to expand his or her career possibilities ("career enhancing strategies": see Bachman, O'Malley, & Johnson, 1978; Feij et al., 1995; Penley & Gould, 1981) and the searching behaviour that a newcomer exhibits. Nevertheless, a high level of job mobility can be explained as both a positive and a negative indicator of successful socialization (Heesink, 1992). Van der Linden and Dijkman (1989) report that there is a case of high-level job mobility among Dutch people. Although many young people enjoy a reasonable amount of job satisfaction, more than 50% of those interviewed thought that they would not remain in the same job. Evidently, aspirations exist among many young people to progress to a better job. A sign of successful socialization!

In this context, it is also worth noting that nowadays there is an increasing number of employees who have a flexible contract. That is, many young people no longer want to have lifelong employment in one single job, but divide their time over different employers and more jobs at a time, or in succession.

5.3 Conformity or innovation?

Feldman (1976) views job innovation, i.e. the testing of new work procedures and making suggestions to do work differently or better, as an important result of the organizational socialization process. If in the early stage of the organizational socialization process expectations are not in agreement with the reality of the job, the newcomer can react in different ways: either the person re-adjusts their expectations and values, or they try to change their situation (or both). Literature suggests that both job change and self-change are feasible means by which new employees adjust to new jobs (Black & Ashford, 1995). In the present view of socialization (see Section 4.2) people are seen as "active" in the sense that they will, in principle, try to influence and modify their work situation, instead of only passively reacting to the situation (Anderson & Thomas, 1996; Graen, 1976; Whitely, 1986). In other words, the newcomer has an active role in negotiating his or her new work environment (Louis, 1980a).

As has been pointed out previously, a distinction can be made between (a) an innovative role orientation, in which a newcomer attempts to alter procedures for performing a role, the purpose of the role itself, or both, and (b) a custodial orientation, in which a newcomer accepts the prescribed limits of a role in an organization (Jones, 1986). Which factors influence the orientation the new employee adopts?

Whether or not a young employee will exhibit innovative behaviour, in Feldman's (1976) opinion, mainly depends on how much the newcomer feels supported and valued. Recent studies show that innovation is related to individualized socialization tactics applied by the organization (see the references given in Section 4.1.2) and to the way newcomers seek information. Mignerey et al. (1995), for example, found that during organizational entry, socialization tactics as well as communication traits, attitudes and values influence informational feedback seeking, resulting in more confidence and less role ambiguity. Newcomers who actively sought information and became critically involved during early employment were more likely to assume an innovative role profile within the organization.

West and Rushton (1989) suggested that adjustment to mismatches following work-role transitions may foster high levels of personal change and attempted role innovation. However, low discretion environments in particular hinder such adjustment, leading to frustration and intention to turnover. Our own research yielded a similar finding: scores on a scale measuring "correspondence" (high scores mean that the job is better, low scores that the job is worse than initial expectations in several respects) were cross-sectionally related to attempted job content innovation, i.e. innovative attempts and decision latitude. Moreover, correspondence was related to newcomers career enhancing strategies, i.e. career planning, seeking help and advice from others, communication of work goals and aspirations, skill development, working extra hours and networking (Feij et al., 1995). Whitely (1986) used the term "interpersonal innovation" to describe this way of influencing the work situation. With this term he means the forming of social networks with an eye on obtaining task information or promotion. Such networks can also serve to give or receive support and advice from others.

In summary, it appears that a good fit between the person and his or her working situation, as well as met expectations or surprise reactions, generally have positive consequences for the employees. They do not only foster commitment (see Section 5.1), but also innovative behaviour. On the other hand, it is generally assumed that too strong an agreement between the needs of the individual and the climate of the organization—resulting from an overly one-sided selection policy—leads to conformism instead of creativity and innovative behaviour (Argyris, 1957; Schein, 1968).

Schein (1968) distinguishes between two kinds

of organizational values to which the newcomer does or does not conform: (a) pivotal values and (b) relevant values. "Pivotal" values are absolutely essential to the survival of the organization, for example, profit making in a commercial company or the transfer of knowledge at school. The "relevant" values of an organization are important, but they are not absolutely necessary for membership. Examples are dress codes and various unwritten rules governing behaviour.

Schein (1968) outlines the presumed consequences that the acceptance or the rejection of the two kinds of values will have for the innovative behaviour of the newcomer. According to Schein the acceptance of (a) in combination with the rejection of (b) will lead to "creative individualists". Rejection of both (a) and (b) will lead to poorly innovative employees: "rebels". But the acceptance of both (a) and (b) is not favourable either, because this only produces "conformists". Wanous (1992) however, points out that there is little empirical data available to support these, in our opinion, somewhat disputable hypotheses. Moreover, Anderson and Thomas (1996) remark that Schein's (1968) paper stems from a time when the focus of socialization research was on the active organization and passive individual.

The answer to the question, can one speak in terms of successful work socialization—concerning the criterion conformity, or innovation—is partly dependent on the nature and level of the job. So, we would expect that the employee would take the initiative and apply themselves with renewed vigour in the case of more autonomous jobs, rather than in the case of systematic, pre-determined work.

Mortimer et al. (1986) have shown how important it is that people are autonomous in their work, are able to make decisions themselves, can carry out innovations and are open to a challenge. These conditions have a positive effect on the psychological development of employees. In the study of Mortimer et al. (1986) it was evident that autonomy at work is conducive to feelings of personal competence and positive attitudes towards work; autonomy increases involvement and intrinsic motivation. In short, "occupational self-direction" appears to be a crucial condition for successful socialization (see Kohn & Schooler, 1973, 1983). Also according to O'Brien (1986), the influence of perceived job attributes on job satisfaction is said to be so strong that the effects of differences in personality and work values disappear.

However, in our opinion this does not mean that jobs in which autonomy is not possible will necessarily lead to stagnation in the socialization process. One should probably apply different criteria, depending on the nature of the job. Roberts (1984, p. 42) suggests: "sometimes recruits learn to identify with employing organizations rather than occupations .... In some occupations recruits learn to value extrinsic rather than intrinsic rewards". Roberts concludes that although details vary from job to job and to a certain extent also from person to person, work socialization, aside from the learning of technical skills, is ultimately concerned with the development of aspirations and self-image, corresponding to the job one holds.

Finally we would like to stress once more that the work socialization process (in the broad definition—see Section 2.1) is never fully complete for most people. Nicholson (1987) points out that for many people socialization has a cyclic character. Presumably totally different indicators are relevant in the diverse phases, in order to be able to judge whether or not the process is successful. One of the starting points of the WOSY research is "recursivity" (WOSY International Research Group, 1989). This means that the results of a certain phase in the work socialization process can be viewed as "input" for a following phase (Whitely et al., 1992). Thus, the combination of various personal characteristics (MOW International Research Team, 1987) and job and work environment characteristics (Banks, Feij, Parkinson, & Pieró, 1992) determine the satisfaction, well-being and career behaviour of the newcomer (Feij et al., 1992, 1995); these outcomes could lead to changes in the person or in the environment, after which the cycle repeats itself.

6 CONCLUSION

The socialization of young people is pre-eminently a multi-disciplinary area of research. An extensive amount of literature exists on the subject, but research is highly fragmented. In spite of the accumulating knowledge, the majority of authors in their field conclude that still very little is known concerning the course of socialization processes. Vondracek et al. (1986, p. 101) conclude for example:

> Our review . . . does not allow us to be especially positive about the quality and extensiveness of extant knowledge about career development in adolescence. We have seen that most research is adevelopmental and that problems of design, method, and analysis plague even much of the research that has the minimal requirements of a study of intraindividual change, i.e., two times of measurement. Moreover, there have been few studies that have gone beyond the description of covariation among some marker variables (e.g., age, sex, SES) and career development related variables.

According to Vondracek et al. (1986), little knowledge about the causal processes in career development can be gleaned from this literature.

Clarke (1980a) is equally pessimistic about the literature in the field of school–work transition. Among other things she points to the all too often insufficient and irregular research methodology and to the use of small-scale or specific research samples.

Fisher (1986, p. 137) concludes, based on a survey of literature on the subject of organizational socialization: "At present the process is poorly understood, yet it is a process which occurs repeatedly throughout most individuals' lives". Later literature reviews also endorse this view (e.g. Anderson & Thomas, 1996; Feldman, 1989; Hall, 1987; Wanous & Colella, 1989).

There are several reasons that can be given for this lack of understanding.

A first explanation is found in the poor research methods employed. The research results are often incomparable because of the difference in the methods used, or impossible to generalize across diverse groups. Moreover, the results are often obsolete too soon as a result of structural changes in society. It is clear that the only way to trace the causal mechanisms that are responsible for successful or unsuccessful socialization is to employ adequately designed multi-variate and longitudinal "panel studies". Until recently, such studies were rare. For a methodological agenda showing how the ideal research should be planned see Vondracek et al. (1986).

A second reason is the previously mentioned multi-disciplinary character of the research area. The literature on socialization is spread across many disciplines (psychology, sociology, communication science, economics) and is related to diverse areas of life (work, relationships, etc.). Nevertheless, many authors agree that socialization in the work process is strongly interwoven with social integration in other areas of life (e.g. Higgins, Duxbury, & Irving, 1992). One needs insights from all these disciplines to fully understand socialization. A further complication is that *the* socialization process is difficult to predict due to the fact that so many factors influence it. On the one hand contingency variables such as social-economic status, level of training, type of work, gender and ethnicity; and on the other hand structural factors such as employment situation, upbringing habits, educational systems, and governmental policy. In short, the ever-changing social-economic, political and cultural factors.

A third and perhaps even more fundamental cause of this inconsistent availability of material on the subject is that one can view "socialization" in two different ways: from the viewpoint of the person or from the context (Eldredge, 1995). Developmental psychologists view socialization as identity or career development; work and organizational psychologists, on the other hand, study the training and introductory procedures involved in developing a newcomer into an accepted "insider". In short, the literature is not very coherent.

There are other reasons for this. One can take the view that the social situation influences personality development; on the other hand, there is also the view that the self-developing person selects, or is selected for, his or her situation. In this context, this is referred to as the "socialization-hypothesis" versus the "selection-hypothesis" (Kohn & Schooler, 1983; Mortimer et al., 1986). Sometimes socialization, i.e. the normative process of adaptation of the individual to the values, demands and expectations of the social structure, is contrasted with "individualization" (the self-realization of the individual) or with personalization (the influencing of the environment by the person).

In this chapter we hope to have made clear that this is a case of two sides of the same coin. Social integration is related to the development of both the personal and social identity (Mael, 1991). Socialization is a constant interaction between a person and his or her social environment and insight into both these factors is therefore essential for a complete understanding of this process (for a discussion, see Dowd, 1990).

In summary, methodological problems, the fact that the literature is scattered across the various disciplines, domain specificity and at the same time the interwoven character of socialization processes, and differences in viewpoint are all factors that make it difficult to determine exactly what is known about socialization. Furthermore, there is a need for more research with an experimental, manipulative character besides the present research which is mainly cross-sectional and correlational. Due to the previously mentioned reasons, there are few "umbrella" theories, in which knowledge about socialization in the diverse areas of life, such as socialization at work or in relationships is integrated. Steps in that direction have been taken by Mortimer et al. (1986) and Tazelaar (1982; see also Tazelaar & Wippler, 1985).

Fortunately, there are also positive developments. Longitudinal research has recently become more popular. In many industrialized countries large-scale longitudinal studies are currently carried out regarding the relation between training, the work career and the experiences of young people in other areas of life. Examples are: Dijkstra (1989, 1993) and Meijers (1989) in The Netherlands; the international comparative WOSY research (WOSY International Research Group, 1989); the Michigan student study (Mortimer et al. 1986), and the extensive "Youth in transition-study" (Bachman et al., 1978, 1984) in the United States. In Germany in particular an important research tradition has evolved (Kohli, 1980, 1986; Blossfeld & Nuthmann, 1991; Heinz, 1991).

Fisher (1986, p. 137) signalled a new trend in organizational socialization research: "The study of socialization seems to be on the brink of adapting a whole new approach—that of seeing the newcomer as an active problem solver and agent of his or her own socialization". Subjects that will demand extra attention from researchers in the near future are, according to her: the selection of "socializing agents" by young people, and furthermore the way in which "individual differences in both dispositions and beliefs effect newcomer *reactions* to socialization pressures and *actions* in self-socialization" (p. 138). As we have made clear in the section on communication and information processing (Section 4.2), much of this "agenda" is still a topic in current socialization research. With regard to the individual differences mentioned by Fisher (1986), it seems appropriate that attention should be paid to motivational determinators of the socialization process in future research. In our opinion, "mismatch", i.e. incongruity, dissonance, or other terms that say something about the discrepancy between expectations and reality, is an important motivating factor. As Wanous (1992) also points out, "mismatch" can form a key term in theories on work motivation, satisfaction, mobility and stress. Important topics in both work psychology and organizational psychology such as selection of personnel, training, work socialization and career planning can all be regarded from one perspective: the optimal fit between the person and his or her environment.

One must realize, however, that the assumption that important transitions should go hand in hand with "disequilibrium" or "reality shock" (in which psycho-analytical thinking in terms of stages and crises reverberates) is certainly not always realistic. For a majority of young people, transitions progress automatically, as it were (see Clarke, 1980a). This image corresponds with the recent vision of young people actively creating their own future, instead of passively reacting to what happens to them.

Furthermore, the mismatch does not always have to be negative: a job can also be better than the newcomer had thought. In our research we found that this is connected to intensive career enhancing strategies of the new employee, signalling the wish to seek promotion (Feij et al., 1992, 1995).

But just how relevant is the information on the work socialization process for the practical domain?

It is clear that the acquisition of insight into the development of young people roughly between the ages of 18 and 30 is of great scientific importance. In comparison with the adolescence phase about which much has been written (Jepsen, 1984; Tinsley & Heesacker, 1984), this period of life has seen comparatively little research, probably because people view the age groups within young adulthood as not being problematic. Yet, this phase with its many simultaneous status transitions, is of crucial importance for an individual's further career and work socialization.

The scientific knowledge on the work socialization process can be used in two ways. On the one hand there is institutional application, i.e. usage for the benefit of organizations, governmental departments and policy forming; and on the other hand individual application: usage focusing on the improvement of career choice and the well-being of the individual.

One can think of the following institutional applications:

- By the government: guidance for graduates; improvement of the educational system and improvement of the fit between school and work; employment policy, e.g. the creation of places where young people can gain job experience.
- By schools and training institutes: adjustment of the training demands and questions from society (the organization); improvement of career advice and career guidance.
- By companies: improvement of recruitment and selection methods and the information given to newcomers; the establishment or refinement of company training and development activities concerning the new employees' technical as well as social skills. In The Netherlands, for instance, issues like information for new employees and the education of new employees are explicitly reported in the Work Legislation Act of 1983 (the Dutch Arbo-law).

These institutional targets will mainly be similar to those of the individual. A characteristic of the current situation is a "once again" growing job market. However, great shifts in the nature of the work are also taking place. This is a consequence of the ever-increasing roles of automation and information (De Keyser, Qvale, Wilpert, & Ruiz Quintanilla, 1988). Therefore, it is important for young people to choose the optimal direction and course of both training and work in good time, and integrate smoothly and quickly with colleagues. On the other hand, there is a strong increase in the number of part-time jobs and flexible contracts, which stimulates frequent job change. Most young people no longer aspire to lifelong employment in the same job or company. At the same time, the bond between education, vocational training and job choice is loosened. These developments might be a reason to drastically change our concept of work socialization in the near future.

In summary, for both the individual and the organization it is of great importance that the socialization process progresses successfully. For the individual, because successful socialization is advantageous for his or her well-being and contentment at work; and for the organization, as part of a broader "human resource management" policy. Knowledge of what employees expect of their job (and how these expectations change during the early part of their career) helps organizations in the design of tasks, reward systems, leadership styles and personnel policies, in order to improve contentment to the work and motivation (Wiersma, 1988).

Moreover, insight into the progression of socialization or the social integration of the "average" young person in our present society can help to understand and reduce the deficit of socially less fortunate groups, for example, the physically and/or mentally handicapped, and ethnic minorities. Based on literature reviews, Swanson (1992) and Watkins and Subich (1995) concluded that the career experiences of racial-ethnic minorities remain underrepresented in research and poorly understood.

Finally, the increasing number of working

mothers and dual-earner/career couples also forms an important reason why research into the socialization process should be intensified. The study of the work-family conflict, and of the influence that working mothers have on the development of their children, is still in its "infancy" (see Gottfried & Gottfried, 1988; Higgins et al., 1992; Scar et al., 1989; Watkins & Subich, 1995). Present social developments can be expected to have significant repercussions on the upbringing and the socialization of the next generation.

ACKNOWLEDGEMENTS

The author wishes to thank Klaartje Bleeker, Michael Burke and Dr Deanne den Hartog for their assistance in translating the Dutch text on which this chapter is based.

NOTES

1. Several publications mentioned in this chapter are part of the research programme "The process of social integration of young adults", which is being conducted by the department of Methods and Techniques (the Faculty of SCW), and the department of Work and Organizational Psychology (the Faculty of FPP) at the Vrije Universiteit in Amsterdam. It is a longitudinal study among 1775 young Dutch people aged 18, 22 and 26 (see Dijkstra, 1989; 1993). Publications from this project are: Heesink (1992); Taes (1989); Taris et al. (1991, 1994, 1995a,b); Van der Velde and Feij (1995); Van der Velde et al. (1995).
2. The data used in the following publications were drawn from the Work Socialization of Youth (WOSY) International Research Project (see WOSY International Research Group, 1989): Banks et al. (1992); Feij et al. (1992, 1995); Van Gastel and Feij (1989a,b)); Van Gastel et al. (1991); Taris et al. (1992); Touzard (1992); Whitely et al. (1992).
3. These stages were defined as: entre/encounter stage (in the organization for less than one month); metamorphosis (in the organization for between one and six months); post-metamorphosis (in the organization for more than six months). Other authors, however, have suggested other time criteria (e.g. Nelson, 1987; see also Vandenberg & Self, 1993).

REFERENCES

Adkins, C.L. (1995). Previous work experience and organizational socialization: A longitudinal examination. *Academy of Management Journal, 38*, 839–862.

Ajzen, I. (1985). From intention to actions: A theory of planned behavior. In J. Kuhl & J. Beckman (Eds.), *Action control: From cognition to behavior* (pp. 11–39). Berlin: Springer Verlag.

Allen, N.J., & Meyer, J.P. (1990a). The measurement and antecedents of affective, continuance and normative commitment to the organization. *Journal of Occupational Psychology, 63*, 1–18.

Allen, N.J. & Meyer, J.P. (1990b). Organizational socialization tactics: A longitudinal analysis of links to newcomers' commitment and role orientation. *Academy of Management Journal, 33*, 847–858.

Allen, V.L., & Vliert, E. van de (Eds.) (1984). *Role transitions. Explorations and explanations.* New York: Plenum Press.

Anderson, N., & Thomas, H.D.C. (1996). Work group socialization. In M.A. West (Ed.), *Handbook of work group psychology* (pp. 423–450). Chichester: Wiley.

Archer, S.L. (1985). Career and/or family: The identity process for adolescent girls. *Youth and Society, 16*, 289–314.

Argyris, C. (1957). *Personality and organization.* New York: Harper.

Ashford, S.J. (1986). The role of feedback seeking in individual adaptation: A resource perspective. *Academy of Management Journal, 29*, 465–487.

Ashford, S.J., & Black, J.S. (1996). Proactivity during organizational entry: The role of desire for control. *Journal of Applied Psychology, 81*, 199–214.

Ashford, S.J., & Cummings, L.L. (1985). Proactive feedback seeking: The instrumental use of the information environment. *Journal of Occupational Psychology, 58*, 67–79.

Ashforth, B.E., & Saks, A.M. (1995). Work-role transitions: A longitudinal examination of the Nicholson model. *Journal of Occupational and Organizational Psychology, 68*, 157–175.

Ashforth, B.E., & Saks, A.M. (1996). Socialization tactics: Longitudinal effects on newcomer adjustment. *Academy of Management Journal, 39*, 149–178.

Astin, H.S. (1984). The meaning of work in women's lives: A sociopsychological model of career choice and work behavior. *Counseling Psychologist, 12*, 117–126.

Bachman, J.G., & O'Malley, P.M. (1984). The youth in transition project. In S.A. Mednick, M. Harway, & K.M. Finello (Eds.), *Handbook of longitudinal research* (Vol. 2, pp. 121–140). New York: Praeger.

Bachman, J.G., O'Malley, P.M., & Johnston, J. (1978). *Youth in transition, Vol. VI. Adolescence to adulthood—change and stability in the lives of young men.* Ann Arbor, MI: University of Michigan, Institute for Social Research.

Baker, H.E. (1992). Employee socialization strategies and the presence of union representation. *Labor Studies Journal, 17*, 5–17.

Baker, H.E., & Feldman, D.C. (1990). Strategies of organizational socialization and their impact on newcomer adjustment. *Journal of Managerial Issues, 2*, 198–212.

Baker, W.K. (1995). Allen and Meyer's 1990 longitudinal study: A reanalysis and reinterpretation using structural equation modeling. *Human Relations, 48*, 169–181.

Bakke, E.W. (1953). *The fusion process.* New Haven: Yale University, Labor and Management Center.

Baltes, P.B. (Ed.) (1978). *Life span development and behavior, Vol. 1.* New York: Academic Press.

Bandura, A. (1977). *Social learning theory.* Englewood Cliffs, NJ: Prentice Hall.

Banks, M.H., Feij, J.A., Parkinson, B., & Peiró, J.M. (1992). National and occupational differences in work content and environment of job entrants. *Revue Internationale de Psychologie Sociale, 5*, 61–79.

Bauer, T.N., & Green, S.G. (1994). Effect of newcomer involvement in work-related activities: A longitudinal study of socialization. *Journal of Applied Psychology, 79*, 211–223.

Berg, J. van den, & Tillaart, H. van den (1986). *Nieuwe werknemers. Een onderzoek naar rekrutering en introduktie van nieuwkomers in bedrijven.* Nijmegen: Instituut voor Toegepaste Sociale Wetenschappen.

Bergh, N. van den (1990). Managing biculturalism at the workplace: A group approach. *Social Work with Groups, 13*, 71–84.

Black, J.S. (1992). Socializing American expatriate managers overseas: Tactics, tenure, and role innovation. *Group and Organization Management, 17*, 171–192.

Black, J.S., & Ashford, S.J. (1995). Fitting in or making jobs fit: Factors affecting mode of adjustment for new hires. *Human Relations, 48*, 421–437.

Blair, S.L. (1992). Children's participation in household labor: Child socialization versus the need for household labor. *Journal of Youth & Adolescence, 21*, 241–258.

Blau, G. (1988). An investigation of the apprenticeship organizational socialization strategy. *Journal of Vocational Behavior, 32*, 176–195.

Bleichrodt, N., & Leest, P. van (1987). *Van werkloze naar informaticus: Werving en selectie.* Amsterdam: Stichting Promotie Informatica Omscholing Nederland.

Blossfeld, H.P., & Nuthmann, R. (1991). Transition from youth to adulthood as a cohort process in the Federal Republic of Germany. In H.A. Becker (Ed.), *Life histories and generations*, Vol. 1 (pp. 185–217). Utrecht: ISOR.

Boerlijst, G., & Aite-Peña, A. (1989). Loopbaanontwikkeling en -begeleiding. In P.J.D. Drenth, H. Thierry & C.J. de Wolff (Eds.), *Nieuw handboek arbeids- en organisatiepsychologie*, Vol. 2.8 (pp. 1–41). Deventer: Van Loghum Slaterus.

Borman, K.M., & Reisman, J.R. (Eds.) (1986). *Becoming a worker.* Norwood, NJ: Ablex Publishing Corp.

Bretz, R.D., & Judge, T.A. (1994). Person-organization fit and the theory of work adjustment: Implications for satisfaction, tenure and career success. *Journal of Vocational Behavior, 44*, 32–54.

Breukelen, J.W.M. van (1990). Organizational commitment. Een bruikbaar begrip voor onderzoek in organisaties? *Gedrag en Organisatie, 3*, 264–286.

Bronfenbrenner, U. (1979). *The ecology of human development.* Cambridge, MA: Harvard University Press.

Bullis, C. (1993). Organizational socialization research: Enabling, constraining and shifting perspectives. *Communication Monographs, 60*, 10–17.

Caldwell, D.F., Chatman, J.A., & O'Reilly, C.A. (1990). Building organizational commitment: A multifirm study. *Journal of Occupational Psychology, 63*, 245–261.

Chao, G.T., O'Leary-Kelly, A.M., Wolf, S., Klein, H.J., & Gardner, P.D. (1994). Organizational socialization: Its content and consequences. *Journal of Applied Psychology, 79*, 730–743.

Chao, G.T., Walz, P.M., & Gardner, P.D. (1992). Formal and informal mentorships: A comparison on mentoring functions and contrast with nonmentored counterparts. *Personnel Psychology, 45*, 619–636.

Chapman, M. (1990). "Ever since Durkheim: The socialization of human development": Commentary. *Human Development, 33*, 165–168.

Chatman, J.A. (1991). Matching people and organizations: Selection and socialization in public accounting firms. *Administrative Science Quarterly, 36*, 459–484.

Clarke, L. (1980a). *The transition from school to work: A critical review of research in the United Kingdom.* London: Her Majesty's Stationery Office, Careers Service Brand, Department of Employment.

Clarke, L. (1980b). *Occupational choice: A critical review of research in the United Kingdom.* London: Her Majesty's Stationery Office, Careers Service Brand, Department of Employment.

Coetsier, P., Claes, R., & Berings, D. (1987). *Socialisatie van jongeren met werken inzonderheid in verband met nieuwe technologieën.* Rapporten van het laboratorium en seminarie voor toegepaste psychologie. Report No. 51. Gent, Belgium: Rijksuniversiteit Gent.

Cohen, A. (1991). Career stage as a moderator of the relationships between organizational commitment and its outcomes: A meta-analysis. *Journal of Occupational Psychology, 64*, 253–268.

Colella, A. (1994). Organizational socialization of employees with disabilities: Critical issues and implications for workplace interventions. *Journal of Occupational Rehabilitation, 4*, 87–106.

Comer, D.R. (1991). Organizational newcomers' acquisition of information from peers. *Management Communication Quarterly*, *5*, 64–89.

Crites, J.O. (1969). *Vocational psychology*. New York: McGraw-Hill.

Crites, J.O. (1973). *Career maturity inventory*. Monterey, CA: California Test Bureau/McGraw-Hill.

Crites, J.O. (1981). *Career counseling: Models, methods and materials*. New York: McGraw-Hill.

Dijkstra, W. (Ed.) (1989). *Het proces van sociale integratie van jongvolwassenen: De gegevensverzameling voor de eerste hoofdmeting*. Amsterdam: VU Boekhandel/Uitgeverij.

Dijkstra, W. (Ed.) (1993). *Het proces van sociale integratie van jongvolwassenen: De gegevensverzameling voor de tussenmeting en de tweede hoofdmeting*. Amsterdam: VU Boekhandel/Uitgeverij.

Dowd, J.J. (1990). Ever since Durkheim: The socialization of human development. *Human development*, *33*, 138–159.

Dunnette, M.D., Arvey, R.D., & Banis, P.A. (1973). Why do they leave? *Personnel*, *50*, 25–39.

Edwards, J.R. (1991). Person-job fit: A conceptual integration, literature review, and methodological critique. In C.L. Cooper & I.T. Robertson (Eds.), *International Review of Industrial and Organizational Psychology*, Vol. 6 (pp. 283–357). New York: Wiley.

Eldredge, B.D. (1995). Some things not considered: Evaluation of a model of career enhancing strategies and content innovation with respect to organizational socialization. *Journal of Vocational Behavior*, *46*, 266–273.

Erikson, E.H. (1968). *Identity: Youth and crisis*. New York: Norton.

Etzioni, A. (1964). *Modern organizations*. Englewood Cliffs, NJ: Prentice-Hall.

Featherman, D.L., & Sørensen, A. (1984). Societal change and role transitions into adulthood. In V.L. Allen, & E. van de Vliert (Eds.), *Role transitions. Explorations and explanations* (pp. 137–149). New York: Plenum Press.

Feij, J.A. (1985). Persoonlijkheidspsychologie. In J.F. Orlebeke, P.J.D. Drenth, R.H.C. Janssen & C. Sanders (Eds.), *Compendium van de psychologie*, Vol. V (pp. 139–253). Muiderberg: Coutinho.

Feij, J.A. (1987). Procesos de socialización de los jovenes consideraciones teoicas. In J.M. Peiró, & I.D. Moret (Eds.), *Socialización laboral y desempleo juvenil: La transición de la escuela al trabajoc*. Valencia: Nau llibres.

Feij, J.A., Banks, M.H., Parkinson, B., & Whitely, W. (1992). Work socialization: In search of the person-environment interaction. *Revue Internationale de Psychologie Sociale*, *5*, 137–150.

Feij, J.A., Whitely, W.T., Peiró, J.M., & Taris, T.W. (1995). The development of career-enhancing strategies and content innovation: A longitudinal study of new workers. *Journal of Vocational Behavior*, *46*, 231–256.

Feldman, D.C. (1976). A contingency theory of socialization. *Administrative Science Quarterly*, *21*, 433–452.

Feldman, D.C. (1981). The multiple socialization of organization members. *Academy of Management Review*, *6*, 309–318.

Feldman, D.C. (1989). Socialization, resocialization and training: Reframing the research agenda. In I.L. Goldstein (Ed.), *Training and development in organizations* (pp. 376–416). San Francisco: Jossey-Bass.

Fine, S., & Wiley, W. (1971). *An introduction to functional job analysis: A scaling of selected tasks from the social welfare field*. Kalamazoo, MI: W. E. Upjohn Institute for Employment Research.

Fishbein, M., & Ajzen, I. (1975). *Belief, attitude, intention and behavior*. Reading, MA: Addison-Wesley.

Fisher, C.D. (1986). Organizational socialization: An integrative review. In K.M. Rowland & G.R. Ferris (Eds.), *Research in personnel and human resources management*, Vol. 4 (pp. 101–145). Greenwich, CT: JAI Press.

Frese, M. (1982). Occupational socialization and psychological development: An under-emphasized research perspective in industrial psychology. *Journal of Occupational Psychology*, *55*, 219–224.

Fryer, D. (1989). Ervaringen met werkloosheid. In P.J.D. Drenth, H. Thierry, & C.J. de Wolff (Eds.), *Nieuw handboek Arbeids- en Organisatiepsychologie*. Deventer: Van Loghum Slaterus.

Gastel, J. van, & Feij, J.A. (1989a). *Werksocialisatie van jongeren. Eerste tussentijds rapport van het onderzoek naar de work socialization of youth*. (SI-report WE–89/35). Amsterdam: Vrije Universiteit, Department of Work and Organizational Psychology.

Gastel, J. van, & Feij, J.A. (1989b). *Werksocialisatie van jongeren. Tweede tussentijdse rapport van het onderzoek naar de work socialization of youth: De metaalindustrie*. (SI-report WE–89/36). Amsterdam: Vrije Universiteit, Department of Work and Organizational Psychology.

Gastel, J. van, Feij, J.A., & Staarman, I. (1991). *Jongeren in de beginfase van hun eerste baan. Een onderzoek naar de relatie tussen baankenmerken en werkwaarden enerzijds en welbevinden anderzijds*. (technical report). Amsterdam: Vrije Universiteit, Department of Work and Organizational Psychology.

Gecas, V. (1981). Contexts of socialization. In M. Rosenberg & R.H. Turner (Eds.), *Social psychology: Social perspectives* (pp. 165–199). New York: Basic Books.

Gottfried, A.E., & Gottfried, A.W. (Eds.) (1988). *Maternal employment and children's development:*

Longitudinal research. New York: Plenum Publishing Corporation.

Graen, G. (1976). Role making processes within complex organizations. In M.D. Dunnette (Ed.). *The handbook of industrial and organizational psychology* (pp. 1201–1246). Chicago: Rand McNally.

Greenberger, E. & Goldberg, W.A. (1989). Work, parenting, and the socialization of children. *Developmental Psychology, 25,* 22–35.

Grotenhuis, H. te, & Dronkers, J. (1989). Enkele gevolgen van werkloosheid en arbeidsongeschiktheid in de verzorgingsstaat. Ongelijke kansen van kinderen. *Amsterdams Sociologisch Tijdschrift, 15,* 634–651.

Guimond, S. (1995). Encounter and metamorphosis: The impact of military socialisation on professional values. *Applied Psychology: An International Review, 44,* 251–275.

Hackman, J.R., & Oldham, G.R. (1975). Development of the job diagnostic survey. *Journal of Applied Psychology, 60,* 159–197.

Hackman, J.R., & Oldham, G.R. (1980). *Work design.* Reading, MA: Addison-Wesley.

Hall, D.T. (1976). *Careers in organizations.* Pacific Palisades, CA: Goodyear.

Hall, D.T. (1987). Careers and socialization. Special Issue: Yearly review of management. *Journal of Management, 13,* 301–321.

Hautaluoma, J.E., Enge, R.S., Mitchell, T.M., & Rittwager, F.J. (1991). Early socialization into a work group: Severity of initiations revisited. *Journal of Social Behavior & Personality, 6,* 725–748.

Heesink, J.A.M. (1992). *Uitgeschoold, ingeschaald: Loopbaanontwikkeling en psychisch welzijn van jong-volwassenen.* Dissertation. Vrije Universiteit, Amsterdam, The Netherlands.

Heesink, J.A.M., & Feij, J.A. (1992). Loopbaanontwikkeling en welzijn bij jong-volwassenen. *Gedrag en Organisatie, 5,* 343–365.

Heinz, W.R. (1991). Labour market entry and the individualization of the life course. In H.A. Becker (Ed.), *Life histories and generations,* Vol. III (pp. 563–579). Utrecht: ISOR.

Helbing, H. (1987). *The self in career development. Theory, measurement and counseling.* Dissertation. Amsterdam, The Netherlands: University of Amsterdam.

Hellman, C.M. & McMillin, W.L. (1994). Newcomer socialization and affective commitment. *Journal of Social Psychology, 34,* 261–262.

Herriot, P. (1984). *Down from the ivory tower: Graduates and their jobs.* Chichester: Wiley.

Hess, J.A. (1993). Assimilating newcomers into an organization: A cultural perspective. *Journal of Applied Communication Research, 21,* 189–210.

Higgins, C.A., Duxbury, L.E., & Irving, R.H. (1992). Work-family conflict in the dual career family. *Organizational Behavior & Human Decision Processes, 51,* 51–75.

Holland, J.L. (1973). *Making vocational choices: A theory of careers.* Englewood Cliffs, NJ: Prentice-Hall.

Hurrelmann, K. (1988). *Social structure and personality development: The individual as a productive processor of reality.* Cambridge: Cambridge University Press.

Jablin, F.M. (1984). Assimilating new members into organizations. In R.N. Bostrom (Ed.), *Communication Yearbook 8* (pp. 594–626). Beverly Hills, CA: Sage.

Jablin, F.M. (1987). Organizational entry, assimilation, and exit. In F.M. Jablin, L.L. Putnam, K.H. Roberts, & L.W. Porter (Eds.), *Handbook of organizational communication: An interdisciplinary perspective* (pp. 679–740). Newbury Park, CA: Sage.

Jepsen, D.A. (1984). The developmental perspective on vocational behavior: A review of theory and research. In S.D. Brown, & R.W. Lent (Eds.), *Handbook of counseling psychology* (pp. 178–215). New York: Wiley.

Jones, G.R. (1983). Psychological orientation and the progress of organizational socialization: An interactionist perspective. *Academy of Management Review, 8,* 464–474.

Jones, G.R. (1986). Socialization tactics, self-efficacy and newcomers' adjustments to organizations. *Academy of Management Journal, 29,* 262–279.

Katz, R. (1980). Time and work: Toward an integrative perspective. In B.M. Staw & L.L. Cummings (Eds.), *Research in Organizational Behavior,* Vol. 2 (pp. 81–128). Greenwich, CT: JAI Press.

Katz, R. (1985). Organizational stress and early socialization experiences. In T. Beehr, & R. Bhagat (Eds.), *Human stress and cognition in organizations: An integrative perspective* (pp. 117–139). New York: John Wiley.

Katz, D., & Kahn, R.L. (1978). *The social psychology of organizations* (2nd Ed.). New York: Wiley.

Kelley, H.H. (1967). Attribution theory in social psychology. In D. Levine (Ed.), *Nebraska symposium on motivation,* Vol. 15 (pp. 192–238). Lincoln, NE: University of Nebraska Press.

Kelley, S.W. (1992). Developing customer oriention among service employees. *Journal of the Academy of Marketing Science, 20,* 27–36.

Keyser, V. de, Qvale, T., Wilpert, B., & Ruiz Quintanilla, S.A. (Eds.). (1988). *The meaning of work and technological options.* Chichester: Wiley.

Kidd, J.M. (1984). The relationship of self and occupational concepts to the occupational preferences of adolescents. *Journal of Vocational Behavior, 24,* 48–65.

Kohli, M. (1980). Lebenslauftheoretische Ansätze in

der Sozialisationsforschung. In K. Hurrelmann & D. Ulich (Eds.), *Handbuch der Sozialisationsforschung* (pp. 299–320). Weinheim: Beltz.

Kohli, M. (1986). Social organization and subjective construction of the life course. In A.B. Sørensen, F.E. Weinert, & L.R. Sherrod (Eds.), *Human development and the life course* (pp. 271–292). Hillsdale, NJ: Lawrence Erlbaum Associates Inc.

Kohn, M.L. (1977). *Class and conformity: A study in values* (2nd Edn.). Chicago: University of Chicago Press.

Kohn, M.L. (1981). Personality, occupation and social stratification: A frame of reference. In D.J. Treiman, & R.V. Robinson (Eds.), *Research in social stratification and mobility*, Vol. 1 (pp. 267–297). Greenwich, CT: JAI Press.

Kohn, M.L., & Schooler, C. (1973). Occupational experience and psychological functioning: An assessment of reciprocal effects. *American Sociological Review, 38*, 97–118.

Kohn, M.L., & Schooler, C. (1982). Job conditions and personality: A longitudinal assessment of their reciprocal effects. *American Journal of Sociology, 87*, 1257–1285.

Kohn, M.L. & Schooler, C. (1983). *Work and personality: An inquiry into the impact of social stratification.* Norwood, NJ: Ablex.

Kram, K.E. (1985). *Mentoring at work: Developmental relationships in organizational life.* Glen View, IL: Scott, Foresman.

Kram, K.E., & Isabella, L.A. (1985). Mentoring alternatives: The role of peer relationships in career development. *Academy of Management Journal, 28*, 110–132.

Kristof, A.L. (1996). Person-organization fit: An integrative review of its conceptualizations, measurement, and implications. *Personnel Psychology, 49*, 1–49.

Krumboltz, J.D. (1981). A social learning theory of career selection. In D.H. Montross, & C.J. Shinkman (Eds.), *Career development in the 1980s: Theory and practice* (pp. 43–66). Springfield, IL: Charles C. Thomas.

Linden, F.J. van der, & Dijkman, T. (1989). *Jong zijn en volwassen worden in Nederland.* Nijmegen: Hoogveld Instituut.

Louis, M.R. (1980a). Surprise and sense making: What newcomers experience in entering unfamiliar organizational settings. *Administrative Science Quarterly, 25*, 226–251.

Louis, M.R. (1980b). Toward an understanding of career transitions. In C.B. Derr (Ed.), *Work, family and the career: New frontiers in theory and research* (pp. 200–218). New York: Praeger.

Louis, M.R., Posner, B.Z., & Powell, G.N. (1983). The availability and helpfulness of socialization practices. *Personnel Psychology, 36*, 857–866.

Lueptow, F.B., McClendon, M.J., & McKeon, J.W. (1979). Father's occupation and son's personality: Findings and questions for the emerging linkage hypothesis. *The Sociological Quarterly, 20*, 463–475.

Lytton, H., & Romney, D.M. (1991). Parents' differential socialization of boys and girls: A meta-analysis. *Psychological Bulletin, 109*, 267–296.

Maanen, J. van (1976). Breaking in: Socialization to work. In R. Dubin (Ed.), *Handbook of work, organization and society* (pp. 67–130). Chicago: Rand McNally.

Maanen, J. van (1978). People processing: Strategies of organizational socialization. *Organizational Dynamics, 14*, 19–36.

Maanen, J. van, & Schein, E.H. (1979). Toward a theory of organizational socialization. In B.M. Staw (Ed.), *Research in organizational behavior*, Vol. 1 (pp. 209–264). Greenwich, CT: JAI Press.

Mael, F.A. (1991). A conceptual rationale for domains and attributes of biodata items. *Personnel Psychology, 44*, 763–792.

Mael, F.A., & Ashforth, B.E. (1995). Loyal from day one: Biodata, organizational identification, and turnover among newcomers. *Personnel Psychology, 48*, 309–333.

Marcia, J.E. (1980). Identity in adolescence. In J. Adelson (Ed.), *Handbook of adolescent psychology* (pp. 158–187). New York: Wiley.

Marsh, K.A., Dobos, J., & Brown Zahn, S. (1988). *Acquisition of member integration and competitive strategy information in organizational socialization.* Paper submitted to the International Communication Association, 1 November.

McCarthy, H. (1986). Making it in able-bodied America: Career development in young adults with physical disabilities. *Journal of Applied Rehabilitation Counseling*, 17, 30–38.

Meijers, F. (Ed.) (1989). *Jongeren op weg. Eerste onderzoeksverslag uit het project "Jongeren en Arbeid".* Leiden: Rijksuniversiteit, Vakgroep Andragogiek, sectie Jongerenstudies.

Meyer, J.P. & Allen, N.J. (1988). Links between work experiences and organizational commitment during the first year of employment: A longitudinal analysis. *Journal of Occupational Psychology, 61*, 195–209.

Meyer, J.P., & Allen, N.J. (1991). A three-component conceptualization of organizational commitment. *Human Resource Management Review, 1*, 61–89.

Meyer, J.P., & Allen, N.J. (1993). Commitment to organizations and occupations: Extension of a three-component conceptualization. *Journal of Applied Psychology, 78*, 538–551.

Mignerey, J.T., Rubin, R.B. & Gorden, W.I. (1995). An investigation of newcomer communication behavior and uncertainty. *Communication Research, 22*, 54–85.

Miller, V.D. (1989). *A quasi-experimental study of newcomers' information seeking behaviors during organizational entry.* "Top three" paper presented at the 37th International Communication Association Convention, Organizational Communication Division, San Francisco, CA: May 26–29.

Miller, V.D., & Jablin, F.M. (1991). Information seeking during organizational entry: Influences, tactics, and a model of the process. *Academy of Management Review, 16*, 92–120.

Mobley, W.H. Griffith, R.W., Hand, H.H., & Meglino, B.M. (1979). Review and conceptual analysis of the employee turnover process. *Psychological Bulletin, 86*, 493–522.

Moreland, R.L., & Levine, J.M. (1982). Socialization in small groups: Temporal changes in individual-group relations. *Advances in Experimental Social Psychology, 15*, 137–192.

Morrison, E.W. (1993a). Longitudinal study of the effects of information seeking on newcomer socialization. *Journal of Applied Psychology, 78*, 173–183.

Morrison, E.W. (1993b). Newcomer information seeking: Exploring types, modes, sources and outcomes. *Academy of Management Journal, 36*, 557–589.

Mortimer, J.T., Lorence, J., & Kumka, D.S. (1986). *Work, family and personality: Transition to adulthood.* Norwood, NJ: Ablex.

MOW International Research Team (1987). *The meaning of work: an international perspective.* London: Academic Press.

Mulford, C.L., Klongan, G.E., Beal, G.N., & Bohlen, J.M. (1968). Selectivity, socialization, and role performance. *Sociology and Social Research, 53*, 68–77.

Neimeyer, G.J., Brown, M.T., Metzler, A.E., Hagans, C., & Tanguy, M. (1989). The impact of sex, sex-role orientation, and construct type on vocational differentiation, integration and conflict. *Journal of Vocational Behavior, 34*, 236–251.

Nelson, D.L. (1987). Organizational socialization: A stress perspective. *Journal of Occupational Behaviour, 8*, 311–324.

Nelson, D.L., Quick, J.C., & Joplin, J.R. (1991). Psychological contracting and newcomer socialization: An attachment theory foundation. *Journal of Social Behavior & Personality, 6*, 55–72.

Nicholson, N. (1984). A theory of work role transitions. *Administrative Science Quarterly, 29*, 172–191.

Nicholson, N. (1987). Work-role transitions: Processes and outcomes. In P.B. Warr (Ed.), *Psychology at work* (3rd Ed., pp. 160–177) Harmondsworth: Penguin.

O'Brien, G.E. (1986). *Psychology of work and unemployment.* Chichester: Wiley.

Orpen, C. (1993). The effect of organizational cultural norms on the relationships between personnel practices and employee commitment. *Journal of Psychology, 127*, 577–579.

Ostroff, C., & Kozlowski, S.W.J. (1992). Organizational socialization as a learning process. The role of information acquisition. *Personnel Psychology, 45*, 849–874.

Ostroff, C., & Kozlowski, S.W.J. (1993). The role of mentoring in the information gathering processes of newcomers during early organizational socialization. *Journal of Vocational Behavior, 42*, 170–183.

Owens, T.J. (1992). The effect of post-high school social context on self-esteem. *Sociological Quarterly, 33*, 553–577.

Paludi, M.A. (1990). Sociopsychological and structural factors related to women's vocational development. *Annals of the New York Academy of Sciences, 602*, 157–168.

Pence, L.J. (1995). Learning leadership through mentorship. In D.M. Dunlap & P.A. Schmuck (Eds.), *Women leading in education* (pp. 125–144). Albany, NY: State University of New York Press.

Penley, L., & Gould, S. (1981). *Measuring career strategies: The psychometric characteristics of the career strategies inventory.* San Antonio, TX: The University of Texas, Center for Studies in Business, Economics and Human Resources.

Porter, L.W., Lawler, E.E., & Hackman, J.R. (1975). *Behavior in organizations.* New York: McGraw-Hill.

Premack, S.I., & Wanous, J.P. (1985). A meta-analysis of realistic job preview experiments. *Journal of Applied Psychology, 70*, 706–719.

Reese, H.W., & Overton, W.F. (1970). Models of development and theories of development. In L.R. Goulet & P.B. Baltes (Eds.), *Life-span developmental psychology: Research and theory* (pp. 116–145). New York: Academic Press.

Reichers, A.E. (1987). An interactionist perspective on newcomer socialization rates. *Academy of Management Review, 12*, 278–287.

Roberts, K. (1984). *School leavers and their prospects. Youth and the labour market in the 1980s.* Milton Keynes: Open University Press.

Roe, A. (1956). *The psychology of occupations.* New York: Wiley.

Rosenberg, M. (1981). The self-concept: Social product and social force. In M. Rosenberg & R.H. Turner (Eds.), *Social Psychology: Sociological perspectives* (pp. 593–624). New York: Basic Books.

Rousseau, D.M. (1989). New hire perceptions of their own and their employer's obligations: A study of psychological contracts. *Journal of Organizational Behaviour, 11*, 389–400.

Saks, A.M., & Ashforth, B.E. (1996). Proactive socialization and behavioral self-management. *Journal of Vocational Behavior, 48*, 301–323.

Saks, A.M., & Ashforth, B.E. (1997). Socialization tactics and newcomer information acquisition. *International Journal of Selection and Assessment, 5*, 48–61.

Scarr, S., Phillips, D., & McCartney, K. (1989). Working mothers and their families. *American Psychologist, 44*, 1402–1409.

Schaufeli, W. (1988). *Unemployment and psychological health. An investigation among Dutch professionals.* Dissertation. Groningen, The Netherlands: University of Groningen.

Schein, E.H. (1968). Organizational socialization and the profession of management. *Industrial Management Review, 9*, 1–16.

Schein, E.H. (1978). *Career dynamics: Matching individual and organizational needs.* Reading, MA: Addison-Wesley.

Schneider, B. (1987). The people make the place. *Personnel Psychology, 40*, 437–453.

Schultz, J.F.H., & Buunk, A.P. (1990). Dissatisfactie, perceptie van alternatieven en zoekgedrag op de arbeidsmarkt. *Gedrag en Organisatie, 31*, 236–252.

Stradling, S.G., Crowe, G., & Tuohy, A.P. (1993). Changes in self-concept during occupational socialization of new recruits to the police. *Journal of Community and Applied Social Psychology, 3*, 131–147.

Super, D.E. (1955). The dimensions and measurement of vocational maturity. *Teachers College Record, 57*, 151–163.

Super, D.E. (1957). *The psychology of careers.* New York: Harper & Row.

Super, D.E. (1980). A life-span, life-space approach to career development. *Journal of Vocational Behavior, 16*, 282–298.

Super, D.E. (1981). A developmental theory: Implementing a self-concept. In D.H. Montross & C.J. Shinkman (Eds.), *Career development in the 1980s: Theory and practice* (pp. 28–42). Springfield, IL: Charles C. Thomas.

Swanson, J.L. (1992). Vocational behavior, 1989–1991: Life-span career development and reciprocal interaction of work and nonwork. *Journal of Vocational Behavior, 41*, 101–161.

Taes, C. (1989). *Perceptie van de arbeidsmarkt bij MBO-schoolverlaters.* Amsterdam, the Netherlands: Vrije Universiteit. Department of Work and Organizational Psychology. (Technical report.)

Tajfel, H. (1978). *Differentiation between social groups. Studies in the social psychology of intergroup relations.* London: Academic Press.

Taris, T.W., Bok, I.A., Feij, J.A., & Heesink, J.A.M. (1994). Opleiding en de ontwikkeling van de beroepsloopbaan van jonge mannen en vrouwen: Een longitudinale analyse. *Pedagogische Studiën, 71*, 353–365.

Taris, T.W., Heesink, J.A.M., & Feij, J.A. (1995a). The evaluation of unemployment and job-searching behavior: A longitudinal Study. *The Journal of Psychology, 129*, 301–314.

Taris, T.W., Heesink, J.A.M., & Feij, J.A. (1995b). De continuiteit van de arbeidsloopbaan van vrouwen na het eerste kind. De effecten van kenmerken van de werkloopbaan. *Mens en Maatschappij, 70*, 54–64.

Taris, T.W., Heesink, J.A.M., Feij, J.A., Velde, M.E.G. van der, & Gastel, J.H.M. van (1991). Arbeidsmobiliteit van jongeren: De invloed van persoons- en werkkenmerken. *Gedrag en Organisatie, 4*, 444–463.

Taris, T.W., Velde, M.E.G. van der, Feij, J.A., & Gastel, J.H.M. van. (1992). Young adults in their first job: The role of organizational factors in determining job satisfaction and turnover. *International Journal of Adolescence and Youth, 4*, 51–71.

Tazelaar, F. (1982). From a classical attitude behavior hypothesis to a general model of behavior, via the theory of mental incongruity. In W. Raub (Ed.), *Theoretical models and empirical analysis* (pp. 101–128). Utrecht: Rijksuniversiteit, Vakgroep Theoretische Sociologie en Methodologie.

Tazelaar, F., & Wippler, R. (1985). Problemspezifische Anwendungen der allgemeine Theorie mentaler Inkongruenzen in der empirischen Sozialforschung. In G. Büschges & W. Raub (Eds.), *Soziale Bedingungen-Individuelles Handeln-soziale Konzequenzen* (pp. 117–179). Frankfurt: Verlag Lang.

Tiggemann, M., & Winefield, A.H. (1984). The effects of unemployment on the mood, self-esteem, locus of control, and depressive affect of school-leavers. *Journal of Occupational Psychology, 57*, 33–42.

Tiggemann, M., & Winefield, A.H. (1989). Predictors of employment, unemployment and further study among school-leavers. *Journal of Occupational Psychology, 62*, 213–221.

Tinsley, H.E.A. & Heesacker, M. (1984). Vocational behavior and career development, 1983: A review. *Journal of Vocational Behavior, 25*, 139–190.

Toffler, B.L. (1981). Occupational role development: The changing determinants of outcomes for the individual. *Administrative Science Quarterly, 26*, 396–417.

Touzard, H. (Ed.) (1992). Work socialization of youth. *Revue Internationale de Psychologie Sociale, 5*, Whole number 1, 1–157.

Turner, J.C. (1984). Social identification and psychological group formation. In H. Tajfel (Ed.), *The social dimension*, Vol. 2 (pp. 518–538). Cambridge: Cambridge University Press.

Vandenberg, R.J., & Self, R.M. (1993). Assessing newcomers' changing commitments to the organization during the first 6 months of work. *Journal of Applied Psychology, 78*, 557–568.

Velde, M.E.G. van der, & Feij, J.A. (1995). Change of work perceptions and work outcomes as a result of voluntary and involuntary job change. *Journal of Occupational and Organizational Psychology, 68*, 273–290.

Velde, M.E.G. van der, Feij, J.A., & Taris, T.W. (1995). Stability and change of person characteristics among young adults: The effect of the transition from school to work. *Personality and Individual Differences, 18*, 89–99.

Verijdt, H., & Diederen, J. (1987). *Determinanten van beroepskeuze.* OSA-Werkdocument no. W.39. Nijmegen, The Netherlands: ITS.

Vianen, A.E.M. van, & Bruggencate, M. ten (1995). Persoon-klimaat-congruentie van nieuwkomers in de organisatie [Person-climate fit of newcomers in the organization]. *Gedrag en Organisatie, 8*, 30–49.

Vondracek, F.W., Lerner, R.M., & Schulenberg, J.E. (1986). *Career development: A life-span developmental approach.* Hillsdale, NJ: Lawrence Erlbaum Associates Inc.

Wanous, J.P. (1992). *Organizational entry. Recruitment, selection, orientation, and socialization of newcomers* (2nd Edn.). Reading, MA: Addison-Wesley.

Wanous, J.P., & Colella, A. (1989). Organizational entry research: Current status and future directions. In G. R. Ferris & K. M. Rowland (Eds.), *Research in personnel and human resources management*, Vol. 7 (pp. 59–120). Greenwich, CT: JAI Press.

Warr, P.B. (1987). *Work, unemployment and mental health.* Oxford: Oxford University Press.

Waterman, A.S. (1982). Identity development from adolescence to adulthood: An extension of theory and a review of research. *Developmental Psychology, 18*, 341–358.

Watkins Jr., C.E., & Subich, L.M. (1995). Annual review, 1992–1994: Career development, reciprocal work/nonwork interaction and women's workforce participation. *Journal of Vocational Behavior, 47*, 109–163.

Waung, M. (1995). The effects of self-regulatory coping orientation on newcomer adjustment and job survival. *Personnel Psychology, 48*, 633–650.

Weiss, H.M. (1978). Social learning of work values in organizations. *Journal of Applied Psychology, 63*, 711–718.

Werff, J.J. van der (1985). *Zelfbeschouwing in de psychologie.* Muiderberg: Coutinho.

West, M., & Rushton, R. (1989). Mismatches in the work-role transitions. *Journal of Occupational Psychology, 62*, 271–286.

Whitely, W. (1986). *Background and significance of the problem of the socialization of youth to work.* Research proposal and bibliography. Gent: Rijksuniversiteit Gent.

Whitely, W., Peiró, J.M., & Sarchielli, G. (1992). Work socialization of youth theoretical framework, research methodology and potential implications. *Revue Internationale de Psychologie Sociale, 5*, 9–35.

Wiersma, U.J. (1988). Rolconflict als een mediërende variabele: Over verschillen tussen mannen en vrouwen en hun voorkeuren voor functiekenmerken. *Gedrag en Organisatie, 1*, (5), 3–21.

WOSY International Research Group (1989). Socialización laboral del joven: Un estudio transnacional. *Papeles del Psicologo, 39/40*, 32–35.

Zahrly, J., & Tosi, H. (1989). The differential effect of organizational induction process on early work role adjustment. *Journal of Organizational Behavior, 10*, 59–74.

11

Management Development

Gary P. Latham and Gerard H. Seijts

INTRODUCTION

Management development has become a multi-billion dollar undertaking for organizations world-wide. Evidence from North America alone suggests that more than 90% of organizations engage in developmental activities for their managers (Loo, 1991; Saari, Johnson, McLaughlin, & Zimmerle, 1988). The growing interest within academic circles in management development has resulted in three literature reviews (Baldwin & Padgett, 1993; Keys & Wolfe, 1988; Wexley & Baldwin, 1986). Wexley and Baldwin (1986) defined management development broadly as "the process by which individuals learn, grow, and improve their ability to perform professional management tasks" (p. 277). Similarly, Baldwin and Padgett (1993) described management development as "the complex process by which individuals learn to perform effectively in managerial roles" (p. 25). Keys and Wolfe (1988) defined management development as "any process whereby managerial knowledge and skills are attained from non-credit programs or on-the-job experiences" (p. 205).

Generally, a distinction is made between management education, management training, and planned as well as unplanned on-the-job training. Together these three concepts form the core of what is currently referred to as management development.

Management education includes those activities conducted by business schools that focus on the development of managerial knowledge and conceptual skills. It is "the acquisition of a broad range of conceptual knowledge and skills in formal classroom situations in degree-granting institutions" (Keys & Wolfe, 1988; p. 205). Management training encompasses activities designed to inculcate specific skills that are "positionally and organizationally specific to those already in the ranks of management" (Keys & Wolfe, 1988, p. 206). Examples include leadership, problem solving and decision making, interpersonal effectiveness, self-awareness, motivation of self and others and rater training (Burke & Day, 1986). On-the-job training refers to the lessons directly learned from one's everyday experiences in the role of a manager (McCauley, Ruderman, Ohlott, & Morrow, 1994). Examples include job assignments, job rotation, and mentoring that is done for the specific purpose of developing the effectiveness of the manager.

The purpose of this chapter[1] is four-fold. First, taxonomies of core competences that define what a manager must do to be effective are described. Special attention is given to the competency-based management development movement and the criticisms that surround this movement. Second, the methods used to develop managers are examined with regard to their strengths and weaknesses. Third, the importance of the trainer to the management development process is emphasized. Fourth, ways of improving management development are discussed. The theme underlying this chapter is that the management development process must be linked closely to an organization's strategy.

MANAGEMENT EDUCATION

Taxonomies of critical managerial skills and models of effective management have attracted the attention of scholars for the past 25 years (e.g. Campbell, Dunnette, Lawler, & Weick, 1970; Kotter, 1982; McCall, Lombardo, & Morrison, 1988; Mintzberg, 1973, 1989; Powers, 1987; Whetten & Cameron, 1991; Yukl, Wall, & Lepsinger, 1990). In general, these taxonomies emphasize three core competencies, namely: (1) motivating, rewarding, delegating to, and developing subordinates; (2) interpersonal skills that enable one to manage conflict and build teams; and (3) problem-solving skills (Baldwin & Padgett, 1993).

Implicit in the position of the "competency-based management development movement" is that: (1) managerial competencies can be identified; (2) managers and potential managers can be trained to acquire and perfect managerial competences; and (3) competent managers make a difference in the level of organizational performance (Albanese, 1989). Two factors have played a key role in providing the context in which the competency-based management development movement has developed. First, in the 1970s and 1980s, many North American businesses declined *vis-à-vis* international competitors. Much of the decline was attributed by scholars as well as senior level executives to the lack of effective management. Second, the rapidly escalating costs of a university education combined with the anxiety of Americans regarding the declining position of the United States as an economic leader, brought strident calls for business schools to show that graduating students are well educated (Albanese, 1989).

The criticism of the curriculum offered in American business schools was fueled by a group of researchers known as the "competency-based management development movement" (e.g. Behrman & Levin, 1984; Waters, 1980). They argued that managers and managers-to-be emerged from business schools ill-prepared in that the students were insensitive to the nuances of organizational culture, they lacked genuine interest in managing, and hence they were deficient in the skills necessary for effectively managing subordinates (Heisler & Lasher, 1986). Practical application with regard to ways of leading, managing, and working effectively with others was said to be missing from the classroom (Stuller, 1993).

In their book, *Management Education and Development: Drift or Thrust into the 21st Century*, Porter and McKibbin (1988) placed strong emphasis on the need to provide systematic, well-planned, lifelong managerial education. Specifically, six areas were highlighted as receiving insufficient attention from business schools: (1) breadth of curriculum and pedagogical techniques to broaden the scope of the interests of business-school students; (2) attention to the external environment (government relations, societal trends, legal climate, and international developments) of business and management; (3) consideration of international dimensions; (4) recognition that society is becoming increasingly service and information driven; (5) integration of curricula across functional areas; and (6) education in interpersonal and communication skills. In cooperation with the American Assembly of Collegiate Schools of Business, the European Foundation for Management Development issued a report entitled *Manager for the 21st Century: Their Education and Development* (Finney & von Glinow, 1988) that supported the conclusions reached by Porter and McKibbin.

The competency-based management development movement has been endorsed by the American Management Association. They too have developed a generic model of the competent manager (Keys & Wolfe, 1988; Wexley & Baldwin, 1986) that emphasizes five core competences: (1) goal and action management; (2)

leadership; (3) human resources management; (4) subordinate direction; and (5) a focus on others.

The response of business to the perception of an inadequate education provided by business schools was two-fold (Wexley & Baldwin, 1986). First, some organizations, such as the Bank of Montreal, General Electric, General Motors, Holiday Inn, McDonalds, Polaroid and Texas Instruments, took it upon themselves to create their own "universities" to educate their managers in the skills perceived to be essential for implementing the organization's strategy. Management education is viewed by these companies as results-oriented and organizationally specific. Education is aimed at teaching their managers ways to implement specific business strategies to attain specific corporate objectives (Bolt, 1985).

A second approach taken by companies has been to form partnerships with business schools to create education programmes tailored to specific organizational issues. The partnership between Stentor, the alliance of Canadian telephone companies, and the University of Toronto is one such example (Latham, Daghighi, & Locke, in press). This partnership is aimed at enabling the Canadian telecommunications industry to create a national organization that provides "seamless service with a local touch" to customers. This is being accomplished by teaching managers the knowledge and skills necessary for understanding a customer's financial ability to form a partnership with them, discovering ways that they can enhance the customer's ability to attain its strategy, and creating ways to put together teams of people who will allow the preceding to occur effectively. Consistent with Porter and McKibbin's fifth recommendation, previously cited, the management development programme integrates curricula from three functional areas, namely finance/accounting, strategic management and business policy, and organizational psychology/human resource management. Fuchsberg (1993) reported that in North America three of every four executive education dollars are now spent on company-tailored programmes rather than on the open-enrollment managerial courses traditionally offered by business schools.

Criticisms of an education that focuses on competency-based management, however, are not lacking. This is because most taxonomies are based primarily on speculation and opinion; empirical support of them is largely non-existent. Managerial competences need to be identified through systematic research (i.e. job analysis). Then, empirical tests of the link between the demonstrated competences and indices of managerial effectiveness should be conducted to test their validity. The level of mastery with which a behaviour is performed rather than the frequency of managerial behaviour should also be considered (Baldwin & Padgett, 1993). This is because an increase in frequency of a particular behaviour, with no increase in mastery, may have little or no positive effect on a manager's performance (Shipper, 1991).

Leading business schools such as Harvard and Stanford view customized business education programmes "as a kind of intellectual slumming" (Stuller, 1993). This is because the course content in such programmes can become too narrow; the role of education is viewed by those two universities as much broader than merely teaching specific competences. Moreover, it is questionable whether a skills-list definition of competences reflects how managers actually function in the workplacc (Stcwart, 1989; Vaill, 1989). The present taxonomies, for the most part, fail to differentiate the knowledge and skills required at the different managerial levels (Blakely, Martineau, & Lane, 1992). Most developmental activities are currently directed at lower-level management. Thus Werther (1993) argued that there is a "senior management developmental gap".

Kraut, Pedigo, McKenna, and Dunnette (1989) identified tasks that are important regardless of whether the person is a first-line supervisor or a senior executive. In addition, their survey showed that the relative importance of the tasks differed as one moved up the management hierarchy. Specifically, their data showed that managing an individual's performance was perceived to be important for entry-level managers, managing group performance was perceived to be important for middle managers, and monitoring the external environment was perceived to be important for senior-level managers. Thus it would appear that management education should continue to focus on such basics of management as the motivation of a subordinate, and ways of giving performance feedback. As people move up the management hierarchy, refresher training in these areas is appropriate. Educational programmes for middle managers, however, should emphasize the skills needed for designing and implementing effective group and intergroup work, diagnosing and resolving problems within and among work groups, negotiating with peers and supervisors, and so on. The training of senior executives should focus on broadening their understanding of the organization's competition, world economies, and politics. In other words, education of managers should be targeted, and it should be targeted to their hierarchical level of responsibilities.

Empirical research is also needed to determine the extent to which managers in other parts of the world have, or are in need of, managerial competences other than those of their North American counterparts. All too often it is assumed that there is only one recipe for management development, namely that which works in the United States (Hofstede, 1993; Maruyama, 1990; McNulty, 1992). The validity of some management education principles may be constrained by national borders. Currently, we do not know which principles generalize to which countries. Yet the need to identify them grows continuously with the North American Free Trade Agreement and the formation of the European Economic Community, and the increasing globalization of business.

COURSE DELIVERY

Inherent in management education is the issue of how instructors can bring about a relatively enduring change in managers' behaviour that will increase an organization's effectiveness. Keys (1989) argued that an instructional style includes a proper balance among three factors, namely: (1) the dissemination of ideas, principles or concepts; (2) an opportunity to apply the content in an experientially controlled environment; and (3) feedback as to the results of the actions taken. The teaching methods that instructors can use to achieve this balance include: lectures, group discussions, teleconferencing and videos, case studies, simulations and microcomputers, behaviour modelling and role playing, and outdoor experiences.

Lectures

The strengths and weaknesses of the lecture as a method of educating managers have been outlined by Griffin and Cashin (1989). The advantages include the fact that: (1) a lecture can be given to many managers at one time; (2) material can be presented in an economical, straightforward, and integrated manner; (3) the lecture ensures that core subjects are covered; and (4) a lecture poses minimal threat to managers in that their attention can be directed to what is being taught rather than to feelings of intimidation from fear of being asked by an instructor to do something before being ready to do so.

The shortcomings of the lecture include the fact that feedback is often lacking for both the manager and the lecturer. In a lecture, it is difficult to discern whether the managers do in fact understand the issues that are being addressed, and whether they can apply what is being taught to their job. A further drawback to a primary reliance on lectures is that they are unsuitable for higher forms of learning such as diagnosing and analysing particular situations or problems. Finally, managers tend to forget information presented in lectures if they are not soon given the opportunity to practise what was taught to them.

Group Discussion

Encouraging group discussion can be a powerful way of enriching a lecture. Managers' understanding of the material presented can be checked through questions and comments. Through discussion, ideas presented in the lecture are explored and refined. In this way, the managers become active participants in the learning process relative to the lecture. Because the managers have work experience, this method allows them to test whether they can relate the lecture material to their job. Group discussion is appropriate for teaching higher-order cognitive material involving application, analysis, synthesis and evaluation (Gronlund, 1987).

Teleconferencing and Videos

Teleconferencing involves the use of technologies such as computer terminals, telephones, and video cameras that allow information to be shared instantaneously with distant locations. This form of technology is especially useful for large companies who wish to train managers simultaneously in branches in different cities and countries. This technology obviously saves time and travel costs because it makes the learning material accessible to a large number of people/groups who hear the same thing at the same point in time. The technology is especially valuable for companies who lack the subject-matter-expertise in given locations. In short, it allows an organization to "take the mountain to Mohammed".

The United States Air Force Institute of Technology, for example, established a "Teletech Program" which provides training for 4,500 students. Queens University in Kingston, Ontario is offering an Executive MBA to managers across Canada using this technology. People from Halifax, Nova Scotia to Vancouver, British Columbia will be able to interact with the instructor and one another through the use of this medium. In the UK, the Open University also uses this medium to teach managerial skills.

A drawback of this method is that the informal interactions among the educator and the managers are reduced. The cameras cannot be on all groups at one time. There is currently a noticeable time-lag between the spoken and heard word. Thus communications among students sometimes lack spontaneity. These limitations can reduce the feedback necessary for enhancing learning and motivation.

Video (tape and disc) as well as teleconferencing have become important educational media. A major benefit of using video tapes is recording managers in action. In this way feedback can be given easily, and the strengths and areas of improvement for the manager can be easily analysed and discussed (Wells, 1989).

Prerecorded video-tapes allow educators to bring outstanding presenters to the classroom for a comparatively small financial investment. Business schools such as Wharton have entire courses that are available on video-tape.

Video-disc technology is still in its infancy. The required expenses are substantial because of the cost of the equipment (hardware) and prerecorded material (software). Two basic formats that have been used for video-disc training are interrupted video and interactive video. Both allow individuals to learn at their own pace. Interrupted video returns the manager to the same material if incorrect answers are given. The interactive form, on the other hand, provides the manager with further explanations of the topic in a manner different from how it was originally presented. As of 1986, the lecture fell to second place behind videotechnology in terms of the number of firms who use it as a teaching tool (Lee, 1987).

Cases

Two approaches to case studies include those that are long, complex and rich in detail, versus the critical incident that is precise, relatively short, and typically does not contain all the necessary information for solving a problem situation thoroughly. The advantages of this method of teaching managers is that it: (1) focuses on "doing" in a classroom setting as a way to improve managerial skills; (2) enhances development of verbal and written communication skills; (3) possesses an illustrative quality; (4) exposes managers to a wide range of true-to-life organization problems; (5) inspires managers' interest in otherwise theoretical and abstract material; and (6) provides concrete reference points that foster learning by association and thus bridge the gap between theory and practice (Osigweh, 1989). Drawbacks to a primary emphasis on using cases as a teaching methodology are that it: (1) focuses on past and static considerations; (2) minimizes double-loop learning; (3) can lead to inappropriate generalizations; and (4) can foster groupthink. The latter can occur when people, whose comments depart from the norm, become silent or move toward the "average response" for fear of being labelled as deviant.

Simulations and Microcomputers

Business games range from the simple to the complex, computerized to non-computerized, interactive to non-interactive, and single participant to multiple participants. They have been developed for low, middle and upper management. They can focus on a specialized single decision to multiple business decisions, and they can be customized for an organization. Examples of business games include the leaderless group discussion, in-basket techniques, complex decision-making simulations, and large-scale behavioural simulations.

Faria (1989) examined the growth in usage of business games in training programmes within organizations and business schools in the United States. Conservative estimates indicate that 55% of large organizations are currently using business games in their training programmes; 86% of business schools use business games in their own programmes; and 45% of the business schools indicated that business games are used in their management development programmes.

The advantages of business games or simulations is that they allow for active experience, or practice on the part of managers. They thus facilitate skill development (Keys, 1989). Outcomes of one's actions occur much faster in a simulation than in the real world, where outcomes can be slow or ambiguous (Senge, 1990). Moreover, a simulation is a safe place where managers can practice without causing risk for the firm (Faria, 1989); thus the managers can experiment in ways that may not be possible in the real world. Future consequences of one's actions can therefore be evaluated (Senge, 1990).

Another advantage of using a simulation for developing a manager's skills is the transfer of what is learned to the job (Baldwin & Ford, 1988; Wexley & Latham, 1991). This is because the newly-acquired behaviours can be practised in the context of other managerial activities and responsibilities (Thornton & Cleveland, 1990). Stentor, in Canada, uses a simulation exercise developed by the University of Toronto to assess how well managers have mastered the knowledge and skills taught in the classroom. Specifically, actual data on potential customers are presented to managers who work in simulated account teams to determine whether the customer has the financial strength to be turned into a partner with the telecommunications industry, if so, how the telecommunications industry can help the partner achieve its strategic goals, and how individuals in the telecommunications industry can work effectively as a team to bring this about.

The microcomputer revolution has had a significant effect on business simulations. Microcomputers allow managers to make a series of decisions (Curry & Moutinho, 1982; Wells, 1989) at multiple points in time and, as a result, both the immediate and the long-range impact of a decision can be examined. They allow the teaching of analytical and diagnostic skills. They provide a framework for understanding and integrating concepts. The manager is drawn into the educational process by being required to actively participate in making decisions, hence there is learning by doing. Through computer simulations, managers experience situations that they might not normally encounter. Introduction of uncertainties helps to ensure realism. Finally, computer simulations allow the individual to learn in small steps, and more importantly permit repetition of the material. Repetition and continuous practice is a *sine qua non* for retention. In short, simulations compress space and time thus allowing managers to experience the long-term and distant side effects of their actions. Simulations provide a practice field in which people can explore alternative policies, learn about extreme situations, and develop a shared understanding of business dynamics (Senge, 1990).

The drawbacks of simulation-based teaching are three-fold. First, they can foster a misleading impression of precision and certainty by presenting an overly structured and simplified view of business. Although there are often no "right answers" to managerial problems, and no "right way" to manage in the real world, computer-based simulations can inadvertently suggest otherwise (Linstead, 1990). Moreover, they can inflate beliefs about the accuracy with which uncertain events can be predicted (Kottemann, Davis, & Remus, 1994). Second, models are sometimes chosen because of convenience at the expense of realism (Sterman, 1989a; 1989b). A third potential drawback is that not all material is amenable to structuring (Linstead, 1990). Knowledge that is to be built into a computer-based simulation may be bedevilled by technical ambiguity and phenomenological ambiguity. Both ambiguities are related to the difficulties of representing human expression. Technical ambiguity refers to a lack of linguistic clarity or imperfect logic. Phenomenological ambiguity concerns both the disagreement in the interpretation of relationships among terms or events, and outputs that are subject to multiple interpretation.

In general, most business games do exhibit external validity in that the simulations capture the essence of the real world environment that they are attempting to replicate (Keys & Wolfe, 1990; Norris, 1986). However, they should not be used as a substitute for other course delivery methods. Simulations are most effective when they are used in conjunction with structured training delivery methods such as lectures, group discussion, reading assignments, and demonstrations that provide an important conceptual framework that highly participative methods often lack (Curry & Moutinho, 1992; Linstead, 1990).

For managers to experience the full benefits of business games the instructor should not overlook the post-game period as a time for participants to acquire knowledge and skills (Faria, 1989). The post-game period should be used for analysis and critiques of what has happened or not happened and the reasons for it. Too often instructors only provide a brief summary or overview.

Role Playing and Behaviour Modelling

This method of developing managers has been used by such diverse companies as AT&T, Ford, and IBM. Weyerhaeuser Company (Latham & Saari, 1979) used behaviour modelling to train managers how to interact effectively with their employees. Their nine training modules focused on the following topics: (1) orienting a new employee; (2) giving recognition; (3) motivating a poor performer; (4) discussing poor work habits; (5) discussing potential disciplinary action; (6) reducing absenteeism; (7) handling a complaining employee; (8) reducing turnover; and (9) overcoming resistance to change. The training programme was designed to include the components of effective modelling, namely, attentional processes, retentive processes, motor reproduction processes, and motivational processes.

The trainees met for two hours each week for nine weeks. Each training session followed a similar format:

1. Introduction of the topic by the trainers (attentional processes).
2. Presentation of a film that depicts a supervisor modelling effectively a situation based on a set of three to six learning points that were shown in a film immediately before and after the model was presented (retention processes).
3. Group discussion of the effectiveness of the model in exhibiting the desired behaviours (retention processes).
4. Actual practise in role-playing the desired behaviours in front of the training class (retention processes; motor reproduction processes).
5. Feedback from the training class on the effectiveness of each trainee in demonstrating the desired behaviours (motivational processes).

In each practice session, one trainee took the role of manager and the other trainee assumed the role of an employee. No set scripts were used. Instead, the two trainees were asked to recreate an incident relevant to the film topic for that week which had occurred to at least one of them within the past year.

The learning points in the film were posted in front of the trainee playing the role of supervisor. For example, the learning points for handling a complaining employee included: (1) avoid responding with hostility or defensiveness; (2) ask for and listen openly to the employee's complaint; (3) restate the complaint for thorough understanding; (4) recognize and acknowledge his or her viewpoint; (5) if necessary, state your position nondefensively; and (6) set a specific date for a follow-up meeting. These learning points provided one of the key components of coding and retention.

At the end of each of the nine training sessions, the supervisors were given copies of the learning points for that session. They were asked to use the managerial skills they had learned in class with one or more employees on the job within a week's time period. In this way, transfer of training from the classroom to the job was maximized. The managers were also asked to report their successes and failures to the training class the following week.

To further ensure that the manager would be reinforced for demonstrating on-the-job behaviours that were taught in class, their supervisor attended an accelerated programme designed to teach them the importance of praising a manager, regardless of whether he or she was in the training or control group, whenever they saw him or her demonstrate a designated behaviour. This procedure enhanced the motivational processes of the training.

An evaluation of this behaviour modelling training included four types of measures: reaction, learning, behaviour, and performance criteria. The training programme produced highly favourable trainee reactions, which were maintained over an eight-month period. Moreover, the performance of the managers was significantly better than that of managers in a control group on a learning test administered six months after training, and on performance ratings collected on the job one year after training.

The practical significance of this study is that it supports earlier applications of behaviour modelling for training managers. These studies taken together indicate that certain leadership skills can be taught, provided that: the manager is given a model to follow; is given a specific set of goals or learning points; is given an opportunity to perfect the skills; is given feedback about the effectiveness of his or her behaviour; and is reinforced with verbal praise for applying the acquired skill on the job (Latham & Saari, 1979). A meta-analysis of 70 studies on the effectiveness of management training found that behaviour modeling was among the most effective of all training techniques (Burke & Day, 1986).

Outdoor-centered training

Organizations are increasingly using outdoor-centered exercises to teach team-building skills. The activities typically involve an increasing level of challenge and risk that requires a concomitant increase in the participants' trust in and dependence on one another (Galagan, 1987; Long, 1987). The effectiveness of these programmes comes primarily from anecdotal evidence (Newstrom, 1985). For example, Zwieten (1984) wrote that "what companies get from the climbing experiences is turned-on people, people with heightened self-awareness, a sense of control and competence and a willingness to be receptive to the environment in which they work" (p. 33). Wagner, Baldwin, and Roland (1991) reported that outdoor programmes had a positive effect on individual problem-solving behaviour and the participant's perception of group awareness.

Both Gall (1987) and Mol and Vermeulen (1988) identified two important components of outdoor programmes that are frequently lacking, namely: (1) the development of action plans for transferring the learning from these exercises to the workplace; and (2) follow-up on the success of the programme. Despite the high monetary costs of participation in outdoor programmes, many organizations do not define the objectives of the outdoor training beforehand, nor do they evaluate its effectiveness after training has taken place. But, with the exception of behaviour modelling and role playing, these two criticisms apply to virtually all training activities (Wexley & Latham, 1991). Keys (1989) noted that assessment and feedback are essential steps for learning, and yet assessment and feedback are usually the neglected elements in all development programmes. This is unfortunate because goal setting and feedback in relation to goals are critical to increasing one's performance (Locke & Latham, 1990).

On-the-Job Learning

Three formal techniques for on-the-job learning are action learning, mentoring, and job rotation. Action learning, developed in Europe, has only recently become a popular method for developing managers in North America (Mumford, 1987). This method was originally used in the British coal mines shortly after the Second World War. Currently, organizations such as AT&T, Ford, and Royal Dutch Shell use this method (De Geus, 1988).

Action learning is a developmental technique that entails: (1) learning from one's experience; (2) sharing that experience with others; (3) asking colleagues to critique and to offer advice on possible future actions; (4) taking that advice and implementing it; and (5) reviewing with colleagues the action taken and the lessons that were learned (Enderby & Phelan, 1994; Margerison, 1988; Revans, 1982, 1984). With this method, managers face real-time management problems for which there is no readily known answer, and for which an answer is urgently needed. Rather than the "there and then" case examples from another time and place, the "here and now" examples of problems that managers currently are experiencing are discussed. The tasks that are explored are neither trivial nor are they so complex that it would take an extensive time period to generate plausible solutions (Margerison, 1988). The University of Toronto's Management Executive Programmes uses this method with its partner Domtar to teach Domtar's managers ways of developing and implementing strategic planning concepts.

The underlying assumption of this developmental technique is that a manager learns to be a manager by taking responsibility for action rather than by talking about it, or listening to someone else talk about it. Managers, organized into groups of five to ten, who are faced with a common problem, work to find a solution to that problem by learning from one another in a climate of support and encouragement.

As Antal (1993) noted, mentors provide a protégé career support (e.g. coaching, protection, challenging assignments, exposure, and visibility), as well as psychosocial support (e.g. serving as a role model, as a friend, or as a counsellor). Two processes explain why mentoring is so beneficial to a protégé's success (Dreher & Ash, 1990). First, a mentor provides a special form of entry into important social networks. This in turn provides the protégé with opportunities to show talent and competence to upper management, and to acquire important information through informal communication (Berstein & Kaye, 1986; Kram, 1985; Zey, 1985). Second, a mentor serves as a model and as a source of vicarious reinforcement for the protégé (Bandura, 1986). In this way, a protégé acquires important managerial skills from observing an effective model. Thus, the protégé's sense of competence, identity, and effectiveness in a managerial role is enhanced (Bandura, 1986). In addition, mentoring relationships can alleviate the stress that occurs during times of organizational change (Kram & Hall, 1989).

Empirical evidence suggests that those people who had extensive experience as protégés in mentoring relationships received more promotions, earned higher incomes, and were more satisfied with their pay and benefits than individuals who did not have a mentor (Dreher & Ash, 1990; Scandura, 1992; Turban & Dougherty, 1994; Whitely & Coetsier, 1993). Moreover, no evidence was found that the sex of either party moderated the relationship between mentoring and career outcomes (Dreher & Ash, 1990).

Job rotation is receiving increasing recognition as a form of management development (Baldwin & Padgett, 1993; Feldman, 1988; Heisler & Benham, 1992; McCauley et al., 1994). The downside to this approach to development is the increase in costs associated with the person's learning curve, the increase in workload and decrease in productivity for the person and for co-workers, and a decrease in motivation of co-workers. Nevertheless, managers report that the most significant learning experiences that have contributed to their development is in fact on-the-job experiences (Davies & Easterby-Smith, 1984; McCall et al., 1988; Mumford, 1988). This is because on-the-job challenges can force a manager to cope with organizational stresses and problems (Ohlott, Ruderman, & McCauley, 1994), and as such can teach managers the skills necessary for performing future jobs (Donnel & Hall, 1980).

Research indicates that on-the-job development is most likely to occur when the participant is placed in challenging situations (McCauley et al., 1994; McCauley, Ohlott, & Ruderman, 1989; Ohlott et al., 1994). Under such circumstances, managers are required to solve problems and to make choices in a dynamic situation under conditions of risk and uncertainty. As noted by Ohlott et al. (1994) "exposure to such situations can produce changes in the way the manager approaches problems, handles risks, makes decisions, or takes actions" (p. 48).

Three developmental components of on-the-job experiences have been identified (McCauley et al., 1994). These include: (1) job transitions; (2) task-related variables; and (3) obstacles. Job transitions are changes in job content, job status, or job location. A move to a new organizational unit or geographical location, for example, is a job transition. Under such circumstances, managers must learn new skills and strategies to adapt successfully (Davies & Easterby-Smith, 1984). Task-related variables refer to problems and dilemmas inherent in the job itself. The manager must learn to employ different actions or strategies to deal with these situations, and learn from the consequences (Davies & Easterby-Smith, 1984).

These developmental opportunities stimulate learning because the: (1) transitions require managers to fill the gap between their current skills and perspectives and those required by the situation; (2) task-related challenges require them to respond to problems and dilemmas stemming from the critical features of tasks; and (3) obstacles create the motivation and drive to overcome a challenging situation (Davies & Easterby-Smith, 1984; McCauley et al., 1994). McCall and Lombardo (1983) found that having had different work experiences was a key factor that differentiated successful from derailed executives.

The effectiveness of on-the-job learning methods is dependent upon the effectiveness of the trainer/supervisor. This illustrates the point raised by Blum (1989) who argued that there has been an overemphasis on course materials and techniques that are used for management development. Significant improvements in learning effectiveness will be made, he argued, when attention is devoted to the trainer. Trainers must become highly skilled in consulting and counseling others if managers are to be developed in the classroom, let alone on the job.

Although the selection of qualified people for developing managers is critical for management development, Wexley and Latham (1991) reported that the selection process is frequently treated too lightly by many organizations. There are at least four basic requirements of people who develop managers (Stuart & Burgoyne, 1978; Wexley & Latham, 1991). First, the person must be an expert in the knowledge that is to be imparted. Second, the person must have knowledge of, and ability to use the various learning principles and training methods. Third, the person must be well grounded in organization, task, and person analyses. Fourth, the individual must possess the personal qualities that facilitate learning. These qualities include flexibility, enthusiasm, and a sense of humour. Blum (1989) argued that the person must also be able to convince managers that the subject matter or skill being taught is important for them to learn. The persuasion skills of the trainer can influence the trainee's self-efficacy and hence behaviour on the job (Eden & Ravid, 1982; Eden & Shani, 1982). Finally, Latham and Crandall (1991) argued that the person must be able to communicate with top management the ways that the training is consistent with the long-range strategy of the firm, and ensure that steps are taken to remove situational constraints preventing a manager from applying the newly-acquired knowledge and skills to the job.

CONCLUSION

The distinction made in the introduction to this chapter between management education and management training is likely to become increasingly blurred in the future. Virtually all business schools in Canada and the United States are undertaking thorough reviews of their existing programmes. This is due in large measure to the extraordinary changes that have affected the business environment in the past decade, including the questioning of the value of an MBA education. The majority of business schools are introducing a management skills development course. Academics are writing books on this subject (e.g. Mealiea & Latham, in press). These courses teach the skills, and the theories underlying them, for leadership, problem solving and decision making, interpersonal effectiveness, and motivation of self and others.

Executive education is also being reshaped. Business schools in North America and the United Kingdom have experienced a significant drop in the number of participants in their open-enrollment management development programmes. Consequently, business schools are actively seeking partnerships with organizations to develop the latter's managers. Those schools that are doing this successfully are those that develop a curriculum that is tailored to the partner's strategic plan. That is, the curriculum is designed to provide people with the knowledge and skills necessary to implement and achieve the organization's plan. Only high-profile universities such as INSEAD, Harvard and Stanford are likely to downplay this trend because of the cachet that executives continue to place on simply being able to state that they attended classes at these universities. Moreover, it is high-profile schools such as these that provide opportunities for managers to network effectively with and learn from their counterparts in other organizations from around the world. Such networks and their concomitant power relationships have been shown to be a key factor that distinguishes successful from unsuccessful managers (Gunz, 1989).

The necessity for presenting customized management development activities within the context of the organization's goals has been emphasized by Brown and Read (1984). They argued that the productivity gap between the UK and Japanese companies can be closed by taking a strategic view of training policies. This should be done by ensuring that the developmental plan for managers is constructed in the same context and by the same process as the organization's strategic plan, and that it is viewed in direct relationship to it. Thus achievement of management development goals should be regularly monitored and subjected to a thorough annual review alongside an organization's business plan.

Hussey (1985) too has argued that the objectives of management development should be reviewed by top management whenever a major shift in the organization's strategic emphasis is planned. However, his survey of UK companies revealed that only one-third of the respondents saw the necessity for doing so because they felt that training objectives should be tailored to the person rather than to corporate needs. Hussey argued that training should not be done for the improvement of the individual with the hope that it will benefit the organization; training should be provided for the benefit of the firm, knowing that this in turn will benefit the individual.

Domtar's partnering with the University of Toronto's Executive Development Program reflects this philosophy. The week-long management development programme focuses on the communication of Domtar's strategy, and the multiple ways of implementing it effectively throughout the organization. The programme makes explicit to the course participants that the financial, strategic, organizational, and team-building skills that they are acquiring will increase their value as managers both internally and externally to the world of Domtar.

Three types of competitive strategies are innovative strategy, quality enhancement strategy, and cost reduction strategy. Schuler and Jackson (1987) argued that organizations with an innovative strategy should teach managers ways of dealing effectively with ambiguity and unpredictability. Organizations with quality-enhancing strategies should focus on teaching employees to identify ways to improve the process by which goods and services are made and delivered. An organization pursuing a cost-reduction strategy should teach managers how to implement tight controls without hurting employee morale.

There is an overemphasis in the management development literature on taxonomies of core competences. Managers undoubtedly must understand finance, marketing, logistics, strategic planning, organizational behaviour, human resource management, and governmental, societal and ethical issues. These courses are taught thoroughly in most business schools. The relative emphasis in skill mastery for a particular position in an organization can be identified through job analysis. This methodology is well known to organizational psychologists and human resource management specialists. The key to effective management development programmes therefore is not to develop another taxonomy of competences, but rather to show how to link the knowledge and skill gained in management development programmes to an organization's overall goals and its plan for attaining them. In this way, the difficulties that Werther (1993) reported in obtaining senior executive support for management development activities should disappear.

Similarly, too much emphasis in the literature on management development is placed on the "bells and whistles" of various teaching techniques, especially simulations. As Kearsley (1991) has pointed out, the type of behaviour or skills to be learned should dictate the type of teaching medium that is appropriate. For example, if the behaviour to be learned calls for an auditory stimulus or response, then a medium with audio capability is needed. Similarly, if the knowledge to be acquired involves visual images, then a medium capable of presenting pictures or graphics is required. If the learning involves the mastery of procedures, the use of a dynamic medium such as video or computer simulations may be useful. But in addition, the aptitude of the managers who are being taught must also be taken into account. If the people have poor reading skills, an emphasis should be placed on visual rather than textual presentations. If they are known to have low motivation to learn what is to be taught, then a stimulating medium such as videos or computers might be selected. The idea that there is one best medium for management development does not make a lot of sense. The sequence of developmental media proposed by Thornton and Cleveland (1990) begins with didactic forms of learning such as lectures and readings, proceeds to the use of simple demonstrations and controlled group discussions, and then involves the use of simple simulations to practise isolated, basic tasks. Only then are complex simulations used to assist managers in acquiring complicated skills. Supervised on-the-job experience should then allow the manager to put the skills into practice on an on-going basis.

Research is needed on how managers learn. Interviews conducted by Hill (1991) suggests that the process of becoming a manager is primarily one of learning from experience. Through trial and error, observation and interpretation, newly-appointed managers learn what it takes to become effective in their respective organizations. Rather than embarking on a quest for a perfect mentor, Hill argued that new managers should pursue a strategy of building a network of developmental relationships that includes peers. Access to a network of peers is a key ingredient to a manager's success because peers provide a supportive forum in which one's thoughts and feelings can be explored regarding existing and anticipated challenges. Similarly, Kram and Isabella (1985, p. 129) found that peers:

> provide a forum for mutual exchange in which an individual can achieve a sense of expertise, equality, and empathy that is frequently absent from [relationships with senior people]. In addition, peer relationships appear to have a longevity that exceed that of [relationships with senior people]. Several of the peer relationships we studied had lasted about thirty years. Thus these relationships can provide continuity over the course of a career, seeing individuals through change and transition, as well as through the day-to-day tasks of work life.

The latest trend in management development education encompasses much of what has been described in this chapter. It is teaching managers ways of creating a learning organization. Such an organization is continually expanding its capability to shape its future as a result of looking at the world in new ways, whether in its understanding of the latent need of customers in terms of what they might truly value but would never think to ask for, or in understanding ways to increase the effectiveness and efficiency of the business.

A leading proponent of this education process is Senge (1990, 1991). The core competencies that Senge argued that a manager must possess to facilitate the design of a learning organization are threefold: the ability to (a) continually refine a shared vision; (b) bring to the surface and challenge prevailing mental models; and (c) foster systemic patterns of thinking.

A mission statement in most organizations lacks the vitality and excitement of a shared vision statement that comes from people asking, "Why do we exist?" "Who would miss us if we were gone?" "What is it that we truly want to achieve?" "What is our primary source of discontent?" Responding to such questions is a never-ending process as the world of business becomes increasingly dynamic.

A vision creates constructive tension between where the organization is versus where employees want it to be. It gives them a cause to rally around. Thus managers learn ways of helping people gain insight into current reality relative to their vision. They do this by encouraging employees to articulate their mental models of key assumptions. This is an important skill to acquire because one's mental models influence how problems and opportunities are perceived, courses of action are identified, and one's choices are made. For example, Ian Mitroff, in his study of General Motors, found that the mental model GM executives had of customers was that cars serve primarily as status symbols. Therefore styling was believed to be more important to customers than quality. Because mental models usually remain unspoken or tacit, there is little or no possibility of challenging the validity or updating the accuracy of such assumptions until they are actually articulated.

Working with mental models requires going beyond identifying and articulating them. Managers learn to help employees restructure their views of reality to see the underlying causes of problems, and hence the myriad possibilities of shaping the organization's future. Managers are taught to teach people to look at (1) events (e.g., The Dow Jones average went up 16 points because high fourth quarter profits were announced yesterday); (2) patterns of behaviour (e.g., the newspaper editorial that explains the fluctuations in the market in the context of historic trends); and (3) systemic thinking (e.g., focusing on what causes the pattern or trend). They learn to search for interrelationships rather than to react to each move as an isolated event. For example, rather than looking for ways to blame others or to find plausible circumstances beyond one's control as explanatory factors, they learn to look for poorly-designed systems as explanations for organizational problems. They then learn to identify leverage points whereby small well-focused actions can produce significant, enduring organizational change.

To teach such principles, Senge and his colleagues have argued for the use of job simulations that allow managers to learn together within teams where the simulation combines meaningful business issues with meaningful interpersonal dynamics. The participants are able to experience the long-term systemic consequences of key strategic decisions. Through role playing exercises they are given multiple opportunities to practise surfacing mental models within the context of a low-risk setting.

The underlying assumption or mental model of this approach to management development is that learning is a continuous process of discovering new insights about the world, inventing possibilities for action, producing those actions, and then reflecting on the outcomes in order to lead to new discoveries. The Massachusetts Institute of Technology, where Senge is a faculty member, is forming partnerships with a consortium of organizations to explore the usefulness of this approach to management development.

What is sadly missing from the management development literature is rigorous systematic empirical evaluations of the extent to which management development programmes attain the objectives for which they have been designed. This is puzzling because it is well known that feedback in relation to goals is critical for learning and motivation. Evaluation is a form of feedback to the trainees, the trainer, and the sponsoring organization that supports management development. The mental model of the present authors is that evaluation must consist of more than an action research model based on a participant observer approach, whereby the people who implement the development programme along with the participants provide anecdotal evidence of what has occurred as a result of the training. Organizational psychologists possess the knowledge to conduct evaluative research properly through the use of experimental and quasi-experimental design. As Senge (1991) pointed out, knowledge is the capacity for effective action. It is time for organizational psychologists to move from exhortations of the effectiveness of management development to determining if, how, and under what conditions, management development truly develops managers in enduring ways. In the absence of systematic evaluations that are relatively objective and unbiased, the question can be asked as to how long organizations will continue to support management development primarily on the basis of faith.

NOTES

1. This chapter was supported by a Social Sciences and Humanities Research Council grant to the first author. The authors are grateful to Joseph D'Cruz, Soosan Daghighi,

Martin Evans, Hugh Gunz, and Michael Jelland for their helpful comments on this chapter.

REFERENCES

Albanese, R. (1989). Competency-based management education. *Journal of Management Development*, *8*, (2), 66–76.

Antal, A.B. (1993). Odysseus' legacy to management development: Mentoring. *European Management Journal*, *11*, 448–454.

Baldwin, T.T., & Ford, J.K. (1988). Transfer of training: A review and directions for future research. *Personnel Psychology*, *41*, 63–105.

Baldwin, T.T., & Padgett, M.Y. (1993). Management development: A review and commentary. In C.L. Cooper and I.T. Robertson (Eds.), *International review of industrial and organizational psychology* (vol. 8, pp. 35–86). New York: Wiley.

Bandura, A. (1986). *Social foundations of thought and action: A social-cognitive view*. Englewood Cliffs, NJ: Prentice-Hall.

Behrman, J.N., & Levin, R.I. (1984). Are business schools doing their job? *Harvard Business Review*, *6*, (21), 140–147.

Berstein, B.M., & Kaye, B.L. (1986). Teacher, tutor, colleague, coach. *Personnel Journal*, *65*, (11), 44–51.

Blakely, G.L., Martineau, C.L., & Lane, M.S. (1992). *Management development programs: The effects of management level and corporate strategy*. Unpublished manuscript, Morgantown, WV: West Virginia University.

Blum, A.A. (1989). The teacher as the technique in training. *Journal of European Industrial Training*, *13*, (1), 19–22.

Bolt, J.F. (1985). Tailor executive development to strategy. *Harvard Business Review*, *63*, (6), 168–176.

Brown, G.F. & Read, A.R. (1984). Personnel and training policies—some lessons for Western companies. *Long Range Plan*, *17*, (2), 48–57.

Burke, M.J., & Day, R.R. (1986). A cumulative study of the effectiveness of managerial training. *Journal of Applied Psychology*, *71*, 232–245.

Campbell, J.P., Dunnette, M., Lawler, E.E., & Weick, K. E. (1970). *Managerial behavior, performance and effectiveness*. New York: McGraw-Hill.

Carnevale, A.P. (1989). The learning enterprise. *Training and Development Journal*, *43*, (2), 26–33.

Curry, B., & Moutinho, L. (1992). Using computer simulations in management education. *Management Education and Development*, *23*, 155–167.

Davies, J., & Easterby-Smith, M. (1984). Learning and developing from managerial work experiences. *Journal of Management Studies*, *21*, 169–183.

Donnel, S.M., & Hall, J. (1980). Men and women as managers: A case of no significant differences. *Organizational Dynamics*, *8*, (4), 60–77.

Dreher, G.F., & Ash, R.A. (1990). A comparative study of mentoring among men and women in managerial, professional, and technical positions. *Journal of Applied Psychology*, *75*, 539–546.

Eden, D., & Ravid, G. (1982). Pygmalion vs. self-expectancy effects of instructor and self-expectancy on trainee performance. *Organizational Behavior and Human Performance*, *30*, 351–364.

Eden, D., & Shani, A.B. (1982). Pygmalion goes to boot camp: Expectancy, leadership, and trainee performance. *Journal of Applied Psychology*, *67*, 194–199.

Enderby, J.E. & Phelan, D.R. (1994). Action learning groups as the foundation for cultural change. *Asia Pacific Journal of Human Resources*, *32*, (1), 74–82.

Faria, A.J. (1989). Business gaming: Current usage levels. *Journal of Management Development*, *8*, (2), 58–65.

Feldman, D.C. (1988). *Managing careers in organizations*. Glenview, IL: Scott, Foresman.

Finney, M. & Glinow, M. A. von (1988). Integrating academic and organizational approaches to developing the international manager. *Journal of Management Development*, *7*, (2), 115–128.

Fuchsberg, G. (1993). Executive education: Taking control. *The Wall Street Journal Reports*, 10 September.

Galagan, P. (1987). Between two trapezes. *Training and Development Journal*, *41*, (3), 40–53.

Gall, A.L. (1987). You can take the manager out of the woods, but ... *Training and Development Journal*, *41*, (3), 54–61.

Geus, A.P. de (1988). Planning as learning. *Harvard Business Review*, *66*, (2), 70–74.

Griffin, R.W., & Cashin, W.E. (1989). The lecture and discussion method for management education: Pros and cons. *Journal of Management Development*, *8*, (2), 25–32.

Gronlund, N.E. (1987). *Stating objectives for classroom instructions*. New York: Macmillan.

Gunz, H. (1989). *Careers and corporate cultures: Managerial mobility in large corporations*. Oxford: Basil Blackwell.

Heisler, W.J., & Benham, P.O. (1992). The challenge of management development in North America in the 1990s. *Journal of Management Development*, *11*, (2), 16–31.

Heisler, W.J., & Lasher, H.J. (1986). A call for increased cooperation in the business of management development and management education. *Journal of Management Development*, *5*, (2), 62–73.

Hill, L.A. (1991). *Beyond the myth of the perfect mentor: Building a network of developmental relationships*. Boston: Harvard Business School.

Hofstede, G. (1993). Cultural constraints in management theories. *Academy of Management Executive*, *7*, (1), 81–93.

Hussey, D.E. (1985). Implementing corporate strategy: Using management education and training. *Long Range Plan, 18*, (5), 28–37.

Kearsley, G. (1991). Training media and technology. In J. E. Morrison (Ed.), *Training for performance* (pp. 231–255). Chichester: Wiley.

Keys, J.B. (1989). The management of learning grid for management development revisited. *Journal of Management Development, 8*, (2), 5–12.

Keys, J.B., & Wolfe, J. (1988). Management education and development: Current issues and emerging trends. *Journal of Management, 14*, 205–229.

Keys, J.B. & Wolfe, J. (1990). The role of management games and simulations in education and research. *Journal of Management, 16*, 307–336.

Kottemann, J.E., Davis, F.D., & Remus, W.E. (1994). Computer-assisted decision-making: Performance, beliefs, and the illusion of control. *Organizational Behavior and Human Decision Processes, 57*, 26–37.

Kotter, J.P. (1982). *The general managers.* New York: Free Press.

Kram, K.E. (1985). *Mentoring at work: Developmental relationships in organizational life.* Glenview, IL: Scott Foresman.

Kram, K.E., & Hall, D.T. (1989). Mentoring as an antidote to stress during corporate trauma. *Human Resource Management, 28*, 493–510.

Kram, K.E., & Isabella, L.A. (1985). Mentoring alternatives: The role of peer relationships in career development. *Academy of Management Journal, 28*, 110–132.

Kraut, A.I., Pedigo, P.R., McKenna, D.D., & Dunnette, M.D. (1989). The role of the manager: What's really important in different managerial jobs. *Academy of Management Executive, 3*, (4), 286–293.

Latham, G.P., & Crandall, S. (1991). Organizational and social factors affecting training effectiveness. In J.E. Morrison (Ed.), *Training for performance* (pp. 259–285). Chichester: Wiley.

Latham, G.P., Daghighi, S., & Locke, E.A. (in press). Educational applications of goal setting theory. In J.L. Bess (Ed.), *Teaching well and liking it: Motivational perspectives.* San Francisco, CA: Jossey Bass.

Latham, G.P., & Saari, L.M. (1979). The application of social learning theory to training supervisors through behavior modeling. *Journal of Applied Psychology, 64*, 239–246.

Lee, C. (1987). Where the training dollars go. *Training and Development Journal, 24*, (10), 51–65.

Linstead, S. (1990). Beyond competence: Management development using computer-based systems in experiential learning. *Management Education and Development, 21*, 61–74.

Locke, E.A., & Latham, G.P. (1990). *A theory of goal setting and task performance.* Englewood Cliffs, NJ: Prentice-Hall.

Long, J.W. (1987). The wilderness lab comes of age. *Training and Development Journal, 41*, (3), 30–39.

Loo, R. (1991). Management training in Canadian organizations. *Journal of Management Development, 10*, (5), 660–72.

Margerison, C.J. (1988). Action learning and excellence in management development. *Journal of Management Development, 7*, (5), 43–53.

Maruyama, M. (1990). Some management considerations in the economic reorganization of Eastern Europe. *Academy of Management Executive, 4*, (2), 90–91.

McCall, M.W., & Lombardo, M.M. (1983). What makes a top executive? *Psychology Today*, February, 26–31.

McCall, M.W., Lombardo, M.M., & Morrison, A.M. (1988). *The lessons of experience: How successful executives develop on the job.* Lexington, MA: Lexington Books.

McCauley, C.D., Ohlott, P.J., & Ruderman, M.R. (1989). On-the-job development: A conceptual model and preliminary investigation. *Journal of Managerial Issues, 1*, 142–158.

McCauley, C.D., Ruderman, M.R., Ohlott, P.J., & Morrow, J.E. (1994). Assessing the developmental components of managerial jobs. *Journal of Applied Psychology, 79*, 544–560.

McNulty, N.G. (1992). Management education in Eastern Europe: 'fore and after. *Academy of Management Executive, 6*, (4), 78–87.

Mealiea, L., & Latham, G.P. (in press). *Skills for managers in organizations.* Burridge, IL: Irwin.

Mintzberg, H. (1973). The nature of managerial work. New York: Harper & Row.

Mintzberg, H. (1989). *Mintzberg on management: Inside our strange world of organizations.* New York: Free Press.

Mol, A.J., & Vermeulen, L.P. (1988). Is management development worth the effort? *Human Resources Management Australia, 26*, (3), 18–29.

Mumford, A. (1987). Action learning. *Journal of Management Development, 6*, (2), 1–70.

Mumford, A. (1988). *Developing top managers.* Aldershot: Gower.

Newstrom, J.W. (1985). "Mod" management development: Does it deliver what it promises? *Journal of Management Development, 4*, (1), 3–11.

Norris, D.R. (1986). External validity of business games. *Simulation and Games, 17*, (4), 447–459.

Ohlott, P.J., Ruderman, M.N., & McCauley, C.D. (1994). Gender differences in managers' developmental job experiences. *Academy of Management Journal, 37*, 46–67.

Osigweh, C.A.B. (1989). Casing the case approach in management development. *Journal of Management Development, 8*, (2), 41–57.

Porter, L.W., & McKibbin, L.E. (1988). Management education and development: Drift or thrust into the 21st Century. New York: McGraw-Hill.

Powers, E.A. (1987). Enhancing managerial competence: The American Management Association competency programme. *Journal of Management Development, 6*, (4), 7–18.

Price Waterhouse Cranfield project on international strategic management (1991). Bedford: Cranfield University.

Revans, R. (1982). What is action learning? *Journal of Management Development, 1*, (3), 64–75.

Revans, R. (1984). *The origins and growth of action learning*. Lund: Chartwell Bratt.

Saari, L.M., Johnson, T.R., McLaughlin, S.D., & Zimmerle, D.M. (1988). A survey of management training and education practices in US companies. *Personnel Psychology, 41*, 731–743.

Scandura, T.A. (1992). Mentorship and career mobility: An empirical investigation. *Journal of Organizational Behavior, 13*, 169–174.

Schuler, R.S., & Jackson, S.E. (1987). Linking competitive strategies with human resource management practices. *Academy of Management Executive, 1*, (3), 207–219.

Senge, P.M. (1990). *The fifth discipline: The art and practice of the learning organization*. New York: Doubleday.

Senge, P.M. (1991). *Transforming the practice of management*. Paper presented at the Systems Thinking in Action Conference, November.

Shipper, F. (1991). Mastery and frequency of managerial behaviors relative to subunit effectiveness. *Human Relations, 44*, 371–388.

Sterman, J.D. (1989a). Misperceptions of feedback in dynamic decision making. *Organizational Behavior and Human Decision Processes, 43*, 301–335.

Sterman, J.D. (1989b). Modeling managerial behavior: Misperceptions of feedback in a dynamic decision making experiment. *Management Science, 55*, 321–339.

Stewart, R. (1989). Studies of managerial jobs and behavior: The ways forward. *Journal of Management Studies, 26*, (1), 1–10.

Stuart, R., & Burgoyne, J. (1978). Teachers and trainers: their skills. In J. Burgoyne and R. Stuart (Eds.), *Management development: Context and strategies*. Farnborough: Gower Press.

Stuller, J. (1993). Practical matters. *Across the Board, 30*, (1), 36–40.

Thornton, G.C., & Cleveland, J.N. (1990). Developing managerial talent through simulation. *American Psychologist, 45*, 190–199.

Turban, D.B., Dougherty, T.W. (1994). Role of protégé personality in receipt of mentoring and career success. *Academy of Management Journal, 37*, 688–702.

Vaill, P. (1989). *Managing as a performing art: New ideas for a world of chaotic change*. San Francisco, CA: Jossey Bass.

Wagner, R.J., Baldwin, T.T., & Roland, C.C. (1991). Outdoor training: Revolution or fad? *Training and Development Journal, 45*, (3), 50–57.

Waters, J.A. (1980). Managerial skills development. *Academy of Management Review, 5*, 449–453.

Wells, R.A. (1989). A review of educational technology for management development. *Journal of Management Development, 8*, (2), 33–40.

Werther, W.B. (1993). A university/corporate solution to closing the executive development gap. *Journal of Management Development, 12*, (8), 61–68.

Wexley, K.N., & Baldwin, T.T. (1986). Management development. *Journal of Management, 12*, 277–294.

Wexley, K.N., & Latham, G.P. (1991). *Developing and training human resources in organizations*. Glenview, IL: Scott Foresman.

Whetten, D.A., & Cameron, K.S. (1991). *Developing management skills*. New York: Harper Collins.

Whitely, W.T. & Coetsier, P. (1993). The relationships of career mentoring to early career outcomes. *Organization Studies, 14*, 419–441.

Yukl, G.A., Wall, S., & Lepsinger, R. (1990). Preliminary report on the validation of the management practices survey. In K.E. Clark & M.B. Clark (Eds.), *Measures of leadership*. West Orange, NJ: Leadership Library of America.

Zey, M.G. (1985). Mentor programs: Making the right moves. *Personnel Journal, 64*, (2), 53–57.

Zwieten, J. van (1984). Training on the rocks. *Training and Development Journal, 38*, (1), 26–33.

12

Career Development and Career Guidance

Johannes Gerrit Boerlijst[1]

INTRODUCTION

Since the publication of the first edition of this handbook (Drenth, Thierry, Willems, & De Wolff, 1984), career development, career planning and career guidance have become part and parcel of personnel work in organizations. The career of individual employees now forms an integrating theme in personnel procedures employed at present (Gutteridge, Leibowitz, & Shore, 1993). Progress has also been made in scientific terms. This is particularly apparent in the extension of familiar theoretical paths, such as those of Super (1957), Super, Starishevsky, Matlin, and Jordaan (1963), Holland (1985a), Dawis and Lofquist (1984, 1993), Crites (1981) and Osipow (1983). Arthur, Hall, and Lawrence (1989) and Montross and Shinkman (1992) provide a summary of this.

This chapter will proceed on the following lines. Section 1 discusses the growing interest within organizations for career studies and career guidance. This interest is attributed to the issues raised by the increased dynamics of organizations (Section 1.1). The problems first manifested themselves at the top of organizations. They then extended to affect an ever increasing group of personnel. The "management development" or MD approach dating from the 1960s has been replaced in a number of organizations by that of "human resources management" (Section 1.2). At the heart of this issue is the increasing necessity to take into account the individual's own potential for development and change in the long term. It has, in fact, become a psychological issue. This aspect is elucidated in Section 2. Theory-development in the area of careers has taken place most particularly within W&O psychology. A shift in emphasis has occurred (Section 2.1). Originally, attempts were made to predict careers on the basis of historical facts pertaining to persons and their situations. This type of thinking is being replaced by attempts to develop models of career processes. An insight into this can be useful for strategic, specifically-oriented influencing of individual careers, for example via management interventions. The significance of the theoretical orientations developed thus far appears to be restricted at the present time. Integration with concepts originating from the so-called life-span developmental psychology is the obvious course and may well culminate in a more workable career theory (Section 2.2). The changes in the management issue experienced by people in organizations, as outlined in Section 1, have been accompanied by a change in the definitions of the concept "career". This is the theme of Section 3. The different definitions have gradually acquired a more dynamic and broader character. The multitude of accepted meanings presents a handicap for the forming of theories on careers and for career guidance in the practical situation (Section 3.1). An attempt will be made to formulate an all-inclusive definition (Section 3.2). The aspect-variants or "facets" of this definition will be dealt with one by one in Section 4. In Section 5, the influencing of careers in the practical situation will be discussed. First, the policy side will be elucidated (Section 5.1) followed by various intervention possibilities (Section 5.2). Finally, in Section 6 attention will be drawn to some societal developments that will be likely to have a far-reaching effect on careers, namely the ageing of the working population and the increase in the number of working women.

1 CAREERS AS A PROBLEM IN ORGANIZATIONS

1.1 Careers: a management problem

The growing interest displayed by organizations in the career issue is comparatively recent. We must begin by noting that the significance of increased knowledge on the subject of careers is not favoured everywhere equally highly. Static organizations, for example, show little interest in individual careers; at most there is an interest in the more formal aspects relating to the career issue. Such organizations are characterized by a rather invariant organizational structure, a more or less unchanging package of objectives and an equally rigid set of measures to achieve these objectives. Priority is not given to research and development. These organizations are usually of a rather bureaucratic nature and can be efficiently run by application of the classical principles of "scientific management", which includes a division of labour carried to extremes. As many different types of work and functions as possible are created, requiring only a limited amount of ability and effort from a person in the course of time.

The major problem in this connection experienced by such organizations is finding people willing and able to perform the tasks required of them satisfactorily, year in year out. Selection, placement and training for a required function area are here of greater importance than consideration of people's potential for development and change. Their career generally has a predictable character and will be relatively easy to steer within hierarchically-laid beaten tracks. As a rule the division of work within these organizations is geared to a fixed careers structure, with its social foundation in the classical, but still prevalent, forms of professional training. Although the running of this type of organization may be very demanding, this is counteracted by the stability of the management and the administration.

The form of organization outlined here predominated in our society for a long time. Over the last 20 years, it has increasingly made way for a type of organization which is much more dependent on the requirements and changing needs of the environment. This environment is necessary as a market for the products supplied by the organization. On the other hand, that same environment offers certain resources to the organization, such as raw materials, ideas, services, and so on. Organizations must be continuously capable of timely adjustment to changes in their environment and of making the most of the new opportunities thereby provided. They must be able to change their targets and products according to the needs of the market, and to live with uncertainty and the chance of success or the risk of failure. Not only is there a need for adjustment, but also, very often, for creative innovation in terms of targets, means and products in order to be able to combat the sometimes fierce competition from other organizations. They must also be able to influence their environment in their own favour. The success of this complex programme depends among other things on the unchanging suitability and the continuing versatility of people present in the organization. All this requires higher standards than is the case in the static organizations that have just been referred to. The management of a dynamic organization should be alert to the latent capacities, development potential and interests of their employees (and of itself!). It is no wonder that this has led to a need for an increase in knowledge regarding the development and influencing possibilities of careers. Indeed, the general opinion is that the possession of this knowledge will probably enable the progress of management and employees to be monitored and stimulated better and more systematically. Specific career interventions and career steering could lead to the creation of a pool of flexible human ingenuity and accumulated experience, which the organization can draw on in changing circumstances and which it can count on in the planning and execution of strategic policy (Mulder, Romiszowski, & Van der Sijde, 1990; Rothwell, 1991).

1.2 From "management development" to "human resources management"

As emerged in the previous Section, in modern, dynamic organizations a strong emphasis is placed on people's potential for development and change during the entire course of their career. Initially, around 1960, attention was centred on the top management of organizations and on the policy sectors immediately below. In the lower echelons the work could, to a certain extent, still continue along the old lines. Here, management was able to carry on applying classical organization principles and skilful division of work. Although the demand for modernization increased in these areas as well (for example in the area of "work structuring"), the long-term development of lower-level personnel was not yet a key issue. One question which was, however, a subject of interest was that of how the manifested strength and quality of the top management could be consolidated when the persons in question left the organization, for example on retirement. In connection with the issue of top people leaving, a need arose in many large companies for instruments to find out who might be suitable successors and how their necessary extension of knowledge and mobility could be enhanced. Such policy instruments and the activities resulting from them are generally referred to by the term "management development" (MD).

The emphasis within MD is on the collection of facts, based on which the "management potential" of the organization on an individual level can be assessed. An example of this is a register of positions filled by employees during their former career, their particular achievements, their interest in other positions, and so on.

A second area of attention is the development of tests that could predict this management potential. The stimulation of management potential by means of training is obviously one of the core activities of MD. A product of this is the great number of internal and external management training courses that have mushroomed since 1960. The instrumental part of MD does not appear to be particularly successful. The emergence of computers with a large memory capacity enabled a vast amount of historical data on persons to be recorded. Such data files have, however, proved to be very difficult to keep up to date and are often difficult to access at the moment they are needed. Moreover, there is not uncommonly a lack of insight into the relevant interrelation and validity of such data when taking particular decisions. More or less the same can be said of the tests developed for the assessment of management potential. A drawback of such instruments is that they were not originally designed to be used for the development of career theory.

In many organizations, MD is no longer confined to the management, but is often provided to all categories of personnel. (The middle and higher echelons of personnel are given, relatively speaking, the most individual attention anyway. In the case of lower placed categories, the activities are generally more categorially oriented). What were initially rather disconnected activities relating to personnel work in the area of selection, introduction, placing, training and education, and so on, are now gradually making way for a coherent, integrated system of career development, career planning and career guidance, where a mutual matching of the different needs and potentials of organization and personnel is the aim (Schein, 1978; Boerlijst & Meijboom, 1989). Both parties, organization and individual, are held responsible for the realization of this. In modern standard works on personnel work (e.g. Bennett, 1992; Hodgetts & Kroeck, 1992) this integrated approach to "human resources development" has been given a prominent place.

The increasing interest in integrated career management for all sections is tied up with the problems resulting from the far-reaching effects of automation and computerization. Reacting alertly and creatively to new requirements and developments is by definition a necessity for every dynamic organization. In the 1960s, essential changes took place at a much slower pace than at present. The gradual introduction of powerful computer networks and computer-backed technology has made possible the acceleration of all kinds of organizational and production processes. An organization can supply its markets at a much greater speed. This, in turn, has facilitated an accelerated shift in market demands. As an example of this one can cite the development, production and sale of sound media, such as radios and tape recorders. Nowadays, the total life-cycle of any type of sound medium is very short. Within a period of a year or less all the initial expenses, which are often very steep, must be recovered. This not only places great pressure on the effectiveness and efficiency of research and development, but obviously also on the production and commercial circuits. The integration between all parties involved—which the traditional organization-theory classifies as separate management positions—must be intensified in the interests of gaining time. The management of a production and marketing organization must conform to high standards. Not only must it possess much wider insight and experience than previously, but it must also be capable of a greater speed of decision making and reaction. At the same time a strategic line must be consistently adhered to, for example regarding the efforts and development of the necessary personnel. Control and command can no longer operate only from the top, either. It is, after all, possible for something to go wrong at any point in an organization, however careful the procedures. All the personnel members involved should react adequately and inventively to perceived disorders, without being hindered by bureaucratic principles. Moreover, the potential flexibility of software and means of production can only be used to advantage when the necessary "know how" and knowledge based on practical experience are readily available. This implies a decentralization of management and supervision. For many of the personnel this will mean an expansion of their responsibilities. The effects of this in a modern flexible organization will be that the demand for personnel with progressively higher qualifications will increase at all levels, and that provision for the further development of that same personnel is high on the agenda of personnel policy.

Adequate functioning in an organization requires more than a suitable educational background. The utmost care and attention should be given to the introduction and coaching of newcomers as well as continuing training and guidance during the subsequent stages of their career. This attitude has resulted in the development of activities that we at present summarize with the term "training and development of human resources" (Wexley & Latham, 1991) and with a still broader term, "career management". The management of human resources within an organization calls for an individual approach, which extends far beyond the approach of the former customary "personnel management". Promotion of the long-term interests of the organization and of the employees go hand in hand. Possibilities for the design of systems for career management, practical applications of this and suggestions for the necessary training of personnel officials, management and employees for their implementation, have been described by Gattiker & Larwood (1988), Lengnick-Hall & Lengnick-Hall (1990), and Gutteridge et al. (1993); their contributions are geared to practical application though embedded in a theoretical context (see Cascio, 1991).

Although terms such as career development, career planning and career guidance have in the meantime become generally accepted in many organizations, there appears to be very little implemented operational career management going on in practice, for this requires time and attention, which an organization often does not have at its disposal. Companies that pursue an expansive policy in the field of advanced technology and automation and where the utmost is demanded of the available human resources are those very ones where there is the danger of insufficient or inadequate care and attention to the introduction and guidance of new employees. This is certainly so if those designated with this task cannot find the time to do so, because of their absorption in another task; for instance recovering the costs of the often gigantic investments in new technology.

If, for those same reasons, newcomers are burdened with a full, complicated and responsible task immediately on arrival, the risk of "teething troubles" is most definitely very great indeed (Boerlijst, Smit, & Vermeulen, 1987).

2 CAREER PSYCHOLOGY

2.1 Career as a theme in W&O psychology: a change in orientation

Since time immemorial, W&O psychology has concerned itself with careers. However, a change in orientation has occurred in the course of time. Attention was initially directed to helping solve career issues as they presented themselves in traditional organizations. As already stated, this traditional type of organization is typified by a certain degree of stability in its division of work and in the nature of the functions performed by a large section of its personnel. The division of labour relates to a careers structure supported by the community, mainly via education. In earlier views expressed by W&O psychologists and sociologists, a career was often defined as "adjustment to an occupation". What was meant by this was an occupation as performed and developed in traditional, relatively static work organizations. This interpretation of careers entailed an emphasis on educational and vocational information and guidance and on the prediction of the suitability of people to adjust to the execution and development of a career. This latter activity is part and parcel of the circuit of selection and placement within the organization. Extensive literature is available on the measuring and significance of individual career preferences and individual decision making on the choice of an occupational career. Helbing (1987) provides a clear summary of this, and it would be beyond the scope of this publication to expand on it here. On the one hand, the range of the subject matter is rather restricted—namely, to the preparatory phase and, at most, the initial phase of pursuance of a career. The individual career as a process, sometimes lasting more than 40 years, is not covered in sufficient depth at all. On the other hand, there is an over-assumption of the static and stable nature of the career being pursued. It is much more difficult to predict careers in modern organizations on the basis of historical facts concerning qualities, views and experiences of people before they have even embarked on a career.

The more the importance of development of individuals within their career was recognized and the need for a means of influencing individual careers became greater, the more interest W&O psychologists took in individual career processes. Researchers started looking for suitable models and theories for describing them.

2.1.1 Importance of occupational theories and concepts for the formation of career process models

Certain theoretical notions and concepts relating to career preferences and career choice are useful for the formation of theories and models relating to career processes.

If it is a question of personal preferences and development of preferences, then several authors point to the necessity of congruence. The image that individuals have of themselves must be congruous with the image that they have of the object of preference, for example an occupation, a position or a particular career (Super, 1986). Some theoreticians consider the congruence of the perceived career image with the "ideal" self-image to be the prime motivating factor. This view reflects the idea that choices of a particular career path are one of the factors that determine the formation and change in the "self" (see Hall, 1976, p. 31). This matches the assumption of Holland (1985a) that certain personality types only feel at home in a certain type of work environment (see also Subsection 5.3.1). This view is obviously of great importance in career counselling and career guidance. Holland assumes that the degree of congruence between personal orientation and work environment is not only important in the choice of an occupation or career, but also for a successful progression of a career. The findings of Adler and Aranya (1984) in a study among accountants, revealed, however, that they started to show more deviations in later stages of their careers, as compared to their "ideal" personality types (according to Holland); the congruence that may exist at the start of a career does not therefore always appear to be lasting. Holland's theory certainly forms a good starting point for empirical research (Spokane, 1985).

It is striking that, both in examinations of career preferences and of decision making as to career choice, cognitive and social comparison processes and social identifications are given prominence (Osipow, 1983). The self-image is placed on one side, and the image of certain environmental aspects, on the other. Such comparisons undoubtedly play an important part in making choices during the course of one's career. In this context, we may draw attention to Schein's "career anchor" concept (1978). He assumes that everyone, at least in principle, is capable of developing an awareness of his or her own abilities, motives, attitudes, needs, values, and the like. This awareness will be derived from experiences in the practice of his or her actual career. Schein calls this insight into oneself a "career anchor" because it gives the person something to hold onto in the process of transitions and changing circumstances during his or her career. It enables individuals to reaffirm themselves continuously in any new life situation. The "career anchor" of individuals is the crystallized set of self-reflections on their own personal attitudes, emotions, and actual behaviour in different situations during their career on the one hand, and of the self-experiences of the outcomes of these attitudes, emotions and behaviour on the other. Were individuals to have a different working environment than their present one, their career anchor might also be different. That is why Schein believes that individual career anchors cannot be predicted by means of tests early on. They acquire stability only in the middle phase of the career. Awareness of one's career anchor may form a foundation for conscious career choices and decisions. In the framework of career guidance, this concept deserves more attention from personnel managements than it is currently receiving.

2.1.2 Individual development during the career: the time perspective

In the classical views on careers, little attention is paid to the time dimension. There are, of course, exceptions. Super (1957) was the first to describe the development of career-relevant self concepts as a maturation or unfolding process in age-related stages. Within each stage, the individual is confronted with specific requirements, tasks, problems and changes in his or her living environment, which he or she must cope with somehow or other. The transition to each new phase requires an adjusted "career maturity" of the self-insight or self-concept of the individual. This must grow, as it were, towards a new phase in which new tasks and responsibilities must be assumed. Super is of the opinion that the degree of maturity for the various different phases of an occupational career can be measured and that this measurement is a valid indicator of the successful progression of the next phase. He and his co-workers have formulated a theory on this that has also acquired empirical support, at least regarding the early phases of different occupational careers (Super, 1981, 1986; Super et al., 1963). A number of authors have embroidered on this theme of age-related, phasic development (Levinson, 1978, 1986; Schein, 1978; Van Maanen, 1977). We will return to this in Subsection 2.2.2.

Within W&O psychology, the middle phase or climacteric of the career (the so-called "mid-career") has received special attention (Hunter & Sundel, 1989). This is the phase in which a person can no longer consider himself or herself to be young, and in which the realization dawns that he or she will soon be counted as belonging to the category of older people. It is, in any case, a phase that everybody must experience; the phase in which the individual is confronted with their own finiteness (Jacques, 1965). A further factor coming to the fore in this phase is the realization that a person's career is going to end and that the time left for further achievements is about to run out (Kalish, 1989). This phase calls for a drastic re-orientation of the individual in terms of remaining career opportunities or those still to be newly developed (Hall, 1986b; Katchadourian, 1987; Sherman, 1987) and is often accompanied by the frustrating feeling that these opportunities may have gone for good. This may result in stress at work and in the work relations, with negative consequences not only for the individuals concerned but also for those around them, at work, in the family, among their friends, and so on (Janssen, 1992). Career guidance will have to be geared to steer management and personnel through this phase with the minimum of difficulty (Benner, 1984). This is to the benefit not only of the person concerned but the whole organization (see also Section 6.1).

In the theories mentioned so far, the phasic progression is of a generally applicable nature. What any individual may expect in a particular phase can be predicted to a greater or lesser degree, within a particular population. There are also theories in which the progression of the career is described as a development that could very well have a general structure, but whose content is highly individual. This assumes that within the individual career, predictions are possible but that they are not necessarily relevant to other peoples' careers. In such theories, career development is seen as a time-related process of interactions or transactions between the individual and the work organization, whose success is in the interests of both parties (London & Wueste, 1992). Such theories emphasize the importance of acquiring experience and learning through experience for the further development of the individual (see Kolb, 1984).

It is not possible within the scope of this chapter to discuss all the theoretical models that have been put forward in the field of career development within W&O psychology. Some of them will, however, be raised in the course of the following Sections. Here, we will make only one or two general comments.

Most of the views on career development are of an exploratory nature. In so far as the hypotheses put forward are not trivial, they have not been sufficiently tested, not so much because this would basically not be feasible, but because it is extremely difficult to find or hold onto a suitable and willing environment for empirical research. Research of this sort calls for a longitudinal and multivariate approach, and this is liable to be confronted by many problems in design and execution.

In a critical evaluation, Schein (1986) draws attention to the lack of interrelationship between the various different theories and models, and, additionally, to their often prejudiced orientation to the prediction of organization-dependent criteria of success and progress. Finally he also draws attention to the insensitivity of these models to the sometimes very large differences between the organization cultures in which careers unfold. In this context, Bakker (1987) found that, in a prominent machine factory, the traditional conception of the career of skilled workers with secondary-school education formed a barrier to certain investments in modern means of production, which were seemingly desirable from a strategic point of view. Although such means of production call for continuous attention and presence of more highly qualified personnel "on the shop floor", the organizational culture in this particular case stipulated that highly qualified workers should be placed in a managerial position at an early stage. Strong tradition dictated that the handling of machinery and tools should be left to highly experienced, but somewhat less-qualified skilled workers.

2.2 Careers and life-span psychology

In the last Section we drew attention to models and theories involving a time-bound, phasic career development. In general this presupposes a particular, fixed sequence of situations that a person is confronted with in the course of his or her career. As a rule, it is assumed that the complexity of the situations in the first phase of the career increases progressively to reach a peak somewhere halfway through. There then generally follows a phase of stable complexity, which in its turn is followed by a decrease. The first phases are characterized by the acquisition of skills, which might be handed on to young adults at later phases.

It is sometimes explicitly or implicitly assumed that adults experience a further cognitive, emotional, or more broadly expressed, personality development, as is the case with children and adolescents. This development is indicated in very rough lines, probably because still so little is known about it. It is only recently that development psychology began to become interested in adults. For a long time the prevailing view in society was that the intellectual and emotional development of people comes to an end relatively early on, at some point in the course of the second decade of life, and that after that ensues a longer or shorter period of decline. Curiously enough it took a long time for psychologists to begin to mistrust this hypothesis. This can probably be attributed to the fact that empiric research on adults is by no means as easy to organize as it is on children. Nevertheless, the situation has changed in the meantime. Nowadays many researchers focus their attention on life-span psychology and the developments taking place in adults (see Kastenbaum, 1993; Smolak, 1993). Opinions originating in developmental psychology, which were considered to be more or less established, are now no longer accepted. A detailed discussion of this is given by Datan, Rodeheaver, and Hughes (1987), from whom a number of the following facts have been derived.

2.2.1 Doubt as to the feasibility of a generally applicable theory on the subject of the individual life-span

A number of authors entertain the view that a general theory formulated with the help of statistical models is very unlikely to have the result of enlightening our understanding of the individual life-span. They advocate a personological approach (Rodeheaver & Datan, 1985). In this, the researcher takes into account the fact that a person's interpretation of the events and circumstances occurring during the course of his or her life will be subjective and idiosyncratic. Furthermore, that these individual interpretations are not only able to influence the behaviour of the person but also their environment. Such interpretations can for example contribute to the forming of ideas and plans relating to that person's own future. These, in turn, may result in self-influencing or influencing their own situation. These views could lead one to draw the conclusion that theory formation pertaining to careers should be of a descriptive rather than of a prescriptive or predictive nature (Freeman, 1993). The subtleties of the combination of the many factors that may influence and determine an individual career would then not easily be overlooked as is often the case in an experimental testing of more generally formulated career hypotheses. The question remains of course as to how such research can best be organized and to what types of generalization it could lead (see Vondracek, Lerner, & Schulenberg, 1986).

2.2.2 Doubt as to the choice of development models

It is generally assumed that the life of an individual progresses in stages. For the 0–20 age group these stages are fairly clearly defined. They are closely connected to the natural development of the bio-psycho-social system "man". Certain changes and reorganizations of that system are age-related. Social institutions that have been established for young people take this into account. A characteristic of young people's development is growth on all fronts. Institutions such as the family, the school, the youth organization, and so on, focus on this growth and impose their own system of phases on young people which matches the natural "organic" growth phases as closely as possible. For example, a school employs a hierarchically phased structure in age-related classes or levels. In this way, education is tailored to the phase of growth of the average pupil of that age. In adults the problem may be that a natural phasing is less manifest. Usually there is no longer any clear growth in those human functions that were in the forefront in one's youth, in family and school situations. However, practically everyone recognizes that stages do nonetheless occur in adult life. Organizations, therefore, take this as a basic supposition, usually explicitly or tacitly. For instance, it is generally assumed that for younger employees growth of experience is the dominating factor, that there then occurs a stage of stability, followed by a period of diminished activity. This also presupposes vague age limits. Schein (1978, p. 40) gives us a typical example. He distinguishes nine successive stages in a work career, each of which is characterized by (rough) age limits, particular roles in the work situation and certain specific problems and tasks for those in that stage of their career. Schein determines these stages as follows:

1. A period of growth, exploration and development of the imagination (this takes place before adulthood).

2. The entry into the world of work.
3. A period of basic training on the job.
4. Full temporary employment in the first part of the career.
5. Full permanent employment in the first part of the career.
6. A period of crisis in the middle part of the career.
7. Later stage of the career, either in a managerial or in a non-managerial position.
8. A period of demotion, detachment and decline.
9. The retirement stage.

The model suggests a continuity in development and transition from one phase to another, at least seen from the point of view of the organization. Schein, however, draws attention to the fact that the transitions may be discontinuous for the person in question and may give rise to all sort of problems of adjustment. Many people in employment will be able to recognize their own experiences in such a model. Others, however, will have the feeling that such a system of phases has, as it were, been imposed on them from above. Schein notes that not everybody passes through all the stages and that their sequence, too, is not always the same.

Among developmental psychologists, discussion is taking place on the forming of models based on stages. There are theoretical models that assume an individual goes through a cumulative, "natural" or otherwise, life development towards a progressively higher state of adulthood (which may in some cases be followed by a phase of stability and a decline at a later age). The findings of research into the concept of continuous development (growth, later followed by stabilization and/or decline) are varied. The view is sometimes even expressed that the idea of a "stage of development during adulthood" should be abandoned and the history of an individual life should be seen as a succession of entirely person-related actions and reactions of that person in relation to the circles in which he or she moves (see Neugarten, 1984). In any case it has become evident that classification into stages is a complicated matter for any single individual.

Virtually any other social context imposes on the individual its own life stages, as it were, in the sense that at a given moment important changes may occur in tasks, requirements and roles that the individual must adapt to. The pattern of actions, interactions and transactions that the individual develops in one social context (the family for example) will not always be easy to combine with the pattern that fits another context (work for example). Transitions from one stage to another often call for an adjustment and reorientation of the individual to his or her environment, which cannot always be realized at the due time. The person must be "ready" for them, as it were.

In this connection we refer to Levinson's theory (1986), which characterizes every human life by what he terms, a certain "life structure" and postulates that this structure is both universal—meaning that it applies to everybody—and age-dependent. According to Levinson, life proceeds in a series of alternating phases. Each time one can distinguish a certain "formation phase", followed by a "transitional phase", which is the bridge to the next "formation phase". In every formation phase the person is part of a certain system of relations and transactions with his or her social environment, geared to an optimum adaptation of the individual to circumstances and problems which occur in the period of life in question. If these circumstances and problems are changed in any way, whether drastically or not, then in the following transitional phase, the previously-formed system of relations and transitions is gradually transformed or demolished and the ground is laid for the formation of a new system. After this, a new formation phase dawns. In this way, periodic change in "life structure" becomes a fact. From research into biographical material, Levinson (1978) draws the conclusion that formation and transitional phases are related to modal "natural" age limits. Each formation phase generally lasts for 5–7 years and each transitional phase, about 5 years. This theory provides no clear explanation for these periodic occurrences anchored in human nature. Levinson's indication of the successive phases is extremely general and therefore rather meaningless, for example:

17–22 = "early adult transition";
22–28 = "entry life structure for early adulthood";

28–33 = "age 30 transition";
33–40 = "culminating life structure for early childhood";
40–45 = "mid-life transition".

Levinson states further that within each phase the individual may experience the occurrence of growth and stability phenomena as well as decline, and that the successive phases are not necessarily regulated according to some sort of hierarchy. He prefers to compare the various formation phases with different "seasons", each of which has its own characteristics. What each individual is actually undergoing in the different phases contentwise remains virtually unanswered by this theory. How people experience their life-events and personal development is to a large extent individual and cannot really be classified under the same heading.

If Levinson's theory were correct, what might the consequences be for an organization? As an example we will put forward the case of an organization imposing a particular type of phasing on its employees' careers by means of a system of periodic job-rotation. According to the theory under discussion, any transition to a new job should take place in a "natural" transition phase and not halfway through a formation phase, because this would then result in serious disruptions to the development of the employee concerned, frustrations, symptoms of stress, and so on. Anthropological, sociological and clinical-psychological observations of transitional symptoms ("career transitions") show that phase transitions do not often take place without a struggle and that some individuals succeed only partially, or not at all, in coping with such transitions. Sheehy (1976) even talks in this connection of "crises of adult life".

2.2.3 Doubt as to the primacy of "formal reasoning" in the field of cognitive development

For a long time empirical findings led to the assumption that one of the characteristics of the development of a person is a relatively rapid increase in all kinds of cognitive skills, followed by a steady decrease of those same skills with increasing age (Botwinick, 1967). In particular, Lehman's research (1964) on the relationship between age and creativity in scientific researchers strengthened this view. Refining of research methodology has resulted in a partial revision of this point of view. This in turn resulted in intellectual abilities being generally measured in relation to certain achievements. This incurs the risk that, under certain circumstances, achievements will not be a correct representation of the actual abilities. Circumstances that have a negative effect on a person's performances are: a poor state of health, difficult living conditions, and deficiencies in the education received. These occur more frequently among older people than young people. Moreover, older people in research situations are handicapped by a relatively low speed of reaction and inexperience with psychological methods of measuring (Reese & Rodeheaver, 1985). If one adjusts for these factors, the achievements measured with increasing age remain the same for a long time and a decline in most of the cognitive functions does not set in before the age of 65 or 70, which is of course above the normal age of retirement! (Birren & Bengtson, 1988; Birren & Schaie, 1990; see also Volume 2, Chapter 8 of this Handbook).

Until relatively recently, the emphasis in research into the development of cognitive abilities lay primarily in certain forms of formal, logical reasoning. These are the forms of reasoning that are usually given the greatest priority in the education of young people and that also come most succinctly to full development in one's youth. Each person develops these abilities to his or her own, distinctive level, which can be evaluated by observing the average degree of difficulty of the tasks and problems that the person in question is able to solve. These are also the forms of reasoning that the standard intelligence tests call upon. Research has shown (Labouvie-Vief, 1985) that most people continue to possess these abilities to their own distinctive average level for virtually the whole of their working lives. This is enough for them to cope with their "daily work". However, they are usually only able to attain maximum or peak achievements at a younger age (here too there are exceptions: "stayers" and "late-developers").

In recent years more attention has been paid to higher forms of "coordinating" reasoning, which surpasses this type of "school" intelligence (Commons, 1990; Stevens-Long & Commons, 1992). These are the very forms of reasoning that develop in mature and older people in particular and enable them to make associations between the substance of various types of knowledge and to produce conclusions and generalizations about them. Moreover, more research is being carried out into those forms of functioning of a cognitive content that enable a person to continue to hold his or her own in the broad social context of day-to-day life. Acquiring experience and developing expertise in a multitude of fields play an important part in this. Exposés on this subject may be found, *inter alia*, in Dittmann-Kohli and Baltes (1985), Chi, Glaser, and Farr (1988), Sinnott and Cavanaugh, (1991) and Ericsson and Smith (1991). The interesting thing about these aspects of cognitive functioning is that they continue to develop for many years and that they make it possible to find compensations for decreasing cognitive functions which are, indeed, susceptible to the effects of age (for example certain short-term memories). The development of these higher skills, which are more closely related to life experience, is undervalued by education and society alike, compared to "logical" reasoning. Many people are not given the chance to develop them to an adequate level. Their life situation, for example at work and in their organization, offers too few points of departure and stimuli for this (Boerlijst & Aite-Peña, 1989).

A number of authors (Datan et al., 1987, p. 167; Munnichs, Mussen, Olbrich, & Coleman 1985) point to the plasticity of the functioning of adults and older people that equips them, sometimes better than younger people, to be able to estimate the social implications of solutions to problems value-wise, to think of a variety of solutions for the same problems, to allow their intuitions and feelings to be brought to bear on the problem, and so on. In the same types of area, the development of valid strategies is left to the individual. School, work organizations and society hardly concern themselves with this at all. During the course of their careers, adults and older people have in principle a host of opportunities for carrying on with their own development and coping with new situations (Morrison & Adams, 1991; Morrison & Hock, 1986). They can also find compensations for those abilities and skills that recede with the increase in age. The problem is, however, that up to now little attention has been paid to a conscious and specific stimulation of them—even on the part of the individuals concerned.

3 DEFINITIONS OF CONCEPTS

3.1 The concept "career": a multitude of meanings

Terms such as career, career planning, career guidance and career development are gradually becoming generally accepted. However there is little agreement among (and sometimes also in) organizations about the meaning of these concepts or how they should be given substance. Both in everyday speech as well as in the professional jargon of experts on organization and personnel work, we find a multitude of descriptions. If we are to arrive at a unification of the different career theories that are at present still very disparate, it is in our opinion important to find a way of connecting the different meaning-variants. We have thus far given a survey of general definitions which in principle cover all the common and less-common meaning-variants.

3.2 A coordinating definition for the concepts of "career", "career development" and "career guidance"

We have construed these definitions on the lines of a so-called "facet-analytical model" developed by Louis Guttman and his coworkers (see for structuring definitions Foa, 1965; Levy, 1994). Such a definition should include, in terms as abstract as possible, all logically distinguishable features or facets that implicitly or explicitly play a part in making up the current definitions of a concept. From this coordinating definition, all possible definition-variants can, in principle, be derived. This is achieved by giving various interpretations to the facets referred to in the definition. In other words, every facet represents a collection of interpretations of a particular feature of the concept in question.

A coordinating definition is effected by an

analysis and comparison of different definitions of a concept. To give an example, in a somewhat older definition, a career is described as: "adjustment to the requirements of an occupation" (see Section 2.1). A number of explicit and implicit facets can be distinguished here. These are shown in italics. The term "occupation" denotes a *context* in which the career is exercised. "Requirements" refer to certain *aspects* of the occupation that are found to be *relevant* (that is to say important, essential, functional, or similar). In this definition, the aspects in question and their relevance, thus two facets, are not referred to explicitly. Nevertheless it seems to be assumed that certain aspects in the execution of an occupation are so important that norms of adjustment can be set. The term "adjustment" denotes a *change of position* in one or more variable aspects, in this case a shift in direction of the norms set, from "less adjusted" to "more adjusted". A number of facets have not been specifically mentioned, but are nevertheless assumed. For example the adjustment takes place in a particular *period of time* that may extend over a number of years. Furthermore, it concerns the adjustment of *people or groups who follow or pursue the career*. Not referred to, but none the less very important, is the question as to what point of view a career is examined from, in other words who the *observing agency* is. An employee, for example, observing and describing his or her own career, will often consider different aspects to be important than a manager or board of directors, for example. In the one case, the career is seen from an internal point of view, in the other case from an external position and therefore probably defined or interpreted differently (Campbell & Moses, 1986).

The following coordinating definition is the result of analyses such as these. The various facets are shown in italics and indicated by a letter in bold type.

A career **L** is a representation of the sequence of *successive positions* **S** as ascertained by an *observing agency* **A**, that a *career occupant* **O** has held or acquired within a certain *period of time* **T** on *aspect-variables* **V** that have a certain *relevancy* **R** to a certain *context* **C**.

There are many methodological and meta-theoretical advantages attached to the use of such a form of definition (Runkel & McGrath, 1972). For instance, the structure of the definition contains points of departure for all sorts of plans for empirical research relating to careers. The different facets, indeed, denote all those factors that could be involved in research of this type, whether as peripheral conditions or as independent or dependent variables. It may be useful to describe the career in general as the representation of the logical product of the different facets:

$$\{S \times A \times O \times T \times V \times R \times C\} \rightarrow L$$

This formulation betrays the great complexity of the concept and therefore that of systematically setting up research on the subject. In Section 4 we will discuss briefly the role that the different facets play in the theory and practice of career development and career guidance. First, however, we will give a coordinating definition for both these concepts.

The concept career development has two connotations: (1) the natural development of the career; and (2) the active development of the career. In interpretation (1) "career development" can be defined as the actual realization of the career, **L**. This, therefore, requires no new definition. In interpretation (2), the definition is as follows:

A career development $\mathbf{D_L}$ is a representation of the *interventions* **I** of a *person or body* **B**, geared to the application of *determinants* **D** for the influencing of the *career* **L**, consistent with certain *policy objectives* **P**.

Career guidance is a form of career development as in the second interpretation, because here it involves interventions by a guiding body. No separate definition is therefore required for career guidance.

4 FACETS OF THE CONCEPT "CAREER"

In this Section the various facets of the concept of career **L** (see Section 3.2) will be examined further.

4.1 Career occupants (facet O)

Any specific definition or description of a career requires an identification of the person or persons occupying it. This can be done in two ways: (1) simply by the naming and (2) by a specification of the (possibly varying) characteristics of the person or persons in question.

We refer to an "individual career" in the case of one specific career occupant and of a "collective" or "categorial career" in the case of a group or category of people, whose careers have a number of essential points in common.

4.1.1 *Individual careers*

We must make a distinction between descriptions of individual careers of an idiographic type and those of individual careers of a model type. An example of the first sort is formed by (auto) biographies, descriptions that reflect the specific individuality of the development of the person in a detailed and "true-to-life" manner. The second sort concerns a description whose idiosyncratic outlines have been rubbed out and have been abstracted to such an extent that the individual career of the person in question becomes comparable with that of other people. Organizations are usually more interested in formal descriptions of the latter type, because they enable a comparison to be made between persons. An example of this is the curriculum vitae in connection with a job application. It is, for that matter, curious that organizations often forget to enlighten applicants sufficiently on the frameworks of comparison that the "curricula" to be supplied by them must fit into. Because of this, the probable advantage of easy mutual comparison is lost.

4.1.2 *Categorial careers*

The best-known example of these is probably the "modal" career of a particular occupational group. This assumes that the individual careers of the members of such a group will deviate little one from another.

In a psychological and social respect, the existence of categorial careers has certain advantages. A person can make a specific choice from among the range of careers available and can receive information on the consequences of such a choice career-wise. The preparation (training, education, etc.) for a categorial career can be organized structurally (vocational training for example). An organization knows in advance what it may and can expect of a member of the category concerned, and which career perspective it should offer him or her. A clear division of work is possible. The mutual relationships in terms of status are fixed a priori.

Recently it has become apparent that clear disadvantages are attached to this situation. These have been observed in particular in organizations which must appeal to flexibility, innovative ability and a readiness to change on the part of their management and personnel. Here, the difficulty arises that existing managerial norms and customs pertaining to careers within a categorial occupational group are as a rule not compatible with the versatility deemed to be necessary and which the career occupants in question should in fact manifest. In other words, standard managerial views and prevailing expectations pertaining to a career may contribute to conformism and a certain degree of fossilization (Bakker, 1987).

4.2 Context of a career (facet C)

Every career is associated with a certain situational context, which can be specified in facet **C**. Examples of this are the work organization or the working environment, and also family, relatives, school, friends and acquaintances, community life and so on. Since each individual takes part in different social relationships, he or she is pursuing different careers, usually simultaneously; a family career, a school career, a work career, a social career, and so on. Every social context sets its own requirements and is also subject to its own typical changes. These have consequences for the role behaviour that is expected and required of the participants (Shull & McIntyre, 1984). Following different careers simultaneously calls for multiple forms of actions and reactions from the individual that are often difficult to combine. This may easily result in inner conflicts and stresses, unless people have developed a mainstay in themselves, an identity of their own with a clear course (see the comments in Subsection 2.1.1. on Schein's career anchor-concept; also Buunk, Doosje, Jans, & Hopstaken, 1993). Participation in different social contexts may of course provoke conflicts with the person's environment. In this context, the relationship between family and work in particular deserves attention (Burke, 1986; Jackson, Zedeck, & Summers, 1985; Zedeck, 1992). Super (1986) has devoted a descriptive study to combining roles in work and "spare" time.

4.3 Career aspects (facet V) and their contextual relevance (facet R)

Facet **V**, the collective career aspects, is a co-element along with facets **S** and **T** still to be discussed, which together form the core of the career concept. Facet **V** covers all variable dimensions on which an individual may hold variable positions or values (**S**) in the course of time (**T**). These aspects or dimensions are referred to in every definition or description of a career. Normally however, some kind of restriction is applied to them. The choice of aspects, the interpretation and the weight given to each of them, very much depend on the context in which the career takes place. In a family career, for example, one aspect of interest will be the degree of attachment to the parents; in a work career, this attachment will as a rule play no part.

An aspect that is a factor in virtually every career context is the variable position of the career occupant in the contextual structure (the position in the family, in the organization, in society, and so on). The substance of the meaning or interpretation of such a pluricontextual aspect may vary greatly, not only between the different contexts, but also within them. As far as the latter is concerned, let us take the aspect "mobility" as an example. In a bureaucratic organization, mobility will often be interpreted in company-hierarchical or geographical terms (the faster a person can rise up a hierarchical ladder or the greater the variety of countries he or she can work in successively, the more mobile he or she is). In a dynamic organization geared to innovation, decisiveness, competitive power, and such like, the tendency will be to think of mobility as its horizontal variant (being able to carry out different functions in the organization at one and the same level within a certain period), or mental mobility (being capable of keeping pace with different kinds of changes in objectives or ways of working). In some of these types of organizations, mobility will probably be understood in a motivational sense (the will or the readiness of a person to change his or her position many times).

In any career definition, therefore, a more detailed explanation of facet **V** must be provided. Different career types can never simply be treated as if they were alike. We can never refer to the career of anyone, if we do not know what variable aspects have been allowed for and what interpretations should be ascribed to it.

Not all aspects play an equally important part in a career. Some are more significant or relevant for the (continuing) existence of the social context in question than others. In the course of time, there may also be a change of relevance in respect of the relative or absolute value of a particular career aspect. An example of this is the status-hierarchy dimension. In its original "bureaucratic" sense, status has, in the course of time, lost relevance in many organizations. For a correct understanding of a career in a particular context, we should also have a correct picture of the contextual relevance of the aspects included in facet **V**. This contextual relevance is specified in facet **R**.

4.4 Career dynamics: time (facet T) and change of position (facet S)

An essential element of the career concept is the fact of its being both time- and duration-bound (facet **T**). A career has a beginning and an end in time. Within this period occur the successive registrations of the positions that a person holds on different aspect variables. The results of these full-time registrations are included in facet **S**.

Facet **S**, then, comprises the results of what takes place in the career, what developments the career occupant experiences, what actions he or she undertakes, what interactions and transactions with his or her environment the person becomes involved in, and so on.

Each of these registrations takes place at a certain point in time. This necessitates a certain time reference. There are a number of possibilities for this. Facet **T** comprises the specification of the time references that have been used in a particular definition or description of a career. We shall now summarize some of these possibilities. As more or less neutral time references, calendar time and the age of the career occupant may be denoted. A less neutral reference is the so-called "historical time" in which the career evolves. This refers to historical, time-bound events and circumstances in the context, which have a normative influence on the career of all the contemporaries in that context (London & Wueste, 1992). An example of this is the description of careers in an organization by means of the points in time at which fundamental reorganizations or changes in the prevailing context have occurred. These points in time may be indicated not only in years but also in terms of significant events (for example a change in the board of directors, or the takeover of the company). A time reference of an entirely different nature is bio-psychosocial time. Here, the emphasis is placed on those points in time at which particular fundamental changes in the pattern of life of each person occur, to a varying degree independent of that person's historical context. This time reference is used in surveys on careers, in which a division into "natural" age-bound phases is assumed (see Levinson, 1986). Finally, a time reference allied to this is "the subjective experience of time", by means of which a career occupant divides his or her own career or life into periods.

The description of an actual career is based primarily on combinations of the facets **V**, **S** and **T**.

4.5 Career observers (facet A)

Careers are defined or described from the viewpoint of a particular observer. Usually this observer or observing agency has a particular business or personal interest in the career in question. In the case of work careers, a distinction is usually made between the so-called "external" career, that is the career as seen and defined from the managerial point of view (Campbell & Moses, 1986), and the "internal" career as it is described and experienced by a career occupant. It is self-evident that the "external" and the "internal" careers of one and the same career occupant may diverge considerably. This could be a source of conflicts between the career occupant and his or her environment. Any form of career guidance should take into account the possibility of such differences of opinion. It sometimes even happens, for instance in a job application, that the career occupant describes his or her own career as an outsider, thus adopting an external viewpoint.

4.6 Career theory and career determinants (facet D)

Every career theory tries to provide explanations for what goes on within the province of careers. The explanatory factors are referred to as "career determinants". These are specified in facet **D**. A distinction should be made between outer- and inner-contextual determinants. In a school career, there may, for example, be a sudden change of course, owing to an earthquake or the outbreak of war (outer-contextual). A change of course can also occur as a consequence of a change in performance on the part of the career occupant (inner-contextual). Inner-contextual determinants may sometimes correspond to certain facets of the career **L** itself. In the example given here, the quality of the career occupant's performance may on the one hand form a characteristic aspect of his or her career. On the other hand that same performance may influence the next period in the career occupant's career. The performance belongs, therefore, within the provinces of both facet **V** and facet **D**, but has a different role in each.

5 INFLUENCING OF CAREERS IN THE PRACTICAL SITUATION

In practice, "career development" and "career guidance" are performed via interventions by people or agencies. These interventions are aimed at the application of certain career determinants (see Section 4.6) and the realization of certain policy objectives.

5.1 Career policy (facet P)

There are three forms of policy that should be borne in mind in career development or career guidance in the practical situation. Analogous to the distinction already made between "internal" and "external" careers, we can also distinguish "internal policy" (1) and "external policy" (2 and 3):

1. An "internal or personal career policy" of the career occupant refers to objectives that

the career occupant is striving to attain personally.

2. An "external or institutional career policy, tailored to the individual" refers to career objectives of the organization that the career occupant is a part of, but in which the specific possibilities, needs and interests of the individual career occupant have also, to a certain extent, been allowed for.
3. An "external or institutional, supra-personal career policy" refers to a policy that is geared to a whole category of career followers, in which the main objectives of personnel policy aspired to by the organization are expressed.

Many activities in the area of "management development", "education and training", and such like are the result of suprapersonal policy. Occasionally career occupants do not deem such activities to be adequate and would prefer to see a different, more personal approach. In such a case, it is a short step to a discussion being started about who "is actually responsible" for the career; the organization or the individual, or both (Bolyard, 1981). Hall (1976) gives a list of strategies that the organization and the career occupant may follow in order to arrive at what he terms "more effective careers". He warns, and rightly so, against the parties involved sometimes taking too little account of the fact that the future of an organization is very difficult to predict. We ourselves were given to understand in (unpublished) conversations with personnel officials from a multinational company, that career plans drawn up by them often exceeded the maximum possible planning term of their company segment by many years. Hall (1976) also observes that career interventions may result in mounting, though unreal, expectations pertaining to career possibilities. Frustrations may run high if those expectations are not fulfilled.

5.2 Career interventions (facet I)

A lot is being published on intervention possibilities for career influencing. Reviews of these can be found in Hall and Goodale (1986), Walsh and Osipow (1990), Spokane (1991), and Montross and Shinkman (1992). Exposés by Hall (1976) and Burck and Reardon (1984) are instructive for those involved in career guidance. Hall devotes ample attention to the possibility of stimulating the career occupant to plan and steer their own career, as a supplement to career planning and career guidance on the part of the organization. As is the case in careers and career policy, we can therefore differentiate between "external" and "internal" interventions. A combination of both provides a good opportunity for increasing the effectiveness of a work career.

5.3 Instruments and aids

5.3.1 Tests and questionnaires

In the framework of career planning and career guidance in the different phases of a person's lifetime, interest tests may prove a great help. So-called "career interest questionnaires" have been developed in the framework of occupational and career choice. Those most used are the Strong-Campbell Interest Inventory, the Kuder Occupational Interest Survey, the Jackston Vocational Interest Survey and the Self-Directed Search (SDS) by Holland (1985b). Psychometrically speaking, the quality of these tests is satisfactory. In general, however, the structure of these instruments lacks an explicit theoretical foundation, except in the case of SDS. The latter is based on Holland's theory (1985a), which assumes that certain personality types are drawn to specific work and occupational climates and that they feel more at home there than in other occupations (Gottfredson, Jones, & Holland, 1993). Holland therefore looks on interest questionnaires as personality tests. An affinity of some Strong-Campbell scales with personality tests has been demonstrated in the meantime. This appears to be in line with Holland's theory (Johnson, Flammer, & Nelson, 1975).

Measured vocational interests do not only reflect an orientation towards occupational environments, social climates, and such like. Our own research (Boerlijst, 1974) made the idea plausible that such interest measurements are also related to preferences for certain existing work "packages" within a company or for certain function areas. In the framework of the theories discussed earlier from the circles of Super and others, Helbing has designed a self-discovery test called the "Personal and Role Characteristics Test" (Helbing, 1987). For the determination of one's own "career anchor" (see Subsection 2.1.1.) Schein (1978) has compiled a "Career Anchor Self-analysis Form". Apart from tests and questionnaires, there are also many kinds of exercises and games to promote "insight into oneself" (see Hall, 1976, p. 182 for references).

5.3.2 Training

Training is probably the main aid in influencing careers. A discussion of this subject can be found elsewhere in this Volume (see Chapter 9). Relevant to our theme are the surveys of Wexley and Latham (1991) on "human resources" training and development, by Wexley (1984, p. 543), and Brislin and Yoshida (1994) on "cross-cultural" training, for example by means of job rotation or "sabbaticals" taken in a completely different environment, or via preparation for a new career. In connection with the discussion on the meaning of "learning by experience" for cognitive development, it would probably be useful to start a debate on the question as to whether current training methods in organizations make sufficient use of these opportunities for development (see Subsection 2.2.3).

5.3.3 Computer systems to aid career management and career planning

Since the 1970s, many kinds of computer-controlled systems have been developed, containing a wealth of easily accessible information to aid career choice, career development and career guidance. They were, in fact, designed especially for use by schoolchildren and students and their application in industry is still very limited.

Such systems can be divided into two categories:

1. Occupation information systems, which comprise a variety of information on occupations regarding content and functioning, such as: the required training programmes available, work situations that one may come across, jobs and positions available in different organizations, salary scales and possible developments in them, possible professional career paths, etc.
2. Career development information systems, for the purposes of interpretation and evaluations of needs, interests, attitudes and aspirations of prospective career occupants, in terms of career opportunities within existing occupations or occupation families.

In a number of countries, for example the USA and Canada, extensive information banks and programs have been developed for nationwide use. Most of these are, in fact, a combination of the previously mentioned two categories. Some of them permit interactive communication between the system and the users. The acquired information can then be tailored to fit the person in question. More detailed information on this can be found in Minor (1986), Peterson, Sampson, and Reardon (1991) and Peterson and Ryan-Jones (1994). It is likely that with the boom in "personal computers" the area of application of such information systems will be extended quite considerably. A correct interpretation is absolutely dependent on the inclusion of occupation or career advisers' expertise regarding the information system's program. In this way, the system can act as an "external expert system", accessible to the lay person.

What is, then, the value of such information systems in the whole career issue? There is no simple answer to this. Recommendations are given by Forrer and Leibowitz (1991). There are many snags in the development and use of such instruments in a methodological sense (Boerlijst, 1987a). The existing systems have invariably been developed for purposes other than career guidance and the like (Van Rienen, 1983) and within this context, cannot be used at all, or at any rate less effectively. In many cases there has often been a disregard for scientifically acceptable rules of system design, as described by Roe (1986) and others. Moreover, the norms for validity and reliability are not taken seriously. In an ideal situation, an occupation or information system is geared to providing as correct and reliable as possible an understanding of the actual processes involved in the pursuance of occupations or functions. Such a system "represents" the reality of the pursuance of the occupation or function. The realms of "reality" which, theoretically, should be "represented" by the information system are, however, remarkably complex and obscure as a rule. This makes it virtually impossible to observe and describe the aggregate of relevant relations within the empirical system. Representative models and measurements can generally not be realized. So-called "indexing" methods and measurements are then usually resorted to (Dawes, 1972). Indexing systems do not claim to give a simulation or accurate portrayal of the empirical system. Their intention is only to generate data that will enable reasonably accurate predictions to be made pertaining to the procedures within that system. Such data are often recorded in the form of "indices", which accounts for the term "indexing information systems".

Nearly all existing occupation and function information systems are, in this sense, indexing. In practice, however, indexing systems very often come into being intuitively, that is to say without any underlying theory as a point of departure. In such cases, the indices in question should not be trusted. If we look at systems available on the market, we find many more information systems dealing with occupations than with functions or positions in organizations. In designing the latter, one is presumably confronted with the difficulty that functions and positions are usually not invariant. Occupations generally have a more stable structure. It is noteworthy that in most of the available systems, the dynamic characteristic of occupations and functions in practice is not at all evident. This problem is encountered in the case of information systems to aid MD, for example in a "register of interests". An additional problem is the fact that such systems tend to become quickly out of date (see Section 1.2).

6 SOME DEVELOPMENTS TO BE EXPECTED

During recent years, things have become somewhat quieter on the front of theory development pertaining to careers. It may well be a case of consolidation. However, developments can again be expected in the not too distant future. There are sufficient reasons to suppose this.

In the first place, the use of very sophisticated, flexible computerized information and production systems in organizations (see Section 1.2) requires a thorough reconsideration of the part to be played by human labour and human thinking, and, in addition, a reconsideration of the content of tasks and careers. On the one hand, it is likely that a great number of traditional and relatively highly-qualified jobs will disappear with the arrival of computer systems. On the other hand, these call for a complicated mental effort in terms of command and control, which, in turn, gives rise to a need for new forms of highly flexible and creative labour tasks. The traditional applications of hierarchically organized, functionally divided work within organizations, going back to Taylor's principles of scientific management, will have to be drastically reconsidered if our society is to maintain its versatility and productivity (see Kern & Schumann, 1984).

In the second place, the next half century will be characterized by fundamental shifts in demographic relations in our hemisphere. The consequence of this will be a gradual ageing of the working population, hitherto unknown (Boerlijst, 1987b; also Chapter 8, Volume 2 of this Handbook).

In the third place, we can expect women to enter the labour market in increasing numbers.

London and Stumpf (1986) referred to a number of trends which called for a new orientation within the theory and practice of career development in the future and which are partly related to or are the result of the points outlined here. Nowadays these points are still relevant. They are:

1. More and different kinds of specialists with different values, career insights, and technical languages.
2. More people working away from the traditional office setting.
3. More flexible approaches to work (such as flexible hours, job sharing, and part-time employment).
4. Decreased loyalty to companies (people will change jobs and careers more often).
5. Formal organizational structures giving way to project teams, task forces, matrix structures, and interdependent units.

6. An increasing need to train and retrain people at different career stages in order to maintain job security.
7. Changes in how people relate to each other (for instance, communication via computer lacks nonverbal cues and displays no emotions).
8. More collaborative and cooperative work, including involvement in decision making (see Hall, 1992).
9. Pressure to increase job satisfaction by changing job content." (London & Stumpf, 1986, p. 25).

6.1 Careers in an ageing society

The relative ageing of the working population, not only in many countries of Western Europe but also in the USA, Canada, and in Japan, is beginning to attract the attention of policy makers. In Japan in particular, both the government and the business community have already become aware that an end should come to the low productivity of older employees and the no-longer working, if this group—as such representing a major part of those still in possession of great purchasing power—is not to lapse into a state of poverty (Boerlijst, 1987b). A research institute, sponsored by the Japanese government, is engaged in application-oriented research into the specific ways for older people to keep mentally and physically fit and to slow down the process of degeneration (Boerlijst, Van Dijk, & Van Helvoort, 1987). A few of the large Japanese companies have incorporated their employees' transition to "growing old" in a career guidance programme. Their measures vary, but include:

- Preparation for a "second" career after their 45th year. The new career path seen not as an extension of that of younger employees but one that can be embarked on precisely because of the previous experience of the older person concerned.
- "Outplacement" of the over-45s to businesses of small or medium-sized supply companies, insofar as those suppliers are in need of qualified and experienced middle management.
- Employment in a business unit within the company specially created for older people, intended for the renovation of complicated products or systems produced by those employees at an earlier stage in their career.

Obviously, the maintenance of productivity and efforts of the older people concerned is a particularly stubborn problem, because classical culture patterns have to be broken. Although the Japanese organization culture does have certain advantages in this respect over that of Western Europe and the USA, including the salary system, in which the level of the salary is determined to a great extent by the length of service (Ministry of Labour, Japan, 1985), and much less by the position held), it is to be recommended that the solutions being sought in Japan are not disregarded. We, too, will have to search for effective means to keep the vitality of the working community at as high a level as possible. An increase in the impoverishment of society may well be avoidable. However, in order to achieve this, in the first decade of the next century, organizations will have to make a much greater appeal to their employees than at present. We must ensure that young people are, and continue to be, equipped for this by offering them a wide range of learning experience and expertise (Boerlijst & Aite-Peña, 1989; see also Subsection 2.2.3.) Experience teaches us that "if the dominant life activities of a given person do not contain a sufficient amount of cognitive demands and supports, cognitive structures and functions will tend to regress" (Dittmann-Kohli & Baltes, 1985). It will also be advisable to investigate exactly why there is still an increasing trend in our society to push older people out of the production process. It is likely that it could be a question of a collection of stereotyped views, which perceive an incompatibility between growing older and innovation or progress. Finally, it should be considered whether it is not possible to remove the mental or physical blockages that people experience sometimes all too early, but as a rule in the middle of their career, feeling themselves confined and in a dead end (Sinick, 1984). This phenomenon is mostly designated as "mid-life crisis".

6.2 Careers and changing man-woman relations

In the next few decades a structural shortage of well-qualified young people is likely to arise in our organizations in connection with the demographic development just referred to. One of the possible solutions to this "dejuvenization issue" is an increase in the number of women entering the production process (Sekaran, 1992). In a certain sense, women are a new phenomenon in the labour market, insofar as they are at present applying for the sort of function and position that used to be occupied almost exclusively by men. We may presume that a considerable number of research projects and theories in this area will have to be repeated or revised, because most of them are related almost exclusively to men (Stromberg & Harkess, 1988). The position of women and their opportunities in the labour market and within organizations are less favourable for them than for men, but there are nevertheless changes in the air (Meulders, 1993). The status of women, especially that of younger women, is slowly gaining recognition in many areas of work. In many countries where most work is traditionally done by men, women find themselves in a difficult situation. They often experience unpleasant treatment and a lack of incentives in their work and career (Ott, 1985; Van Doorne-Huiskes, 1986). Gibbons and Murphy (1991) stress the relevance of making optimal incentive contracts in the presence of career concerns.

Although anti-discrimination acts guarantee their income position to be similar to that of comparable male workers, in practice women are still less well off. This is of course a de-motivating factor for entering the labour-market (Blau & Ferber, 1990; Ferber, 1987). But still, changes in national opinion and attitude are beginning to take place. For instance in The Netherlands in 1965 only 16% of the population accepted the idea of "working mothers". In 1975 this percentage had already risen to 56% (De Rijk, 1984). Here, as in many other countries, there is a steady increase in the number of "dual-career" families, in which both husband and wife work (Sekaran, 1986). Another change concerns the occupation and study choice made by women. This is moving more and more in the direction of traditional male occupations (Blau & Ferber, 1985), though this change is slow in gathering momentum. Women are still avoiding the technical courses of study, and new subjects such as information technology are not attracting much attention on the part of women (Davidson & Cooper, 1987).

It is, in the meantime, a fact that more men than women are ending up in newly-created occupations. The entry of women into management functions is progressing slowly and laboriously (Davidson & Cooper, 1993). MD programmes usually take too little account of the specific difficulties of, and problems experienced by, women (Bennett, 1986). Practically all the studies existing on the subject of women in management positions emphasize the difficulties experienced by them in connection with segregation, discrimination, underpayment, lack of understanding of the family situation, preconceptions, and so on (Ferber & O'Farrell, 1991). The paradox is clear: half of the human race is treated as if it were a minority. The signs are becoming manifest that a change in that minority position is on the way, as is evident from the annual review on "women and work" (Larwood, Stromberg & Gutek, 1985), studies on the careers and career development of women appear nowadays with great regularity.

NOTE

[1] The author kindly acknowledges Anjelica Aite-Peña for her great help in searching literature for the 1989 version of this review, published in the First Edition of this *Handbook*.

REFERENCES

Adler, S., & Aranya, N. (1984). A comparison of the work needs, attitudes, and preferences of professional accountants at different career stages. *Journal of Vocational Behavior*, *25*, 45–57.

Arthur, M.B., Hall, D.T., & Lawrence, B.S. (Eds.) (1989). *Handbook of career theory*. Cambridge: Cambridge University Press.

Bakker, B.A. (1987). *Benutting van competenties van Werktuigbouw-MTS-ers in Philips' Machinefabriek M bij de doorvoering van flexibele produktieautomatisering* [Utilizing competences of technical school mechanical engineering pupils at Philips' engineering factory M, in the implementation of flexible production automation]. Study report. Enschede: University of Twente.

Benner, P.E. (1984). *Stress and satisfaction on the job: Work meanings and coping of mid-career men*. New York: Praeger.

Bennett, R. (1986). How performance appraisals hurt women managers. *Women in Management Review*, 2.
Bennett, R. (1992). *Dictionary of personnel and human resources management*. London: Pitman.
Birren, J.E., & Bengtson, V.L. (Eds.) (1988). *Emergent theories of aging*. New York: Springer.
Birren, J.E., & Schaie, K.W. (Eds.) (1990). *Handbook of the psychology of aging* (2nd Edn.). San Diego: Academic Press.
Blau, F.D., & Ferber, M.A. (1985). Women in the labor market: The last twenty years. In L. Larwood, A.H. Stromberg, & B.A. Gutek (Eds.), *Women and work: An annual review* (Vol. 1.) Beverley Hills, CA: Sage.
Blau, F.D., & Ferber, M.A. (1990). *Career plans and expectations of young women and men: The earnings gap and labor force participation*. Cambridge, MA: NBER.
Boerlijst, J.G. (1974). *Werk met perspectief: Instrumentontwikkeling ten behoeve van functie-en loopbaanonderzoek*. [Work with a perspective: Development of instruments in aid of job position- and career research]. Amsterdam: Academische Pers.
Boerlijst, J.G. (1987a). *De beoordeling van beroepen-en functie-informatiesystemen*. [The assessment of career-and function information systems]. Report commissioned by the Stichting Leerplanontwikkeling. Enschede: University of Twente.
Boerlijst, J.G. (1987b). Veroudering van de beroepsbevolking in Nederland en Japan. [Ageing of the working population in Holland and in Japan]. *Cahiers Biowetenschappen en Maatschappij*, *11*, 3.
Boerlijst, J.G., & Aite-Peña, A. (1989). *Does the ageing of the working population really pose a threat?* Paper presented at the 4th West European Congress on The Psychology of Work and Organisation, Cambridge (UK), April.
Boerlijst, G., Dijk, N. van, & Helvoort, E. van (1987). Japans personeelsbeleid en de oudere werknemer [Japanese personnel policy and the older employee]. *M&O, Journal for Organization Theory and Social Policy*, *41*, 338–350.
Boerlijst, G., & Meijboom, G. (1989). Matching the individual and the organisation. In P. Herriot (Ed.), *Assessment and selection in organizations* (pp. 25–44). London: Wiley.
Boerlijst, J.G., Smit, E.A., & Vermeulen, J. (1987). *De aansluitingsproblematiek tussen het hoger onderwijs (technisch universitair en –beroepsonderwijs) en de telecommunicatie-sector* [Problems of linking higher education and the telecommunication sector]. Final report commissioned by FME Netelcom and PTT Telecommunicatie. Enschede: University of Twente.
Bolyard, C.W. (1981). Career development: Who's responsible in the organization. In D.H. Montross, & C.J. Shinkman (Eds.), *Career development in the 1980s: Theory and practice* (pp. 292–299). Springfield, IL: Thomas.
Botwinick, J. (1967). *Cognitive processes in maturity and old age*. New York: Springer.
Brislin, R.W., & Yoshida, T. (Eds.) (1994). *Improving intercultural interactions: Modules for cross-cultural training programs*. Thousand Oaks, CA: Sage.
Burck, H.D., & Reardon, R.C. (1984). *Career development interventions*. Springfield, IL: Thomas.
Burke, R.J. (1986). Occupational and life stress and the family: Conceptual frameworks and research findings. *International Review of Applied Psychology*, *35*, 347–369.
Buunk, B.P., Doosje, B.J., Jans, L.G.J.M., & Hopstaken, L.E.M. (1993). Perceived reciprocity, social support, and stress at work: The role of exchange and communal orientation. *Journal of Personality and Social Psychology*, *65*, 801–811.
Campbell, R.J., & Moses, J.L. (1986). Careers from an organizational perspective. In D.T. Hall (Ed.), *Career development in organizations* (pp. 274–309). London: Jossey-Bass.
Cascio, W.F. (1991). Applied psychology in personnel management (4th Edn). Englewood Cliffs, N.J: Prentice-Hall.
Chi, M.T.H., Glaser, R., & Farr, M.J. (1988). *The nature of expertise*. Hillsdale, N.J: Lawrence Erlbaum Associates Inc.
Commons, M.L. (Ed.) (1990). *Adult development*. (Presentations made at the Beyond Formal Operations Conference 2: The Development of Adolescent and Adult Thought and Perception Symposium, held at Harvard University). New York: Praeger.
Crites, J.O. (1981). *Career counseling: Models, methods, and materials*. New York: McGraw-Hill.
Datan, N., Rodeheaver, D., & Hughes, F. (1987). Adult development and aging. *Annual Review of Psychology*, *38*, 153–180.
Davidson, M.J., & Cooper, C.L. (Eds.) (1987). *Women and information technology*. Chichester: Wiley.
Davidson, M.J., & Cooper, C.L. (1993). *European women in business and management*. London: Chapman.
Dawes, R.M. (1972). *Fundamentals of attitude measurement*. New York: Wiley.
Dawis, R.V., & Lofquist, L.H. (1984). *A psychological theory of work adjustment*. Minneapolis: University of Minnesota Press.
Dawis, R.V., & Lofquist, L.H. (1993). From TWA to PEC. *Journal of Vocational Behavior*, *43*, 113–121.
Dittmann-Kohli, F., & Baltes, P.B. (1985). Toward a neofunctionalist conception of adult intellectual development: Wisdom as a prototypical case of intellectual growth. In C. Alexander, E. Langer, & M. Oetzel (Eds.), *Higher stages of human development: Adult growth beyond formal operations*. New York: Oxford University Press.

Doorne-Huiskes, J. van (1986). *Loopbanen van vrouwen en mannen* [Careers of women and men]. Utrecht: Institute of Sociology.

Drenth, P.J.D., Thierry, H., Willems, P.J., & Wolff, C.J. de (Eds.) (1984). *Handbook of Work and Organizational Psychology*. New York: Wiley.

Ericsson, K.A., & Smith, J. (1991). *Toward a general theory of expertise: Prospects and limits*. Cambridge: Cambridge University Press.

Ferber, M.A. (1987). *Women and work, paid and unpaid: A selected, annotated bibliography*. New York: Garland.

Ferber, M.A., & O'Farrell, B. (Eds.) (1991). *Work and family: Policies for a changing workforce*. Washington: National Academy Press.

Foa, U.G. (1965). New developments in facet design and development. *Psychological Review, 72*, 262–274.

Forrer, S.E., & Leibowitz, Z.B. (Eds.) (1991). *Using computers in human resources: How to select and to make the best use of automated HR systems*. San Francisco: Jossey-Bass.

Freeman, M. (1993). *Rewriting the self: History, memory, narrative*. London: Routledge.

Gattiker, U.E., & Larwood, L. (Eds.) (1988). *Managing technological development: Strategies and human resources issues*. Berlin: de Gruyter.

Gibbons, R., & Murphy, K.J. (1991). *Optimal incentive contracts in the presence of career concerns: Theory and evidence*. Cambridge, MA: NBER.

Gottfredson, L.S., Jones, E.M., & Holland, J.L. (1993). Personality and vocational interests: The relation of Holland's six interest dimensions to five robust dimensions of personality. *Journal of Counseling Psychology, 40*, 518–523.

Gutteridge, T.G., Leibowitz, Z.B., & Shore, J.E. (1993). *Organizational career development: Benchmarks for building a world-class workforce*. San Francisco: Jossey-Bass.

Hall, D.T. (1976). *Careers in organizations*. Santa Monica, CA: Goodyear.

Hall, D.T. (1986a). An overview of current career development theory, research, and practice. In D.T. Hall (Ed.), *Career development in organizations* (pp. 1–20). London: Jossey-Bass.

Hall, D.T. (1986b). Breaking career routines: Midcareer choice and identity development. In D.T. Hall (Ed.), *Career development in organizations* (pp. 120–159). London: Jossey-Bass.

Hall, D.T. (1992). Career indecision research: Conceptual and methodological. *Journal of Vocational Behavior, 41*, 245–250.

Hall, D.T., & Goodale, J.G. (1986). *Human resource management: Strategy, design, and implementation*. Glenview, IL: Scott Foresman.

Helbing, H. (1987). *The self in career development*. Ph.D. thesis. Amsterdam: author.

Hodgetts, R.M.L., & Kroeck, K.G. (1992). *Personnel and human resources management*. Fort Worth, TX: Dryden Press.

Holland, J.L. (1985a). *Making vocational choices*. Englewood Cliffs, N.J: Prentice-Hall.

Holland, J.L. (1985b). The self-directed search: professional manual. Odessa, FL: Psychological Assessment Resourcing.

Holland, J.L., Magoon, T.M., & Spokane, A.R. (1981). Counseling psychology: Career interventions, research and theory. *Annual Review of Psychology, 32*, 279–305.

Hunter, S., & Sundel, M. (Eds.) (1989). *Midlife myths: Issues, findings and practice implications*. Newbury Park, CA: Sage

Jackson, S.E., Zedeck, S., & Summers, E. (1985). Family life disruptions: Effects of job-induced structural and emotional interference. *Academy of Management Journal, 28*, 574–586.

Jacques, E. (1965). Death and the mid-life crisis. *International Journal of Psycho-analysis, 41*, 502–514.

Janssen, P.P.M. (1992). *Relatieve deprivatie in de middenloopbaanfase bij hoger opgeleide mannen* [Relative deprivation in the middle phase of the career of highly educated men]. Maastricht: Universitaire Pers.

Johnson, R.W., Flammer, D.P., & Nelson, J.J. (1975). Multiple correlations between personality factors and SVIB occupational scales. *Journal of Counseling Psychology, 22*, 217–223.

Kalish, R.A. (Ed.) (1989). *Midlife loss: Coping strategies*. Newbury Park, CA: Sage.

Kastenbaum, R. (Ed.) (1993). *Encyclopedia of adult development*. Phoenix, AZ: Oryx Press.

Katchadourian, H. (1987). *Fifty: Midlife in perspective*. New York: Freeman.

Kern, H., & Schumann, M. (1984). *Das Ende der Arbeitsteilung? Rationalisierung in der industriellen produktion: Bestandsaufnahme, trend-bestimmung*. München: Beck.

Kolb, D.A. (1984). *Experience as the source of learning and development*. Englewood Cliffs, NJ: Prentice-Hall.

Labouvie-Vief, G. (1985). Intelligence and cognition. In J.E. Birren, & K.W. Schaie (Eds.), *Handbook of the psychology of aging* (2nd Edn, pp. 500–530). New York: Van Nostrand Reinhold.

Larwood, L., Stromberg, A.H., & Gutek, B.A. (Eds.) (1985). *Women and work: An annual review* (Vol. 1). Beverley Hills, CA: Sage.

Lehman, N.C. (1964). The relationship between chronological age and high level research output in physics and chemistry. *Journal of Gerontology, 19*, 157–164.

Lengnick-Hall, C.A., & Lengnick-Hall, M.L. (1990). *Interactive human resource management and strategic planning*. New York: Quorum.

Levinson, D.J. (1978). *The seasons of a man's life.* New York: Knopf.

Levinson, D.J. (1986). A conception of adult development. *American Psychologist, 41*, 3–13.

Levy, S. (Ed.) (1994). *Louis Guttman on theory and methodology: Selected writings.* Aldershot: Dartmouth Publishing Co.

London, M., & Stumpf, S.A. (1986). Individual and organizational career development in changing times. In D.T. Hall (Ed.), *Career development in organizations* (pp. 21–49). London: Jossey-Bass.

London, M., & Wueste, R.A. (1992). *Human resources in changing organizations.* New York: Quorum Books.

Maanen, J. van (1977). Experiencing organization: Notes on the meaning of careers and socialization. In J. van Maanen (Ed.), *Organizational careers: Some new perspectives* (pp. 15–48). New York: Wiley.

Meulders, D. (1993). *Position of women on the labour market in the European Community.* Aldershot: Dartmouth Publishing Co.

Ministry of Labour, Japan (1985). *Yearbook of labour statistics, 1983.* Policy Planning and Research Department, Tokyo: Minister's Secretariat.

Minor, F.J. (1986). Computer applications in career development planning. In D.T. Hall (Ed.), *Career development in organizations* (pp. 202–235). London: Jossey-Bass.

Montross, D.H., & Shinkman, C.J. (Eds.) (1992). *Career development: Theory and practice.* Springfield, IL: Thomas.

Morrison, R.F., & Adams, J. (Eds.) (1991). *Contemporary career development issues.* Hillsdale NJ: Laurence Erlbaum Associates Inc.

Morrison R.F., & Hock, R.R. (1986). Career building: Learning from cumulative work experience. In D.T. Hall (Ed.), *Career development in organizations* (pp. 236–273). London: Jossey-Bass.

Mulder, M., Romiszowski, A.J., & Sijde, P.C. van der (Eds.) (1990). *Strategic human resource development.* Amsterdam: Swets & Zeitlinger.

Munnichs, J., Mussen, P., Olbrich, E., & Coleman, P. (Eds.) (1985). *Life-span and change in a gerontological perspective.* New York: Academic Press.

Neugarten, B.L. (1984). Interpretive social science and research on aging. In A. Rossi (Ed.), *Gender and the life course.* Chicago: Aldine.

Osipow, S.H. (1983). *Theories of career development* (3rd Edn.). Englewood Cliffs, NJ: Prentice-Hall.

Ott, M. (1985). *Assepoesters en kroonprinsen: Een onderzoek naar de minderheidspositie van agentes en verpleegsters* [Cinderellas and crown princes: Research into the minority position of policewomen and nurses]. Doctoral thesis. Amsterdam: University of Amsterdam.

Peterson, G.W., Ryan-Jones, R.E. (1994). A comparison of the effectiveness of three computer assisted career guidance systems: DISCOVER, SIGI and SIGI PLUS. *Computers in human behavior, 10*, 189–198.

Peterson, G.W., Sampson, J.P., & Reardon, R.C. (1991). *Career development and services: A cognitive approach.* Pacific Grove, CA: Brooks/Cole.

Reese, H.W., & Rodeheaver, D. (1985). Problem solving and complex decision making. In J.E. Birren, & K.W. Schaie (Eds.), *Handbook of the psychology of aging* (2nd Edn, pp. 474–499). New York: Van Nostrand Reinhold.

Rienen, G.L.M. van (1983). *Beroepeninformatie en onderwijsprogrammering* [Occupational information and educational programing]. Rapport AN I.104.2986. Enschede: Stichting voor de Leerplanontwikkeling.

Rijk, T. de (1984). Women at work in Holland. In M.J. Davidson & C.L. Cooper (Eds.), *Working women: An international survey.* New York: Wiley.

Rodeheaver, D., & Datan, N. (1985). Gender and the vicissitudes of motivation in adult life. In M.L. Kleiber & M.L. Maehr (Eds.), *Advances in motivation and achievement*, (Vol. 4, *Motivation and adulthood*, pp. 169–187). Greenwich, CT: JAI Press.

Roe, R.A. (1986). *A technological view on personnel selection.* Invited lecture: Colegio Official de Psicólogos de Madrid. Delft: Technische Universiteit.

Rothwell, S. (Ed.) (1991). *Strategic planning for human resources.* Oxford: Pergamon Press.

Runkel, P.J., & McGrath, J.E. (1972). *Research on human behavior: A systematic guide to method.* New York: Holt, Rinehart & Winston.

Schein, E.H. (1978). *Career dynamics: Matching individual and organizational needs.* Reading, MA: Addison-Wesley.

Schein, E.H. (1984). Culture as an environmental context for careers. *Journal of Occupational Behaviour, 5*, 71–81.

Schein, E.H. (1986). A critical look at current career development theory and research. In Hall D.T. (Ed.), *Career development in organizations* (pp. 310–331). London: Jossey-Bass.

Sekaran, U. (1986). *Dual career families: Contemporary organizational and counseling issues.* San Francisco: Jossey-Bass.

Sekaran, U. (Ed.) (1992). *Womanpower: Managing in times of demographic turbulence.* Newbury Park, CA: Sage.

Sheehy, G. (1976). *Passages: Predictable crises of adult life.* New York: Dutton.

Sherman, E. (1987). *Meaning in mid-life transitions.* Albany, NY: State University of New York Press.

Shull, F.A., & McIntyre, J.R. (1984). Organizational role differentiation and individual propensity for role changes. In V.L. Allen & E. van de Vliert (Eds.), *Role transitions: Exploration and explanation.* New York: Plenum.

Sinick, D. (1984). Problems of work and retirement for an aging population. In N. Gysbers (Ed.), *Designing careers* (pp. 532–557). San Francisco: Jossey-Bass.

Sinnott, J.D., & Cavanaugh, J.C. (Eds.) (1991). *Bridging paradigms: Positive developments in adulthood and cognitive aging*. New York: Praeger.

Smolak, L. (1993). *Adult development*. Englewood Cliffs, NJ: Prentice-Hall.

Spokane, A.R. (1985). A review of research on person-environment congruence in Holland's theory of careers. *Journal of Vocational Behavior, 26*, 306–343.

Spokane, A.R. (1991). *Career interventions*. Engewood Cliffs, NJ: Prentice-Hall.

Stevens-Long, J., & Commons, M.L. (Eds.) (1992). *Adult life: Developmental processes* (4th Edn). Mountain View, CA: Mayfield.

Stromberg, A.H., & Harkess, G. (Eds.) (1988). *Women working: Theories and facts in perspective* (2nd Edn) Mountain View, CA: Mayfield.

Super, D.E. (1957). *The psychology of careers*. New York: Harper.

Super, D.E. (1981). A developmental theory: Implementing a self-concept. In D.H. Montross & C.J. Shinkman (Eds.), *Career development in the 1980s: Theory and practice* (pp. 28–42). Springfield, IL: Thomas.

Super, D.E. (1986). Life career roles: Self-realization in work and leisure. In D.T. Hall (Ed.), *Career development in organizations* (pp. 95–119). London: Jossey-Bass.

Super, D.E., Starishevsky, R., Matlin, N, & Jordaan, J.P. (Eds.) (1963). *Career development: Self-concept theory*. New York: College Entrance Examination Board.

Vondracek, F.W., Lerner, R.M., & Schulenberg, J.E. (1986). *Career development: A life-span developmental approach*. Hillsdale, NJ: Lawrence Erlbaum Associates Inc.

Walsh, W.B., & Osipow, S.H. (Eds.) (1990). *Career counseling: Contemporary topics in vocational psychology*. Hove, UK: Lawrence Erlbaum Associates Ltd.

Wexley, K.N. (1984). Personnel training. *Annual Review of Psychology, 35*, 519–551.

Wexley, K.N., & Latham, G.P. (1991). *Developing and training human resources in organizations* (2nd Edn). New York: Harper Collins.

Zedeck, S. (1992). *Work, families, and organizations*. San Francisco: Jossey-Bass.

13

Participative Management

P.L. Koopman and A.F.M. Wierdsma

1 INTRODUCTION

Participative management, defined as joint decision making or at least shared influence in decision making by a superior and his or her employees (Wagner & Gooding, 1987), is still a central theme of research in the organizational sciences. Many studies have yielded a positive, although sometimes weak, correlation between participation and matters such as motivation, satisfaction and task performance (e.g. Heller, Drenth, Koopman, & Rus, 1988; Miller & Monge, 1986; Rooney, 1993; Strauss, 1982). However, these results are also open to some criticism, one aspect of which is methodological (Wall & Lischeron, 1977; Wagner & Gooding, 1987; Whyte, 1987). Other authors state that a better distinction should be made between the effects of the various types of participation (Cotton, Vollrath, Frogatt, Lengnik-Hall, & Jennings, 1988; Long & Warner, 1987). And, during the past decade, a good deal has changed in the socio-economic context of most organizations (Lammers & Széll, 1989). What significance does this have for experiences with and possibilities of participative management?

Since the Second World War, the theory and practice of participative management has known varying emphases. Post-war reconstruction dominated labour relations until far into the 1950s. Efforts were concentrated on rebuilding The Netherlands and on acquiring a position in the international market. When, in the 1960s, emphasis shifted from jointly increasing the size of the pie to how it was to be divided, a turn-about also occurred in labour relations. The new generation—much better educated and without the experience of the depression years and the Second World War—made other demands of hierarchical relations. The late 1960s and early 1970s were thus dominated by a reorientation in societal relations. In politics and in the trade unions, the "ideological" component waxed. In The Netherlands, work consultation (started for a multitude of reasons) was largely approached from and assessed on its contribution to change in labour relations and power relations. Research issues were formulated in a one-sided manner, so that evaluation studies aroused the impression that the reason behind work consultation was an endeavour to achieve democracy. As a consequence, the effects that were found on this dimension were disappointing.

The international economic crisis in the 1970s caused a switch of attention towards the issues of survival; increasing the size of the pie once again came to be of current interest. Entrepreneurship and leadership were placed in a different light. "Poised for action" and "purposive" became popular concepts. Strict hierarchical relations between the no-nonsense manager who rode out the crisis and his or her dedicated employees again became acceptable. Once again the "ideological" component waxed, but this time under the pressure of international competition. Small, decentralized units or companies proved to be very successful. The dedication of employees to the organizational goals again seemed important. Market relations and the growing demand for flexibility and concern for quality required a high degree of commitment from employees to their work. Participation of employees in the decision making within the organization, often expressed in terms of organizational culture, was increasingly seen as a strategic asset. The contribution of Japan, with a social order that greatly differs from the individualist cultures of the industrialized West, drew attention to the link between social policy and economic success (Lodge & Vogel, 1987). Because of this, participative management was once again the focus of attention (Wilkins & Ouchi, 1983).

Another stream of literature that places participation of employees more in the centre of attention of management was the recognition of the various ways in which the organization can be evaluated. Morgan (1986) brought the concept of paradigm from the philosophy of science (Kuhn, 1970) within the focus of managers. His metaphors of organizations and underpinning of the relevance of multi-paradigmatic thinking brought about an interest in assessing the different viewpoints within an organization. Bolman & Deal (1991) talk about the necessity for conceptual pluralism. The literature on sociorationalism and emerging postmodern thinking on organizations again stimulated a perspective on organizations in which the joint construction of reality and the importance of language is stressed (Czarniawska-Joerges, 1988; Gergen, 1994; Reed & Hughes, 1992; Shotter, 1993; Tsoukas, 1994). The myth of the rational organization with a known set of objectives and a cohesive culture is being challenged (Meyerson & Martin, 1987).

This chapter begins by discussing the primary motives for and forms of participative management (Sections 2 and 3), followed by a discussion of its effects, which will primarily be considered in terms of work consultation and quality circles (Section 4). In search of the conditions for success, a model is presented in Section 5. Sections 6 and 7 treat the relationship to the organizational structure and the organizational culture. Finally, in Section 8, it is argued that the possibilities of participative management are largely determined by the general company policy and by the personnel management philosophy.

2 WHY PARTICIPATIVE MANAGEMENT?

The motives for participative management can broadly be classified into three categories (Dachler & Wilpert, 1978; Erez, 1993; Heller et al., 1988; Lammers, 1973; Long & Warner, 1987; Strauss, 1982):

- Participation as a right.
- Participation as a means to greater commitment and better work performance.
- Participation as a means to better coordination and control of company operations.

In the first category, participative management is explicitly seen in the context of co-determination and industrial democracy (IDE International Research Group, 1981, 1993; Poole, 1986). The redistribution of power within the organization forms an important point of view in this category. The second category places participative management in the context of the quality of work life. Different emphases can be recognized here. Sometimes the emphasis lies on humanization and combating alienation (Davis, 1977), sometimes on the better utilization of employee knowledge and on reaching better decisions (Heller, 1988; Likert, 1967). The third category views participation as a coordination mechanism (Johnson & Gill, 1993; Mintzberg, 1979). The question is; under what circumstances an organization can profit from it?

Participation as a right

In contrast to the other approaches, which emphasise the instrumental nature of participative management, here participation is regarded as a value in itself. Having a say in matters relating to one's own work and its context are seen as a right or as an obligation. Lammers and Széll (1989) speak in this context of *structural* democratization (in contrast to *functional* democratization). Especially during the 1970s, proponents of this approach could be found in socialist parties, the trade union movement and among left-wing social scientists. In The Netherlands, this loose "coalition" brought about legislation aimed at achieving greater participation in company decisions (e.g. Works Council Act, Working Conditions Act) and a series of experiments with participation (De Man, 1988). One important conclusion from these experiments was that any form of participation can only take root when it fits within and makes a real contribution to business operations. This often proved to be hardly the case (De Man & Koopman, 1984). Viewed in retrospect, this is perhaps not so surprising. The initiators were often primarily interested in the issue of the redistribution of power. As a result, they devoted much attention to the aspect of formalization; forms of participation such as work consultation were encompassed by extensive rules to safeguard the position of the less powerful as much as possible. Less attention was paid to the contingency problem—the question whether the new forms of participation fitted in a particular situation. Forms of influence without codified rules were not recognized and largely ignored (Boisot, 1987).

With the passing of the 1970s, the environment became much more threatening for most organizations. The economic recession, rapidly progressing automation and increased demands from the market put many companies under pressure. No-nonsense management dominated the spirit of those times. Achievers were once again valued. Functional demands were also made of participation and consultation. These changes weakened support for participation as a right. Nowadays, one-sided attention to structuring the relations within organizations has been supplemented by an orientation to the organizational design in order to continue to meet changing environmental demands.

Greater commitment, higher achievement

In many cases participative management is advocated and introduced in the context of the quality of working life. Sometimes the concept of humanization is central. In contrast to the Taylorian mode of operation (short-cycle tasks, separation of execution and planning) with its alienating effect (Blauner, 1964; Hackman & Oldham, 1976; Chapter 2 in Volume 4 of this handbook), this school advocates task enrichment and the restructuring of work groups into semi-autonomous units (Davis, 1977; Chapter 4 in Volume 4 of this handbook), in the expectation that the climate will thus improve, commitment will increase and—as a result—performance will improve (see the "Human Relations" model of Miles, 1965). Other publications stress such concepts as expertise and utilization of capacities (Heller & Wilpert, 1981; Likert, 1967). Because it utilizes the knowledge and experience of the employees, participative management is primarily seen as a means to arrive at qualitatively better decisions and at the better implementation of those decisions. One condition here is that those involved possess the relevant expertise; otherwise any consultation is a waste of time, resulting in pseudo-participation. Because the utilization of human capacities is central here, it is sometimes termed the "Human Resources" model (Miles, 1965). The literature gives numerous examples of wasted human capacities in organizations (Heller, 1988), and many "classical" sources have already pointed this out (Argyris, 1964; Herzberg, Mausner, & Snyderman, 1959; Likert, 1967; McGregor, 1960). The research literature reveals that the effect of participation in goal-setting on performance is mediated by goal-commitment. However, this effect is not consistent across studies. On possible explanation for the lack of consistency is that cultural values moderate the effect of participation on performance (Erez, 1994).

An emerging line of thinking related to the commitment and achievement argument comes from the employees' desire to be part of an organization that offers learning possibilities (Swieringa & Wierdsma, 1992). With a decreasing self-evident loyalty within organizations and an increasing awareness of the significance of the protection of their market position, employees are getting more alert to the possibilities for growth and learning.

Better coordination and control

Some tools of management can be used both to stimulate greater commitment and for a better coordination and control of work behaviour (Koopman, 1991). Participative management is no exception. It is like two sides of a coin. Whether making use of it will benefit the effectiveness of the organization depends on the type of organization. Mintzberg (1979) has shown that—depending on the type of environment, the prevailing technology and the task content—different sorts of coordination mechanisms take on greater or lesser importance. For instance, the *adhocracy* with its dynamic environment needs more fine tuning and consultation than the mechanistic bureaucracy with its great routine and predictability. In the latter case, coordination largely takes place by means of rules and regulations, which are increasingly interwoven in the operating instructions of the new technological systems. So although the contribution of participative management in a classical bureaucracy is generally modest, it can have a certain compensatory effect. However, it generally does no more than serve as a fairly non-committal channel of communication. The chance of continuity in such circumstances is not great (Sassoon & Koopman, 1988). But the preference for a certain form of coordination in an organization is not only a result of the task requirements. It also depends upon the prevailing views and basic values: the organizational culture. Not every organizational culture readily lends itself to participative management, as we will demonstrate in Section 7 (Deal & Kennedy, 1982; Handy, 1985; Harrison, 1972; Pheysey, 1993).

Conflict between goals

We have seen that the motives for participation can be very divergent. To a certain extent, the goals can co-exist and strengthen one another. On the other hand, certain goals are quite obviously mutually incompatible. For example, there is a conflict between the view of those who primarily see participative management as a means to acquire greater acceptance of the organizational goals and those who primarily see it as a "counterbalancing power" to management (Strauss, 1982).

Perhaps, on the basis of all experiences with participative management during the past two decades, we must also say that not all motives are equally realistic. Heller (1988) argues that, in complex organizations, changes in exchange rates, costs of raw materials, tax rates, pressure from competitors, and so on, have much more influence on operating results than changes in participation are ever capable of having. Thierry and De Jong (1979) came to similar conclusions in a study of conditions for systems of participation and payment by results (the Scanlon plan). This makes it difficult to prove the statement that the economic functioning of the entire organization can be demonstrably strengthened by participative management. Many studies of the effects of participation have yielded highly unconvincing results because the research design or methodology did no justice to the complexity of the subject and the number of relevant variables. Initiatives in participation are therefore often a question of outlook and policy (Lawler, 1986, 1989; Walton, 1985).

We have also seen that the "participation as a right" motive resulted in all manner of regulations at a national and company level, but that this motive—due in part to the changed economic context—has lost much of its significance. The long-term effect of the present trend towards deregulation may even be that legislation on participation is soon unnerved or repealed. This means that the foundation for participative management will increasingly have to be found in a fairly functional, pragmatic motivation, as advocated in 1973 by Vroom and Yetton (Vroom & Yetton, 1973), and partly confirmed by research (Vroom & Jago, 1988). As a political instrument for achieving greater industrial democracy, participative management has disappeared from the scene (Rosenstein, Ofek, & Harel, 1987). In the words of Lammers and Széll (1989, p. 321): "We cannot escape the impression that in the 1980s forms and processes of participation were in the vast majority of cases presented, set up, and evaluated as 'functional' programmes and practices". In order to survive, consultation and participation must ultimately make a contribution—one that is recognized by management—to the proper functioning of the organization. Its contribution may have various aspects, such as better communication, better quality of decisions, more commitment, more flexible innovation, better performance, and so on.

Among different perspectives on participation the common thread is the acceptance of the "hierarchy and control" way of thinking about organizing. From the control perspective, machine metaphor, participation can be looked upon as supporting the end-goals of the organization. When the perspective changes toward organizing as a process, brain or culture metaphor on organization, participation becomes one of the ingredients of the organizing process (Morgan, 1986; Weick, 1979). In this chapter we will summarize the literature on participation from the more "traditional" perspective. That is to say, participation as a way of getting a say in the decision-making process of those who are dominant in the design of the organization. In the process approach on organizing, participation is the essence of organizing and all organizational members are partners in the construction of meaning and reality (Cooperrider & Srivastva, 1987; Gergen, 1994). The focus is on conditions that block the process of construction of reality.

3 FORMS OF PARTICIPATIVE MANAGEMENT

As this section will show, the results of participative management are linked to the form it takes. Various authors have attempted to develop a taxonomy based on a number of characteristics. Dachler and Wilpert (1978) named three main dimensions:

1. Formal versus informal (whether or not it is regulated).
2. Direct versus indirect (self-participation or via representatives).
3. More versus less influence (foreknowledge, taking part in discussions, participating in decisions).

Locke and Schweiger (1979) added to this a fourth aspect: the subject matter of the decision. They distinguished routine personnel decisions, matters relating to the actual work, terms of employment and company policy. Cotton et al. (1988) named yet a fifth dimension: the time horizon. They approvingly cited Lawler's (1986) view that, in the introduction of participative management, organizations must take a long-term approach, because the short-term results can often be invisible or even negative. Combining these dimensions leads to a large number of possible types of participative management, the following six of which occur most frequently in practice (Cotton et al., 1988):

1. Participation in decisions about the work itself (with, as characteristics: formal, direct, long-term, much influence).
2. Consultative participation (as in 1, but with slight influence).
3. Short-term participation (formal, short duration, direct, work oriented, much influence).
4. Informal participation (informal, direct, much influence).
5. Employee ownership (formal, indirect, many subjects, much influence in principle).
6. Representative participation (formal, indirect, influence moderate or slight).

More or less similar taxonomies can be found in Strauss (1982), Jain and Giles (1985), Long and Warner (1987), and Levine and Tyson (1990). We will now give a few examples of each category. A typical example of the first category is the autonomous work group, in so far as it has the final say on decisions involving its own work. In some cases the participation is limited to certain aspects of the work, such as merit pay (Jenkins & Lawler, 1981).

Many forms of participative management belong in the second category. Some examples are work consultation, quality circles, Scanlon plan committees, and so on. Work consultation is a "regular and regulated form of consultation between a superior and his or her employees as a group, involving participation in and exerting influence on the decision making about the work and the working conditions in particular" (Koopman & Wierdsma, 1984, p. 643). This form of consultation enjoyed immense popularity in The Netherlands during the 1970s, when it was generally introduced with great pretentions and high expectations of its contribution to industrial democracy. There were bound to be disappointments. In many places work consultation died an untimely death; however, this form of consultation is still frequently seen in Dutch organizations. By now, expectations have been aligned with realistic possibilities. Often the experiences with work consultation were used as a base for quality circles and other forms of total quality management practices on the shop floor.

Quality circles are along more or less the same line (Drenth & Koopman, 1983; Sassoon & Koopman, 1988). A common definition is: "a small group of people who perform similar work and who meet voluntarily at a fixed time to discuss, analyse and solve problems in their work" (Marks, Mirvis, Hackett, & Grady, 1986, p. 61). In comparison to work consultation, the approach often leans more to the functional, aiming at the solution of practical problems. These groups often have better support in using work methods. Training in the use of statistical techniques to identify problems and to track down the causes of defects helps to keep the consultation focused on shared problems at work. A disadvantage is perhaps that integration in day-to-day company routine is very limited; quality circles are the dessert, as it were. If this is the case, then quality circles encounter the same problems as work consultation. They are viewed as supplementary to the work rather than as a part of it. As a result, their continuity rapidly becomes problematic. Any influence on day-to-day routine is then slight (see Section 4).

The Scanlon plan provides financial bonuses for ideas and suggestions that improve productivity (Thierry, 1987). The bonuses are awarded to groups, with each member receiving the same percentage of the bonus. In order for the groups to function well, there must be real opportunities to influence the company system via participation, benefits that are set periodically and can be quantified in an economic sense, and an adequate link between participation and a group's award (Thierry & De Jong, 1979). When the relationship between participation and its economic effects is clear—which is often the case in practice—it may be difficult to find a suitable productivity formula. There are many variants of the Scanlon plan. To increase the chances of success, the plan chosen must be closely attuned to the specific work situation (Miller & Schuster, 1987; see also Chapter 2 in Volume 4 of this handbook).

Participation in the third category ("short-term" participation) has primarily become known from the experiments on training effects in laboratory situations, varying from a single session to a few days. An example would be goal-setting experiments, in which the effect on performance of participation in the formulation of goals is studied (Latham & Marshall, 1982). Another form of participation can be found in project teams and task forces of different kinds. Issue or project-bound participation allows workers to be creative and to use their experience even within a "prescriptive" bureaucratic organization (Bushe & Shani, 1991; Hirschhorn, 1991; Swieringa & Wierdsma, 1992).

Many organizations, primarily in the United States, have no formal systems of participation. None the less, the *informal relations* and the manner of cooperation between superiors and employees can sometimes very well be typified as participative management. This is category four. Categories five (co-ownership) and six (representative participation) fall outside of the scope of this chapter. When employees are co-owners of a company, they can theoretically exert great influence on top management in the shareholders' meeting and/or the Board of Directors (or a similar body). However, this often turns out to be disappointing in practice (Keil, 1983; Long, 1983; Rooney, 1993; Russell, 1983, 1996). Many countries, especially in Europe, have forms of representative participation in "ordinary" organizations. The most common forms are the Works Councils (several countries), Joint Consultation Committees (England), the Board of Directors (West Germany and others), the Workers' Council (former Yugoslavia) and collective negotiations by trade union representatives (most countries). For experiences of these see Poole (1986) and Chapter 16 in Volume 4 of this handbook.

4 EFFECTS OF PARTICIPATIVE MANAGEMENT

With the rise of participative management during the 1960s and 1970s, the number of studies of its effects grew. Initially, the manuscripts were highly speculative and normative, based upon hopes and expectancies. The stream of empirical studies grew, reporting mainly positive results (e.g. Blumberg, 1968; Lowin, 1968). Later authors were critical of these studies, especially on methodological grounds (e.g. Wall & Lischeron, 1977; Wagner & Gooding, 1987). Finally, from a number of more recent sources it has appeared that the results are greatly determined by factors such as the specific form of participation (e.g. Cotton et al., 1988; Strauss, 1996), the phase of decision making in which participation takes place (Heller et al., 1988; Rus, 1996), the expertise of the participants, and the structural and cultural context of the organization and the environment (De Man, 1988; Drenth & Koopman, 1984; Erez, 1994; Maczynski, Jago, Reber, & Böhnisch, 1994).

4.1 Satisfaction and productivity

As a group, the first empirical studies reported mainly moderate to very positive results (Coch & French, 1948; Marrow, Bowers, & Seashore, 1967; Morse & Reimer, 1956; Strauss, 1963) on the relationship of participation both to satisfaction and to productivity. Explanations for this differ per author. Sometimes emphasis is placed on the presumed improvement in the communication with—as a result—qualitatively better decisions and more flexible implementation. Sometimes it is assumed that participation contributes to better goal setting and greater acceptance of the goals thus formulated.

The review by Filley, House, and Kerr (1976) still reported positive results. They investigated 32 studies of the effects of participative leadership. In 20 of these studies—including laboratory experiments, correlational studies and field experiments—the satisfaction of the participants was measured. A positive relationship was established between participation and satisfaction in 19 of the 20 cases. The relationship between participation and group productivity was investigated in 23 studies. It turned out to be positive in 16 cases; in the other 7 studies no relationship was found.

A more ambiguous picture was sketched in the literature study by Locke and Schweiger (1979). They discussed 43 studies of the relationship between participation and satisfaction, 26 (60%) of which yielded a positive relationship. In 13 cases there was no clear relationship, while in 4 cases it was even negative. The results from 46 studies of the relationship between participation and productivity were even more unclear. In 26 cases (56%) there was no relationship, in 10 cases the relationship was positive and in another 10 cases it was negative. Another review by Lock, Feren, McCaleb, Shaw, and Denny (1980) found very diverse relationships between participation and productivity.

On the basis of a review of the literature as well as their own research, Wall and Lischeron (1977) came to the conclusion that some of the results, particularly those based on correlational studies, might perhaps be attributed to methodological flaws. In their own experiments they could find no systematic relationship between participation and satisfaction. The authors did not feel that the fact that most correlational studies found consistent results was any proof of a positive effect of participation on satisfaction, for the following reasons:

- The direction of the effect may well be the other way round: more satisfied employees may participate more. In addition, the relationship between participation and satisfaction may be caused by a third variable, for example, hierarchical level.
- Often participation is merely one element on scales that measure several aspects of leadership. These scales also contain elements such as warmth, openness, and trust. Great satisfaction with more 'participative' leadership could be caused by these other elements as well.
- Scales that measure leadership often contain

evaluative elements. For a study of the effect of participation on satisfaction, however, a descriptive measure is needed to avoid the danger of tautology (Wall & Lischeron, 1977, pp. 20–23).

The conclusions of Wagner and Gooding (1987) are along the same lines. They performed a meta-analysis on 118 correlational studies of the relationship between participation and various dependent variables. The mean correlation with these variables turned out to be .32. The 118 studies were subsequently divided into two groups. For the 47 studies with "perception-perception" correlations—based on questionnaires that were administered to respondents at the same point in time—a mean correlation was found of .39. The mean correlation from the other 71 studies—which made use of various methods of data collection—turned out to be only .12. These results seem to indicate that the empirical evidence for the positive effects of participation are at least partly due to methodological artefacts.

There are other methodological problems as well. The work of Guzzo, Jette, and Katzell (1985) is an example. Using meta-analysis, the authors investigated the effectiveness of socio-technical interventions in achieving improved productivity. Participants in the experimental groups indeed showed higher productivity than participants in the control groups. And because participation is a dominant element of socio-technical interventions, the results seem to confirm the relationship of participation to productivity. The trouble is—and this is also true of other participation experiments—that a great many other organizational measures generally accompany the introduction of participation (Wagner & Gooding, 1987). This makes it very difficult to determine precisely what effect should be ascribed to what variable.

The picture thus remains somewhat unclear. The most recent reviews seem to indicate that, generally speaking, participative management nevertheless has a limited positive effect. Miller and Monge (1986) found a mean correlation of .34 between participation and satisfaction and a mean correlation of .15 between participation and productivity. The results of Wagner and Gooding (1987) are of the same order, although the method of study makes a considerable difference (see Table 13.1).

A separate remark should be made about the relationship between participation and goal setting. Numerous experiments and field studies have shown that, for good task performance, it is important to formulate difficult and specific goals (Locke et al., 1980; Locke & Latham, 1984, 1990; Miner, 1984; see also Chapter 11 in Volume 4 of this handbook). Naturally, the goals must be accepted by the participants. In most laboratory experiments this causes few problems. Goal acceptance is generally so great that there is hardly any variance on this variable. The result is that goal acceptance or commitment shows scarcely any relationship to performance (Locke & Henne, 1986). But it is not implausible that in social situations with a somewhat longer time horizon—as most work situations have—commit-

TABLE 13.1

The influence of different methods of study on the relationships between participation and effects.

Dependent variables	Mean correlations			
	Percept-percept		Multi-source	
Task performance	.45	(4)*	.11	(25)
Decision performance	—	—	.21	(12)
Motivation	.35	(3)	.25	(3)
Satisfaction	.42	(27)	.11	(23)
Acceptance	.35	(13)	.09	(8)

* Figures in brackets indicate the number of studies.
Source: Wagner & Gooding (1987, p. 532).

ment is much more difficult to achieve, and participative management might well be able to play an important role here (Austin & Bobko, 1985). Also Erez (1994) claims that the effect of participation on performance can only be observed if it has an advantage in strengthening the level of goal commitment, self-efficacy (Bandura, 1986), and shared knowledge. When these factors are high regardless of participation, as is often the case in research experiments but also in specific work situations (Locke et al., 1984), participation has no superiority over non-participation. But, for example, in the case of resistance to change participation has an advantage over non-participation in enhancing commitment through attitude change. The review by Cotton et al. (1988) seems to offers indications in this direction. As previously mentioned, these authors distinguished various forms of participation as gleaned from 91 studies. Table 13.2 gives a summary of their primary conclusions.

The conclusion is clear: the effects of participative management are determined in part by the form of participation. It should be noted that the dimensions "direct versus indirect", "amount of influence" and "duration" are of primary importance. But other context factors are important as well. This is the subject of the second part of this chapter. But before going into this, we would first like to consider somewhat more extensively the effects of two specific forms of participative management: work consultation and quality circles.

4.2 Work consultation and quality circles

Numerous organizations in The Netherlands introduced work consultation, especially during the 1970s. As described earlier, the motives of the groups involved were very different. It is therefore interesting to investigate which of these divergent objectives were achieved in practice. A nice illustration is given in Figure 13.1, showing the results of work consultation in three very different organizations.

According to these findings, which are in general agreement with what has been found elsewhere, the "immediate" participants see work consultation primarily as an instrument to improve the information flow, especially from the bottom up. To a somewhat lesser extent they also feel that people are better informed and that the interests of the employees are better promoted. Results such as better decisions and greater acceptance of decisions are also sometimes mentioned. They do not feel work consultation is a waste of time.

The participants much less frequently named an increased influence on departmental policy or even on day-to-day routine. Points such as increased work satisfaction and better utilization of knowledge and experience were seldom mentioned. The work consultation chairpersons

TABLE 13.2

Form of participation	Effects on performance	Effects on satisfaction
1. Participation in work decisions	Positive*	Mixed
2. Consultative participation	Inconclusive**	Inconclusive
3. Short-term participation	No effect	No effect
4. Informal participation	Positive	Positive
5. Employee ownership	Positive	Positive
6. Representative participation	No effect	Mixed

* "Positive" means that more than ⅔ of the studies in this cell showed positive results. "No effect" means that fewer than ⅓ showed positive results. "Mixed" means that more than ⅓, but fewer than ⅔ were positive.

** Although results were positive, called "inconclusive" in relation to imperfections in methodology.

Source: Cotton et al. (1988, p. 11)

Effects of participation on performance and satisfaction.

FIGURE 13.1

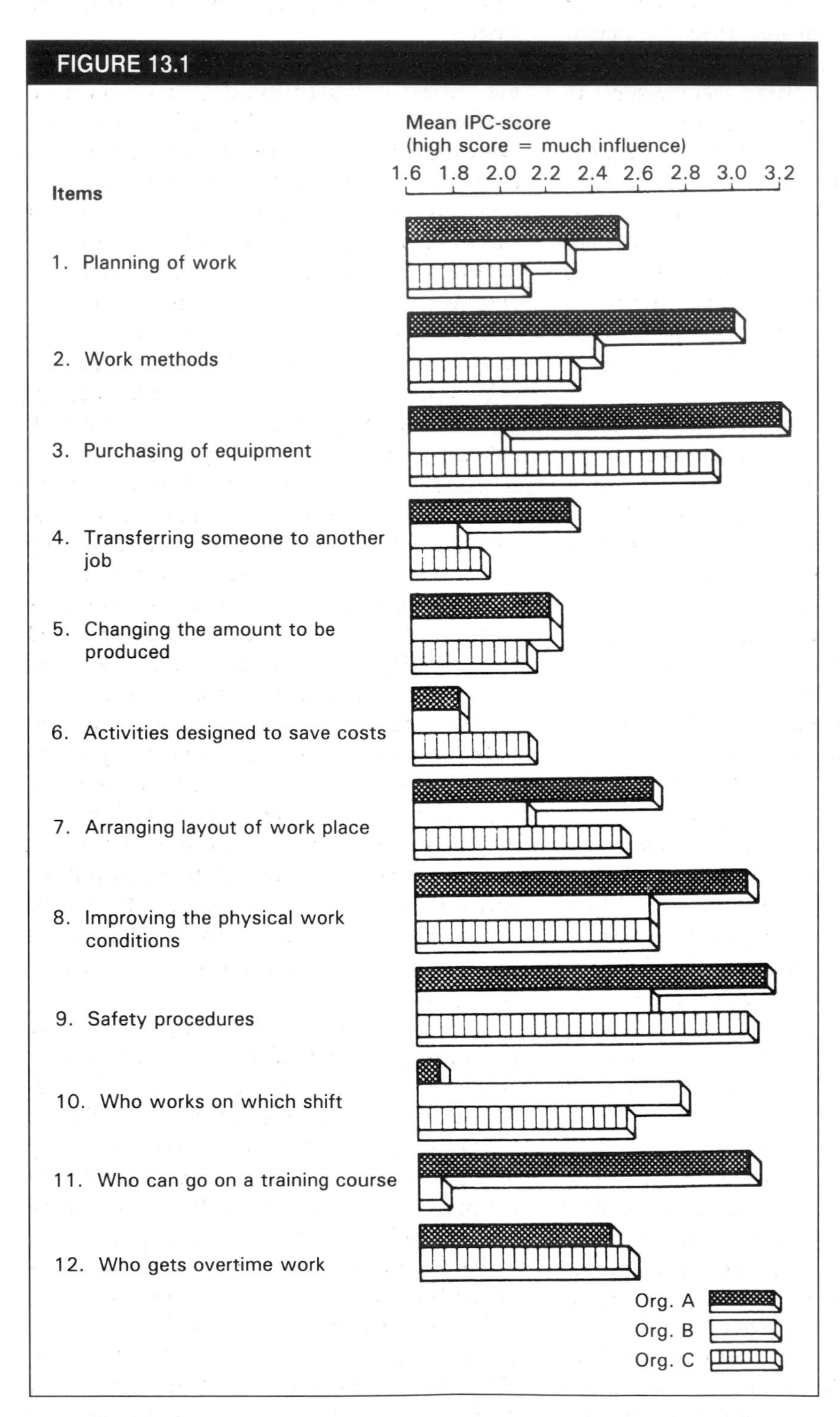

Results of work consultation according to the participants in three organizations. From Drenth and Koopman, (1983, p. 65).

largely felt the same about the results of work consultation as the employees. The most important difference was in the absolute level of the scores. The chairpersons were more positive in their evaluation than the group members on almost all points. They principally observed more influence of the group members on day-to-day routine than the group members themselves. Almost without exception, the conclusions from most research reports confirm that the contribution of work consultation to greater actual influence – frequently the original intention—has remained extremely modest (Koopman, Drenth, Heller, & Rus, 1993; De Man, 1988).

Experiences with quality circles are rather varied. To be sure, many success stories are found in the literature—not always from entirely unimpeachable sources—but more serious evaluation studies are still fairly rare (Sassoon & Koopman, 1988). Some authors report improvements in productivity and efficiency, a decrease in absenteeism (Aloni & Gonen, 1986; Marks, Mirvis, Hackett, & Grady, 1986) and an increase in proposals to solve problems (Hattem, 1987). Others report more mixed results. For instance, Goodfellow (1981), who studied 29 companies in the United States, found that only 8 of them were successful in terms of productivity and efficiency. Cox and Norris (1983) found no difference in performance and absenteeism before and after the introduction of quality circles. Lehman (1986) reported that, although participants in quality circles indeed declared that the production level had risen, this could not be confirmed by objective measurements. In short, although here and there positive experiences are reported, the general results with respect to productivity seem to be on the modest side. However, the situation in Japan seems to be somewhat different. Here, group goals were found to be more effective than in the West (Matsui, Kakuyama, & Onglatco, 1987). Erez (1994) argues, therefore, that it is reasonable to propose that the cultural background can either support or inhibit the effectiveness of participatory management. In individualistic cultures, like the USA, group goals very often result in social loafing and free riding because group members in individualistic cultures do not share responsibility to the same extent as group members in collectivistic cultures, like Japan and China.

According to Wood, Hull, and Azumi (1983), the effects of quality circles should sooner be sought in the direction of the quality of the work. We should think of job enrichment, the acquisition of problem-solving skills, communication, feedback, and so on. Various studies have indeed shown such relationships. Mohrman and Novelli (1985), for example, found a relationship with feedback on work results. Rafaeli (1985) found relationships with task variety, with autonomy and with influence. Gantos (1987) reported relationships with task satisfaction, with team development and with group cohesion, but none with autonomy, challenge or training possibilities.

Marks et al. (1986) also studied the relationship between participation in quality circles and various aspects of the quality of work life. They found a relationship with satisfaction with promotion possibilities, but not with task characteristics such as importance, challenge and responsibility. The researchers concluded that participation in quality circles is not anchored in the organization. Finally, a study by Hattem (1987) showed that participation in quality circles had a positive effect on the perceived autonomy and the subjective value of the task. However, there appeared to be no influence on the task characteristics of variation, identification, importance and feedback. Nor were there positive effects on general satisfaction, intrinsic motivation and satisfaction with promotion opportunities, salary, colleagues and superiors.

In conclusion, we may state that, although here and there positive results are reported, quality circles do not seem to be a method for task enrichment. In the view of Lawler and Mohrman (1985), a quality circles programme is more likely to create a parallel organization alongside the existing one. Bushe and Shani (1991) elaborate on the possibilities of parallel learning structures within bureaucratic organizations. Because they do not become an integral part of the day-to-day task of the participants, quality circles are perceived as an external factor (see also Bradley & Hill, 1987). This makes continuity in quality circles, as in work consultation, frequently a problem. Blair and Whitehead (1984) stated that

75% of the programmes for improvement of the work—of which quality circles are a part—that had functioned in the United States were no longer in existence, and that only one-third of the circles were successful in Japan. In the aircraft construction company, Lockheed, a pioneer in the field of quality circles in 1974, the circles disintegrated once their founders left the company (Bruck, 1985). Klein reported in 1984 that the majority of the circles in which she had performed her research were no longer in existence by then (Klein, 1984). In the company studied by Mohrman and Novelli (1985), the programme was a failure and the quality circles were stopped after a short time. On the other hand, more successful programmes are known that have been in operation longer (e.g. Marks et al., 1986; Rafaeli, 1985). This brings up the question of the conditions for success. This is discussed in Section 5.

5 A MODEL FOR PARTICIPATIVE MANAGEMENT

In this section, participative management will be approached from the point of view of an exchange process, using elements from exchange theory (Chadwick-Jones, 1976; Shaw & Constanzo, 1970, pp. 69–116) and from the point of view of cognitive expectancy theory (Lawler, 1973; Vroom, 1964; see also Chapter 11 in Volume 4 of this handbook). We will assume that the introduction and the functioning of participative management is impossible without clear extra efforts—over a longer period of time—by company management, department heads and employees, sometimes with temporary support by staff groups. The extra effort or investment on the part of management may involve making time and facilities available for participative management, ensuring rapid and adequate feed-back to the questions and suggestions that arise in the sessions, and so on. The department heads also face additional requirements. They will have to consult regularly with their employees as a group. They are also expected to exhibit a participative style, which demands different attitudes and capacities from those on which people were often selected in the past. From the employees, finally, greater involvement is expected in the functioning of the organization, as well as an active contribution of ideas. This is no small threat, for the withdrawal of their involvement is often the only road open to employees against the much more powerful management.

In our model we assume that the various groups will only want to make this extra effort if there is sufficient confidence that it will lead to an improvement in their own position, or—in terms of expectancy theory—to outcomes with a positive valence (Kipnis, 1976; Pollard & Mitchell, 1972). Each group makes its own assessments. Management wonders what the potential contribution is from the employees via participative management to the organizational goals as formulated by management. The employees regularly make their further cooperation dependent on expected successes. Figure 13.2 shows a flow chart of our model. To simplify the presentation, only two groups are distinguished here, management and employees. This is a very simplified version of the complex reality but it allows us to work with results of the research that evaluates participation as a means to gain influence or as a right. The main objective of the model is to create language that facilitates a debate about participation in which the interdependent relationship between workers and management is placed in the context of the realization of different objectives.

Let us take a closer look at Figure 13.2. We speak of a cyclic model, by which we mean a dynamic process in which expectancies, choices, behaviour and reinforcement take place in succession, and tomorrow's choices are determined in part by the experiences of today. Behaviour frequently precedes a change in attitude (Bem, 1970; Pfeffer, 1982). The continuity of the consultation is determined by the extent to which both groups see their primary goals and interests strengthened as a result (Boissoneau, 1987; Sell, 1986). This statement implies that we do not believe in the continuity of participative management if it is only instrumental for the interests of one of the partners. The frequent debate in the literature on the "true" managerial motives in introducing participative management (e.g. Cole & Byosiere, 1986) is therefore of limited value.

FIGURE 13.2

A cyclic model for participative management.

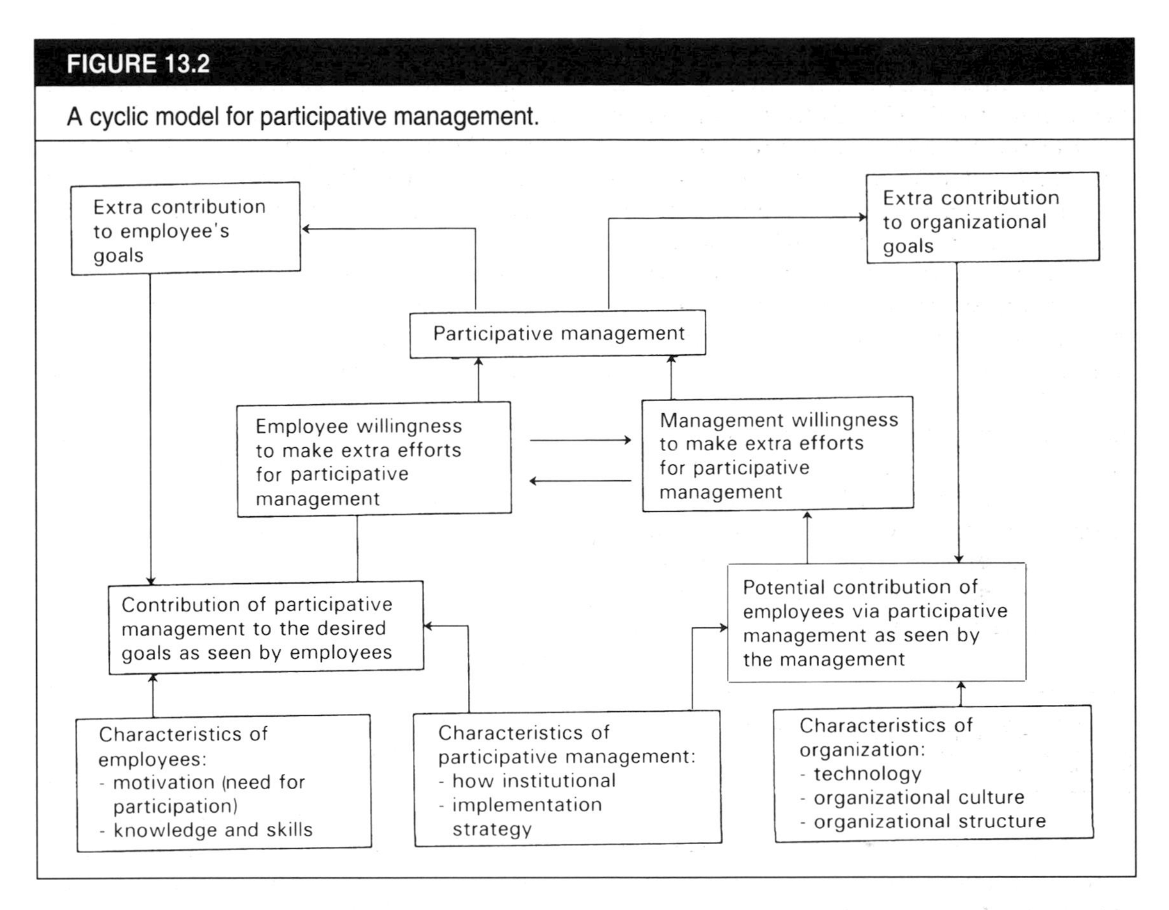

The implication this has—that participative management offers less chance of increasing influence if management sees it primarily as their own tool—seems to us only partly true. This view is based upon the assumption that management is the only party which is in a position to determine the nature of participative management. But participative management that does not have the endorsement of the employees involved has no way to maintain itself or to develop. In Section 6 we shall try to demonstrate that it is precisely when management expects to gain from participative management that the employees' chances to legitimise their "definition of the situation" increase. If, in the eyes of management, the employees have some contribution to make, then withholding it becomes an interesting option and a negotiating situation ensues. The extent to which the situation assumes a negotiating nature is partly determined by the extent to which management is dependent upon the efforts of the employees and the opportunities employees have to wield their influence. Participation is a relational concept and therefore the mutual circular influence of actions of each group upon the other is crucial.

Following Watson (1986), we assume that the employment strategy will be a reflection of dominant values and attitudes of management on the one hand, and on the other, the circumstances perceived by management as making the relationship to the labour factor problematic, in the sense that operating results depend to a large extent on the efforts of the employees. The literature gives a number of circumstances or context factors that can increase the relative power position of employees. Examples are: a complex organizational structure, complex tasks for which much knowledge is required, a tight labour market with as a consequence high labour costs, stringent social legislation, a high level of unionization, and finally, a society friendly to democracy, as it was in Western Europe in the 1970s (see also Mintzberg, 1979, 1983; Robbins, 1990).

The assumption of the model in Figure 13.3 is

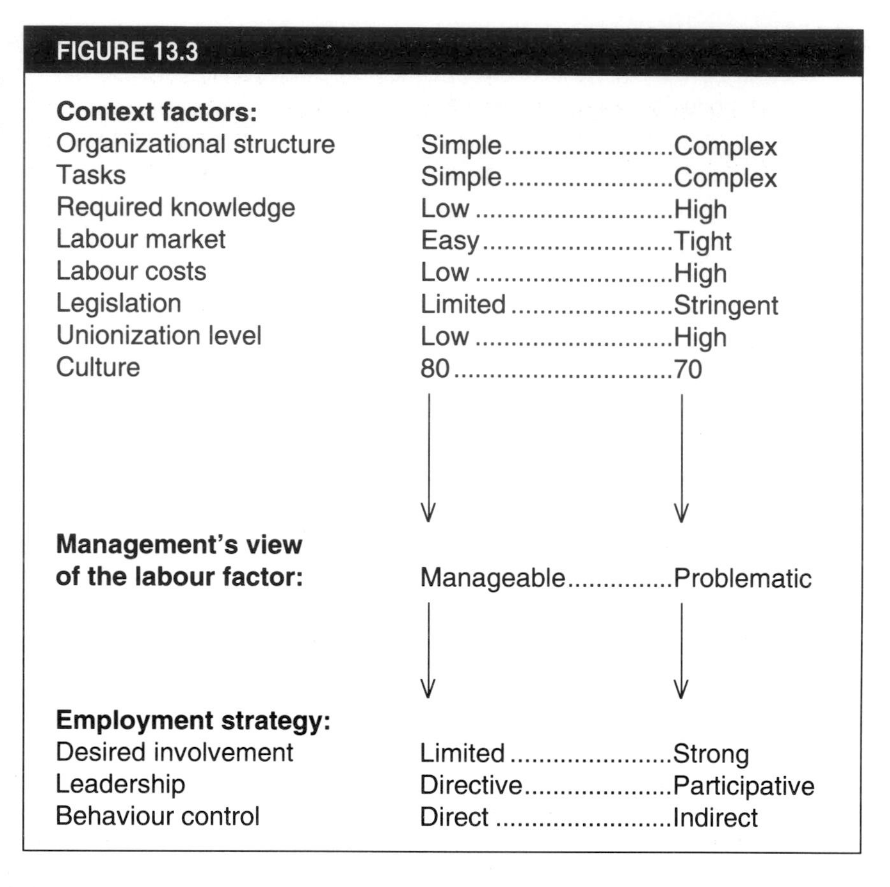

Factors that influence the employment strategy. Adapted from Watson (1986, p. 169).

that the factors in the right-hand column promote the adoption of an employment strategy which places strong emphasis on participative procedures and of an approach aimed at increasing involvement. Dominant values, preferences and views of management, however, determine or temper the strength of this relationship. A few of the factors cited will now be explored. First of all attention is paid to structural factors such as task characteristics, organizational structure and environment, and subsequently to cultural factors, including aspects of the *Zeitgeist* and overall policy.

6 RELATIONSHIP TO ORGANIZATIONAL STRUCTURE

In *The Structuring of Organizations* Mintzberg (1979) distinguishes five ideal configurations: the simple structure, the mechanistic or machine bureaucracy, the professional bureaucracy, the divisional organization, and the adhocracy. The form each type takes and the manner in which coordination takes place is strongly intertwined with the nature of the environment, primarily its stability and complexity (see Figure 13.4).

In a simple, stable environment, internal processes take a predictable course. This leads to routinization and formalization. Tasks are highly specialized and short-cycled. Coordination takes place via standardization of procedures. There is little need for participative management: the functioning of the organization does not ask for it and the potential contribution of the employees is generally modest. In such a situation participative management at best serves the purpose of a somewhat non-committal "channel of communication" (Koopman & Wierdsma, 1984). It may make a limited contribution to the atmosphere or offer a certain compensation for frustrating aspects of the task or the work situation.

In an organization with a complex, dynamic

FIGURE 13.4

Simple environment	Complex environment
Mechanistic Bureaucracy Centralized High formalization Stable environment Standardized rules and procedures	*Professional Bureaucracy* Decentralized Low to moderate formalization Stable environment Standardization of skills and values
Simple Structure Centralized Low formalization Dynamic environment Direct supervision of top management	*Organic Form (Adhocracy)* Decentralized Low formalization Dynamic environment Mutual adjustment

The relation between organization structure and environment in the typology of Mintzberg (1979).

environment, the possibilities of participative management are entirely different. The functioning of such an organization or a network of organizations (Andriessen, 1996; Miles, 1996) is entirely dependent on good vertical as well as horizontal consultation. Good results are conditional upon utilization of all available employee expertise. Participative management is not a mere accessory, but is an integral "coordination mechanism" in the organization (see Figure 13.5). The other configurations in Figure 13.5 can be seen as transitional forms in which participative management has a role of greater or lesser importance depending on other conditions, which will be discussed next.

One determinant of the leeway for participative management in a particular unit is the organizational design, and specifically whether it has a process or a product structure. Before a product is ready to leave the plant, usually a large number of operations will have taken place. The organization of these operations (what order, who does what, etc.) can vary greatly. Broadly speaking, two different structures can be distinguished: a process-oriented and a product-oriented set-up of operations. We may speak of a process orientation (or functional set-up) when similar operations are brought together as much as possible in departments or within individual tasks (for example, welding, work preparation). With each step, the product to be manufactured moves to another department to undergo the next type of operation. When tasks and departments are thus structured, it is entirely consistent with classical organizational theory: highly specialized tasks and functional units. On the other hand, we may speak of a product orientation if all actions that are necessary to make a certain product are brought together as much as possible in a particular work unit. There, as complete as possible a product is made, and a customer is served as fully as possible by a department or in each task.

What are the consequences for task structuring and work consultation? With a process orientation, the possibilities to structure tasks within a production department are limited to an enlargement of responsibilities. This involves an extension of the old task with similar elements, for example the preliminary treatment of product 1 alongside that of product 2. In the product orientation, on the other hand, some task enrichment can be introduced. Preliminary operations,

FIGURE 13.5

Participative management as a channel of communication and as a coordination mechanism.

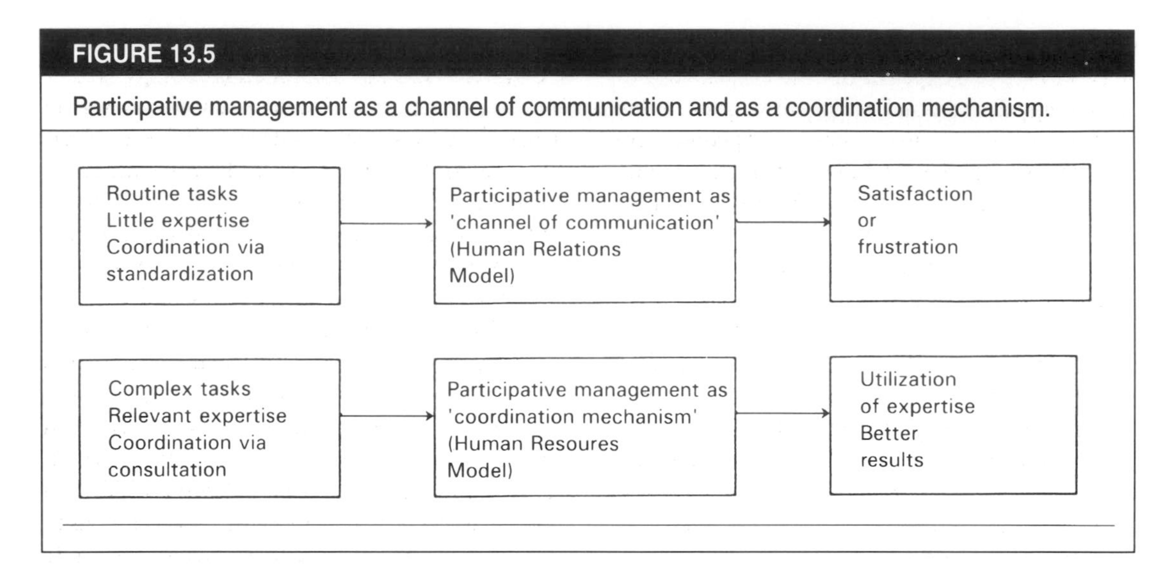

assembly and finishing can then be performed by a single work unit or even by a single person. In relation to the possibilities for work consultation in a production department, it is important to establish where the coordination of production problems takes place, for this largely determines the extent to which such problems can be effectively handled during work consultation. For work consultation, the product orientation offers two important advantages: horizontal communication lines are shorter (and so the feedback is faster), and the topics of consultation are broader and more relevant to the work itself.

7 RELATIONSHIP TO ORGANIZATIONAL CULTURE

For the sake of continuity, any form of participative management should be related to the organizational culture. Participative management is based on the "responsible" or "self-actualizing" person. Swieringa & Wierdsma (1992) elaborate on situations in which incongruency between insights and principles block renewal and development within organizations. Essential for the development of a learning climate are change strategies that foster learning. New insights on managing and organizing should become congruent with a change in the deep-seated principles of the "taken for granted" reality of the organizational culture. If basic views in the organization do not encompass this, then participative management is doomed to founder or to pass into oblivion. Sooner or later it will clash with the assumptions at the heart of the organization. Successful experiments with work structuring, quality of work life and work consultation illustrate that changes in the task content or the consultative structure do not remain confined to the experiment. These experiments resulted in attempts by those involved to extend the experimental starting points to aspects of the work situation that had remained unchanged. Work structuring experiments led to requests to adapt the task content to the degree of employee involvement and responsibility demanded by the consultation (De Man, 1988). Often this was not in accordance with existing structures, which—especially in the 1960s and 1970s—were strongly determined by the mechanistic paradigm in which domination, control and separation of ideas and action were basic assumptions (Morgan, 1986). The opposite of this form of control is control by the beliefs and values that people adopt in the course of time: the organizational culture.

Organizational culture is all the views and values shared by the members of an organization and which distinguish it from other organizations (Czarniawska-Joerges, 1992; Schneider, 1990; Triandis, 1994 ; Trice & Beyer, 1993; see also

Chapter 6 in Volume 4 of this handbook). Hofstede (1991, p. 5) speaks of "the collective programming of the mind which distinguishes the members of one group or category of people from another". At the heart of the organizational culture are the basic values, surrounded by the norms with respect to desired behaviour. The norms as operationalizations of the values are reinforced by rituals, stories, myths, symbols and language which are the forms of expression in which the culture presents itself to an outsider (Dandridge, Mitroff, & Joyce, 1980; Morgan, Frost, & Pondy, 1983). Several authors have likened the organizational culture to an onion, in which the outer layers are the heroes, stories, and so on, and the centre is formed by the views, values and assumptions (Neuijen, 1992; Schein, 1992).

The organizational culture develops over time and in relation to the environmental demands and the matter of internal integration. Its beginnings lie in the views and values of the founder. Around his or her mission, the founder gathers people who are willing to work for the organization. The borderline between the personal goals of the founder and the organizational goals is vague. From the start, the workers usually see the founder as the personification of the organization. The founder steers and controls his or her company via a network of faithful supporters, often family members. In this phase the foundation is laid that will determine the culture for a long time to come. Later come the stories and anecdotes about earlier days, confirming the essential values (Adams, 1972; Clarke, 1972; Dandridge et al., 1980; Mintzberg, 1983; Wilkins, 1983). These stories, sagas and myths are an interpretation of past events (Berg, 1985) and serve an important purpose in the retention of shared experiences—they are the "memory" of the organization (Wilkins, 1979).

The culture is learned and passed on to new members, and manifests itself in shared views, behaviour patterns, objects and feelings (Sathé, 1985). Typically, an organizational culture is so self-evident that its influence is difficult to recognize by members of the organization. Culture is taken for granted reality. Ganzevoort (1981) termed it "fictional rationality". He spoke of organizational culture only when the values and views influence behaviour or structures. This division of culture into "idea system" and "adaptive system" has its roots in anthropology (Keesing, 1974), but can also be found in views on management and organization (Allaire & Firsirotu, 1984). Because views and values influence the choice processes within the organization, a culture influences the organizational structure, the management systems, the perception of the environment and thus the choices with respect to technology and strategy. The relationship between culture and structure is of a circular causal nature (Wierdsma, 1985). Various typologies have attempted to order the variety of organizational cultures (Boisot, 1986; Deal & Kennedy, 1982; Harrison, 1972; Pheysey, 1993; Quinn, 1988; Van Muijen & Koopman, 1994). A frequently used typology is that of Harrison, which is quite consistent with Mintzberg's structural configurations discussed in Section 6. Here, we will briefly discuss the characteristics of each type and then indicate possibilities and problems for participative management.

The *power culture* is characterized by an orientation to a single leader, often the founder/owner. There is a clear power centre: the leader dominates and controls the organization via a network of confidants in key positions. Coordination primarily takes place through personal contacts and informal mutual adjustment. Rules and procedures are less important or absent, because they would limit the degrees of freedom and would thus erode the power position of the "powerful". The main thing is the effectiveness of the organization as a whole. Loyalty to the top is a *sine qua non* for a career in the company. Mintzberg's "simple structure" corresponds best to this type of culture.

The *role culture* is characterized by great confidence in rules and procedures. The position a person holds is essential; the person is of less importance. There is a strong tendency to observe agreements and to respect one another's authority and responsibilities. Outward characteristics of positions and roles such as titles and seniority are very important. Caution, avoidance of conflict and of personal ties are essential. Relations are of an instrumental nature (Katz & Kahn, 1978): they are relations between functionaries rather than between persons. The attention of employees is strongly focused on their position in the network of relations. It is important to make sure that existing relations are not disturbed. The role culture sometimes leads to excessive concern for what is not done. Initiatives can be blocked or delayed at an early stage without a rule being violated (if the customs officers go on strike, or they work to rule). This type of culture is strongly related to the machine bureaucracy. In trying to ban personal arbitrariness and nepotism, the bureaucracy acquires a different form of arbitrariness in that a functionary in the network can decide whether a request will be honoured immediately or with a delay.

The *task culture* is characterized by an orientation to the fulfilment of a task. Due to the changing demands of the environment and the high level of employee expertise, there is often no time, no need or no desire to set down the manner in which the work is done in rules and procedures. The capacities of the participants are primary, and power is concentrated where these capacities come together: in project teams and coordinators. The norm is that information is shared. We frequently see this type in an adhocracy.

Finally, Harrison distinguishes the *person culture*. A characteristic of this culture is that the participants work primarily for themselves and regard the organization as a network of facilities. Management concerns itself with setting contingencies and safeguarding the basic conditions. The participants choose the organization for pragmatic reasons, because it makes a good context for their actual goal: professionalism. Among the structural configurations, the professional bureaucracy comes the closest to this type of culture. The employees are very well educated and often maintain a "clientele" or task domain of their own. Some staff departments or R&D departments in large organizations have such a culture. These combinations of the types of culture and the structural configurations occur often, but there are also situations in which the characteristics of the culture do not correspond to the structural characteristics and the environment. In many a large organization in which we might well expect to find characteristics of the role culture, the power culture predominates (Handy, 1985). Rules and procedures are not the mode of operation. The informal networks "control" the decisions which relate to the identity and the strategy of the organization. Working with both cultural and structural typologies enriches the possibilities for analysis. As a result of its scale, a large organization may acquire more role culture elements, but they will not necessarily dominate the culture. A dynamic environment encourages flexibility and a task culture. Again, an organization can react with a power culture. Wilkins (1983) warns against too facile a diagnosis of the organizational culture. Sackman (1991) shows the preference within the management literature to treat organizational culture as a unifying concept. Meyerson and Martin (1987) distinguish between three views or paradigms in the approach of organizational culture. The integration paradigm stresses the shared goals, beliefs and values that hold a potentially diverse group of organizational members together like a social or normative glue. The differentiation paradigm accepts inconsistency within a culture and focuses on the identification of subcultures. The third paradigm stresses the lack of clarity within organizations and considers the organization to be a "jungle" in which ambiguity "overrules" consistency. What possibilities does participative management have in the cultural types Harrison described?

At an organizational level, the *power culture* has many characteristics in common with the collectivist cultures that we see at a macro level in Asian countries. In a collectivist society, emphasis is on the group, and the individual must know his or her place within the group (Wierdsma, 1988). Self-image and self-respect are anchored in the collective in that its members give an individual his or her "face". Maintaining harmony with others is of vital importance. Disturbance of the relations can lead to loss of face. The manners and the communication style are intended to prevent this happening. Indirect communication and great trust in a shared pattern of views and values mean that much need not be said explicitly. The communication shows a low degree of codification (Boisot, 1983). Ambiguity is functional because it provides leeway. Later, when circumstances have changed, a person can again be in harmony with the whole by adopting a different interpretation. There is a big distance between the leaders and the followers, and loyalty is given in exchange for safety within the order thus created. Much information is withheld; knowledge is not freely shared. The borders between "in-group" and "out-group" are largely determined by access to information. A power culture offers hardly any room to participative management. Only those who shape and transmit the culture may participate in the decisions that concern the entire organization. At best, people in the lower echelons have some say in carrying out these decisions. Requests by them for a say in formulating goals and setting contingencies within which they must work will not be honoured. Any structuring or regulations would place too many restrictions on the power of decision and room to manoeuvre of the key figures. As long as the basic views are not up for discussion, work consultation can serve as a channel of communication.

In much of Japanese business and industry, employees show a relatively high degree of involvement in their organizations, and forms of participative consultation such as quality circles have flourished. Among the collectivist cultures, however, Japan occupies a place all its own (Hofstede, 1991). The predominant characteristic is the "clan culture" in which the decisive factor is the distinction between "insiders" and "outsiders" (Boisot, 1986). Such organizations, together with the government and the financial world, make up "Japan Ltd" Lifelong employment, for all practical purposes, makes closed social systems of the organizations, in which relations often find their origins in old feudal traditions.

The wish to institutionalize participation and consultation is in keeping with a *role culture*. But the sum total of regulations can deteriorate into a ritual of carefully coordinated meetings, detailed minutes and even officials at a central staff level to monitor progress on decisions made and action to be taken. An impressive framework of regulations and procedures becomes a caricature if it is still the focus of activity after the start-up phase. In a stable and relatively simple market, a bureaucracy often results, with a network of participatory forms tailored to the formal organization. In such large-scale bureaucracies, we often find a paradoxical situation: the formal organization has become so opaque that the work can only be done through a network of people who know the rules and can interpret them, bending them if necessary. The formal organization is the basis for a network of informal contacts by means of which a great deal can be achieved, as long as the rules are not violated. The organization is incapable of linking a type of participation based on formal regulations to the "true" decision making. The paradox—in point of fact, very many matters are impossible, but if you know the way, suddenly very much is possible—is resolved by the informal network; on trust, a balance is kept of services owing. The basis of trust, which makes it possible to postpone a "return favour" in the exchange relationship, stands in opposition to the formal relations, which exclude such a thing. Just as in the power culture, withholding information or giving it selectively is often the norm. Sharing information is a prerequisite for participation, and is itself a result of individualist western cultures.

The views and values of the *task culture* show the most correspondence to the norms of the individualist cultures that we find in many western countries; they are strongest in North America (Hofstede, 1991). The individual is the basic unit of such a culture. Individuals operate in a market situation in which they are rewarded on the basis of their contribution and depending on the competition. Equal opportunities and competition are important. The object is to achieve synergy from the antithesis between differences. Conflicts between people are allowed and they are manageable because people accept the rules of the game: laws and regulations. These laws and regulations are based upon abstract truths and must be applied without respect to persons. The communication style is direct and explicit, and information should be freely available to all. The task culture is far and away the best environment for many types of formal and informal participation. Emphasis is on informal consultation based upon the needs of the participants. The norms encourage sharing information with others to lighten the collective task. The cultural preference in which to make transactions is the "market" and not the "bureaucracy" (Williamson, 1975; Williamson & Ouchi, 1981).

In a *person culture*, the main problem is to motivate those involved to make efforts for the goals of the whole. Involvement in administrative decisions is often felt to be a distasteful task. On the other hand, if management seems to want a say in how the work is done, it is scarcely tolerated by the professionals. Participation in managerial situations is concentrated on jointly increasing the available resources and on their distribution. Participation is often even limited to the allocation of resources.

Various authors consider employee participation in the decision making on matters relating to their own work important in achieving the desired level of flexibility. Both in production companies and in the service sector, the involvement of the employees is seen as a condition for the achievement of the required customer orientation. In the service sector, the attitude of employees is an essential facet of the service provided (Sadler, 1988). Quality control, then, is primarily preventive and aimed at avoiding mistakes, since they can be rectified only with difficulty or not at all. Management tries to influence the behaviour of the employees by stressing the basic values and views of the company. If the market situation makes it necessary to delegate matters, a strong organizational culture can be a strategic asset. A strong organizational culture makes it possible to react quickly and flexibly, and be geared to the market, because the organizational members have sufficiently internalized the organizational values and are able to use them as guidelines in their decision making (Deal & Kennedy, 1982). Mechanistic organizations frequently have to contend with problems in involving the employees in the work and in the organization as a whole. The stringent separation of ideas and actions, and the strict hierarchical relations in which control plays an important role, often result in a passive, defensive or rebellious attitude. The clash between the interests of the organization and those of the employees, combined with the frail employee power position, invites an attitude of observance of rules and procedures (Argyris, 1964). The means become more important than the end. Employees resist control by incorporating what De Sitter (1977) termed "defensive leeway". The group norms ensure that outsiders—in this case, the management—do not get the information they need to remove the "stretch" from the work. Attempts to achieve this by applying more control are only counter-productive. Such attempts to "crack down" (Watzlawick, Beauin, & Jackson, 1974) do not bring a solution. As long as the underlying views and values are not negotiable, any attempts at improvements remain within the existing frame of reference: single loop learning (Argyris, 1992; Argyris & Schön, 1978). The defensive routines that people have learned protect them from criticism.

If participation is to be a part of the coordination mechanisms in the organization, and to contribute to increasing flexibility and quality, then it must be compatible with the organizational culture and the underlying cultural preferences in a country or region. It is essential for organizations to come full circle from single loop to double loop learning: the behavioral norms and the assumptions underlying mutual relations then come up for discussion. (In double loop learning not only the behaviour itself, but also the relevance of the norms may be debated, see Argyris, 1985.) Swieringa and Wierdsma (1992) developed a conceptual frame and an intervention method of collective learning to initiate and facilitate dialogue and debate when deep-seated "principles" have to be reconsidered. Mechanisms that give rise to single loop learning are: one-sided control of the agenda by the powerful party, zero sum thinking (one party's gain is the other's loss), and rationalizing. Characteristics of organizations that break down these barriers are two-way communication, openness on the basis of equality, respect for the other person and a problem-solving approach.

Argyris thus avows the values of American culture, and his assumption is that most organizational members share these values with respect to equality and openness. Cultures show strong differences as regards these values. The phenomenon of participative management in itself is an affirmation of a cultural preference. But participative management in its various forms is linked to specific cultural preferences. In America, participation is primarily found in the form of quality of work life and in forms in which part of the proceeds from the "participation profit" are passed on to the participants, who are entitled to their share of this profit. In Europe, with its predominantly individualist culture, we find more characteristics of a collectivist culture. There, participative management much more strongly takes the shape of "bureaucratic/organizationally embedded" forms of representative consultation, where transactions are regulated by an organizational form. Mobility is lower, and employees tend to be members of a workers' community which exhibits a stronger link between the development of an organization and a of person. In Japan this link is even stronger.

If participation is to take root, then it will have to be so embedded in the organization that it can withstand the hesitancy and resistance that is to be expected on the part of employees and managers. The introduction of quality circles or other forms of consultation can be supported by intensive campaigns to draw the attention of the entire staff. Many quality programmes utilize large-scale campaigns to convince employees of the necessity of the programme. Stickers and folders support this process. The danger inherent in this approach is that it remains limited to the outer layer of the organizational culture. If the message does not relate to the views and values of the organization, any change will not be permanent.

8 A QUESTION OF POLICY

Is the extent of participation determined by environmental circumstances and organizational characteristics or is it a matter of outlook and policy?

Long and Warner (1987) pose the question whether direct relationships can be found between the changes in the economic conditions in the period from 1975–1985 and experiences with participative management. Due to increasing unemployment and a decreasing level of unionization, the relative power position of worker representatives also decreased (see also Pankert, 1985; Thompson, 1987). Did this lead to the relinquishment of rights acquired earlier? Here and there this seems to be the case; however, the researchers emphasize that there are great differences between companies. And there are differences between various forms of participation. Sometimes an economic crisis forms the occasion to bypass participatory bodies, sometimes it acts as a platform where temporary harmonization takes place, or at least joint attempts are made to avert the common danger as far as possible (Backhaus, 1987; Thierry & De Jong, 1979; Wood, 1986). The researchers found that a wide variety of reactions were possible. They concluded that participative management is not so much related to the economic circumstances in themselves, but rather to the stability of the environment, the complexity of the technology, the educational level of the personnel and, especially, to the desire of management to involve personnel in policy to a greater or lesser degree. All kinds of circumstances can promote the use of participation or increase the chance of success; in the final examination it is primarily a matter of the views and the outlook of management.

Walton (1985) distinguished two management models that are illustrative in this connection, the control model and the commitment model (see Table 13.3). In the control model, employees are seen as performers of closely defined, highly fragmented tasks. The minimum requirements are precisely formulated. Rewards are linked to variance in individual performance. Involvement in higher organizational goals is not expected. Participation is not encouraged. The labour factor is seen as a variable cost item. Control and efficiency are dominant criteria.

In the commitment model, broader tasks are designed, combining aspects of planning and execution. Individual responsibilities often change with changing circumstances and are therefore flexibly formulated (Morgan, 1986). Often teams are responsible for a particular product. Performance requirements are derived from higher organizational goals. A market orientation and an attitude of constant improvement are essential. The organizational design is relatively flat. Much of the coordination is trusted to mutual adjustment, based on expertise and information, rather than on control from above. The reward system also reflects shared responsibilities and achievements. Collective, not individual, bonuses are part of policy. Participation and involvement in all manner of fields is encouraged, even if it

TABLE 13.3

Two management models.

	Control model	Commitment model
1. Job design	Everyone is responsible for his or her own precisely described task; work is highly fragmented	Broader tasks, flexible description of responsibilities, teamwork
2. Performance requirements	Calculated standards define minimum requirements	Emphasis on higher goals, dynamic and market oriented
3. Organizational design	Steep organization steered from above, coordination and control via rules and procedures; emphasis on positional power	Flat organization with mutual adjustment, coordination and control via common goals and values; emphasis on relevant information and expertise
4. Reward system	Reward for individual performance	Group rewards or profit sharing
5. Job security	Employees are seen as variable costs	Priority given to additional training and transfer
6. Participation	In delimited areas, risks emphasized; only strictly necessary information is disseminated	Broader participation encouraged; information widely spread
7. Labour relations	Emphasis on matters of discord in contacts with works council and trade unions	Attention is also paid to shared problems and interests
8. Management philosophy	Management stresses its own prerogatives and obligations to shareholders	Employee representatives seen as legitimate stakeholders

Source: Walton (1985, pp. 250–251).

involves taking certain risks. This is offset by the guarantee that participation will not threaten job security. Personnel is not the final item on the budget; it is working capital that must be kept intact through schooling and training. Employee representatives are considered legitimate stakeholders, alongside shareholders, customers and the public.

It will be clear that overall company policy, as indicated previously in two contrasting models, is a strong determinant of the possibilities for participative management in a certain department. Of course these are black-and-white portrayals. The reader will have noted a certain parallel with the previously discussed Figure 13.5. Walton's (1985) description, however, places strong emphasis on the separate and independent value of the management outlook alongside or even in contrast to the circumstances. As Child (1972) also stated, the relationship between external circumstances and internal policy always runs via the link of the "strategic choice". Whether the choice made was correct can often only be established in the long run, and sometimes not at all.

Contingency theory is nowadays everywhere accepted in the organizational sciences. Contingency theory makes no statements about the "one best way", but specifies the conditions in which a particular choice is effective. Such theories stimulate a manager not to be dogmatic or adamant, but to let his or her choices depend on the current circumstances, to allow the circumstances to determine what course of action is the most adequate. Pfeffer (1982), however, stated that the concepts are ambiguous and not free of tautology. The scientific research inspired by contingency theory offers the manager contradictory advice. Pfeffer observed a contrast between the popularity of the theory and the—limited—applicability and consistency of research results. The complexity of management in actual practice and the influence of perceptions on the assessment of context variables make the results less readily applicable in a real situation. Surely a manager will allow his or her decisions to be influenced by "objective" circumstances, but—especially with time pressure—he or she will also resort to intuition and perception in determining the right course (see also Chapter 14 in Volume 4 of this handbook). Management is more than problem solving; it also demands pathfinding, a vision and the capacity to formulate inspiring goals (Leavitt, 1986). So it is not merely the circumstances which determine whether participative management is desirable. The views of management are another significant factor. The literature on organizational culture advocates stability and consistency in a manager's choices and behaviour. A manager whose behaviour pattern is extremely pragmatic and dependent on circumstances evokes uncertainty among his or her employees because his or her identity is too erratic. Pfeffer (1981) draws attention to the role of the manager in interpreting ambivalent situations. In organizations, defining reality is also a process of consultation and negotiation in which management occupies a central position (Weick, 1979). Management has an important task in reducing ambiguity and elucidating the situation. New developments in organizational thinking show convincing arguments that the rationality of "one best way" and contingency approaches should be counterbalanced by the view of organizing as a process of meaning creation, social construction, enactment and map making (Gergen, 1994; Reed & Hughes, 1992; Shotter, 1993; Tsoukas, 1994; Weick, 1979, 1994). Providing a semantic framework and, to a certain extent, aligning the various views and values of organizational members, are key tasks of management.

So, although it is influenced by the circumstances, participative management is primarily a question of outlook and policy. If its form is not consistent with the views and values of management, the change will not be permanent. A call for participation that is incompatible with one's own convictions can never be communicated in a convincing manner to the employees. Visible non-verbal behaviour is extremely revealing (Peters, 1978). The way in which an action is performed has great communicative value and can be in sharp contrast to the stated views. Management shows its views and values in all manner of routine choices.

Changing circumstances can greatly stimulate a transition of the organization from the control model to the commitment model. Swieringa and Wierdsma (1992) talk about a shift from "prescriptive" to learning organizations. Semler (1994) gives an excellent example of a self-organizing organization in which workers manage "themselves". Recent developments with respect to customer and market orientations, the emphasis on quality control by preventing mistakes and the demand for quality in services, presume an increased leaning in the direction of the commitment model of Walton (1985). Increased employee involvement in the organizational goals can give a decisive edge over the competition in the market. But the pace and the intensity of the process of increasing employee commitment to the work and to the organization will have to be attuned to the relative inertia of variables such as structure, culture, management systems and the technological choices of yesteryear. Participative management is often approached as a way of integrating the thinking capacities and decision preferences of workers in the management-dominated "machine" way of thinking about organizations. A emerging shift is toward thinking about organizations as coalitions of individuals and groups which collectively create a more of less shared reality. From the perspective of organizing as a process, participation is the key ingredient. Consensus or the ability to create committed collective action to reach goals depends on the quality of the process or the construction of reality. Introducing or intensifying participative management should result in a lengthy and intensive process of change, one in which outlook and policy will be decisive. Only consistency over a longer period of time between behaviour and the views and values expressed by management is convincing enough to tap the thinking of the workers and give substance to participative management. In the final analysis, it is primarily a question of outlook and policy on the balance between organizing and organization and the balance between control and commitment.

REFERENCES

Adams, R. (1972). *Watership down.* London: Rex Collings.

Allaire, Y., & Firsirotu, M. (1984). Theories of organizational culture. *Organization Studies, 5,* 193–226.

Aloni, M., & Gonen, M. (1986). Clear skies for Israel aircraft. *Quality Circles Digest,* 60–70.

Andriessen, J.H.E. (1996). The introduction of networking technology in organizations: Increasing freedom and control. In P.J.D. Drenth, P.L. Koopman, & B. Wilpert (Eds.), *Organizational decision making under different economic and political conditions* (pp. 127–138). Amsterdam: North-Holland.

Argyris, C. (1964). *Integrating the individual and the organization.* New York: Wiley.

Argyris, C. (1985). *Strategy, change and defensive routines.* Boston: Pitman.

Argyris, C. (1992). *On organizational learning.* Cambridge, MA: Blackwell.

Argyris, C., & Schön, D. (1978). *Organizational learning.* Reading: Addison-Wesley.

Austin, J.T., & Bobko, P. (1985). Goal-setting theory: Unexplored areas and future research needs. *Journal of Occupational Psychology, 58,* 289–308.

Backhaus J. (1987). The emergence of worker participation: Evolution and legislation compared. *Journal of Economic Issues, 21,* 895–910.

Bandura, A. (1986). *Social foundations of thoughts and actions: A social cognitive theory.* Englewood Cliffs, NJ: Prentice-Hall.

Bem, D.J. (1970). *Beliefs, attitudes, and human affairs.* Belmont, CA: Brooks/Cole.

Berg, P.O. (1985). Organization change as a symbolic transformation process. In P.J. Frost, L.F. Moore, M.R. Louis, C.C. Lundberg, & J. Martin (Eds.), *Organizational culture.* Beverly Hills: Sage.

Blair J.D., & Whitehead, C.J. (1984). Can quality circles survive in the USA? *Business Horizons, 27,* 17–23.

Blauner, R. (1964). *Alienation and freedom.* Chicago: University of Chicago press.

Blumberg, P. (1968). *Industrial democracy.* London: Constable.

Boisot, M.H. (1983). Confidence revisited: The codification and diffusion of knowledge in the British and the Japanese firm. *Journal of Management Studies, 20,* 159–190.

Boisot, M.H. (1986). Markets and hierarchies in a cultural perspective. *Organization Studies, 7,* 135–158.

Boisot, M.H. (1987). *Information and organizations.* London: Fontana.

Boissoneau, R. (1987). The importance of Japanese management to health care supervisor: Quality and American circles. *Health Care Supervisor, 5,* (3), 28–38.

Bolman, L.G., & Deal, T.E. (1991). *Reframing organizations.* San Francisco: Jossey-Bass.

Bradley, K., & Hill, S. (1987). Quality circles and managerial interests. *Industrial Relations, 26,* 68–82.

Bruck, C.G. (1985). What happens when workers manage themselves? *Fortune, 104,* (2), 62–69.

Bushe, G.R., & Shani, A.B. (1991). *Parallel learning structures.* Reading: Addison-Wesley.

Chadwick-Jones, J.K. (1976). *Social exchange theory: Its structure and influence in social psychology.* London: Academy Press.

Child, J. (1972). Organization structure and strategies of control: A replication of the Aston study. *Administrative Science Quarterly, 17,* 163–177.

Clarke, B.R. (1972). The organizational sage in higher education. *Administrative Science Quarterly, 17,* 178–184.

Coch, L., & French, J.P.R. (1948). Overcoming resistance to change. *Human Relations, 1,* 512–533.

Cole, R.E., & Byosiere P. (1986). Managerial objectives for introducing quality circles: An US–Japan comparison. *Quality Progress, 19,* (3), 25–30.

Cooperrider, D.L., & Srivastva, S. (1987). Appreciative inquiry in organizational life. *Research in Organizational Change and Development, 1,* 129–169.

Cotton, J.L, Vollrath, D.A., Frogatt, K.L., Lengnick-Hall, M.L., & Jennings, K.R. (1988). Employee participation: Diverse forms and different outcomes. *Academy of Management Review, 13,* 8–22.

Cox, J.F. & Norris, D.R. (1983). Measuring quality circles' effectiveness. *Proceedings of the American Production and Inventory Control Society*, 178–181.

Czarniawska-Joerges, B. (1988). *To coin a phrase*. Stockholm: Stockholm School of Economics.

Czarniawska-Joerges, B. (1992). *Exploring complex organizations*. London: Sage.

Dachler, H.P. Wilpert, B. (1978). Conceptual dimensions and boundaries of participation in organizations: A critical evaluation. *Administrative Science Quarterley*, *23*, 1–39.

Dandridge, T.C., Mitroff, I., & Joyce, W. (1980). Organizational symbolism. *Academy of Management Journal*, *5*, 77–82.

Davis, L.E. (1977). Evolving alternative organization designs: Their sociotechnical bases. *Human Relations*, *30*, 261–273.

Deal, T., & Kennedy, A. (1982). *Corporate cultures*. Reading, MA: Addison-Wesley.

Drenth, P.J.D., & Koopman P.L. (1983). Experiences with "werkoverleg": Implications for Quality Circles. *Journal of General Management*, *9*, 57–73.

Drenth, P.J.D., & Koopman, P.L. (1984). A contingency approach to participative leadership: How good? In J.G. Hunt, D.M. Hosking, C.A. Schriesheim, & R. Stewart (Eds.). *Leaders and managers: International perspectives on managerial behavior and leadership* (pp. 303–315). New York: Pergamon.

Erez, M. (1993). Participation in goal-setting: A motivational approach. In W.M. Lafferty, & E. Rosenstein (Eds.), *International handbook of participation in organizations* (Vol. 3). Oxford: Oxford University Press.

Erez, M. (1994). Towards a model of cross-cultural industrial and organizational psychology. In H.C. Triandis, M.D. Dunnette, & M.H. Leaetta, (Eds.), *Handbook of industrial and organizational psychology* (2nd Edn, Vol. 4). Palo Alto, CA: Consulting Psychologists Press.

Filley, A.C., House, R.J., Kerr, S. (1976). *Managerial process and organizational behavior*. Glenview, IL: Scott Foresman.

Gantos, L.A. (1987). Quality Circles: An exploratory study of their efficacy for improving school decision structures. *Dissertation Abstracts International*, *48*, (2), 265(A).

Ganzevoort, W. (1981). Organisatie-ideologieën: De fictie van de rationaliteit van het organiseren [The fiction of rationality in organizing]. *Intermediair*, *17*, No. 36.

Gergen, K.J. (1994). *Towards transformation in social knowledge* (2nd Edn). London: Sage.

Goodfellow, M. (1981). Quality control circles programmes: What works and what doesn't. *Quality Progress*, 14, August, 30–33.

Guzzo, R.A., Jette, R.D., & Katzell, R.A. (1985). The effects of psychologically based intervention programs on worker productivity: A meta-analysis. *Personnel Psychology*, *38*, 275–291.

Hackman, J.R. & Oldham, G.R. (1976). Motivation through the design of work: A test of a theory. *Organizational Behavior and Human Performance*, *16*, 250–279.

Handy, C.B. (1985). *Understanding organizations*. New York: Penguin.

Harrison, R. (1972). Understanding your organization's character. *Harvard Business Review*, *50*, 119–128.

Hattem, E. (1987). *The effect of participation in quality circles on employee attitude, behavior and productivity*. Final Thesis for the M.Sc. Degree in Management Science Organizational Behavior. Tel Aviv University, Israel.

Heller, F.A. (1988). Participation and competence: A necessary relationship. In R. Russell & V. Rus (Eds.), *International handbook of participation in organizations*. Chichester: Wiley.

Heller, F.A., Drenth, P.J.D., Koopman, P.L., & Rus, V. (1988). *Decisions in organizations: A three-country comparative study*. London: Sage.

Heller, F.A. & Wilpert B. (1981). *Competence and power in managerial decision-making*. Chichester: Wiley.

Herzberg, F., Mausner, B., & Snyderman, B.B. (1959). *The motivation to work*. New York: Wiley.

Hirschhorn, L. (1991). *Managing in the new team environment*. Reading, MA: Addison-Wesley.

Hofstede, G. (1991). *Cultures and organizations: Software of the mind*. London: McGraw-Hill.

IDE International Research Group (1981). *Industrial democracy in Europe*. Oxford: Clarendon Press.

IDE International Research Group (1993). *Industrial democracy in Europe revisited*. Oxford: Oxford University Press.

Jain, H.C., & Giles, A. (1985). Worker's participation in western Europe: Implications for North America. *Industrial Relations*, *40*, 747–772.

Jenkins, G.D. & Lawler, E.E. (1981). Impact of employee participation in pay plan development. *Organizational Behavior and Human Performance*, *28*, 111–128.

Johnson, P., & Gill, J. (1993). *Management control and organizational behaviour*. London: Paul Chapman.

Katz, D., & Kahn, R.L. (1978), *The social psychology of organizations*. New York: Wiley.

Keesing, R. (1974). Theories of culture. *Annual Review of Anthropology*, *3*, 73–79.

Keil, T.J. (1983). *The formation of worker consciousness in a producer cooperative*. International Workshop: "Future Prospectives of Economic and Industrial Democracy", Dubrovnik.

Kipnis, D. (1976). *The powerholders*. Chicago: University of Chicago Press.

Klein, J.A. (1984). Why supervisors resist emoployee involvement. *Harvard Business Review*, *62*, 5, 87–95.

Koopman, P.L. (1991). Between control and commitment: Management and change as the art of balancing. *Leadership and Organization Development Journal, 12*, (5), 3–7.

Koopman, P.L., Drenth, P.J.D., Heller, F.A. & Rus, V. (1993). Participation in complex organizational decisions: A comparative study of the United Kingdom, The Netherlands, and Yugoslavia. In W.M. Lafferty, & E. Rosenstein (Eds.), *International handbook of participation in organizations (Vol. 3)*. Oxford: Oxford University Press.

Koopman, P.L., & Wierdsma, A.F.M. (1984). Work consultation as a channel of communication and as a consultative framework. In P.J.D. Drenth, H. Thierry, P.J. Willems, & C.J. de Wolff (Eds.), *Handbook of Work and Organizational Psychology* (Vol. 1, pp. 643–661). Chichester: Wiley.

Kuhn, T.S. (1970). *The structure of scientific revolutions.* Chicago: University of Chicago Press.

Lammers, C.A. (1973). Self-management and participation: Two concepts of democratization in organizations. In E. Pusic, (Ed.), *Participation and Self-management* (Vol.4). Zagreb: Institute for Social Research.

Lammers, C.J., & Széll, G. (1989). Concluding reflections organizational democracy: Taking stock. In C.J. Lammers, & G. Széll, (Eds.), *International handbook of participation in organizations* (Vol. 1). Oxford: Oxford University Press.

Latham, G.P., & Marshall, H.A. (1982). The effects of self-set, participatively set and assigned goals on the performance of government employees. *Personnel Psychology, 35*, 399–404.

Lawler, E.E. (1973). *Motivation in work organizations*. Monterey: Brooks/Cole.

Lawler, E.E. (1986). *High-involvement management: Participative strategies for improving organizational performance*. San Francisco: Jossey-Bass.

Lawler, E.E. (1989). Participative management in the United States: Three classics revisited. In C.J. Lammers, & G. Széll (Eds.), *International handbook of participation in organizations* (Vol. 1). Oxford: Oxford University Press.

Lawler, E.E., & Mohrman, S.A. (1985). Quality circles after the fad. *Harvard Business Review, 63*, (1), 65–71.

Leavitt, H.J. (1986). *Corporate pathfinders*. Homewood, IL: Dow Jones-Irwin.

Lehman, M.E. (1986). An evaluation of the effect of quality circles program on productivity in health care facility. *Dissertation Abstracts International, 47*, (5).

Levine, D, & Tyson, L. (1990). Participation, productivity, and the firm's environment. In A. Blinder (Ed.), *Paying for productivity*. Washington DC: Brookings Institution.

Likert, R. (1967). *The human organization: Its management and value*. London: McGraw-Hill.

Locke, E.A., Feren, D.B., McCaleb, V.M., Shaw, K.N., & Denny, A.T. (1980). The relative effectiveness of four methods of motivating employee performance. In K.D. Duncan, M.M. Gruneberg, & D. Wallis (Eds.), *Changes in working life*. London: Wiley.

Locke, E.A., Frederick, E., Lee, C., & Bobko, P. (1984). Effect of self-efficacy, goals, and task strategies on task performance. *Journal of Applied Psychology, 69*, 241–251.

Locke, E.A., & Henne, D. (1986). Work motivation theories. In C.L. Cooper, & I. Robertson, (Eds.), *International review of industrial and organizational psychology*. London: Wiley.

Locke, E.A., & Latham, G.P. (1984). *Goal setting: A motivation technique that works*. Englewood Cliffs, NJ: Prentice-Hall.

Locke, E.A., & Latham. G.P. (1990). *A theory of goal setting and risk performance*. Englewood Cliffs, NJ: Prentice-Hall.

Locke, E.A., & Schweiger, D.M. (1979). Participation in decision-making: One more look. In B.M. Staw (Ed.), *New directions in organizational behavior* (pp. 265–339). Greenwich, CT: JAI Press.

Lodge, G.C., & Vogel, E.F. (1987). *An ideology and national competitiveness*. Boston: Harvard Business School.

Long, R.J. (1983). *Employee ownership: The North American experience.* International Workshop: "Future Prospectives of Economic and Industrial Democracy", Dubrovnik.

Long, R.J., & Warner, M. (1987). Organizations, participation and recession: An analysis of recent evidence. *Industrial Relations 42*, 65–88.

Lowin, A. (1968), Participatory decision-making: A model, literature critique and prescription for research. *Organizational Behavior and Human Performance, 3*, 68–106.

Maczynski, J., Jago, A.G., Reber, G., & Böhnisch, W. (1994). Culture and leadership styles: A comparison of Polish, Austrian, and U.S. managers. *Polish Psychological Bulletin, 25*, 303–315.

Man, H. de (1988). *Organizational change in its context*. Delft: Euron.

Man, H. de, & Koopman, P. L. (1984), Medezeggenschap tussen ideologie en bedrijfspraktijk [Co-determination between ideology and practice]. *M&O, Tijdschrift voor Organisatiekunde en Sociaal Beleid, 38*, 471–480.

McGregor, D.M. (1960). *The human side of enterprise*. New York: McGraw-Hill.

Marks, M.L., Mirvis, P.H., Hackett, E.J., & Grady, F.J (1986). Employee participation in a quality circle programme: Impact on quality of work life. *Journal of Applied Psychology. 71*, 61–69.

Marrow, A.J., Bowers, D.G. & Seashore, S.E. (1967). *Management by participation*. New York: Harper & Row.

Matsui, K., Kakuyama, T., & Onglatco, M.L. (1987). Effects of goals and feedback on performance in groups. *Journal of Applied Psychology, 72*, 407–415.

Meyerson, D., & Martin, J. (1987). Cultural change:

An integration of three different views. *Journal of Management Studies*, *24*, 623–647.

Miles, R.E. (1965). Human relations or human resources. *Harvard Business Review*, *43*, 148–163.

Miles, R.E. (1996). Participative management: From idealistic ought to economic must. In P.J.D. Drenth, P.L. Koopman, & B. Wilpert (Eds.), *Organizational decision making under different economic and political conditions* (pp. 21–28). Amsterdam: North-Holland.

Miller, C.S., & Schuster, M.H. (1987). Gainsharing plans: A comparative analysis. *Organizational Dynamics*, *16*, 44–67.

Miller, K.L., & Monge, P.R. (1986). Participation, satisfaction and productivity: A meta-analytic review. *Academy of Management Journal*, *29*, 727–753.

Miner, J.B. (1984). The validity and usefulness of theories in an emerging organizational science. *Academy of Management Review*, *9*, 296–306.

Mintzberg, H. (1979). *The structuring of organizations*. Englewood Cliffs, NJ: Prentice-Hall.

Mintzberg. H. (1983). *Power in and around organizations*. Englewood Cliffs, NJ: Prenctice-Hall.

Mohrman, S.A., & Novelli, L.J. (1985). Beyond testimonials: Learning from a quality circles programme. *Journal of Occupational Behavior*. *6*, 93–110.

Morgan, G. (1986). *Images of organization*. London: Sage.

Morgan, G., Frost, P.J., & Pondy, L.R. (1983). Organizational symbolism. In L.R. Pondy, P.J. Frost, G. Morgan, & T.C. Dandridge (Eds.), *Organizational symbolism* (pp. 3–39). Greenwich, CT: JAI Press.

Morse, N.C., & Reimer, E. (1956). The experimental change of a major organizational variable. *Journal of Abnormal and Social Psychology*, *52*, 120–129.

Muijen, J.J., & Koopman, P.L. (1994). The influence of national culture on organizational culture: A comparative study between 10 countries. *European Work and Organizational Psychologist*, *4*, 367–380.

Neuijen, J.A. (1992). *Diagnosing organisational cultures*. Groningen: Wolters-Noordhoff.

Pankert, A. (1985), Recent developments in labour relations in the industrialised market economy countries: Some bench-marks. *International Labour Review*, *124*, 531–544.

Peters, T. (1978), Symbols, patterns and settings. *Organizational Dynamics*, *7*, Autumn, 3–23.

Pfeffer, J. (1981). "Management as symbolic action" In L. Cummings, & B. Shaw, (Eds.), *Research in organizational behavior*. Greenwich CT: JAI Press.

Pfeffer, J. (1982). *Organizations and organization theory*. Boston: Pitman.

Pheysey, D.C. (1993). *Organizational cultures: Types and transformations*. London: Routledge.

Pollard, W.E., & Mitchell, T.R. (1972). Decision theory analysis of social power. *Psychological Bulletin*, *78*, 433–446.

Poole, M. (1986). *Towards a new industrial democracy: Workers participation in industry*. London: Routledge & Kegan Paul.

Quinn, R.E (1988). *Beyond rational management*. San Francisco: Jossey-Bass.

Rafaeli, A. (1985). Quality circles and employee attitudes. *Personnel Psychology*, *38*, 603–612.

Reed, M., & Hughes, M. (1992). *Rethinking organizations*. London: Sage.

Robbins, S.P. (1990). *Organizations theory: Structure, design, and applications* (3rd Edn.). Englewood Cliffs, NJ: Prentice-Hall.

Rooney, P.M. (1993). Effects of worker participation in the USA: Managers' perceptions vs. empirical measures. In W.M. Lafferty, & E. Rosenstein, (Eds.), *International handbook of participation in organizations* (Vol. 3). Oxford: Oxford University Press.

Rosenstein, E., Ofek, A., & Harel, G. (1987). Organizational democracy and management in Israel. *International Studies of Managenent and Organization*, *17*, 52–68.

Rus, V. (1996). The quality of decision-making. In P.J.D. Drenth, P.L. Koopman, & B. Wilpert (Eds.), *Organizational decision making under different economic and political conditions*. Amsterdam: Koninklijke Nederlandse Akademie van Wetenschappen.

Russell, R. (1983). Employee ownership in the services. International Workshop: "Future Prospectives of Economic and Industrial Democracy". Dubrovnik.

Russell, R. (1996). The limits of workplace democracy. In P.J.D. Drenth, P.L. Koopman, & B. Wilpert (Eds.), *Organizational decision making under different economic and political conditions* (pp. 59–70). Amsterdam: North-Holland.

Sackmann, S.A. (1991). *Cultural knowledge in organizations*. London: Sage.

Sadler, P. (1988). *Managerial leadership in the post-industrial society*. Aldershot: Gower.

Sassoon, M., & Koopman, P.L. (1988). De kwaliteit van kwaliteitskringen: Een tussentijdse evaluatie [The quality of quality circles]. *Gedrag en Organisatie*, *1*, (5), 22–37.

Sathé, V. (1985). *Culture and related corporate realities*. Homewood: Irwin.

Schein, E. (1992). *Organizational culture and leadership* (2nd Edn). San Francisco: Jossey-Bass.

Schneider, B. (1990). The climate for service. In B. Schneider (Ed.), *Organizational climate and culture*. San Francisco: Jossey-Bass.

Sell R. (1986). The politics of workplace participation. *Personnel Management*, *18*, (6), 34–37.

Semler, R. (1994). Why my former employees still work for me. *Harvard Business Review*, *72*, (1), 64–74.

Shaw, M.E. & Constanzo, P.R. (1970). *Theories of social psychology*. New York: McGraw-Hill.

Shotter, J. (1993). *Conversational realities*. London: Sage.

Sitter, L.U. de (1977). *Productieorganisatie en arbeidsorganisatie in sociaal economisch perspectief.* Den Haag: Nive.

Strauss, G. (1963). Some notes on power-equalization. In H.J. Leavitt (Ed.), *The social science of organizations* (pp. 41–84). Englewood Cliffs, NJ: Prentice-Hall.

Strauss, G. (1982). Workers participation in management: An international perspective. In L.L. Cummings & B.M. Staw (Eds.), *Research in Organizational Behavior, 4* (pp. 173–265). Greenwich, CT: JAI Press.

Strauss, G. (1996). Some selected problems associated with formal workers' participation. In P.J.D. Drenth, P.L. Koopman, & B. Wilpert (Eds.), *Organizational decision making under different economic and political conditions.* (pp. 117–126) Amsterdam: North-Holland.

Swieringa, J., & Wierdsma, A.F.M. (1992). *Becoming a learning organization.* Reading: Addison-Wesley.

Thierry, H. (1987). Payment by results systems: A review of research 1945–1985. *Applied Psychology: An International Review, 36*, 91–108.

Thierry, H., & Jong, J.R. de (1979). *Naar participatie en toerekening*. Assen: Van Gorcum.

Thompson D. (1987). New role for labor unions. *Industry Week, 23*, (3), 30–38.

Triandis, H.C. (1994). Cross-cultural industrial and organizational psychology. In H.C. Triandis, M.D. Dunnette, & M.H. Leaetta (Eds.). *Handbook of industrial and organizational psychology* (2nd Edn, Vol. 4). Palo Alto, CA: Consulting Psychologists Press.

Trice, H.M., & Beyer, J.M. (1993). *The cultures of work organizations.* Englewood Cliffs, NJ: Prentice-Hall.

Tsoukas, H. (1994). *New thinking in organizational behaviour*. Oxford: Butterworth-Heinemann.

Vroom, V. (1964). *Work and motivation*. New York: Wiley.

Vroom, V.H., & Jago, A.G. (1988). *The new leadership: Managing participation in organizations.* Englewood Cliffs, NJ: Prentice-Hall.

Vroom, V.H., & Yetton, P.W. (1973). *Leadership and decision-making*. Pittsburgh: University of Pittsburgh Press.

Wagner, J.A. & Gooding, R.Z. (1987). Shared influence and organizational behavior: A meta-analysis of situational variables expected to moderate participation-outcome relationships. *Academy of Management Journal, 30*, 524–541.

Wall, T.D., & Lischeron, J.A. (1977). *Worker participation*. London: MacGraw-Hill.

Walton, R.E. (1985). From control to commitment: Transforming work force management in the United States. In K.B. Clark, R.H. Hayes, & C. Lorenz (Eds.), *The uneasy alliance*. Boston: Harvard Business School Press.

Watson, T.J. (1986). *Management, organization and employment strategy: New directions in theory and practice*. London: Routledge & Kegan Paul.

Watzlawick, P., Beavin, J.H., & Jackson, D.D. (1974). *De pragmatische aspecten van de menselijke communicatie*. Deventer: Van Loghum Slaterus.

Weick, K. (1979). *The social psychology of organizing.* Reading, MA: Addison-Wesley.

Weick, K.E. (1994). Cartographic myths in organizations. In H. Tsoukas, (Ed.), *New thinking in organizational behaviour*. Oxford: Butterworth-Heinemann.

Wexley, K.N., & Yukl, G.A. (1984). *Organizational behavior and personnel psychology*. Homewood: Irwin.

Whyte, W.F. (1987). From human relations to organizational behavior: Reflections on the changing scene. *Industrial and Labor Relations Review, 40*, 487–500.

Wierdsma, A.F.M. (1985). Comparatief management: Ontwikkelingen en relevantie. *M&O, Tijdschrift voor Organisatiekunde en Sociaal Beleid, 39*, 136–155.

Wierdsma, A.F.M. (1988). Interculturele communicatie. In C. Korswagen, J. Kolkhuis Tanke, & S. Verrept, (Eds.), *Handboek taalhantering*, Vol. 17, IV, 1,1–28.

Wilkins, A. (1979). *Organizational stories and third-order controls*. Utah: Brigham Young University.

Wilkins, A.L. (1983). Organizational stories as symbols which control the organization. In L.R. Pondy, P.J. Frost, G. Morgan, & T.C. Dandridge (Eds.), *Organizational symbolism*. Greenwich CT: JAI press.

Wilkins, A.L. & Ouchi, W.G. (1983). Efficient cultures: Exploring the relationship between culture and organizational performance. *Administrative Science Quarterly, 28*, 468–481.

Williamson, O.E. (1975). *Market and hierarchies*. New York: Free Press.

Williamson, O.E., & Ouchi, N.W.G. (1981). The markets and hierarchies program of research: Origins, implications, prospects. In A.H. van der Ven & W.S. Joyce (Eds.), *Prospectives in organization design and behavior*. (pp. 347–370). New York: Wiley.

Wood. S. (1986). Researching the new industrial relations. *Employee Relations* (UK). *8*, 5, 23–30.

Wood, R., Hull, F., & Azumi, K. (1983). Evaluating quality circles: The American application. *California Management Review, 26*, (1), 37–53.

14

Negotiation

Evert van de Vliert and Willem F.G. Mastenbroek

INTRODUCTION

Possibly the most important form of cooperation takes place when members of an organization or their representatives attempt to agree about sharing or exchanging something among themselves. This behaviour is known as negotiation, irrespective of whether the agreement aimed for concerns money, aims, procedures, personnel, influence, work, resources, time or other things. This list immediately emphasizes the fact that no one can fulfil an organizational function without continually having to negotiate. Moreover, many organizations are tending towards forms of decentralization whereby vertical control via assignments is being replaced by horizontal agreement by means of negotiation. This chapter will shed light on the background of the process and the outcome of negotiations. However, an account of the chosen restrictions, definitions and theoretical elaborations will first be given.

BASIC ASSUMPTIONS

An organization is such a complex phenomenon that a scientist will preferably study only one specific aspect of it. In our case this is the behaviour by which individuals look after their own or others' interests by means of making agreements. It is assumed that different people and groups often have conflicting interests and that one then usually turns to negotiation. One attempts to make one or more mutual agreements about, for example, criteria, the nature of assignments, a plan, a sale, or rights and duties. Seen in this way an organization can be defined as a jumble of negotiations and agreements between different members of the organization and with people outside the organization.

For convenience of comparison, the majority of researchers concentrate on negotiations between just two people. Here we presume that their results can also be applied to situations including at least three negotiators, and no special attention is paid to this. Negotiations between groups are not dealt with either. As far as collective negotiations between employees and employers are concerned, we have limited ourselves to individual representatives who attempt to do business for third parties (for collective labour negotiations between groups see the journals *Industrial and Labor Relations Review* and *Journal of Collective Negotiations in the Public Sector* as well as Himmelmann, 1971; Lipsky & Donn, 1987; Morley & Stephenson, 1977; Putnam, 1994; Wall, 1977; Wolters, 1989).

The key concepts "interest" and "negotiation" can be defined as follows. An *interest* is something that touches and motivates someone, since an outcome is linked to it. Chapter 11 in Volume 4 of this handbook makes it clear that an infinite number of positive and negative outcomes, and therefore interests, exist. It also makes clear that people attempt to look after their interests in many different ways. Our chapter is limited to those situations in which members of an organization experience conflicting interests, either between themselves or with outsiders. Moreover they believe or hope that negotiation will lead to better results than letting the situation take its course, by "fighting", or other reactions.

Negotiation is the behaviour of parties concerned when tuned towards one another, while they attempt agreement on the distribution or exchange of benefits or costs. Five explanations may help to clarify this definition:

1. One can only speak of negotiation if the parties have opposite interests when determining their outcomes.
2. The aim of agreement implies that the parties are dependent on one another for their own outcomes.
3. Outcomes can be seen as benefits or costs.
4. Negotiation aims towards agreement and not necessarily the achievement of agreement. This aim can lead to a compromise, or to the creative neutralization of the conflicting interests, complete capitulation by one of the parties, a temporary stalemate, or a definitive split.
5. Last but not least, agreement may be achieved on the division of yields or costs (for example, money, debts, raw materials, working hours, environmental measures, obligations to third parties), or the exchange of certain yields or costs for others (for example, money for raw materials, working hours for environmental measures).

In addition, it is important to note that the concepts of distribution and exchange used in our definition of negotiation do not refer to the well known types of distributive and integrative bargaining respectively (Thomas, 1992; Walton & McKersie, 1965). Distributive bargaining represents the extent to which a party minimizes or maximizes its relative gain or loss of outcomes *vis-à-vis* the other party. Put another way, the size of each party's proportion of a fixed pie is at stake. In contrast, integrative bargaining represents the extent to which a party minimizes or maximizes outcomes for both parties. The size of the joint pie is at stake.

Following Lax and Sebenius (1986), we view distributive and integrative bargaining as different aspects of, rather than different types of, negotiation. We will argue that distributive and integrative processes are entwined in a symbiotic bonding that pervades all negotiation behaviours, rather than excluding one another (see Putnam, 1990). A better basis for a typology of negotiations are the actual and potential "ownership" of a disputed benefit or cost, because there is usually a clear boundary between mine and yours. It is believed that the interests promoted and the negotiation tactics employed are dependent on whether the wished benefits or the rejected costs already belong to the other party. We will look at this more closely in a taxonomy of negotiations.

TYPES OF NEGOTIATION

If one sees negotiations as a process of conveyance of property between parties, it is possible to differentiate between two main types and one subtype of negotiation, on the grounds of the following prototypical situations.

1. The available outcome belongs to no one, at least no one in particular (for example, potential clients, the duty timetable, apparatus, a certain habit, speaking time, integrity). One generally turns to negotiation when another party lays a claim to certain yields or on exemption from certain costs. Since the negotiators are not the exclusive owner, they make use of a division criterion. When doing so they will claim a share of the outcome which is as favourable as possible. However, in the end they will usually agree to a less favourable division,

since they need to come to agreement with the other party. Their tactical interaction is characterized by the pursuit of a so-called *claim negotiation*. Theories about joint decision making are perfectly applicable to this sort of negotiation (Gulliver, 1979; Neale & Bazerman, 1991; Pruitt & Carnevale, 1993).

2. Each party is the formal or informal owner of yields desired or costs rejected by the other party (for example, a designated budget, debt, signing rights, usable personnel, break-time, a scandalous policy memorandum, someone's work station). Since it is difficult or impossible to make a claim, it is obvious that an attempt should be made to "buy" the desired goods from the other party or to "sell" the undesired goods to the other party. One can pay using every means of exchange acceptable to the other, irrespective of whether one is the formal or informal owner of the means of exchange. Since this is in fact a buyer-seller relationship, we call this tactical transaction *trade negotiation*. Exchange theories related to the exchange of promises, services or other means, are particularly applicable to this type of negotiation, on the grounds of an "exchange rate" agreed on by the negotiators (Anzieu, 1974; Wall, 1985).
3. In the previous two main types of negotiation, the negotiator is the potential owner of the disputed outcome. However this is not necessarily the case in interests looked after by third parties. In this case one has an essentially different interaction with the other party, from whom one claims or buys while acting as a representative. We use the term *representative negotiation* for both subtypes of claim and trade negotiation.

Table 14.1 summarizes the characteristic differences between claim and trade negotiations. These differences indicate that it is possible to recognize a claim negotiation and a trade negotiation by looking at their introductory period, course and end result. This does not mean that the interests and tactics of claim and trade negotiations do not overlap. Neither does this deny the fact that the different types of negotiation sometimes shade into one another, or intertwine. The situation in which the parties first have to exert a lot of energy to aquire a financial, personnel or organizational yield from others, which must then be shared out, also often takes place. This is a complex combination of the three types of negotiation dealt with. After or during the representative claim or trade negotiations with the outsiders, an internal claim or trade negotiation will take place. This chapter will discuss the interests and tactics characteristic of claim negotiations, trade negotiations and representative negotiations respectively.

CLAIM NEGOTIATIONS

This section deals with the pursuance of an agreement on the division of one or more yields or costs when an owner does not yet exist or when the owner is not present. We include those situations in which the negotiators are the joint owner rather than individual owner of something. One can think along the lines of a discussion between two people concerning the distribution of an allocated budget

TABLE 14.1

Characteristic differences between claim negotiations and trade negotiations.

Characteristic	*Claim negotiations*	*Trade negotiations*
Ownership	No owners	Owners
Basis	Criterion	Means of exchange
Agreement	Distribution	Rate of exchange
Theoretical framework	Decision theories	Exchange theories

or a promised increase in man hours, or colleagues among whom no one wants to be responsible for a new project which needs to be carried out, or two managers in a functionally organized business who need to discuss the claims they are each going to make on the central department of logistics in the coming year. In each case their key aim appears to be agreement on a criterion or criteria to achieve division. In each case the criteria for decision play a key role in their interests and tactics.

Interests

An interest touches and motivates someone, because it leads to an outcome. Psychologists call this type of interest "need" or "motive". Thus it is not surprising that Lewicki and Litterer (1985), referring to Maslow, classify interests on the grounds of the following needs: physiological satisfaction, safety and security, love and belonging, esteem, self-actualization, knowledge and understanding, and aesthetic appreciation. Unfortunately they do not indicate how these needs influence the negotiators. Differentiation between main interests and additional interests may provide more insight. Using our starting points it is possible to classify three main interests: *one's own interest*, the *opponent's interest* which is incompatible with one's own interest, and the superordinate *joint interest* of the agreement. Lax and Sebenius (1986) also recognize three additional interests: *process interests* such as someone's reputation as a negotiator, *relational interests* such as a pleasant understanding with the opponent, and *interests in principles* such as justice (see, for a similar categorization, Roloff & Jordan, 1992). Even though we believe every outcome to represent both a main and an additional interest, we will stick to Lax and Sebenius's (1986) classification for convenience of comparison. We will discuss the joint interest and the additional interest, paying a relatively large amount of attention to the interests in principles, which can come in useful as decision criteria during claim negotiations.

The fact that the experienced joint interest can sometimes be interpreted in different ways, whereby it becomes somewhat ambiguous, can lead to complications. Are we talking about the division of a cake of fixed size, whereby the agreement leads to each individual getting what the other does not get? Or is it possible to increase the size of the cake by joint actions, so that all parties get what they want? If, during the division of a jointly allocated and too small increase in personnel, the heads of departments A and B realize that A actually needs more staff during the autumn and winter while B needs more staff in the winter and spring, then they will increase the size of their cake. If, on top of this, they make a plan in which they can make more effective use of their staff in the winter, or can allow some work to be carried out in the summer, it may be possible to honour both claims completely. Lax and Sebenius (1986) believe that the joint interest is rarely ambiguous, and that every manager knows that it is necessary to choose between a compromise in which the cake is divided or a solution in which the cake is enlarged. In fact their whole book is based on the proposition that "negotiators must manage the inescapable tension between cooperative moves to create value for all and competitive moves to claim value for each" (Lax & Sebenius, 1986, p. 6).

The importance which the parties attach to the value of their main outcomes must not be overestimated. Observers of actual negotiations continually emphasize the fact that the progress of the process is crucial, and that those involved also find the course of the process important (Dupont & Faure, 1991; Gulliver, 1979; Mastenbroek, 1987, 1989; Zartman & Berman, 1982). If the process is well-organized, and at the same time flexible and flowing, and one has the possibility of showing what one is worth, this is seen as an additional yield. During official negotiations, such as collective wage claims, the procedures are usually promoted to an additional main interest. In this case negotiations about the rules and the method by which the further negotiations must be conducted take place first: place and time of the meetings, participants, agenda, decision making, time limits, and so on.

Relational interests are looked after if one aims towards discussions that take place pleasantly and in which the working atmosphere is improved rather than worsened. This is less important during one-off claim negotiations. However in an organizational context, in which the parties are continually dependent on one another, the future relationship almost always plays a role (Donohue & Ramesh, 1992). Women find this even more important than men (Greenhalgh, 1987). The negotiation may be a flash in the pan, but the mutual relationship is seldom so. Even so, very little research has been carried out into the link between these relational interests and behaviour during negotiation. This is due to the large influence that game theoretics orientated towards economics have on the paradigms to study negotiations, and due to the dominance of laboratory experiments as a research method (e.g. Murnighan, 1991; Roth, 1991).

A claim negotiation often includes the criteria by which the allocation of the yields or costs are made. This brings us to interests in principles. Fisher and Ury (1981) are very motivated by principled negotiation, in which the parties insist that decisions are made on the grounds of objective criteria, such as tradition, precedent, equal opportunities or professional ethics. This sounds wonderful, but in practice it means that one no longer claims on the basis of outcomes but on the basis of favourable principles. Thus negotiators often conveniently appeal to previously-made policy agreements, in the interests of the business, or in a more general social interest. A very different criterion is that one wants to remain honest and one wants to be treated honestly. Another favourite is the *status-quo principle* (Lewicki & Litterer, 1985; Pruitt, 1981) in which none of the parties involved must become worse off in the future. This principle may prevent a decrease in salary or position, or a change in the nature of the work. It is not without reason that a union negotiator sometimes attempts to create a new status quo via a precedent by entering into a favourable collective labour agreement for a particular branch of industry.

Many divisions take place on the basis of opinions about what is and what is not fair. The four most important principles of distributive justice are those of equality, equity, need, and opportunity (Albin, 1993; Deutsch, 1985; Kabanoff, 1991; Pruitt, 1981; Pruitt & Carnevale, 1993; Zartman & Berman, 1982). The *equality principle* is the most simple, since it does not refer to a criterion beyond the here and now of the negotiations. Everyone gets equal amounts. It is a salient and powerful principle, as long as it is possible to halve the sum of the yields or costs. In general, equal payoffs are preferred over inequity, especially disadvantageous inequity (Loewenstein, Thompson, & Bazerman, 1989). A book on negotiation even has the principle of equality as its title: *The 50% Solution* (Zartman, 1976). Even if a 50/50 division is not decided on, this does not mean that the 50/50 principle will no longer be applied. If, during a negotiation, A claims 90% of the yield while B claims 40% then it may be in the interest of A or B for them both to make equally large concessions. Sharing the pain can be an effective way of preventing the joint interests of the agreement from being in danger, especially towards the end of tiresome negotiations.

Naturally the use of the principle of equality is not in the interest of those who believe that they have good reasons not to apply it. One such reason is, for example, the unfairness of the 50/50 rule. The *equity principle* involves division occurring on the basis of each person's merits. The greater the contribution towards the size and the utility of the outcomes to be shared, the more one receives. The parties find this fair because they acquire equal outcomes in proportion to their sacrifices, profit or accountability. Once they are in agreement that the equity principle should be used, this does not guarantee that they will apply the same criteria to determine the size of each person's contribution (for example, invested means, time, ideas, effort), let alone that the results of their measurements will be equal. On top of this, agreement must also be achieved as to whether the proportion between contributions and outcomes of the one party is the same as the proportion between contributions and outcomes of the other. In short, a compromise based on fairness is an achievement of exceptional like-mindedness.

Equality and equity do not take into account the extent to which each of the negotiators benefits from the outcomes. Two other rules use this as their starting point. According to the *principle of need*, a division dependent on the size of the legitimate interests of each party is justified. People who are able to show to need more of something, get more. The *principle of opportunity* states that people must receive more yield the better they can make use of it. This is, for example, the case if someone can make use of it straight away or can demonstrably create more return than the other. However, as is the case for the degree of equity, the level of need or opportunity is not easily determined. This can also become the subject of negotiation. However the greatest problem is most probably the level to which each of the four principles of righteousness are acceptable to both parties.

Some authours believe that in the case of hierarchic negotiation relations, the superior party usually has more interest in applying the principle of equity (e.g. Bacharach & Lawler, 1981). A more general tendency is that successful members of an organization tend to choose equity while unsuccessful members choose equality. In agreement with this, Beer and Gery (1972) found that productive workers tended to support performance related pay, while unproductive workers preferred general pay raises. Furthermore, Deutsch (1985, p. 44) has developed the hypothesis that "the tendency for economically oriented groups will be to use the principle of equity, for solidarity-oriented groups to use the principle of equality, and for caring oriented groups to use the principle of need as the basic value underlying the system of distributive justice."

In summary, at least one's own and a joint main interest are at issue during a claim negotiation, while process interests, relational interests and interests in principles usually also play a role. The status quo, equality, equity, need and opportunity have been discussed as the most important principles of distributive justice. The more and stronger people experience these interests, the more dependent they are on their own and the other party's tactical position (Bacharach & Lawler, 1981).

Tactics

We understand negotiation tactics to be every action that aims at agreement with the other party about the mutual allocation of the yields or costs. Tactics are strung together to form strategies which, according to Thomas (1992), are directed at the other's rational/ instrumental reasoning, the other's normative reasoning, or the other's emotions. Wall (1985) has made an inventory of 169 modes of behaviour and has categorized them as aggressive tactics, nonaggressive tactics, posturing tactics, debate tactics and irrational tactics. On the grounds of this he has developed a normative theory which specifies the circumstances necessary to weave the different categories of tactics together into a strategy. In the case of simple negotiations this is dependent on whether the opponent is engaged in inappropriate behaviour, whether the opponent is contingently cooperative, whether future negotiation is important, and whether the opponent has limited alternatives. Our objection to this theory is the tacit presumption that the parties will either have to promote their own interests, or those of the other party, or their joint interests. Pruitt (1981, p. 16) bases his strategic choice model on the same presumption, but then explicitly states: "Conditions that enhance (or diminish) the probability of adopting one strategy diminish (or enhance) the probability of adopting the others".

We believe that behavioural conceptualizations in terms of forced choices misunderstand the essence of negotiations. One of our starting points is, after all, that there are always at least two interests which are present simultaneously, which are inseparable and do not exclude one another. One's own interests and the joint interests are always inextricably tangled in negotiations. Therefore negotiation is both competitive and cooperative, with both characteristics often combined within the same behaviour (Mastenbroek, 1980, 1987; Putnam, 1990). In formulating this proposition we distance ourselves from not only Wall (1985) and Pruitt (1981), but also those who have followed Walton and McKersie (1965) and treat distributive and integrative negotiation separately (e.g. Dupont, 1986; Fisher & Ury, 1981; Jandt, 1985; Lewicki & Litterer, 1985; Lewicki, Weiss, & Lewin, 1992; Roloff, Tutzauer, & Dailey, 1989). In all types of negotiation, distributive aspects of behaviour are tied up with integrative aspects.

The dual character of claim negotiation can be understood if one looks for a built-in tension between distributive claims and integrative agreements, which forms a balance within each tactic. The balance will shift towards claiming or towards sharing, and sometimes towards both claiming and sharing, dependent on the situation and that stage of the negotiation. There is a dynamic balance. According to Mastenbroek (1980, 1987), who proposed and elaborated on this hypothesis, peaks to each pole are possible now and then, but only during certain episodes. Instead the key characteristic is the actual balance between the poles, so that each negotiation tactic is in fact the effective employment of a *dilemma between competition and cooperation*. It is a skill not to be overpowered by the "either-or" nature of the dilemma, but to choose for "both this and this" behaviour. Mastenbroek (1980, 1987, 1991) points out that the dilemma manifests itself in the contents of the negotiation, the power balance between the parties, the climate, and the procedures. According to Putnam (1990), tactics must serve both distributive and integrative functions through wording, and proposal generation has to merge attacking arguments with developing alternatives.

If a teacher does not agree with his or her headmistress about a ban on smoking in the school, his or her negotiation tactics will comprise the use of facts, arguments, proposals, standpoints, required changes, proposals on a compromise and concessions, among other things. The dilemma between competitive-distributive and cooperative-integrative aspects of behaviour can be found in each of these elements. The teacher can give information that is more or less in his or her favour, can choose a more or less radical standpoint, and can concede more or less rapidly. Obviously the same applies to the headmistress. Both parties' behaviour is aimed at agreement, although each of them can form the aimed-for agreement more or less in his or her interest. A large amount of research has been carried out into the effect of the basis of the contents of tactics and the choice of more or less persistent, hard or soft tactics (good surveys are given by Carnevale & Pruitt, 1992; Gulliver, 1979; Morley & Stephenson, 1977; Pruitt, 1981; Pruitt & Carnevale, 1993; Raiffa, 1982; Rubin & Brown, 1975).

Although this is not surprising, it appears that good preparation pays off, since one is able to claim more realistically and more convincingly as well as being able to undermine claims (distributive) and because one has better insight into which compromises or win-win solutions are possible (integrative). Thus being able to see through both one's own and the opponent's situation is a primary tactical instrument. Lewicki and Litterer (1985) see the following as subjects of effective planning: understand the nature of the conflict; specify the goals and objectives; clarify how to manage the negotiation process (identify, prioritise, and package the issues, and establish an agenda); understand the opponent's current resources and needs as well as the history of his or her bargaining behaviour. They have published a checklist of 27 questions to help negotiators prepare themselves sufficiently beforehand. Experienced negotiators recommend that the collection of information and planning should be continued at the beginning of the negotiations, by asking as many questions as possible. In fact, questions are also a tactic to communicate information about one's own claim and other own interests, to maintain the initiative and to keep the other party busy with things other than thinking (Rackham & Carlisle, 1978a).

A consequent tough tactic is to start with a large claim which is just about defendable at the beginning, signals of determination, few or minor concessions, and exaggeration of these small concessions. Arguments about fairness can play a part. Bargainers who do not overdo the tactical exaggeration, so that the other party drops out, will achieve a better agreement (Chertkoff & Esser, 1976; Hamner & Yukl, 1977; Pruitt, 1981; Rubin & Brown, 1975; Wall, 1985). The main explanation for this is that the opponent party will lower her or his aspirations. From a psychological point of view this is a somewhat poor explanation of the accommodating behaviour of the opponent, since a link is missing between the low level of aspiration and more concessions. A possible link is the experience of the anticipated negotiation outcomes as involving gains and profits, or as involving losses and costs.

If we presume that negotiators experience results above their level of aspiration as gains and results below their level of aspiration as losses, then a decrease in their level of aspiration will be linked to an enlargement of the domain of gains and a reduction of the domain of losses. This is most relevant, because a gain prospect is less attractive than an objectively equivalent loss prospect is aversive (Kahneman & Tversky, 1979; Tversky & Kahneman, 1981) to the effect that gain framed negotiators demand less, concede more, and settle easier than loss framed negotiators (Carnevale & Pruitt, 1992; De Dreu, 1993; De Dreu, Carnevale, Emans, & Van de Vliert, 1994; De Dreu, Emans, & Van de Vliert, 1992; Neale & Bazerman, 1991; Thompson, 1990). Thus it would be sensible for negotiators to give the opponent a lower level of aspiration and therefore a larger gain perspective. This can be achieved by the consequently tough position which has already been described. A second way is by decreasing the interests of the opponent by relativising the value of its results, or by arguing that the results will not lead to the results expected (Lewicki & Litterer, 1985; Wall, 1985). In this way the teacher could try to convince the headmistress that a ban on smoking in the school could actually stimulate the pupils to smoke more rather than less, or that they will switch to more damaging stimulants.

Another much-used way of decreasing the aspirations of the opponent and therefore of increasing his or her experience of gains is by emphasizing the fact that one is going to suffer a loss oneself. De Dreu (1993; De Dreu et al., 1992, 1994) has however shown that this tactic can also work contrary to expectations. The opponent appears to adopt the communicator's loss frame. As a consequence, in reaction to the communicator's loss frame, the opponent will demand more rather than less, will concede less rather than more, and will probably tend to prefer stalemate to settlement. De Dreu (1993) also showed that this process of frame adoption by an opponent occurs regardless of the cooperative or competitive intention of the communicator, as evident in the communications during the negotiation.

The tactic of rapidly providing the opponent with a gain perspective by manipulation is not without disadvantages to the functioning of the organization. Deception can undermine the mutual relationship and it also damages the principle interests (Lewicki, 1983). Emotional manipulation by praising or flattering, or by condemning and disapproving can actually provoke suspicion, irritation and antipathy rather than lenience (Baron, Fortin, Frei, Hauver, & Shack, 1990; Mastenbroek, 1989). However a popular opposite of manipulation, taking a tough position, is not without disadvantages either. A definitive choice of position, take it or leave it, blocks the progress of the joint process, forces the other into the defence and risks the pleasant working relationship (Dupont, 1986; Fisher & Ury, 1981).

A tactic in which relatively equal amounts of attention are paid to both one's own and the joint interest is to prevent one's own claims and manoeuvres from causing the other to lose face. Loss of face occurs if one experiences a decrease in status, if one feels personally rejected and if one's own freedom of action is hurt by someone else (Pruitt, 1981). According to the theory on gain and loss perspectives just discussed, the opponent will adopt a far tougher position by more loss of face than by less gain of face (Brown, 1977; Tjosvold & Huston, 1978). Pruitt (1981) deals with the following tactics to ensure that the opponent does not lose face and may gain face: support the other's desired image another time, use of disclaimers that deny relevance to the other's sensitivities, use of indirection in the statement of demands, diminish the size or significance of what is being done or asked, blame external forces for behaviour or demands, shift responsibility for behaviour to acceptable motives, encourage a belief that the other party has participated in the decision making, and employ sanctioned forums (see also Folger & Poole, 1984; Wilson, 1992).

In fact limiting the opponent's loss of face is a special case of the rule that tactics of *firm flexibility* serve all interests the best (Fisher & Ury, 1981; Pruitt, 1981). This rule has been proved by empirical research and entails that one should hold onto one's own main interests and goals for as long as possible, combined with flexibility as far as taking standpoints and exploring ways of figuring out agreement are concerned. This will be easier if it is possible to differentiate between main interests and additional interests and if one is able to imagine a number of alternative final outcomes te serve one's own interest. Such a tactic of firm flexibility is an interesting combination of the distributive/claiming and the integrative/agreeing aspects of negotiation. While a close watch is kept on one's main interest, one is willing to exchange information, review an earlier point of view, look at new ideas, accept a change in procedure or a different dividing principle, allow the other to take the initiative, and so on. This implies that the opponent has every chance of looking after at least their additional interests. The chance of lasting deadlocks is minimalized in this way.

Firm flexibility also prevents the joint interest from only being meagrely realized as a cake of fixed size, even though the cake could have been enlarged. Bazerman (1983) presumes that the members of a competitive society are prejudiced in that they think in terms of winning and losing. This means that when one is confronted with a negotiation situation, it is often wrongly presumed that the yields or costs to be shared out are of a fixed size. This promotes application of the principles of dividing, such as the 50/50 rule on the grounds of the principle of equality. This leads to lean compromises. It also curbs creativity and the solution of problems, which are both necessary to come to a solution that is totally satisfactory to both parties. In short, negotiating members of an organization often do not function optimally because of the "fixed-pie-bias". Other reasons to choose the clear and fast path of compromising above the less clear and time-consuming path of total problem solving are a low level of aspiration, fear of a serious conflict, the chance of an impasse coming ever closer and a lack of time (Rubin, Pruitt, & Kim, 1994). All in all organization members do not pay enough attention to the possibilities of more integrative negotiations (Fisher & Ury, 1981; Jandt, 1985; Lax & Sebenius, 1986; Pruitt, 1983).

In summary, each tactic forms a dynamic balance between claiming and looking for agreement. Good preparation allows one to operate more successfully between these poles. The tactics used influence the gain or loss prospects and therefore the irreconcilable or lenient reaction of the opponent. A tactic of holding on to one's own aims while at the same time being flexible with respect to the joint route, serves all the interests best.

TRADE NEGOTIATIONS

If the real or imaginary owner of yields or costs tries to come to an agreement on the transfer of these to the opponent, one cannot speak of parties with comparable claims. In this case it is possible to differentiate between a seller and a buyer, who are both trying to achieve an optimal exchange of the one outcome against the other. A businessman or woman and their client are a good example of this. However, trade negotiations can also be applied to colleagues who have to be seduced into doing something, the boss who wants to know the advantages to the group of joining in with something, the member of staff who sets the shop floor manager conditions when carrying out a plan, two directors who want to redefine their responsibilities, as well as many other situations. They must all come to an agreement about the sort of outcome which they themselves will get, the sort of outcome which the other will get in return, the mutual weighing up of the outcome and the counter outcome and the size of the conveyance of property. In fact three independent partial agreements are made: about the means of exchange, the rate of exchange and the size of the exchange. If money or another means of exchange is obvious, the first partial agreement is already fixed. If on top of this there is also a fixed rate of exchange then the second partial agreement is also fixed. In the last case there is little discussion with respect to, for example, a stamp which costs 20 pence. In all other cases interests are served by means of tactics.

Interests

The same types of main and additional interests are of importance in trade negotiations as in claim negotiations, even though they are interpreted differently (for an overview see Table 14.2). First, the main interests of both parties are such that they (a) exchange a relatively worthless yield or a relatively important cost to themselves against a relatively valuable outcome which the other party owns, (b) against an exchange rate which is as lucrative as possible and (c) in a most satisfactory size. Therefore it is strictly possible to differentiate between three outcome elements in each sale agreement. Of these components, the means and the rate of exchange require further attention.

In their elaboration of the exchange theory Foa and Foa (1980) propose that interpersonal yields differ from one another in the extent to which they are concrete and particularlistic, respectively. Goods and services are very concrete, with goods being much less personal than services. Money is moderately concrete and absolutely not personal. Information and status are hardly concrete, with information being much less personal than status, and so on. The main hypothesis states that more comparable yields, in terms of concreteness and particularism, can be exchanged better. Thus people prefer to exchange goods for other goods or services, prefer to exchange money for goods or information, and information for information or status. This hypothesis is at odds with the fact that negotiating members of an organization often also request or offer financial or other somewhat incomparable compensation in exchange for certain contributions (Lawler, 1981; Pruitt, 1981).

As well as being more or less concrete and particularistic, means of exchange can also be more or less intrinsic or instrumental. Someone's interest in an outcome is intrinsic if one is only interested in the valued outcome. However it is instrumental if the outcome is of value because of its influence on further developments. Given the fact that intrinsic outcomes are more final than instrumental outcomes, we presume that it is more difficult to substitute one's own yields and costs when these are intrinsic then when they are instrumental. Consequently we additionally presume that one is more likely to exchange instrumental yields and costs than intrinsic ones. If both parties request and offer outcomes which are of instrumental importance to everyone (for example time and means of production) agreement on the means of exchange will be reached more easily than when the exchange of more intrinsic outcomes is wished for (for example confidential information and feelings of sympathy).

TABLE 14.2

Types of interest.

Main interests
- One's own interest
- Opponent's interest
- Joint interest

Additional interests
- Process
- Relation
- Principles

In order to determine the rate of exchange, most members of organizations usually have to compare apples and oranges. When is the rate of exchange fair and when is the one rate of exchange better than the other? Since it is difficult to determine this precisely, each person's intended rate of exchange is usually fairly broad rather than sharply defined. If one finds a certain inequality desirable or acceptable, one may sometimes broaden the intended rate of exchange. Thus an aspiration zone is created per party with an upper limit (maximal exchange rate) and a lower limit (minimal exchange rate). In a claim negotiation the maximal and minimal claim will form the aspiration zones of each party.

The area between the lower limits of the two parties is called the *settlement range* (Thomas, 1992; Walton & McKersie, 1965) or the *zone of agreement* (Raiffa, 1982). It is positive if the aspiration zones overlap, whereby both parties find each rate of exchange between their lower limits acceptable (for example the seller wants to receive at least £120 while the buyer wants to knock down the price to at least £140). However, it is negative if the aspiration zones do not overlap, in which case both parties reject each rate of exchange between their lower limits (for example the seller wants to receive at least £140 while the buyer wants to knock down the price to at least £120). One's own interests are served most at one's own upper limit, while the joint interest is served most midway between both lower limits (in both examples this is £130). It is noteworthy that Walton and McKersie (1965), who have a predominantly economic approach, ignore the fact that the range of the rate of exchange is often determined by the size of the exchange (e.g. quantity rebate). More understandable is the fact that as non-psychologists they ignore the fact that negotiators have both main interests and side interests.

If against the background of a negative settlement range, the distance between the lower limits cannot be bridged during a negotiation, the sale will not take place. Pulling out will be seen as the best way of coming up for one's own interests. This is because each party will remain the owner of a relatively attractive outcome, which makes it possible to sell to someone else. An example of such *ownership interest* is the boss who does not get permission to replace an employee who does not function well. This boss keeps the employee and thus also the possibility of replacing the employee at some point. Therefore it is in his or her interest that agreements under his or her minimal rate of exchange are not made. On the one hand the boss has to take care to not receive an employee who is even worse, while on the other hand an attempt can be made to strike a bargain at another point in time.

This combination of aspects of interests has been called "Best Alternative To a Negotiated Agreement" (BATNA) by Fisher and Ury (1981). It is in one's own interest to have alternatives. The more good alternatives one has at one's disposal, the less dependent one is (Bacharach & Lawler, 1981). One can speak of the power of the good alternative (Fisher, 1983) which even allows one to set a higher lower limit (Lax & Sebenius, 1986). Pinkley, Neale, and Bennett (1994) showed that having an alternative increases one's own outcome as well as the joint outcome; the more attractive or valuable the alternative, the greater one's own and joint benefits. With this we end our discussion of the main interests.

One of the most important process interests is concerned with the phases of a negotiation. The literature on descriptive and prescriptive phase models of negotiation has been summarized by Holmes (1992). Research in the field (Douglas, 1962; Putnam, Wilson, & Turner, 1990) and a simulation experiment (Morley & Stephenson, 1977) have demonstrated that during successful trade negotiations the dynamic equilibrium between competition and cooperation mentioned earlier shifts from mainly competition to mainly cooperation. During the initial choice of position one allows one's own upper limit to remain dominant. However in the following exploratory phase attempts are made to learn about the settlement range of the opponent, by means of pressure or questions and tentative suggestions. This phase is so action-packed that it is sometimes possible to differentiate between three subphases, namely detailed consultation including large doses of pressure, then a phase of maturation, and finally a phase of joint search for ways out of the blind alley (Himmelmann, 1971). During the last phase the joint determination of a joint final position between the two lower limits becomes of importance, while the upper limits disappear. The agreement will be improved if all three phases are completed (for a more detailed list of eight phases, see Gulliver, 1979). It may be of importance that the whole process takes a large amount of time, since this implies or conjures up visions of tiresome negotiations, which in turn convince the parties that the final agreement was the maximum they could achieve.

Relational interests will play an important role particularly during repeated trade negotiations. If the different participants meet one another frequently then more will be at stake during the transaction. One may for example like the opponent, or may not want to be made a fool of in the presence of the opponent. Negotiators who contribute to the joint interest and stick to the rules of the game in doing so will gain credit, which means that they will be in the opponent's good books during future negotiations. The credit can then be used to insist on a favourable rate of exchange. In negotiation literature one speaks of a relationship of mutual trust, even though the meaning of this is not specified. Does it refer to serving the joint interest, being open and honest, or to observing the agreement? Too much emphasis is placed on trust being a sort of magical power and too little on trust being a scientific and unambiguous operational concept.

As far as the principle interests are concerned, the principle of equal concessions is perfectly applicable to the joint determination of the rate of exchange. It is seen as just if both parties take equally-sized steps to bridge their differences. Research has shown that negotiators tend to translate equality in the frequency rather than the size of the concessions (Wall, 1985). One tends to experience injustice if concessions are not rewarded by any counter-concessions at all. However injustice can also be felt if an unsuitable action is expected in return (Foa & Foa, 1980), because one is cheating the opponent, or because one wants to renegotiate an original concession or sale agreement. This can lead to feelings of guilt or shame about one's own behaviour and it is usually in one's own interst to avoid it, if at all possible.

In summary, during a trade negotiation one exchanges outcomes with another party, in such a way that both parties value that which they acquire more than that which they have to give up. Each person's interests lie primarily and especially in a suitable means of exchange, an acceptable exchange rate and the absence of a better alternative agreement. At the same time the progress from a more competitive to a more cooperative process, the future mutual relationship and decent sales behaviour are also of importance.

Tactics

As has already been stated; buyer and seller pursue a mutual agreement about the exchange of outcomes of a particular size and against a particular rate of exchange. In this process a balance in their tactical behaviour must be found between promoting, on the one hand the competitive own interest in the exchange and on the other hand the cooperative joint interest of a successful exchange. This dilemma between competition and cooperation is inherent in all negotiations and has already been discussed with respect to the aspiration level of the parties, the loss and gain of face and the tactic of tenacious flexibility.

Since the literature has demonstrated a lack of differentiation between claim and trade negotiations, attention has never been paid to the tactics which negotiators apply to define their situation as a claim or trade situation. A new line of research could look at the tactics which aim at converting a claim negotiation to a trade negotiation, or vice versa. We have in mind behaviour such as denying that one is the owner of costs (a bad plan, an unpleasant chore, the wrong tools, a debt, a backlog), the appropriation of outcomes (a promising idea, a pleasant chore, good tools, credit, a lead), disputing that the opponent is the owner of yields, or labelling the opponent as the owner of costs. A fertile area of theory building and intervention is that situation in which one of the parties does not see any owners and thus wants to pursue a claim negotiation on the grounds of arguments of justice, while the other party believes there to be owners and therefore wishes to pursue a trade negotiation on the grounds of exchange.

If both parties define their activities as a trade negotiation, their tactics will be aimed at the means and the rate of exchange. We will first concentrate on the means of exchange, after which we will look at the rate of exchange. As an example we will take a member of an organization who sometimes has to work overtime in order to make a deadline. The reward can be in the form of money, extra time off, special working hours, more participation, exemption from other work, and a better place to work, among other things. At the same time the board of directors may believe that this member of the organization should be promoted to a managerial position, while the person in question would rather become more specialized. Much research has been inspired by the question as to what would be best for this person; to tackle a single issue with a specific counter achievement, or to include a package of issues with a diversity of outcomes in return, in the negotiation (Fisher, 1964; Lax & Sebenius, 1986; Mannix, Thompson, & Bazerman, 1989; Pruitt, 1981, 1983; Raiffa, 1982).

During a discussion on four different subjects, one can obviously pursue four different negotiations. We speak of a package negotiation only when these subjects are linked to one another. Even though package negotiations can be more complex, they increase the chance of a satisfactory result if the outcomes differ in their subjective value and if a combination of outcomes yields more than the sum of the individual outcomes (Lax & Sebenius, 1986). Thus the organizational member in question could buy time to study during the day in exchange for overtime and, on top of this, could also attempt to link a future managerial job to the completion of the proposed specialism. Diverse issues even apply to something as simple as buying some new apparatus; for example, quality, make, service, discount or delivery time.

Competent negotiators appear to prefer package

negotiations. Compared with less skilful negotiators they plan subnegotiations concurrently instead of following on from one another (Rackham & Carlisle, 1978b). The advantage of this is that each party has more chance of exchanging an outcome which is hardly valued for an outcome which is valued greatly. The package allows one to map one's own as well as the other's use of the diverse outcomes and counter-achievements, so that more insight is gained into everyone's priorities and what each person can best "give and take". However, package negotiations do decrease the chance of an agreement if sensitive or complex issues are included.

A popular tactic is to include several less important demands in the package in order to facilitate later concession behaviour (Gulliver, 1979). If the bidder links two demands, then granting the one demand serves as a condition for the other also being granted. Conversely, the recipient of an offer can switch to a package negotiation by attaching one or more conditions to a concession or to the complete acceptance of the offer. In this last case these form a disbanded condition, for example if the overtime is dependent on agreement at home or one's own private agenda. A precondition is always used to safeguard an extra main or additional interest. Even though this behavioural pattern of setting conditions often takes place, we are as yet unsure as to when negotiators switch to this type of behaviour.

A negotiator who stipulates a precondition brings an extra means of exchange into the discussion and thereby usually creates a promise or a threat. If the opponent complies with the precondition, a reward will be given by means of a concession or consent to an agreement. If this does not occur, punishment will follow in the form of no concessions or rejection of the agreement. We are intrigued by the fact that the same precondition is more effective when it is clothed with a promise than with a threat. Rubin and Lewicki (1973) have proved that the statement "If you do not do X, I will reward you" evokes more compliance and a more positive mutual relationship than the phrase "If you do not do X, you will not be punished, if you do X, I will not reward you" and "If you do X, you will be punished". Naturally these effects only occur when the receiver of the message is convinced that the sender can and will do what is said, and will for example actually call a strike (Bacharach & Lawler, 1981; Brett, 1984).

As well as agreeing on the means of exchange, agreement must also be reached on the rate of exchange. Above the actual rate of exchange was described as a point between the two parties' minimal exchange rates. The package negotiations just discussed demonstrate that it is often much more complicated than this. This emphasizes the tactical importance of collecting information on possible means of exchange, compromises and solutions, and the value which those involved place on them, prior to the negotiations. Raiffa (1982) reported that bank employees who negotiate loans find the most important characteristics of an effective negotiator to be the ability to prepare and plan well beforehand, and to know precisely what is of importance to the different parties. It has been demonstrated that more successful negotiators collect more information (Rackham & Carlisle, 1978a). Experienced negotiators spend slightly more time on diagnosis than inexperienced negotiators (25% versus 16%), spend much more time on the alternatives (25% versus 8%), spend much less time on goal setting (16% versus 33%) and a little less time on the tactics and strategy (32% versus 41%) (Dupont, 1986, p. 68; see also Bass, 1966; Thomas, 1992).

Since the rate of exchange is determined by the level to which the means of exchange are seen as scarce, and by the value which these have for the parties, the following tactical tasks are of importance during the first phase of a trade negotiation (Emans, 1988; Fisher & Ury, 1981; Lewicki & Litterer, 1985; Mastenbroek, 1989): (a) underpinning the alternatives for acquisition or sales which one has oneself (for example, by mentioning other suppliers or buyers); (b) undermining the opponent's alternatives (for example, by organizing a collective boycott); (c) giving well-founded reasons for the value that one's own means of exchange will have for the other (for example, by demonstrating the value of an article); and (d) undermining the value that one attaches to the other party's means of exchange (for example, by showing little interest, or by waiting for a considerable amount of time before reacting). Both the main interests and the additional interests need to be promoted via these tactical tasks. This makes the negotiation task complex. However it is made slightly easier if it is possible to generalize Bacharach and Lawler's (1981) findings. They say that it is easier to get a more favourable rate of exchange by undermining the other party's alternatives than by giving good arguments for one's own alternatives. For that matter, carrying out the tactical tasks (a) to (d) in the start phase will advance the realization of an agreement in later phases.

A negotiator who begins by asking for a high price communicates trust in his or her own alternatives and in the correctness of the proposed rate of exchange. Furthermore one creates the possibilities of future concessions between the two parties, one masks one's own lower limit, and one influences the lower limit of the opponent towards one's own upper limit. The same applies to the tactics of very limited concessions, even though in this case the opponent may prepare themselves for this. The fact that concession behaviour may lead to the expectation of further concessions can be overcome by stating that the standpoint being held is definite, or that the concession is a one-off and has been made for a specific reason (for example, because of a miscalculation or other new information) or by linking the concession to a threat (Pruitt, 1981). One also often applies principle interests to create a firm and credible impression. However, one risks the fact that this may lead to loss of face or a deadlock (Lax & Sebenius, 1986; Wilson, 1992).

During a deadlock the buyer and seller still aim towards agreement, but without further progress. Standpoints are repeated and meetings are suspended, among other things. This may be a deliberate action to create time to think things over, to make it clear that many more concessions cannot be expected, or to test the other's determination. Fells (1985) differentiates between three types of deadlock, the *process impasse* when negotiators do not succeed in taking up standpoints which create a positive "settlement range", the *issue impasse* in which attempts to find acceptable compromises or solutions keep failing, and the *loss of face impasse* when the agreement aimed for seems to ask unreasonable concessions from one of the parties. This typology suggests that process, relational and principle interests lead to deadlocks more easily than main interests.

Impasses strengthen the need for an approach that will lead to agreement (Douglas, 1962; Morley & Stephenson, 1977). The following tactics have been successfully applied to end deadlocks: breaking the spiral of attacks and defence by making a summary; by putting forward a small alteration or chance of concession; by asking questions; or by focusing on the underlying interests (Fisher & Ury, 1981; Mastenbroek, 1989; Rackham & Carlisle, 1978a); immediately answering a gesture of concession with an equal concession (Esser & Komorita, 1975; Hamner, 1974); inserting an informal brainstorming session to look for possible solutions (Lax & Sebenius, 1986). Similarly, stalemates can also be overcome by increasing the time pressure by using, for example, a deadline, the cost of the deadlock or an alternative sales transaction (Carnevale, O'Connor, & McCusker, 1993; Pruitt & Drews, 1969; Rubin & Brown, 1975; Walton & McKersie, 1965); agreement on a cooling down period (Pruitt, 1981); using a mediator or arbitrator (Bercovitch, 1984; Prein, 1982; Touzard, 1977).

In summary, the integrating power of trade tactics usually increases when one negotiates on a more extensive package of issues and uses promises rather then threats. As negotiators become more competent, they will pay more attention to each party's alternatives, will undermine the alternatives of the other party more strongly and will be less compliant at the beginning of the discussion. Process, issue and loss of face impasses exist, as well as a considerable number of tactics to break these deadlocks. One of these tactics is to allow someone else to take over the rest of the deliberation.

REPRESENTATIVE NEGOTIATIONS

Our perspective of pursuing agreement on transfer of ownership also draws attention to the negotiator who claims, buys or sells on behalf of another person or on behalf of a group. One often sees both parties promoting the interests of ownership of others instead of those of themselves. This "on behalf of" construction may be by virtue of one's profession, as is the case with an estate agent, a trader or a solicitor (Rubin & Sander, 1988). A more common situation is that in organizations spokesmen, delegates, substitutes or mediators are used (D. Friedman, 1986; R. A. Friedman & Podolny, 1992; Pruitt & Carnevale, 1993). Managers continually act in all directions on behalf of their subordinates, colleagues or superiors. This is why Lax and Sebenius (1986) finish their book *The manager as negotiator* with the chapter "The manager is always in the middle". All these representatives have to work with both constituents and opponents. This requires tactics that take into account the often incompatible interests of at least three parties, namely the negotiating representative, the constituency and the opponent.

Interests

Previous sections discussed which main and additional interests are involved when one holds a claim or trade negotiation respectively (see Table 14.2). If one represents one or more others, the own interest, the joint interest and the possible extra process, relational, and principle interests will be placed in a slightly different triadic perspective. For organizations this triadic perspective is somewhat more realistic, given the fact that members of an organization seldom negotiate alone and almost always have to consider relevant wishes from other people (Adams, 1976; Frey & Adams, 1972). This can be seen most clearly in the model of the organization as a system of interlocking roles (Kahn, 1991; Katz & Kahn, 1978). In this framework the negotiating representative is known as a "linking pin" and as the fulfiller of a "boundary role".

The own interest of the negotiating representative is strongly influenced by two implications of taking a position between the constituency and the opponent. In the first place the representative will experience stress and will have to learn to get rid of this stress or be able to control it (Driscoll, 1981; Dupont, 1986). In the second place the representative will be confronted with opposing role expectations, and with the question which then arises as to which behavioural choice will lead to the most favourable personal outcome (Carnevale, 1985; Druckman, 1977; Dupont, 1986; Turner, 1992). This internal conflict, which may especially be concerned with what issues one must discuss, how, against whom, where, and when, will be mainly discussed along with the tactics of representative negotiations.

It is in the personal interest of the negotiator to please the constituents since this can lead to rewards and can prevent reproval. Such positive and negative outcomes of sanctions especially take place if the constituents can monitor not only the final result but also the unfolding of the negotiation process (Adams, 1976; Carnevale, Pruitt, & Seilheimer, 1981; Smith, 1987). However this interest of the negotiator is not isolated and absolute. It will be weighed against the possible rewards and reproval by the satisfied or disappointed opponent (Adams, 1976; Walton & McKersie, 1965). In other words, it is of great importance to the representative negotiator to calculate his or her power relationship with the constituents and the opponent.

Experienced negotiators prefer a delegate opposite them who is as powerful and competent as possible. This would appear to be to their disadvantage, since they cannot trounce such an opponent. However the advantages are: (a) the responses and the ultimate negotiation results are better; (b) the negotiations can be completed more rapidly (Jackson & King, 1983; Klimoski & Asch, 1974); (c) the opponent does not have to consult with the constituents (Bartunek, Benton, & Keys, 1975; Klimoski & Asch, 1974; Kogan, Lamm, & Trommsdorff, 1972); and (d) the chance is greater that the opponent will stick to the agreement instead of being called back by his or her constituents. It can be concluded that experienced negotiators see a good relationship with their opponent and his or her supporters as a joint interest.

In general, representatives place more importance on this joint interest with the opponent than do their constituents. According to Pruitt (1981) there are three reasons for this. First, representatives often believe that they must reach agreement. Second, they have a more realistic view of the priorities of the opponent and of the difficulties of getting them to concede still more. Third, the relationship between the representative and the opponent is more intimate than that between the constituents and the opponent, to the effect that the former is less inclined to carry out tough negotiations than the latter. A possible fourth reason is that the discussions among the constituents lead to group polarization; that is, the members of the group develop more extreme ideas about the negotiation process and its potential outcomes (Rabbie, Visser, & Tils, 1976).

The effectiveness of organizations is increased when negotiators place more importance on the joint interest with the opponent than on the constituents' interest. After all, the continued existence of every organization is put in danger if it does not enter into agreements with outgroups. Additionally, Wall (1985) views representative negotiation as the perfect means by which internal integration can be created, both on a horizontal level between groups and on a vertical level between hierarchical layers. The production manager consults the head of administration, the station sergeant consults the picket officer, the member of the works council consults the director, the supervisor consults the subcontractor, and so on. Horizontal negotiation avoids overburdening higher management and forces those involved to look at the limiting circumstances, uncertainties and the opponent's interests. Vertical negotiations avoid the cost of use of power and loss of face and involve both subordinates and superiors in each other's goals, values, time perspectives and specific problems.

If the constituents are able to keep a close eye on the negotiator, it is yet more important that the steps in the negotiation process are both clear and acceptable. This is because the constituents will assess the loyalty and conformity of the representative on the grounds of the process (Adams, 1976). A recent field of interest is the interaction between process and principle interests in the form of so-called *procedural justice* (Albin, 1993; Deutsch, 1985; Folger, 1986; Karambayya & Brett, 1989; Sheppard, Lewicki, & Minton, 1992; Sheppard, Saunders, & Minton, 1988; Tyler, 1986). A procedure is justifiable as long as the right people negotiate, in an open and honest manner and in agreement with the valid rules of play. One sometimes appears to find the justice of the procedure more important than the justice of the resulting outcome. Thus unpublished research has shown that those Dutch soldiers who are given a bad assessment by their commander are much more likely to complain about the procedure followed than about the negative outcome.

Also, with respect to the importance of the relationship with the opponent, the representative cannot handle things independently of the constituents. According to Strauss (1978) it is of considerable importance whether one is being forced to represent people or is chosen or named, and whether the constituents know and acknowledge this. Managers appear to be able to distance themselves from the constituents more easily than other representatives (Morley & Stephenson, 1977). However, as far as this is concerned southern Europe differs from northern Europe. In countries such as Greece and Spain the relationships with the constituency and the opponent are of main importance rather than additional importance, while in Scandinavia and The Netherlands the tasks and the final agreement are more important than the relationships (Hofstede, 1984). During negotiations between the representatives of the EC countries this cultural difference is a continual source of misunderstanding and fustration (G.O. Faure, personal communication).

Naturally there is a connection between the importance of relational interests and the sort of principles that one applies to the procedure and the agreement. It would be an endless task to scientifically chart all these and other principles. It makes more sense to apply the concept of *legitimacy* to cover the various grounds on which the representative justifies the role expectations received from both the constituency and the opponent. These legitimacy judgments may be founded on the formal or traditional position of the grass roots or the opponent, the appreciation or admiration which they elicit, their expertise or level of knowledge, and also on the accuracy of their standpoints or the adequacy of their tactics. It has been proved that the representative will weigh up the legitimacy of the constituents' role expectations against the legitimacy of the opponent's incompatible role expectations (Van de Vliert, 1981b).

In summary, the self-interest of someone who negotiates for others overlaps the main and additional interests of both the constituency and the opponent. Sanctions can be expected from the parties on both sides; both will keep an eye on the level of procedural justice. The relationship with both people or groups can be of importance and both sides will be more or less in the right. Representatives experience the integrating joint interest with their opponent—including a good relationship between the opponent and his or her own supporters—more strongly than their constituents.

Tactics

We have proposed that all negotiation tactics have a double character, because a dynamic balance exists between promoting the competitive own interest and the cooperative joint interest. During representative negotiations, competition and cooperation are usually anchored in the constituents and the other negotiator(s) respectively. As the negotiations progress the representative will become more and more the "person in the middle", wedged between the demand from the grass roots to fight and the demand from the opponent to cooperate. Little attention has been paid to these conflicting loyalties on the tactics to be applied. If any attention is paid at all, the line of Walton and McKersie (1965) is blindly followed. They deal with the negotiations with the constituents and the negotiations with the opponent separately (e.g. Turner, 1992). Thus these "backwards" and "forwards" types of negotiation have been separated in the same way as distributive and integrative negotiation have been separated. Hence, once again, we come across a misunderstanding of the essence of negotiations, given that one breaks the unbreakable.

Paradoxically this misunderstanding of bilateral negotiations goes back to Walton and McKersie (1965), who were the first to study the tactical role conflict of the representative in depth. They have even published a "model for role conflict resolution", but introduce this with an implausible presumption: "we assume that the negotiator has explored all the possibilities for changing the expectations of the opponent, and we focus here on his mechanisms for dealing with only one source of pressure—his own organisation" (Walton & McKersie, 1965, p. 303). In short the most essential aspect of the conflict between the incompatible role expectations of the constituents and the opponent are reasoned away. While Walton and McKersie ignore negotiating "forwards", Carnevale (1985) ignores "backwards" negotiation two decades later. He discusses determinants of four strategies for reacting to the opponent without recognizing that these are inextricably linked to the strategies directed at the constituency.

Our criticism even applies to Druckman's (1977) well thought out contribution "Boundary role conflict: Negotiation as dual responsiveness". In this article he elaborates that two sorts of function must be fulfilled during representative negotiation: monitoring one's own side for evidence of preferences and monitoring the other side for evidence of movement. These are seen as fundamentally different processes of information-processing. When dealing with the constituents the representative would weigh up and maximize the value of the outcomes, emphasizing identification with them and their priorities. When dealing with the opponent the representative would gradually react to the concessions made by both parties and to his or her own anticipations and evaluations. After having developed very different models, Druckman observes that the two processes nevertheless unfold simultaneously and complement one another. Thus information from the constituents would determine which concessions are preferable, while information about tactical interactions with the opponent will determine whether or not concessions are made.

It is not difficult to question this, given the fact that information from the own ranks will often determine whether conceding behaviour is desired, while information about the tactics being applied by the negotiators will often determine which concessions will have effect. One important point of criticism is that Druckman (1977) assumes there to be two independent processes that form a precondition for each other's effect. However the dual nature of negotiation means that only one process exists, in which the constituents and the opponent exert influence on the same dynamic equilibrium between competition and cooperation simultaneously. When, for example,

Frey and Adams (1972) conclude that their representatives are much tougher bargainers when the constituents are suspicious and the opponent is cooperative, then we interpret this as the result of one process and not of two separate complementary processes.

If we return to the point at which previous authors have lost track of the role conflict, we come across the question of how the representative can react to the dilemma which the constituency and the opponent create. According to Walton and McKersie (1965) a relevant answer to this question can be found in Gross, Mason, and McEachern's (1958) theory of role conflict resolution, which Van de Vliert (1975, 1981a, 1981b, 1984) has since elaborated on (see also Laskewitz, Van de Vliert, & De Dreu, 1994). During repeated tests of the theory, information has been gathered about the reactions of representatives to the conflicting expectations of their role behaviour as accountant, policeman, administrator, personnel manager, organization consultant, school superintendent or industrial manager. It appears possible to differentiate between primary tactics and various secondary tactics. The primary reaction to the role conflict is to collect information to lessen the ambivalence. Before doing anything else the representative will collect information on, for example, the composition of the constituency and the opponent, their precise role expectations, the reasons why they have these expectations and the positive and negative consequences of alternative behaviours.

The secondary tactics can be clearly described by using the bipartite definition of the situation which is forced on the representative: there is a conflict between what the constituents and what the opponent expect of me as negotiator; I will have to choose between these conflicting negotiation behaviours (see Table 14.3). The representative who feels wedged between the two and totally accepts the somewhat compelling definition of the situation, will side with either the constituency or the opponent. If the conflict is accepted, while the choice is only accepted temporarily, a compromise of alternating choice behaviour will be manifested. If the representative accepts the conflict, while partially rejecting the choice, the compromise will form a middle course, a mixture instead of an alternation. The negotiator who accepts the conflict and totally rejects the forced choice, will display avoidance by taking it lying down. The opposite of this, that is, total rejection of the conflict and acceptance of the choice, characterizes directed attempts to put an end to the role conflict by altering the opinion of either the constituents or the opponent. Finally, if both parts of the definition of the situation are rejected, a solution is usually found by rolling the ball back to the two parties. The secondary tactics will now be handled in more detail, in the order given in Table 14.3.

Side with constituency. At the start of negotiations one usually complies with the wishes of the constituents, especially if: a strict mandate has been prepared; one has to give account later; the negotiator still has to prove themselves and if the constituents can follow the negotiations closely (Bass, 1966; Ben-Yoav & Pruitt, 1984; Pruitt & Carnevale, 1993). If the principal party wants to

TABLE 14.3

Eight tactics of representative negotiations as typified by the acceptance or rejection of the conflict and the choice between constituency and opponent.

Tactics	*Acceptance of*	
	Conflict?	*Choice?*
Side with constituency	Yes	Yes
Side with opponent	Yes	Yes
Compromise: alternation	Yes	Yes (temporarily)
Compromise: mixture	Yes	No (partially)
Avoid	Yes	No
Change constituency	No	Yes
Change opponent	No	Yes
Resolution	No	No

have its own way and if the negotiator remains on its side this will result in an issue impasse, or a fairly unsatisfactory agreement (Fells, 1985; Friedman, 1986; Lamm, 1978; Neale, 1984; Tjosvold, 1977). In this way the "best" and most loyal representatives become the worst negotiators (Lamm, 1978; Lamm & Kogan, 1970; Vidmar, 1971). More constructive are "double track negotiations" with the representative taking the side of the constituents both formally and verbally while informally and nonverbally making it apparent to the opponent that concessions can be expected (Wall, 1985; Walton & McKersie, 1965). During such double-track negotiations, *conformity with respect to behaviour* is usually demonstrated to the constituents on the grounds of probable sanctions, while there is *nonconformity with respect to opinions* on the grounds of legitimacy judgements. Identification with militant constituents is sometimes pretended to win time or to be persistent without this being taken personally.

Judging by the theory on choosing sides (Van de Vliert, 1981b), the representative will allow the definition of the situation in Table 14.3 to be strongly dependent of two factors, namely sanction power and legitimacy power in a broad sense. The negotiator will side with the constituents if their reaction is more appreciative or more reproving than the opponent (expected sanctions) and/or if they have more right to a choice of their side than the opponent (legitimacy). We recognize the own interests and the relational interests in the expected sanctions, and the legitimacy includes procedural justice and other principle interests. Thus the theory implies that the representative tactically chooses for the party that has the power to satisfy the most interests.

The following three hypotheses can be derived from the last paragraphs:

1. As the negotiations proceed the constituents' power decreases and the opponent's power increases, to the effect that the representative sides more with the opponent and less with the constituents (cf. Bacharach & Lawler, 1981).
2. To the extent that the representative ascribes less power to the constituents than to the opponent, the effectiveness of the representative negotiation increases.
3. To the extent that the representative ascribes more sanction power and less legitimacy power to the constituents than to the opponent, the level of double-track negotiating by the representative increases (that is, conformity with respect to behaviour, nonconformity with respect to opinions).

Side with opponent. In general, when the representative and the constituents have different goals, the negotiator tends to agree with, or build upon ideas and proposals from the opponent or from those ideas generated during the bargaining itself (Turner, 1990, 1992). Furthermore, when the representative and the constituents agree that a coalition with the opponent yields the best outcomes, the negotiator tends to choose tactics such as siding and cooperating with the opponent (Enzle, Harvey, & Wright, 1992). In particular, relational and principle interests can cause the representative to actually change his or her mind, even though this will often be concealed from the constituents by manipulating the supply of information in the case of goal incongruency (Driscoll, 1981; Lax & Sebenius, 1986). This secrecy is often a dire necessity because of the following self-destructing course of affairs: a representative given freedom of action will be more cooperative than competitive, which makes the constituents suspicious, in which case they will begin to monitor their negotiator, which makes her or him feel distrusted, and leads him or her to depart from the more cooperative attitude (Adams, 1976). In short, constructive cooperation with the opponent tends to be ruined because of the counter forces it evokes in the constituents.

If two representatives face one another, it is not uncommon that one of them will make a gesture that provides a gain of face for the other party, or will give the opponent chances to let off steam to avoid losing face (Mastenbroek, 1989; Wilson, 1992). Sometimes one can also achieve a victory by allowing the opponent a pyrrhic victory.

That which has been said about siding with the constituency on the grounds of sanction and legitimacy power, applies, *mutatis mutandis*, to siding with the opponent.

Compromise: alternation. The representative who sometimes goes along with the constituents and at other times with the opponent develops a Janus face. Illustrative are internal functionaries such as work and organization psychologists, organization consultants, personnel officers and company doctors, who sometimes have to advise and guide the employees and at other times have to control them. Successively conforming "backwards" and "forwards" with the constituents' and the opponent's incompatible role expectations, for example by so-called "shuttle diplomats", is an example of this (Lax and Sebenius, 1986). In this case the boundary between representative negotiation and mediation fades (see also Pruitt, 1981). This type of tactic changes over to leading a double life once both the constituents and the opponent are misled by misusing the fact that they are not quite sure of what is precisely happening. This increases the chance of an agreement, but one risks the chance of being caught out sooner or later.

Compromise: mixture. When using the option of a 50/50 settlement, or another middle course tactic, one partly conforms with the role expectations of both the constituents and the opponent. More than any other reaction, this type of behaviour makes it clear that Walton and McKersie (1965), Druckman (1977) and Carnevale (1985) have contributed to a theoretical deviation. The tactic of a middle course demonstrates that representative negotiation is concerned with one process with one equilibrium between competition and cooperation, not with two separate processes. The middle course leads to one distribution or one exchange rate. A completely different illustration of this is given by the representative who does not pass on confidential information from one side to the other, but does give the other party the tenor of the information.

Again reasoning along the lines of the theory on choosing sides, a compromise will mainly occur in those situations in which the representative believes that the constituency and the opponent both have just as much relevant sanction and/or legitimacy power. Under these circumstances of a balance of power between "in front" and "behind" there is an increased chance of a longitudinal compromise of alternation or a transversal compromise of mixture.

Avoid. Rubin et al. (1994) differentiate between two types of avoidance: permanent withdrawal and temporary inactivity. Permanent withdrawal takes place, among other things, if a named negotiator returns the assignment. Temporary inactivity may be associated with well-known tactics such as gaining time and letting the situation sort itself out. Empirical indications exist that suggest the tactic of avoidance becomes more attractive as the behavioural rules used by both sides are found more illegitimate, irrespective of whether sanctions can be expected (Van de Vliert, 1981b). Avoidance can also be the result of the representative lapsing when concentrating on the promotion of the own interests instead of those of the constituents or the opponent (Friedman, 1986). Lastly, Friedman and Podolny (1992) have shown that the boundary-spanning role in representative negotiations is a differentiated function that is not necessarily loaded onto one person, and that role conflict can be avoided if several people take on different aspects of the boundary-spanning function.

Change constituency. After discussing the previous tactics of fairly passive acceptance of the incompatible role expectations ("role taking"), we have now come to the more active tactics of rejecting the conflict ("role making"; see Graen, 1976; Strauss, 1978). The role expectations from one's own camp can be altered by giving a certain impression of the opponent's position, by adjusting the interests of the partners via communication with the opponent, or through direct use of one's influence by persuasion or enforcement (Lax & Sebenius, 1986; Turner, 1990, 1992; Walton & McKersie, 1965). Driscoll (1981) reported that the negotiators of both employers and employees often use these tactics and that their role conflict diminishes by doing so. Their most proactive strategy is to alter the composition of the constituency by recruiting members or manoeuvring them onto another track.

Change opponent. These tactics have already been discussed in previous sections, except that attention was paid to the fact that they can be inspired by constituents who have made more legitimate claims and have more means of sanctioning than the opponent.

Resolution. A less directional solution is to bring the constituents and the opponent into contact with one another, with the aim of them neutralizing their conflicting role expectations (Driscoll, 1981; Walton & McKersie, 1965). This is both a more agreeable and a more effective mode of conflict management than compromising (Van de Vliert & Euwema, 1994; Van de Vliert, Euwema, & Huismans, 1995). An example is the head of the department who insists that the directors and the works council come to an agreement about the nature and size of a computerization project, before giving it the go-ahead. This can be successful because those directly involved will come to realize the true nature of the interests and will give up unrealistic expectations (Lax & Sebenius, 1986). In fact, the representative will eliminate the intermediation so that the multi-stage negotiation is converted into a direct claim or trade negotiation, at least temporarily or partially. A more active variation is that the representative serves as a quasi mediator (Colosi, 1983) trying to reconcile the differing views of the constituents and opponent.

As is the case with compromise reactions, tactics leading to role conflict resolution occur most frequently when the constituents' and the opponent's power over the representative are more or less balanced (Ben-Yoav & Pruitt, 1984; Carnevale, 1985). This compares well with the fact generally agreed on that a deadlock increases the desire for an approach that will lead to an agreement (Douglas, 1962; Morley & Stephenson, 1977) and that a power balance between the negotiators enhances the effectiveness of negotiations (Bacharach & Lawler, 1981; Mastenbroek, 1987, 1989, 1991). However, at the same time behaviour leading to solutions requires room to manoeuvre, and this can come under threat when the opponent and the supporters are both very powerful.

In summary, progress has been made if the process of representative negotiation is no longer split into negotiation with the constituents and negotiation with the opponent. The conflicting role expectations of the constituents and the opponent have a central position. The representative will choose more reactive or more proactive tactics depending on the sanction power and the legitimacy power of each of the role senders. Reactive tactics of "role taking" notably include siding with the constituency, siding with the opponent, compromise through alternation, and compromise through mixture and avoidance. Proactive tactics of "role making" include attempts to change the constituents or the opponent, and the resolution of the role conflict.

CONCLUSION

The most important contributions of this chapter on negotiations in organizations appear to us to be: (a) the differentiation between claim and trade negotiations; (b) the special attention paid to the relationship between interests and tactics; and (c) the view of the effect of negotiation dilemmas. In this final section we will take a short look at the significance of each of these points for theory building and practical application.

One of our points of departure was that distributive and integrative bargaining are different *aspects* rather than different *types* of negotiation. For that reason we have proposed the dichotomy of claim negotiation versus trade negotiation. Each claim and trade negotiation reflects a symbiotic bonding of distributive and integrative processes. The border area in which the negotiator can determine whether either a claim or a trade negotiation will be started or continued appears most interesting, both theoretically and practically. In the part on trade negotiations we have initiated some brainstorming on the tactics that one can apply to convert one type of negotiation into another. It was implied that a claim negotiation automatically converts into a trade negotiation if one of the parties sets a precondition. The question arose as to what happens when one of the parties does not believe there to be owners and therefore wants to hold claim negotiations on the grounds or reasons of justice, while the other party does believe there to be owners and therefore wants to hold trade negotiations on the grounds of things being done in return.

A second contribution of this chapter is that

interests have been presented as the determinant of tactics. This point acquires body only once one realizes that almost all the mainly experimental research into negotiation ignores process, relational and principle interests, while the practical negotiator tends to overlook these additional interests far too often as well. Consequently it was difficult to say much about the precise relationships between interests and tactics during claim and trade negotiations. Only two clusters of interests (sanction power and legitimacy power) could be indicated as global determinants of some tactics during representative negotiations. It is high time that social organizational psychology starts delivering knowledge on how to recognize and manage the yields and the costs which are involved with, for example, deception, social credit, loss of face, norms and stress.

The third contribution that we wanted to make in this review is our own outlook on the effects of the dilemmas that are so characteristic of negotiations. These dilemmas are concerned with the simultaneous operation of the own interest and the joint interest and consequently the simultaneous realization of competitive and cooperative behaviour. Other authors divide the dilemma into its separate processes of distributive versus integrative negotiation, and negotiation with the opponent and the constituency respectively. Insight into the fact that competitive and cooperative negotiation are intertwined with one another, and therefore always lead to tension, may perhaps help the members of an organization to approach negotiations in a more realistic manner.

AUTHORS' NOTE

Dr Evert van de Vliert is Professor of Organizational and Applied Social Psychology at the University of Groningen, The Netherlands. Dr Willem F.G. Mastenbroek is a director of the Holland Consulting Group and Professor of Organizational Culture and Communication at the Free University in Amsterdam, The Netherlands.

Preparation of this chapter was sponsored by Grant 560–271–011 from The Netherlands Organization for Scientific Research (NWO), awarded to Evert van de Vliert and Carsten K.W. de Dreu. We gratefully acknowledge the comments of Carsten K.W. de Dreu and Ben J.M. Emans on previous versions of this chapter.

REFERENCES

Adams, J.S. (1976). The structure and dynamics of behavior in organizational boundary roles. In M.D. Dunnette (Ed.), *Handbook of industrial and organizational psychology* (pp. 1175–1199). Chicago: Rand McNally.

Albin, C. (1993). The role of fairness in negotiation. *Negotiation Journal, 9*, 223–244.

Anzieu, D. (1974). Introduction de la psychologie de la négociation [Introduction of the psychology of negotiation]. *Bulletin de Psychologie, 28*, 759–774.

Bacharach, S.B., & Lawler, E.J. (1981). *Bargaining: Power, tactics, and outcomes.* San Francisco, CA: Jossey-Bass.

Baron, R.A., Fortin, S.P., Frei, R.L., Hauver, L.A., & Shack, M.L. (1990). Reducing organizational conflict: The role of socially-induced positive affect. *International Journal of Conflict Management, 1*, 133–152.

Bartunek, J.M., Benton, A.A., & Keys, C.B. (1975). Third party intervention and the bargaining of group representatives. *Journal of Conflict Resolution, 19*, 532–557.

Bass, B.M. (1966). Effects on the subsequent performance of negotiators of studying issues or planning strategies alone or in groups. *Psychological Monographs, 80*, 1–31.

Bazerman, M.H. (1983). Negotiator judgment: A critical look at the rationality assumption. *American Behavioral Scientist, 27*, 211–228.

Beer, M., & Gery, G.J. (1972). Individual and organizational correlates of pay system preferences. In H.L. Tosi, R.J. House, & M.D. Dunnette (Eds.), *Managerial motivation and compensation.* East Lansing, MI: Michigan State University.

Ben-Yoav, O., & Pruitt, D.G. (1984). Accountability to constituents: A two-edged sword. *Organizational Behavior and Human Performance, 34*, 283–295.

Bercovitch, J. (1984). *Social conflicts and third parties: Strategies of conflict resolution.* Boulder, CO: Westview.

Brett, J.M. (1984). Managing organizational conflict. *Professional Psychology: Research and Practice, 15*, 664–678.

Brown, B.R. (1977). Face-saving and face-restoration in negotiation. In D. Druckman (Ed.), *Negotiations: Social-psychological perspectives* (pp. 275–299). Beverly Hills: Sage.

Carnevale, P.J. (1985). Accountability of group representatives and intergroup relations. In E.J. Lawler

& B. Markovsky (Eds.), *Advances in group processes* (Vol. 2 pp. 227–248). Greenwich, CT: JAI Press.

Carnevale, P.J., O'Connor, K.M., & McCusker, C. (1993). Time pressure in negotiation and mediation. In O. Svensson & J. Maule (Eds.), *Time pressure and stress in human judgment and decision making* (pp. 117–127). New York: Plenum Press.

Carnevale, P.J., & Pruitt, D.G. (1992). Negotiation and mediation. *Annual Review of Psychology, 43*, 531–582.

Carnevale, P.J., Pruitt, D.G., & Seilheimer, S. (1981). Looking and competing: Accountability and visual access in integrative bargaining. *Journal of Personality and Social Psychology, 40*, 111–120.

Chertkoff, J.M., & Esser, J.K. (1976). A review of experiments in explicit bargaining. *Journal of Experimental Social Psychology, 12*, 464–487.

Colosi, T. (1983). Negotiation in the public and private sectors: A core model. *American Behavioral Scientist, 27*, 229–253.

Deutsch, M. (1985). *Distributive justice: A social-psychological perspective*. New Haven: Yale University Press.

Donohue, W.A., & Ramesh, C.N. (1992). Negotiator-opponent relationships. In L.L. Putnam & M.E. Roloff (Eds.), *Communication and negotiation* (pp. 209–232). Newbury Park, CA: Sage.

Douglas, A. (1962). *Industrial peacemaking*. New York: Columbia University Press.

Dreu, C.K.W. de (1993). *Gain and loss frames in bilateral negotiation: Concession aversion following the adoption of other's communicated frame*. Unpublished doctoral dissertation, University of Groningen, The Netherlands.

Dreu, C.K.W. de, Carnevale, P.J., Emans, B.J.M., & Vliert, E. van de (1994). Effects of negotiator frames: Loss aversion, mismatching, and frame adoption. *Organizational Behavior and Human Decision Processes, 60*, 90–107.

Dreu, C.K.W. de, Emans, B.J.M., & Vliert, E. van de (1992). The influence of own cognitive and other's communicated gain or loss frame on negotiation behavior. *International Journal of Conflict Management, 3*, 115–132.

Driscoll, J.W. (1981). Coping with role conflict: An exploratory field study of union-management cooperation. *International Review of Applied Psychology, 30*, 177–198.

Druckman, D. (1977). Boundary role conflict: Negotiation as dual responsiveness. *Journal of Conflict Resolution, 21*, 639–661.

Dupont, C. (1986). *La négociation: Conduite, théorie, applications* [Negotiation: Behavior, theory, applications] (2nd Edn). Paris: Dalloz.

Dupont, C., & Faure, G.O. (1991). The negotiation process. In V.A. Kremenyuk (Ed.), *International negotiation: Analysis, approaches, issues* (pp. 40–57). San Francisco: Jossey-Bass.

Emans, B.J.M. (1988). *Machtgebruik: Onderzoek naar empirisch onderscheidbare soorten van machtgebruik* [Power use: An empirical classification of types of power use]. Unpublished doctoral dissertation, University of Groningen, The Netherlands.

Enzle, M.E., Harvey, M.D., & Wright, E.F. (1992). Implicit role obligations versus social responsibility in constituency representation. *Journal of Personality and Social Psychology, 62*, 238–245.

Esser, J.K., & Komorita, S.S. (1975). Reciprocity and concession making in bargaining. *Journal of Personality and Social Psychology, 31*, 864–872.

Fells, R.E. (1985). *The industrial relations process*. Unpublished manuscript, University of Western Australia, Department of Industrial Relations.

Fisher, R. (1964). Fractionating conflict. In R. Fisher (Ed.), *International conflict and behavioral science: The Craigville papers* (pp. 91–109). New York: Basic Books.

Fisher, R., & Ury, W. (1981). *Getting to yes: Negotiating agreement without giving in*. London: Hutchinson.

Fisher, R.J. (1983). Negotiating power: Getting and using influence. *American Behavioral Scientist, 27*, 149–166.

Foa, E.B., & Foa, U.G. (1980). Resource theory: Interpersonal behavior as exchange. In K.J. Gergen, M.S. Greenberg, & R.H. Willis (Eds.), *Social exchange: Advances in theory and research* (pp. 77–94). New York: Plenum Press.

Folger, J.P., & Poole, M.S. (1984). *Working through conflict: A communication perspective*. Glenview, IL: Scott, Foresman.

Folger, R. (1986). Mediation, arbitration, and the psychology of procedural justice. In R.J. Lewicki, B.H. Sheppard, & M.H. Bazerman (Eds.), *Research on negotiation in organizations* (Vol. 1, pp. 57–79). Greenwich, CT: JAI Press.

Frey, R.L., & Adams, J.S. (1972). The negotiator's dilemma: Simultaneous in-group and out-group conflict. *Journal of Experimental Social Psychology, 8*, 331–346.

Friedman, D. (1986). The principal-agent problem in labor-management negotiations. In E.J. Lawler & B. Markovsky (Eds.), *Advances in group processes* (Vol. 3, pp. 89–106). Greenwich, CT: JAI Press.

Friedman, R.A., & Podolny, J. (1992). Differentiation of boundary spanning roles: Labor negotiations and implications for role conflict. *Administrative Science Quarterly, 37*, 28–47.

Graen, G. (1976). Role-making processes within complex organizations. In M.D. Dunnette (Ed.), *Handbook of industrial and organizational psychology* (pp. 1201–1245). Chicago: Rand McNally.

Greenhalgh, L. (1987). Interpersonal conflicts in organizations. In C.L. Cooper & I.T. Robertson (Eds.), *International review of industrial and organizational psychology* (pp. 229–271). Chichester: Wiley.

Gross, N., Mason, W.S., & McEachern, A.W. (1958).

Explorations in role analysis: Studies of the school superintendency role. New York: Wiley.
Gulliver, P.H. (1979). *Disputes and negotiations: A cross-cultural perspective*. San Diego, CA: Academic Press.
Hamner, W.C. (1974). Effects of bargaining strategy and pressure to reach agreement in a stalemated negotiation. *Journal of Personality and Social Psychology, 30*, 458–467.
Hamner, W.C., & Yukl, G.A. (1977). The effectiveness of different offer strategies in bargaining. In D. Druckman (Ed.), *Negotiations: Social-psychological perspectives* (pp.137–160). Beverly Hills: Sage.
Himmelmann, G. (1971). *Lohnbildung durch Kollektivverhandlungen* [Wage base determination through collective bargaining]. Berlin: Duncker & Humblot.
Hofstede, G. (1984). *Culture's consequences*. Beverly Hills, CA: Sage.
Holmes, M.E. (1992). Phase structures in negotiation. In L.L. Putnam & M.E. Roloff (Eds.), *Communication and negotiation* (pp. 83–105). Newbury Park, CA: Sage.
Jackson, C.N., & King, D.C. (1983). The effects of representatives' power within their own organizations on the outcome of a negotiation. *Academy of Management Journal, 26*, 178–185.
Jandt, F.E. (1985). *Win-win negotiating: Turning conflict into agreement*. New York: Wiley.
Kabanoff, B. (1991). Equity, equality, power, and conflict. *Academy of Management Review, 16*, 416–441.
Kahn, R.L. (1991). Organizational theory. In V.A. Kremenyuk (Ed.), *International negotiation: Analysis, approaches, issues* (pp. 148–163). San Francisco: Jossey-Bass.
Kahneman, D., & Tversky, A. (1979). Prospect theory: An analysis of decisions under risk. *Econometrica, 47*, 263–291.
Karambayya, R., & Brett, J.M. (1989). Managers handling disputes: Third-party roles and perceptions of fairness. *Academy of Management Journal, 32*, 687–704.
Katz, D., & Kahn, R.L. (1978). *The social psychology of organizations* (2nd Edn). New York: Wiley.
Klimoski, R.J., & Asch, R.A. (1974). Accountability and negotiatior behavior. *Organizational Behavior and Human Performance, 11*, 409–425.
Kogan, N., Lamm, H., & Trommsdorff, G. (1972). Negotiation constraints in the risk-taking domain: Effects of being observed by partners of higher or lower status. *Journal of Personality and Social Psychology, 23*, 143–156.
Lamm, H. (1978). Group-related influences on negotiation behavior: Two-person negotiation as a function of representation and election. In H. Sauermann (Ed.), *Bargaining behavior* (pp. 284–309). Tübingen: Mohr.
Lamm, H., & Kogan, N. (1970). Risk taking in the context of intergroup negotiations. *Journal of Experimental Social Psychology, 6*, 351–363.
Laskewitz, P., Vliert, E. van de, & Dreu, C.K.W. de (1994). Organizational mediators siding with or against the powerful party? *Journal of Applied Social Psychology, 24*, 176–188.
Lawler, E.E. (1981). *Pay and organizational development*. Reading, MA: Addison-Wesley.
Lax, D.A., & Sebenius, J.K. (1986). *The manager as negotiator: Bargaining for cooperation and competitive gain*. New York: Free Press.
Lewicki, R.J. (1983). Lying and deception: A behavioral model. In M.H. Bazerman, & R.J. Lewicki (Eds.), *Negotiating in organizations* (pp. 68–90). Beverly Hills, CA: Sage.
Lewicki, R.J., & Litterer, J.A. (1985). *Negotiation*. Homewood, IL: Irwin.
Lewicki, R.J., Weiss, S.E., & Lewin, D. (1992). Models of conflict, negotiation and third party intervention: A review and synthesis. *Journal of Organizational Behavior, 13*, 209–252.
Lipsky, D.B., & Donn, C.B. (Eds.) (1987). *Collective bargaining in American industry: Contemporary perspectives and future directions*. Lexington, MA: Heath.
Loewenstein, G.F., Thompson, L.L., & Bazerman, M.H. (1989). Social utility and decision making in interpersonal contexts. *Journal of Personality and Social Psychology, 57*, 426–441.
Mannix, E.A., Thompson, L.L., & Bazerman, M.H. (1989). Negotiation in small groups. *Journal of Applied Psychology, 74*, 508–517.
Mastenbroek, W.F.G. (1980). Negotiating: A conceptual model. *Group & Organization Studies, 5*, 324–339.
Mastenbroek, W.F.G. (1987). *Conflict management and organization development*. Chichester: Wiley.
Mastenbroek, W.F.G. (1989). *Negotiate*. Oxford: Basil Blackwell.
Mastenbroek, W.F.G. (1991). Development of negotiating skills. In V.A. Kremenyuk (Ed.), *International negotiation: Analysis, approaches, issues* (pp. 379–399). San Francisco: Jossey-Bass.
Morley, I., & Stephenson, G. (1977). *The social psychology of bargaining*. London: Allen & Unwin.
Murnighan, J.K. (1991). *The dynamics of of bargaining games*. Englewood Cliffs, NJ: Prentice Hall.
Neale, M.A. (1984). The effect of negotiation and arbitration cost salience on bargainer behavior: The role of arbitrator and constituency in negotiator judgment. *Organizational Behavior and Human Performance, 34*, 97–111.
Neale, M.A., & Bazerman, M.H. (1991). *Cognition and rationality in negotiation*. New York: Free Press.
Pinkley, R.L., Neale, M.A., & Bennett, R.J. (1994). The impact of alternatives to settlement in dyadic negotiation. *Organizational Behavior and Human Decision Processes, 57*, 97–116.

Prein, H.C.M. (1982). *Conflicthantering door een derde partij* [Conflict handling by a third party]. Lisse: Swets & Zeitlinger.

Pruitt, D.G. (1981). *Negotiation behavior*. New York: Academic Press.

Pruitt, D.G. (1983). Strategic choice in negotiation. *American Behavioral Scientist, 27*, 167–194.

Pruitt, D.G., & Carnevale, P.J. (1993). *Negotiation in social conflict*. Buckingham: Open University Press.

Pruitt, D.G., & Drews, J.L. (1969). The effect of time pressure, time elapsed, and the opponent's concession rate on behavior in negotiation. *Journal of Experimental Social Psychology, 5*, 43–60.

Putnam, L.L. (1990). Reframing integrative and distributive bargaining: A process perspective. In B.H. Sheppard, M.H. Bazerman, & R.J. Lewicki (Eds.), *Research on negotiation in organizations* (Vol. 2, pp. 3–30). Greenwich, CT: JAI Press.

Putnam, L.L. (1994). Productive conflict: Negotiation as implicit coordination. *International Journal of Conflict Management, 5*,

Putnam. L.L., Wilson, S.R., & Turner, D.B. (1990). The evolution of policy arguments in teacher's negotiations. *Argumentation, 4*, 129–152.

Rabbie, J.M., Visser, L., & Tils, J. (1976). De vertegenwoordiger en zijn achterban [The representative and his constituency]. *Nederlands Tijdschrift voor de Psychologie, 31*, 253–268.

Rackham, N., & Carlisle, J. (1978a). The effective negotiator: The behaviour of successful negotiators. *Journal of European Industrial Training, 2* (6), 6–11.

Rackham, N., & Carlisle, J. (1978b). The effective negotiator: Planning for negotiations. *Journal of European Industrial Training, 2*, (7), 2–5.

Raiffa, H. (1982). *The art and science of negotiation*. Cambridge, MA: Harvard University Press.

Roloff, M.E., & Jordan, J.M. (1992). Achieving negotiation goals: The "fruits and foibles" of planning ahead. In L.L. Putnam & M.E. Roloff (Eds.), *Communication and negotiation* (pp. 1–45). Newbury Park, CA: Sage.

Roloff, M.E., Tutzauer, F.E., & Dailey, W.O. (1989). The role of argumentation in distributive and integrative bargaining contexts. In M.A. Rahim (Ed.), *Managing conflict: An interdisciplinary approach* (pp. 109–119). New York: Praeger.

Roth, A.E. (1991). An economic approach to the study of bargaining. In M.H. Bazerman, R.J. Lewicki, & B.H. Sheppard (Eds.), *Research on negotiation in organizations* (Vol. 3, pp. 35–67). Greenwich, CT: JAI Press.

Rubin, J.Z., & Brown, B.R. (1975). *The social psychology of bargaining and negotiation*. New York: Academic Press.

Rubin, J.Z., & Lewicki, R.J. (1973). A three-factor experimental analysis of promises and threats. *Journal of Applied Social Psychology, 3*, 240–257.

Rubin, J.Z., Pruitt, D.G., & Kim, S.H. (1994). *Social conflict: Escalation, stalemate, and settlement* (2nd Edn). New York: McGraw-Hill.

Rubin, J.Z., & Sander, E.A. (1988). When should we use agents? Direct vs. representative negotiation. *Negotiation Journal, 4*, 395–401.

Sheppard, B.H., Lewicki, R.J., & Minton, J.W. (1992). *Organizational justice: The search for fairness in the workplace*. New York: Lexington Books.

Sheppard, B.H., Saunders, D.M., & Minton, J.W. (1988). Procedural justice from the third-party perspective. *Journal of Personality and Social Psychology, 54*, 629–637.

Smith, W.P. (1987). Conflict and negotiation: Trends and emerging issues. *Journal of Applied Social Psychology, 17*, 641–677.

Strauss, A. (1978). *Negotiations: Varieties, contexts, processes, and social order*. San Francisco: Jossey-Bass.

Thomas, K.W. (1992). Conflict and negotiation processes in organizations. In M.D. Dunnette & L.M. Hough (Eds.), *Handbook of industrial and organizational psychology* (2nd Edn, Vol. 3, pp. 651–717). Palo Alto, CA: Consulting Psychologists Press.

Thompson, L.L. (1990). Negotiation behavior and outcomes: Empirical evidence and theoretical issues. *Psychological Bulletin, 108*, 515–532.

Tjosvold, D. (1977). Commitment to justice in conflict between unequal status persons. *Journal of Applied Social Psychology, 7*, 149–162.

Tjosvold, D., & Huston, T. (1978). Social face and resistance to compromise in bargaining. *Journal of Social Psychology, 104*, 57–68.

Touzard, H. (1977). *La médiation et la résolution des conflits* [Mediation and the resolution of conflicts]. Paris: Presses Universitaires de France.

Turner, D.B. (1990). Intraorganizational bargaining: The effect of goal congruence and trust on negotiator strategy use. *Communication Studies, 41*, 54–75.

Turner, D.B. (1992). Negotiator-constituent relationships. In L.L. Putnam & M.E. Roloff (Eds.), *Communication and negotiation* (pp. 233–249). Newbury Park, CA: Sage.

Tversky, A., & Kahneman, D. (1981). The framing of decisions and the rationality of choice. *Science, 211*, 453–458.

Tyler, T.R. (1986). When does procedural justice matter in organizational settings? In R.J. Lewicki, B.H. Sheppard, & M.H. Bazerman (Eds.), *Research on negotiation in organizations* (Vol. 1, pp. 7–23). Greenwich, CT: JAI Press.

Vidmar, N. (1971). Effects of representational roles and mediation on negotiation effectiveness. *Journal of Personality and Social Psychology, 17*, 48–58.

Vliert, E. van de (1975). Gross, Mason and McEachern have not really verified their theory of role conflict resolution. *Journal for the Theory of Social Behaviour, 5*, 225–234.

Vliert, E. van de (1981a). A three-step theory of role

conflict resolution. *Journal of Social Psychology, 113*, 77–83.

Vliert, E. van de (1981b). Siding and other reactions to a conflict: A theory of escalation toward outsiders. *Journal of Conflict Resolution, 25*, 495–520.

Vliert, E. van de (1984). Role transition as interrole conflict. In V.L. Allen & E. van de Vliert (Eds.), *Role transitions: Explorations and explanations* (pp. 63–79). New York: Plenum.

Vliert, E. van de, & Euwema, M.C. (1994). Agreeableness and activeness as components of conflict behaviors. *Journal of Personality and Social Psychology, 66*, 674–687.

Vliert, E. van de, Euwema, M.C., & Huismans, S.E. (1995). Managing conflict with a subordinate or superior: The effectiveness of conglomerated behavior. *Journal of Applied Psychology, 80*, 271–281.

Wall, J.A. (1977). Intergroup bargaining: Effects of opposing constituent's stance, opposing representative's bargaining, and representative's locus of control. *Journal of Conflict Resolution, 21*, 459–474.

Wall, J.A., Jr. (1985). *Negotiation: Theory and practice*. Glenview, IL: Scott Foresman.

Walton, R.E., & McKersie, R.B. (1965). *A behavioral theory of labor negotiations: An analysis of a social interaction system*. New York: McGraw Hill.

Wilson, S.R. (1992). Face and facework in negotiation. In L.L. Putnam & M.E. Roloff (Eds.), *Communication and negotiation* (pp. 176–205). Newbury Park, CA: Sage.

Wolters, T. (1989). *Onderhandeling en bemiddeling: Een studie op het terrein van de arbeidsverhoudingen* [Negotiation and mediation: A study in the area of industrial relations]. Amsterdam: VU Uitgeverij.

Zartman, I.W. (Ed.) (1976). *The 50% solution*. New Haven: Yale University Press.

Zartman, I.W., & Berman, M.R. (1982). *The practical negotiator*. New Haven: Yale University Press.

15

Conflict and Conflict Management

Evert van de Vliert

INTRODUCTION

In recent decades, conflict, especially the parties' behaviour in a conflict, has been attracting increasing academic attention. The results of these efforts are considered here in the light of the so-called *escalation model*. To begin with, some restrictions on this survey will be discussed as well as definitions of conflict and conflict management, and my own view of the customary approaches to conflict.

POINTS OF DEPARTURE

In constructing their theories, organizational psychologists usually restrict themselves to conflicts between two individuals or groups. Following in their footsteps, I shall not consider purely intrapersonal conflicts or conflicts among three or more parties. And, except for a typology of intervention strategies in the last section, conflict management by an intervening third party will not be discussed either.

Two individuals, an individual and a group, or two groups, are said to be in conflict when and to the extent that at least one of the parties feels it is being obstructed or irritated by the other (for other definitions, see Fink, 1968; Rahim, 1992; Rubin, Pruitt, & Kim, 1994; Schmidt & Kochan, 1972). Important aspects of this definition are:

1. The frustration is a subjective experience and does not necessarily have an objective basis.
2. The nature of the frustration may be cognitive or affective, or both (sensations of blocked goals, or feelings of repulsion, hostility, fear).
3. The frustration is blamed on the other individual or group.
4. The magnitude or intensity of the frustration may vary: usually the conflict de-escalates or escalates.
5. The frustration is not necessarily coupled with particular conflict behaviour toward the other party. The reaction to the frustration as well as all secondary reactions to that primary reaction come under the heading of conflict management, irrespective of

whether the reactions are those of the frustrated party or of the opposite party.

6. The conflict can be one-sided. One-sided conflicts occur, in particular, when only one party feels frustrated but avoids any verbal or nonverbal communication about the issue, or when only one of the frustrated parties attributes its frustration to the other. The existence of such one-sided conflicts asks for a conceptualization of conflict management in terms of personal action rather than social interaction.

In the study and management of conflicts two kinds of approaches or models have been used: process models and structural models. Process models are oriented primarily toward the cyclical and dynamic courses of conflicts where one event follows another, such as frustration, conceptualization of the issue, action, reaction, consequence, and renewed frustration (Filley, 1975; Lewicki, Weiss, & Lewin, 1992; Pondy, 1967; Rahim, 1992; Thomas, 1992; Walton, 1987). Structural models, on the other hand, are oriented primarily toward factors influencing the issues and the behaviour of the parties: the parties' predispositions, the degree of mutual dependence and incompatibility of interests, pressure from others, rules and procedures (Katz & Kahn, 1978; Lewicki et al. 1992; Thomas, 1992; Walton & Dutton, 1969). Process models pay little attention to the causes of conflicts; structural models on the other hand neglect the dynamics and consequences of conflicts. Organizational problems tend to place the conflict parties in both a sequence of events (process model) and a constellation of forces (structural model). In this chapter I shall attempt, therefore, to integrate the two models rather than differentiate them any further.

A disadvantage of both the process approach and the structural approach is their lack of systematic concern for the central mechanisms of escalation and de-escalation, and for the extent to which conflict management constitutes a strategic choice. Therefore, the intention is to blend the process model and the structural model into what is called the *escalation model*. This compound model not only does justice to the sequence of events (process model) and to the constellation of forces (structural model), but it also emphasizes the de-escalating or escalating nature of all kinds of spontaneous and strategic conflict management. From the models it integrates, it adopts the assumption that the causes, characteristics, and consequences of interpersonal conflicts do not differ essentially from the causes, characteristics, and consequences of intergroup conflicts (see Lewicki et al. 1992). A last point of departure is that the escalation model involves an heuristic framework. It has not been formulated with a view to deduce testable hypotheses from it.

ESCALATION MODEL

As depicted in Figure 15.1, there are characteristic phenomena underlying a conflict, referred to as the *antecedent conditions*. These potential determinants of conflict are sometimes called latent conflicts. For at least one of the parties involved they may cause certain cognitive or affective frustrations, referred to as the perceived *conflict issues*. Because what one author calls "antecedent condition" is called "conflict issue" by another, the explicit criterion chosen here is that of feeling obstructed or irritated. The conflict management subsequent to this experience represents the model's essence. Numerous behaviours exist that are capable of handling conflict. For example, Roloff (1976) reported 44 conflict response modes, and Wall (1985) listed and categorized 169 tactics. The central issue here is to be sure to distinguish between mainly spontaneous or strategic de-escalative behaviour on the one hand, and mainly spontaneous or strategic escalative behaviour on the other.

De-escalative behaviour involves a range of actions, including:

- Reducing the chances of the other party also getting frustrated.
- Reducing the chances of a related conflict in the future.
- Resolving the current conflict.
- Reducing or preventing the intensification of the current conflict.

FIGURE 15.1

Escalation model.

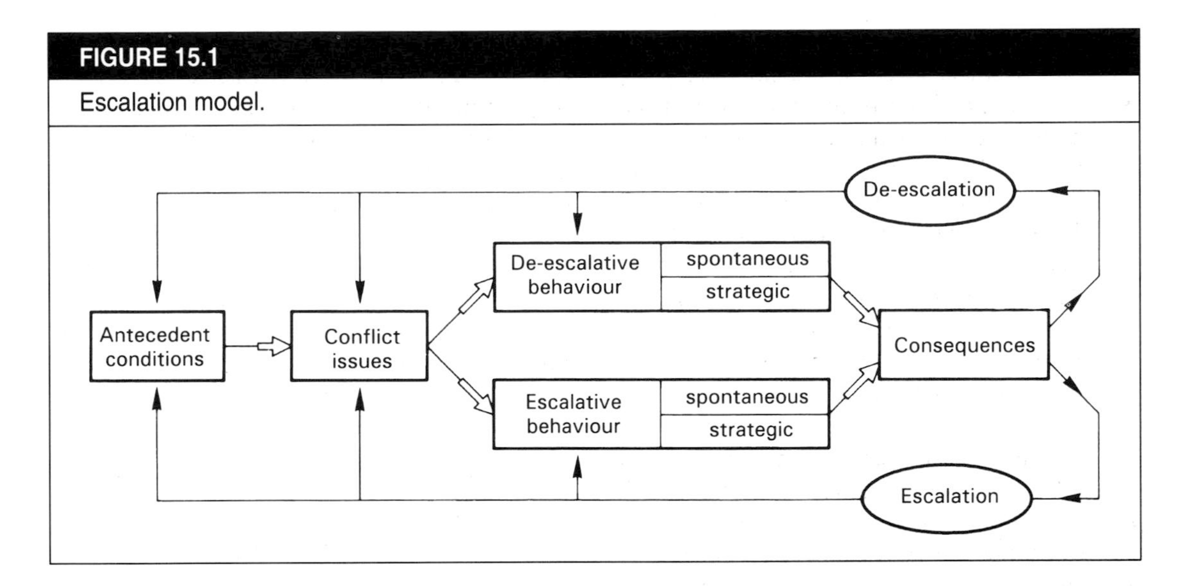

Obviously, the opposite is *escalative behaviour*. All such behaviour is *spontaneous* inasmuch as it is not intentional. It is *strategic*, however, inasmuch as it forms part of a conscious plan either to prevent or to stimulate conflict or intensification of conflict. Spontaneous or strategic conflict management has de-escalating or escalating *consequences* for the antecedent conditions, the conflict issues, or the parties' subsequent behaviour, as well as for the accompanying opinions, feelings and behavioural tendencies. With direct consequences this feedback is immediate (e.g. conflict resolution or vengeful behaviour). With indirect consequences conflict management first influences other variables, such as positive or negative feelings, which in their turn influence the antecedent conditions, conflict issues, or subsequent escalative or de-escalative behaviours.

Having presented the escalation model, I shall now discuss the relevant literature, using the constituent parts of the model as a convenient structure.

ANTECEDENT CONDITIONS

A natural classification of the potential causes of conflict would be: organizational characteristics, individual characteristics, and relational characteristics.

Organizational characteristics

It is a precarious job to indicate which organizational characteristics may be a source of conflict. In the first place, potential conflict is inherent in the phenomenon of organization: "every aspect of organizational life that creates order and coordination of effort must overcome other tendencies to action, and in that fact lies the potentiality for conflict" (Katz & Kahn, 1978, p. 617). Second, depending on context and kind of conflict, the same organizational characteristics may be related to conflict in different ways. For example, standardization reduces conflict, but at the same time it is attended by role prescriptions and performance registrations which enlarge the chances of conflict (Child, 1973). And third, correlation does not necessarily imply causality.

We would do well to keep all this in mind when learning that, apparently, conflict is related to structural aspects such as number of hierarchical levels, number of departments, decentralization, deconcentrated specialization and heterogeneity among members of the organization (Corwin, 1969; Hage, 1980; Naase, 1978; Nachmias, 1982), and joint resources or means. Ambiguity of tasks, input, or criteria of evaluation also goes hand in hand with conflict (Walton & Dutton, 1969; Walton, Dutton, & Cafferty, 1969). Role conflicts are found especially with incumbents of managing, controlling, and innovative positions, as well as with those in representative or other boundary roles (Miles & Perreault, 1976; Van de Vliert, Visser, Zwaga, Winnubst, & Ter Heine, 1983).

At the same time, conflict appears to be associated with cultural organizational characteristics, such as goals, values, and norms. On the one hand, conflicts prosper by differences in, for instance, goals, reciprocal openness, or tolerance (Lawrence & Lorsch, 1967), and by diversity of values among group members and between the group and governing superiors (Jehn, 1994). On the other hand, conflicts may arise from close supervision, illegitimate rules, the norm that competition is to the benefit of the organization, or from the absence of the norm that quarrelling is "not done" (Blake, Shepard, & Mouton, 1964; Naase, 1978).

The organizational regulation mechanisms constitute a case in their own right. The formal and informal rules influence not the rise of the conflict as such, but rather the form it takes on and the subsequent course of the conflict process: rights and duties, weapons allowed, procedures in cases of disagreements and complaints, possibilities for appeal (Glasl, 1980; Pinkley, 1990; Prein, 1982; Scott, 1965). Ury, Brett, and Goldberg (1988) discussed main principles for designing effective dispute management systems that reconcile underlying interests, which are less costly and more rewarding than systems that determine who is right, which in turn are less costly and more rewarding than systems that determine who has more power. Unfortunately, no one explicitly distinguishes between the rules regulating the management of existing conflicts and the rules preventing or stimulating conflict issues (see, however, Rubin et al., 1994). This is confusing and has undoubtedly slowed down developments in this field.

Individual characteristics

As indicated by a survey of Boekestijn (1979), various explanations of conflict behaviour can be traced to individuals. It is assumed that relationships exist between education and aggression, personal frustration and aggression, polarizing thought processes and conflict, mistaken perceptions and conflict. In view of such explanations, Blake and Mouton (1989) warned against the "psychodynamic fallacy" of unjustifiably ascribing conflicts to individuals. Like Sherif (1966), they believed the extra- and supra-individual determinants of conflict to be much more important than the individual ones. The question is, however, whether the latter is true, since even stimulation of certain parts of the brain may elicit hostile behaviour. Also there is increasing evidence that aggressive behaviour is related to hormonal imbalances and to the configuration of chromosomes (Weitz, 1977).

Researchers have been concerned more with the influence of personality traits and attitudes than with the biological basis of conflicts. Using experimental games, they find a more combative attitude with the increase of, among other things, the need of power, dogmatism, machiavellism, suspiciousness, and a sense of inferiority (Křivohlavý, 1974; Terhune, 1970). In actual organizational situations, conflicts seem to occur more often and to be more serious when the people involved are more neurotic or introvert, or when people have a high degree of intolerance of ambiguity or internal control, and are readier to take risks (Cummings, Harnett, & Schmidt, 1972; Kahn, Wolfe, Quinn, Snoek, & Rosenthal, 1964; Naase, 1978).

One of the most important causes of conflicts between individuals or groups is intrapersonal conflict (Sanford, 1964). Role ambiguity and various kinds of role conflict are especially well known (Van de Vliert et al., 1983 recall that only when one holds others responsible for these frustrations, can a two-sided conflict arise). One could think of the role ambiguity experienced by members of an organization following unexpected disappointment or events they were not told about, or of a department manager who got stuck between the conflicting desires of his supervisors

TABLE 15.1

Antecedent conditions.

Organizational characteristics
Individual characteristics
Relational characteristics

and subordinates, or of the role conflict of a representative having a constituency. Apparently there are at least three ways for such internal tension to become manifest and, thus, to result in external social conflict. First, as a discharging, aggressive explosion in which anger turns inner irritation into outer conflict. Second, as a deliberate attempt at changing role expectations or at foisting the conflict upon others. Third, as some form of non-conforming behaviour, such as innovation, withdrawal, and rebellion (Merton, 1957; Moscovici, 1985).

Individual characteristics influencing the course but not the rise of the conflict include styles of conflict management. Sternberg and Dobson (1987) studied no fewer than 16 of such personal styles of handling conflicts. Common practice distinguishes five styles:

1. *Avoiding*, or withdrawing from, discord and confrontation, because of indifference regarding the relationship with the opposite party.
2. *Accommodating*, or smoothing, in order to retain a good relationship.
3. *Compromising*, in which case each party is partly satisfied.
4. *Problem solving*, so that both parties get rid of their frustrations completely.
5. *Fighting* in order to win and beat the opponent (cf. Blake & Mouton, 1970, 1985; Van de Vliert, 1997a).

These behavioural predispositions are related to various personality dimensions (Chanin & Schneer, 1984; Jones & Melcher, 1982; Schneer & Chanin, 1987). If the mode of conflict management favoured most turns out to be unsuitable or ineffective, one is assumed to fall back upon another personal style, the "back-up" style. However, thorough research into patterns of subsequent conflict behaviours has still to be done (interesting first inputs were given by Morrill & Thomas, 1992; Phillips & Cheston, 1979; Van de Vliert & Euwema, 1994).

Relational characteristics

Because often the characteristics of each party will increase the chances of conflict only when they stand in some relation to one another, it is remarkable that the research tradition of experimental conflict games usually ignores relational characteristics. The most general formulation of relational influence is that perceived inequality of age, education, experience, status or ambition tends to stimulate conflict (Apfelbaum, 1974; Naase, 1978). A well-known illustration is the higher educated employee with less experience versus the lower educated employee with more experience. They differ in power source and, consequently, run a great risk of falling-out over their mutual influence (Kabanoff, 1985). As new social categories enter the workforce, and move up in organizations, conflicts rooted in gender, race, and class differences have become more prominent (Donnellon & Kolb, 1994). The proposition that inequality breeds conflict, however, is rather unsophisticated, as it does not take into account the extent to which perceived differences may be acceptable.

Organizations exist by virtue of some form of accepted inequality that could be associated with harmonious cooperation rather than with conflict—the complementary fulfilment of functions. This acceptance seems to be important also for the research-based viewpoint that relatively small and extremely big differences in power constitute conditions for conflicts (Mulder, 1978). An additional condition seems to be that the parties reject the imbalance of powers, otherwise there would be no basis for conflict. Horwitz's (1964) results and view are more sophisticated: hostility does not result from differences in influence as such but rather from an influence ratio turning out more unfavorably than expected. Raven and Kruglanski (1970) represented a completely different point of view. According to them, conflicts are tempered by possibilities of positive sanctioning, whereas they are intensified by possibilities of negative sanctioning.

A point often mentioned is the extent of mutual dependence among the parties. Yet the opinions are contradictory. On the one hand, there are many who confirm that mutual dependence is a source of conflict, especially if one is very dependent on an unreliable person or group (Prein, 1982; Rubin et al., 1994). On the other hand, Naase (1978) stated that greater dependence fosters conformity and may, therefore, counter conflict. Besides, there is some consensus, based partly on Sherif's (1966) field experiments, that mutual dependence in the form of shared interests prevents or reduces conflict. According to Coser (1956), closer relations may intensify both the existing harmony and the existing conflict. In short, mutual dependence is a double-edged sword. We need exact definitions of dependence and conflict as well as a more precise specification of the conditions under which an association obtains between them.

Deutsch's (1973) distinction between "promotive interdependence", with the parties needing one another to attain their goals, and "contrient interdependence", with the goals being irreconcilable, appears to be a step in the right direction. Recently, Janssen (1994) has shown that promotive or positive task interdependence evokes high concerns about both one's own and the opponent's goals, whereas contrient or negative task interdependence evokes high concern about one's own goals but low concern about the opponent's goals. Note that perceived task interdependence always leads to high concern about one's own goals, and that positive versus negative task interdependence is reflected best in the resulting high versus low degree of concern for the other party's goals. Consequently, if task performers are interrelated, concern for the other's goals is a crucial determinant of the existence and persistence of conflict (for empirical evidence, see Janssen, 1994; Johnson & Johnson, 1989; Sherif, 1966).

Finally, other determinants of conflict, such as communication failures among the parties, mutual prejudices, and mutual suspiciousness, though obvious, are no less important. The relational characteristics could well turn out to be more important than the other antecedent conditions, since they are not restricted to one of the conflict parties, as are individual characteristics, or to a characteristic both parties have in common, as is the case with most organizational characteristics.

CONFLICT ISSUES

According to Walton (1987, p. 68) and Mastenbroek (1987, p. 125) the antecedent conditions may give rise to three kinds of frustrations:

1. Conflicts of interest over scarce resources.
2. Disagreements about collective policies or procedures or individual role behaviours.
3. Social-emotional conflicts whereby a group member's identity comes into question (dozens of similar and other typologies may be found in Coombs, 1987; Deutsch, 1973; Fink, 1968; Glasl, 1980; Prein, 1982; Rahim, 1992).

The *scarce resources* one tries to secure in a conflict of interests may be both material and social. They concern money, equipment, space, and manpower, but also information, attention, prestige, authority, and social power. As long as the conflict parties share the same interests and their conflict is embedded in accepted rules of play, we usually speak of competition.

In the case of disagreements about organizational *policies or procedures*, it is not the available resources but a group's activities, intended or accomplished, that constitute the basis of conflict (Schmidt & Kochan, 1972). The conflict is about the intention, planning, execution, coordination, results, or control of group activities. For example, Wall and Nolan (1986) found that 54% of the conflicts in task groups were described as having their origin in unequal member contributions towards task accomplishment or in procedural matters. Another illustration are decision-making processes, in which most conflict issues crop up in the phase in which alternatives are developed rather than in the phases of start, rounding off, and implementation (Koopman, 1980). According to Brickman (1974), diverging goals or procedures that concern the rules regulating the conflict handling, as previously discussed, represent revolutionary conflicts; haggling about the "appealability" of a case is a good example.

Disagreements about *role behaviours* are concerned with what a member of an organization should or should not do under certain circumstances. Often a task group seeks to find a specialized role for the individual that maximizes his or her contributions to the attainment of organizational goals, whereas the individual attempts to define a specialized role that maximizes the satisfaction of personal needs (Moreland & Levine, 1984). In particular, routine decisions about the scheme of working-hours, the working conditions, transfer, fixing holidays, and the division of tasks appear to be seen as conflictual in many companies (Andriessen, Drenth, & Lammers, 1983). Strangely enough, it is not among the adherents of role theory in the first place where we must look for studies of role conflicts between parties, since they generally concern themselves with intrapersonal role conflicts.

Frustration of an individual's or group's *identity* occurs when others deny the self-image or characteristic identifications, including values and sensibilities. This often occurs when cutting down staff and in mergers. It comprises forms of social competition where one compares oneself or one's own party to another, intending nothing but to come out of it well—to win. Such identity conflicts may be recognized by their intense emotional involvement: feelings of being insulted, of fear, suspicion, resentment, contempt, anger, hate (Mastenbroek, 1987).

It appears that, with escalation, cognitive conflicts of interest and disagreements turn into affective conflicts of identity (Walton, 1987), sometimes called the "personalization of conflict". Conversely, rationalization may turn deeply-rooted affective frustrations partly into manifest surface problems (Deutsch, 1973; Walton, 1987). Colleagues aspiring to the same management function may become so personally involved in that conflict that they begin to obstruct one another in other respects as well. As the social-emotional issues may result both from and in other conflict issues, they have a central function that, to date, has been insufficiently recognized, let alone researched.

The three types of conflict issues are neither mutually exclusive nor exhaustive. Bisno (1988) covered the aforementioned frustrations about scarce resources, collective or individual activities, and personal identity but discussed additional types of conflicts which may mimic, or get entangled with what he termed "the real thing". They included:

1. *Induced conflicts* intentionally created in order to achieve other than explicit objectives.
2. *Misattributed conflicts* involving incorrect attribution as to the behaviours, participants, issues, or causes.
3. *Illusionary conflicts* based on misperceptions or misunderstandings.
4. *Displaced conflicts* in which the opposition or antagonism is directed towards persons or concerns other than the actual offending parties or the real issues.
5. *Expressive conflicts* characterized by a desire to express hostility, antagonism, or other strong feelings.

TABLE 15.2

Conflict issues.

Scarce resources
Goals, procedures, role behaviours
Identity

DE-ESCALATIVE CONFLICT MANAGEMENT

Each direct or indirect reaction of the parties to a conflict issue constitutes conflict management. It is de-escalative if it does not increase or if it decreases either party's frustration. If the adversary becomes more frustrated there is no question of de-escalation. On paper, such a description causes no problems, but in practice it does. Because the amount of frustration perceived is a personal matter, it is not always easy to establish whether a behaviour has a de-escalative effect. Nor is it always easy to establish whether a party's attempt at preventing further frustration is a conscious one (strategic de-escalation) or not (spontaneous de-escalation). But these problems in characterizing certain behaviours would be overrated if, merely because of them, we would ignore such important distinctions as those between de-escalative and escalative behaviour and between spontaneous and strategic behaviour.

Spontaneous de-escalative behaviour

Spontaneous conflict handling of a mainly de-escalative nature consists of rejection or talking down of frustration, of cooperative styles of behaviour, and other automatic reactions to a frustrating situation, such as blindly conforming to organizational regulating mechanisms.

Repression of a minor conflict occurs if one suppresses awareness of it, does not pay any attention to it, or revises one's own perception or opinion regarding the issue immediately (Brown, 1983; Delhees, 1979; Pondy, 1967). It appears that group members, unable to avoid a conflict, will often unconsciously attenuate their frustration by: considering it of minor importance; seeking compensation in pleasant activities; reformulating the issue in such a way as to take the sting out of it; viewing it less egocentrally; or by not attributing any negative intention to the other party (Delhees, 1979; Deutsch, 1973; Thomas & Pondy, 1977).

Of the personal styles of conflict management, avoiding, accommodating, compromising and problem solving usually have at least a short-term de-escalative effect. For example, at a meeting of a works council the closing down of part of a plant is to be discussed. A council member against the management doing so may be absent from that meeting (avoiding), be silent (accommodating), propose to carry out the plan only partially or not until some further date (compromising), or try to find out what the management actually wants to attain and how that can be done without closing down part of the plant (problem solving). These reactions can be spontaneous. At any rate, each of these reactions will decrease rather than increase the council member's frustration, while frustration of the management does not occur or is kept within bounds. Those low on internal control and risk taking will most probably tend to avoid and to accommodate (Cummings et al., 1972). They deny the conflict issues, do not react at all or react minimally to them, use abstract statements, select a semantic or procedural focus, make jokes, pass ambivalent or pessimistic remarks (Hocker & Wilmot, 1991). People predisposed to react in a confronting and problem-solving manner are both more assertive and more cooperative (Prein, 1976) and score higher on internal control and risk taking. Kabanoff (1987) reported that less need of control is related to more de-escalative behaviour in the form of nonconfrontation or integration.

While some view the aforementioned modes of de-escalative conflict management primarily as personality traits (e.g. Filley, 1975), others view them rather as organizational characteristics (following Lawrence & Lorsch, 1967), as conflict behaviours strongly influenced by the type of situation (e.g. Hocker & Wilmot, 1991; Rahim, 1992), or as manifestations of a pattern of social interaction (e.g. Folger & Poole, 1984; Van de Vliert, 1997a). It is likely that each view contains some grain of truth. More certainty about the nature of conflict management modes can be obtained only if the research in this field succeeds in struggling out of the theoretical vacuum in which it still operates (Putnam & Poole, 1987).

Examples mentioned in the literature make it clear that spontaneous de-escalative behaviour is sometimes more determined by the situation. Thus, in certain situations, confrontation is automatically avoided because there is no time for it, or the issue is considered trivial, or one is too much in favour of, too involved with, or has too much in common with the other(s). In an uncertain crisis situation the members of a cohesive and closed group with a directive leader will be inclined to swallow their objections to the plans of the leader (Janis, 1982; for prevention, see Kroon, 't Hart, & Van Kreveld, 1991; Turner & Pratkanis, 1994). But there are also situations in which negotiating about a compromise is just a foregone conclusion, as in the case of a mild conflict of interest about scarce material resources or in conflicts urgently requiring a mutually satisfactory settlement (Blake et al., 1964; Rahim, 1992; Thomas, 1992).

Spontaneous problem-solving behaviour may be expected to occur when the opponent is perceived as equally powerful, when one is able to put oneself in the other party's shoes, or when one: has a positive attitude toward the phenomenon of conflict; does not feel threatened; believes that everyone else is of equal value; appreciates the adversary's contributions; or trusts the other party because one considers it likeminded, reliable, willing, non-manipulative (Deutsch, 1973; Filley, 1975; Musser, 1982). Because of these prerequisites, solution behaviour is unlikely in social-emotional conflicts, where one's own identity is at stake.

A last determinant of spontaneous de-escalative behaviour consists of conflict inhibiting regulation mechanisms—for example, task assignments, delivery dates, backroom consultations, voting in writing, and loyal cooperation—which one obeys without really thinking about it. Murray (1975) noted with amazement that although such customs, rules, and procedures are applied most in organizations, they nevertheless have been studied least.

In conflicts between supervisors and subordinates, the latter will usually unquestioningly comply with the decisions, wishes, or irritating behaviour of their supervisors, as they happen to be in power legitimately (Raven & Kruglanski, 1970), to prevent reprisals (Musser, 1982), or because negotiating and fighting are beyond the subordinates' scope and frame of mind (Van de Vliert, Euwema, Dispa, & Vrij, 1988). If they do not comply, the boss or department manager will usually suppress the conflict promptly and successfully by insisting on his or her rights (Brown, 1983; Shepard, 1964). In a very different way, the hierarchical principle automatically has a de-escalative effect when one reverts to established priorities, such as are often laid down in a hierarchy of role obligations (Merton, 1957).

Strategic de-escalative behaviour

As soon as a conflict party *consciously* pursues prevention or de-escalation, his or her behaviour changes from spontaneous to strategic. With Figure 15.1 as our guide, we can differentiate between strategic conflict management directed mainly towards more de-escalative antecedent conditions, towards eliminating the frustrating issues, or towards promoting further de-escalative behaviour.

The first category of strategic de-escalative behaviour includes, in particular, changing the organizational or relational characteristics, which usually goes beyond an incidental conflict. For example, Fisher (1994) developed 15 generic principles for analysing, confronting, and resolving intergroup conflict, and for creating policy-making procedures and enduring structures that institutionalize equality, autonomy, and respect among contending groups. Structural operations often propagated are: diminishing power differences by institutionalizing joint consultations; explicating the decision-making and executive responsibilities or dividing them up more appropriately; establishing an expert and impartial point of coordination, or establishing or clearing communication channels. A decrease rather than increase of mutual dependence occurs with decentralization, job enlargement or job enrichment, creation of a buffer, or even total separation of roles. When personnel or financial means are involved, further frustration can be prevented by adding personnel, through early retirement, transfers, different working hours, reconsideration of remuneration rules, changing allocated budgets, and the like. Finally, a well-known procedure is to look for superordinate goals to be reached only through the efforts of both parties (Blake & Mouton, 1984; Sherif, 1966). However, it has been demonstrated that this may have an escalating rather than de-escalating effect when the tasks of the conflict parties differ insufficiently (Brown & Wade, 1987), and when, rather than a third party, one of the two parties initiates the superordinate goal (Johnson & Lewicki, 1969).

Basically, this means that arrangements are made that should completely or partly eliminate a current conflict and, at the same time, prevent similar conflicts from occurring in the future. They represent deliberate changes in the antecedent conditions in order to remove the conflict. Further-

TABLE 15.3

De-escalative conflict management.

Spontaneous de-escalative behaviour
Denying the conflict
De-escalating styles of behaviour
Situational determination
Regulation mechanisms
Strategic de-escalative behaviour
Changing antecedent conditions
Problem solving
Re-conceptualization of issues
De-escalating reaction models
Negotiation

more, it turns out that, sometimes, those directly involved introduce formal or informal regulation mechanisms that should ensure more de-escalative conflict management rather than preventing further conflicts. This mostly involves rules concerning the manner in which the parties should deal with one another or the steps they must or are allowed to take externally. For example, "management by exception" contains such a rule, this being that when the members of an organization are in conflict, they should first try everything in their power to find a solution, before calling in the management.

Both the agreements intended to end a conflict and the regulation mechanisms will only have an appeal if they are known, clear, and unprejudiced, if they are supported and adhered to by others and promise to bring about improvement, while at the same time ensuring that deviations will soon come to light (Deutsch, 1973). In this case, rules have the advantage of being impersonal and legitimate, which in itself will have a more de-escalative effect than taking a personal stand or, for instance, applying negative sanctions (Raven & Kruglanski, 1970). Moreover, as elucidated under "Organizational characteristics", eventually regulations often elicit spontaneous de-escalative behaviour. In individual cases, however, rules may discourage problem solving, promote black-white thinking encouraging win-lose competition, and tend to lead to new rules.

The most advocated de-escalative strategy, problem-solving behaviour, is oriented towards the incidental conflict issues themselves instead of towards the antecedent conditions. Filley (1975) in his "win-win method" Gray (1989) in her theory of collaboration, and Rubin et al. (1994) in their "integrative solution" worked out this strategy in detail. In the search for creative resolutions, the following activities may be helpful:

1. Recast an attack on people as an attack on particular problems.
2. Ask whether there is a real rather than an induced, misattributed, illusionary, displaced, or expressive conflict.
3. Analyse the group members' underlying interests, and set reasonably high aspirations with respect to these interests.
4. Inventorize interpersonal differences in valuation, forecast, risk aversion, time preference, capability, constituency.
5. Explore ways to reconcile the conflicting positions.
6. Evaluate alternative solutions and agree on a single solution.

That problem solving is, as a rule, the most effective way of managing conflict is supported by persuasive arguments, anecdotal evidence, and systematic empirical research (Blake & Mouton, 1984, 1985; Burke, 1970; Lawrence & Lorsch, 1967; Likert & Likert, 1976; Rubin et al., 1994). Hocker and Wilmot (1991) emphasized that conflict resolution is time and energy consuming and, consequently, is not worth the effort if the investment in the issue or relationship is low. Moreover, they reasoned that possibilities for integrative conflict handling are bounded by the group characteristics. Integration was assumed to be a functional conflict management choice only if the group is characterized by both an average level of cohesion or social connectedness and an average degree of adaptability to changing conditions. Others have argued that conflict resolution is to be advised only if time pressure is not high, if a win-win outcome is not out of the question, and if the issue is not too sensitive because peoples' identities are involved (Walton, 1972; Walton & McKersie, 1965). As for identity conflicts, Walton stated that any satisfactory resolution will always contain elements of conciliation.

A kind of alternative to conflict resolution is the conscious reconceptualization of a conflict issue in such a way that frustration decreases or even disappears (Filley, 1982; Thierry, 1977; Thomas & Pondy, 1977). Reconceptualization causes one to view a conflict as less abstract and therefore easier to solve, as redeemable, as less threatening to one's identity, less a matter of all or nothing or of "it's me or him", "us or them" (cf. Pinkley, 1990). Much attention has been paid to the approach of Fisher (1964), who divided big conflicts into a number of small ones, each of which involves fewer people, topics, principles, or related issues. Another kind of reconceptualization is to remind oneself that, in spite of the conflict, the relationship with the opposite party is essentially one of cooperation. The attractive thing about these strategies is that they can often dispense with the opposite party. But there is the risk of getting stuck with a shifted conceptualization of the problem, thus obscuring the real conflict. Walton (1987) and Deutsch (1973) did not consider this a very serious drawback, because working on some less threatening manifest problem may often clear the way for and encourage resolution of the more fundamental frustrations. It often happens that both the realization of more preventive conditions and the elimination of the conflict issues themselves is undesirable or impossible. Strategic interventions must then be directed towards stimulating de-escalatve behaviour. There are three frequently verified strategies for changing from hostile behaviour to less frustrating behaviour: Allport's (1979) restoration of contact; Deutsch's (1973) realization of cooperation; and Osgood's (1966) "Graduated and Reciprocated Initiatives in Tension reduction" (GRIT).

The contact hypothesis, formulated by Allport in the 1950s, postulates that restoration of the interaction with members from a group one dislikes, brings about appreciation and respect for that group. However, Sherif (1966) showed that the conflict increases rather than decreases if one arranges for struggling groups to meet each other in pleasant situations. Others have studied which characteristics the contact must have or under which conditions the contact must be made, to be able to produce de-escalation. This resulted in a shopping list of prerequisites for contact restoration to be successful as a de-escalative strategy (Pettigrew, 1986). Stephan (1985) enumerated no fewer than 13 necessary conditions and added that the list, long as it is, is surely incomplete. Hence a more valid hypothesis seems to be that restoration of contact has just the wrong effect.

Through laboratory experiments, Deutsch and his colleagues did research on the usefulness of various strategies in terms of their ability to induce the opponent to more cooperation. The most effective one is to react defensively, always reciprocating an attack with self-defence and never with a counter-attack. The strategy of consistently turning the other cheek apparently stimulates exploitation rather than cooperation. Least effective is a strategy of deterrence in which one does counter-attack. So the most de-escalative strategy is the one where one does not react in a hostile fashion but does not allow intimidation either. This is supported by Axelrod's (1984) finding that the tit-for-tat strategy—that is, matching the opponent's level of (de-)escalative behaviour—usually encourages the opponent to cooperate. It is also in accord with the experimental result that threats—however preventively intended—intensify rather than attenuate the conflict, especially when the adversary deems the threat unwarranted. Making promises, on the other hand, is an effective de-escalative tactic (Deutsch, 1973; Rubin et al., 1994).

Using Osgood's (1966) GRIT strategy, developed in order to realize a step-by-step way to relieve international tension, one expounds one's strategy, then publicly makes some unequivocal conciliatory gesture, and subsequently invites the opposite party to reciprocate. If the opposite party does not reciprocate, these de-escalating initiatives are continued. Attacks are countered by measured retaliation, after which a relieving measure is announced again. Gaining trust and credibility is crucial. According to experimental data, this is a successful strategy that can also be applied by groups or individuals in conflict (Lindskold, 1978; Patchen, 1987).

Negotiation refers to the realisation of a mutually acceptable or mutually satisfactory settlement by dividing or exchanging positive or negative outcomes (see Chapter 14 of this handbook). Among the other activities on behalf of short-term stimulation of de-escalative behaviour are: agreeing on a cooling off period, settling on procedures, deliberately avoiding the opponent or the issue, throwing dice, voting, giving in after mature consideration, and also unexpectedly reacting in a sympathetic way by mild flattery, a small gift or self-depreciating remarks, or in a humorous way (Baron, 1984; Baron, Fortin, Frei, Hauver, & Shack, 1990). If one goes to talk with the opposite party, one may safeguard the reliability of the communication (Burton, 1969; Walton, 1987), replace subjective judgements by objective descriptions (Filley, 1975), and exchange views on and feelings about one's own and the other party (Van de Vliert, 1987; Walton, 1987). The latter three tactics have proved useful, particularly in de-escalating social-emotional conflicts. It is remarkable and disappointing that, for the so important affective conflicts of identity, relatively few de-escalative strategies have been developed.

Consequences of de-escalative behaviour

Consequences may be of longer or shorter duration. Thus, feedback to antecedent conditions is more lasting than feedback to conflict issues or to behaviour. Consequences may also be direct or indirect. De-escalative conflict management may result in a resolution of the problem both directly and through agreement on a decision-making procedure, through joint goals or through more reciprocal empathy. However, the two distinctions have much in common. That is to say, direct or immediate consequences involve a shorter term than do indirect consequences.

A direct consequence of changing the antecedent organizational or relational characteristics is the partial or complete removal of the conflict. For example, the higher the level of value similarity in work groups, the lower the amount of both task and emotional conflict (Jehn, 1994), which in turn has countervailing consequences: whereas task-focused conflict increases decision quality, decision acceptance, and performance, identity-related emotional conflict decreases them (Amason & Schweiger, 1994; Jehn, 1994; Tjosvold, 1991; Van de Vliert & De Dreu, 1994). So, prevention of conflict is a two-edged sword with regard to performance. There also exist various indirect consequences, such as destroying healthy competition and elasticity, about which hardly anything is known. We do not know exactly how the parties experience the various structural operations and cope with them individually and socially. Nor is it clear whether the party taking the initiative for some operation experiences consequences different from those of the opposite party. This lacuna is partly due to the separation, criticized earlier, of the structural and the process approach.

Successful conflict resolution not only removes frustration, according to plan, but also leads to higher effectiveness (Barker, Tjosvold, & Andrews, 1988; Burke, 1970; Euwema, 1992; Johnson, Johnson, & Smith, 1989; Lawrence & Lorsch, 1967; Rubin et al., 1994; Tjosvold, 1991; Tutzauer & Roloff, 1988; Volkema & Bergmann, 1989), trust and openness (Deutsch, 1973, 1980; Zand, 1972), attraction (Johnson et al., 1989), and de-personalization of future conflicts (Filley, 1975). Thomas (1992) suggested that modes of conflict behaviour other than problem solving may be effective short-term approaches that do not move beyond the limitations of the current conditions. Conflict resolution, however, represents the one-best-way long-term approach, which emphasizes that contextual variables are changeable and that the ideal organization should be brought nearer by all manner of means.

It is plausible that the beneficial effects of conflict resolution also hold for an adversary who eliminates the conflict issue through reconceptualization. Furthermore, a negotiator who strives for a compromise is considered to be just as willing and attractive (Rahim & Buntzman, 1989; Ruble & Thomas, 1976), although the compromise may leave both negotiators with some residue of frustration. A hypothesis developed elsewhere (Van de Vliert & Hordijk, 1989) stated that compromising and problem-solving behaviours are different, that their respective direct outcomes in the form of a settlement and a resolution have some common points, and that their final social-psychological consequences tend to be the same.

A much favoured proposition is that de-escalative behaviour in one party will elicit de-escalative behaviour in the other party. Earlier it was shown to be sufficiently likely that this view is generally correct. Here it is more interesting to note that spontaneous or strategic de-escalative behaviour quite often has indirect consequences entailing or realizing escalation of conflict. In hierarchical organizations, de-escalative rules sometimes appear to result in more rather than less frustration (Pondy, 1967). Unilateral openness intended as a de-escalative tactic, drawing attention to overall interests, and tough negotiating all can have a boomerang effect (Filley, 1975; Johnson & Lewicki, 1969; Walton, 1987).

It often occurs that managers who want to prevent further conflict by suppressing the current disagreement in fact attain the opposite result (Deutsch, 1973). It has been mentioned already that threats have an intensifying rather than attenuating effect. In addition avoidance of any confrontation is experienced negatively too (Phillips & Cheston, 1979; Ruble & Thomas, 1976), which often has the consequence that, in the end, a destructive unspoken or underground conflict arises (Glasl, 1980; Hocker & Wilmot, 1991). Thus, like the hierarchical suppression of conflict, avoidance may for a while have a direct, de-escalative effect, but in the long run it will have an indirect, escalating effect.

It may be concluded that the indirect consequences of de-escalative behaviour can be of a de-escalative as well as of an escalative nature, depending on the kind of conflict behaviour and how it is experienced by the opposite party.

ESCALATIVE CONFLICT MANAGEMENT

Any reaction of either party to the conflict issues, or to the other's behaviour, is escalative if it increases one's own cognitive or affective frustration or if it frustrates the other party for the first time or anew and extra. Therefore, anyone familiar with conflict handling will recognize behaviours that are intended to be preventive or de-escalative but are in fact escalative—for instance, threats and suppression. A reaction escalates a conflict if it brings about, directly or indirectly, an expansion of, *inter alia*: "the size and number of the immediate issues involved, the number of motives and participants implicated on each side of the issue; the size and number of the principles and precedents that are perceived to be at stake" (Deutsch, 1973, p. 351). The increased frustration, in its turn, again elicits fresh reactions from the parties. Since, apparently, expanding conflicts tend to become more complex, it is no great step from this line of thinking to the assumption that with continuing escalation the strategic aspects of behaviour will eventually supersede the spontaneous ones.

Spontaneous escalative behaviour

Ways to escalate conflict management, in which spontaneity usually predominates, include magnifying an issue, attacking the adversary, and restricting the amount of interaction. These are particularly characteristic of conflicts with strongly emotional aspects.

In the literature, it is agreed that parties tend to connect a conflict about facts with their own identities and emotions. This may be observed to occur in any strike. According to Walton (1969, p. 87), there are two mechanisms that largely explain this escalation:

> One is the need for consistency. If one dislikes the position another takes, or if he is in competition with him, there is a psychological tendency to develop similar attitudes toward the person. The second mechanism involves the tactics of competition, debate, and bargaining over substantive differences; such tactics contain many points of friction and are likely to result in feelings of being attacked, in perceptions that the other is unfair, etc.

Not only may cognitive conflicts lead to affective identity conflicts. As some issue comes to affect identity more and more, there will, conversely, be a growing tendency to exaggerate the issue (Walton, 1972). This occurs often by unconsciously shifting the problem from, for example, an "and-and" issue to one of "either-or", or from a secondary or isolated position to a central one (Louis, 1977; Thierry, 1977). Because the rules imposing restraints on conflict management constitute an additional source of frustration, the regulation mechanisms themselves will sometimes be challenged (Brickman, 1974), As a consequence of the reduction of their cognitive dissonance (Deutsch, 1973), attributions of cause and intention (Jones & Remland, 1993; Louis, 1977), and simplification of their line of thinking under stress, the parties come to consider themselves as being good, reasonable, cooperative, and victimized, and the opponent as bad, unreasonable, hostile, and instigative. Such black-and-white mirror images constitute stimuli for further escalative behaviour.

In conflicts at work, shouting at others is much more often used than throwing things, pushing, striking, or punching an adversary (Volkema & Bergmann, 1989). The impulsive attack on the opponent is represented by terms such as win-lose fight, dominance, forcing, and competition. It is a power context, in which all the available means of direct influence are brought into play: convincing information, attraction as a relation, legitimate claims, expertise, positive and negative sanctions (Raven & Kruglanski, 1970). The main determinant of this type of spontaneous conflict management is, according to some, personality, according to others the organizational situation. Over the last decade much research has been conducted into the predominantly individual explanation of "conflict entrapment". Whoever falls into this trap, escalates his or her commitment to a failing course of action in order to justify prior investments in the conflict issues and in the previously chosen reactions (Brockner & Rubin, 1985). Rubin et al. (1994) emphasized the influence of a lack of perceived integrative potential, which in its turn is a function of high aspirations of both own party (mainly personal determinants) and rival party (mainly situational determinants). Terhune (1970) concluded that both types of determinants are important, but that certain situations minimize the influence of certain personality traits on conflict management. Going by the results of experimental games, as Terhune did, Kelley and Stahelski (1970) argued that the influence of the perceived social situation can ultimately be traced to personality. This view contains the danger that one may unjustifiably tend to hold individuals too much responsible for the escalation of conflicts.

It is an intriguing fact that frustrated supervisors in hierarchical organizations usually react in a forcing and dominating way. According to Vroom and Yetton (1973) they do this because of the effect that they expect from their behaviour. Supervisors will consult and negotiate with a subordinate only if they expect that the subordinate will not obey a unilateral decision from above. An alternative explanation, the so-called "framing explanation" (Van de Vliert et al., 1988) sees escalative behaviour as less strategic and more spontaneous. It states that the supervisor's hierarchical position frame activates a cognitive frame in which the behavioural alternatives acquire a meaning that encourages escalation and discourages de-escalation. For supervisors the hierarchical context implies that they have a power preponderance that is directly associated with ideas of winning. In any case they do not have to bother about accommodating and losing. In consequence, they will think strongly in terms of fighting or not fighting, as a result of which the distinction between the not-fighting alternatives moves into the undifferentiated background. It is most likely that supervisors experience compromising and resolving as forms of not-forcing and, in large part, losing. On the basis of this frame of mind supervisors will be disposed to force in order not to "lose".

Anyone knows from experience that a deeply-rooted conflict may go hand in hand with a decline in contact between the parties (sometimes starting with avoidance intended as prevention). Relatively often, individuals or groups at war prefer to deal with one another as little as possible. The resulting behaviours are a compound of enforcement and avoidance, including a very disagreeable form of resisting and a less disagreeable form of process controlling by dominating the procedures to one's own advantage (Van de Vliert & Euwema, 1994). In the case of resisting, face-to-face contacts are avoided while one obstructs the other's plans, talks behind the other's back, and forms alliances with other people (Morrill & Thomas, 1992; for empirical evidence, see Volkema & Bergmann, 1989).

Bisno (1988) distinguished the following three types of resisting: *negativism*, when people, by body language or terse verbalization, manifest disagreement or hurt, without overtly engaging in hostility; *non-compliance*, which runs the gamut from simple non-cooperation to the covert sabotage of policies by inadequate implementation; and *stonewalling*, by adamantly refusing to comment about something or to admit to an action or statement. As a more complex combination of escalation and avoidance, sometimes new issues arise from a person's subconscious, ensuring the isolation of the opponent (Walton, 1987). The less contact, however, the less chance of de-escalative reactions and the greater chance of escalating misinterpretations, stereotypes, and distrust (Brown, 1983; Burton, 1969; Deutsch, 1973).

According to Glasl (1980), a conflict increasing in force passes through nine stages of escalation. The first is characterized by incidental frustration which puts a strain on cooperation and mutual understanding. The second stage of escalation entails that the parties have come to think in a polarized way and that their disputes are irrational and unfair. At the third stage readiness to fight, lack of understanding, and nonverbal communication are predominant in both parties: deeds, not words! Escalation stage four involves stereotyped image building, win-lose behaviour, and asking others for support. In the fifth stage, the opponent's immoral character comes to the fore. One tries to expose the other party and make them lose face. Escalation stage six is one of all-pervasive and determined threat. The seventh stage is reached when each party tries to destroy the other's weapons and to inflict more harm than they have suffered themselves. Finally, escalation stages eight and nine represent the splitting up and total destruction of the enemy, respectively; both parties lose or even go to ruin.

Glasl combined the first three stages of escalation into a main phase I, where both parties still consider the substantial aspects of their conflict to be central, while they cooperate to search for agreement. In main phase II, containing escalation stages four through six, the opponents' reciprocal image building and interaction become more of a problem and cooperation turns into obstruction. The last three stages of escalation, constituting main phase III, have in common the opponents' denial of the other's human value, thus clearing the way for manipulation, retaliation, elimination, and destruction. In the first main phase, spontaneous escalative behaviour is predominant, in the second main phase it is strategic escalative behaviour, while in the third main phase the spontaneous and strategic elements are strongly interconnected.

Strategic escalative behaviour

Mainly at Kelly's (1970), Robbins's (1974), and Janis's (1982) instigation, the insight became evident that sometimes work situations elicit too little conflict to be effective (Bartunek, Kolb, & Lewicki, 1992; Brown, 1983; Hage, 1980; Rahim, 1992; Van de Vliert, 1985, 1997b; Van de Vliert & De Dreu, 1994). Such situations call for stimulation of conflict. The goal one may have in mind when applying conscious escalation of conflict varies from conquering or adversely affecting the opposite party to creating a more effective level of tension so as to bring the conflict to an end that is more or less satisfactory to both parties. The first extreme occurs, for example, when an important conflict is considered inevitable and insoluble, because it ran aground on bad people, ideological differences, or scarce resources (Blake et al., 1964). At the other extreme, we are confronted with a restricted escalation to some constructive point of greater intensity (Robbins, 1974), through which the ability of the parties to produce, process, and utilize information increases (Hocker & Wilmot, 1991; Johnson & Tjosvold, 1989; Robbins, 1974; Walton, 1987). Although this may sound fine, compared to the de-escalative strategies discussed, neither the goals nor the means of escalation have been studied satisfactorily. Recently some theory development has been initiated (Van de Vliert & De Dreu, 1994), but empirical research is still lacking. The framework in Figure 15.1 suggests that escalative conflict management may be directed towards changing

TABLE 15.4

Escalative conflict management.

Spontaneous escalative behaviour
Exaggerating the conflict
Attacking the opponent
Restricting contact
Resisting
Strategic escalative behaviour
Changing antecedent conditions
Extension of conflict issues
Re-conceptualization of issues
Escalating reaction models
Fair fighting
Looking for allies
Dialectical inquiry
Devil's advocate

the antecedent conditions or towards extending the issues or promoting further escalative behaviour.

Continuous escalation is a powerful weapon in the hands of those wishing to bring about fundamental changes in existing organizational and relational characteristics. Because in such cases a conflict functions as a lever for changes, it is sometimes called a strategic conflict (Glasl, 1980; Pondy, 1969); it comprises the aforementioned revolutionary conflict. The ever more forcible ways by which certain action groups bring far-reaching demands to the attention of directors and politicians, such as obstruction and even occupation of buildings or terrains, may serve as an illustration. By making use of every conceivable escalative behaviour, they try to bring about other structures and cultures, which, of course, in their turn will serve as antecedent conditions of future conflict. This radical strategy differs from operations that are intended to render the existing antecedent conditions more conflict stimulating. In this case, structural or cultural barriers to escalation will be lowered or potential triggers reinforced (Walton, 1987). Alternatively, the chance of frustration is enhanced through such reorganizations as recommended by Robbins (1974): a more complex organizational structure, irreconcilable collective goals, a changeable style of leadership, carefully contrived transfers, unacceptable role prescriptions.

An extension of issues that is not directed towards fundamental changes often serves some hidden goal. Mulder (1978) mentioned the raising of prestige, diverting attention, and removing internal discord. Here it does not seem to matter very much which frustrations are increased or introduced. The original conflict may be reconceptualized in an intensifying direction and thus be concerned with various other things, become more threatening to identity, or grow into a matter of life and death. But one may also seize upon other fairly arbitrary items, keep back information, or supply threatening intelligence (Robbins, 1974). Creating new issues in order to gain a tactical advantage over the opponent, however, constitutes a different case (Glasl, 1980; Walton, 1987). Then it appears to be important to choose one's main goals carefully.

Finally, deliberate escalation is also possible through influencing further behaviour, that is, without first changing the antecedent conditions or conflict issues. If a party decides on such a course, that decision will most likely be based on one or more of the following factors:

1. Old wounds that were a consequence of earlier conflict.
2. Current frustration.
3. Norms existing as antecedent conditions: one should not be soft-hearted, should fight injustice, etc.
4. The role expectations of a constituency or some other encouraging audience.
5. One's own role expectations: "Being a manager I cannot afford to lose face", "It is my task to interfere now", etc.
6. The imagined hostile intentions of the opponent.
7. The expected benefits after deduction of the expected costs, or the balance of the positive and negative consequences of escalative behaviour, including external and inner sanctions.

The behaviour that characteristically effects further escalative action is familiar to us: twisting information, lying, not listening, ignoring, laughing at someone, interrupting, belittling, accusing, using abusive language. Less well-known is fair fighting. A fight is fair to the extent that the fighters follow agreed rules. Bach and Wyden's (1969) main rule of play, later supported by Deutsch (1973, pp. 384–385) was not to be afraid of struggles but to learn how to fight fairly and constructively. In the short-term this produces escalation, in the long-term de-escalation. Although the authors did not make clear what they meant by a "fair fight", their descriptions indicated that they considered openness, honesty, equality, and reciprocity relevant criteria. The goal should be to pursue better mutual relationships instead of knockouts. The parties must learn not only to communicate better with one another but also to acquire skills in communicating about the following rules laid down for fair conflict management: no bluffing, generalizations, or ultimatums; no underhandedness; no aiming for the opponent's

Achilles' heel; no deliberate actions in the presence or the absence of certain third parties; no physical violence. In the context of the escalation model such rules of fair play constitute regulation mechanisms.

Glasl's (1980) fourth escalation stage, discussed earlier, has come when the parties proceed to the tactic of looking for allies. This refers to trying to improve one's own position and impairing that of the opposing party by obtaining the moral and active support of outsiders. In an industrial conflict, for example, an employee will turn to his trade union or the local employment bureau or may try to get the support of his or her colleagues. Whether such activities will result in victory depends not only on the opponent's conflict handling but also on the kind and amount of power the opponents and their possible allies can, and will, exert over the others (Van de Vliert, 1981). Relatively powerless organization members will prefer more acceptable escalative behaviours, such as arguing and protesting, thus making it all less grim (unless tension has mounted too high; see Mulder, 1978).

A party wanting to create unilaterally a more effective tension level so as ultimately to bring the conflict to an end satisfactory to both parties, will prefer controlled escalation. It will state conditions, emphasize differences, defend its own interests or its being right, undermine the views of the adversary, outline its own identity, vent and clarify feelings. Well-known strategies are aiming for competing proposals of two groups—or dialectical inquiry—and devil's advocacy. Such approaches will benefit the quality of decision making (Amason & Schweiger, 1994; Johnson et al. 1989; Schweiger, Sandberg, & Ragan, 1986; Tjosvold, 1985, 1991). For example, using middle managers from divisions of electronics and medical technology, Schweiger, Sandberg, and Rechner (1989) assessed the effectiveness of both approaches. Compared to consensus-seeking groups, groups using dialectical inquiry or devil's advocacy made significantly higher quality decisions. The results suggested that debate itself, through its presence rather than its format, improves group performance by formalizing and legitimizing escalative behaviours. Therefore, it is sensible to have each de-escalative phase of integration preceded by a controlled phase of sufficient intensification or differentiation of the conflict, during which the issues are defined and analysed (Johnson et al., 1989; Walton, 1987; for more detailed phase theories, see Folger & Poole, 1984).

In retrospect, permanent stimulation of frustration through the antecedent conditions seems a very unsophisticated instrument. Extension of issues emerges as a pivotal subject, because stimulation of escalative behaviour will fairly quickly change into just that. Here the need for research is greatest, especially concerning those points at which conflicts of interest and disagreements come to touch upon the identity of an individual or group.

Consequences of escalative behaviour

Whereas de-escalative behaviour quite often leads indirectly to more rather than less frustration, escalative behaviour does not lead so easily to de-escalation by means of other variables. From the preceding section it is apparent that, in the end, moderate escalation can be conducive to problem-solving behaviour. The price of the better decisions may be that the opponents involved fancy the idea of future cooperation less than before (Schweiger et al., 1986). On the other hand there is Coser's (1956) proposition that conflict brings the parties closer together and that it restores the unity and stability among them unless the relationship is affected in a seriously negative manner. He received support in Bach and Wyden's (1969) practical experience, and in Corwin's (1969) interesting research result that, if the number of minor disagreements increases the number of major clashes decreases.

Johnson et al. (1989) reviewed research evidence on constructive controversy. They concluded that the presence of controversy within decision-making groups results in better ideas and more creative group decisions, more member satisfaction, and a higher degree of emotional involvement in and commitment to the implementations of the decisions. In a similar vein, Van de Vliert and De Dreu (1994) argued that when conflict focuses on task issues, when tension level is low, and when disputants' goals are positively interdependent, conflict stimulation generally increases joint performance (see also Bartunek et al., 1992; Tjosvold, 1991; Walton, 1969).

Direct fighting and indirect fighting by dominating and controlling the process to one's own advantage appear to stand out as, respectively, an ineffective and an effective alternative for getting one's way. Van de Vliert, Euwema, and Huismans (1995, based on Euwema, 1992), who investigated police sergeants handling an escalating conflict with either a subordinate or a superior, reported very negative versus very positive effects on the sergeants' joint outcomes and mutual relationship for direct fighting versus process controlling. Indirect fighting by dominating the process was even more effective than problem solving. The data also suggest that process controlling is so effective because it provides a subtle, indirect way to prevail without creating a disagreeable impression in the eyes of the opponent.

Thanks to the experiments of Sherif (1966) and Blake and Mouton (1989) we know, furthermore, that escalation of a conflict between groups is accompanied by prevention or de-escalation of conflict within those groups. Identification with one's own group, feelings of solidarity, and tractability are found to increase, while internal differences and irritations dissolve. Negotiators with a constituency know this mechanism from experience and will, for that reason, take a more rigorous stand externally (see Chapter 14 of this handbook). However, Doise and Lorenzi-Cioldi's (1989) careful inspection of the relevant experimental findings showed that intergroup hostility can also generate intragroup conflict. When relations between ingroup members are brought into focus, correlations appear that are contrary to the classical hypothesis. Rabbie (1979) has shown that the hypothesis holds only if a group expects to win; if it expects to lose, cohesion will rather diminish, and the trial of strength between the groups will induce intragroup escalation rather than de-escalation (see also Stein, 1976). Indeed, it is not only the group's expectation of losing that may undermine the relation between external escalation and internal de-escalation. An attacked work group will, at the same time, develop a more centralized and task-oriented leadership (Mulder & Stemerding, 1963; Rabbie, 1979) and become less tolerant internally—qualities which increase rather than decrease the chances of internal conflict.

The relationship between the groups will come to be marked more and more by communication distortions, ingroup-outgroup differentiation, exaggerated mutual prejudices and mutual distrust (Deutsch, 1973; Rabbie, 1979; Van de Vliert, 1987). The defeated group grows divided and starts looking for a scapegoat (Blake & Mouton, 1984, 1989; Shepard, 1964). These are all direct or indirect consequences functioning also as antecedent conditions, so that a vicious spiral of feedbacks and further frustration may readily arise. Escalating personal conflicts take the same course. Moreover, they draw attention to the intrapersonal conflicts that result from conflicts between individuals or groups. These intrapersonal conflicts also constitute antecedent conditions for further conflicts. Indeed, social conflicts lead to individual tension experiences, which disturb information processing, elicit black-white thinking, and promote rigid behaviour (Smart & Vertinsky, 1977; Walton, 1987). In this interaction between interpersonal and intrapersonal conflicts we again come upon an important area yet unexamined by organizational psychologists.

Deliberately creating and spontaneously magnifying conflict issues are among the escalative behaviours discussed, which lead to further frustration without mediation of antecedent conditions. Furthermore, extension of conflict issues occurs through the disapproval and disgust as well as the tendencies to blame and to feel threathened evoked in the opponent by escalative conflict management as such (Rubin et al., 1994; Ruble & Thomas, 1976). In particular, ineffective negative feedback, exertion of force, and taking illegitimate steps have such an effect (Baron, 1989; Deutsch, 1973).

Similar to these consequences is the fact that escalative behaviour directly instigates the adversary to defensive and other escalative behaviour. Renwick (1975) found that members of an organization will behave in a hostile way if they think the oppositie party is doing the same. Thus, this readiness to fight that is ascribed to the opponent works as a self-fulfilling prophecy, without this being noticed (Kelley & Stahelski, 1970; Thomas & Pondy, 1977). In a meta-analysis of studies on conflict management it was shown that enforcing behaviour has a more antagonistic meaning for observers than for actors (Van de Vliert & Prein, 1989). In agreement with insights from attribution theory, there appears to exist a tendency to apply double standards to one's own and others' fighting behaviour. Consequently, communication about escalative behaviours is likely to be difficult between actors and their opponents. As a result the odds are that one reacts to another's "more" frustrating fighting behaviour with one's own "less" frustrating fighting behaviour. Most likely such processes of attribution of meaning to verbal and nonverbal escalative behaviour touch on the core of conflict escalation (cf. Jones & Remland, 1993).

When tension emerges between people, there is a tendency for each of the parties to draw an outsider into the encounter as a coalition partner (Smith, 1989). However, looking for allies to help a group member with the trial of strength is a strongly escalating tactic (Van de Vliert, 1981). The immediate consequences are that, by informing an outsider, the conflict issue becomes more defined and that, moreover, the relationships between the conflicting parties and the outsider become a stake in the conflict. If an original outsider does take sides, various indirect consequences are added:

1. Siding implies that the outsider adopts the win-lose conceptualization and thus reinforces it.
2. It creates a winner (the party chosen) and a loser (the party rejected), which also precipitates escalation.
3. It increases the number of individuals actively involved in the conflict.
4. It complicates the conflict issue and the conflict management by adding other views.
5. The energy the outsider invests in the conflict raises the total stake of the conflict.
6. The act of siding encourages the outsider to demonstrate behaviour supporting the correctness of his or her choice.

As is generally known, the escalation process, if not checked, will result in delays, impasses, disintegration of subdivisions, personnel turnover, absenteeism, and other inefficiences in the organization. At the same time, the psychological and physical condition of the organization members deteriorates, which will not fail to have its effect either. They become, for example, inwardly frayed, dependent, indifferent, cynical, oversensitive, restless, or ill (Kahn et al., 1964). Against the background of the above this means that, as a rule, escalation is a self-reinforcing, destructive process, unless the whole system of antecedent conditions and spontaneous or strategic de-escalative conflict management curbs excess escalation.

USE OF THE MODEL

The escalation model developed here has the following advantages:

1. It integrates the customary process and structural approaches.
2. Its focus really consists of the central mechanism of de-escalation and escalation.
3. It may inspire new research on conflict and conflict management.
4. It provides the practising organisational psychologist with a typology of strategies of conflict management.

Of these points, 3 and 4 have not yet been discussed. As for 3, this chapter has already presented some important research questions and assumptions. First, there is the question of the relative influence of the various antecedent conditions on the rise of the three kinds of conflict issues and on the de-escalative or escalative course of conflict processes. The answers to this question also highlight the need for more complex research, simultaneously taking into account more independent, intermediating, moderating, and dependent variables. Next, there are questions regarding the pivotal functions of social-emotional conflicts: when and how does a conflict of interest or a disagreement begin to affect the identity of an individual or group? Conversely, when and how does an affective identity conflict become a source of extra cognitive problems? What role does nonverbal communication play in such spirals of escalation (Jones & Remland, 1993)? What strategic behaviour can control escalation brought about by social-emotional issues?

Furthermore, an important scientific leap forward might be made if more thorough attention were to be paid to the theoretical relations among modes of conflict handling. To be sure, the classification of de-escalative versus escalative conflict behaviours presented here seems to be empirically sound (Van de Vliert & Euwema, 1994; Van de Vliert et al., 1995), but it is confined to the theoretically meagre level of a typology. The same applies to Deutsch's (1973, 1980) cooperation-competition dichotomy, Putnam and Wilson's (1982) trichotomy, Blake and Mouton's (1970, 1985) very well-known five-part taxonomy, and the 16 styles of Sternberg and Dobson (1987; see also Van de Vliert, 1990, 1997a). In a first attempt to address this problem of theoretical scantiness, Van de Vliert and Kabanoff (1990) reinterpreted Blake and Mouton's (1970, 1985) conflict management grid as a model of quantitatively specified interrelations among the five modes of conflict management rather than a five-category scheme for just classifying these behavioural modes.

A related, promising development is to drop the implicit assumption that, at least within one cycle of transaction, each party uses only one de-escalative or escalative mode of conflict behaviour. Actually, mixtures and sequences of, for example, fighting and problem solving seem much more common (Falbe & Yukl, 1992; Rubin et al., 1994; Van de Vliert, 1997a; Van de Vliert et al., 1995). Similarly, it is often taken for granted that distinct modes of conflict behaviour only have a mutually exclusive influence on the outcomes. As evidence to the contrary, some effective ways of conflict management, including constructive controversy discussed in this chapter and firm flexibility discussed in the chapter on negotiation (see Chapter 14), are conglomerations of behavioural components instead of pure behaviours. The effectiveness of conglomerated conflict behaviour may well become a rich research topic in and of itself.

Finally, future research might throw more light on the differences as to the causes and effects between the three feedbacks on the antecedent conditions, conflict issues, and behaviour, respectively. The indirect escalating consequences of de-escalative behaviour and the indirect, de-escalating consequences of escalative behaviour in particular are still a challenging void. Also, very little is known about the interaction between two-party conflicts and intrapersonal conflicts, including one-sided conflicts. If we really want to do something about that, longitudinal studies of conflict processes are urgently necessary. Longitudinal studies may, moreover, improve our insight into the patterns of subsequent conflict behaviours and into the phases of escalating conflicts.

The practising organizational psychologist training clients in constructive conflict management or intervening in conflicts—as a third party—will certainly benefit from the results of such research (point 4). Both the conflict parties and any third party may use the escalation model first as a diagnostic instrument providing questions about causes, issues, reactions and consequences, and subsequently as a means for selecting certain de-escalative or escalative behaviours.

On the basis of the diagnosis, the third party may single out the antecedent conditions, the conflict issues, their conflict behaviour, or the consequences as its point of action for intervention. Regardless of the point of action, the intervention strategy may then be directed towards either de-escalation or escalation. Combination of both choices results in a typology of eight strategies of conflict management, as represented in Figure 15.2 and worked out in more detail elsewhere (Van de Vliert, 1997b). Each of the four de-escalative and four escalative strategies corresponds to the changing of certain aspects of the relationship between the two conflict parties on the one hand, and to certain roles of the intervening party on the other. The former was discussed in the above sections on conflict management, the latter—the roles of the third party—would really require a separate chapter (see Bercovitch, 1984; Brown, 1983; Carnevale, 1986; Carnevale & Pegnetter, 1985; Fisher, 1983; Glasl, 1980;

FIGURE 15.2

Typology of eight strategies of conflict management by a third party.

Conflict management by a third party		Point of action for intervention			
		Antecedent conditions	Conflict issues	Conflict behaviour	Consequences
Intervention strategy	De-escalation	I	II	III	IV
	Escalation	V	VI	VII	VIII

Kaufman & Duncan, 1989; Kolb, 1989; Lewicki et al., 1992; Prein, 1982; Rubin, 1980).

REFERENCES

Allport, G.W. (1979). *The nature of prejudice*. Reading, MA: Addison-Wesley.

Amason, A.C., & Schweiger, D.M. (1994). Resolving the paradox of conflict, strategic decision making, and organizational performance. *International Journal of Conflict Management*, *5*, 239–253.

Andriessen, J.H.T.H., Drenth, P.J.D., & Lammers, C.J. (1983). *Medezeggenschap in Nederlandse bedrijven* [Participation in Dutch companies]. Amsterdam: Noord-Hollandsche Uitgevers Maatschappij.

Apfelbaum, E. (1974). On conflicts and bargaining. *Advances in Experimental Social Psychology*, *7*, 103–156.

Axelrod, R. (1984). *The evolution of cooperation*. New York: Basic Books.

Bach, G.R., & Wyden, P. (1969). *The intimate enemy*. New York: Morrow.

Barker, J., Tjosvold, D., & Andrews, I.R. (1988). Conflict approaches of effective and ineffective project managers: A field study in a matrix organization. *Journal of Management Studies*, *25*, 167–178.

Baron, R.A. (1984). Reducing organizational conflict: An incompatible response approach. *Journal of Applied Psychology*, *69*, 272–279.

Baron, R.A. (1989). Negative effects of destructive criticism: Impact on conflict, self-efficacy, and task performance. In M.A. Rahim (Ed.), *Managing conflict: An interdisciplinary approach* (pp. 21–31). New York: Praeger.

Baron, R.A., Fortin, S.P., Frei, R.L., Hauver, L.A., & Shack, M.L. (1990). Reducing organizational conflict: The role of socially-induced positive affect. *International Journal of Conflict Management*, *1*, 133–152.

Bartunek, J.M., Kolb, D.M., & Lewicki, R. (1992). Bringing conflict out from behind the scenes. In D.M. Kolb & J.M. Bartunek (Eds.), *Hidden conflict in organizations: Uncovering behind-the-scenes disputes* (pp. 209–228). Newbury Park, CA: Sage.

Bercovitch, J. (1984). *Social conflicts and third parties: Strategies of conflict resolution*. Boulder, CO: Westview.

Bisno, H. (1988). *Managing conflict*. Newbury Park: Sage.

Blake, R.R., & Mouton, J.S. (1970). The fifth achievement. *Journal of Applied Behavioral Science*, *6*, 413–426.

Blake, R.R., & Mouton, J.S. (1984). *Solving costly organizational conflicts*. San Francisco, CA: Jossey-Bass.

Blake, R.R., & Mouton, J.S. (1985). *The managerial grid III*. Houston, TX: Gulf.

Blake, R.R., & Mouton, J.S. (1989). Lateral conflict. In D. Tjosvold & D.W. Johnson (Eds.), *Productive conflict management: Perspectives for organizations* (pp. 91–149). Minneapolis, MN: Team Media.

Blake, R.R., Shepard, H.A., & Mouton, J.S. (1964).

Managing intergroup conflict in industry. Houston, TX: Gulf.

Boekestijn, C. (1979). De psychologie van relaties tussen groepen [The psychology of intergroup relations]. In J.M.F. Jaspars & R. van der Vlist (Eds.), *Sociale psychologie in Nederland; Vol. 2. De kleine groep* (pp. 166–189). Deventer: Van Loghum Slaterus.

Brickman, P. (1974). *Social conflict: Readings in rule structure and conflict relationships*. Lexington, MA: D.C. Heath.

Brockner, J., & Rubin, J.Z. (1985). *Entrapment in escalating conflicts: A social psychological analysis*. New York: Springer-Verlag.

Brown, L.D. (1983). *Managing conflict at organizational interfaces*. Reading, MA: Addison-Wesley.

Brown, R., & Wade, G. (1987). Superordinate goals and intergroup behaviour: The effects of role ambiguity and status on intergroup attitudes and task performance. *European Journal of Social Psychology*, *17*, 131–142.

Burke, R.J. (1970). Methods of resolving supervisor-subordinate conflict: The constructive use of subordinate differences and disagreements. *Organizational Behavior and Human Performance*, *5*, 393–411.

Burton, J.W. (1969). *Conflict and communication*. London: MacMillan.

Carnevale, P.J. (1986). Strategic choice in mediation. *Negotiation Journal*, *2*, 41–56.

Carnevale, P.J., & Pegnetter, R. (1985). The selection of mediation tactics in public-sector disputes: A contingency analysis. *Journal of Social Issues*, *41*, 65–81.

Chanin, M.N., & Schneer, J.A. (1984). A study of the relationship between Jungian personality dimensions and conflict-handling behavior. *Human Relations*, *37*, 863–879.

Child, J. (1973). Strategies of control and organizational behavior. *Administrative Science Quarterly*, *18*, 1–17.

Coombs, C.H. (1987). The structure of conflict. *American Psychologist*, *42*, 355–363.

Corwin, R.G. (1969). Patterns of organizational conflict. *Administrative Science Quarterly*, *14*, 507–520.

Coser, L. (1956). *The functions of social conflict*. Glencoe, IL: Free Press.

Cummings, L.L., Harnett, D.L., & Schmidt, S.M. (1972). International cross-language factor stability of personality: An analysis of the Shure-Meeker personality/attitude schedule. *Journal of Psychology*, *82*, 67–84.

Delhees, K.H. (1979). *Interpersonelle Konflikte und Konfliktbehandlung in Organisationen*. Bern: Haupt.

Deutsch, M. (1973). *The resolution of conflict: Constructive and destructive processes*. New Haven: Yale University Press.

Deutsch, M. (1980). Fifty years of conflict. In L. Festinger (Ed.), *Retrospections on social psychology* (pp. 46–77). New York: Oxford University Press.

Doise, W., & Lorenzi-Cioldi, F. (1989). Patterns of differentiation within and between groups. In J.P. van Oudenhoven & T.M. Willemsen (Eds.), *Ethnic minorities: Social psychological perspectives* (pp. 43–57). Amsterdam/Lisse: Swets & Zeitlinger.

Donnellon, A., & Kolb, D.M. (1994). Constructive for whom? The fate of diversity disputes in organizations. *Journal of Social Issues*, *50*, 139–155.

Euwema, M.C. (1992). *Conflicthantering in organisaties: Een onderzoek onder brigadiers van politie naar de invloed van de hiërarchische relatie op het verloop van conflicten over afwijkend gedrag* [Conflict handling in organisations: An investigation into the influence of the formal hierarchical relation between policemen on the conflict process in cases of deviant behaviour]. Amsterdam: VU Uitgeverij.

Falbe, C.M., & Yukl, G. (1992). Consequences for managers of using simple influence tactics and combinations of tactics. *Academy of Management Journal*, *35*, 638–652.

Filley, A.C. (1975). *Interpersonal conflict resolution*. Glenview, IL: Scott, Foresman.

Filley, A.C. (1982). Problem definition and conflict management. In G.B.J. Bomers & R.B. Peterson (Eds.), *Conflict management and industrial relations* (pp. 79–95). Boston: Kluwer/Nijhoff.

Fink, C.F. (1968). Some conceptual difficulties in the theory of social conflict. *Journal of Conflict Resolution*, *12*, 412–460.

Fisher, R. (1964). Fractionating conflict. In R. Fisher (Ed.), *International conflict and behavioral science: The Craigville papers* (pp. 91–110). New York: Basic Books.

Fisher, R.J. (1983). Third-party consultation as a method of intergroup conflict resolution. *Journal of Conflict Resolution*, *27*, 301–334.

Fisher, R.J. (1994). Generic principles for resolving intergroup conflict. *Journal of Social Issues*, *50*, 47–66.

Folger, J.P., & Poole, M.S. (1984). *Working through conflict: A communication perspective*. Glenview, IL: Scott Foresman.

Glasl, F. (1980). Konfliktmanagement: Diagnose und Behandlung von Konflikt in Organisationen. Bern: Haupt.

Gray, B. (1989). *Collaborating: Finding common ground for multiparty problems*. San Francisco, CA: Jossey-Bass.

Hage, J. (1980). *Theories of organizations: Form, process and transformation*. New York: Wiley.

Hocker, J.L., & Wilmot, W.W. (1991). *Interpersonal conflict* (3rd Edn.). Dubuque, IA: William C. Brown.

Horwitz, M. (1964). Managing hostility in the laboratory and the refinery. In R.L. Kahn & E. Boulding (Eds.), *Power and conflict in organizations* (pp. 77–94). London: Tavistock.

Janis, I.L. (1982). *Groupthink* (2nd Edn.). Boston: Houghton-Mifflin.

Janssen, O. (1994). *Hoe interdependentie motiveert tot conflictgedrag* [How interdependence motivates conflict behaviour]. Unpublished doctoral dissertation, University of Groningen, The Netherlands.

Jehn, K.A. (1994). Enhancing effectiveness: An investigation of the advantages and disadvantages of value-based intragroup conflict. *International Journal of Conflict Management*, *5*, 223–228.

Johnson, D.W., & Johnson, R.T. (1989). *Cooperation and competition: Theory and research*. Edina, MN: Interaction Book Company.

Johnson, D.W., Johnson, R.T., & Smith, K. (1989). Controversy within decision making situations. In M.A. Rahim (Ed.), *Managing conflict: An interdisciplinary approach* (pp. 251–264). New York: Praeger.

Johnson, D.W., & Lewicki, R.J. (1969). The initiation of superordinate goals. *Journal of Applied Behavioral Science*, *5*, 9–24.

Johnson, D.W., & Tjosvold, D. (1989). Constructive controversy: The key to effective decision-making. In D. Tjosvold & D.W. Johnson (Eds.), *Productive conflict management: Perspective for organizations* (pp. 46–68). Minneapolis, MN: Team Media.

Jones, R.E., & Melcher, B.H. (1982). Personality and the preference for modes of conflict resolution. *Human Relations*, *35*, 649–658.

Jones, T.S., & Remland, M.S. (1993). Nonverbal communication and conflict escalation: An attribution-based model. *International Journal of Conflict Management*, *4*, 119–137.

Kabanoff, B. (1985). Potential influence structures as sources of interpersonal conflict in groups and organizations. *Organizational Behavior and Human Decision Processes*, *36*, 113–141.

Kabanoff, B. (1987). Predictive validity of the MODE conflict instrument. *Journal of Applied Psychology*, *72*, 160–163.

Kahn, R.L., Wolfe, D.M., Quinn, R.P., Snoek, J.D., & Rosenthal, R.A. (1964). *Organizational stress: Studies in role conflict and ambiguity*. New York: Wiley.

Katz, D., & Kahn, R.L. (1978). *The social psychology of organizations* (2nd Edn.). New York: Wiley.

Kaufman, S., & Duncan, G.T. (1989). Third party intervention: A theoretical framework. In M.A. Rahim (Ed.), *Managing conflict: An interdisciplinary approach* (pp. 273–289). New York: Praeger.

Kelley, H.H., & Stahelski, A.J. (1970). Social interaction basis of cooperators' and competitors' beliefs about others. *Journal of Personality and Social Psychology*, *16*, 66–91.

Kelly, J. (1970). Make conflict work for you. *Harvard Business Review*, *48*, (4), 103–113.

Křivohlavý, J. (1974). *Zwischenmenschliche Konflikte und experimentelle Spiele*. Bern: Huber.

Kolb, D.M. (1989). Labor mediators, managers, and ombudsmen: Roles mediators play in different contexts. In K. Kressel & D.G. Pruitt (Eds.), *Mediation research: The process and effectiveness of third-party intervention* (pp. 91–114). San Francisco: Jossey-Bass.

Koopman, P.L. (1980). *Besluitvorming in organisaties* [Decision-making in organizations]. Assen: Van Gorcum.

Kroon, M.B.R., 't Hart, P., & Van Kreveld, D. (1991). Managing group decision making processes: Individual versus collective accountability and groupthink. *International Journal of Conflict Management*, *2*, 91–115.

Lawrence, P.R., & Lorsch, J.W. (1967). *Organization and environment: Managing differentiation and integration*. Boston: Harvard University.

Lewicki, R.J., Weiss, S.E., & Lewin, D. (1992). Models of conflict, negotiation and third party intervention: A review and synthesis. *Journal of Organizational Behavior*, *13*, 209–252.

Likert, R., & Likert, J.G. (1976). *New ways of managing conflict*. New York: McGraw-Hill.

Lindskold, S. (1978). Trust development, the GRIT proposal, and the effects of conciliatory acts on conflict and cooperation. *Psychological Bulletin*, *85*, 772–793.

Louis, M.R. (1977). How individuals conceptualize conflict: Identification of steps in the process and the role of personal/developmental factors. *Human Relations*, *30*, 451–467.

Mastenbroek, W.F.G. (1987). *Conflict management and organisation development*. Chichester: Wiley.

Merton, R.K. (1957). *Social theory and social structure*. New York: Free Press.

Miles, R.H., & Perreault, W.D. (1976). Organizational role conflict: Its antecedents and consequences. *Organizational Behavior and Human Performance*, *17*, 19–44.

Moreland, R.L., & Levine, J.M. (1984). Role transitions in small groups. In V.L. Allen & E. van de Vliert (Eds.), *Role transitions: Explorations and explanations* (pp. 181–195). New York: Plenum Press.

Morrill, C., & Thomas, C.K. (1992). Organizational conflict: Management as disputing process. *Human Communication Research*, *18*, 400–428.

Moscovici, S. (1985). Social influence and conformity. In G. Lindzey & E. Aronson (Eds.), *The handbook of social psycholology* Vol. 2, (3rd Edn., pp. 347–412). New York: Random House.

Mulder, M. (1978). *Conflicthantering: Theorie en praktijk in organisaties* [Conflict management: Theory and practice in organizations]. Leiden: Stenfert Kroese.

Mulder, M., & Stemerding, A. (1963). Threat, attraction to group, and need for strong leadership: A laboratory experiment in a natural setting. *Human Relations*, *16*, 317–334.

Murray, V.V. (1975). Some unanswered questions on

organizational conflict. *Organization and Administrative Science, 5*, 35–53.

Musser, S.J. (1982). A model for predicting the choice of conflict management strategies by subordinates in high-stakes conflicts. *Organizational Behavior and Human Performance, 29*, 257–269.

Naase, C. (1978). *Konflikte in der Organisation*. Stuttgart: Enke.

Nachmias, D. (1982). Organizational conflict in public bureaus: A model. *Administration and Society, 14*, 283–298.

Osgood, C.E. (1966). *Perspective in foreign policy*. Palo Alto, CA: Pacific Books.

Patchen, M. (1987). Strategies for eliciting cooperation from an adversary. *Journal of Conflict Resolution, 31*, 164–185.

Pettigrew, T.F. (1986). The intergroup contact hypothesis reconsidered. In M. Hewstone & R. Brown (Eds.), *Contact and conflict in intergroup encounters* (pp. 169–195). Oxford: Blackwell.

Phillips, E., & Cheston, R. (1979). Conflict resolution: What works? *California Management Review, 21*, 76–83.

Pinkley, R.L. (1990). Dimensions of conflict frame: Disputant interpretations of conflict. *Journal of Applied Psychology, 75*, 117–126.

Pondy, L.R. (1967). Organizational conflict: Concepts and models. *Administrative Science Quarterly, 12*, 296–320.

Pondy, L.R. (1969). Varieties of organizational conflict. *Administrative Science Quarterly, 14*, 499–505.

Prein, H.C.M. (1976). Stijlen van conflicthantering [Styles of conflict management]. *Nederlands Tijdschrift voor de Psychologie, 31*, 321–346.

Prein, H.C.M. (1982). *Conflicthantering door een derde partij* [Conflict management by a third party]. Lisse: Swets & Zeitlinger.

Putnam, L.L., & Poole, M.S. (1987). Conflict and negotiation. In F.M. Jablin, L.L. Putnam, K.H. Roberts, & L.W. Porter (Eds.), *Handbook of organizational communication: An interdisciplinary perspective* (pp. 549–599). Newbury Park, CA: Sage.

Putnam, L.L., & Wilson, C.E. (1982). Communicative strategies in organizational conflicts: Reliability and validity of a measurement scale. In M. Burgoon (Ed.), *Communication Yearbook* (Vol. 6, pp. 629–652). Newbury Park, CA: Sage.

Rabbie, J.M. (1979). Competitie en coöperatie tussen groepen [Competition and cooperation between groups]. In J.M.F. Jaspars & R. van der Vlist (Eds.), *Sociale psychologie in Nederland; Vol. 2. De kleine groep* (pp. 190–226). Deventer: Van Loghum Slaterus.

Rahim, M.A. (1992). *Managing conflict in organizations* (2nd Edn.). Westport, CT: Praeger.

Rahim, M.A., & Buntzman, G.F. (1989). Supervisory power bases, styles of handling conflict with subordinates, and subordinate compliance and satisfaction. *Journal of Psychology, 123*, 195–210.

Raven, B.H., & Kruglanski, A.W. (1970). Conflict and power. In P.G. Swingle (Ed.), *The structure of conflict* (pp. 69–109). New York: Academic Press.

Renwick, P.A. (1975). Perception and management of supervisor-subordinate conflict. *Organizational Behavior and Human Performance, 13*, 444–456.

Robbins, S.P. (1974). *Managing organizational conflict: A nontraditional approach*. Englewood Cliffs, NJ: Prentice-Hall.

Roloff, M.E. (1976). Communication strategies, relationships, and relational change. In G.R. Miller (Ed.), *Explorations in interpersonal communication* (pp. 173–196). Beverly Hills, CA: Sage.

Rubin, J.Z. (1980). Experimental research on third-party intervention in conflict: Toward some generalizations. *Psychological Bulletin*, 87, 379–391.

Rubin, J.Z., Pruitt, D.G., & Kim, S.H. (1994). *Social conflict: Escalation, stalemate, and settlement* (2nd Edn.). New York: McGraw-Hill.

Ruble, T.L., & Thomas, K.W. (1976). Support for a two-dimensional model of conflict behavior. *Organizational Behavior and Human Performance, 16*, 143–155.

Sanford, R.N. (1964). Individual conflict and organizational interaction. In R.L. Kahn & E. Boulding (Eds.), *Power and conflict in organizations* (pp. 95–104). London: Tavistock.

Schmidt, S.M., & Kochan, T.A. (1972). Conflict: Toward conceptual clarity. *Administrative Science Quarterly, 17*, 359–370.

Schneer, J.A., & Chanin, M.N. (1987). Manifest needs as personality predispositions to conflict-handling behavior. *Human Relations, 40*, 575–590.

Schweiger, D.M., Sandberg, W.R., & Ragan, J.W. (1986). Group approaches for improving strategic decision making: A comparative analysis of dialectical inquiry, devil's advocacy, and consensus. *Academy of Management Journal, 29*, 51–71.

Schweiger, D.M., Sandberg, W.R., & Rechner, P.L. (1989). Experiential effects of dialectical inquiry, devil's advocacy, and consensus approaches to strategic decision making. *Academy of Management Journal, 32*, 745–772.

Scott, W.G. (1965). *The management of conflict: Appeal systems in organizations*. Homewood, IL: Irwin-Dorsey.

Shepard, H.A. (1964). Responses to situations of competition and conflict. In R.L. Kahn & E. Boulding (Eds.), *Power and conflict in organizations* (pp. 127–135). London: Tavistock.

Sherif, M. (1966). *In common predicament*. Boston: Houghton Mifflin.

Smart, C., & Vertinski, I. (1977). Designs for crisis decision units. *Administrative Science Quarterly, 22*, 640–657.

Smith, K.K. (1989). The movement of conflict in organizations: The joint dynamics of splitting and triangulation. *Administrative Science Quarterly*, *34*, 1–20.

Stein, A.A. (1976). Conflict and cohesion: A review of the literature. *Journal of Conflict Resolution*, *20*, 143–172.

Stephan, W.G. (1985). Intergroup relations. In G. Lindzey & E. Aronson (Eds.), *Handbook of Social Psychology*, (Vol. 2, pp. 599–658). New York: Random House.

Sternberg, R.J., & Dobson, D.M. (1987). Resolving interpersonal conflicts: An analysis of stylistic consistency. *Journal of Personality and Social Psychology*, *52*, 794–812.

Terhune, K.W. (1970). The effects of personality in cooperation and conflict. In P.G. Swingle (Ed.), *The structure of conflict* (pp. 193–234). New York: Academic Press.

Thierry, H. (1977). *Organisatie van tegenstellingen* [The organisation of antitheses]. Assen: Van Gorcum.

Thomas, K.W. (1992). Conflict and negotiation processes in organizations. In M.D. Dunnette & L.M. Hough (Eds.), *Handbook of industrial and organizational psychology* (Vol. 3, 2nd Edn., pp. 651–717). Palo Alto, CA: Consulting Psychologists Press.

Thomas, K.W., & Pondy, L.R. (1977). Toward an "intent" model of conflict management among principal parties. *Human Relations*, *30*, 1089–1102.

Tjosvold, D. (1985). Implications of controversy research for management. *Journal of Management*, *11*, 221–238.

Tjosvold, D. (1991). *The conflict-positive organization: Stimulate diversity and create unity*. Reading, MA: Addison-Wesley.

Turner, M.E., & Pratkanis, A.R. (1994). Social identity maintenance prescriptions for preventing groupthink: Reducing identity protection and enhancing intellectual conflict. *International Journal of Conflict Management*, *5*, 254–270.

Tutzauer, F., & Roloff, M.E. (1988). Communication processes leading to integrative agreements: Three paths to joint benefits. *Communication Research*, *15*, 360–380.

Ury, W.L., Brett, J.M., & Goldberg, S.B. (1988). *Getting disputes resolved: Designing systems to cut the costs of conflict*. San Francisco, CA: Jossey-Bass.

Vliert, E. van de (1981). Siding and other reactions to a conflict: A theory of escalation toward outsiders. *Journal of Conflict Resolution*, *25*, 495–520.

Vliert, E. van de (1987). Behandeling van conflict tussen groepen [Intervening in conflicts between groups]. In F.W. Winkel (Ed.), *Relaties tussen groepen: Sociaal-psychologische analyses en interventies* (pp. 7–20). Alphen a/d Rijn: Samsom.

Vliert, E. van de (1990). Sternberg's styles of handling interpersonal conflict: A theory-based reanalysis. *International Journal of Conflict Management*, *1*, 69–80.

Vliert, E. van de (1997a). *Complex interpersonal conflict behaviour: Theoretical frontiers*. Hove, UK: Psychology Press.

Vliert, E. van de (1997b). Enhancing performance by conflict-stimulating intervention. In C.K.W. de Dreu & E. van de Vliert (Eds.), *Using conflict in organizations* (pp. 208–222). London: Sage.

Vliert, E. van de, & Dreu, C.K.W. de (1994). Optimizing performance by conflict stimulation. *International Journal of Conflict Management*, *5*, 211–222.

Vliert, E. van de, & Euwema, M.C. (1994). Agreeableness and activeness as components of conflict behaviors. *Journal of Personality and Social Psychology*, *66*, 674–687.

Vliert, E. van de, Euwema, M.C., Dispa, J.J., & Vrij, A. (1988). Een "framing-verklaring voor conflictgedrag van boven-en ondergeschikten [A framing explanation for conflict behaviour of supervisors and subordinates]. *Gedrag en Organisatie*, *1*, 47–57.

Vliert, E. van de, Euwema, M.C., & Huismans, S.E. (1995). Managing conflict with a subordinate or a superior: Effectiveness of conglomerated behavior. *Journal of Applied Psychology*, *80*, 271–281.

Vliert, E. van de, & Hordijk, J.W. (1989). A theoretical position of compromising among other styles of conflict management. *Journal of Social Psychology*, *129*, 681–690.

Vliert, E. van de, & Kabanoff, B. (1990). Toward theory-based measures of conflict management. *Academy of Management Journal*, *33*, 199–209.

Vliert, E. van de, & Prein, H.C.M. (1989). The difference in the meaning of forcing in the conflict management of actors and observers. In M.A. Rahim (Ed.), *Managing conflict: An interdisciplinary approach* (pp. 51–63). New York: Praeger.

Vliert, E. van de, Visser, A.P., Zwaga, P.G.J., Winnubst, J.A.M., & Ter Heine, E.J.H. (Eds.) (1983). *Rolspanningen* [Role strains]. Meppel: Boom.

Volkema, R.J., & Bergmann, T.J. (1989). Interpersonal conflict at work: An analysis of behavioral responses. *Human Relations*, *42*, 757–770.

Vroom, V.H., & Yetton, P.W. (1973). *Leadership and decision making*. Pittsburgh, PA: University of Pittsburgh Press.

Wall, J.A., Jr. (1985). *Negotiation: Theory and practice*. Glenview, IL: Scott Foresman.

Wall, V.D., Jr., & Nolan, L.L. (1986). Perceptions of inequity, satisfaction, and conflict in task-oriented groups. *Human Relations*, *39*, 1033–1051.

Walton, R.E. (1969). *Interpersonal peacemaking: Confrontations and third party consultation*. Reading, MA: Addison-Wesley.

Walton, R.E. (1972). Interorganizational decision making and identity conflict. In M. Tuite, R. Chisholm & M. Radnor (Eds.), *Interorganizational decision making* (pp. 94–111). Chicago: Aldine.

Walton, R.E. (1987). *Managing conflict: Interpersonal dialogue and third-party roles* (2nd Edn.). Reading, MA: Addison Wesley.
Walton, R.E., & Dutton, J.D. (1969). The management of interdepartmental conflict: A model and review. *Administrative Science Quarterly, 14*, 73–84.
Walton, R.E., Dutton, J.M., & Cafferty, T.P. (1969). Organizational context and interdepartmental conflict. *Administrative Science Quarterly, 14*, 522–542.
Walton, R.E., & McKersie, R.B. (1965). *A behavioral theory of labor negotiations: An analysis of a social interaction system*. New York: McGraw Hill.
Weitz, S. (1977). *Sex roles: Biological, psychological and social foundations*. Oxford: Oxford University Press.
Zand, D.E. (1972). Trust and managerial problem solving. *Administrative Science Quarterly, 17*, 229–239.

16

Women and Work

Marlies Ott

INTRODUCTION

A marked increase in the number of women on the labour market, alterations to the law, positive actions; the whole field of women and work is in a flux, which is also reflected in the research that has assumed enormous proportions. The subjects are diverse and the separate fields of study widely branched out. A study of man-woman communication on the workfloor in itself would be well worth writing an article about. Therefore, a chapter on "women and work" cannot be anything more than a rather limited selection of research results.

Studies on "women and work" differ from standard surveys implicitly or explicitly referring to men, in a number of ways (Gutek, Larwood, & Stromberg, 1986). First, more attention is paid to demographic data, such as the number of working women, which women have jobs, and where. This is not merely done in order to get a picture of the labour market, but also because the number and division of women working entail important psychological, sociological and policy-making implications. Second, research on "women and work" is nearly always meant to improve the position of women. It may deal with problems working women have to cope with, such as sexual harassment, dead-end careers and effects of a minority position ("tokenism"). Surveys are also held to contradict stock remarks that women are ignorant or indifferent.

This chapter pays a lot of attention to demographic data such as labour participation, unemployment, and so on. Attention is given to a group The Netherlands still have, a category quite often ignored: housewives. In a later section I will present a number of research results on the basis of two questions:

1. Do men and women differ as to individual characteristics that are more often than not considered to be the determinants of working behaviour?
2. Are the situational characteristics different for men and women?

I will then show how research may lead to erroneous interpretations, when the aforementioned differences are not recognized.

In Section 3 a number of disadvantages of the existing division of work are mentioned followed by a debate on the policy of the Dutch Government.

1 WHAT WORK IS DONE BY WOMEN?

In The Netherlands one and a half to two times more unpaid work than paid work is done, and most of the unpaid work is carried out by women. Therefore, in Section 1.1 the category of housewives and household work is discussed. Section 1.2 gives demographic data about women working outdoors. As a matter of course paid and unpaid work is related. Theories taking into account shifts between paid and unpaid work are called buffer theories. As early as 1941 Kuznets already indicated the importance of production in the household sector (Oudijk, 1983). He assumes that production in the household sector shrinks in times of a boom and grows in a slump.

1.1 Housewives

The group of women occupied full-time with household chores, the housewives, has been strongly on the decrease over the last few years, but still makes up a large proportion of working women. Exact figures are lacking, but this can be inferred from the data about the working population. In 1960, 74% of all women aged between 15 and 64 did *not* belong to the working population, whereas in 1993 that percentage had gone down to 47% (Sociale en Culturele Verkenningen, 1994). For the married women with children under 3 years old, the percentage of 82% in 1982 has fallen to 73% in 1988 (Sociaal en Cultureel Rapport, 1988; Sociaal-economische Maandstatistieken, 1990). It cannot be suggested, however, that all these women are full-time housewives, since students and people working less than 15 hours a week also fall within this category. Another indication of the size of the group of housewives is that in 1985, 46% of the women between the ages 18 and 64 had no source of income of their own (Sociaal en Cultureel Rapport, 1988). It is expected that in the future the group of housewives will become even smaller. The Dutch Government's endeavours to further the economic self-reliance of the future generations of women will be an accelerating factor of this decline. The 1990-generation is often taken to be the starting-point, i.e. the generation that is or will be 18 years old after 1990.

The very large group of housewives form a forgotten group: relatively little research is done on the subject. Household work is not considered to be "real" work, and there is little interest in the organization of housekeeping or in the required skills. Work and organizational psychologists have, so far, paid little attention to housewives and housekeeping. One exception is the ergonomist Grandjean (1973), who studied what prerequisites a house, a kitchen, and so on, should meet in order to satisfy a housewife's needs.

Many definitions as to what housekeeping involves are current. Here follows the derived definition by Spaander and Van Houten (taken from De Monchy, 1981). "Householding" involves the following tasks:

- Cleaning the home.
- Taking care of meals, clothes, pets and garden.
- The organization and planning of these activities.
- Taking care of partner and children.

It is particularly the last two categories that are underestimated. Men in particular are inclined to underestimate household work (Komter, 1985). Although the group occupied full-time with these activities is getting smaller and smaller, this does not imply that the need for household work will disappear altogether. A lot of time is spent on it. Table 16.1 shows that adult women work 26.5 and men 10.4 hours per week on average. This table also shows that people with a paid job of more than 20 hours spend much time on household activities: women 16.4 and men 8.4 hours a week on average.

1.2 Women working outside the home

More data are known on women working outside the home, such as participation in the labour market, level of work, and so on.

1.2.1 Participation in the labour market

In 1991, 56% of the women aged 15 to 64 formed part of the working population; for men this percentage was 82% (Enquête Beroepsbevolking, 1991). In 1960 this percentage for women was a mere 26%, showing how many more women have started working outside the home over recent decades. Table 16.2 shows that, in addition,

TABLE 16.1

Average time spent by adults on housekeeping and caring 1985–1990 (on a weekly basis).

Total			*No children under 15*	*One or more children under 15*
	1985	**1990**	**1985**	**1985**
Women	28.3	26.5	25.1	34.0
Working[1]	16.9	16.4	15.0	25.2
Not working[2]	30.8	*	28.2	35.3
Men	10.3	10.4	10.4	9.9
Working[1]	8.2	8.4	7.1	9.5
Not working[2]	12.7	*	13.7	10.1

[1] People performing paid labour in the week of survey.
[2] People not performing paid labour in the week of survey.
* Data unknown.

Source: Hooghiemstra and Niphuis-Nell (1993).

women with young children are going into the labour market. In 1975 only 12% of married women with children aged from 0–3 formed part of the working population. In 1985 the percentage proved to have gone up to 27%.

Table 16.3 shows the extent of employment among various groups of ethnic minority women to be greatly different and lower than for native women. For both groups it is valid that women with a lower education level are working less outside the home than those with a higher level of schooling.

Seen from an international perspective The Netherlands are still scoring low where women working in jobs are concerned (see Table 16.4). Of all twelve Western industrial countries only Ireland, Italy and Belgium are behind The Netherlands in this respect.

Why there is such a low percentage of women working in The Netherlands is unkown. The reasons sometimes given are that the rate of individual income in The Netherlands is in accordance with the needs of a family, and that the social security system functions in such a way that the need for women to go out and work is not as strong as in the surrounding countries. Another explanation sometimes given is the negative attitudes in the past of the political parties, both denominational and progressive, and the unions. Whereas the denominational parties did not accept women manifesting themselves in public life on religious grounds, the progressive parties and the trade unions based their objections primarily on the deplorable conditions of working-class families at the end of the 19th century, when child labour and woman labour were widespread phenomena.

1.2.2 Part-time labour

Table 16.4 gives information about working part-time in various countries. The Netherlands has the highest percentage of women working part-time: 62%, whereas the percentage for men is only 16%; part-time work being defined as up to 35 hours a week. If labour participation were not represented in persons but in labour years the female labour participation would be lagging behind even further in The Netherlands than in other countries, as shown in Table 16.4. Part-time work clearly meets the needs, but brings with it some risks such as a reduced chance of career opportunities.

In her thesis *Labour Duration, Organization and Emancipation* (1989) Demenint-de Jongh

TABLE 16.2

Married women belonging to the working population, according to age of youngest child still at home, 1975–1988 (in percentages of all married women with a youngest child still at home relating to age category).

Date	Age youngest child still at home: 0–3 years	4–12 years	No children at home	Total
1975	12	21	28	22
1977	13	22	30	24
1979	16	25	31	26
1981	19	30	32	29
1983	23	32	33	32
1985	25	31	32	32
1988	27	35	*	*

* Data unknown.

Sources: Central Bureau of Statistics, Counting of Labour Force, 1975, 1977, 1979, 1981, 1983 and 1985
Hooghiemstra and Niphuis-Nell (1993).

states that employment for women in the past and nowadays but also in the future will lastingly be linked to part-time work. It is therefore important to create conditions to make part-time work possible at every level in the organization. On the basis of her study Demenint-de Jongh arrives at the conclusion that the psychological resistance against part-time work at the higher levels is probably "harder" than the so-called "hard" impediment in the field of an organization; apparently these obstacles could always immediately be cleared.

1.2.3 Level of jobs

The Dutch Wage Administration Control Department in its supervisory task concerning the Act on Equal Pay and Equal Treatment, quite regularly investigates the market sector. Data from these surveys sometimes tell us something about the division of women and men over the job levels for a more or less representative part of this sector. Over a number of years the Home Ministry has studied the position of female and male civil servants in the departments. These studies provide the data shown in Table 16.5.

The table shows women to be over-represented at the lower levels and under-represented at the higher levels. At the highest level in the market-sector not a single woman is to be found. This lopsided division can only partly be due to the difference in schooling between men and women (Sociaal en Cultureel Rapport, 1988).

Women earn 23% less than men as an average gross hourly rate. The greater part of this may be due to differences between the job levels, but this is not the only reason. In spite of the Act on Equal Pay of 1975 it still turns out that women get less pay then men in the same or equivalent job. A survey of Loontechnische Dienst (LTD) (1985) showed that women earn 5% less on an average in equivalent jobs. Labour market influences are mentioned as one of the reasons.

1.2.4 Occupation categories

In 166 out of the 285 classified occupations in The Netherlands no or very few women (less than 10%) are working. Only 9 occupations are held almost exclusively by women (90–100%; see Table 16.6).

In Table 16.7 the occupations with the largest number of women are shown.

Eighteen per cent of the female workforce is employed in only two occupations, a quarter of the total in three, one third in four and more than half in eight occupations. The concentration is far less

TABLE 16.3

The extent of employment of ethnic minority and native women, according to level of schooling, 1991 (in percentages)[1].

Level of schooling	*Turks*	*Moroccans*	*Surinamese*	*Antilleans*	*Native*
No complete schooling	13	2	16	9	*
Completed elementary education	19	13	32	16	36
Lower vocational education	33	20	46	38	48
Advanced elementary education	29	24	46	39	60
Intermediate vocational education	42	*	65	48	67
Higher general secondary education	18	*	65	61	65
Total	19	8	43	34	

[1] Number of working people as a percentage of 15–65-year-old people, excluding schoolgoing children. In The Netherlands there is a population of 10.5 million 15–65-year-old people, of which more than 1 million are ethnic minorities, persons not having the Dutch nationality or not born in The Netherlands (Sociale en Culturele Verkenningen, 1994).
* Fewer than 25 respondents in all.

Source: ISEO (SPVA, 1991), in: "Sociale en Culturele Verkenningen, 1994".

strong among men. Only half of the total is to be found in 30 occupations.

Until 1983 the division of work according to sex for occupations rose slightly in the labour market, but has been gradually diminishing since then (Groot, 1990). It is true to say that quite a few men went into occupations in which women were over-represented, but the opposite hardly occurred. Of the absolute increase of the male occupational population of 607,000, 105,480 men started careers in which women were over-represented. Only 60,890 women out of a total increase of female workers of 1,276,000 went into jobs in which men were over-represented. This implies that twice as many men made a non-traditional choice of profession (Hooghienstra & Niphuis-Nell, 1993). Evidently, the increasing supply of women on the labour market still focuses to a large extent on the traditional "women's jobs".

This development also led to the so-called redress Bill, introduced to revise the legislation on equal treatment. One of the alterations was that preferential treatment or positive action was only allowed for women and no longer for men. An advertisement by FNV (one of the trade unions) some years ago, stated that "in view of the structure of our staffing, the preference for men that was expressed for administrative vacancies is no longer permitted" (De Wildt, 1989).

The steeply rising line of the number of unemployed in the early half of the 1980s did not develop further. Between 1985 and 1987 there was

TABLE 16.4

Labour market participation[1] and part-time workers in a number of OESO-countries, 1990.

	Labour market participants[1]		*Part-time workers*[2]			
	Women	Men	All workers	Women	Men	% women of part-time workers
The Netherlands	51.5	78.1	33.0	62.0	16.0	70.0
Belgium	45.2	69.9	10.0	25.0	2.0	90.0
Denmark	76.6	85.8	24.0	42.0	9.0	79.0
France	56.9	75.1	12.0	24.0	4.0	83.0
Great Britain	65.0	85.3	22.0	44.0	5.0	87.0
Ireland	40.7	76.5	8.0	17.0	4.0	68.0
Italy	42.4	75.4	6.0	11.0	3.0	65.0
W. Germany	56.8	55.6	13.0	31.0	2.0	91.0
Australia	52.2	75.7	21.0	*	*	*
New Zealand	63.8	84.3	20.0	*	*	*
United States	57.5	76.1	14.0	*	*	*
Canada	68.3	84.8	15.0	*	*	*

[1] Defined as working population in percentages of the population of 15–64-year-old people.
[2] In percentages of categories concerned.
* Data unknown.

Sources: OECD Economic Surveys Australia, New Zealand, United States, Canada (1990–1994)
OECD (1991: 46), cited in Hooghiemstra and Niphuis-Nell (1993).
CBS, Statistisch Jaarboek 1994.

even a slight decline. In 1988 another method of calculating unemployment figures was started. Up to 1988 the registration at the employment bureaus was used, but these accounts were not correct any more as was proven, among other things, because a number of the people registered as "unemployed" had jobs. After 1988 figures were based on data from both the "Enquête Beroepsvolking" (Survey on Working Population) and the registration at the employment bureaus, and are called "Geregistreerde werkloosheidscijfers" (GWL). Table 16.8 shows that the distortion of figures was stronger in the data for women than for men. Before 1988 there was a marked discrepancy in unemployment figures, whereas from 1988 onwards these figures are almost equal for women and men. Over the last few years the unemployment figure for women has been diminishing.

Table 16.9 shows that unemployment among allochthonous women differs considerably and that the extent of this unemployment is substantially larger than among autochthonous women. In Table 16.8 the "Geregistreerde werkloosheidscijfers (GWL)" (Registered unemployment figure) after 1988 was used. In Table 16.9 the CBS '81/EBB figure is used, referring to all individuals who are out of work and/or who are registered with the employment bureaus, are actively seeking work, or who are on unemployment benefits. This goes to explain the difference between the unemployment figures shown in Table 16.8 and those shown in Table 16.9.

TABLE 16.5

Participation of female workers in (part of) the market sector and in the departments according to job levels, 1987, 1988 (in percentages).

	Job levels as applied by the LTD								
	I	*II*	*III*	*IV*	*V*	*VI*	*VII*	*VIII*	*Total*
Participation of women in the market sector, 1988	71	47	31	28	14	7	1	0	33
	Job levels as applied by the departments								
	I	*II*	*III*	*IV*	*V*	*VI*			*Total*
Participation of women at departments, January 1987	40	31	12	11	5	4			24

Source: LTD 1988.

TABLE 16.6

Percentage of women among the total number of workers in that occupation	*Number of occupations*	*Percentages of working women out of the total number of working women*
0–10	166	3.6
10–20	29	2.4
20–40	34	13.3
40–60	27	24.3
60–80	12	20.5
80–90	8	15.6
90–100	9	20.4

Source: Van Mourik and Siegers (1988).

Division of women in occupations, according to the percentages of women in those occupations, 1985.

TABLE 16.7

Occupations with the largest number of women, 1985.

Name of occupation	*Number of women working in that occupation (in 1000s)*	*Percentage of total female working force*	*The same cumulated*[1]
Shop assistants and other (excluding sales representatives)	163.3	9.9	9.9
Correspondents, clerical staff (not mentioned above)	133.7	7.9	17.8
Service staff (not mentioned above)	132.2	7.8	25.6
Secretaries, typists, teletexists	125.3	7.4	33.0
Charwomen, window-cleaners etc.	99.5	5.9	38.9
Book-keepers, cashiers, counter clerks	94.3	5.6	44.5
Other domestics	67.8	4.0	48.6
Trained nurses	64.7	3.8	52.4
Teachers at schools etc.	51.5	3.1	55.4
Waitresses, barmaids and others	47.5	2.8	58.3
Household staff etc.	41.8	2.5	60.7

[1] Differences by rounding off.

Source: Van Mourik and Siegers (1988).

2 DETERMINANTS OF WORKING BEHAVIOUR

With respect to the determinants of working behaviour a distinction is usually made between individual characteristics and situational characteristics. One must bear in mind that these characteristics may be correlated; they mutually influence each other and rarely have independent effects on working behaviour. The following questions are essential for work and organizational psychologists:

1. Are the individual characteristics different for men and women?
2. Are the situational characteristics different for men and women?

An elaborate answer to these questions is beyond the scope of this work, as it would involve many areas of psychology. However, these questions provide the background for a number of interesting research results.

2.1 Individual characteristics

Questions about the differences in individual characteristics between men and women have interested many psychologists. In their book *The Psychology of Sex Differences*, now a classic, Maccoby and Jacklin (1975) survey the research results up to 1975. After 1975 this type of research has become less frequent. The question of sex differences is considered somewhat taboo. This is understandable, though not very sensible. It is understandable because data on sex differences have more than once been abused to legitimize the

TABLE 16.8

Registered unemployed individuals, yearly average as a percentage of the dependent working population[1].

Unemployed	*1975*	*1985*	*1986*	*1987*	*1988*	*1989*	*1990*	*1991*	*1992*
Men	5.0	14.8	13.4	12.6	6.7	5.7	4.9	4.3	4.4
Women	5.0	18.5	17.7	17.4	6.0	5.7	5.0	4.7	4.0
Men and women	5.0	15.9	14.7	14.1	6.4	5.7	5.0	4.5	4.2

[1] The term "dependent working population" refers to the working population with the exception of the self-employed. The registered unemployed group consists of people who are available for paid work in full-time service, i.e. with a minimum of 15 hours a week. Until January 1978 the minimum was 30 hours a week.

Sources: Statistisch Zakboek (1988)
Sociaal Economisch Maandstatistiek, 1990
CBSS 1992, in: Hooghiemstra and Niphuis-Nell (1993).
Statistisch Jaarboek (1994).
Social Monthly Statistics, February and August 1990, published by CBS, Annual 7, no. 2 and 8 and Statistics Pocket Book

existing role division between men and women, with total disregard for the interactions between situation and person. It is not sensible because strategies of change need to be based on insight into these interactions and thus also into their separate factors. We will deal with the question of individual characteristics as used by Roe in Chapter 2, Volume 3 of this Handbook. He mentions three categories: dispositional characteristics, habitual characteristics and motivational characteristics. These categories can be distinguished according to the degree of assumed stability. Dispositional characteristics, also called traits, are considered to be most constant. They originate in hereditary factors and/or past experiences. Examples are: various intellectual abilities and styles. It is assumed that habitual characteristics are acquired through environmen-

TABLE 16.9

Position of ethnic minorities according to sex, in percentages, 1993.

	Turks	*Moroccans*	*Surinamese*	*Antilleans*	*Native*
Women					
Employment[1]	18	6	38	36	43
Labour participation rate[2]	25	12	50	46	48
Unemployment[3]	32	50	22	17	10
Men					
Employment rate	43	29	56	60	73
Labour participation rate	59	50	68	71	77
Unemployment	27	44	18	14	5

[1] Employment rate: percentages of working individuals of population between 15–65 years old.
[2] Labour participation rate: percentages of working and unemployed individuals of population between 15–65 years old.
[3] Unemployment: unemployment individuals in percentage of number of working and unemployed individuals.

tal influences, namely through learning, practise and habituation. Examples are: various kinds of knowledge, skills, attitudes, expectations and habits. Motivational characteristics refer to temporary or more permanent conditions of (or in) any individual, which bring about a particular level of activity and a specific directness of behaviour. Examples are: needs such as hunger and thirst, but also the level of ambition, cognitive dissonance, and so on.

Obviously, there are differences between men and women with respect to the motivational characteristics, for these are the most unstable and depend on the situation. In view of the fact that women as a rule find themselves in different situations, and do work quite different from men's work, differences are bound to occur in this respect. An example to illustrate this is when we consider the levels of ambition among male and female employees. These levels are also influenced by the expected career opportunities. The greater the chance of promotion, the more probably one will develop a high level of ambition. The fact that women are mainly employed in jobs providing limited career opportunities makes a relatively low level of ambition more likely (Kanter, 1977). Such phenomena are discussed elaborately in reflections on "female achievement" (see Frieze, Parsons, Johnson, Ruble, & Zellman, 1978; O'Leary, 1977).

It is to be expected that, among the habitual characteristics, differences will be formed, because upbringing and learning experiences play an important role. We have been made aware of the influence of the expectation that women will, in due course, become mother and housewife, and of the interactions between upbringing, education and choice of a career. In a girl's upbringing sometimes more emphasis is laid on house keeping and motherhood and on the personal qualities required for such a position, than on how to survive as well as possible in an organization. This difference of "career" intentions is very likely to influence men and women's interest, values, knowledge and skills in their development.

It is true that many more girls are intending to participate in the labour market all their lives, yet the differences in learning experiences are still very great. Girls of the 1990 generation (aged 12 and 13 in 1985) for example spend twice as much time on household chores on average than boys of that same generation, namely 5.6 hours a week as against 2.9 hours a week (Sociaal en Cultureel Rapport, 1988). As far as education is concerned the difference in education *level* is disappearing, but there are still marked differences in the *course* of education. At a lower vocational training level most boys go to school for elementary technical training and most girls go to a lower domestic science school or technical education establishment (Sociaal en Cultureel Rapport, 1988)

Hennig and Jardim (1977), two American researchers, have given many courses for personnel in trade and industry aimed at developing an awareness of the effects differences in upbringing have on working behaviour. During those courses they asked people what they had learned, when engaged in team sports in childhood. Among other responses they answered as follows: you learned how to compete and cooperate with boys (girls) whom you would not choose as friends; you learned what losing is like; you learned to take criticism from the coach, from fellow-players, and from spectators; you learned that you had to make plans and that others refused to help you if you put yourself in the limelight too often; you learned that you had to know the rules thoroughly, in case you wanted to influence the referee's decisions; you found out that some people are better than others, but that they nevertheless need each other; and you noticed that the coach was important for the group's morale.

According to Hennig and Jardim it is because of women's lack of experience of team sports that they are insufficiently aware of the importance of the informal system of relationships, shared information, loyalties, dependence, mutual advantage and protection. For that matter, Hennig and Jardim's approach is aimed at adapting women to the situation as it is. Nowadays we realize that the specific skills women acquire through their upbringing can be effective and efficient in an organization as well, though it is necessary to stay alert for the confusion that may result when women participate in their own way in organizations in which the "rules of the game" have previously been determined primarily by men.

One of Henley's studies (1977) shows that a

difference in upbringing can directly cause a difference in working behaviour. This study was mainly concerned with non-verbal behaviour. The fact that women and men learn, and also apply, different forms of non-verbal communication, apparently has a great influence on the position they attain in society. Most of the studies on non-verbal communication do no more than establish the differences between men and women. According to Henley, however, there is a highly important intermediating variable, namely power. Her study shows that much of the behaviour between a subordinate and his or her superior bears a resemblance to the conduct between husband and wife. Not only are these actions caused by the difference in power, but the difference is emphasized and even increased by this. Moreover, Henley is convinced that from early childhood on, women are taught feminine, i.e. subordinate, behaviour. When women start behaving as superiors, it is regarded as male conduct, or it is ignored, punished or interpreted sexually. For a woman supervisor this implies that either she cannot really behave as a supervisor, that is, show behaviour connected with coordinating, delegating, criticizing and so on, or she will be looked upon as unfeminine.

Fewest differences were found among the *dispositional* characteristics, which are considered to be the most constant. As a group, boys have higher scores on spatial insight and physical aggression. Women score higher on verbal skills; this difference, however, is not found among children (Maccoby & Jacklin, 1975).

2.2 Situational characteristics

The focal question in this section will be whether the situational characteristics are different for men and women?

These characteristics too can be manifold among themselves. In a material sense, one could consider the place where one works, the machinery, and the pace of work; in an immaterial sense there are such factors as the presence of other people and their expectations. Earlier in this chapter it was mentioned that there are considerable differences in the kinds of work and in the conditions under which work is done. Some other examples of differences in situational characteristics follow here.

First, there is this characteristic which as such is not different for men and women, yet has different *effects* on men and women. As a rule, organizations are based on a 38-hour working week, the assumption being that the employees all have someone to take care of them at home. This is not true for all male employees. However, for women this is hardly ever true. Since women employees are in charge of the greater part of household work, a 38-hour working week will more often cause them strain.

Another situational characteristic concerns staffing policy. Those who create such a policy may use stereotyped images of men and women, and so develop different policies for men and women. Many personnel managers take for granted the stereotype that women will continue to work until the birth of their first child and then leave the organization. This may lead to their employing women exclusively in jobs that are

TABLE 16.10

	Man should be promoted	*Woman should be promoted*	*Should make no difference*
1978	34	2	64
1981	17	1	82
1985	12	1	87
1987	10	2	89
1991	8	3	89

Source: SCP 1975–1991, in: Hooghiemstra and Niphuis-Nell (1993).

Views on different treatment of the woman 1978–1991 in percentages. *"Suppose there are two employees and only one can be promoted; they are equal in all respects except for their sex. Who should get the promotion?"*

characterized by monotony and a lack of career opportunities, sometimes assessing the women's achievement lower than the men's. This phenomenon, shown in many of the studies (e.g. Nieva & Gutek, 1980) is one of the causes of indirect differences in wages. These differences are found in situations in which women have had better schooling and/or working experience than their male colleagues and are paid the same wages (Schippers, 1987). The views held by those in charge of personnel policy can also play a role, when it comes to chances for promotion. To illustrate this, Table 16.10 contains the answers to the following question: "Suppose there are two employees and only one can be promoted; they are equal in all respects except for their sex. Who should get the promotion?"

We can see that in 1991, 8% of the respondents favoured men for the promotion, against 3% who favoured women. Eighty-nine percent feel that it should not make any difference. This contrasts sharply with the figures for 1978, when the opinions were far more often to the advantage of men.

Finally, an important situational characteristic is that the majority of organizations consist primarily of men. This characteristic also has different effects for men and women. First, women in men's occupations or in higher-level positions often find themselves on their own. This can provoke processes as described by Kanter (1977) under the heading of "tokenism". Kanter referred to these people belonging to a tiny minority on the workfloor (15%) as "tokens". She predicted that these individuals: would become "extra-conspicuous"; are left out of the informal system; and experience a strong stereotyping of their role, which will mean extra interference with their work and experience greater pressure. Indeed, this theory was supported for women being in such a token position (Izraeli, 1983; Ott, 1985; Spangler, Gordon, & Pipkin, 1978). It appeared that male individuals in a minority group on the other hand experienced more advantages than disadvantages (Ott, 1985). Ott's research also showed the inconsistent functioning of the so-called critical mass. It appeared that a male majority would rather not see a female minority increase up to approximately 25%, whereas a female majority had no problems whatsoever with such an increase of the male minority. Both "tokenism" as well as critical mass refer to mechanisms leading to the fact that men are entering into women's jobs quickly, whereas this process is slow and laborious for women entering into men's jobs. This is an extra impediment because the generally traditional men's jobs are better paid and provide more autonomy (Kauppinen-Toropainen, 1983).

Another effect of the fact that organizations primarily consist of men is that women are frequently confronted with sexual harassment, mostly in the form of verbal and physical "womanizing" behaviour. Sexual harassment makes women feel ill at ease at work, and as a result they achieve less than they are capable of, and more often than not they fall ill. This sort of behaviour towards women is definitely not only limited to the lowest job levels. Power often appears to be an important factor. A survey of the Ministry of Social Affairs and Employment in a municipal organization, an industrial firm and a number of smaller firms, shows that 33% of the "annoyers" are superiors or bosses. Sexual harassment particularly takes place when women are in the minority in jobs traditionally occupied by men. (De Rijk, 1989). Gutek & Morasch (1982) assumed sexual harassment also to take place in women's jobs, but that this isn't recognized as such because women take for granted that this behaviour may be part and parcel of that occupation.

The relationships between colleagues at work also affect women more negatively. Led by the observation that amorous relationships are not appreciated at work and that they affect personnel policy with regard to women, Quinn (1977) made a study of romance on the job. One remarkable conclusion in his study is that, in the case of affairs, women are dismissed twice as often as men.

In the last few years there has been a study on the working relationships among women. O'Leary's survey (1987) shows that contrary to what is assumed women think it an advantage to work under a female superior.

2.3 Interactions between individual characteristics and situational characteristics

It is a well-known fact that the structure of an organization influences individual characteristiscs. Thus, career opportunities affect the ways people regard themselves and their jobs; possibilities of promotion influence the attitude towards work, the level of ambition and the sense of responsibility. Conversely, those who have "fallen behind" behave in a different way to people with successful careers, which further limits their possibilities. When examing the problem of why particularly women hold lower positions in organizations, one is hampered by the question to what extent this could be explained by either situational characteristics or rather by individual characteristics. The study of De Jong (1983) shows that women employees view the problem as resulting from unequal treatment in the promotion policy, and that the management attributes it to women's lack of motivation. Both viewpoints can be supported by the results of research. Information on the relative influence can be gained only from longitudinal studies, which, unfortunately, are rare due to practical difficulties.

2.4 Erroneous interpretations

Frieze et al. (1978) provide a survey of the one-sided approaches in psychological research, which may lead to erroneous interpretations. Three types of errors are mentioned here:

1. The use of concepts which have been applied with respect to male employees only.
2. Ascribing the differences found among employees to the situation in an organization without taking into account the differences between male and female employees, which may have been caused by the difference in role attitudes with regard to men and women.
3. Ascribing the differences between male and female employees to their respective sexes regardless of the differences of the positions they hold in an organization.

The "reality shock" (Hall, 1976) may serve as an example of the first type of error. When a man starts in his first job he will have a number of expectations, for example, intrinsically satisfying work, an inspiring employer, good pay and possibilities of promotion. When these expectations turn out to be unrealistic, he will have to remodel his expectations. The company too, has expectations regarding the new employee, such as competence, acceptance of the standards of the organization and its informal power system, loyalty, and so on. During the first period the socializing influence of the company will be strongest and most frustrating for the new employee. It is not certain whether this "reality shock" also happens to women. In a case-study in which 25 women at the levels of "vice-president" or "president" of an organization were extensively interviewed, Hennig and Jardim (1977) found that none of the 25 women appeared to have suffered such a "reality shock". They were highly pleased with their first jobs, and their expectations had not run high. As a matter of fact, the starting period had been the reverse of a "reality shock" to the women. They found the work enjoyable, and realized that they were sometimes doing better than their colleagues. This example goes to show that having high hopes is an essental condition for a "reality shock" to occur. Owing to the fact that women generally do not prepare themselves for a long career in an organization, their expectations, for the most part, will not be high.

The second type of error can be illustrated by the results of an imaginary study on satisfaction concerning career opportunities. If research were to be done among male and female constables in a police force, it might turn out that those working in the reporting post and those working on the vice-squad are more satisfied with their career opportunities than those in the traffic department or mounted police. This might be attributed to the actual career opportunities for these positions. However, closer investigation might show that this result is caused by the fact that women are over-represented in those two formerly-mentioned jobs. Women who tend to work for a few years only, tend to be more satisfied with their career opportunities.

The third error relates to the fact that within organizations one frequently finds a preference for male managers, among men as well as among women. More often than not this is attributed to the difference in management styles between men and women. Kanter (1977) reports studies which demonstrate that styles of management may vary according to the manager's power and career opportunities, and that there is a general preference for those management styles that prevail in positions offering a great deal of power and many career opportunities. Such positions, however, are held relatively more often by men. This might imply that it is not so much a question of preference for men, as for managers with power and career opportunities.

3 THE DIVISION OF WORK ACCORDING TO SEX

From the previous sections it has become quite clear that, in The Netherlands, there is a rather stringent division of work, namely into household work and occupational work, and that this division is consistent in the general line with the division of work according to sex. Housekeeping is mainly women's work. But also in paid work there is a segregation between "men's jobs" and "women's jobs". By the term "division of work according to sex" we mean both segregational phenomena. This division of work according to sex has far-reaching consequences for the role attitudes of men and women and for the personal characteristics they may develop. It affects the mutual (power) relationship between the sexes as well as the relationships men/society/family and women/society/family.

The following negative aspects of this situation can be mentioned:

- Women are under-represented in those key-positions from which our society is formed. Hence, the experiences of women in particular are insufficiently included in the process.
- Husband and wife are mutually dependent. He depends on her for his basic needs; her standard of living depends on his income. This may easily cause conflicts. Moreover, when a relationship is not clearly defined because there is no contract, conflicts are hard to deal with.
- When, in the case of a conflict, a family is confronted with outside officials, these are mostly men. The odds are that such an official will sooner identify with the man and fail to see the woman's problems in the right perspective.
- The media pay little attention to the views of women. Usually women are described and filmed by men, which puts them into the position of "the other". It is expecially this aspect that Simone de Beauvoir dealt with in her famous book *The Second Sex*.
- Whenever women deviate from the traditional path and, for example, start working in a man's job, they remain dependent on men's acceptance.
- It is the cumulation of all these aspects that increases women's liability to become alienated.

During the last few years awareness has been growing that the division of work according to sex contributes to these negative aspects. Re-distribution of unpaid and paid work is supported by many people nowadays. In 1961, 61% of the Dutch population between the ages of 16–80 were in favour of men and women sharing in paid work equally. Only twenty percent did not support this opinion. Seventy-two percent of women and men agreed with the suggestion that men and women should equally divide the household chores (Sociaal Cultureel Rapport 1991). Unfortunately, there is still a discrepancy between opinion and behaviour. The picture that emerges from the figures as to the time men and women really spend on household work is less rosy than the results of opinion polls want us to believe.

The Dutch Government sees: "The emancipation process, leading to equal social positions of women and men as an irreversible, and in view of righteousness, laudable development" (Sociaal Cultureel Rapport, 1988). Recently emancipation policy has been strongly emphasized as to the future. The main objective is for the generation that will be 18 after 1991 to become economically self-reliant. Two components can be attributed to the concept of economic self-reliance: financial independence, and the so-called care-independence. Financial independence means having sufficient financial means of one's own to be able to provide for oneself, irrespective of personal, emotional ties and/or way of life. Care-independence means taking care of oneself as regards maintenance and household chores, and sharing the care of others equally between men and women (Werkgroep Vrouw en Werk, 1987, p. 26).

Thinking in terms of "the 1990-generation" is to be found in various government policy-making articles. However, there is a real danger that by the proposed changes women will be ill-treated and their weak social position will be undermined even more.

In their chapter "Emancipation" from the Social and Cultural Report 1988, Niphuis-Nell and Van Delft (1988) deal with the question: is it reasonable to take for granted this economic independence for the 1990-generation? They mention hopeful as well as alarming aspects. A hopeful aspect is the disappearance of differences in education-level between the sexes and the increase of labour participation of women. It is alarming, however, to have to predict that the differences in training courses won't change, that the segregation of occupations won't decrease, and that the 1990-generation will have to cope with a great shortage of day-nursery facilities.

Affirmative action is one of the ways in which women's positions in organizations can be improved. This is generally seen as a coherent entity of measures that are taken in an organization, with a view to achieving proportional representation of women in all occupations within a reasonable time span. In recent years the Dutch Government has tentatively taken the initiative with such projects. The trial project "Affirmative Action for Women in Government Departments" led to the start of affirmative-action programmes in all Departments in 1988. Such policy schemes consist of the following items (De Jong et al., 1983):

1. An analysis of the register of personnel and labour situation.
2. A declaration of intent.
3. Plans relating to informing employees as well as the public about policy.
4. Allocation of the responsibility of the execution of this policy.
5. An inventory of bottlenecks and a survey of the measures to remove them.
6. Procedures for evaluation and internal policy supervision.

The most important item of the policy scheme is the analysis of the personnel register. In the analysis a comparison is made between the build-up of the personnel register according to sex and function, and the data on the supply of the various categories of employees on the labour market. The comparison shows in which groups of jobs women are under-represented. We speak of under-representation when the number of women in a function group is smaller than may be expected from their availability in the occupational population. For each group of employment in which women are under-represented, goals should be formulated. Also a forecast should be made indicating the time needed to reach the objectives.

From discussions in the media it is sometimes feared that affirmative action will lead to a lowering of the quality of staffing. Whether this is true or not will depend upon the definition of "proportional representation". Within the Positive Action Project the parameter was the share of women in the occupational population, in so far as they are sufficiently qualified for the job at hand. For choosing this criterion for the drawing up of target figures, account is taken of differences in occupational training and experience, as well as of the difference in labour market participation between men and women. By applying this criterion there is little chance of degradation of quality in staffing.

Although activity is discernible on many fronts, it will take many more years to reach proportional representation of paid and unpaid work. Some movement is detectable at the level of action groups, trade unions, political parties, and also in the world of science. Over the last few years many fields of study have directly or indirectly been engaged in looking into the consequences of the division of work. As a matter of course the social sciences are among them, but also economics, law and the study of history. There is hardly any field of learning or science which is not involved in this discussion, not even philosophy, medical science, architecture, literature or theology.

4 TASKS FOR WORK AND ORGANIZATIONAL PSYCHOLOGY

The pervasive consequences of the division of work according to sex have already been discussed. It also appeared that the ultimate goal, namely redistribution of work, is endorsed by many people. In striving to achieve change all sorts of questions arise:

- What forms of reduction of working time promote a process of redistribution of labour?
- How can a policy of selection and promotion without discrimination be encouraged?
- How can equal treatment be ensured? For example, what possibilities are offered by the various systems of job evaluation? (See also Chapter 8, Volume 3 of this Handbook.)
- How can an organization help remove the resistance to women in higher positions and men's occupations?
- Under what conditions can women be introduced into men's occupations, such as the navy, the fire brigade and the police force?
- How can women be assisted when resuming paid work after having raised children for a number of years?

Over the last few years, work and organizational psychology has provided some contributions, such as Tijdens' study, "Automation and Women's Labour" (1989), Ott's research on the minority position of policewomen and male nurses (1985), and Demenint-de Jongh's study, "Labour Duration and Emancipation" (1989). More contributions, however, are urgently needed. Work and organizational psychology could serve the purpose of emancipation. It could apply the theories of social psychology, which include a lot of knowledge on sex-role stereotypes and discrimination. Sociology, whose researchers have been trying for quite some time to explain the origins of segregational phenomena also has a part to play. Work and organizational psychology has access to and experience with policies of change in organizations. Undoubtedly a great deal of information provided by this handbook, even if it is not specifically applied to the redistribution of work, can be useful in this context. Therefore, we may justifiably expect that work and organizational psychology can provide a momentous contribution to this new and challenging field of study.

REFERENCES

Beauvoir de, S. (1949), *Le deuxième sexe*. Paris: Éditions gallimard.

Brouns, M., & Schokker, A. (1990). *Arbeidsvraagstukken en sekse* [Questions on labour and sex]. The Hague: Centre for Distribution DOP.

Central Bureau of Statistics, Counting of labour force (1975). Author.

Central Bureau of Statistics, Counting of labour force (1977). Author.

Central Bureau of Statistics, Counting of labour force (1979). Author.

Central Bureau of Statistics, Counting of labour force (1981). Author.

Central Bureau of Statistics, Counting of labour force (1983). Author.

Central Bureau of Statistics, Counting of labour force (1985). Author.

Demenint-de Jongh, M. (1989). *Arbeidsduur, organisatie en emancipatie* [Labour duration, organization and emancipation]. Culemborg, The Netherlands: Lemma B.V.

Economic Survey Australia 1994 (1994). Paris: Organization for Economic Cooperation and Development.

Economic Survey Canada 1990/1991 (1991). Paris: Organization for Economic Cooperation and Development.

Economic Survey New Zealand 1993 (1993). Paris: Organization for Economic Cooperation and Development.

Economic Survey United States 1993 (1993). Paris: Organization for Economic Cooperation and Development.

Enquête Beroepsbevolking [Survey on working population] (1991). The Hague: Central Bureau of Statistics.

Frieze, I.H., Parsons, J.E., Johnson, P.B., Ruble, D.N., & Zellman, G.L. (1978). *Psychological perspective*. New York: W.W. Norton & Company.

Grandjean, E. (1973). *Ergonomics of the home.* London: Taylor & Francis.

Groot, L. (1990). De onderwijs-en beroepssegregatie

tussen mannen en vrouwen in de eerste helft van de jaren tachtig [Segregation of education and occupation between men and women in the early eighties]. *Tijdschrift voor arbeidsvraagstukken* [Periodical for Labour Questions], *6*, (4) 5–25.

Gutek, B.A., Larwood, L., Stromberg, A. (1986). Women at work. In C.L. Cooper, & I. Robertsson (Eds.), *Review of industrial and organizational Psychology*. New York: Wiley.

Gutek, B.A. & Morasch, B. (1982). Sex-role spillover, and sexual harassment of women at work. *Journal of Social Issues*, *38*, (4), 55–74.

Hall, D.T. (1976). *Careers in organizations*. Pacific Pallisades: Goodyear Publications.

Henley, N.M. (1977). *Body Politics: Power, sex and nonverbal communication*. Englewood Cliffs, NJ: Prentice-Hall.

Hennig, M., & Jardim, A. (1977). *The managerial woman*. New York: Anchor Press/Double Day.

Hooghiemstra, B.T.J., & Niphuis-Nell, M. (1993). *Sociale atlas van de vrouw* [Social atlas of women], *Volume II*. The Hague: VUGA.

Izraeli, D.N. (1983). Sex effects or structural effects? An empirical test of Kanter's theory of proportions. *Social Forces*, *62*, 153–165.

Jong, A. de (1983). *Gelijke behandeling en het personeelsbeleid* [Equal treatment and personnel policy]. Deventer: Kluwer.

Kanter, R.M. (1977). *Men and women of the corporation*. New York: Basic Books.

Kauppinen-Toropainen, K. et al. (1983). Job dissatisfaction and work-related exhaustion in male and female work. *Journal of Occupational Behavior*, *4*, 193–207.

Komter, A.E. (1985). *De macht van de vanzelfsprekendheid: Relaties tussen vrouwen en mannen* [The power of the matter-of-course: Relationships between women and men]. The Hague: VUGA.

Loontechnische Dienst [Wage Administration and Control Dept.], Ministry of Social Affairs (1978). *Rapport gelijke kansen voor vrouwen en mannen* [Report on equal opportunities for women and men]. The Hague: Ministry of Social Affairs.

Loontechnische Dienst [Wage Administration and Control Dept.] (1978). *De positie van mannen en vrouwen in het arbeidsproces*. Der Haag: Ministerie van Sociale Zaken en Werkgelegenheid.

Maccoby, E.E., & Jacklin, C.N. (1975). *The psychology of sex differences*. London: Oxford University Press.

Ministry of Social Affairs and Employment (1986). *Ongewenste intimiteiten op het werk: Onderzoek naar ongewenste omgangsvormen tussen de seksen in arbeidsrelaties* [Sexual harassment at work: Study on unwanted manners between the sexes in labour relationships]. The Hague: Ministry of Social Affairs and Employment.

Monchy, C. de (1981). *Gedeelde smart is halve smart (huisvrouw, huishouden en A&O psychologie)* [A sorrow shared is a sorrow halved (housewife, household and W&O psychology]. Doctoral thesis: University of Amsterdam.

Mourik, A. van, & Siegers, J.J. (1988). Ontwikkelingen in de beroepensegregatie tussen mannen en vrouwen 1971–1985 [Developments in job segregation between men and women], 1971–1985. *Economisch-Statistische Berichten (Economic-Statistical Information)*.

Mourik, A. van, & Siegers, J.J. (1982). *Ontwikkelingen in de beroepssegregatie tussen mannen en vrouwen in Nederland 1973–1979* [Developments in job segregation between men and women in the Netherlands] 1973–1979. Research report, University of Utrecht, Economics Institute.

Nieva, V.F., & Gutek, B.A. (1980). Sex effects in evaluation. *Academy of Management Review*, *5*, 267–276.

Niphuis-Nell, M., & Delft, X. van (1988). In *Sociaal en cultureel rapport, 1988*. The Hague, Staatsuitgeverij.

O'Leary, V.E. (1977). *Toward understanding women*. Monterey: Brooks/Cole.

O'Leary, V.E. (1987). Women's relationships with women in the workplace. In B. Gutek, A. Stromberg, & L. Larwood (Eds.), *Women and work* (Vol. 3), Beverly Hills: Sage.

Ott, E.M. (1985). *Assepoesters en kroonprinsen: Een onderzoek naar de minderheidspositie van agentes en verplegers* [Cinderellas and Crown Princes: survey on the minority position of policewomen and male nurses]. Amsterdam: SUA.

Oudijk, C. (1983). *Sociale atlas van de vrouw* [Social atlas of women]. The Hague: Staatsuitgeverij.

Quinn, R.E. (1977). Coping with cupid: The formation, impact and management of romantic relationships in organizations. *Administrative Science Quarterly*, *22*, 30–45.

Rijk, T. de (1989). Ongewenste intimiteiten [Sexual harassment]. *Magazine voor Personeelsmanagement [Magazine for Personnel Management]*, *13*, (3).

Roe, R.A. (1983). *Grondslagen der personeelsselectie* [Foundations of personnel selection]. Assen: Van Gorcum.

Schippers, J.J. (1987). *Beloningsverschillen tussen mannen en vrouwen: Een economische analyse* [Differences in remuneration between men and women; An economic analysis]. Groningen: Wolters Noordhoff.

Sociaal-economische Maandstatistieken [Social-economic monthly statistics] (1990). (pp. 90–92). The Hague: Central Bureau for Statistics.

Sociaal en cultureel rapport [Social and cultural report] *1978* (1978). The Hague: Staatsuitgeverij.

Sociaal en cultureel rapport [Social and cultural report] *1988* (1988). The Hague: Staatsuitgeverij.

Sociaal en cultureel rapport [Social and cultural report] *1991* (1991). The Hague: Staatsuitgeverij.

Sociale en culturele verkenningen [Social and cultural Explorations] *1994* (1994). The Hague: VUGA.

Spangler, E., Gordon, M.A., & Pipkin, R.M. (1978). Token women: An empirical test of Kanters's hypothesis. *American Journal of Sociology, 84,* 160–170.

Statistisch jaarboek [Statistics annual] *1994* (1994). The Hague: SDU publishers.

Statistisch zakboek [Statistics pocket book] *1981* (1981). The Hague: Staatsuitgeverij.

Statistisch zakboek [Statistics pocket book] *1988* (1988). The Hague: Staatsuitgeverij.

Tijdens, K. (1989). *Automatisering en vrouwenarbeid* [Automation and women's labour]. Utrecht: Jan van Arkel.

Werkgroep vrouw en werk [Study group: woman and work]. *Programmeringsstudie vrouwen en economische zelfstandigheid* [Programming study on women and economic self-reliance]. Amsterdam: Amsterdam University.

Wildt, J. de (1989). Samen werken met vrouwen: Ervaringen van een man in vrouwenorganisaties [Working together with women: A man's experiences in working in women's groups]. *Intermediair,* Seminar Affirmative Action.

17

Work and Health Psychology: Methods of Intervention

J.A.M. Winnubst and R.F.W. Diekstra

1 INTRODUCTION

Work and health psychology, a young discipline that has attracted considerable interest over the past decade, originally developed as an offshoot of clinical psychology and industrial and organizational psychology. The rise to prominence of this discipline in the mid-1980s can be at least partly attributed to the rapid increase in industrial absenteeism, and the wastage and early retirement that took place during those years—the results of an organizational revolution that were accentuated by the radical changes that took place in business management.

Mintzberg's characterization of professional bureaucracies increasingly seems apt for many of these new organizations: there is less hierarchy, and greater emphasis on individual responsibility; there is greater freedom to work in one's own way; organization is more flexible; more work is assumed under group tasks, and work itself has become more interesting and yet also more demanding (Mintzberg, 1979; Winnubst, 1993).

In addition to this, continual reorganizations, mergers and changes have an effect on both managers and employees alike. Some observers also identify a profound change in the values and norms that govern people's communal lives, claiming that the protestant work ethic has lost its hegemony and that the significance of working in organizations has concomitantly diminished. It is no longer unusual for people to take voluntary early retirement from their work (Furnham, 1990).

If we add to this the "greying" of the population, it becomes clear that there may well come a time when younger, highly motivated workers are in short supply, with increasing reliance on the older workforce. It is therefore of the utmost importance to ensure that this workforce remains in good health: hence the increasingly high profile and the significance attached to work and health psychology.

The profession could be described as a practical sub-discipline of psychology, concerned with the promotion of health and the ability of people to function effectively in working organizations. The following are important aspects of this sub-discipline:

1. Diagnostics: to identify problems and pressure points by means of observation, questionnaires, interviews and personal conversation.
2. Anamnesis, coaching, counselling and therapy; giving professional assistance to individual employees with problems concerning their health and healthy functioning.
3. Research: the building up of a tradition of research into fatigue and stress.
4. Training and professional education: basic university courses, post-academic and postdoctoral training to be set up and a system of certification and quality control developed.
5. Consultancy: the provision of advice on work and health in a multidisciplinary context.

As a distinct professional field, work and health psychology was given prominence in The Netherlands by the publication of a handbook in two volumes (Schabracq & Winnubst, 1993; Winnubst & Schabracq, 1992). An English language *Handbook of Work and Health Psychology*, with mainly international authors, appeared in 1996, edited by Schabracq, Winnubst, and Cooper. A Polish language version will be published in 1998. The field has been in existence much longer than this, however. *Clinical Psychology in Industrial Organizations*, for instance, was published in the United States in the early 1970s (Abt & Riess, 1971). Since the professional opportunities for these psychologists depend partly on developments in Dutch legislation and partly on the role of the work and organization consultants, we shall first look at current legislation and its consequences. Turning to the theoretical side, we shall then look at a model framework with which we hope to be able to underpin this field of study: the work stress model. Following this, various approaches to preventive and curative intervention will be outlined.

2 WORK, HEALTH AND WELFARE: LEGISLATION

In 1996 in The Netherlands, out of a population of 15 million people, 1 million were in one way or another unfit for work. In addition to this, there was a high level of unemployment and the level of absenteeism through illness, certainly in an international perspective, was also relatively high. Within the frame of existing social legislation (disablement, illness absenteeism and unemployment) this cost the country, in 1994, around 50 thousand million guilders. The Dutch community can no simply longer afford such sums. As a consequence, the government now pursues a dual policy aimed at reducing the flood of workers signing on for social disablement benefit. On the one hand, by means of new legislation, they are attempting to make the flight from working life far less attractive and so curb the level of this unsuitability for work, and on the other hand, by adjusting existing legislation, they are attempting to improve working conditions (Amendment ARBO law, 1994).

It is now legally required of all employers that they must make use of an ARBO service (a new Dutch socio-medical service). The employer is now compelled to implement a policy that deals with illness absenteeism (Reduction of Illness Absenteeism Law, 1994). The employer is encouraged—indeed urged—to treat more seriously the questions of the quality of work and the welfare of the workers in his or her company.

Similar legislation is being introduced in more and more countries to regulate working conditions. The "Occupational Safety and Health Act" has been in operation in the USA since 1970; the "Norwegian Working Environment Act" in Norway since 1977; the "Swedish Work Environment Act" in Sweden since 1977 also; and in Germany since 1981 the "Centre for Accident Prevention and Occupational Medicine".

The Dutch health and safety (ARBO) legislation stipulates four areas of necessary expertise: the work and health doctor, the safety consultant, the work hygienist and the work and organization consultant. These together constitute the core of the new ARBO service. Of these, the work and health psychologist identifies emphatically with the fourth role, that of the work and organization consultant.

For the purposes of this chapter, the point to

emphasize is that the government has recently taken the initiative in attaching much more significance to policy and legislation in the area of work, health and welfare, and that the employer, albeit sometimes reluctantly, is following. In the context of the possible role of psychologists, it is significant that a large percentage of the disabled are laid off on grounds of psychological problems (40%) or of mobility complaints (40%). These latter complaints frequently also include a psychological component, as is also the case with heart and other vascular illnesses, asthma, and so on.

The work and health expert can play an important role both in tracking down work problems and in their prevention and treatment. After first looking at an organizing theoretical framework, various aspects of its application will be dealt with.

3 A FRAMEWORK: THE WORK STRESS APPROACH

A number of different approaches to work stress can be identified in the literature of work and health psychology. According to many researchers, stress is a normal phenomenon in organizations (see, for example, Karasek & Theorell, 1990; and Chapter 7 in Volume 2 of this handbook). For a healthy and satisfying life, a certain degree of tension is essential. It is rather the continuous lack of tension or challenge or, on the other hand, the continuous subjection to excessive stress or pressure that can undermine one's pleasure in life, one's work, and health. A certain tension or discrepancy between the demands of a job and the available skills and means (personal, material and social) are associated with a relatively high level of welfare. It is where the level of such tension or discrepancy is too high or too low that problems appear. In the literature, these extremes are known respectively as BOSS (Burn Out Stress Syndrome) or ROSS (Rust Out Stress Syndrome), syndromes characterized by symptoms or complaints that are in large part identical. These typically include such feelings as lack of motivation and worry, but also physical symptoms like sleep, stomach and muscle complaints, headaches, and high blood pressure. Changes in behaviour also associated with the syndrome include poor performance, an increased consumption of addictive substances, a higher chance of falling victim to accidents, and suchlike.

The optimal level of stress, or the amount of pressure and tension under which a person functions optimally, not only differs from one individual to another, but also changes significantly for the same individual over time. In this context, not only do the characteristics of individuals play a significant role, but also the various characteristics of the situation or the environment in which the person concerned has to function.

It follows from this that the degree to which work stress erodes a worker's well-being or leads to health problems is determined by the way in which work-specific factors, individual characteristics and social factors or environmental characteristics interact. This insight, which is widely acknowledged these days (Health Council, 1992), has spawned a number of so-called interactional, or relational models of work stress, all of which share more points of correspondence than difference.

In this chapter, we shall use the term "work stress" in the restricted sense of *distress*, i.e. dysfunctional stress or stress which manifests itself in physical, psychological or social dysfunction (we shall leave out of consideration here the function-enhancing *eustress*). We thus follow a definition of work stress consistent with that of the World Health Organization (WHO), which says that work stress is the negatively experienced condition which follows from the fact that someone is not in a state, or does not deem him- or herself to be in a state to fulfil the demands or expectations placed on him or her by the work situation; and which is coupled with complaints or physical, psychological and/or social dysfunction. Implicit in this definition, of course, is the further definition of health formulated in the constitution of the WHO (1987), which reads: "Health is not merely the absence of disease, but a complete state of physical, mental and social wellbeing".

Consonant with this definition, therefore, work stress is to be seen and studied as the result of the interaction of a series of factors or causes of stress, designated here as *stressors*, the most notable being the following (see also Janman, Jones, Payne, & Rick, 1988; Karasek & Theorell, 1990; Kompier & Marcelissen, 1990; Matteson & Ivancevich, 1987):

1. Job demands (their number, nature and pattern). In the first place, this is a matter of the content of work, including the amount of that work, the work rate, the level of responsibility and the extent of conflict and inconsistency in the demands of the job. This also includes the extent of freedom of decision making, and the possibilities available for carrying out the work and for resolving work problems.
2. The available backup or social support for coping with the demands of the job. Industrial relations are involved here: the management methods employed by managerial heads and supervisors, relations with colleagues, available structures for consultation. Social support in relation to work can also come from other sources than the work situation itself, and can take different forms. For this reason, several authors (e.g. Karasek & Theorell, 1990) draw a distinction between three types of backup: support in the emotional sense, informational assistance, and assistance in the adaptive modification of behaviour.
3. The material resources available for coping with job demands: we refer to particular aspects of the working conditions, such as availability of the necessary material and personal resources to satisfy the job demands adequately. Is the strength of personnel adequate for the tasks assigned? Is the equipment provided and the available space adequate? Are they both suitable and operational? Are the technical provisions for summoning assistance adequate in case of either danger or the threat of danger?
4. Personal attitude to the demands of the job, plus the personal qualities and skills a person can command in relation to those demands. One might think here of a person's estimation of whether the job is worthwhile, his or her degree of self-confidence and his or her self-image, belief in his or her own competence and coping ability. The presence or absence of personality traits or disorders that could interfere with the fulfilment of job demands is also relevant here. And finally, there is the question of whether or not a person possesses the social, communicative, problem-solving and intellectual skills that are either necessary or desirable in order to do the job.
5. A person's physical suitability to the task of satisfying job demands: the questions of whether someone has a physical/sensory disease or handicap, what is his or her general condition of physical health, the extent of any stress sensitivity (also hereditary sensitivity to stimuli).
6. The organizational and extra-organizational social context in which the job has to be carried out: this includes not only the general characteristics of the company or working organization but also the living conditions of the workers.

Within the framework of this way of thinking, work stress, as the dependant variable, can be explained as the consequence of the discrepancies (which differ from one person to another, from one department to another, from firm to firm and family to family) between the demands of a job (factor 1) on one side, and the available social backup, resources, personal attitudes and skills, physical characteristics and general organization and social environmental characteristics (factors 2–6) on the other.

The further point that should be emphasized here is that work stress, according to this approach, is not to be explained a priori, or even exclusively, in terms of the demands made in the workplace itself. There are other demands upon individuals whose source lies not in the workplace but in other areas of life, such as the family, relations with partners, and the neighbourhood a worker lives in (i.e. the so-called "extra-organizational stressors": see Matteson & Ivancevich, 1987) that can all play a significant role.

The more the number of potentially stressful tasks in different compartments of an individual's life increase, the greater is the risk that the resources and support available will be inadequate to take care of all the demands imposed, including work, with the inevitable result that either particular responsibilities are neglected in favour of others, or that all obligations are carried out at an unsatisfactory level. The person concerned then finds him or herself saddled with the further load of countermanding the specific stressful consequences of his or her neglect, and with this increased load of responsibility in the face of inadequate backup, resources and skills, the whole problem—and crucially the work stress—can of course only be exacerbated. A downward spiral gradually supervenes, a spiral of worsening functioning in the workplace, in the person's private situation and other social networks, leading ultimately to a breakdown in health.

4 THE IMPORTANCE OF DIAGNOSTICS

In any organization, an adequate "work and health" policy has to begin with a sound diagnostic provision for its employees. "Risk analysis" is the term that regularly surfaces in the legislation. The employer must ascertain which operations and workplaces entail a higher risk to health and safety. In this chapter, we shall concentrate on that area where work and health psychology can make its pre-eminent contribution, the field of health and welfare, ignoring for the most part such other aspects as work hygiene and company safety.

Diagnostics can be practised at different levels: the individual level, the level of the department and at the level of the organization as a whole.

Psychodiagnostics plays an important role in the selection of personel. It is essential, before appointing someone to any operation, to give full attention to the question of whether that particular person is suited to the particular operation. Some occupations demand a great deal of resilience from the employee.

The culture, structure and design of the organization form the subject matter of more integrated diagnostics. Many organizations are these days engaged in the processes of re-engineering. Consultants seldom realize, however, that there is a price to pay for novel methods of organization, in the sense that these often lead to dramatic increases in illness, absenteeism and early retirement as a result. Not every individual can tolerate the high rates of change within and without organizations to the same degree (see also Chapter 9 in Volume 4 on the assessment of organizational change). It may therefore be desirable to begin any such re-engineering project on the basis of a properly constituted organizational diagnostics.

Meulenbeld and Van Lingen (1993) discuss an interesting survey of diagnostic instruments employed in the field of work and health, carried out by the Dutch Institute for Working Conditions in collaboration with the Dutch Institute for Preventive Health Care (TNO). Out of 225 instruments, around 50 were described and evaluated. At the end of their book, the authors set out their "top 10": those identified as the most widely used diagnostic instruments in industrial healthcare in The Netherlands:

- Periodic medical investigation.
- Welfare at work.
- Inspection of working conditions.
- Reports of occupational illness.
- Qucstionnaires on health experience.
- Advice about lifting.
- Sick building syndrome.
- General road transport and haulage business reconnaissance.
- Periodic investigation of operations.
- Questionnaires on organizational stress.

5 TOWARDS A MULTI-DISCIPLINARY APPROACH

According to Schabracq (Winnubst & Schabracq, 1992), the work and health psychologist is a more generally oriented psychologist whose expertise embraces organization theory and industrial psychology, group dynamics, psycho- and organizational diagnostics, stress intervention, psychopathology and advice on social security.

In the organizational context, his or her role is within a team of specialists. As we shall explain in Section 7, his or her co-specialists comprising this team include the company doctor and company social worker, the line head and engineer, the head of personnel and the manager. He or she is also a member of the previously mentioned ARBO team, along with the company doctor, the work hygienist and the safety consultant. It is therefore essential that he or she should be able to cooperate well with others.

Many psychologists commit the beginner's error of overestimating their own importance, thus making their position impossible from the outset. The psychologist must realize that he or she is a relative latecomer to the organization; the industrial medical expert specifically plays a far more central role in the field of power in question, and next to them the manager, engineer and head of personnel also occupy more central positions in the organization than the psychologist. Tobias (1990) and Nathans (1991) give a highly engaging account of how consultant relations can be developed within a company, what problems of prejudice and bias one can encounter, what confusions of role are possible and what pitfalls should be avoided. The consultant must acquire insight into his or her own functioning and develop his or her own advisory strategies.

Whereas the consultant who works in relation to a team is mainly confronted with general questions of prevention and health and welfare problems, the independently-established work and health psychologist is much more concerned with their cure.

6 PREVENTION OR CURE?

The interventions open to the work and health psychologist who works in collaboration with professionals from other disciplines either within a company or an ARBO service, are preventive interventions. They are part of a policy whose aim is to promote the better, healthier functioning of the employee through information and advice, by means of periodic testing, risk analysis, organizational design, the re-designing of jobs and operations, by having a policy for career and ageing, and so on. Preventive intervention of this kind is naturally best implemented before damage is done, but where from time to time problems do arise, such as stress, burnout or conflict, more curative interventions are undertaken.

In the following sections, several possibilities for both preventive and curative intervention will be dealt with.

7 THE WORK AND HEALTH PSYCHOLOGIST AS CONSULTANT IN PREVENTIVE INTERVENTION

The health and welfare of employees are strongly correlated with adequate industrial health care, with the way their function is articulated within the organization, with the way that management operates, and with the opportunities available for building a career within the organization. The work and health psychologist has an advisory role to play in relation to all these matters.

7.1 Socio-medical counselling and industrial health programmes

Psychological complaints and disorders that arise in the workplace can be dealt with by counselling under the sponsorship of a socio-medical team, which might consist of a doctor specializing in work and health, a manager, a personnel functionary, an industrial psychologist and an industrial social worker. The function of the team is to give an early warning of any possible problems that may arise in the work situation. In the first instance, the team should as far as possible try to prevent problems from arising, and then to deal with them if they do. If an employees's psychological problems are so complex that the team cannot adequately handle them, the individual can be refered to a Regional Mental Welfare Institute (in The Netherlands), a specialist psychotherapeutic agency or an independent psychologist. Whether such ideal practice obtains in reality, of course, is another question. Schröer (1993) carried out an interesting investigation in this area, looking at the nature of nervous exhaustion, what help was available and the extent of absenteeism. In the case of nervous strain, those concerned first sought the help of their general practitioner. Sometimes this was followed by referral to a Regional Mental Welfare Institute or to general social work. But what is striking is that the industrial and the insurance medical consultancy sector was never involved. Schröer recommends that this sector should be involved to a much greater extent than hitherto.

Another problem to which Van der Klink and Sijtsma (1993) draw attention is that there may well be discrepancies between the prevailing values of a socio-medical team and those held by an external assistance agency. For the team, health is always connected with a person's ability to function effectively, whereas this is not always the case with external therapists. A team should ensure as a matter of priority that such discrepancies between internal and external values are kept to a minimum.

Another area in which the work and health psychologist can make his or her presence felt is that of the company's welfare programmes. Such programmes are introduced to promote the health of employees by appealing to their way of living, and to deal with tension and other factors that constitute a health risk. The basic idea of company welfare programmes is that they should help to keep medical costs within limits, that the application of workers should improve, that illness absenteeism be reduced and productivity raised. The last of these objectives in particular has evoked some criticism (Schreurs & Winnubst, 1992). Within the framework of such programmes, the interventions (sometimes with a curative aspect) that have most frequently been developed have been in the areas of:

- Weight reduction: obesity is a risk factor for both heart and vascular diseases. Such programmes are often behavioural-therapeutic in nature and are even more often set up as mutual competitions. The great problem with weight reduction is the difficulty of achieving a permanent change in people's harmful eating habits.
- Stopping smoking: smoking is an important risk factor, both for heart and vascular diseases and for cancer. It is found to be very difficult to stop smoking and the rate of recidivism is a further problem here.
- Reducing alcohol intake: excessive consumption of alcohol at work is a growing problem; "employee assistance" programmes, supervised by a work and health psychologist or a clinical psychologist are increasingly coming into fashion.
- Fitness: a greater degree of physical fitness leads to a reduction of risk factors for heart and vascular problems, illness absenteeism and over-consumption of medical drugs.

Organizations are increasingly providing the facilities for such initiatives, and insurance companies too are showing more interest in the possibility of achieving a reduction in premiums and in the promotion of health; all of which indicates that we have now entered the stage where it is essential that these programmes should be evaluated. Positive gains have been clearly demonstrated in the form of employees' enhanced awareness of their own welfare and in the fact that that such an industrial welfare policy has also encouraged the introduction of other forms of health promotion (Schreurs, Keilman, Severijnen, & Winnubst, 1993), which focus specifically on:

- Hypertension: high blood pressure is also an important risk factor for heart and vascular disease. Measuring blood pressure, setting dietary regimes and remedial therapy are employed alongside relaxation exercises and courses in stress management. The programmes of this kind are generally successful and lead to genuine reductions in blood pressure (De Mey, 1992; Van Dixhoorn, 1990);
- Back pain: chronic back pain is an important root cause of absenteeism and early retirement. The introduction of back training, which includes information, physiotherapy and psychological counselling, is most important. Critical evaluation, however, leads to the disappointing conclusion that, in general, only short-term benefits are achieved (Schreurs et al., 1993).
- Health education: health eduation in the workplace is an area that for the most part remains to be developed. It is anticipated, however, that once the proper health and safety legislation is in force, progress will rapidly follow.

An interesting investigation undertaken by Maes, Kittel, Scholten, & Verhoeven (1994) looked into the effects of a total industrial health programme implemented by Brabantia, a Dutch manufacturing firm making household articles. The authors found that this kind of programme led both to a definite gain in health and a fall in illness absenteeism. The health gains were evident in a greater participation in fitness classes, a healthier diet and lower levels of smoking and alcohol intake; but once the novelty faded and the employees' enthusiasm lapsed, illness absenteeism rose once more. The interest of the employees also dwindled if no official time was allotted to the programme, demanding that they devote more of their own free time. In short, a rather patchy picture was presented of the success of such a programme.

7.2 Quality of work and organizational design

A question that is increasingly raised in this area concerns the notion of "healthy" work and "healthy" jobs. It has been obvious for many years that monotonous work in short cyclical tasks can cause intolerably high levels of both physical and mental wear and tear, whereas giving employees more responsibility and more autonomy makes their work more interesting and more challenging. There are indications that increased control over their work not only mitigates stress, but also has positive aspects with regard both to the general state of health and specifically to the functioning of the immune system (Furda & Meijman, 1992). The role played by tiredness is also significant, both at work and in employees' recovery time, i.e. the time needed to recuperate after a working week (Meijman, 1993).

Irrespective of the design of the task and whether or not the work is interesting, it is just as important to determine employees' level of tolerance of work stress. There is a suggestion that more recent forms of organization give rise to new forms of stress. The flat, open, flexible organization in which integrated, autonomous tasks play a great role can lead to feelings of insecurity and overload (Winnubst, 1993). As part of a multidisciplinary team, the work and health psychologist gives advice in the area of operation planning and the quality of work. What he or she must always bear in mind is that work, as well as being interesting, autonomous and varied, must be so organized as to be able to sustain a working life of many years.

7.3 Management Development

Koopman (1993) points out that the manager of the future will have to deal with the following developments:

- The product is becoming ever more intangible, as a result of which the emphasis comes to lie on the provision of services, with a strongly enhanced client-orientation.
- The emphasis increasingly—and increasingly strongly—falls on information technology, with concomitant loss of many operations and the appearance of new ones.
- Organizations are increasingly becoming managed in a professional manner.
- More prominence is given these days to the ability to influence the culture of an organization. Motivating the employee and creating a product-image and an organization's own culture have become more important considerations.

Managers must, to an increasing extent, operate in a context of decentralized forms of organization, in business units with a strong emphasis on internal entrepreneurship, in a context of horizontal leadership and team management. All these aspects place high demands on the selection and training of management. For a more extensive treatment of this theme of Management Development, refer to Chapter 11 in this Volume.

In the same context, coaching and psychological counselling for managers is in the ascendant. Tobias (1990) discusses this trend from a clinical psychological perspective. Because of the multiplicity of changes and the rate of change, managers need to have access to personal counselling, for there are often too few suitable persons in their working environment to whom they can turn.

7.4 Human Resource Management

Schalk (1992) and Mensink (1993) make an explicit connection between Human Resource Management (HRM) and work and health psychology. HRM is the primary area of personnel policy, whose central underlying principle is that the top management of an organization should honour the philosophy that the optimal use of the human factor leads to better performance by the organization as a whole. In this sense, HRM meshes perfectly with the objectives of modern management development. The HRM policy integrates easily into the strategic management of the organization.

Within HRM, Mensink particularly sees a distinctive role for the work and health psychologist in consultancy. He recognizes a distinction between:

- Consultation with managers; over how to conduct discussions about absence, how to participate in socio-medical teams, and how to supervise the return from long illness.
- Straightforward consultation with fellow-workers, concerning careers, absence through illness, and such problems as rejection and burnout.

The work and health psychologist also has a contribution to make in the specific areas dealt with in Section 8.

8 CURATIVE INTERVENTIONS BY THE WORK AND HEALTH PSYCHOLOGIST

The expertise of the work and health psychologist, at both basic and more advanced levels and in addition to diagnostics and research, includes consultancy, anamnesis (functional analysis), coaching, counselling and therapy; all of which focus on work and the organization. Before looking in more detail at the latter four approaches in turn, we shall first say something about the differences between them.

Anamnesis (functional analysis) is the systematic charting of the background to problems at the personal level (and therefore differs from organizational diagnostics).

Coaching is the systematic supervision of workers and managers in their functioning and with specific reference to problems that arise in and through their work.

Counselling as a term has here (perhaps more strongly than is usually the case) the connotation of assistance, where problems are of such a nature as to threaten serious dysfunction.

Psychotherapy is the professional help offered by specially-trained psychotherapists to overcome problems of dysfunction and emotional disturbance (anxieties, phobias, obsessions).

8.1 Stress management

Working in an operational organization always causes stress. Diekstra, De Heus, Schouten, and Houtman (1994) have shown in an investigation involving 15,000 employees in The Netherlands that the following measures are adopted, either by individuals or by companies, to combat stress.

The top ten measures adopted by individual persons to combat stress were:

1. Talking, most importantly with colleagues, in order to cultivate an equable social climate.
2. Involvement in active sport, including cycling, speed walking and fitness programmes.
3. Maintaining a certain distance, becoming less involved in the work.
4. Trying to relax by walking, doing yoga, self-training.
5. Getting things in proportion, finding significance in other things outside work.
6. Engaging in a hobby, such as gardening, reading, listening to music.
7. Ensuring a fair sharing of the work, setting one's own limits.
8. Leading a healthy life: sleeping more, getting adequate rest and eating a healthy diet.
9. Changing one's job; resigning.
10. Planning work activities.

The top ten measures adopted by firms to combat stress were:

1. The regular, structured holding of work consultations; team meetings.
2. Taking on and making available more personnel; hiring temporary workers.

3. Holding discussions with management; holding operational discussions.
4. The redistribution of activities, better coordination, limiting activities.
5. Informal discussions, looking after colleagues, and promoting frank contact and exchange.
6. Promotion of a friendly social climate, creating a sociable working atmosphere and a good team spirit.
7. Setting priorities among activities; attending to clarity, firm arrangements, planning.
8. Openness and straightforwardness over the way the affairs of the organization are going; supplying information.
9. Flexible working hours; adapting times of work, creating possibilities for part-time work.
10. Giving responsibility and gearing operations to the worker.

This inventory says little about the effectiveness of the measures identified, but that was not its aim; nor does the survey say anything about the frequency of incidence of stress. What it does make clear, however, is the preferences of both personnel and organizations when it comes to dealing with stress.

Some employees show stress reactions only occasionally; for example, only when deadlines have to be met or when exceptional circumstances obtain, such as when the apparatus that has to be used is faulty. Others wrestle constantly with difficult working conditions and with the stress reactions that result. Sources of stress include monotony, exclusion from decisions over one's own task, disturbed working rhythm, overwork, conflicts, reorganizations, and threat of dismissal (Cooper & Davidson, 1987).

Stress reactions appear more often among workers of type A behavioural style (hasty, competitive, slightly hostile), and of these mainly among those who work in the middle to lower echelons of the company. Stress reactions appear less often among workers in the middle to lower sections of a company where they enjoy the adequate support of their section-head (Marcelissen, 1987).

The considerable research on stress undertaken over the last 25 years (Karasek, 1992) teaches that interventions can be effectively aimed at

- The level of organization: the design of sociotechnical alternatives in production; new ways of managing; more involvement and greater scope for employees.
- The level of the production group (or department): working in autonomous groups; enriching work tasks; working in teams.
- The level of the individual: cognitive restructuring; relaxation techniques; individual supervision; resolution of conflicts; raising motivation; healthier living (fitness).

Karasek (1992) reviews 19 case studies of stress prevention through the reorganization of work. What struck him most forcibly was that in one of the careers generally considered most stressful, that of the miner, the physical demands constituted only 25% of the cited sources of stress considered most threatening, whereas the psychological demands constituted 75% of the stress sources considered most threatening. His conclusion is that far more attention should be paid to psychosocial causes of stress.

The literature in this field is so extensive that it not feasible to summarize it here. (The reader is referred to reviews by Karasek & Theorell, 1990; Schreurs & Winnubst, 1992; Van der Klink, 1993; and Chapter 7 of Volume 2 of this handbook). Effect studies, however, are for the most part lacking; this is an area that calls out for serious investigation.

Van der Hek and Klomp (in preparation) have recently carried out a meta-analysis of the effects of interventions designed to counteract work stress. Their review, which covers the period between 1987 and 1994, critically compares the results of 26 investigations on the basis of a number of methodological and statistical criteria such as presence of a control group, the kind and number of interventions, assignment of participants to groups on a random basis, data collection prior to the interventions, the method of data analysis and reported efficacy of interventions. With regard to efficacy, the interventions turn out to be interchangeable: relaxation exercises appear to be no more effective than training in social skills or assertivity. The majority of studies report on the efficacy of the interventions, with improvements registered in such dimensions as emotional fatigue, anger, illness absenteeism, anxiety, work stress, psychological complaints, assertivity, depression, hostility and blood pressure. The authors explicitly state that future research should take cost effectiveness as an important theme. All studies report at least some of the dimensions cited above, but it should be emphasized once again that in general it remains unclear which interventions are responsible for improvements in which dimensions.

Psychologists of various backgrounds—work and organization psychologists, clinical psychologists, and more recently work and health psychologists—have all been active in this area of stress management.

8.2 Dealing with conflict

Prein (1993) also sees intervention in conflict explicitly as an area of work for the work and health psychologist. The psychologist can act as a third party, i.e as a bystander who is not primarily involved in the conflict, to alter the course of a potentially highly negative spiral through a process of problem resolution (see also Chapter 15 in this Volume). The research of Prein and Van der Vliert has shown that this can have important positive effects on health and can also lead to a reduction in the levels of illness absenteeism and early retirement.

8.3 Burnout

Terluin and Van der Klink (1993) describe overwork or nervous exhaustion as a sudden decompensation resulting from the psycho-social overload of an individual who was previously functioning normally. Other terms employed for this condition are "burnout", "hyperesthetic-emotional syndrome", "neurasthenia", "reactive depression". These conditions occur more frequently among middle-aged persons who work in a very conscientious manner, who invest a great deal in their work and in courses and who suffer from overload, particularly in situations of conflict. The phenomenon is more frequently seen among police officers, nurses, and educators, but also in professions involving a high degree of monotony in the work.

Schaufeli (1990) deals with a number of interventions in cases of nervous exhaustion: these interventions can be individual or interpersonal, directed either at the workplace or at the level of organization. For the most part, these interventions correspond with those work routines generally identified under stress management. Schaufeli also deals with a burnout treatment programme of his own, mainly based on directive behavioural therapy. The treatment focuses initially on the personal complaints, then subsequently on problems at work and finally on the more fundamentally significant problems. Because nervous exhaustion is so overwhelmingly a preliminary to early retirement it needs very careful handling.

8.4 Post-traumatic stress syndrome (PTSS)

Kleber (1986, 1992) describes post-traumatic stress disturbances as blockages in the normal processes of coming to grips with life's experiences. PTSS has been found to originate increasingly often in events caused by or at work. For instance counter personnel who witness or experience robberies; machinists and drivers who experience suicides and accidents; pilots, pursers and stewardesses who may have survived air accidents. If the traumatized employee is unable to put these terrible experiences behind them, the trauma is continually revisited, the person withdraws, is unable to sleep properly, becomes depressed and no longer functions properly in his or her job. Not infrequently, this situation leads on to more serious problems, such as resort to drink, phobias, somatic or sexual problems—such as impotence, frigidity and emotional blockage in intimate relations (Carlier & Gersons, 1993).

Psychologists have an important role to play, both in the preventive training of employees who run considerable risks, and in the initial reception of potential victims of trauma. Trauma desensitization, hypnotherapy and psychodynamic therapy are all employed in the treatment of PTSS. Such treatments call for great care, a high degree of training and considerable expertise.

9 CONCLUSION

There are of course other areas where the expertise of the work and health psychologist is called upon, such as counselling employees with career problems, providing the help and support needed to work through loss, for example, mourning the death of a loved one, training in self-efficacy, improving self-management and correcting unproductive personal styles. Personal counselling in cases of absence due to illness should perhaps be noted here as a function of special significance. In the context of the present chapter, however, it is not feasible to give a complete account of these further areas; the reader is referred to the handbooks cited in Section 1.

To summarize a rather rapid account of the identity and function of this developing professional discipline, we can assert with confidence that work and health psychology represents the first response to the demand for more expertise and professionalism wherever questions concerning the health and welfare of working individuals are raised. The work stress model suggests both a theoretical framework and a point of departure for future research: a site to build upon a tradition of work and health psychology that has been established for several decades.

The new Dutch legislation offers a framework for the work and health psychologist to collaborate with other professionals. In cases where curative interventions are required, work and organizational psychology again offers an excellent starting point. When it comes to the improvement of the quality of work, the work and health psychologist will necessarily play a supplementary rather than a leading role, since the company doctor, manager, engineer and head of personnel have all already been involved with this issue for a considerable time. Where the issue turns on the treatment of health problems that have arisen at work, however, the roles are different. Here, the clinical added value of the work and health psychologist is more obvious, particularly if he or she is willing to undertake further training and qualification and actually to participate in the shop-floor world of industrial health and welfare.

REFERENCES

Abt, L.E., & Riess, B.F. (1971). *Clinical psychology in industrial organizations.* New York: Grune and Stratton.

Buunk, B., & Wolff, C.J. de (1988). Sociaal psychologische aspecten van stress op het werk. In P.J.D. Drenth, H. Thierry, & C.J. de Wolff (Eds.), *Nieuw handboek arbeids-en organisatie-psychologie.* Deventer: Van Loghum Slaterus.

Carlier, I.V.E., & Gersons, B.P.R. (1993). Posttraumatische stress-stoornissen. In J.J.L. van der Klink (Ed.), *Psychische problemen en de werksituatie. Handboek voor een actieve sociaal-medische begeleiding.* Amsterdam: NIA.

Cooper, C.L., & Davidson, M. (1987). Sources of stress and their relation to stressors in non-working environments. In R. Kalimo, M.A. El-Batawi, & C.L. Cooper (Eds.), *Psychosocial factors at work.* Geneva: World Health Organization.

Diekstra, R.F.W., Heus, P. de, Schouten, M., & Houtman, I.L.D. (1994). *Werken onder druk: Een onderzoek naar omvang en faktoren van werkstress in Nederland.* Den Haag, Ministerie van Sociale Zaken en Werkgelegenheid: VUGA.

Diekstra, R.F.W., & Moritz, B.J.M. (1982). De ontredderende werkloosheid. In A. Heertje & E. van der Wolk. *Werkloosheid: Verwording en verwachting.* Amsterdam: Keesing.

Dixhoorn, J. van (1990). *Relaxation therapy in cardiac rehabilitation.* Proefschrift, Rotterdam: Rotterdam Universiteitsdrukkerij.

Furda, J., & Meijman, T. (1992). Druk en dreiging, sturing of stress. In J.A.M. Winnubst & M.J. Schabracq (Eds.), *Handboek arbeid en gezondheid psychologie: Hoofdthema's (Vol I).* Utrecht: Lemma.

Furnham, A. (1990). *The Protestant Ethic: The psychology of work-related beliefs and behaviours.* London: Routledge.

Gehrels, C.G., & Lemmens, R.H.M.M. (1993). *Handboek verzuimmanagement.* Utrecht: De Tijdstroom.

Gezondheidsraad: Commissie Stress en Gezondheid (1992). *Stress en Gezondheid.* Den Haag: Gezondheidsraad. Publicatie nr A92/2.

Hackman, J.R., & Oldham, G.H. (1980). *Work redesign.* Reading, MA: Addison-Wesley.

Healey, C.C. (1982). *Career development.* Boston: Allyn & Bacon.

Hek, H. van der, & Klomp, H.N. (in preparation). The impact of occupational stress management programmes: Practical overview of research.

Horowitz, M.J. (1976). *Stress response syndromes.* New York: Jason Aronson.

Janman, K., Jones, J.G., Payne, R.L., & Rick, J.T. (1988). Clustering individuals as a way of dealing with multiple predictors in occupational stress research. *Behavioral Medicine, 14,* 17–29.

Karasek, R.A. (1992). *Conditions of work digest: Preventing stress at work.* Geneva: International Labour Office.

Karasek, R.A., & Theorell, T. (1990). *Healthy work: stress, productivity and the reconstruction of work life.* New York: Basic Books.

Keirse, E.A.C.G. (1993). Rouw. In J.J.L. van der Klink (Ed.), *Psychische problemen en de werksituatie: Handboek voor een actieve sociaal-medische begeleiding.* Amsterdam: NIA.

Kelley, H.H. (1973). The processes of causal attribution. *American Psychologist, 28,* 107–128.

Kleber, R.J. (1986). *Traumatische ervaringen, gevolgen en verwerking.* Lisse: Swets & Zeitlinger.

Kleber, R.J. (1992). Acute stress in de werksituatie. In J.A.M. Winnubst & M.J. Schabracq (Eds.), *Handboek arbeid en gezondheid psychologie: Hoofdthema's (Vol. I).* Utrecht: Lemma.

Klink, J.J.L. van der (Ed.) (1993). *Psychische problemen en de werksituatie.* Amsterdam: NIA.

Klink, J.J.L. van der, & Sijtsma, F.M. (1993). Strategisch netwerk; systeemdenken. In J.J.L. van der Klink (Ed.), *Psychische problemen en de werksituatie: Handboek voor een actieve sociaal-medische begeleiding.* Amsterdam: NIA.

Kompier, M.A.J., & Marcelissen, F.H.G. (1990). *Handboek werkstress.* Amsterdam: NIA.

Koopman, P.L. (1993). Management development. In M.J. Schabracq & J.A.M. Winnubst (Eds.), *Handboek arbeid en gezondheid psychologie: Toepassingen (Vol. II).* Utrecht: Lemma.

Lambeck, J. (1990). *Outplacement.* Den Haag: Nijgh & Van Ditmar.

Lazarus, R.S. (1984). On the primacy of cognition. *American Psychologist, 39,* 124–129.

Loo, E.L.H.M. van de, & Jong, R.D. de (1993). Stressverwerking en –hantering. In J.J.L. van der Klink (Ed.), *Psychische problemen en de werksituatie: Handboek voor een actieve sociaal-medische begeleiding.* Amsterdam: NIA.

Maes, S., Kittel, F., Scholten, H., & Verhoeven, C. (1994). *Gezonder werken bij Brabantia.* Den Haag: Sdu.

Marcelissen, F.H.G. (1987). *Gangmakers van het stressproces.* Leiden: NIPG/TNO.

Marcelissen, F.H.G., Winnubst, J.A.M., Buunk, B., & Wolff, C.J. de (1988). Social support and occupational stress: A causal analysis. *Social Science and Medicine, 26,* 365–373.

Matteson, M.T., & Ivancevich, J.M. (1987). *Controlling work stress.* San Francisco: Jossey-Bass.

Meijman, T. (1993). De vermoeidheidsbeleving: Beschouwingen over het begrip en de meting ervan. In M.J. Schabracq & J.A.M. Winnubst (Eds.), *Handboek arbeid en gezondheid psychologie: Toepassingen.* Utrecht: Lemma.

Mensink, J.C.M. (1993). Human Resource Management and consultancy. In M.J. Schabracq & J.A.M. Winnubst (Eds.), *Handboek arbeid en gezondheid psychologie: Toepassingen (Vol. II).* Utrecht: Lemma.

Meulenbeld, C., & Lingen, P. van (1993). *Instrumenten op het terrein van arbeid en gezondheid.* Amsterdam: NIA.

Mey, H.R.A. de (1992). Essential hypertension: A matter of life-style. In J.A.M. Winnubst & S. Maes (Eds.), *Lifestyles and stress and health.* Leiden: DSWO Press.

Mintzberg, H. (1979). *The structuring of organizations.* Englewood Cliffs, NJ: Prentice-Hall.

Nathans, H. (1991). *Adviseren als tweede beroep.* Deventer: Kluwer.

Newton, T.J., & Keenan, A. (1990). The moderating effect of the type A behavior pattern and locus of control upon the relationship between change in job demands and change in psychological strain. *Human Relations, 43,* 1229–1255.

Odink, K.S., & Smeets, R.M.W. (1993). Persoonlijkheidsstoornissen. In J.J.L. van der Klink (Ed.), *Psychische problemen en de werksituatie: Handboek voor een actieve sociaal-medische begeleiding.* Amsterdam: NIA.

Payne R.L., & Jones, J.G. (1987). Measurement and methodological issues in social support. In S.V. Kasl, & C.L. Cooper (Eds.), *Stress and health: Issues in research methodology.* New York: Wiley.

Peel, M. (1992). *Career development and planning. A guide for managers, trainers and personnel staff.* London: McGraw-Hill.

Prein, H. (1993). Interventie bij conflicten: de 'Arbeid en Gezondheid'-psycholoog als derde partij. In M.J. Schabracq & J.A.M. Winnubst (Eds.), *Handboek arbeid en gezondheid psychologie: Toepassingen.* Utrecht: Lemma.

Schabracq, M.J., & Winnubst, J.A.M. (1993). *Handboek arbeid en gezondheid psychologie: Toepassingen (Vol. II).* Utrecht: Lemma.

Schabracq, M.J., Winnubst, J.A.M., & Cooper, C. (1996). *Handbook of work and health psychology.* Chichester: Wiley.

Schalk, M.J.D. (1992). Human Resource Management en de Arbeid en Gezondheid Psychologie. In: J.A.M. Winnubst & M.J. Schabracq (1992). *Handboek arbeid en gezondheid psychologie: Hoofdthema's (Vol. I).* Utrecht: Lemma.

Schaufeli, W. (1990). *Opgebrand.* Rotterdam: Donker.

Schreurs, P.J.G., Keilman, M., Severijnen, J., & Winnubst, J.A.M. (1993). Bedrijfsfitness in Nederland.

In M.J. Schabracq & J.A.M. Winnubst (Eds.), *Handboek arbeid en gezondheid psychologie: Toepassingen*. Utrecht: Lemma.

Schreurs, P.J.G., & Winnubst, J.A.M. (1992). Bedrijfswelzijnsprogramma's. In J.A.M. Winnubst & M.J. Schabracq (Eds.), *Handboek arbeid en gezondheid psychologie: Hoofdthema's (Vol. I)*. Utrecht: Lemma.

Schröer, K. (1993). *Verzuim wegens overspanning*. Maastricht: UPM.

Storr, A. (1989). *Solitude*. London: Collins.

Stewart, M.J. (1989). Social support: Diverse theoretical perspectives. *Social Science and Medicine, 28*, 1275-1282.

Terluin, B., Gill, K., & Winnubst, J.A.M. (1992). Hoe zien huisartsen surmenage? *Huisarts en Wetenschap, 35*, 311-315.

Terluin, B., & Klink, J.J.L. van der (1993). Surmenage. In J.J.L. van der Klink (Ed.), *Psychische problemen en de werksituatie: Handboek voor een actieve sociaal-medische begeleiding*. Amsterdam: NIA.

Tobias, L.L. (1990). *Psychological consulting to management: A clinician's perspective*. New York: Brunner/Mazel.

Winnubst, J.A.M. (1993). Burnout, social support and organizational structure. In W.B. Schaufeli, T. Marek, & C. Maslach (Eds.), *Professional burnout: Recent developments in theory and research*. Washington: Hemisphere.

Winnubst, J.A.M., Buunk, B.P., & Marcelissen, F.H.G. (1988). Social support and stress: Perspectives and processes. In S. Fisher & J. Reason (Eds.), *Handbook of life stress, cognition and health*. New York: Wiley.

Winnubst, J.A.M., & Bout, J. van den (1989). Sociale steun en depressie. In B.P. Buunk & A.J. Vrugt (Eds.), *Sociale psychologie en psychische klachten*. Assen: Dekker & Van de Vegt.

Winnubst, J.A.M., Schabracq, M.J., & Jong, R.D. de (1993). De diagnostiek van rolspanningen op het werk: De Vragenlijst Organisatie-Stress (VOS). In M.J. Schabracq & J.A.M. Winnubst (Eds.), *Handboek arbeid en gezondheid psychologie: Toepassingen*. Utrecht: Lemma.

Winnubst, J.A.M., & Marcelissen, F.H.G. (1992). Type A behavior and occupational stress: A causal analysis. In J.A.M. Winnubst & S. Maes (Eds.), *Lifestyles, stress and health: New developments in health psychology*. Leiden: DSWO Press.

Winnubst, J.A.M., & Schabracq, M.J. (1992). *Handboek arbeid en gezondheid psychologie: Hoofdthema's (Vol. I)*. Utrecht: Lemma.

World Health Organization (WHO) (1987). Constitution of the World Health Organization. In *Basic Documents* (36th Edn). Geneva: WHO.

Author Index

Subject Index